# ESSAYS IN
# ECONOMIC HISTORY

# ESSAYS IN ECONOMIC HISTORY

## VOLUME ONE

*Reprints edited for*
*The Economic History Society*

*by*

## E. M. CARUS-WILSON

*Professor of Economic History*
*in the University of London*

NEW YORK
ST. MARTIN'S PRESS
1966

**Made and printed in Great Britain by**
Percy Lund, Humphries & Co. Ltd, London and Bradford

# PREFACE

THE growing interest in economic history early in the present century, among both historians and economists, was marked by the appearance in England of two new periodicals wholly devoted to the subject—*Economic History*, launched in 1926 by the Royal Economic Society as a supplement to the *Economic Journal*, and the *Economic History Review*, launched in 1927 by the newly founded Economic History Society. In 1941 *Economic History* was discontinued, but after the war, in 1948, the Royal Economic Society gave financial support to the Economic History Society and was accorded representation on the editorial board of the *Economic History Review*.

It is to the files of these two journals that the student must turn for the results of much of the research that has been done in the field of economic history since 1926. Complete sets of them are not, however, always available in libraries, nor can they now be made up, since many back numbers are today out of print. The aim of the present collection is therefore to make readily accessible in one volume a selection of those articles which have proved most in demand among students. The selection has been made by a sub-committee appointed for this purpose by the Council of the Economic History Society. In making its choice the sub-committee has restricted itself to the files of the first twenty years, and account has been taken only of articles which have not been substantially incorporated in later published work. For these reasons alone, and because of the many new contributions to the subject which have been published elsewhere, the volume should not be regarded as offering a representative view of recent work in economic history.

The essays here reprinted have been reproduced unaltered, save for a few minor amendments and the correction of occasional misprints. They therefore reflect the views of their authors at the time that they were written. Each author has, however, been invited to add a brief note, should he so wish, about any points to which he would like to call attention in the light of later research; such notes appear as postscripts to the articles in question.

Thanks are due to the Royal Economic Society for permission to reprint articles first appearing in *Economic History*, and to Miss Olive Coleman for much help in the preparation of the volume for the press.

E. M. CARUS-WILSON.

# CONTENTS

# THE RISE OF A MONEY ECONOMY

## M. M. POSTAN

### I

T HE " rise of a money economy " is one of the residuary hypotheses of economic history: a *deus ex machina* to be called upon
when no other explanation is available. The subject of economic
history is sufficiently new to contain problems which economic historians
have not yet had time to resolve, and problems which have not yet been
resolved lend themselves only too easily to generalized explanations.
These stop-gap generalities have not so far been described or catalogued.
But a critical reader would probably recognize them without the aid of
a cautionary table. For most of them are little more than invocations of
sociological theories underlying the Victorian idea of progress.

One such invocation is the so-called " rise of the middle classes ".
Eileen Power and others have already pointed out how frequently the
middle-class formula has been used to bridge gaps in historical knowledge. The recipe has been to credit the rising middle classes with
almost every revolutionary event of European culture to which a more
specific cause has not yet been assigned. If towns grew in the eleventh
and twelfth centuries, this was due to the rise of the middle classes; if
lay culture and religious dissent flourished in the late twelfth and the
early thirteenth centuries, this was also due to the rise of the middle
classes. So, if we are to believe some writers, was the consolidation of
national monarchies in England and France in the later Middle Ages,
the dissolution of feudal power in the fifteenth century, the Reformation,
the Tudor despotism, the Elizabethan renaissance, the scientific development of the seventeenth century, the Puritan revolution, the economic
liberalism and the sentimental novel of the eighteenth century. In fact
the martyrdom of Poland and the Russian revolution are very nearly
the only historical phenomena which nobody has yet thought fit to lay
at the door of the newly born bourgeoisie.

The very range of the occasions on which the formula has been
employed is sufficient to warn us against its employment. Yet *au fond*
its applications are not as absurd as they appear when strung together.
Like most current sociological generalizations, the middle-class formula
contains a modicum of truth without which it would not have found its
way into otherwise creditable writings. At one time or another the
middle classes must have risen; at some time or other they must have
grown; and from their rise or their growth historical consequences were
bound to follow. There is, therefore, nothing *a priori* wrong in an

attempt to consider the rising middle classes as an important historical event. What is wrong is the frequent assumption that the middle classes rose suddenly at a clearly recognizable point in the past, and that, having risen, they went on growing in number and strength all through subsequent history. Equally erroneous is the notion that the most significant feature in the history of the middle classes was their increase. Eileen Power has shown that in the English Middle Ages the birthday of the bourgeoisie, the precise century or year when it first made its appearance, is impossible to discover. The English middle classes are as old as English history, and their record is not one of continuous and uninterrupted growth. Gauged by their power and wealth they were more prominent in the early fourteenth century than in the fifteenth, and were more " capitalistic " in the free conditions of the early Middle Ages than they were to become in the more rigidly regulated economy of the later Middle Ages.[1] Indeed, students will find that the changes in the structure, outlook and behaviour of the middle classes are much more significant than the mere swelling of their numbers or the inflation of their power through consecutive centuries of English history.

## II

Another such formula is the "rise of a money economy". Ever since the days of Cunningham and Thorold Rogers money economy has been repeatedly called in to help in dealing with recalcitrant problems of economic history—sometimes the same kind of problems as those which had elsewhere been "palmed off" on the middle classes.[2] Historians have frequently taken it for granted that a money economy, like the bourgeoisie, arose at a single point of English history, usually at a point best suited to their argument. They have thus been able to ascribe to the rising money economy an infinite variety of phenomena: the transformation of the Anglo-Saxon society in the tenth and the eleventh centuries, the rise of towns in the eleventh and twelfth, the development of royal taxation in the twelfth and thirteenth, the commutation of services in the thirteenth and fourteenth, and several features of the English renaissance in the sixteenth. All these and many other events, widely separated in time and space, have been explained as due to the rise of money economy.

Needless to say, in some contexts the formula is more convincing than in others. Its term—the words "money economy" and more still

---

[1] Eileen Power, *The Wool Trade in English Medieval History* (Oxford, 1941), chap. vi.

[2] *E.g.* W. Cunningham, *The Growth of English Industry and Commerce* (5th edn., Cambridge, 1910), I, 22, 242, 458, 546, etc.; E. Lipson, *The Economic History of England* (7th edn., 1937), I, 94, 102, 105, 608. On the other hand, Ashley, when he wrote his famous text-book, refused to be drawn into the prejudices of his time, and did not even mention money economy by name.

the word "rise"—have been used in many different senses; but it is only in one of its many connotations that it has a meaning sufficiently clear, and some foundation in fact. In all its other senses it is more or less untrue, and from the point of view of European and English history more or less irrelevant.

It is least relevant when it happens to be used in its simplest and most direct sense. If the word rise is taken to mean the birth or the first appearance, and the term money economy is employed to point the contrast with economies in which trade is altogether absent or else is conducted without money, the formula cannot be of much importance. It could mean nothing to medieval historians, who have used it most often, even if it might mean something to archaeologists, who have hardly used it at all.

I do not want to deny that a money economy in this sense must have appeared at one time or another on the continent of Europe, and that at some primitive stage in their development the European peoples were innocent of trade, or at least unfamiliar with the use of money. But this condition, if it ever existed, must have disappeared earlier than the earliest point at which European history can be said to begin. Have not the archaeologists traced interregional trade into neolithic days and was not at least one pre-historic civilization—the Bronze Age—dependent on international exchanges for the very metal from which it derived its name?[3] The use of money in trade may have been more recent than trade itself, but, however recent, it goes far beyond the beginnings of European civilization and is probably older than the oldest of the written records.

Money had apparently been current on this island long before the Romans came, and had been known to Angles, Saxons and Jutes before they invaded this country. Since then their institutions, their pattern of obligations and their economic life never ceased to reflect their familiarity with money. The oldest Anglo-Saxon laws, those of the sixth-century kings of Kent, fix murder fines in money terms, and so do the Anglo-Saxon laws of the subsequent centuries. And blood fines were not the only payments and obligations to be expressed in Anglo-Saxon documents in money terms. Professor Stenton has recently reminded us that one of the earliest payments to the Church, the plough-penny, may date back to as early as the seventh century.[4] The most important

[3] The only comprehensive account of prehistoric trade in all its aspects is that given by W. Stein in Ebert's *Reallexikon der Altertumskunde*. But since Stein wrote, very numerous studies of a prehistoric trade in different regions of northern Europe have appeared in various archaeological publications. In these studies the vital importance of long-distance trade in the Bronze Age has been brought out very clearly. On the part played in this trade by the British Isles see S. Pigott, " The Early Bronze Age in Wessex ", *Proceedings of the Prehistoric Society* (1938).

[4] F. M. Stenton, *Anglo-Saxon England* (Oxford, 1943), 152. Here, as elsewhere in his book, Professor Stenton has shown that it is possible to deal with the economic phenomena of the distant past without invoking the money economy in general.

Anglo-Saxon payment to the Church, that of churchscot, may have been paid in kind, for it was similar to the tithe of later centuries.   But this was not a mark of natural economy, for failure to pay churchscot was apparently punished by a money fine.   The principal agricultural imposts payable to the king were food rents from his estates and were, therefore, for a long time paid in kind.   But long before the Conquest some of these rents had been paid in money.[5]   Revenues, such as the gelds for specific purposes, and above all the Danegeld, were expressed in money units; so also were various payments between private persons. Men buying estates paid for them with lump sums of money.   A payment of a thousand shillings for an estate has been recorded as early as Offa's reign.[6]   The innumerable customary payments of ancient origin listed by Miss Neilson[7] appear for the first time in English records as " pennies " of one kind or another, or in other words, as cash payments. There were numerous public payments, or to be more exact royal dues, which had become assimilated to feudal rent: the hidage, the cornage, the sheriff-silver, the wardpenny.   And there were also payments in lieu of obligations more purely manorial: the heddornwerch, the woodpenny, the shernsilver, the hedgingsilver, the bedripsilver, the averpenny, and numerous other pennies and silvers in lieu of ancient labour services on land.   Few of them are mentioned in documents before the twelfth century, but their character as well as their etymology are clearly Anglo-Saxon.

All this evidence of pre-medieval money payments has been known to historians since the very beginnings of medieval scholarship; yet it has not prevented them from placing the rise of a money economy centuries later than the recorded dates of Anglo-Saxon money transactions.   This inconsistency has sometimes been justified on theoretical grounds.   In accordance with the terminological distinctions of modern economics, some historians have been inclined to explain away the early references to money on the ground that in the Anglo-Saxon period, as in the early centuries of the Middle Ages, money units were employed to measure obligations and not to make payments.   In the jargon of the economist, money was a unit of account and not a medium of exchange.

For this distinction no historical proof has so far been adduced. What the facts tell us is that certain payments were reckoned in money, and unless the contrary is proved the conclusion must be that payments

---

[5] The story of the commutation of the royal farms into money derives from the author of *Dialogus de Scaccario*, Bishop Richard, who himself got it from hearsay. But his dates, if not his other details, are somewhat doubtful. *Cf.* R. L. Poole, *Exchequer in the Twelfth Century* (Oxford, 1912), 27.  In fact, as Professor Stenton points out, the traces of an organized financial system in England are "unexpectedly remote". There were rudiments of a national treasury in the ninth century (*op. cit.* 645.) See also E. Lipson, *op cit.* 602.

[6] W. de G. Birch, *Cartularium Saxonicum*, I (1885), no. 271.

[7] N. Neilson, *Customary Rents* (Oxford Studies in Social and Legal History, II, 1910), 50 *et seq.* and 114 *et seq.*

would not be thus reckoned unless they were also thus discharged. Other facts tell us that in this country gold was coined and circulated before the Roman Conquest. Anglo-Saxon money was coined at least as early as the sixth century and was received, exported and hoarded by foreigners trading with England at least as early as the eighth century.[8] There can thus be no doubt that money was in fact employed in payment, and was not an abstract standard of value.

The whole argument that the use of money and coins for reckoning came sooner or easier to the primitive man than the handing over of coins in payment is not borne out by either archaeological or anthropological evidence, and is a pure piece of *a priori* reasoning. And until a better argument is found or better evidence is adduced, references in early documents to money payments must be understood in their literal sense. The onus of proof belongs to those who believe that obligations, though expressed in money, were discharged in other ways.

Thus, from the point of view of English history, and even from that of medieval and Anglo-Saxon history, the rise of a money economy in the sense of its first appearance has no historical meaning. Money was in use when documented history begins, and its rise cannot be adduced as an explanation of any later phenomenon.


# III

The formula means more when used in its vaguer and more general sense. The expression " money economy " can be taken to mean the relative frequency of money payments, while the word " rise " can be used to denote not their birthday but their general expansion. In this sense the growth of a money economy means merely an increase in the relative volume of money payments and is something economists can understand and historians can test. For in this sense the process is historically not very different from what other historians prefer to describe as the rise of exchange economy and the decline of a natural economy.

Recently historians have cast some doubt and even a little aspersion upon the notion of a natural economy. It is now usual to argue that in all periods of recorded history men depended upon trade and markets, and that " pure " natural economy was never known in Europe. Nevertheless, the fundamental principle underlying the distinction has not been wholly destroyed. Even if economies wholly natural never existed, economies partly natural did. The economic condition of European

---

[8] Though in Professor Stenton's words " the continuous history of English currency begins with Offa " (*op. cit.* 220), some Anglo-Saxon coins are much older. C. F. Keary, *A Catalogue of English Coins in the British Museum* (1887), I, vi. See also H. A. Grueber, *Handbook of the Coins of Great Britain and Ireland in the British Museum* (1889), pp. i-x.

societies at every stage of their existence was more or less natural and
more or less self-sufficient; sometimes more and sometimes less. And
it is in these changes towards or away from natural economy that the real
meaning of the rise of a money economy will be found.

Indeed, the history of mankind, and still more the history of Europe,
is marked by recurrent phases of active exchanges. No student of the
thirteenth century will fail to notice not only an over-all increase in
agricultural and industrial production, but also a greater emphasis on
production for sale and the spread of more or less capitalistic agriculture
on large estates, and the consequent growth of towns, markets and
mercantile classes. Similar changes in the sixteenth or the eighteenth
centuries are so familiar that some historians find them too trivial even
to be worth mentioning. Used in this sense, the formula of the rise of
money economy points to a real social process, easy to identify and
dangerous to miss.

Yet even in this sense the formula is sometimes wrapped up in a great
deal of theory and mysticism, or else hitched to irrelevant facts. The
most irrelevent of the facts with which it is sometimes identified is the
so-called increase of money. How often are we told that the rise of
money economy followed the influx of precious metals from this and that
corner of the world? And yet how seldom are we told how and why
this should have happened. The growth of money economy, if it is to
mean anything at all, signifies an increase in payments, not an increase
in bullion or paper money. Needless to say, a growing quantity of
money can have and has had important consequences. Historians and
economists will easily find instances of social transformations brought
about by additions to the mere volume of the circulating medium,
Situations of this kind recurred several times in the course of the
eighteenth and nineteenth centuries. There was the well-known and
much publicized increase in bullion in the sixteenth century, and a
similar influx may also have occurred in the late twelfth and the thirteenth centuries. Yet by no means all these events necessarily led to
any of the consequences with which the rise of money economy is
commonly credited.

The influx of bullion could have different effects at different times.
In periods and societies unaccustomed to money but otherwise fond of
gold, an increase in the supply of precious metals would only make plate
and gold buckles more abundant. In periods when gold and silver were
mainly used as mediums of exchange, the chief effect of their increase
would be to raise the level of prices.[9] As prices rose and fell, social
relations—and money economy with them—were bound to change. Yet
at the cost of a little pedantry historians will do well to consider such

---

[9] Even that was by no means inevitable, for new bullion was sometimes absorbed
without raising prices, and conversely, prices could rise independently of supplies of
gold and silver.

changes as products of price revolutions, not as consequences of more abundant bullion.

To say, therefore (as it is sometimes said), that in the thirteenth century commerce grew because the money economy was rising, and then to proceed to account for the latter by the influx of gold and bullion from the east, is to be wrong not only in fact (throughout the Middle Ages trade with the east set up bullion movements flowing from west to east, not from east to west) but also in logic. Prices were apparently buoyant all through that period, and as they rose some people may have felt inclined to use their money more frequently or else to produce for sale more than they would otherwise have done. But it is not at all certain that the rise in prices was due to an influx of precious metals, and it is certain that the expansion of trade was not solely due to the rise in prices. Peace, the growth of population, the expansion of settlement, the improvements in commercial and financial technique, all played their part in breaking up the self-sufficiency of local markets and in commercializing the economic activities of men.

What is true of the thirteenth century is also true of many other periods. Some of the best-known instances of commutation, i.e. of transition from payments in kind to payments in money, occurred at the time when prices were falling and the quantity of circulating medium presumably declined. In the fourteenth and fifteenth centuries substitution of money payments for labour services followed from the falling agricultural prices and from the general agricultural depression of the times. A still earlier wave of commutations, that of the early twelfth century, was not, apparently, preceded by any clearly defined movements of prices and possibly " straddled " across two contrary cycles—a fall followed by a rise. Its explanation will probably be found in the general economic and political insecurity of the age, which made it difficult for landlords to control production in their outlying estates, to exact labour services and to move large quantities of agricultural produce across the country.

In short, the rise of a money economy in the sense of greater preponderance of money payments is not identical with the greater abundance of money itself. More gold and silver could sometimes result in higher prices; higher prices could sometimes raise the relative volume of money transactions. But in general the volume of money transactions was an historical phenomenon of composite origin and reflecting an infinite variety of causes, social, economic and political.

## IV

Thus the rise of a money economy has a meaning wider and more general than that of mere currency inflation. Yet it is also possible to view it in too broad and too diffuse a light, or, as I have said elsewhere, to wrap it in too much sublimity and metaphysics. Now and again it has been interpreted as one of those inexorable tendencies of human progress of which the nineteenth century sociologists—Spencer, Buckle, Marx and Comte—were inordinately fond. In some writings, and especially in some German writings, the rise of money economy figures as a permanent tendency of historical development and as an ever-unfolding manifestation of the progressive destinies of humanity.

In reality it is none of these things. It is certainly not uninterrupted and in that sense not progressive. Until the Industrial Revolution it was nothing more than a recurrent economic phenomenon unconnected with any elemental and mystical tendencies of human history or with secular changes of human behaviour. The history of western Europe, and for that matter the history of the world, is not a continuous record of expanding exchanges. The unbroken growth of world trade between the beginning of the eighteenth century and the end of the nineteenth has misled historians into believing that the growth of world trade had been equally unbroken in the past. Medievalists and historians of the sixteenth and the seventeenth centuries should be guilty of no such delusion. In so far as growing money economy depended on growing production, it could not possibly be continuous, for the simple reason that world production itself did not grow progressively or continuously. In this country there was a protracted slump in the late fourteenth and the fifteenth centuries; possibly also a slump at the turn of the Anglo-Saxon and Norman periods. I do not know whether anything in the nature of an economic recession intervened in the middle decades of the seventeenth century, but there is no doubt that the rate of growth, if growth there was, was at that time much retarded. Abroad, the history of the last twelve hundred years was repeatedly punctuated by local falls in production and incomes. In short, cumulative increases in world production, now taken for granted by economists and politicians, are all too recent to be considered eternal, still less primeval.

It will, of course, be argued (and this also happens to be my view) that a money economy in the true sense of the term depended for its development not so much on a general increase in production as on those subtler historical changes which led men away from domestic self-sufficiency and directed them towards shops and market places. But changes of this character were even less continuous and less progressive than the purely material record of world output. No historian will be unhistorical enough to lump together all the occasions when humanity forsook the habits of natural economy and showed a preference for buying and selling. This may have happened in the twelfth and the early thirteenth centuries because peace reigned, because law was observed, because prices were buoyant, population was rising and more mouths had to be fed. This may have happened in the sixteenth century because prices were rising, but also because new riches were brought in by English merchants from abroad, and because new needs were following in the wake of the renaissance. Commercial production may have expanded in the eighteenth century because population was growing, because international trade was bringing in new wealth, while human ingenuity was finding new and profitable ways for employing capital in commercial production. American farmers may have gone over to cash crops in the second half of the nineteenth century because the very condition of their settlements in the middle west forced them to produce for sale; also because the virgin prairie made it possible for them to produce cheaply, while the new railways made it possible for the produce to be carried away; but chiefly because for political and social reasons the cash nexus had begun to penetrate the entire social fabric of the United States. The African natives may be producing for the market because of the incidence of colonial taxation; the Russian peasants because of the state policy of capital accumulation. From this point of view there was not one rise of money economy but several rises of several money economies. There was a series of independent peaks with a different road to each, and no peak except the last ever opened the prospect of continuous rises unbroken by descents.

For descents there doubtless were, and I have already mentioned some of them. In France at the end of the eighteenth century, in Germany during and after the Thirty Years' War, all over the Continent during the religious wars, during the troubles of the fifteenth century, during the conquests and migrations of the ninth and tenth centuries; at all these places and times economic activity declined or remained stagnant, and material life became more local and self-sufficient. These were times of a more or less general retreat from a money economy.

## V

"More or less general": the reason why I am reluctant to commit myself to a more sweeping statement is that movements towards greater money economy, as well as movements away from it, were not only less continuous than people imagine but also less general. General recessions or general expansions of economic activity affecting every branch of agriculture, industry and trade were common enough, but general changes in the relative volume of money transactions were much less common. I doubt whether history could show a single example of the use of money expanding, so to speak, all along the line, unchecked and unbroken by local retreats. Let us look again at the English medieval examples which I have already mentioned. I have cited the fifteenth century as a period of declining trade, of growing self-sufficiency and, therefore, a good example of declining money economy. But while this generalization holds good of most departments of fifteenth-century life

2

and justifies my general verdict on the epoch, it does not apply to the labour market. For, as I have already pointed out, and as every school-boy knows, the fifteenth century was also the time when labour services were being commuted and money payments were being substituted for labour dues. No wonder the economic historians who approached the period entirely from the point of view of agricultural labour jumped to the conclusion that the age was one of a rising money economy.[10] A clear contrast to the fifteenth century was presented by the thirteenth. At that time the general movement was towards bigger and better trade; more was produced and a greater share of what was produced went to the market. Yet in the employment of labour a contrary tendency prevailed. The lords endeavoured to enforce labour services to their legal maximum, to exact them in kind wherever their sales were optional, and to impose new services wherever the legal position was vague enough to permit it.[11] To an historian looking at the period from the point of view of labour it might well appear as one of a declining money economy.

Similar examples could be found in other periods and other countries. They all suggest that the changes in the so-called " money economy " have been less uniform than the formula of money economy would suggest to the uninitiated. But nothing reveals the complexity of the process and the dangers of the formula better than the so-called " farm ".

In present-day language the word "farm" connotes the typical English unit of agricultural enterprise, but it derives from the more restricted term which was used in the later Middle Ages and in the early centuries of the modern era to denote a common type of contractual tenancy. It was a form of lease established on land (usually on the demesne) which had previously yielded to the lord a fluctuating income, in order to provide him with a stable, i.e. " firm ", annual income. In this sense a " farm " was not a purely agricultural term, but applied to all transactions of "farming out ", i.e. letting out a fluctuating source of income for a fixed annual sum. There was a sheriff's farm, whereby a fixed annual sum was substituted for the hitherto variable revenues from royal vills and from other miscellaneous sources; the firma burghi, by which boroughs undertook to discharge their many and various payments to their overlord, usually the king, in a fixed annual sum; " farms " of customs and so forth. Thus, on the whole, the creation of a " farm " indicated a desire on the part of the owner to stabilize his income; a desire which would be most acutely felt at times when the revenues fluctuated unduly or else showed a tendency to fall. And this would, as a rule, suggest conditions of an economic slump and could be interpreted as a superficial symptom of an economic depression. But

---

[10] E.g. A. E. Levett, *The Black Death on the Estates of the See of Winchester* (Oxford Studies in Social and Legal History, V, 1916), *passim*, but especially 154-8.
[11] M. Postan, "The Chronology of Labour Services", in *Transactions of the Royal Historical Society*, 4th Ser., XX (1937), 169-93.

it cannot be safely used as a symptom of either a rising or a declining money economy.

On some manors of the late fourteenth and the early fifteenth centuries, farms were created on demesnes which had previously provided the lord's household with its provisions.  These farms clearly meant a change towards a money economy and a further step towards the commercialization of agriculture.  But they meant nothing of the sort when they happened to be introduced, as they were now and again throughout the Middle Ages, in outlying manors in substitution for fluctuating rents and money payments.  And they may mean all sorts of things when they appeared in the garb in which we meet them in the eleventh and the early twelfth centuries—that of manorial and monastic *feorms*.

In the earliest manorial surveys available to us, mostly those of the twelfth century, and in all other documents dealing with the financial organization of large estates in the closing century of the Anglo-Saxon era and the first century of the Norman rule, we invariably find some if not most manors held by *firmarii* for a payment of a time-farm, *i.e.* a fixed payment representing the landlord's sustenance for a definite period—a month, a week, a day.  This might be a *firma unius noctis* on royal manors or a week's *feorm* in a manor belonging to the canons of St. Paul's or the monks of Christchurch, Canterbury.  But in each case the arrangement would be roughly the same; a fixed payment, largely in kind, but often also in money, would be due from the manor at a fixed date.

This arrangement has been known to historians ever since the days of Spelman and Dugdale; more recently it was described by E. H. Hale in his introduction to the Domesday of St Paul's; and more recently still by several students of early monasticism.[12]  Yet I doubt whether the historical and economic meaning of the transaction has always been understood.  Historians have sometimes been misled by the deliveries in kind which characterize the Benedictine method of estate management into believing that what they are dealing with is a primitive stage in manorial economy: a stage still characterized by direct payments in produce.  The end of this stage is usually described as a " commutation " of direct deliveries of produce, and as a substitution of a money economy for payments in kind.

This interpretation of the *feorm* is not wholly wrong, but it is certainly out of focus.  The fact that some or most monastic *feorms* were fixed in kind was not the only element of the transaction.  In fact many of them were paid in money, or at least in both produce and money.

[12] *E.g.* N. Neilson, *Economic Conditions on the Manors of Ramsey Abbey* (Philadelphia, 1899), and R. A. L. Smith, *Canterbury Cathedral Priory* (Cambridge, 1943).  More synoptic accounts, both free from economic preconceptions, will be found in D. Knowles, *The Monastic Order in England* (Cambridge, 1940), 441-4 ; and in F. M. Stenton, *op. cit.* 476-8.

The Benedictine landlords always ran their "headquarter estates" for the sake of their produce. But on all other estates the characteristic feature of the payments was not that they were made in kind but that they were fixed and firm. At the time when they were established they denoted not so much a choice between produce and money as a choice between fluctuating income and fixed income; and the historical situation they represented was not that of natural economy but that in which landlords happened to prefer fixed yield to fluctuating profits from rent and cultivation.

From this point of view the *feorm* of the eleventh century is not fundamentally different from the "farm" of the fifteenth.[13] Neither can be represented as in any way primitive or in any way concerned with the general development of a money economy. Both are natural re-actions of landlords to a combination of circumstances unfavourable to direct exploitation of estates: political unsettlement, or difficulties of transport and communications, or falling prices. And both could be followed and preceded by periods of direct exploitation for fluctuating income. That in the twelfth and thirteenth centuries direct exploitation as a rule followed the *feorms* of the eleventh century is now generally regarded as certain. Historians are not so certain about what condition preceded the *feorm*. But then, nothing is certain about the large estates in the Anglo-Saxon era, least of all their economic organization. In the absence of proof we are all thrown back on probabilities, and, to my mind, the probability of an earlier agricultural boom—a time when estates were managed by speculative landlords in expectation of rising incomes—is very high indeed. Without an earlier phase of this kind most features of the eleventh- and twelfth-century manor would be impossible to explain. For how could we otherwise explain the juxta-position on so many manors of "old demesne" and "new demesne", of new holdings with old, of ancient holdings with new ones; and how can we account for the innumerable signs of an earlier expansion and colonization?

To conclude. The rise of a money economy does not mean the rise of money. It may mean an increase in the relative volume of money payments, as distinct from the increase in money itself. Yet even in this sense it is not a continuous process of human evolution. Increases in the relative volume of money transactions could reflect a whole variety of economic changes and were little more than passing, and sometimes recurrent, historical phenomena, which combined with other phenomena to create unique and unrepeatable historical situations.

[13] *Cf.* the early and the late references to farms in R. A. L. Smith, *op. cit.* 128-33, 201-3.

# THE YIELD AND PRICE OF CORN IN
# THE MIDDLE AGES

## LORD BEVERIDGE

THE great series of the account rolls of the Bishopric of Winchester, extending from 1208 to 1453, suggested to Dr Hubert Hall and myself some years ago the possibility of constructing a new table of medieval prices in England longer and more continuous than that of Thorold Rogers. Further examination of the sources has shown this hope to be justified. Delay in the preparation and publication of such a table has been due mainly to the wealth of new material continually unearthed by Dr Hall and his assistants, and the end is not yet. Meanwhile the Winchester Rolls with which our investigation began can be used to throw light incidentally on another economic problem, that of the productivity of medieval agriculture as judged both by the yield per acre and by the yield per quarter of seed used. The present paper gives some preliminary results which are subject to revision in detail.

The information used relates to nine out of the fifty or more manors included in the Winchester Rolls. They have been selected geographically—one from each of the counties of Somerset, Wilts, Oxford, Berks, Bucks and Surrey, and three from northern, central and southern Hampshire respectively. Similar information could be obtained for many or most of the other manors of the Bishopric, but it has not seemed worth while to extract it all. One of the manors—Esher in Surrey—proved to be a rye manor, growing little wheat, and for that grain eight manors alone are used. Bearing in mind the types of soil in these manors there seems to be no reason for suspecting that they are exceptional.

At the end of the grange account for each manor the total quantity of grain is given with details of the following items: grain produced, grain brought forward from a previous year, grain bought during the year. In addition there are in some manors and some periods other entries, such as " church seed ", " allowances to servants " at Downton and Witney, " increment of the granary " to about 1318, and charges *super compotum* after about 1288. These entries are followed by the acreage and the seed sown for the next year, and occasionally by the rate of seed used per acre. The yield per quarter of seed used and the yield per acre have to be calculated by comparing the produce in one roll with the acreage and the seed in the preceding roll. Dependence on two successive rolls for each year's figures means that there are more gaps in the series of yields than in the series of prices, and that there is occasional risk of putting together produce and seed or acreage which do not relate to the same area. For each of the manors, however, other than Esher, yield figures of wheat are available for from 106 to 143 separate years. Possibilities of error, through the cause named and through other more important causes, though they cannot be eliminated completely, have, it is hoped, been reduced to harmlessness. The main difficulties presented by the records are dealt with in a note at the end of this article.

Generally, it may be said, the figures of yield per quarter of seed are more trustworthy than those of yield per acre. The former, indeed, appear to be better than anything available for any other period in English history, not excluding the most modern times. The amount of grain actually used for seed today is not recorded in England, as it is in Australia, and agricultural textbooks contain widely varying rules as to how much seed should be applied to each acre. For the comparisons made below I have used the estimates adopted for statistical purposes by the Ministry of Agriculture of 2¾ bushels of wheat per acre, 3 bushels of barley, and 4¾ bushels of oats.

It is possible that in another respect also the medieval figures are better than the modern ones. The produce in the former is the measured amount for which the bailiff accounted; modern figures of produce are based on estimates and, as Mr J. A. Venn has pointed out, may now err systematically by defect.[1]

Table I gives the location of each of the manors, the number of separate years for which yield figures of wheat can be given, and the areas covered by the returns in the first and the last half-century under review.

The material for examination is not spread evenly over the whole period. During the first half of the thirteenth century and after 1425 there are more gaps in the series of rolls than during the fourteenth century. Moreover, the acreage to which the returns relate diminishes from the beginning to the end of the period, as more and more of the land is let at a rental or otherwise disposed of in place of being worked directly on the Bishop's account. Thus the total wheat area covered in the eight manors, excluding Esher, begins at about 1,400 acres for the first half of the thirteenth century, and falls in successive half-centuries to 885, 682, 559 and 465 acres (in 1400-49). That for barley in nine manors goes from 500 to 253 acres; that for oats from about 1,550 to 293 acres. Though some decline of wheat acreage is found in almost every manor, except where the acreage at the beginning was already small, both the rate of decline and the acreage covered vary considerably from one manor to another. It may be added that, taking the manors as a

[1] *The Economic Journal*, September 1926.

## TABLE I

### Manors, Acreage and Years Included

| Manor | County | Average acreage covered in returns | | | | | | Years covered for Wheat |
|---|---|---|---|---|---|---|---|---|
| | | Wheat | | Barley | | Oats | | |
| | | 1200–49 | 1400–49 | 1200–49 | 1400–49 | 1200–49 | 1400–49 | |
| Nailsbourne | Somerset | (87)[2] | 36 | (7)[2] | 2 | (117)[2] | 32 | 106 |
| Downton | Wilts | 314 | 53 | 181 | 69 | 234 | 27 | 125 |
| Witney | Oxon | 292 | 40 | 72 | (56)[1] | 212 | (38)[1] | 111 |
| Wargrave | Berks | 20 | 38 | 20 | 42 | 94 | 13 | 109 |
| Wycombe | Bucks | 156 | 59 | 22 | 33 | 160 | 37 | 116 |
| Ecchinswell | Hants (N.) | 90 | 45 | 13 | 18 | 93 | 29 | 140 |
| Overton | Hants (Mid.) | 43 | 41 | 49 | 44 | 182 | 42 | 143 |
| Meon | Hants (S.) | 371 | 153 | 144 | 45 | 467 | 113 | 137 |
| Esher | Surrey | — | — | 29 | — | 94 | — | — |

[1] 1350-99.    [2] 1250-99.

whole, the decline of acreage covered by the returns proceeds steadily. There is no sudden jump at the Black Death or at any other point. In this respect the present inquiry confirms Miss Levett's conclusion that " the estates of the Bishop of Winchester during the fourteenth century show no revolution either in agriculture or in tenure, but changes are effected by a continuous economic evolution " [2] It is perhaps possible to trace in the figures for twenty-five years after the Black Death a slight check in the rate at which the acreage directly farmed for the Bishop declined, but that is all.

The results for the period from 1200 to 1450 as a whole are summarised in Table II, and the mean of the nine manors (eight only for wheat) is compared so far as possible with modern experience, that is to say, with the average for England in the twenty years from 1895 to 1914. The average yield per acre in the seven counties in which the manors lie is slightly but not significantly less than that for England as a whole. The latter has been used here as presumably better for comparison with the Ministry of Agriculture's estimates of seed used.

The seed used per acre in the Middle Ages is for wheat and oats much the same as, though slightly less than, the modern estimate of the Ministry of Agriculture. For barley it is considerably more; whether this difference is due to a real change of practice, or to the manors not being typical of the whole country, or through error in the Ministry of Agriculture's estimate cannot be said with certainty.

The yield per quarter of seed used is very much less than in modern times. On the average of the eight or nine manors as compared with modern England, the productivity of wheat has gone up from 3·89

[2] Oxford Studies in Social and Legal History, V, 142.

## TABLE II

### Yield of Corn in Certain Manors between 1200 and 1450

| Manor | Seed in quarters used per acre | | | Yield in quarters per quarter of seed | | | Yield in quarters per acre | | |
|---|---|---|---|---|---|---|---|---|---|
| | Wheat | Barley | Oats | Wheat | Barley | Oats | Wheat | Barley | Oats |
| Nailsbourne .   . | 0·22 | 0·37 | 0·44 | 4·10 | 4·45 | 2·76 | 0·89 | 1·66 | 1·21 |
| Downton   . | 0·32 | 0·46 | 0·50 | 3·01 | 3·62 | 2·52 | 0·96 | 1·68 | 1·27 |
| Witney   . | 0·32 | 0·47 | 0 61 | 2·97 | 3·78 | 2·18 | 0·96 | 1·76 | 1·33 |
| Wargrave   . | 0·38 | 0·49 | 0·63 | 3·91 | 4·13 | 2·11 | 1·48 | 2·04 | 1·34 |
| Wycombe   . | 0·35 | 0·50 | 0·61 | 3·33 | 3·95 | 2·49 | 1·16 | 1·98 | 1·53 |
| Ecchinswell . | 0·28 | 0·45 | 0·49 | 4·98 | 4·27 | 2·81 | 1·37 | 1·94 | 1·38 |
| Overton   . | 0·29 | 0·47 | 0·55 | 3·85 | 3·87 | 2·52 | 1·13 | 1·83 | 1·38 |
| Meon .   . | 0·28 | 0·51 | 0·55 | 5·00 | 3·59 | 2·71 | 1·38 | 1·82 | 1·50 |
| Esher .   . | — | 0·49 | 0·51 | — | 2·72 | 1·81 | — | 1·34 | 0·92 |
| Mean of all Manors | 0·31 | 0·47 | 0·54 | 3·89 | 3·82 | 2·43 | 1·17 | 1·79 | 1·32 |
| England 1895–1914 | 0·34 | 0·38 | 0·60 | 11·40 | 10·99 | 8·57 | 3·92 | 4·12 | 5·09 |

quarters of yield for each quarter of seed to 11·40, or nearly three times; the productivity of barley has gone up from 3·82 to 10·99—also just under three times; the productivity of oats has gone up from 2·43 to 8·57, or three and a half times. It may be added that the eleven and a half fold yield of wheat in modern England corresponds to what is achieved in newer countries like Australia, where the seed is sown much more thinly and the yield per acre is less.[3] A threefold increase in productivity of seed seems to measure broadly the difference between medieval and modern farming.

The average yield per acre comes out for wheat at 1·17 quarters or 9·36 bushels; for barley, 1·79 quarters or 14·32 bushels; and for oats, 1·32 quarters or 10·56 bushels. The yield in modern times is about three and a third times as great for wheat, two and a third times as great for barley, and three and three-quarters times as great for oats. These figures understate the advantage of modern times for three reasons. First, the medieval yields are for the areas actually cultivated. If the acres were reckoned " as they lie ", i.e. including presumably all the space wasted for various reasons under the open-field system, the acreage would be nearly doubled and the yield per acre approximately halved. The waste in modern cultivation is much less. Second, as has been stated above, there is ground for supposing that modern estimates of yield may habitually tend to be too low. Third, the modern quarter, partly owing to its slightly greater size and partly owing to the higher specific gravity of the grain, contains probably a substantially greater weight of wheat than did the medieval quarter. According to Steffen the difference is that between 480 and 395 lb. avoirdupois, i.e. an increase of over

[3] See note at end.

21 per cent. It is impossible, without much fuller inquiry, to make accurate allowance for all these factors, but it seems likely that the weight of wheat got from any given area today may be from six to eight times, rather than three and a third times, what it was in the Middle Ages.

The individual manors show considerable differences, ranging for wheat from a threefold to a fivefold yield, and from about 7 to nearly 12 bushels per acre. Meon, Ecchinswell and Nailsbourne have high productivity in relation to seed used for all three crops, except barley at the first-named; Witney, Downton and Wycombe are below or close to the average in every case. In yield per acre Wargrave stands out with Ecchinswell and Meon; while Downton and Witney and the lightly sown Nailsbourne are below the average. These differences appear to be related to the predominating type of soil in the various manors today, so far as that can be ascertained.

In the results given above the stretch of two and a half centuries from 1200 to 1450 has been treated as a whole. The next stage in the inquiry is to divide the whole period chronologically, so as to see whether any marked trend either of declining or of increasing productivity of agriculture can be discovered. This is done in Table III, giving for each manor figures similar to those in Table II, in five successive half-centuries.

The material, as stated, is not equally good in all half-centuries. Averages based on less than ten years' figures—as for Witney, Wargrave and Wycombe wheat between 1400 and 1450—are shown in brackets and should be disregarded; the marked fluctuation of yields from one harvest to another makes it unsafe to rely upon a few years only. For this and a number of other reasons already indicated—the different levels of productivity in particular manors, and their unequal and changing representation in the returns—it is difficult to combine their results into any one average figure which shall not be misleading. The figures given at the foot of each section of Table III, being the arithmetic means of the five manors—Nailsbourne, Downton, Ecchinswell, Overton, Meon—which run pretty well throughout the period, are probably open to less objection than most other averages that can be constructed. Looking at these, and disregarding for the moment the doubtful first half-century, two results seem to stand out pretty clearly for wheat:

First, the productivity of seed tends on the whole to rise a little. Second, the productivity of land has no significant movement either of increase or decline.

Barley and oats show increasing productivity of seed a little more markedly than does wheat, and with barley there seems to be an increase also in the productivity of land.

The second of the facts noted above for wheat is perhaps the most striking result of the whole inquiry. Broadly, over the whole range of 250 years from the beginning of the thirteenth to the middle of the fifteenth century, the productivity of the soil under wheat shows no

## TABLE III

### Use of Seed and Yield of Corn in Nine Winchester Manors from 1200 to 1449

#### A. Quarters of seed used per acre

| | Wheat | | | | | | Barley | | | | | | Oats | | | | | |
|---|---|---|---|---|---|---|---|---|---|---|---|---|---|---|---|---|---|---|
| | 1200–49 | 1250–99 | 1300–49 | 1350–99 | 1400–49 | 1200–1449 | 1200–49 | 1250–99 | 1300–49 | 1350–99 | 1400–49 | 1200–1449 | 1200–49 | 1250–99 | 1300–49 | 1350–99 | 1400–49 | 1200–1449 |
| 1. Nailsbourne* | — | 0·24 | 0·23 | 0·19 | 0·19 | 0·22 | — | 0·30 | 0·42 | 0·38 | 0·41 | 0·37 | — | 0·48 | 0·46 | 0·38 | 0·38 | 0·44 |
| 2. Downton* | 0·33 | 0·31 | 0·32 | 0·31 | 0·31 | 0·32 | 0·46 | 0·40 | 0·50 | 0·50 | 0·50 | 0·46 | 0·52 | 0·50 | 0·50 | 0·50 | 0·50 | 0·50 |
| 3. Witney | 0·26 | 0·37 | 0·33 | 0·30 | 0·30 | 0·32 | 0·36 | 0·49 | 0·45 | 0·50 | — | 0·47 | 0·60 | 0·72 | 0·54 | 0·51 | — | 0·61 |
| 4. Wargrave | [0·36] | 0·37 | 0·38 | 0·38 | [0·29] | 0·38 | [0·48] | 0·48 | 0·50 | 0·50 | [0·50] | 0·49 | [0·65] | 0·66 | 0·62 | 0·62 | [0·58] | 0·63 |
| 5. Wycombe | 0·38 | 0·37 | 0·34 | 0·31 | [0·31] | 0·35 | 0·49 | 0·50 | 0·50 | 0·50 | [0·50] | 0·50 | 0·61 | 0·75 | 0·58 | 0·50 | [0·50] | 0·61 |
| 6. Ecchinswell* | 0·22 | 0·26 | 0·28 | 0·30 | 0·28 | 0·28 | 0·40 | 0·40 | 0·44 | 0·47 | 0·50 | 0·45 | 0·44 | 0·50 | 0·50 | 0·50 | 0·49 | 0·49 |
| 7. Overton* | 0·31 | 0·32 | 0·28 | 0·30 | 0·26 | 0·28 | 0·40 | 0·69 | 0·51 | 0·49 | 0·50 | 0·47 | 0·54 | 0·63 | 0·51 | 0·50 | 0·50 | 0·55 |
| 8. Meon* | 0·23 | 0·38 | 0·29 | 0·25 | 0·25 | 0·28 | 0·36 | 0·50 | 0·49 | 0·50 | 0·50 | 0·51 | 0·50 | 0·67 | 0·53 | 0·50 | 0·50 | 0·55 |
| 9. Esher | | | | | | | 0·48 | 0·50 | — | 0·50 | — | 0·49 | 0·50 | 0·50 | 0·51 | 0·51 | — | 0·51 |
| *Mean of 5 manors | (0·26) | 0·30 | 0·28 | 0·27 | 0·26 | 0·28 | (0·38) | 0·46 | 0·46 | 0·47 | 0·48 | 0·45 | (0·49) | 0·56 | 0·50 | 0·48 | 0·47 | 0·51 |

#### B. Quarters of produce per quarter of seed

| | Wheat | | | | | | Barley | | | | | | Oats | | | | | |
|---|---|---|---|---|---|---|---|---|---|---|---|---|---|---|---|---|---|---|
| | 1200–49 | 1250–99 | 1300–49 | 1350–99 | 1400–49 | 1200–1449 | 1200–49 | 1250–99 | 1300–49 | 1350–99 | 1400–49 | 1200–1449 | 1200–49 | 1250–99 | 1300–49 | 1350–99 | 1400–49 | 1200–1449 |
| 1. Nailsbourne* | — | 3·07 | 4·33 | 4·58 | 4·31 | 4·10 | — | 3·55 | 4·86 | 4·67 | 4·10 | 4·45 | — | 2·35 | 2·82 | 2·95 | 3·49 | 2·76 |
| 2. Downton* | 2·73 | 2·48 | 3·43 | 3·41 | 3·29 | 3·01 | 4·53 | 2·55 | 3·90 | 3·83 | 3·94 | 3·62 | 2·87 | 1·97 | 2·64 | 2·74 | 3·10 | 2·52 |
| 3. Witney | 2·94 | 2·80 | 3·01 | 3·27 | [2·63] | 2·97 | 4·40 | 3·86 | 4·25 | 3·32 | — | 3·78 | 2·29 | 2·19 | 2·06 | 2·31 | [3·04] | 2·18 |
| 4. Wargrave | [5·81] | 3·98 | 4·06 | 3·72 | [3·28] | 3·91 | [5·63] | 3·77 | 3·77 | 4·11 | [3·36] | 4·13 | [2·96] | 1·95 | 1·71 | 2·34 | — | 2·11 |
| 5. Wycombe | 3·74 | 2·91 | 3·04 | 3·78 | [2·51] | 3·33 | 4·69 | 3·53 | 2·94 | 4·20 | [4·06] | 3·95 | 3·23 | 2·17 | 2·13 | 2·88 | [2·65] | 2·49 |
| 6. Ecchinswell* | 5·67 | 4·50 | 4·46 | 4·90 | 6·10 | 4·98 | 4·45 | 4·10 | 3·54 | 4·22 | 5·00 | 4·27 | 3·12 | 2·32 | 2·25 | 3·01 | [4·33] | 2·81 |
| 7. Overton* | 3·69 | 4·24 | 3·66 | 3·55 | 4·33 | 3·85 | 4·15 | 3·59 | 3·24 | 3·93 | 4·61 | 3·87 | 2·57 | 2·47 | 2·07 | 2·80 | 3·38 | 2·52 |
| 8. Meon* | 5·19 | 4·44 | 5·26 | 5·25 | 4·66 | 5·00 | 3·89 | 3·56 | 3·47 | 3·42 | 3·89 | 3·59 | 3·05 | 2·53 | 2·43 | 2·86 | 3·63 | 2·71 |
| 9. Esher | | | | | | | 3·12 | 2·78 | 2·72 | 2·42 | — | 2·72 | 1·65 | 1·74 | 1·88 | 1·80 | — | 1·81 |
| *Mean of 5 manors | (4·14) | 3·75 | 4·23 | 4·34 | 4·54 | 4·19 | (4·28) | 3·47 | 3·80 | 4·01 | 4·31 | 3·96 | (2·92) | 2·33 | 2·44 | 2·87 | 3·59 | 2·66 |

#### C. Quarters of produce per acre

| | Wheat | | | | | | Barley | | | | | | Oats | | | | | |
|---|---|---|---|---|---|---|---|---|---|---|---|---|---|---|---|---|---|---|
| | 1200–49 | 1250–99 | 1300–49 | 1350–99 | 1400–49 | 1200–1449 | 1200–49 | 1250–99 | 1300–49 | 1350–99 | 1400–49 | 1200–1449 | 1200–49 | 1250–99 | 1300–49 | 1350–99 | 1400–49 | 1200–1449 |
| 1. Nailsbourne* | — | 0·75 | 0·98 | 0·87 | 0·81 | 0·89 | — | 1·07 | 2·02 | 1·77 | 1·68 | 1·66 | — | 1·13 | 1·30 | 1·11 | 1·31 | 1·21 |
| 2. Downton* | 0·90 | 0·77 | 1·10 | 1·07 | 1·02 | 0·96 | 2·07 | 1·02 | 1·96 | 1·91 | 1·97 | 1·68 | 1·48 | 0·99 | 1·31 | 1·38 | 1·55 | 1·27 |
| 3. Witney | 0·77 | 1·04 | 0·98 | 0·97 | [0·76] | 0·96 | 1·58 | 1·91 | 1·92 | 1·66 | — | 1·76 | 1·37 | 1·57 | 1·12 | 1·17 | [1·75] | 1·33 |
| 4. Wargrave | [2·09] | 1·49 | 1·53 | 1·42 | [1·21] | 1·48 | [2·71] | 1·81 | 2·12 | 2·04 | [1·68] | 2·04 | [1·92] | 1·29 | 1·06 | 1·44 | [1·33] | 1·34 |
| 5. Wycombe | 1·41 | 1·09 | 1·04 | 1·18 | [0·79] | 1·16 | 2·30 | 1·76 | 1·46 | 2·11 | [2·03] | 1·98 | 1·97 | 1·62 | 1·23 | 1·52 | [2·14] | 1·53 |
| 6. Ecchinswell* | 1·23 | 1·18 | 1·24 | 1·49 | 1·69 | 1·37 | 1·75 | 1·64 | 1·56 | 1·98 | 2·49 | 1·94 | 1·37 | 1·17 | 1·12 | 1·52 | 1·69 | 1·38 |
| 7. Overton* | 1·15 | 1·34 | 1·04 | 1·08 | 1·13 | 1·13 | 1·65 | 1·75 | 1·43 | 1·92 | 2·29 | 1·83 | 1·38 | 1·55 | 1·06 | 1·40 | 1·69 | 1·38 |
| 8. Meon* | 1·17 | 1·67 | 1·52 | 1·33 | 1·16 | 1·38 | 1·40 | 2·46 | 1·78 | 1·72 | 1·94 | 1·82 | 1·53 | 1·70 | 1·28 | 1·44 | 1·81 | 1·50 |
| 9. Esher | | | | | | | 1·50 | 1·38 | 1·32 | 1·21 | — | 1·34 | 0·83 | 0·87 | 0·96 | 0·92 | — | 0·92 |
| *Mean of 5 manors | (1·02) | 1·14 | 1·18 | 1·17 | 1·16 | 1·15 | (1·59) | 1·75 | 1·86 | 1·86 | 2·07 | 1·79 | (1·40) | 1·31 | 1·21 | 1·37 | 1·70 | 1·35 |

general change of level.[4]   In one particular manor—Ecchinswell—there seems to be an upward tendency; in another—Meon—there seems to be a downward tendency.   The general impression is one of stability and stagnation.   There is little sign either of material advance in agricultural methods or of that declining fertility of the soil which some writers have discovered in the later Middle Ages.

The result suggests inquiry as to when and how the threefold increase in the productivity of seed between medieval and modern times took place.   The material for answering that question, not on generalisations as to yield at various dates by agricultural writers, but from actual farming records, has not yet been discovered and is probably not to any large extent in existence.   Some farming records scattered through the centuries between the fifteenth and the nineteenth there must be, and search for them might be repaid.   The difficulty would be to get enough of them to be sure that they presented a fair picture; since the Winchester Rolls ended, the farmer who kept accounts has not been typical. Two seventeenth-century accounts examined for me by Dr Hall yield interesting but discrepant results.   One account,[5] kindly communicated by Captain Loder Symonds, R.N., gives for the nine years 1612 to 1620 a yield of 11·83 quarters of wheat and 7·14 quarters of barley for each quarter of seed used; in the best year the wheat yield was more than twentyfold.   These results clearly represent exceptionally good farming; wheat is just above the modern figure.   Another account, apparently for newly enclosed woodlands at Peckham, covers three or four years only between 1639 and 1651.   The yield of wheat per quarter of seed ranges from 3·90 quarters to 5·55, and per acre from 1·46 quarters to 1·83; the advance on medieval times is much less.

All the figures given above are averages taking in many years together. They are based on separate figures for single years which it is proposed to publish later.   Meanwhile it may be stated that the yearly figures show, as might be expected, a marked variation of yield according to harvest conditions. and that their movement shows a strong negative correlation with the movement of prices.   Analysis of the yearly figures should yield interesting comparisons as to the range of variation from good to bad harvests in medieval and modern times respectively.

The present article is concerned primarily with the yield of corn. Detailed examination of prices would not be worthwhile in view of the fuller information now in course of preparation.   Certain figures, however, may be worth giving, even at this stage, and are set out in Tables IV and V.

[4] This statement brings in the first half-century for which no satisfactory mean figure can be given for comparison with the other half-centuries.   From 1200-49 to 1250-99 four of the manors show a decline and three an increase of yield per acre.   Looking at all three crops the hundred years from 1250 to 1349 appear as a period of markedly low productivity of seed, a fact which may perhaps be evidence of exceptional climatic stress.

[5] For Wargrave in Berkshire.

The first of these tables shows, for successive half-centuries from 1200 to 1450, the average prices of grain, livestock, wool and salt as derived from the records of the nine Winchester Manors and from Thorold Rogers. The second table represents some of the same prices as index-

## TABLE IV

### Prices of Commodities 1200 to 1450 (in shillings)

| Commodity | Unit | 1200–49 | 1250–99 | 1300–49 | 1350–99 | 1400–49 | 1200–1449 [6] |
|---|---|---|---|---|---|---|---|
| | | Nine Winchester manors | | | | | |
| Wheat | Qr. | 4·01 | 5·52 | 6·33 | 6·89 | 6·34 | 6·05 |
| Barley | ,, | 2·66 | 3·88 | 4·48 | 4·59 | 3·74 | 4·05 |
| Rye | ,, | 3·68 | 4·68 | 5·29 | 5·34 | — | 4·87 |
| Oats | ,, | 1·60 | 2·35 | 2·63 | 2·72 | 2·05 | 2·36 |
| Salt | ,, | 1·87 | 2·60 | 3·62 | 6·05 | 4·68 | 4·11 |
| Wool (Great)[1] | Clove | 1·42 | 1·86 | 2·31 | 1·85 | 2·04 | 1·92 |
| ,, (Lambs)[2] | ,, | 1·10 | 1·55 | 1·99 | 1·38 | 1·20 | 1·43 |
| Oxen | Each | 7·97 | 10·46 | 13·30 | 14·92 | 14·19 | 12·76 |
| Cows | ,, | 7·05 | 8·55 | 9·18 | 10·40 | 9·02 | 9·24 |
| Sheep (Muttons) | ,, | 1·15 | 1·33 | 1·32 | 1·79 | 1·71 | 1·53 |
| Ewes | ,, | 1·04 | 1·13 | 1·21 | 1·49 | 1·35 | 1·28 |
| Hoggasters | ,, | 0·64 | 1·01 | 1·24 | 1·47 | 1·37 | 1·28 |
| Lambs | ,, | 0·28 | 0·58 | 0·70 | 0·90 | 0·93 | 0·81 |
| Rams | ,, | — | 1·27 | 1·64 | 1·83 | 2·08 | 1·75 |
| | | Rogers' general averages | | | | | |
| Wheat | Qr. | | 5·35 | 6·01 | 6·13 | 5·77 | 5·83 |
| Barley | ,, | | 3·91 | 4·25 | 4·08 | 3·67 | 3·97 |
| Rye | ,, | | 4·39 | 4·60 | 4·24 | 4·07 | 4·32 |
| Oats | ,, | | 2·19 | 2·48 | 2·61 | 2·17 | 2·37 |
| Salt | ,, | | 2·77 | 3·87 | 6·40 | 4·82 | 4·55 |
| Wool [3] | Clove | | 2·14 | 2·14 | 2·11 | 1·77 | 2·03 |
| Oxen | Each | | 10·75 | 13·05 | 14·87 | 18·45 [4] | 14·44 [4] |
| Cows [5] | ,, | | 7·43 | 9·94 | 10·62 | — | 9·55 |
| Sheep (Muttons) | ,, | | 1·68 | 1·92 | 2·06 | 2·11 | 1·97 |

[1] Rarely more than one entry in a year after 1325.
[2] Before 1375 very few entries each year.
[3] Great wool to 1401, mixed thereafter.
[4] 1400-49—"Highest price".
[5] "Highest prices of." This is the only set which runs through the two volumes of Rogers.
[6] Rogers' figures are for 1259-1449.

numbers on the basis: Mean of 1300-49 = 100; in this table the Winchester Manor prices (W) are given in roman type and Rogers' prices (R) are given just below in italics. Wool and livestock other than oxen and sheep are omitted from this table, as the material is less satisfactory than for the articles. On the other hand, there is added an index-number based on Roger's figures for a number of articles not of an agricultural character.[6] Table V presents several suggestive results which may be briefly indicated.

First, there is a satisfactory general agreement between Rogers' figures and mine, though the material used is entirely different. The mean of the former as given at the foot of the table runs 87, 100, 112, 99, and that of the latter 86, 100, 119, 104; the last figures in each list would be closer together if it had not been necessary to omit rye from my figures and oxen from Rogers'. The correspondence is closest where the material is best—as for wheat, barley, oats, oxen and salt. The most

### TABLE V

### *Index Numbers of Prices, 1200 to 1450*

#### (Mean of 1300-49 = 100)

|  |  |  | 1200–49 | 1250–99 | 1300–49 | 1350–99 | 1400–49 |
|---|---|---|---|---|---|---|---|
| Wheat . . | { | W | 63 | 87 | 100 | 109 | 100 |
|  | { | R | — | 89 | 100 | 102 | 96 |
| Barley . . . | { | W | 59 | 87 | 100 | 102 | 83 |
|  | { | R | — | 92 | 100 | 96 | 86 |
| Oats . . . | { | W | 61 | 89 | 100 | 103 | 78 |
|  | { | R | — | 88 | 100 | 105 | 87 |
| Rye . . . | { | W | 70 | 88 | 100 | 101 | — |
|  | { | R | — | 95 | 100 | 92 | 88 |
| Oxen . . . | { | W | 60 | 79 | 100 | 112 | 107 |
|  | { | R | — | 82 | 100 | 114 | — |
| Sheep . . . | { | W | 87 | 101 | 100 | 136 | 130 |
|  | { | R | — | 88 | 100 | 107 | 110 |
| Salt . . . | { | W | 52 | 72 | 100 | 167 | 129 |
|  | { | R | — | 72 | 100 | 165 | 125 |
| Mean of above articles . . | { | W | 65 | 86 | 100 | 119 | 104 |
|  | { | R | — | 87 | 100 | 112 | 99 |
| Other articles . | | R | — | 84 | 100 | 177 | 174 |

W = Mean of nine Winchester manors; R = Rogers.
For sheep, Rogers' prices are the "highest prices".

striking case is that of salt, where the abnormal rise in the half-century after the Black Death and the decline thereafter are recorded in all but identical figures.

Second, there is a rapid rise of prices between the first two periods taken, that is to say, from the first half to the second half of the thirteenth century. This is only the slackening end of a movement which other figures show beginning about the middle of the twelfth century and which, when fully examined, may prove to have been one of the most violent price revolutions in English history, comparable in speed to the revolution of the sixteenth century, though not having equal social

[6] Lime, laths, plain tiles, wrought iron, canvas, cloth, board nails, lath nails, shirting, candles, slates, charcoal, paper (the last five only after 1400, the first eight throughout the period 1260-1450).

and economic consequences.[7]   The mean figures show a further increase
at a slower rate from the second to the third and from the third to
the fourth of the periods taken, and a decline to the last (1400-49).   But
whereas the movements up to 1300-49 are much the same for all the
articles, those after it are divergent.   The use of the mean is dangerous;
still more is the use of the price of any one article as a guide to the
general purchasing power of money.

This is the third and most important point to be made.   Comparisons
of money wages with the price of wheat have led to the building up of a
theory of a "golden age" for the labourer in the fifteenth century,
between the rapid rise of wages following the Black Death and the rise
of prices following the discovery of America.   A well-known and impressive chart in Steffen's *Studien zur Geschichte der Englischen Lohnarbeiter* [8] shows the labourer's daily wage in terms of wheat rising swiftly
from the first half of the fourteenth century, and between 1450 and 1500
ranging at heights never approached again till the last quarter of the
nineteenth century.   Steffen's chart, coupled with the evidence now
adduced as to the unchanged productivity of agriculture at least up to
1450, might even be taken as a great historic illustration of Malthusian
truths.   Might it not appear as if, after the Black Death had bene-
ficently halved the population, the standard of real wages, though there
was no increase of technical skill, rose rapidly, that there were then two
or three happy generations, but that, alas! they generated too freely, so
that, even before the great rise of prices in the sixteenth century, real
wages began to fall headlong till they reached starvation level about
1600, and stayed at or little above it till about 1830.

Serious examination of this or other theories of the "golden age" is
beyond the scope of this article, and must wait on fuller information.
All that can be done here is to call attention to the discrepant movements of the prices of different articles in the later part of Table V, that
is to say after the Black Death.   Wheat, on the average of half-centuries,
remains near the general level of 1300-49; the other grains—barley, oats
and rye—show a decline; wool also, though the figures need further
examination, almost certainly shows a decline.   On the other hand, salt
and livestock of all kinds (except cows) are more costly in the first half
of the fifteenth than in the first half of the fourteenth century.   So,
most markedly, are the non-agricultural articles from Rogers' work
included in the last row of Table V.   How closely the prices for these
articles at different times are comparable with one another, *i.e.* how far
they represent equivalent articles, it is impossible without further investigation to say.   But the rise of 77 per cent shown from the first half to

---

[7] Preliminary results suggest that the prices of wheat and livestock of all kinds
doubled or trebled in fifty years from the third quarter of the twelfth to the first quarter
of the thirteenth century.
[8] I, 112 of the German edition of 1901.

the second half of the fourteenth century is so great that it can hardly be unreal.

With figures such as these, the movements of any general index-number of prices will depend very much upon the weights assigned to different articles. The construction of such an index-number must wait till more and better material has been made available, and the actual turning-points in price movements need to be examined more closely than by half-centuries. The present figures of price are put forward to serve mainly a negative and warning purpose.

### NOTES ON MATERIAL AND TABLES

Apart from the causes of occasional error noted later, the two main difficulties in interpreting the material arise from (a) variations in the mode of reckoning the acreage and (b) the entries of charges *super compotum*.

Acres in the accounts are reckoned either " by the perch ", representing apparently a true measurement of the land actually cultivated, or " as they lie ", representing apparently an estimate in which might be included all the land wasted as balks, grass patches, field roads and the like under the open-field system. In two of the manors (Wargrave and Wycombe) the acres are expressly given by the perch throughout, and in two others (Downton and Esher) they clearly are so reckoned throughout though it is not always expressly stated. In Nailsbourne the reckoning, though never expressly defined, is obviously on the same basis throughout, and has been taken as a measurement by the perch; it is possible but not likely that this is wrong and that the error accounts for the low seed and yield per acre. In the other four manors the method of reckoning varies, being sometimes " by the perch " and sometimes " as they lie ". Fortunately the giving of the seed used makes it possible to control this, and by a very simple calculation to get back in practically every case with reasonable accuracy to the true acreage. The seed used for any given area does not vary rapidly from one year to the next. The reckoning of acres " as they lie " is practically confined to years between 1283 and 1318 and to the three Hampshire manors and Witney. For Ecchinswell from 1283 to 1318, Overton 1302 to 1318, Meon 1302 to 1318 and Witney 1306 to 1318, the nominal acreage " as they lie " has been re-calculated by reference to the seed used.[9]

The entries of charges *super compotum* relate to an interesting procedure, under which the Bishop's auditors apparently fixed the rate of

---

[9] For some other years, *e.g.* Witney 1299 to 1305, 1367 to 1388, and Overton 1291 to 1301, the acres are given " as they lie ", or " as they lie in the fields ", but the seed figures show that the calculation was substantially by the perch. It may be added that in most cases the correction has amounted roughly to halving the acres " as they lie ", though for wheat and oats at Meon the reduction is greater—to one-third. Halving corresponds well with an actual figure in a rental of 1458 found by Dr Hall, where the same area is 32 acres " by the perch " and 61 acres " as they lie ".

yield to be expected; the difference between the produce at that rate and the actual produce is entered, *plus* or *minus*, as something with which the bailiff is charged at the end of his account. The difference between the rated and the actual produce, whether *plus* or *minus*, is not as a rule great, and the latter has normally been used here as representing the achieved rather than the estimated results. Occasionally, however, the actual produce is much below the rated produce, and gives an impossible yield figure. In such cases it is clear that part of the actual produce must have been brought into account for special reasons (*e.g.* late returns or damage to crops by trespass), after the account was closed; the rated produce has been taken accordingly. The rates of yield set by the auditors furnish an interesting supplement to the other figures. They suggest, for instance, that the apparent increase in the productivity of Ecchinswell towards the end of the period was real and does not arise through error in the figures; the rates set, so far as they have been extracted, are definitely higher between 1400 and 1450 than before.

In addition the following minor difficulties occur:

1. Grain remaining from a previous year does not often occur, and if it does is noted, so that it does not enter into the produce of the current year. But in some cases at least it may have been brought in after the previous year's account was made up, and so may have been excluded wrongly from that year's produce.

2. The sowing of more than one variety of the same grain, *e.g.* winter and palm barley, or lesser and great oats, in the same manor in the same year sometimes causes uncertainty.

3. "Increment of the granary" is always about one-eighth of the other produce. Apparently heaped bushels went into the granary, and this is the difference between the heaped and the rased bushel. Such entries have been included throughout.

4. "Church seed", not being produce, has been excluded throughout.

5. Acreage sown for servants' allowances appears in the Downton and Witney accounts in certain periods. It has been excluded throughout, as the produce is entered always at an arbitrary low rate.

Generally the points mentioned above, while they have given much trouble in the preparation of the statistics and while they make it impossible absolutely to rely on the figures for each individual year, are not such as to throw doubt on the substantial accuracy of the main results.

The seed per acre for each manor both for the whole period and for the successive half-centuries has been got not as an average of annual figures, but by dividing total seed by total acreage, omitting years in which acres are reckoned "as they lie".

The yield per seed in each manor is got by dividing total produce by total seed for all years.

The yield per acre in each manor is got by dividing total produce by total acreage for all years (acres "as they lie" being reduced to correct acres by reference to the seed used in the years of correct acreage in the same period).

The means are the arithmetic means of eight or nine manors (Table II) or five manors (Table III).   For 1200-49 the mean of the five manors has been deduced from that for 1250-99 in the ratio of the means including and excluding Nailsbourne; it is shown in brackets in Table III.

The following notes apply to Table III.

Downton (for wheat 1306-1449) and Witney (for wheat 1325-1449) have been corrected by omitting acreage sown for servants.

Witney (for wheat and oats 1300-49), Ecchinswell (for all grains 1250-1349), Overton and Meon (for all grains 1300-49) have been corrected in " A. Quarters of seed used per acre " by excluding the years in which acres are reckoned " as they lie ", and in " C. Quarters of produce per acre " by deducing acreage for these years from seed used.

The bracketed figures for certain manors in certain periods are averages for less than ten years.

In Australia the seed used per acre in the decade 1905-14 averaged 0·938 bushel and the produce 10·22 bushels, an elevenfold yield.   For 1915-24 the productivity is nearly fourteenfold, with seed 0·921 bushel and produce 12·79 bushels per acre.

### Postscript—July 1953

In welcoming the republication of the article above, I should like to draw attention to the fact that it represents a very early stage of the investigations of Price History undertaken by Hubert Hall and myself and many others in collaboration.   The amount of first-rate new material that we discovered for medieval Price History was immense and gives every opportunity of comparing different series of prices and drawing general conclusions.   I have now deposited the bulk of this material in the Institute of Historical Research in London and I hope that in due course it will be worked over fully.

# ASSARTING AND THE GROWTH OF THE OPEN FIELDS [1]

## T. A. M. BISHOP

CENTRAL and eastern Yorkshire offers a uniquely suitable field for the study of certain problems of twelfth- and thirteenth-century agrarian history. The basin of the Ouse, as opposed to the moors of the west and north-east, forms part of the central and eastern English plain; and of the whole region treated in the classical accounts of medieval agrarian history it is, perhaps, the only part which has not been subjected to detailed study. There is a special affinity between the plain of Yorkshire and the region between Welland and Trent; [2] that the rural organisation of Yorkshire after the Conquest has not been studied in conjunction with that of the central Danelaw is due to an event which modified, temporarily or perhaps permanently, the development of the northern district. [3] The devastation of 1069, more extensive in some districts than in others, left about half the Yorkshire plain entirely waste in 1086, and had evidently affected many districts in which the Domesday commissioners found some surviving population. There can be no doubt of the intensity and lasting effects of the devastation. In many vills, seventeen years later, no population was recorded, and no income even from woods or rough pasture; over large parts of Yorkshire the cultivation of the soil was entirely suspended, perhaps for a generation or longer. [4] It is, therefore, reasonable to look for the mature post-Conquest development of Yorkshire at a somewhat later date than for that of the region illustrated by *Danelaw Charters*, and to place it in the thirteenth and perhaps the late twelfth century. The evidence for this period consists chiefly of some thousands of charters surviving in various forms; and with the methods of using charter material elaborated by Professor Stenton the reader must here be assumed to be familiar. I wish to use this material at present only in so far as it relates to the distribution and organisation of arable land. There should be something more than a local interest in relating the

[1] I am obliged to Professor Stenton for kindly reading and criticising this paper.

[2] F. M. Stenton, *Types of Manorial Structure in the Northern Danelaw*, 3, 4; *Danes in England*, 14.

[3] *Danelaw Charters*, ed. F. M. Stenton, Introduction, p. xiii.

[4] It may be argued that *vastum* did not mean wholly depopulated. But the fact that "waste" vills were seldom manorialised in the thirteenth century suggests that they did not contain, at the date of the Norman-French occupation, any population to be brought under manorial discipline.

agrarian institutions of thirteenth-century Yorkshire to those of the rest
of England.    Whatever agrarian system we find existing in thirteenth-
century Yorkshire, it will be one which had in many parts of the county
to be entirely created, or restored, after the Conquest, during a period
for which some documentary evidence survives; and we may learn, in a
study of this evidence, something of the process by which analogous
systems came into being elsewhere.

The majority of the villages in this district are shown in the one-inch
ordnance map to be of the nucleated type.   In nucleated villages, during
the medieval period, we expect to find the greater part of the arable land
lying in large open fields, divided into *culturæ* and subdivided into strips.
For particular forms of the open-field system in Yorkshire there is not,
perhaps, such overwhelming evidence as that which illustrates the two-
field system of the typical Lincolnshire village.[5]   The charters in which
we must study the post-Conquest institutions of Yorkshire are mostly of
the thirteenth century; and though, as Professor Stenton has pointed
out, the conveyancers of the thirteenth century were more careful than
their predecessors to attribute strips to the cultures in which they were
situated,[6] they usually omitted those ingenuous references to agricultural
routine which make earlier charters interesting and valuable.   Professor
Gray has collected, however, sufficient instances of field systems in the
Yorkshire plain to place it definitely within the open-field area;[7] references exist by which his lists could be greatly lengthened; and their
tendency is to show that among the wolds of the East Riding a two-field
system prevailed, while most villages in the vale of York lay under a
system of three great fields.   Direct references to some form of the open-
field system occur alike among villages continuously cultivated since
before the Conquest, and among villages which were devastated and
recolonised.   Throughout the district, moreover, charters describe land
as lying in strips and cultures, and show that some variety of the system
was everywhere normal.   There seem to be no instances from the thirteenth century of vills, fully illustrated by charter material, where the
main arable territory did not consist of open-field land.

It has been suggested that in twelfth-century Yorkshire tenements
were larger than in the central Danelaw.[8]   But much of the period which
is illustrated in *Early Yorkshire Charters*[9] must, I think, be regarded as
transitional; documents of the thirteenth century reveal a tenemental
system not unlike that of Lincolnshire.   In certain vills we find more or
less large manorial demesnes;[10] associated with them are groups of

    [5] *Danelaw Charters*, pp. xxx-xxxii.
    [6] *Ibid.* pp. xlvii, xlviii; *Gilbertine Charters*, ed. F. M. Stenton (Linc. Rec. Soc.),
Introduction, pp. xix, xxi.
    [7] H. L. Gray, *English Field Systems*, 504 *et seq.*
    [8] *Danelaw Charters*, pp. xiii, xxi.                    [9] Ed. W. Farrer, 3 vols.
    [10] Cf. *English Historical Review*, XLIX, 386.   My paper covered the area between
York and the Tees.

villein holdings, almost always measured in bovates, and usually of one or two bovates in size.[11] About half the vills in this district were not manorialised; and in those of them which are illustrated in charters we find large groups of freeholders[12] who are also present, in considerable numbers, in the non-manorialised parts of vills in which manors occur. It is important to notice the tenurial organisation of the free tenants in any one vill. They are not as a rule to be found holding at an equal degree from some external lord or soke; such groups may exhibit, on the contrary, a most complex system of feudation, culminating in some one inhabitant who is, in the feudal sense, " lord " of the vill.[13] The feudal organisation of these groups may, as I suggest below, reveal the process by which they were formed; it must be noted now as affecting the evidence for the size of tenements.[14] The amounts which charters attribute to free tenants may often be suspected of being fees or freeholds rather than holdings in actual economic occupation; and the danger of exaggerating the amount of land which a man possesses and cultivates is greatest in the case of the tenant whose fee is the whole vill, and to whom we should perhaps be inclined to ascribe a holding considerably larger than that of any of his tenants. Again, the amounts which are attributed to tenants in such feudal documents as Kirkby's Inquest are to be regarded as feudal rather than economic conceptions, representing, not the real area of holdings, but fractions of knight's fees. I therefore base the statement that tenements of one or two bovates were normal among freeholders in this district on the following considerations: (a) Holdings of one and two bovates prevail among the villeins; and, in

[11] For villein holdings c. 1250-1300 cf. Yorkshire Inquest, ed. W. Brown (Yorks. Arch. Soc.), pp. i-iv, passim. An extent, c. 1295, of the prebends of York Cathedral, describing thirty-six manors in southern and eastern Yorkshire, mentions 407 arable tenements in villenage, of which 87 per cent are of one or of two bovates. Tenements of one bovate prevail in three, and of two bovates in fifteen manors; in others they are equally prevalent. Brit. Mus. Cotton MS. Claud. B. iii, ff. 166 et seq.

[12] For the distribution of non-manorialised vills in the vale of York, cf. English Historical Review, XLIX, 399, 400.

[13] Thus Ernald of Dromonby, Adam of Cowton, William of Kirkby and Baldwin of Bramhope were lords of Dromonby, North Cowton, Kirkby Wiske and Dishforth c. 1180, 1200, 1210 and 1230. They may have possessed slightly larger holdings than other inhabitants in these vills, which were, however, fully taken up by their free tenants Chartulary of Fountains, ed. W. T. Lancaster, I, 280 et seq., 173 et seq., 380 et seq., 218 et seq. Note the complex tenurial arrangements among at least twenty-four free tenants in Dishforth c. 1225-50, in charters of that period forming the majority of groups of nearly two hundred deeds. Cf. Kirkby's Inquest, ed. R. H. Skaife (Surtees Soc.), 93 et seq., 148 et seq., 174 et seq., for some highly subinfeudated vills; but its account of feudation is often a summary one. Nearly all free tenants seem to hold by forinsec service.

[14] For the recognition of free tenements, cf. Danelaw Charters, pp. xix-xxi. The inter-relation of large numbers of contemporary charters dealing with single vills reveals more difficulties, in the use of charters as evidence for tenemental organisation, than appear in the study of comparatively isolated texts. Cf. the varying references to the holdings of Thomas son of Udard, and Richard son of Hugh, in Dishforth. Chartulary of Fountains, I, 218 et seq., passim.

partly manorialised vills, villein and free tenements must be supposed to have been subjected to the same agrarian routine. (*b*) In large groups of charters related to single vills, amounts of one and sometimes of two bovates recur as highest common factors of the amounts attributed to tenants. (*c*) Amounts of one or of two bovates form the majority of those which were accompanied by appurtenant tofts.[15] The symmetry which charters reveal among the holdings in non-manorialised vills is also shown in the evidence of the Lay Subsidy of 1301; evidence which suggests, moreover, that few inhabitants of such vills did not possess full arable holdings.[16] Large groups of one and two bovate tenements are found in vills which are not mentioned in Domesday, and which were presumably first settled after the Conquest.[17] In nearly all villages in the plain of Yorkshire for which there is any considerable amount of charter evidence, we find, in the thirteenth century, a normal tenement of one or two bovates; in all of them we find the bovate used as a measure of the majority of tenements. A tenemental system based on the bovate is thus co-extensive in this district with an open-field system of cultivation; we may therefore fairly assume that, like the bovates and virgates of the central English plain, the bovate in Yorkshire consisted, as to its main arable land, of a bundle of strips in the open fields.[18]

Thus by the thirteenth century there had been restored, in Yorkshire, a rural organisation resembling that which had survived the Conquest in the central Danelaw. In both districts a characteristic tenement of one or two bovates was made up of strips in open fields; the two-field system of the Yorkshire wolds matches that of the very similar country south of the Humber; and if it is true that the three-field system was merely a variant from that of two open fields,[19] there is nothing remarkable in the prevalence of the more complex routine in the fertile vale of York. That the settlers who recolonised a large part of Yorkshire tended to revert to tradition is further shown by the fact that they did not found many new villages, or create a new type of village settlement considerably larger or smaller than had existed before the Conquest.[20] To show how the bovates and open fields of Yorkshire were created might throw light on the development of arable organisation in large districts and remoter

[15] Cf. *Danelaw Charters*, pp. xxxv, xxxvi.

[16] Cf. *English Historical Review*, XLIX, 391, 399, 400. J. F. Willard, *Parliamentary Taxes on Personal Property, 1290-1334*, 175, points out that though there were no exemptions from this subsidy, in certain parts of Yorkshire few low payments occur; and he suggests that a large number of poor inhabitants escaped taxation. But the all-round level of payments in these districts was very high.

[17] Cf. Greenbury, *Chartulary of Fountains*, I, 330 *et seq.*

[18] Gray, *op cit.* 29, 40, 41, points out the connection of open field systems with such regular tenemental units as the bovate or virgate.

[19] Gray, *op cit.* 31, 72, 73, 81.

[20] Few thirteenth-century vills are not named, and fewer not identifiable, in Domesday. A. H. Smith, *Place Names of the North Riding* (English Place Name Soc.); " Domesday Book for Yorkshire ", ed. and trans. W. Farrer, *V.C.H.* For the disappearance of certain vills and the obliteration of boundaries the Cistercians were responsible.

periods than those with which we are immediately concerned. Now for a period of two or three generations after the devastation, during which the foundations of arable organisation in Yorkshire may be supposed to have been laid, there is, unfortunately, little evidence; charters showing the distribution of arable land among cultivators do not begin to be frequent until late in the twelfth century, when the subsequent character of this distribution was already well marked. For many generations after the devastation, however, Yorkshire must have remained thinly populated; there was plenty room for expansion; and we can observe the clearing of new land going on throughout the thirteenth century. I wish here to describe the clearing which was carried on among groups of free tenants, to whom may be ascribed a comparatively unrestricted power of reclaiming the waste, and who were in any case the normal inheritors of the devastated parts of Yorkshire. Since such groups existed in greater or less numbers in nearly every Yorkshire vill, there is no need to confine the inquiry to wholly non-manorialised vills. It may be that the clearings of free tenants, in the thirteenth century, involved a gradual departure from the system of open fields and bovates described above; it is possible that a study of them will show how the system was created and maintained.[21]

It has been shown that by the thirteenth century the open-field system was fully established in this district; accordingly, within every vill in which we can observe clearing in progress during this period, the assarts are centred upon the subsidiary to a core of open-field land. Thus a grant of one-third of the vill of Sowerby carries with it one-third of the assarts appurtenant to the vill.[22] Twenty acres of land in Bramley are said to lie in *pertinenciis de Bramlei in essartis*.[23] Land to be assarted is limited and assigned by arrangements between feudatories on behalf of themselves and their tenants;[24] and assarting, carried on by groups of cultivators, often seems to be a communal activity tending

[21] Variously spelt terms and terminations denoting assarted land include: *assartum, brek, broc, brote, intake, newbigging, ovenama, ridding, rode*; the last, as Mr Clay points out, *Yorkshire Deeds* (Yorks. Arch. Soc.), V, 6 n., has often no connection with the lineal and superficial measure. Farrer, *Early Yorkshire Charters*, II, vii, suggests that *cultura* usually refers to newly improved land; and this seems to be so when tenements are described as consisting both of bovates and *culturæ*. *Flat* seems to be sometimes used of a severally cultivated assart; thus the demesne of Barmby included six bovates, and *tres flattos* not apparently organised within the open fields. Cotton MS. Claud, B. iii, f. 179. *Butt, headland, gare*, must sometimes be understood as referring to land newly brought into cultivation. For *tofts* and *crofts* as severally cultivated assart land, *cf. infra*, 32. Note that, while charters may locate land in various ways, in the majority of cases quoted and referred to below land is said to lie " in ", " at " or " on " the place to which it is assigned. [22] Bodleian Library MS. Dodsworth vii, f. 139.
[23] *Kirkstall Coucher*, ed. W. T. Lancaster and W. P. Baildon (Thoresby Soc.), 259. Land in Hutton Colswayn is described as lying in the *broces de hoton'*. Cotton MS. Claud. D. xi, f. 71.
[24] *Cf. Chartulary of Bridlington*, ed. W. T. Lancaster, 102; *Early Yorkshire Charters*, I, 380: *Chartulary of Fountains*, II, 815, 816, 826, 833; Bodleian Library MS. Fairfax ix, f. 36; Brit. Mus. Egerton MS. 2827, f. 18.

to the enlargement of the common fields. An Everley deed of *c.* 1200 refers to the grantor's share in the newly assarted land; a tenant in Shipton holds a share of the "intake"; a tenant in Burton Leonard holds land in the new assart.[25] So it is often difficult to make any distinction between assarted and open-field land; much of what is described as assart land appears to be simply open-field land which has been comparatively recently brought into cultivation. Thus there was a *Ridding* and a *Neubigging* in the west field of Bramham, and a culture called *Rodes* in each of the three fields of this vill.[26] Several Hutton Rudby charters (*c.* 1220) ascribe land to three main fields called South Field, Middle Field, and *Northbrockes*; and the last seems to be a third field created, by comparatively recent clearing, in a vill formerly organised under the two-field system.[27] Besides such examples of clearing proceeding in a particular quarter of a vill, we may observe widely scattered clearings made between and at the heads of existing cultures, and giving rise to new cultures—the headlands and gares so often mentioned in charters.[28] A Kirkleatham charter of *c.* 1200 refers to three acres of newly improved land *super buttas*; and *c.* 1213 tenants in Easby came to an arrangement about assarting between their cultures.[29] In every vill, moreover, for which we possess any considerable body of charter evidence, very large numbers of culture names are recorded; the names of no fewer than one hundred and sixty cultures in the fields of Barton occur in the charters and extent of this small vill, and many of them cannot have contained more than a few acres.[30] Thus the open-field system of the

[25] *Yorkshire Deeds*, V, 42; Dean and Chapter Library, York, Register of St Mary's Abbey, f. 115; Bodleian Library MS. Rawlinson B. 455, f. 18. *Cf. Chartulary of Fountains*, II, 636 (grantor's land in an assart in Skipton); *Ibid.* II, 522 (shares in assarts in Marston); *Kirkstall Coucher*, 92 (shares of two tenants in an assart in Stubhouse). The bondmen of Stillington, besides their bovates, held in common four arable tracts called *Riding, pitflatte, clausum paytesyn* and *drescenape.* Cotton MS. Claud. B. iii, f. 188. Possibly they co-operated in cultivating them, and shared the produce.

[26] Cotton MS. Vesp. E. xvii, ff. 82, 83, 89, 152, 153, 159-61. *Cf.* a grant in Shipton of *quandam terram in Intak, quantam* (sic) *pertinet ad unam bovatam terre in illa cultura*, Register of St Mary's f. 115. *Smalebrot* was a late twelfth-century field name in Broughton; *Brokes* and *Stanbreck* occur in the open fields of Hutton Rudby, *c.* 1220; *Old Dreches, New Dreches* on the demesne of East Cowton in 1241; *Drechte* and *Hangbreck* in the fields of Barton in 1309. *Chartulary of Rievaulx*, ed. C. T. Atkinson (Surtees Soc.), 76, 77; *Calendar of Charter Rolls, 1300-1326*, 145; *Yorkshire Fines, 1232-1246*, ed. J. Parker (Yorks. Arch. Soc.), 104; "Extent of Barton", *Yorkshire Archaeological Journal*, XXXII, 91, 95.

[27] *Calendar of Charter Rolls, 1300-1326*, 145. Gray, *op. cit.* 72, 81, supposes such a progress from the two- to the three-field system.

[28] *Cf.* a grant in Hudswell of *omnia vasta mea arata et non arata in les brokes, sicut iacent per particulas in territorio de Hodeswel.* Egerton MS. 2827, f. 220. For cultivated headlands and gares in the fields of Barton, *cf. Yorkshire Archaeological Journal*, XXXII, 91, *et seq.*

[29] *Early Yorkshire Charters*, II, 69; Egerton MS. 2827, f. 18. *Neuchiftdales* was the name of certain arable land abutting on a culture in the fields of Bramham. Cotton MS. Vesp. E. xvii, ff. 160, 161.

[30] Egerton MS. 2827, ff. 63-84, 328-30.; Cotton MS. Claud. B. iii, ff. 55, 109, 116, 117; *Yorkshire Archaeological Journal*, XXXII, 86.

typical Yorkshire vill has not the appearance of having simply survived
from some period when it was created by a large group of settlers; it
seems, on the contrary, to be the result of successive accretions of freshly
cleared land, and to have expanded with the expanding numbers of the
village community.[31]

But though the open fields of this district were undoubtedly being
continuously enlarged during the late twelfth and thirteenth centuries,
by much of the clearing which was going on during this period there
seems to have been created a certain amount of severally cultivated land.
Some Ribston charters refer to land known as the great assart;[32] this
was not simply a newly created part of the open fields, nor was it a tract
held by some less stable form of communal ownership;[33] it seems, on
the contrary, to have consisted of a number of distinct plots held, or at
any rate made, by individual cultivators.[34] Examples of assarts of
which shares were held by numbers of tenants are less frequent, on the
whole, than instances of clearings held by individuals; indeed, by the
majority of references to *unum* or *quoddam assartum* we are to understand a plot of perhaps three or four acres cultivated by a single tenant.[35]
The names of such plots are often prefixed by personal names.  Roger
de Triberg held an assart in Hooton Pagnell called *Tribergridding*.[36]  A
tenant in Sproxton inherited, from one Siwine, asserted land called
*Siwinesriding*.[37]  Now a distinction must be made between an assart
which may simply be a newly created part of the open fields, and a plot
which is described as an assart and held by an individual tenant; and
the latter can hardly have formed part of the open-field system.  With
such individually cultivated assarts may be compared a very similar
form of severally cultivated arable land; I refer to the tofts and crofts,
freqently mentioned in charters, which seem to have consisted, not of
cottages and the enclosures around them,[38] but simply of enclosed plots
of arable land.  Thus the demesne of the manor of Ampleforth included
four acres of arable land in a croft.[39]  Land in Brandesburton is indifferently referred to, in a thirteenth-century deed, as a toft and as a
close.[40]  *Westcroft, Neucroft, Kirkcroft* are names of arable closes

[31] Farrer, *Early Yorkshire Charters*, II, vii, outlines this process.
[32] MS. Rawlinson B. 455, ff. 98, 99.
[33] Such as the plots in Stillington mentioned *supra*, 31 n. 25.
[34] Among them were *Thoriridding, Ulkilridding, Raufridding*; the personal names
suggest that these plots were made and tilled by individual tenants.
[35] *Cf. infra*, 37 n. 68 for examples.
[36] Brit. Mus. Add. Ch. 21268.
[37] *Chartulary of Rievaulx*, 292. *Baldwynrode* in Dishforth was probably made by
Baldwin (1) de Irton, a twelfth-century tenant. *Chartulary of Fountains*, I, 234, 253. *Cf.*
such assart-names as *Swainesridding, Walthefridding, Laisingrode, Kelkirode. Ibid.* I,
27; II, 680; *Early Yorkshire Charters*, I, 383.
[38] For tofts and crofts, *cf. infra*, 33 n. 43.
[39] Cotton MS. Claud. B. iii, f. 181.
[40] *Yorkshire Deeds*, I, 36. Bodleian Library MS. ch. Yorks. 47 records a demise
(1197) by Ralph Atwell of four acres of arable land *in medio crofto suo*; this does not

mentioned in charters of our period;[41] and in such examples as *Gamels-croft* and *Stevincroft* the names of individual tenants are involved in the designations of isolated plots and closes.[42] Between severally cultivated assarts and closes of arable land little distinction can be made;[43] both seem to result from clearing undertaken by individuals, and not directly tending to the enlargement of the open-field land. Did such clearings form an accumulating amount of arable land permanently outside the open fields?[44]

The disadvantages of open-field cultivation suggest that it would not be spontaneously adopted by farmers who could dispose of something more than their own labour. Cistercian monasteries, with their large staffs of *conversi*, preferred directly to reclaim some of the fertile but uninhabited tracts which existed in twelfth-century Yorkshire, and to cultivate them in severalty. The manorial demesnes which were re-created in Yorkshire after the Conquest were normally restricted to vills in which some population existed in 1086; many of these vills, however, were only sparsely populated at the end of the eleventh century; and the opportunity of bringing waste land into cultivation seems to have allowed the lords to create partly consolidated demesnes.[45] But with tenants dependent on their own labour it may be doubted whether the disadvantages would outweigh the advantages of communal methods of agriculture; and there is, besides, no evidence of any such customary or fiscal conditions attaching to assarts as would tend, while promoting fresh clearing, to keep assarted land permanently distinct

---

seem to be the enclosure round his cottage, since land in the fields was later to be substituted for it. Brit. Mus. Topham ch. 16 refers to the right of common in a croft in Hooton Pagnell which Henry le Templer held. An enclosure round a cottage could hardly be subject to common rights.

[41] *Chartulary of Bridlington*, 275, 338; *Early Yorkshire Charters*, I, 55. A partly enclosed culture in Potter Brompton was called *Caluecroft*. *Chartulary of Bridlington*, 143. There was a close in Hovingham called *Humecroft*. *Pedes Finium Ebor. Regnante Johanne* (Surtees Soc.), 65.

[42] MS. Dodsworth xci, f. 96; *Yorkshire Deeds*, I, 9. Cf. *Pincuncroft* in Pinching-thorpe, *Chartulary of Guisborough*, ed. W. Brown (Surtees Soc.), I, 222.

[43] For cases in which the terms toft, croft, close and assart seem to be used indifferently, cf. *Early Yorkshire Charters*, I, 388; MS. Fairfax ix, f. 92; *Yorkshire Deeds*, I, 9; *Chartularies of Monk Bretton*, ed. J. W. Walker (Yorks. Arch. Soc.), 18. Five acres of land in Crambe are described as lying in tofts outside the vill. *Early Yorkshire Charters*. I, 449. A close in Hertburn was called *Hutland*. MS. Fairfax ix, f. 91.

[44] Describing similar assarting in Lincolnshire, Professor Stenton writes: "There is no doubt that these assarts were all intended for several cultivation, and that a considerable step towards the establishment of individualistic husbandry was taken in this way". *Danelaw Charters*, xlii.

[45] Demesne in East Cowton in 1241, consisting chiefly of small and widely scattered strips, included blocks of ten and fourteen acres. *Pedes Finium Ebor*, 104. The demesne of Thrintoft, c. 1295, consisted of a block of forty-one acres and a large number of small strips. *Yorkshire Deeds*, V, 169. The demesne of Ampleforth included a hundred acres in a severally tilled assart. Cotton MS. Claud. B. iii, f. 181. For the origin of some wholly consolidated manorial demesnes, cf. *English Historical Review*, XLIX, 405.

from the open fields.[46] Now it must often happen that names record a state of things which no longer exists. There can be no doubt, for instance, that the terms toft and croft properly refer to forms of en-closure;[47] nevertheless they are often applied to cultures in the open fields. *Toftes* is a common open-field name;[48] four selions lie in a toft in Edenham, six selions in a croft in Marston;[49] *Oxintoftes, Brunetoftes, Barliccroft, Rucroft* are among innumerable examples of the termina-tions -toft and -croft combined in the names of open-field cultures.[50] We have seen that these terminations were often combined with personal names; but *Oretoftes* and *Levenadtoftes* in Ormesby, *Ketelcroft* and *Ulkilcroft* in Deighton and Hudswell refer, not to closes held by indi-viduals, but to cultures containing the strips of numbers of tenants.[51] Again, terms and terminations denoting assarted land, and combined with personal names, frequently indicate not individually held clearings, but cultures in the open fields. Thus in the open fields of Bramhope we find land described as lying in Hugh's assart, *Wimunderidding* and the assart called *Neuintak* formerly held by Henry Northiby.[52] *Wluerik-ridding, Holbernrode, Dunlangabrotes* were field names in Kirkby Knowle, Darthington and Broughton.[53] These names suggest that much of the land afterwards incorporated in the open fields was originally cleared and cultivated by individuals. With such field names may be compared those in which other terminations denoting arable land are combined with personal names. At least three tenants held (1279) land in *Bernolfflat* in the fields of Wombleton; *Osmundflat* and *Edricflat* were field names in North Cowton; *Lefsiflat, Wymundeker, Arkilland* are types of culture names occurring everywhere in the open fields of this district.[54] In some villages field names preserve the names of men who can be identified as early tenants; thus tenants in Balderby cultivated

[46] Farrer, *Early Yorkshire Charters*, II, vii, points out that the clearing of land was not accompanied by a proportionate increase in feudal burdens. Thus *c.* 1170 Agnes Paynel granted, for the forinsec service of half a carucate, four bovates in Bramham together with forty acres *ad exsartandum. Ibid.* II, 345. *Cf.* Cotton MS. Claud. D. xi, f. 89; *Chartulary of Fountains*, I, 12.

[47] On the normal employment of these terms, *cf. Danelaw Charters*, xxxv; D. C. Douglas, *Medieval East Anglia*, 32, 33; *Huntingdon Feet of Fines*, ed. G. J. Turner, lvii.

[48] *Cf.* Egerton MS. 2827, ff. 10, 11, 20, 97; *Yorkshire Deeds*, V, 42, 53, 169; VI, 46; *Chartulary of Fountains*, I, 92; *Pedes Finium Ebor*, 108, 138.

[49] *Chartulary of Bridlington*, 401 (*cf.* 67, 130); *Chartulary of Fountains*, II, 534 (*cf.* I, 317, 423). *Cf. Yorkshire Deeds*, II, 78. Bovate tenements in Cave had appurtenant roods in *magno crofto. Pedes Finium Ebor*, 73.

[50] *Chartulary of Guisborough*, I, 261; *Chartulary of Fountains*, II, 859 (*cf.* I, 317, 423; II, 787, 843-59); *Chartulary of Bridlington*, 379, 418 (*cf.* 317, 352, 382). *Cf.* MS. Fairfax ix, ff. 12, 59, 66.

[51] *Chartulary of Guisborough*, I, 261, 278; MS. Rawlinson B. 455, f. 30; Egerton MS. 2827, f. 206.

[52] MS. Rawlinson B. 455, ff. 2, 3, 6, 7.

[53] *Yorkshire Deeds*, IV, 85; MS. Rawlinson B. 455, f. 28; *Chartulary of Rievaulx*, 76.

[54] MS. Dodsworth xci, f. 37; *Chartulary of Fountains*, I, 184, 391, 398. For other field names of this type, *cf. Place Names of the North Riding*, 325, 332, 333.

certain strips in *Gikelflat*; Gikel held land in Balderby in the middle of the twelfth century, and was no doubt responsible for bringing into cultivation this part of the fields.[55] The significance which I would find in the presence of personal names in the names of cultures is analogous to that which Professor Stenton attaches to the frequent occurrence, in the northern Danelaw, of personal names in the names of vills.[56] How, it is asked, are we to reconcile the prevalence of such village names as Thormanby and Wigganthorpe with the view that vills in this part of England were occupied by groups of free settlers? The problem in the case of field names is a similar one. How are we to reconcile the presence of personal names in the names of cultures with the fact that these cultures contained the strips of a community of tenants? The answer is that they were originally cleared and cultivated by individuals. To suggest that such tracts were divided up by being shared among the heirs of the original assarters is no more, of course, than to connect the growth of communal agriculture with the natural increase of the community. Neither the tenurial organisation of many Yorkshire vills nor the appearance of their open fields suggest that they were settled, after the devastation, by groups large enough to put the open-field system into full operation; on the contrary, the thirteenth-century "lord" of a non-manorialised vill would seem to have inherited his position from an isolated colonist to whom the entire vill had been granted after the devastation; and the feudally dependent population to have been formed by the other descendants of this colonist, together with such newcomers and their descendants as were enfeoffed, from time to time, in shares of the vill.[57] In vills for which much twelfth-century evidence survives we often find that an open-field system was not yet in existence at that period. Mid-twelfth-century charters relating to Balderby and its neighbourhood show much land lying in enclosed clearings, the bovate as a measure of tenements not appearing until the beginning of the thirteenth century.[58] In Bramham, where a three-field system was worked in the thirteenth century, all the cultivated land mentioned in early charters consisted of assarts, tofts, crofts, and isolated plots.[59] In Osgodby, Kirkby Knowle, and Dalton, which were full of selions and bovates in the thirteenth century and later, early charters reveal a severally cultivated ridding as the normal tenement.[60] It may be conjectured that the use of the term toft to denote a full arable holding

[55] *Early Yorkshire Charters*, I, 79, 80. Land in *Murdacflat* was demised by Geoffrey Murdac. MS. Fairfax ix, f. 9. *Barbotflad* in Kirkby Wiske may have been originally held in severalty by a tenant named Alan Barbot. *Chartulary of Fountains*, I, 391, 398.
[56] *Types of Manorial Structure*, 91.
[57] Cf. *infra*, 38-9, for a hypothetical account of this process.
[58] *Chartulary of Fountains*, I, 90-109; II, 802.
[59] Cotton MS. Vesp. E. xvii, ff. 80-93, 151-62; *Early Yorkshire Charters*, II, 340-56.
[60] MSS. Dodsworth vii, ff. 149, 150; xci, ff. 5, 8, 62; cxxB, f. 65. Brit. Mus. Add. MS. 26736, ff. 64, 101. Egerton MS. 2823, f. 84. *Pedes Finium Ebor*, 97. *Percy Chartulary*, ed. M. Martin (Surtees Soc.), 117, 180.

properly belongs to a period when tenements were not yet organised in open fields.[61]  We may conclude, then, that while the open-field system was maintained and enlarged throughout our period, both the formation and the growth of the open fields were largely preceded by a temporary stage of individual clearing and several cultivation.

Such was the place of assarted land within the arable territory of the vills of this district.  How was constant reclamation consistent with the maintenance of a regular tenemental system?  We have seen that by the thirteenth century holdings in this district were usually of one or of two bovates; we must now consider a few cases of holdings apparently less regular.  Some of these are entirely measured in acres; more often the irregular holding consists of one or two bovates together with some odd acres.  Thus a number of tenants mentioned in the Guisborough rental (c. 1280) held, over and above their bovates, amounts of two or three acres each; and it is to be noted that these amounts are, in every case, separately entered and appear to form accretions on integral bovates.[62]  The integrity of the bovate as a tenemental unit is further shown by the fact that a stated fraction of a tenement—the share, for instance, withdrawn by the tenant's widow—is usually measured in fractions of bovates;[63] and even when the tenement consists of one or two bovates together with some odd acres, a fraction of it may be expressed in some such awkward formula as $\frac{1}{3}$ (2bov. + 6a.), instead of being reduced to acres.[64]  Thus, where entire tenements are contemplated, the bovate does not seem to be simply a convenient multiple of the acre, but to possess an integrity of its own; and in tenements consisting of bovates and odd acres it is not altogether fanciful to represent the bovates and acres as incommensurable, and used to measure two different kinds of arable land.  It has been shown that of the bovate-tenements of this district the main arable land lay in open fields; the index of the size of a tenement seems to be afforded by its share of open-field land, to which all other parts of the tenement are normally considered as secondary and appurtenant.[65]  The nature of the odd acres sometimes attached to bovates is shown by the innumerable instances of newly cleared land attached to holdings in the open fields.  Thus two carucates in Ingleby Greenhow were associated, in a grant, with twenty-eight acres of land in "intakes";[66] with twelve bovates of demesne in

[61] Cf. Douglas, op. cit. 3i, 34-7; Danelaw Charters xxxix. A Saltfleetby charter, ibid. 394-5, seems to contain an example of this use.

[62] Chartulary of Guisborough, II, 426. Cf. Egerton MS. 2827, f. 34; Cotton MS. Claud. D. xi, f. 89.

[63] Cf. Yorkshire Deeds, I, 212; IV, 93-5; Pedes Finium Ebor, 70; Cotton MS. Claud. D. xi, f. 88.          [64] Cf. MS. Dodsworth clvi, f. 48.

[65] Cf. Douglas, op cit. 35; Danelaw Charters, xxxv, xxxvi.

[66] Early Yorkshire Charters, I, 451. The appurtenances of a carucate in Seacroft included assarts. Kirkstall Coucher, 121. Frussuræ and essarta were annexed to thirteen bovates in Bagby, c. 1198. MS. Dodsworth vii, f. 16. A carucate in Cave had appurtenant land non mensurata et non culta. MS. Fairfax ix, f. 67.

Hutton Rudby were granted some appurtenant enclosed clearings called *ofnama*;[67] and the instances are too many to be quoted of newly cleared land attached to holdings of one or two bovates.[68] It is, on the other hand, unusual for assarted land in the thirteenth century to constitute an entire arable tenement. Just as clearings are considered as appurtenant to systems of open fields, so assarts, shares in assarts, and the right of assarting are normally attached to single tenements as appurtenances of their open-field land. Now the charters in which we must study the tenemental system of this district refer in various ways to the appurtenances of net arable bovates in the fields. It is unusual for all the appurtenances to be detailed; often only the tofts are mentioned, while equally indispensable accessories such as meadow and common rights are not enumerated; again, the appurtenances may be accounted for in an elaborate but purely conventional formula; most frequently tenements are measured in gross bovates in which all the appurtenances of the net arable bovates are left implicit.[69] There is nothing inconsistent in a grant by a tenant in Ingleby Greenhow of half an acre outside the two bovates which he holds; or in the fact that Henry of Kirkby, holding two bovates in Kirkby Wiske, was able to make a grant of two bovates and three acres.[70] A charter of *c*. 1225 records a grant of six bovates and an assart in Kilvington; a contemporary deed, by which this land was quitclaimed, refers to it simply as six bovates with appurtenances.[71] Not merely, therefore, does the assart normally occur as appurtenant to the open-field holding; we are justified, I think, in suspecting that it was a normal appurtenance.

The free tenants of non-manorialised Yorkshire enjoyed and freely exercised the right of alienating their land; from the charters which

[67] *Calendar of Charter Rolls, 1300-1326*, 142. The arable demesne of Barmby in 1295 consisted of six bovates and three " flats " ; that of Grindall contained *xvj. bouatas terre . . . cum le Ouenames*. Cotton MS. Claud. B. iii, ff. 167, 179. Bovates in Little Edston were associated with *ouenama*. MS. Dodsworth vii, f. 157.

[68] *Yorkshire Inquest*, I, 51-65; assarts appurtenant to the majority of bovate holdings on parts of the Lacy estates in 1258. *Cartulary of Fountains*, II, 522; a grant of all the grantor had, by reason of his two bovates, in two new assarts. *Ibid*. II, 667; two bovates with four acres in riddings. *Kirkstall Coucher*, 92, 96, 151, 154, 175, 259-61; numerous tenements, chiefly of two bovates with appurtenant assarts. *Pedes Finium Ebor*, 65; one bovate in the fields with an appurtenant close. Add. ch. 8117 refers to a tenement as *duas bouetas terre . . . et quoddam essartum*. Cotton MS. Claud. B. iii, ff. 187, 188, 192, 193; tenants holding headlands and shares in closes besides their bovates. Claud. D. xi, f. 71; one bovate with 5¾ acres *in broces*. Cotton MS. Vesp. E. xvii, f. 48; half a bovate in Tickhill with appurtenances *in assartis et assartandis*. MS. Rawlinson B. 455, ff. 2, 6, 41, 99; waste and assarted land attached to bovates and acres in open fields. MSS. Dodsworth liii, f. 20, xci, ff. 20, 62, cxxB, ff. 50, 76, clvi, f. 4; two-bovate tenements each with an appurtenant assart. Register of St Mary's, f. 115; land in "intake" belonging to one bovate.

[69] *Cf.* a grant by Richard Lost, *Chartulary of Guisborough*, II, 1.

[70] *Early Yorkshire Charters*, I, 449; *Chartulary of Fountains*, II, 391. A grant of one bovate in Skipton stipulated that the grantees were not to claim anything in a certain assart. *Cf.* a grant of two bovates in Dishforth, less three acres of land lying near the two bovates. *Ibid*. II, 636; I, 218.     [71] MS. Dodsworth xci, ff. 4, 10.

record their grants of land our knowledge of them is chiefly derived. Many thousands of surviving texts record gifts of land by these tenants to monasteries; and, though the great majority of twelfth- and thirteenth-century Yorkshire charters belong to collections of monastic title deeds, and deal with land eventually acquired by monasteries, many of them record antecedent real transactions between peasant freeholders. The holding of any tenant whose wife had brought a few acres of dowry was made up of land derived from at least two different sources; from this holding he might have to provide dowries for his daughters[72] and small holdings for his adult sons;[73] when he died, his sons inherited shares of a tenement which was subject, besides, to the withdrawal of one-third part by his widow, who could do with it as she pleased.[74] Add to this free commerce in land and continual division of tenements a widespread reclamation of the waste, and you have all the conditions which lead economic historians to look for the rapid disappearance of any such tenemental unit as the bovate.[75] It is scarcely possible that the bovates of some original scheme of distribution should have survived, in their integrity, for two generations; and such a hypothesis is not required to explain the maintenance, throughout the thirteenth century, of a tenemental system based on the bovate. The freeholding population of post-Conquest Yorkshire arose in those waste districts which, owing to the absence of a servile population living in or conveniently near them, the Norman-French lords of the late eleventh century were unable to manorialise. We have found reason to believe that large tracts of waste land were granted to isolated colonists. But such a colonist, though he might find himself in possession of the entire territory of a devastated vill, could take up no more land than he could cultivate by his own labour; and it may reasonably be supposed that, while remaining "lord" of the vill, he would endeavour to pass on some of the incidence of forinsec service by enfeoffing other tenants. The descendants of such colonists, augmented, from time to time, by newcomers, I take to have formed the freeholding population of non-manorialised vills in the thirteenth century.[76] That each free tenant, whatever his feudal

---

[72] Thus Geoffrey "lord" of Howe (c. 1260) was able to give his daughter three acres of land as a dowry. MS. Dodsworth, cxxB, ff. 68, 82.

[73] Any large group of charters yields genealogies of peasant families which show that numerous children survived and took up holdings in their native villages. Cf. the descendants of Ernald son of Bence in Dromonby, *Chartulary of Fountains*, I, 280 et seq. There can be no doubt that the rural population of Yorkshire was growing rapidly in the twelfth and thirteenth centuries.

[74] The chartularies are full of grants by widows in *ligia potestate* or *viduitate sua*. It may be suggested that a woman's dowry always remained distinct from her husband's land. But when a widow is said to retain one-third of one bovate (*Yorkshire Deeds*, IV, 94) or one-third of half a carucate (*Pedes Finium Ebor*, 70), it appears that symmetrical holdings have been divided at the death of the husbands.

[75] Cf. *Danelaw Charters*, xxvi, xlix, 1.

[76] The free tenants in certain vills seem to be closely related by blood and marriage, and to have descended from a few early and middle twelfth-century inhabitants whose names suggest native origin.

position, must rely on the labour of himself and his family, would roughly limit the size of arable holdings. That this labour came to be partly exerted through a communal medium would bring about a more exact levelling in their area. The clearing of the large available tracts of waste land, and the incorporation of clearings in the open fields, would permit this level to be maintained among the open-field holdings of a growing population. That assarts in the thirteenth century did not usually constitute distinct tenements, but were annexed to open-field holdings, is a fact of great significance; it permits us to attribute to the latter a power of growth and reproduction; we may say that there was a close symbiosis between assarted land and holdings in the open fields. Thus a perpetual commerce in land and division of tenements would not be inconsistent with a recurrent equalisation in the size of arable holdings. A Thornaby charter of c. 1250 shows how tenements might be broken up, and their fractions recombined with newly cleared land.[77] It shows the distribution, among nine free tenants, of a carucate of land, together with some odd acres which are kept distinct from the carucate and its divisions, and which no doubt consisted of land not yet brought within the open-field system. The charter is drawn up in such a way as to suggest that the whole area had previously consisted of four two-bovate tenements. These had largely disintegrated; of the first, one tenant held two-thirds, another one-third—the latter had no doubt inherited a dower portion in this tenement. The second tenement remained in the hands of a single tenant; the third was divided among two tenants, the fourth among four tenants. Now how much arable land these tenants possessed elsewhere in Thornaby we do not know; but we may remark that share of the land extended in this charter which is attributed to one of them. Henry son of Siward holds $\frac{1}{3}$ (2 bov.) + $\frac{1}{4}$ (2 bov. + 6a.) + 7a.; and whatever the size of the bovate in Thornaby, it is evident that when the odd acres which Henry holds are brought under the open-field system, he will possess a tenement not greatly exceeding or falling short of the two bovates which we know, from this and other sources, to have been a normal tenement in this vill.[78] The size of open-field tenements, limited, maintained, and kept roughly equal by other factors, was more exactly determined by their subjection to the prevailing system of bovates. Why, however, were tenements so organised? The persistence of bovates as tenemental units must be due to the

---

[77] Brit. Mus. Stowe ch. 499. After disposing of a carucate apparently held by two mesne tenants, the charter proceeds to the homage and service of John son of Hamelin for *duabus partibus duarum bovatarum terre cum pertinenciis*, Henry son of Siward for *tercia parte duarum bovatarum*, William Swres for *duabus bovatis*, William Hyll and Thomas of Elmeden each for *una bovata*, Thomas Hors, Robert of Hylton, Robert of Berewyc and Henry son of Siward each for *quarta parte duarum bovatarum terre et sex acrarum*, John of the Moor for *uno tofto et crofto*, Robert Wyctbody for *una acra et una roda terre* and Henry son of Siward for *septem acris terre*.

[78] Cf. *Chartulary of Guisborough*, II, 426.

continued practice of an open-field system of cultivation. We have seen
that the bovate is essentially a measure of open-field arable; the assimila-
tion of assarted land by the open fields afforded an increasing amount of
arable land available for organisation in bovates.

Thus in the holdings of free tenants, found in greater or less numbers
in nearly every Yorkshire vill, there was implicit a power of growth and
reproduction; and in vills where tenants were not prevented by lords
from dividing their tenements and reclaiming the waste we might
expect to observe, over some long period, an increase in the number of
arable bovates. It is, unfortunately, in the nature of non-manorialised
vills that their development should not be illustrated by the extents and
rentals which are necessary to show this increase. I do not here wish
to relate these arable bovates to the fiscal and feudal carucates and
bovates of Domesday and the feodaries; a discussion of this and other
problems would over-elaborate this account, in part a hypothetical one,
of the rural development of the Yorkshire plain after the devastation.
That this development was characterised by a regular agrarian routine
and tenemental organisation may have been due to the lack of capital
and markets; and if this was so, some account of it may throw light on
the development of similar institutions in other parts of England at
remote periods.

# AN INDUSTRIAL REVOLUTION OF THE THIRTEENTH CENTURY [1]

## E. M. CARUS–WILSON

IT has been commonly supposed that the thirteenth century witnessed a decline in the nascent cloth industry of England, a decline which was only to be checked and converted into renewed advance and yet more spectacular progress under the vigorous patronage of Edward III. We read, for instance, of the "impoverished state" of the industry "on the eve of the great experiment"; of how "something was wrong with the industry, and if it was to be given fresh life something must be done".[2] Such a conception of arrested growth and even of decay is not, however, borne out by a close investigation of the sources. On the contrary, they reveal rather the expansion and rapid development of the industry up to the eve of the accession of Edward III. The reason for this discrepancy is not that the sources themselves have been misinterpreted, but that only one group of them, the urban records, has been hitherto explored in this connection. It has been too readily assumed that the history of industry in England at this time was to be found in the history of her towns and their gilds, and that symptoms of decline evident here signified a decline in the industry as a whole. In reality, however, rural records also throw a flood of light on the industrial history of the time, and when they are considered in conjunction with those of the towns it becomes apparent that the century was one of striking progress industrially, though of equally striking change and upheaval. It witnessed, in fact, an industrial revolution due to scientific discoveries and changes in technique; a revolution which brought poverty, unemployment and discontent to certain old centres of the industry, but wealth, opportunity and prosperity to the country as a whole, and which was destined to alter the face of medieval England.

In the early Middle Ages the various processes of cloth-making were all strictly "handcrafts". The chief processes, apart from dyeing and finishing, were four. First the wool was carded or combed by hand; then it was spun on the rock or distaff. Next the yarn thus prepared was woven on a loom worked by hand and foot, and finally the loose

---

[1] Owing to war conditions it proved impossible to check and to complete all the references in this article, particularly those to manuscript sources in the custody of the Public Record Office.

[2] E. Lipson, *The History of the English Woollen and Worsted Industries* (1921), 11; cf. E. Lipson, *The Economic History of England*, 7th edn. (1937), 449-50; L. F. Salzman, *English Industries of the Middle Ages* (1923), 203.

" web " thus made was fulled by hand or foot. The process of fulling, that is to say, of beating or compressing the cloth in water, served first of all to shrink the cloth, reducing it in width by anything from a fifth to a half, and in length to a corresponding extent.[3] This so increased the density and weight per unit of length as to give it much greater resistance to weather and wear. Secondly, it served to " felt " the cloth, so inextricably entangling the fibres that the pattern of the weaving often ceased to be visible. This not only gave the cloth greater fabric strength, but also a smoother and softer surface, and it was an essential preliminary to the finishing processes of raising and shearing applied to the finer cloths. In addition to shrinking and felting the cloth, making it close and firm, the fulling process also scoured it and cleansed it, with the aid of various detergents[4] such as fuller's earth, removing especially the oil with which the wool had been impregnated before spinning. Now the mechanising of the first three cloth-making processes during the eighteenth and nineteenth centuries is a commonplace of history, but the mechanising of the fourth during the thirteenth century, though it gave rise to an industrial revolution not less remarkable, has attracted scarcely any attention. It is with this that the present article proposes to deal.

Three primitive methods of fulling " by might and strength of man ", without any mechanism, have been most commonly used in western Europe: beating with the feet, with the hands, or with clubs wielded by hand. Most suited to long heavy broadcloths is some method of fulling by foot such as is vividly portrayed in the paintings on the piers of the *fullonica* at Pompeii, and in those of the house of the Vettii there. In these we can see the fuller at work, standing almost naked in a trough, trampling the cloth under foot, while his hands rest on low side walls by which he can support and raise himself. Traces of what may have been fulleries such as these in Roman Britain have been revealed in three places: at Titsey and Darenth in Kent, and at Chedworth in Gloucestershire. Here we have found very similar troughs, circular in form, with low side walls and drainage facilities.[5] Their close proximity, in each case, to beds of fuller's earth and to what later became flourishing centres of the industry, would seem to lend some support to the theory that they were fulleries, though the matter cannot be considered as finally determined. From Roman Gaul we have an actual

[3] For the purpose and nature of fulling, see J. and J. C. Schofield, *The Finishing of Wool Goods* (1935), and J. Schofield, *The Science and Practice of Scouring and Milling* (1921). The medieval assize of cloth sometimes quoted a different standard for cloth " watered " and cloth " unwatered ", e.g. 11 Hen. VI, c.9.

[4] *Cf.* G. Espinas, " Essai sur la Technique de l'Industrie Textile à Douai aux xiiie et xive siècles ", *Mémoires de la Société nationale des Antiquaires de France*, t. LXVIII (1909), 42.

[5] *Archaeologia*, LIX (1904), G. E. Fox, " Notes on some probable traces of Roman Fulling in Britain ", 208-9; *Guide to Chedworth Roman Villa* (1926), 12-13.

representation of a fuller at work in a trough, carved on the "fuller's tomb" at Sens.[6] So for a thousand years and more fullers trod the cloth underfoot, as indeed they have continued to do in outlying parts, such as the Hebrides, untouched by the mechanical inventions of the thirteenth or of the eighteenth centuries. The early fourteenth century ordinances of the fullers' gilds both at Lincoln and at Bristol mention this working "in the trough",[7] and later on in *Piers Plowman* we read of cloth that is "fulled under fote".[8]

Sometimes hands were used instead of, or in addition to, feet. A visitor to Skye in 1774 thus described the Luaghad, or fulling of cloth, there: "Twelve or fourteen women, divided into equal numbers, sit down on each side of a long board ribbed lengthways, placing the cloth on it: first they begin to work it backwards and forwards with their hands, singing at the same time as at the quern: when they have tired their hands, every female uses her feet for the same purpose, and six or seven pairs of naked feet are in the most violent agitation, working one against the other: as by this time they grow very earnest in their labours, the fury of the song rises; at length it arrives to such a pitch that without breach of charity you would imagine a troop of female demoniacs to have been assembled."[9]

Hand fulling alone, or fulling with clubs wielded by hand, has probably always been used for smaller articles. Indeed methods of fulling even in the same locality seem commonly to have varied according to the size and character of the articles to be fulled. A traveller to Iceland in 1814-15 thus describes two different methods in vogue there: "Both ends being knocked out of a barrel, it is filled with articles to be fulled, when it is laid on the side, and two men lie down on their backs, one at either end, with their feet in the barrel, and literally *walk* the cloth, by kicking it against each other. Smaller articles they full by placing them between their knees and breast, and then moving backwards and forwards with the body, turning them always with their hands till ready. This accounts for the very awkward motion which the Icelanders almost always fall into when sitting, and from which many of them cannot refrain even in church."[10] In France in the eighteenth century fulling by hand was frequently used for hosiery, and fulling with clubs wielded by hand for hats and caps.[11] We may infer a similar use of clubs in

[6] C. Roach-Smith, *Collectanea Antiqua*, V (1861), plate XX, fig. 1.

[7] Toulmin Smith, *English Gilds* (1870), 180, *in alveo*; *Little Red Book of Bristol*, ed. F. B. Bickley (1900), II, 12, *ouveraunt en le stok*.

[8] *Piers Plowman* (B), XV, 445. Angus Pirie, a skilled weaver of Dornoch, used to full his cloth by foot in a trough but has given up this method as too strenuous and too chilling now that he is old.

[9] Quoted in E. Lipson, *History of the English Woollen and Worsted Industries* (1921), 139.

[10] E. Henderson, *Iceland* (Edinburgh, 1818), I, 365.

[11] Savary des Bruslons, *Dictionnaire Universel de Commerce*, II, 526; Postlethwayt, *Universal Dictionary of Trade and Commerce* (4th edn., 1774): "Fulling".

Roman times from the account of the martyrdom of St James the Less, written in the second century: *Quidam autem ex eis, accepto fuste ex officina fullonis, quo comprimebat vestes, valide infligit ejus capiti.*[12] For this reason the fuller's club became the emblem of St James and is to be seen in many medieval representations of him, as for instance in the east window of Gloucester Cathedral, on the rood screen at Ranworth, on one of the stall panels at Blythburgh, and on the font at Stalham.[13]

In medieval records it is not easy to distinguish this method of using clubs from that of fulling by hand alone, since both could be described as "fulling by hand" in distinction to "fulling by foot". At any rate it seems that in England one or other of these methods of hand fulling was commonly used for hats and caps. Thus in London long after mechanical fulling had commonly been adopted for broadcloths, the Hurers successfully petitioned against this method being allowed for hats and caps, and ordinances were passed to this effect in 1376;[14] several citizens were fined for breach of the ordinance and, during the hearing of a case against one John Godefray, a jury of cappers and hatters declared that caps could not and ought not to be fulled under the feet or in any other way than by the hands of men.[15] It is clear that the hatters and cappers were as much opposed to fulling by foot as to mechanical fulling; thus again in 1404 they petitioned that their work should not be fulled in mills *or by feet,* but only by the hands of men, and again offending citizens were punished.[16] Most probably hand fulling was reserved for small articles such as hats and caps, made usually of felt, while the long, heavy broadcloths which came to form the staple of the English export industry were fulled by foot.

Such were the primitive methods of fulling in use when the English woollen industry was first established. Most important of them is fulling by foot, since this method was applied to the long, heavy broadcloth which came to form the staple of the English export industry.

The mechanical method of fulling invented during the Middle Ages, and in use for many centuries, was evolved from the primitive method of fulling by foot. The invention was a twofold one. In the first place the action of the two feet was replaced by that of two wooden hammers, alternately raised and dropped on the cloth as it lay in the trough, and controlled probably by a revolving drum on the tilt- or lift-hammer system.[17] In the second place this revolving drum was attached to the

---

[12] *Acta Sanctorum*, XIV, 35.

[13] For other examples, see C. Cahier, *Caractéristiques des saints dans l'art populaire* (1867), 547; F. C. Husenbeth, *Emblems of Saints*, 3rd edn., ed. A. Jessopp (1882), 110.

[14] *Memorials of London*, ed. H. T. Riley (1868), 400.

[15] *Calendar of Plea and Memoranda Rolls, 1364-1381*, ed. A. H. Thomas (1929), 230, 233; *Memorials of London, ut supra*, 529.

[16] *Ibid.* 667.

[17] This revolving drum could be turned by hand, and such a device may still be seen in use in parts of Scotland today, though it is very heavy to work.

spindle of a water-wheel, and this supplied the motive power.   Thus, by a simple contrivance, water power was made to replace human labour, and a series of hammers could be set to work with but one man standing by to watch the cloth and see that it was kept properly moving in the trough.   The whole was then spoken of as a *molendinum fullericum*, or "fulling mill",[18] since, though it was not strictly a mill (*molendinum*) in that it did not grind (*molere*), it bore a resemblance in one part of its mechanism to the water corn mill.   Indeed the building itself, down by the water, with its leet and its revolving wheel, would be difficult to distinguish externally from a corn mill.   Henceforth, just as there had hitherto been a distinction in rentals, surveys, etc., between the windmill, the watermill and the horse-mill (*molendinum ventricum, molendinum aquaticum* and *molendinum ad equos*), so now there appears a further distinction between the water *corn* mill and the water *fulling* mill (*molendinum aquaticum blaericum* and *molendinum aquaticum fullericum*).

The question now arises as to the date of the invention of the water fulling mill.   This would seem impossible to fix with any certainty. M. Bloch asserts that there was a fulling mill at Grenoble "about 1050",[19] but the actual evidence does not seem to support his conclusion.   The charter to which he refers speaks of certain rights *in unum quodque molendinum, quando edificatur, et in bateorium, similiter quando edificatur.*[20]   Now a *bateorium, battorium, batatorium* or *baptitorium* is certainly a place where beating or hammering is carried on, but we are not justified in assuming that this beating was done by water power, or that it was necessarily the beating of cloth.   Ducange defines *Bateria* as, *Ars tundendi pannos, terendi cortices et alia similia facienda,* and in a charter quoted by him there are enumerated *furnos, torcularia, molendina, baptitoria, et fullonos.*   Clearly, then, a *baptitorium* or *bateorium* is not even synonymous with a fullery, much less with a mechanical fulling *mill*, and there is as yet no evidence that the fulling mill was known on the continent at that date.[21]   In England, at any rate, it seems as though water fulling mills were introduced in the latter part of the twelfth century.   The earliest reference to one so far discovered is that in the survey of the Templars' lands made in 1185.   This mentions a *molendinum fulerez* at Newsham in Yorkshire and another, built by the

[18] While "fulling mill" is the most widely used term, certain parts of England had their own local terms, derived from words of different origins describing the same fulling process.   Thus in the place of "full", "fuller", "fulling mill", we find "tuck", "tucker", "tucking mill" in the west country, especially in Cornwall, Devon and Somerset; and "walk", "walker", "walking mill" (or "walkmill") in the north, especially in the Lake District, while in Wales a fulling mill becomes a "pandy". Many of the sites of these ancient mills can be identified by the fact that they have one or other of these expressions attached to them.

[19] *Annales d'histoire économique et sociale,* no. 36, November 1935, M. Bloch, "Avènement et conquêtes du moulin à eau", 543.

[20] *Cartulaires de l'Église Cathédrale de Grenoble,* ed. M. J. Marion (Paris, 1869), 119.

[21] See Postscript.

Templars themselves, at Barton, close to Temple Guiting, in the Cotswolds.[22] Four years later a charter to the Abbey of Stanley in Wilts speaks of the *molendinum monachorum fullericum*.[23] The absence so far of any earlier references to fulling mills does not, of course, prove their non-existence, and how far the lack of other evidence for the twelfth and other centuries is due to lack of documents comparable to those of later centuries it is impossible to say. But a significant change in nomenclature points also to the change having been introduced in the late twelfth century. For from the opening of the thirteenth century not only do references to such mills increase, but so also does the use of the phrase *corn* mill in distinction to *fulling mill*, while the word *fullonia* disappears, giving place to *molendinum fullericum*. Certainly the fulling mill cannot have been at all widely used until the thirteenth century, and it is in the late thirteenth century that we come across the first evidence of opposition to its use on the part of the handworkers.

The origin of the invention is even more obscure than its date. We know neither in what country, nor by whom, water power was first applied to fulling, nor whether the idea spread from a common source or was evolved independently in different regions. It is conceivable that the Templars may have introduced the fulling mill into England. At any rate the religious orders were among the first to take advantage of it and to develop its possibilities. In monastic cartularies many early references, not all of which can be precisely dated, are to be found to fulling mills. About the year 1200 the Abbey of Winchcomb possessed a fulling mill at "Clively", and when the Abbot made a grant of another mill it was on condition that it should not be converted into a fulling mill to compete with his own.[24] The monks of Evesham held a fullers' mill (*molendinum fullonum*) at Bourton-on-the-Water in Gloucestershire in 1206;[25] the Augustinian friary of St John the Baptist at Ludlow had one before 1221, probably on the Teme;[26] Newminster had one on the Wansbeck very early in its history;[27] St Albans had established one by 1274,[28] and in an extent of the Abbey of Kirkstall of 16 Edward I a fulling mill is mentioned as well as a tanning mill.[29]

[22] R. Dodsworth and Sir W. Dugdale, *Monasticon Anglicanum* (1655-73), II, 540; B. A. Lees, *Records of the Templars in England in the Twelfth Century* (1935), pp. ccxiii, 50, 127, cxxv. There was also a derelict fulling mill at Witham, Essex, in 1308, and this may, it is suggested, represent the " mill " in the survey of 1185, *ibid.* p. lxxix.

[23] W. de G. Birch, *Collections towards the history of the Cistercian Abbey of Stanley, Wilts* (1876), 43, quoting Brit. Mus. Harleian MS. 84, f. 273b; see also 15, 17, 33, for later references.

[24] *Monasterium Beatae Mariae Virginis et Sancti Cenhelmi: Landboc*, ed. D. Royce (1892), I, 195.

[25] *Chronicon Abbatiae Eveshamensis*, ed. W. D. Macray (Rolls Series, 1863), 213.

[26] Harleian MS. 6690, f. 89 *et seq.*, quoted in T. Wright, *History of Ludlow* (1852), 98.

[27] *Newminster Cartulary* (Surtees Soc., LXVI, 1878), 3.

[28] *Walsingham, Gesta Abbatum Monasterii Sancti Albani*, ed. H. T. Riley (Rolls Series, 1867), I, 410 *et seq.*

[29] P.R.O. Ancient Extents 86 (1).

Nor were the great episcopal estates behind the monastic ones. The earliest Pipe Roll of the Bishop of Winchester (1208-9) shows that he then possessed four fulling mills (described as *fulleraticum* and *foleraticum*): at Waltham, Sutton, Brightwell and New Alresford; mills to which Dr Hubert Hall called attention as " perhaps the earliest fulling mills in England of which we have mention ".[30]   Later rolls show the Bishop possessed of a fulling mill at Downton in Wiltshire by 1215, of two in Oxfordshire, at Witney, by 1223, and of one in Somerset, at Taunton, by 1224.[31]   The Bishop of Bath owned a fulling mill at Kidderminster in 1293,[32] while early in the following century the Bishop of Exeter agreed to join with the Mayor and Commonalty of Barnstaple in erecting mills, including fulling mills, on the river which divided their property.[33]

It must not, however, be assumed that, since many of the earliest surviving references are to mills on monastic and ecclesiastical estates, laymen lagged behind.   Indeed in the monastic cartularies themselves we get glimpses of lay owners of fulling mills, for such mills often happened to be part of endowments bestowed by laymen upon a monastery. About the year 1200, for instance, Robert of Seckworth owned two " myllis fuleree " in Seckworth and granted the tithes of them to the nunnery of Godstow.[34]   Godstow also claimed tithes in 1235 of the mill called " pannmylle " (probably a " cloth mill ") at Wycombe.[35]   Again, when Peter Undergod founded the hospital of St John the Baptist near the bridge over the Teme at Ludlow, he endowed it, *inter alia,* with the fulling mill which he had bought from Gilbert de Lacy.[36]

The fulling mills on lay estates for which most early records survive are, not unnaturally, those of the King himself.   One of the first royal mills was that near Marlborough, at Elcot.   This was in existence in the reign of John and was rebuilt by the King's orders in 1237.   The task was entrusted to William de Pretsch and Vincent Carpentar', who had workmen under them, and cost altogether £4 17s. 4d.   Most of this money was spent on felling and carting timber from Savernake forest; the rest on remaking the mill-pond, the weir, the mill-wheel and its enclosure, the mill-race and also the *flagella et baterella*—probably the hammers for beating the cloth.[37]   In 1251 Henry III ordered a fulling

---

[30] *Pipe Roll of the Bishop of Winchester,* ed. Hubert Hall (1903), pp. xxvii, 1, 13, 41, 61.
[31] P.R.O. Ecclesiastical Commission, Various, II, 159273, 159278 *et seq.*   References given by Miss M. Wretts-Smith.
[32] *Inquisitions Post Mortem for the County of Worcestershire,* edited for the Worcester Historical Society by J. W. Willis Bund (1894), I, 43; *Calendar of Inqusitions Post Mortem,* III, 45 (21 Ed. I).
[33] *Reprint of the Barnstaple Records,* ed. J. A. Chanter and T. Wainwright (1900), I, 110, no. 20.
[34] *The Godstow and Oseney Registers,* ed. A. Clark (Early English Text Society, 1905), I, 43.
[35] *Ibid,* 89.                    [36] Wright, *op. cit.* 98.
[37] *Calendar of Liberate Rolls,* I, 278 ; *Great Roll of the Pipe, 1241-1242,* 175 ; *Rotuli Litterarum Clausarum,* ed. T. D. Hardy (Record Commission, 1833-44), II, 23.

mill to be built in his park at Guildford;[38] the royal manor of Steeple
Langford in Wilts had one in 1294,[39] and by the beginning of the follow-
ing century there was a royal fulling mill in the West Riding at
Knaresborough.[40]

When we turn to trace fulling mills on estates other than monastic,
episcopal or royal, there is, unfortunately, no comparable evidence
available. The sources are on the whole later in date and different in
character. The mandates and instructions on Royal Close Rolls and
Liberate Rolls have, for instance, no parallel, and in place of the twelfth
and early thirteenth century monastic cartularies we have only scattered
deeds, scarcely ever so early in date. Nor are there any early consecutive
series of manorial accounts such as those enrolled on the great pipe rolls
of the Bishop of Winchester or on the royal pipe rolls, but only separate
accounts, surviving in fragments. The principal sources are threefold:
first the Inquisitions Post Mortem taken on the death of a supposed
tenant-in-chief for the information of the King; secondly, Rentals and
Custumals of individual manors drawn up for the information of the
lord of the manor and his officials; and, thirdly, year to year Accounts
kept of the administration of such manors and records of their Courts.
These three sources are extensive from the latter part of the thirteenth
century, though not until then. The first is the most accessible in print,
through the *Calendars of Inquisitions Post Mortem*, but these are
deceptive for the present investigation, since they do not always reproduce the detailed extents in which the fulling mills are usually to be
found. In these printed calendars, for instance, no fulling mills appear
for Wiltshire before the reign of Edward III, but the more detailed
*Abstracts of Wiltshire Inquisitions Post Mortem* (1242-1326) give five.[41]
Hence, for counties where we have no such thorough survey, the originals
must constantly be consulted. It must further be remembered that these
inquisitions may not always record the state of affairs at the moment
that the return was actually made; they may reproduce earlier surveys.
Thus when a fulling mill appears we can only be certain that it existed
either at that or at an earlier date. Nor do Rentals and Custumals
always give precise dates; often their date can only be inferred from
their handwriting, and even then it is possible that they are sometimes
copies of earlier surveys. None of these sources is sufficiently comprehensive to form any basis for statistical analysis, but from them and
other records we can at least gain an impression of the rapid extension of
the fulling mill during the thirteenth century and its widespread distribution at the beginning of the fourteenth century. And it must be

[38] *Calendar of Liberate Rolls*, III, 376; T. H. Turner, *Domestic Architecture in
England* (1851), I, 233; (1853), II, 149.
[39] P.R.O. Rentals and Surveys, General Series, portf. 16, no. 66.
[40] *Calendar of Close Rolls, 1302-1307*, 35.
[41] *Abstracts of Wiltshire Inquisitions Post Mortem*, ed. E. A. Fry (1242-1326) (1908),
I, 119, 227, 246, 257, 350.

borne in mind that the mills of which record has survived can be only a small proportion of the total, and that the present investigation cannot claim in any waÿ to be exhaustive.[42]

The accompanying table attempts to set out geographically the evidence which has so far come to light as to the distribution of fulling mills in England before the reign of Edward III. All the mills noted here date from the thirteenth or early fourteenth centuries (before 1327), except for the three already mentioned as dating from the late twelfth century; most of them belong to the reigns of Edward I or Edward II.*

**The Pennines**

*Yorkshire: West Riding*

| | |
|---|---|
| Almondbury | M.A., 29/2 (32-3 Ed. I); 1145/21 (Ed. [II]) |
| Alverthorpe | Yorks Archaeological Soc., Record Series XXIX, *Wakefield Court Rolls*, I, 250 (1296) |
| Bradford | M.A., 29/2, 1145/21 |
| Castleford | M.A., 1145/21 |
| Kirkstall | Anc. Ext., 86 (1) |
| Knaresboro' | *Supra*, 48 |
| Leeds | M.A., 1145/21 |
| Newsham | *Supra*, 45 |
| Rothwell | M.A., 29/2, 1145/21 |
| Thorpe Arch | Cal. I.P.M., IV, 25 (29 Ed. I) |
| Wakefield | *Wakefield, ut supra*, I, 176, 252 (1277, 1296); II, 185 (1316) |

*North Riding*

| | |
|---|---|
| Burton Constable | I.P.M., Ed. II, 63 |
| Masham | Cal. C.R., 1302–1307, 164 |

*Lancashire*

| | |
|---|---|
| Burnley | Chetham Soc., CXII, *Two Compoti of the Lancs and Cheshire Manors of Henry de Lacy, 24 and 33 Ed. I*, 4, 8, 15, 16 |
| Colne | *Ibid.* |
| Manchester | *Ibid.* p. xxii |
| Wyresdale | I.P.M., Ed. II, 69 |

**The Lake District**

| | |
|---|---|
| Applethwaite (Windermere) | I.P.M., Ed. II, 81 |
| Brampton | Cal. I.P.M., III, 184 (23 Ed. I) |
| Carleton | M.A., 824/28 et seq. (1 Ed. I et seq.) |
| Carlisle | C. Gross, *Gild Merchant*, II, 39 |
| Clifton | Cal. I.P.M., III, 432 (28 Ed. I) |
| Cockermouth | Surtees Soc., CXXVI, *Register of St. Bees*, 48, 449 (27 Ed. I); R. & S., 730; M.A., 460/24 |
| Crosthwaite | I.P.M., Ed. I, 32 Ed. II, 81[1] |
| Dacre | I.P.M., Ed. II, 82 |
| Egremont | Cal. C.R., 1288–1296, 402 |
| Embleton | I.P.M., Ed. II, 75 |
| Glassonby | I.P.M., Ed. II, 76 |
| Grasmere | I.P.M., Ed. I, 5, 32; Ed. II, 81[2] |
| Greenriggs | I.P.M., Ed. II, 17 |
| Grizedale | I.P.M., Ed. II, 82 |
| Kendal | P.R.O. Assize Roll, 979, m. 2 (40 Hen. III) |
| Millom | I.P.M., Ed. II, 50 |
| Penrith | M.A., 824/28 et seq. (1 Ed. I et seq.) |
| Sowerby | *Ibid.* |
| Staveley | Lancs & Cheshire Record Soc., vol. 54, *Lancs Inquests, Extents and Feudal Aids*, II, 148 |

**The Midlands**

*Derbyshire*

| | |
|---|---|
| Hartington | Cal. I.P.M., III, 300 (26 Ed. I); M.A., 29/3 (7-8 Ed. II) |
| Wirksworth | Cal. I.P.M., III, 291 (25 Ed. I); M.A., 29/3 |

*Nottinghamshire*

| | |
|---|---|
| Warsop | *Notts I.P.M.*, 128 (1268) |

*Northamptonshire*

| | |
|---|---|
| Wellingboro' | |

*Staffordshire*

| | |
|---|---|
| Barton | M.A., 29/3 (7-8 Ed. II) |
| Himley | Cal. I.P.M., VI, 470 (20 Ed. II) |
| Rolleston | M.A., 29/3 |

[42] Further evidence is constantly coming to light, and collections of local deeds still have much to yield. The writer would welcome information as to other early mills than those listed.

* For abbreviations used in the references. see list at end of article.

**The Midlands**
*Worcestershire*

| | |
|---|---|
| Hartlebury | M.A., 1143/18 (30-1 Ed. I) |
| Kidderminster | Worc. I.P.M., I, 43 (1293); Cal. I.P.M., III, 45 |
| Mitton | J. R. Burton, *Kidderminster*, 21 |
| Overbury (*see* Cotswolds) | |
| Shelsley (*see* Welsh Marches) | |

**The Welsh Marches**

| | |
|---|---|
| Alvington | *Tax. Eccl.*, p. 172 |
| Caerleon | M.A., 1202/6 *et seq.* (7 Ed. II *et seq.*) |
| Ludlow | T. Wright, *Ludlow*, 98; Brit. Mus. Harl. MS. 6690, f. 89 *et seq.* |
| Monmouth | *Tax. Eccl.*, 172 |
| Painscastle | I.P.M., Ed. II, 50 |
| Shelsley | *Worc. I.P.M.*, II, 7 |
| Talgarth | *Cal. C.R., 1307–1313*, 200 |
| Usk | M.A., 1202/6 *et seq.* (7 Ed. II *et seq.*) |
| Wilton | I.P.M., Ed. II, 82 |

**The West of England**
*Cornwall*

| | |
|---|---|
| Heskyn | *E.C.H.*, 207 (1307) |
| Lawhitton | *Mon. Ex.*, 429 (1308) |
| Legha in Buryan | *E.C.H.*, 208, n. 8 (1316-17) |
| Penryn | *Mon. Ex.*, 430 (1308) |
| Sheepstall nr. Ruan | *E.C.H.*, 207 (1260) |
| Talgarrek in Camborne | *E.C.H.*, 206 (1260) |
| Treclego | *E.C.H.*, 207 (1291) |
| Tremodret | *E.C.H.*, 207 (1291) |
| Trewithian in St Wenn | *E.C.H.*, 207 (1313) |
| Tybesta | I.P.M., Ed. I, 95 |

*Devon*

| | |
|---|---|
| Bovey Tracey | I.P.M., Ed. II, 100 (19, Ed. II) [3] |
| Chudleigh | *Mon. Ex.*, 428 |
| Crediton | *Mon. Ex.*, 427 |
| Harpford | I.P.M., Ed. I, 42 (27 Ed. I) |
| Hartland | I.P.M., Ed. I, 32 (27 Ed. I) [3] |
| Molton North | I.P.M., Ed. II, 36, 59 (7 & 10, Ed. II) [3] |
| Molton South | I.P.M., Ed. II, 100 (19 Ed. II) |
| Moreton Hampstead | *Cal. I.P.M.*, III, 282 (25 Ed. I) |
| Sampford Courtenay | I.P.M., Ed. I, 21 (23 Ed. I) [3] |
| Slapton | I.P.M., Ed. I, 32 (35 Ed. I) [3] |

**The West of England**
*Somerset*

| | |
|---|---|
| Cheddar | M.A., 1131/3 (1301) |
| Dulverton | Brit. Mus. Add. MSS. 16332 |
| Dunster | Maxwell-Lyte, *Dunster*, I, 297 |
| Taunton | Eccl. Com. |
| Wells | M.A., 1131/4 (1308-9) |
| Wiveliscombe | *Ibid.* |
| Wookey | *Ibid.* |

**The Cotswold District**

| | |
|---|---|
| Barton-on-Windrush | *Supra*, 46 |
| Bourton-on-the-Water | *Supra*, 46 |
| Hawkesbury | C.R., Gen. Series, 175/41 (19 Ed. [II]) |
| Hinton | *Cartulary of the Monastery of St. Peter of Gloucester* (Rolls Series), III, 60 |
| Overbury | *V.C.H., Worc.*, II, 301 |
| Stanway | *Tax. Eccl.*, 234 (1291) |
| Wheatenhurst | R. & S., 245 (15 Ed. I) |
| Winchcomb | *Supra*, 46 |

**The Middle Thames Region**
*The Kennet Valley*

| | |
|---|---|
| Benham Valence | *V.C.H., Berks*, I, 198 |
| Burghfield | *Ibid.* III, 403; Brit. Mus. Harl. MS. 1708, f. 209 |
| Chilton Foliat | *Wilts I.P.M.*, 350 (1307) |
| Elcot | *Supra*, 47 |
| Hampstead Marshall | *V.C.H., Berks*, IV, 182; I.P.M., 54 Hen. III, 25 |
| Newbury | *V.C.H., Berks*, I, 388, IV, 136 |
| Reading | *Ibid.* III, 344 |
| Speen | *Ibid.* IV, 107; M.A., 750/23 (5-6 Ed. I) |

*The Thames Valley*

| | |
|---|---|
| Medmenham | I.P.M., Hen. III, 30 (1263) |
| Purley | *V.C.H., Berks*, III, 421 |
| Seckworth | *Register of Godstow*, I, 43 |
| Witney | *Supra*, 47 |

*The Chilterns*

| | |
|---|---|
| Wendover | Anc. Ext., 79 (2) (24 Ed. I) |
| Wycombe | *Register of Godstow*, I, 89 (1235) |

**Wiltshire**
*North*

| | |
|---|---|
| Chilton Foliat (*see* Kennet Valley) | |

| **Wiltshire** | | **South-Eastern England** | |
|---|---|---|---|
| Chippenham | *Wilts I.P.M.*, 246, 300 (1300) | Tonbridge | *Hundred Rolls* (Record Comm.), II, 219 |
| Stanley-on-the-Marden | *Supra*, 46 | **The London District** | |
| *South* | | | |
| Downton | Eccl. Com. | Enfield | *Cal. I.P.M.*, V, 192 (5 Ed. II) |
| Harnham | *Wilts I.P.M.*, 227 (1299) | | |
| Mere | *Ibid.* 257; M.A., 1055/21 (1300) | Stratford | *Cal. Letter Books of London*, ed. R. R. Sharpe, C. 51 (1299) |
| Sarum, Old | *Cal. I.M.*, I, 328 (1277-8) | | |
| Steeple Langford | R. & S. Gen. Ser., 16/66 (1294) | **East Anglia** | |
| | | Lawford, Essex | *Cal. I.P.M.*, II, 380 (15 Ed. I) |
| **Hampshire** | | | |
| Alresford, New | *Supra*, 45 (1208-9) | Witham, Essex | *Supra*, 46 [2] |
| Sutton | *Ibid.* | Hadleigh, Suffolk | H. Pigot, *Hadleigh*, 229 (1305) |
| Waltham | *Ibid.* | | |
| Winchester | *Infra*, 52 | Aby (or Strubby), Lincs | *Cal. I.P.M.*, VI, 158 (1321-2) |
| **South-Eastern England** | | | |
| Guildford | *Cal. L.R.*, III, 376 (1251) | Tothill | *Cal. I.M.*, I, 238 (1264-5) |

[1] See also J. Somervell, *Water Power Mills of South Westmorland* (Kendal, 1930), where the probable sites of several of these mills are identified.

[2] *Cf.* M. L. Armitt, " Fullers and Freeholders of Grasmere ", *Westmorland and Cumberland Archaeological Society*, New Series, VIII, 139.

[3] See also *Devon Association for the Advancement of Science, Literature and Art*, XLIV (1912), R. Pearse Chope, " The Aulnager in Devon ".

From this survey, inadequate though it must be, it is evident that the use of the fulling mill had become widespread over England and the borders of Wales between the end of the twelfth and the beginning of the fourteenth century. The fulling mill was, indeed, destined to supersede almost entirely the primitive fulling " under the feet of men ", though its final triumph was not yet assured, and a veritable revolution in one of the chief branches of cloth manufacture was in progress. Foot fulling was giving way to mechanical fulling; human labour was being displaced by water power; the industry was being carried on at the mill rather than in the home; it was dependent as never before upon considerable capital equipment, and was already passing out of the gild system of control. Moreover, changes in technique and organisation, striking enough in themselves to warrant the use of the word revolution, were giving rise to changes in location no less striking—changes which were to affect the distribution of the whole English woollen industry. For the survey, it will be seen, reveals remarkable concentrations of mills in the West Riding of Yorkshire, in the Lake District, in Cornwall, Devon, Somerset and the Cotswolds, in Wilts and in the Kennet Valley, with a corresponding dearth of mills in the eastern parts of England. Further, it shows that the mills were almost entirely in the country districts rather than in the towns. Now in both these respects a startling change has taken place since the twelfth and thirteenth centuries. Then the chief centres of cloth manufacture were not in the hilly northern and western regions of England but in the eastern lowlands; not in the rural districts but in the cities. York, Beverley, Lincoln, Louth, Stamford and Northampton[43] were then famous for their fine quality cloth, and next to them in importance came London, Oxford, Winchester, Leicester and Colchester. In all these cities there was a large-scale industry supplying London and, in many instances which we can trace, the export market, and many have left record of their organised groups of fullers[44] as well as weavers. Now, however, with the invention of the fulling mill, water power was becoming a decisive factor in the location of the industry, and it began to concentrate on the swift, clear streams of the north and west, in remote valleys far beyond the bounds of the ancient chartered cities of the plains.

Hence it comes about that this chapter in the development of England's woollen industry is written largely in the records of the manor rather than of the borough. Indeed, in many instances which we can trace, the initiative in the new developments was taken by the lord of the manor, and the capital equipment provided by him. Thus, as we have seen, King Henry III reconstructed his fulling mill at Elcot, using timber from his forest of Savernake,[45] at a cost of £4 17s. 4d., while the Bishop of Winchester built a new fulling mill at Brightwell costing £9 4s. 4d.[46] Similarly the fulling mill at Burnley was built anew (de novo constructo) for £2 12s. 6d. at the expense of the lord of the manor, and money was also spent on the repair of that at Colne.[47] Such instances could be multiplied.

The incentive to such enterprise on the part of the lord of the manor was that the fulling mill was an investment from which considerable profit could be derived. For, like the corn mill, the oven, the wine press, the dye pan, or any other such equipment erected by the lord, it could be made a manorial monopoly, to which the tenants owed suit.[48] Its

[43] See e.g. Newcastle Records Series, II, Pleas from Curia Regis and Assize Rolls, 307; Calendar of Patent Rolls, 1247-1258, 309; F. D. Swift, The Life and Times of James the First . . . of Aragon (1894), 229; Calendar of Close Rolls, 1234-1237, 73, 301; 1247-1251, 154, 157, 301, 375.

[44] E.g. Lincoln, 1200 (Curia Regis Rolls, I, 259). Stamford, 1182 (F. Peck, The Antiquities of Stamford, 1785, 17). Northampton, 1275 (Hundred Rolls, II, 3). London, 1298 (Liber Custumarum, ed. H. T. Riley, Rolls Series (1860), I, 128). Leicester, 1260 (Records of the Borough of Leicester, ed. M. Bateson (1899), I, 89). Winchester, 1130 (Pipe Roll, 31 Henry III, 37). [45] Supra, 47.

[46] Pipe Roll of the Bishop of Winchester, ut supra, 13: in unum molendino foleratico facto de novo (1208-9).

[47] Two Compoti of the Lancashire and Cheshire Manors of Henry de Lacy, 24 and 33 Edward I, Chetham Soc., New Series, CXII (1907), 15, 16.

[48] On this subject see Beiträge zur Geschichte der Technik (1913), C. Koehne, " Die Mühle im Rechte der Völker "; Annales d'histoire économique et sociale, no. 36, ut supra, and cf. G. Espinas, La draperie dans la Flandre française au moyen age (Paris, 1923), II, 213, n. 6: the Duke of Burgundy writes to his receiver concerning his corn mills at Bruay, suggesting that for his greater profit one of them should be made into a " molin foleur de draps ".

value varied not only according to its own efficiency, but also according to the size, population and industry of the area it served.  Thus, for example, a half share in the fulling mill at Kendal was at one time worth 10 marks a year, but in 1274 its value was considered to have fallen to 8 marks.[49]  The reason alleged was that the tenants at Kentmere no longer did suit to it, and probably what had happened was that the mill at Staveley had now been built;[50] and since Staveley is half-way between Kentmere and Kendal, this would mean for the tenants a journey of only about four instead of eight miles down the Kent valley with their cloths.   It is perhaps not a mere coincidence that the development of the fulling mill took place during the century which saw the crystallisation and culmination of the manorial system with seignurial rights and privileges at their height.

How eagerly such monopolies were coveted may be seen from Jocelin de Brakelond's story of Herbert the Dean, who thought that " the profit which may come from the wind ought to be denied to no man ".   When Herbert excused himself thus for erecting his own windmill the Abbot was speechless with rage, and when Herbert pleaded that it was only to grind his own corn and not other men's, he retorted, " I thank you as much as if you had cut off both my feet; by the face of God, I will never eat bread until that building be overturned ".[51]   If even the wind could be thus monopolised, it was still more easy to enforce control over the water, to insist that the lord alone had the right to use it for profit-making, and that no one else could do so without a licence purchased from him.   Even before the introduction of the fulling mill, the lord claimed the right to dispose of the watercourse as he pleased for fulling and dyeing, reserving it wholly to himself, or leasing it out, often as a monopoly, to others.   Thus for instance at Hadleigh one John Garle-berd was granted for an annual rent 10 feet of land along the bank of the mill-pond, with permission to wash his dyed wool there and draw out water, on condition that no one else should have access there.[52]   Later on two dyers were fined at Hadleigh for washing dyed wool in the lord's pond without licence.[53]   Similarly the cellarer of Bury St Edmunds claimed the right to prohibit the town fullers from using the water.   So profitable were such monopolies that frequently when some measure of freedom was granted to tenants the lord expressly reserved the right to maintain them in his hands.   So, for instance, in the charter of 1228 granted by the Archbishop of York to Sherburn in Elmet, the

<hr/>

[49] P.R.O. Inquisitions Post Mortem, Edward I, 5.

[50] See Table, p. 49.

[51] *Chronica Jocelini de Brakelonda*, ed. J. G. Rokewode (Camden Soc., Old Series, XIII, 1840), 43; *cf.* the dispute at Hesdin-le-Vieux over the fulling mills of the Prior of S. Georges (G. Espinas and H. Pirenne, *Recueil de documents relatifs à l'histoire de l'industrie drapière en Flandre* (Brussels, 1906-23), II, 690).

[52] P.R.O. Ecclesiastical Commission, Various, I, 16/2.

[53] *Ibid.* 16/9.

"burgesses in our borough of Shireburn" were forbidden on pain of forfeiture to have an "oven, dye-pan or fulling stocks". Those who made use of the Archbishop's dye-pan might have, in any week they pleased, "a cartload of dead wood from our wood at Shireburn".[54] Or, again, a charter of King John to Ulverston reserved in the King's hands the oven, dye-pan and fullery (furnum, tinctoriam et fulloniam).[55]

Nor did the lords of the manor claim merely the exclusive right of erecting and possessing such fulleries or fulling mills. They insisted also that all cloth made on the manor must be brought to the manorial mill and there fulled by the new mechanical method, and no longer at home "by hand or foot"; just as they insisted that all corn must be ground in their wind mills or water mills, and not at home by hand mills. Such a claim would seem as difficult to justify as it certainly was to enforce. Never, perhaps, was it wholly conceded, and both manorial court rolls and monastic chronicles bear witness to the constant opposition it aroused, and to the hatred which it inspired. At Hawkesbury, for instance, in 1325-6, one Matilda, daughter of Adam the Carter, was fined for fulling a piece of cloth alibi quam ad molendinum domini.[56] Other such cases occur on manorial court rolls, but most striking is the evidence from monastic sources, and most vivid of all is the account of the struggle over the fulling mills at St Albans in 1274. At this time the abbey of St Albans was evidently as proud of its mills as of its conventual buildings. Abbot John (1235-60) spent, it is said, no less than £100 on their reconstruction, taking them back into his own hands after they had been leased out at farm and allowed to fall into disrepair. His successors were evidently determined to make a goodly profit out of them and claimed that no grinding of corn or fulling of cloth, even of small pieces,[57] could be carried out anywhere except at the abbey mills. The people of St Albans, however, resisted what they considered to be an unwarranted usurpation; they gave the abbey mills a wide berth and preferred to grind and full at home, free of charge, by the primitive old-fashioned methods.[58] In 1274 matters came to a head in what the

[54] Old Yorkshire, 2nd Series, 1885, W. Wheater, "The Ancient Cloth Trade".
[55] T. West, Antiquities of Furness (1813), 85, 418; fulloniam cannot strictly be interpreted as fulling mill as it is here, and often elsewhere, translated: it would seem to denote almost always the primitive non-mechanised fullery, and by the fourteenth century the word has virtually disappeared. Cf. charter, quoted by Ducange, reserving furnos, torcularia, molendina, et fullonos.
[56] P.R.O. Court Rolls, General Series, 175/41.
[57] Pannos viles in contrast to pannos grossos, i.e. probably small pieces woven for use at home rather than whole broadcloths woven for sale; this restriction would be peculiarly irksome.
[58] One of the fullers, Henry de Porta, living in Fullers Street, was accused of erecting in his house a truncum ad fullandum pannos; this may perhaps imply some partly mechanised device such as wooden hammers attached to a revolving drum worked by hand. Such a device is still used today, e.g. in the "Clansman Mills" at Killin. Cf. supra, 44.

chronicler describes as a great insurrection, provoked by the zeal of Abbot Roger in enforcing his monopolies by entering the houses of offenders and levying distraint. The people of St Albans determined to contest the case in the King's court, opened a fighting fund to which rich and poor contributed, and, when Queen Eleanor was passing through St Albans, staged a great demonstration to enlist her support. The Abbot tried to outwit them by diverting the royal route and taking the Queen by a back way to the abbey, but his stratagem failed, and the Queen was intercepted by an angry crowd consisting mainly of women, whose attack, said the monkish chronicler, was formidable " since it is difficult happily to compose the anger of women ". Weeping and lamenting and stretching forth their hands, the women complained bitterly of the Abbot's tyranny, crying " Domina, miserere nobis ". It was not easy, however, for an English mob to make their grievances intelligible to a foreign queen and her entourage, and the sympathy aroused by their tears seems quickly to have been dispelled by the assurances of the astute Abbot that the light words of such women were really unworthy of credence. At any rate when the people of St Albans brought their case into the King's court, judgment was given against them, and, despite an appeal, the Abbot won the day and the judgment was proudly entered in the chronicle for future reference.[59]

The story of the gradual emancipation of the industry from seignurial control does not concern us here, for it belongs to the later Middle Ages and is part of the larger story of the disintegration of the manor and the transition from medieval to modern. Indeed, the development of the cloth industry mirrors the rise and decline of the manor as it does that of the gild. Let us turn rather to consider the effects of the invention of the fulling mill and its extension in rural districts upon the old-established urban centres of the cloth industry.

The development of the fulling mill affected decisively the location of the industry, in that it determined that it should be dispersed over the countryside rather than concentrated in the towns.[60] For though at first these mills, often in remote rural valleys, dealt no doubt with the cloth woven for the needs of the rural population, ultimately they came to cater for the needs of the industrialists. Since cloth could be fulled in the mills mechanically, and therefore more cheaply, inevitably much of the work that had been done in the cities came to be sent out to them, and more and more they took over the fulling branch of the cloth

---

[59] *Gesta Abbatam Monasterii Sancti Albani, ut supra*, I, 323, 410 *et seq.* The struggle continued, here as elsewhere, for more than a century, and was one of the causes contributing towards the Peasants' Revolt. *Cf.* the struggle at Evesham during the fourteenth and fifteenth centuries over ovens and cornmills; in 1307 a private oven erected in his house by William de Tettebury was thrown down by the Abbey steward with the aid of the town bailiffs, and in 1388 the hand mills of other tenants were destroyed, as was a horse mill in 1430. (G. May, *History of Evesham* (1845), 83.)

[60] In this respect the English industry offers a striking contrast to that of Flanders.

industry, threatening the handcraft fullers in the towns with unemployment and starvation. In London, for instance, so serious was the competition of the country fulling mills that complaint was made to the King in 1298. It was said that certain men of the city had sent cloths "outside the city to the mill of Stratford and elsewhere, and caused them to be fulled there, to the grave damage of those to whom the cloth belonged and also of the men using this office in the city ".[61] Round these mills grew up groups of industrial workers entirely outside the jurisdiction of urban gilds. In many little rural hamlets in valleys where water power had been turned to account we find colonies of fullers in the late thirteenth century, working evidently to supply no merely local demand. Thus there were fullers scattered throughout the West Riding valleys; at Calverley, for instance, there seem to have been at least five in about 1257.[62] The tendency for one of the chief branches of the woollen industry to shift from the town to the country gave a great stimulus to the development of the industry as a whole there, and doomed to failure the attempt of the cities to concentrate it within their walls to their own profit. To the advantages of water power were added the advantages of freedom from the high taxation in the towns and from the restrictions of the gilds. Colonies of weavers also began to settle round the fulling mills, and, as the industrial population of the rural regions increased, so that of the cities decreased, and the once mighty weavers' gilds sank into insignificance and poverty. The industry, in fact, was deserting the towns for the countryside. There is clear evidence of this decay in the case of at least seven of the leading cloth-producing cities, and others may yet be found to have been in similar case.

Winchester, for instance, in the twelfth century had a considerable number of both weavers and fullers, each organised in their own gild, and each paying £6 yearly to the crown in the time of Henry I.[63] But by the time of Edward I it was becoming increasingly difficult to collect the money, and the reason given for this was that large numbers of the clothworkers had left the town.[64] At Oxford also there was a weavers' gild paying £6 to the crown in the twelfth century.[65] But in the reign of Edward I they successfully petitioned that the sum should be reduced to 42s. on the ground that, while there used to be sixty or more weavers

---

[61] Liber Custumarum, ut supra, I, 127; Calendar of Letter Books of the City of London; Letter Book C, ed. R. R. Sharpe (1901), 51.

[62] H. Heaton, The Yorkshire Woollen and Worsted Industries (Oxford Historical and Literary Studies, X, 1920), 5, quoting Calverley Charters, Thoresby Society Publications, VI, 8-55.          [63] Pipe Roll 31 Henry I, 37.

[64] V.C.H., Hampshire, V (1912), 477. Complaints of financial stringency are, of course, a commonplace of the public records, but the reason here given for the difficulty, read in conjunction with the Bishop of Winchester's records, seems to bear the stamp of truth.

[65] Pipe Roll 31 Henry I, 2; see also V.C.H., Oxfordshire, II (1907), for an account of the fluctuations of the weavers' gild (242 et seq.).

in the town, there were now only fifteen.   Later they asked for a further reduction to 6s. 8d., since there were only seven weavers left, and those were poor; finally, in 1323, they pleaded that all these were dead and had no successors.[66]   The Lincoln weavers were also finding difficulties about paying their annual £6 to the crown in the early fourteenth century and alleged the same reasons, stating that there were no weavers left in Lincoln between 1321 and 1331 and from then until 1345 only a very few, though when Henry II granted their gild there were more than two hundred.[67]   In London the number of looms was said to have fallen from 380 to 80 early in the fourteenth century.[68]   York was in very similar difficulties.   In the twelfth century its weavers' gild had paid a larger sum than any other—£10 annually, but during the thirteenth century it fell into more and more serious arrears, pleading in excuse that " divers men in divers places in the country, elsewhere than in the city or in the other towns and demesne boroughs—make dyed and rayed cloths ".[69]

The decline of the industry in all these five boroughs is easily apparent, since each had an old-established weavers' gild, paying annually to the crown as lord of the borough.   It is less easy to trace developments in the six other leading cloth-making cities, for four at least of these were not royal boroughs, none of them had privileged early gilds, so far as can be discovered, and comparable evidence is not therefore available. Yet here too we can find signs of decay.   Northampton, for instance, complained in 1334 that formerly 300 clothmakers had worked there, but that now the houses where they used to live had all fallen down.[70] Leicester in 1322 declared that there was only one fuller left in the town " and he a poor man ",[71] and it is significant that from the end of the thirteenth century the very extensive Leicester records contain less and less about the cloth industry and more and more about the marketing of raw wool.

Competition from the country districts was not, of course, entirely new.   Some clothmaking had always been carried on in the villages. But hitherto the " great industry " for export had been to a marked extent concentrated in the cities and controlled by them; there lived the capitalist entrepreneurs, carrying on the dyeing and finishing processes, often in their own houses, and employing the colonies of skilled weavers

[66] Oxford Historical Society, XXXII (1896), 99, 123-4; P.R.O. Ancient Petitions, 132/6569.
[67] Calendar of Close Rolls, 1348-1350, 120 (Petition of 1348); Telariorum, given as " spinners " in the calendar, is a synonym for Textorum " Weavers ".
[68] Lipson, Economic History of England, ut supra, 450, quoting Liber Custumarum, ut supra, I, 416-25.   Other versions give the original number as 280.
[69] Heaton, op. cit. 29 (Petition of 1304).
[70] Rotuli Parliamentorum ut et Petitiones et Placita in Parliamento (Record Commission, 1767-77), II, 85.
[71] Calendar of Inquisitions Miscellaneous, II, 138.

and fullers settled within the walls, though they would also buy the rough unfinished webs brought in for sale by the country people. Now, with the invention of the fulling mill, the balance was tilted in favour of the country districts, and the cities were faced with constantly intensified competition. How then did they strive to maintain or recapture their supremacy?

Where circumstances were favourable some set up their own mills, as did Winchester in 1269, when the town granted permission to nine fullers to construct a fullers' mill.[72]  But the slow-moving courses of the rivers on which most of these towns lay were less adapted to mills than were their swift upper courses, nor can the requisite space for the diversion of the watercourse have been always readily available. Moreover, there would tend to be strong opposition to an innovation which would throw so many out of work, and all the forces of conservatism would be arrayed against it.

Other towns therefore resisted the adoption of the new methods, urging the inferiority of machine work as well as the unemployment it caused. Thus a complaint from certain Londoners to the King in 1298 declared that, according to the accepted custom, cloths should be " fulled under the feet of men of this office, or their servants, in their houses in the city and not elsewhere ", but that certain fullers had sent such cloths " outside the city to the mill of Stratford and elsewhere and caused them to be fulled there, to the grave damage of those to whom the cloth belonged and also of the men using this office in the city ".[73] The petitioners did not, however, secure the prohibition of fulling at mills, but only an ordinance that no cloth should be sent outside the city to be fulled at mills (pur foller as molins) except by those who actually owned the cloth, and that six men should watch at the city gates, arrest the cloths, and keep them until the owners came and avowed them as theirs.[74] Twelve years later one Godfrey de Loveyne was heavily fined for sending three cloths outside the city to be fulled at mills.[75]

Most towns, however, concerned themselves primarily with confining the industry within the city walls. Their own civic ordinances could at least compel clothmakers in the city to employ city labour only and thus to maintain the wealth and prosperity of the city. Thus when the craft ordinances of Bristol were first written down in the city records in 1346, that of the fullers decreed qe nul hom face amesner hors de ceste ville nule manere drap a foler qe home appele raucloth sur peyne de perdre xld. pur chescun drap.[76]  In the same ordinance there is mention of cloth being sent " to the mill " (al molyn), so that clearly the opposi-

---

[72] The Black Book of Winchester, ed. W. H. Bird (1925), 190.
[73] Liber Custumarum, ut supra, I, 127.
[74] Ibid. I, 127, 128; Calendar of Letter Book C, ut supra, 51.
[75] Calendar of Letter Books of the City of London; Letter Book D, ed. R. R. Sharpe (1902), 239 (pannos crudos is probably raw, i.e. unfulled, cloth, not " undyed ").
[76] Little Red Book of Bristol, ed. F. B. Bickley (1900), II, 7.

tion was not to milling as such but to the work going out of the city. The prohibition was repeated later in the century,[77] and similar prohibitions continued to be made in other towns. At Winchester, for instance, in 1402, clothmakers of the town were forbidden to employ either fullers or weavers outside the town.[78] A somewhat similar ordinance seems to have been made at Leicester in 1260, and citizens were punished for breach of it.[79]

Such ordinances might do something to prevent city manufacturers from having dealings with workers outside, but they could not prevent an independent industry from flourishing in the country districts. Some cities therefore turned to an authority higher than that of the city and prayed the King to aid them in securing the monopoly they coveted. The York weavers, with those of other royal boroughs in Yorkshire, had already, by their charter of 1164, been granted a monopoly of making dyed and rayed cloth in all Yorkshire. At the end of the thirteenth century their monopoly was, as we have seen, being seriously infringed, so in 1304 they petitioned the King and he ordered the Exchequer to have enquiries made and to compel all found plying the craft in illegal places to refrain.[80] We do not know what effect, if any, was given to this order, but we do know that it did not, any more than did the cities' own ordinances, succeed in the impossible task of confining the cloth industry within urban walls.

The decline of the industry in the thirteenth century in what had been its most flourishing urban centres is as striking as is its expansion in rural regions during the same period, but it is the urban side of the matter which has hitherto attracted the attention of historians, and from it they have falsely deduced a decline in the industry as a whole. The real significance of this decline now becomes clear. The industry was developing, and developing rapidly, but outside the jurisdiction of those cities that had once taken the lead in it. The decay of the once famous cloth-making cities of the eastern plain and the rise of the country fulling mills shows not only that the rural industry was gaining over the urban, but also, when we consider the preponderance of fulling mills in north and west of England, that the broadcloth industry as a whole was tending to shift from east to west, to new centres in the West Riding, the Lake District and the West of England. For here were to be found ample supplies not only of fine wool but also of water power. In the twelfth and early thirteenth centuries the fine quality English cloths specially in demand abroad were cloths " of Stamford ", " of Lincoln ", " of Louth ", " of Beverley ", " of York "; but in the fourteenth and fifteenth centuries there was no demand at all for these cloths, but much

[77] *Little Red Book of Bristol*, ed. F. B. Bickley (1900), II, 7.
[78] *Black Book of Winchester, ut supra*, 8.
[79] *Records of the Borough of Leicester, ut supra*, I, 91, 347.
[80] Heaton, *op. cit.* 28-9.

for "Kendals". "Ludlows", "Cotswolds", "Mendips", "Castle-combes", "Stroudwaters" or "Westerns", and the primary, though not the only, factor in this change was the invention of the fulling mill.

## Postscript

Since this article was written some twenty-four additional early English fulling mills (pre 1327) have come to light, and I am much indebted to those correspondents who have kindly brought a number of these to my notice. In addition, Mr R. V. Lennard has called attention in the *Economic History Review*, XVII, no. 2 (1947) to the mention of a fulling mill in a charter of the Abbey of St Wandrille in Normandy, calendared by J. H. Round (*Calendar of Documents preserved in France*, no. 166, 58). This document is a seventeenth-century version, in the Bibliothèque Nationale, of a charter ascribed by Round to the years 1060-80. The original charter is in the Archives départementales de la Seine-Inférieure at Rouen (Série H, non coté) and has been published by Ferdinand Lot, who dates it at about 1086-7 (*Etudes critiques sur l'abbaye de Saint-Wandrille*, Bibliothèque de l'Ecole des Hautes Etudes, 204ᵉ fascicule, Paris 1913, 96-7). Even though this too speaks of a *molendino fullonario* and thus seems to prove the fulling mill to have been in existence in the late eleventh century, it in no way invalidates the general conclusions on pages 45-6.

ABBREVIATIONS IN TABLE OF MILLS

M.A.       =Public Record Office, Ministers Accounts.
C.R.        =    „     „     „    Court Rolls.
R. & S.     =    „     „     „    Rentals and Surveys.
Anc. Ext.   =    „     „     „    Ancient Extents.
Eccl. Com.   =    „     „     „    Ecclesiastical Commission, Various, II, 159273
                 *et seq.*
I.P.M.        =Public Record Office, Inquisitions Post Mortem.
Cal. I.P.M.   =*Calendar of Inquisitions Post Mortem.*
Cal. I.M.     =    „    „   *Inquisitions Miscellaneous.*
Cal. C.R.     =    „    „   *Close Rolls.*
Cal. L.R.     =    „    „   *Liberate Rolls*
V.C.H.        =*Victoria County History.*
Tax. Eccl.    =*Taxatio Ecclesiastica, circa 1291* (Record Commission 1802).
Mon. Ex     =Oliver, *Monasticon Exoniensis.*
Wilts I.P.M. =*Abstracts of Wiltshire Inquisitions Post Mortem,* ed. E. A. Fry (1908), 1242-1326.
Worc. I.P.M.=*Inquisitions Post Mortem for the County of Worcestershire,* ed. for the Worcester Historical Society by J. W. Willis Bund (1894).
Notts I.P.M. =Thoroton Soc., Record Series, IV, *Inquisitions Post Mortem for Nottinghamshire,* II (1279-1321), ed. J. Standish (1914).
E.H.C.        =Charles Henderson, *Essays in Cornish History* (1935), 206, "Cornish Tucking Mills and Windmills".[1]

[1] This gives no references, but is based mainly on the author's own extensive collection of Cornish deeds, now in the Truro Museum.

# CREDIT IN MEDIEVAL TRADE [1]

## M. M. POSTAN

THE extent to which medieval trade was based on credit does not figure among the favourite problems of economic history. Not that it has been entirely neglected, since the economic theorists have been busy over it for more than seventy-five years: it is the historian who is guilty of neglect. In his absence the field was entirely appropriated by the economic theorist; and the latter, unsupported and unrestrained by research, inevitably produced notions unrelated to historical facts. These notions spring from the source whence have originated so many current preconceptions about the economic nature of medieval civilization—namely, speculations as to the "stages" of economic development. In the nineteenth century sociologists and economists regarded their age as biologists regard the *homo sapiens,* as the culmination of an evolutionary process. To them epochs of history were successive stages in the uninterrupted ascent of mankind from the crude primitivity of pre-history to the complex perfection of their own age. In accordance with this view, the economists have constructed a number of hypothetical models of the evolutionary ladder, in which every step differed from the one which followed in that it did not contain one or other element of the modern economic system, or else contained it in a less developed and a more imperfect form. Now credit, especially in its alliance with trade, does constitute an essential principle of our present economic system; it was therefore inevitably drawn into the schemes of economic progress. The argument was simple. If mercantile credit was one of the basic principles of our economic civilization, then every successive stage of economic evolution made some contribution towards it, and therefore the further back we went the less important the function of credit became, until we reached a time when there was very little credit or none at all. Hence the prevailing notions of the absence or the undeveloped state of credit in the Middle Ages.

This view was given its clearest and sharpest expression by Bruno Hildebrand, one of the fathers of the "historical" school of Political

[1] The following abbreviations have been used in this Article: E.Ch.Pr. = Public Record Office, Early Chancery Proceedings; M.R. = Public Record Office, K.R. Exchequer Memoranda Rolls; A.V. = Public Record Office, K.R. Exchequer, Accounts Various; L.B. = Calendars of Letter Books (ed. Sharpe); P.M. Rolls = Plea and Memoranda Rolls at the Guildhall; V.S.W.G. = Vierteljahrschrift für Sozial-und-Wirtschaftsgeschichte.

Economy. He believed that the only differences between epoch and epoch which furnished principles of evolutionary classification were those relating to the methods of exchange. And from the point of view of the methods of exchange there were three main stages of economic development: the prehistorical and early medieval stage of natural economy when goods were exchanged against other goods; the later medieval stage of "cash" (money) economy, when goods were bought for ready money; and the modern stage of credit economy when commercial exchange was based on credit.[2] The form in which Hildebrand expressed this view of the Middle Ages as the pre-credit era was too simple and straightforward to find general acceptance among historical economists. Karl Bücher, who on this question had a greater influence than any other of Hildebrand's successors, knew more about the Middle Ages, and was careful not to make the presence or absence of credit the sole *differentia* between the various stages of economic development. But, in regarding the institutions of our civilization as the product of a growth extending over the whole of European history, he was bound to assume that in the earlier stages credit could only play a minor part in economic life. There was some miscellaneous borrowing and lending in the Middle Ages, but it did not testify to the economic importance of credit. Medieval loans were always disguised into, or regarded as species of, other transactions with which the Middle Ages were more familiar, especially those of purchase and sale. Moreover, they were used not for production, but for consumption. "It may even be doubted whether in medieval trade credit operations can be spoken of at all. Early exchange is based on ready payment. Nothing is given except where a tendered equivalent can be directly received."[3]

Bücher's general theory of economic evolution now forms one of the axiomatic assumptions of historical research; and his views on credit were naturally adopted by historians with the rest of his theory. In England Dr Cunningham set out to describe the "growth" of English industry and trade: the story of how England's economic power steadily waxed from the early Middle Ages. On the question of medieval credit he believed that only at the close of the Middle Ages did English foreign trade become important enough to afford an opportunity for the use of credit. Until then, notably in the thirteenth and the fourteenth centuries, the volume of English trade was modest, and its methods primitive; the capital employed in it was very small, and there was hardly any room in it for credit; "the demand for money for com-

---

[2] "Natural- Geld- und Creditwirtschaft" in *Jahrb. Nationalökonomie* (1864). For the theoretical criticism of Hildebrand's scheme, see Gustav Cohn, *System der National-ökonomie* (1885), I, 454-5.
[3] *Economic Evolution* (English trans. by Wickett) (1901), 128 *et seq*. Restated in *Grundriss der Sozialökonomie* (1924), I, i

mercial and industrial purposes, at the only rates at which men were accustomed to lend, was practically nil "; " money-lending had nothing to do with commerce; wealthy men borrowed in emergency, or to equip for a war "; " it is very probable that even in emergency merchants did not often have recourse to borrowing, as the gild merchants made arrangements which enabled them, in some cases at all events, to get temporary aid ". As to " credit as a basis for transactions of other kinds "," there is a striking difference between those times and ours ", as " transactions were carried on in bullion; men bought with coin and sold for coin "—in other words, " dealing for credit was little developed, and dealing in credit was unknown ".[4] These views are still common.[5]

There cannot be many topics in the economic history of the Middle Ages on which the evidence is as copious as on credit. The bulk of the evidence consists of records of debts. Most numerous of all are the records of " recognizances "—*i.e.* debts acknowledged before judicial tribunals and entered upon their rolls. After the passing of the Statute of Burnell, 1283, the entries began to be concentrated on special rolls kept by the authorities empowered by the Act to receive recognizances. But before 1283, and to some extent after, recognizances were also entered on various official registers: the letter books of London, the registers of other municipalities, the memoranda rolls of the exchequer, and occasionally on the close rolls and the other chancery enrolments, or the rolls of the King's courts. The number which has survived amounts to several scores of thousands. The second class of references to debts consists of entries and documents relating to pleas of debt. Of these especially important are the petitions on debts among the early chancery proceedings at the Public Record Office; next come references to cases of debts brought before the municipal authorities for trial, execution, or other purposes, and recorded in various municipal registers, and above all on the plea and memoranda rolls at the Guild-hall. Of considerable importance also are the numerous patent roll entries of pardons for outlawry for not appearing before the royal justices on plaints of debt; and finally comes the uncharted sea of the plea rolls and the various local court rolls.[6] The third class is composed of documents dealing with debts and credits, but not in connection with their recording, enforcement, or adjudication. To this class, in the first instance, belong the valuable inventories of debts and goods of foreign merchants, or lists of their transactions, compiled on several occasions in the thirteenth and the fourteenth centuries and now grouped together in the " accounts various " of the exchequer at the Public

---

[4] I, 362-4, 463.

[5] There are, of course, exceptions. See Thorold Rogers, *Industrial and Commercial History* (1892), 69; E. Lipson, *Economic History* (1915), I, 528 *et seq.*

[6] Strictly speaking, to this class of judicial records belong also the statute staple certificates at the Public Record Office—a multitude of documents judicial in purpose, but identical with ordinary recognizances in content.

Record Office. To these one must add the various collections of non-official documents, illustrating the financial transactions of medieval merchants, such as the Cely accounts in the Chancery Files[7] and their letters in the volumes 53 and 59 of the " ancient correspondence " at the Public Record Office; a ledger of a fourteenth-century merchant, a day book of a fifteenth-century scrivener,[8] and a vast number of other miscellaneous documents at the Public Record Office showing the medieval merchants in their dealings with each other. Lastly, there are numerous references to debts and credit in the more general sources, such as the parliamentary rolls, Statutes of the Realm, Rymer's *Foedera*.

It would be possible to enumerate other documents where medieval borrowing or lending is recorded, mentioned, or described. Not all these references to debts relate to mercantile credit, but the proportion is very high. Many debts were never enrolled or officially recorded, especially in the earlier centuries when the tally was still the commonest financial instrument, and in the later Middle Ages when various forms of informal bonds came into use. It was in the second half of the thirteenth and the first half of the fourteenth century that official enrolments in the shape of recognizances were most commonly used for the recording of debts. And it is just in the recognizances of the thirteenth and early fourteenth centuries that the prevalence of mercantile debts is most clearly marked. The preamble to the Statute Burnell, introducing that system of recognizances which prevailed all through the later centuries, expressly stated that the new order was instituted for the benefit of the merchants. That this remained the avowed object of the reformed recognizance was declared or implied in all the subsequent measures dealing with this financial instrument. Some non-mercantile debts found their way into the recognizance rolls, whereupon the Ordainers commanded in 1311 that the Statute Burnell should not hold " except between merchant and merchant, and of merchandise sold between them ".[9] The ordinance remained in force only until 1326, but even a cursory review of the rolls will show that for a number of years after 1326 they continued to deal chiefly with debts between merchants, which presumably arose out of ordinary mercantile transactions. It is only in the second half of the fourteenth century that a change came over the character of the entries in the recognizance rolls —a change reflecting not the evolution of credit itself, but a certain new departure in the nature of financial instruments.[10]

The conclusions to be drawn from this evidence are obvious. The abundance of mercantile debts clearly demonstrates that credit com-

[7] Public Record Office, Chancery Miscellanea, bundle 37.
[8] A.V. 509/19 and 128/37.
[9] 5 Edw. II, c. 33; L.B.E., 53, 213; *Rotuli Parliamentorum*, I, 457.
[10] This and other questions relating to the employment of financial instruments in the Middle Ages lie outside the present article.

monly entered into the commercial practice of the Middle Ages. At the same time it must not be taken to imply the rare use of cash payments, since debts were recorded while cash transactions were not. It affords, therefore, no indication as to the relative importance of credit in the total volume of medieval trade, or as to its part in the turnover of individual merchants. Nor does it solve any of the problems essential for the correct understanding of the nature and function of mercantile credit. Granted that credit transactions were frequent, does it necessarily follow that there was an organic connection between credit and trade? Did credit enter into the ordinary commercial routine, and was it equally common in every branch and at every stage of business? Was it adapted to the multifarious needs of commerce? Did it fulfil the various functions which mercantile credit is theoretically supposed to fulfil? And was there any connection between its functions, its forms, and its methods? The problems are many, and no attempt will be made here to exhaust them all; neither will it be possible to deal with any of them separately. All it is proposed to do here is to review the chief forms of medieval credit in the hope that this will in itself throw light on the problems enumerated.


## SALE CREDITS

" Sale credits "—that is, credits in the shape of deferred payments for goods sold or advances for future delivery—enter into the actual exchange of goods more directly than loans of money; and it was sale credits, rather than loans, that Hildebrand and his followers had in mind when denying the existence of mercantile credit in the Middle Ages. Fortunately no other form of credit is better served by the surviving evidence, so that even a summary treatment of facts will demonstrate clearly enough the extent to which sale credits were common in the different branches of medieval trade.

We may begin with the trade in goods retailed, as some of the fullest and earliest collections of recognizances, notably those recorded in the early letter books and recognizance rolls of London, consist largely of debts for goods intended for consumption in this country. Some of these goods, whether imported from abroad or produced here, were sold directly to the consumer; but most of them to other merchants. German historians have debated whether the Middle Ages possessed a class of traders who could be labelled as wholesalers. One point, however, was not disputed. Whether a separate class of wholesalers existed or not, wholesale trade was common throughout the Middle Ages. Goods were often handled in bulk and sold, not to the final consumers, but to other merchants, and often changed hands several times before being retailed. Now, the evidence of debts makes it clear that credit was demanded and allowed at every stage through which the goods passed from importer or producer to consumer.

Of the foreign commodities retailed in this country, wine seems to have lent itself best to handling *en gros* and to successive sales on credit. The trade in wine, like that in wool and cloth, attracted a large amount of capital, and was apparently open to all—vintners, cordwainers, drapers, curriers, saddlers, mercers, even princes, nobles and ecclesiastics. Some bought for retail, others for resale to merchants. And whenever wine changed hands an opportunity for credit arose. To begin with, wine was often, though not always, bought on credit from wine growers and wine merchants in Gascony and Poitou. Then the importers. whether English or foreign, sold it on credit to retailers or wholesale merchants in England The transactions recorded in London recognizances show wealthy vintners of the thirteenth or the early fourteenth centuries, like William Barache, Simon of Farnham, Allan of Suffolk and others, regularly buying wine on credit from the importers and reselling it again to taverners and smaller vintners. Occasionally they formed partnerships with taverners, who retailed their wine for a share in the profits. But often the chain between the importer and the retailer consisted of several links; there was more than one middleman, and consequently more than one credit transaction.[11]

Similarly as to other commodities. Goods in common demand, like corn, leather, woad, etc., whether imported from abroad or produced here, and whether sold at fairs or distributed from the larger towns, changed hands several times before reaching the consumer, and every time they changed hands credit could be demanded and conceded.[12]

The terms of payment in the principal export trades were similar to those in the internal trade. Exporters of cloth in the later fourteenth and fifteenth centuries made almost exactly the same use of sale credits, and offered the same scope for them, as the wine trade. In its passage from producer to foreign consumer cloth went through several stages, at each of which credit invariably appeared as the governing principle of the transaction. Clothiers would, as a rule, deliver cloth to drapers and other merchants for export or internal sale on several months' credit. Sometimes an additional middleman would intervene; a wandering chapman who had bought the cloth on his circuit, or a big wholesaler, or, what seems to have been quite usual, occasional speculators drawn from various trades and occupations. A chancery petition

[11] See L.B.A., 6 (Falco), *The Red Register of Lynn*, I, 33; Letter Books A, B, and C, and Guildhall Recognizance Rolls 1-4, *passim*; F. Sargeant in Unwin, *Finance and Trade under Edward III*.

[12] The early Letter Books and Recognizance Rolls at the Guildhall abound with references to chaloners, cordwainers and leathersellers buying leather, yarn and other commodities from foreign importers. For credit in the fourteenth and fifteenth centuries between wholesalers and country retailers, see the very numerous references in the Patent Rolls (Pardons for Outlawry), also E.Ch.Pr. 6/20, 7/122, 9/382, 26/272, 46/144.

of the beginning of the fifteenth century tells an interesting story of a quantity of blankets bought by " certeyn chapmen ", resold by them to two vintners, who in their turn resold it *in solido* to someone else. At each stage, except the first, of which we are told nothing, the cloth was sold on credit. And this was apparently quite an ordinary transaction.[13] Nothing can demonstrate better the dependence of the English cloth trade on the system of postponed payments than the failure of the Act of 1430 as to credit sales to foreigners. It was enacted then that no Englishman should sell his goods to aliens except for ready money and goods. A year later, however, the Commons petitioned and Parliament enacted that it should be lawful to sell cloth to aliens " per apprest de paiement . . . de 6 mois a 6 mois ", as otherwise the cloth " could not be uttered or sold ".[14] But even in this form the Statute could not be enforced. Goods other than cloth continued to be sold to foreigners on credit, while in the sales of cloth the terms often did not conform to the legal " de 6 mois a 6 mois ", and credit was allowed for a period of one, two, and even three years.[15]

It remains to show how this system of sale credits was applied to the wool trade, the oldest and the most important branch of English export trade. The financial methods of the English wool trade in the second half of the fifteenth century have recently been described by Dr Power,[16] whose account is largely based on the Cely accounts and correspondence. The Celys bought the greater part of their wool on credit from wool merchants in the Cotswolds, and in turn sold it on credit to foreigners abroad. This chain of credits, however, commenced before the Celys received the wool, for we know that at least one of their Cotswold woolmen, William Midwinter, himself bought his goods from local men on credit. Neither did the chain come to its end as the wool passed into the hands of wool merchants and clothiers in foreign towns. In other words, from the wool grower in the Cotswolds to the buyer of Dutch cloth in Poland or Spain there was one uninterrupted succession of credit sales. This practice was not confined to the Celys, and it was certainly not a fifteenth-century invention. However different may have been the scope and technique of the wool trade in earlier centuries, the methods of payments remained very largely the same. As far back as we can trace the activities of the English exporters on the foreign wool markets, the transactions were commonly based on credit. That in the second half of the thirteenth century English exporters were in the habit of selling their wool on credit is illustrated by a document in the archives of Ypres recording a debt owed by Boidin, son of Walter de Gaunt, to

[13] E.Ch.Pr. 20/2; the other references are too many to be enumerated.

[14] 8 Hen. VI, c. 24; 9 Hen. VI, c. 2; *Rotuli Parliamentorum*, IV, 377, 509.

[15] Abundantly shown by the cases in the M.R. for 37 and 38 Hen. VI, when the court of exchequer happened to obtain information about the credit transactions of a number of foreigners.

[16] *Cambridge Historical Journal*, 1926.

John Ludlow, an English wool exporter, for wool bought in July 1291. Desmarez, who prints this bond, mentions also a number of other similar documents among the thirteenth-century obligations. One Nicolas Ludlow, of Salisbury, figures often in them: in 1277 he appears as creditor for £34 1s. 6d.; in 1279 he sells wool on credit to the value of £234.[17] In the fourteenth century the experiments with the Staple system several times threatened completely to disorganize the trade; yet so long as the English continued to export their wool themselves they regularly sold it on credit.

This close dependence of the wool trade at the foreign marts on the smooth working of the machinery of sale credits was at times clear even to the blundering governments of the fifteenth century. But what the governments admitted only occasionally, the merchants demanded all the time. We find them in 1410 petitioning the Crown to put an end to the English piracy against the Flemings in the interests of the English merchants who " have communication in the feat of merchandise with the inhabitants of the said country of Flanders, appresting them ' selon la cours de la monde ' their wool and merchandise, which cannot and never could be delivered at their true value to the common profit of the whole Realm without that they be apprested in instalments ".[18] And declarations of a similar nature occur over and over again in the fifteenth century in connection with the frequent interruptions of trade by war or the equally frequent anti-credit measures of the Crown. The failure of these measures, more than anything else, reveals the extent to which credit permeated the sale of wool abroad. The attempts to regulate credit in the wool trade of Calais had a greater chance of success than in other trades, since the wool sales abroad were centralized and rigidly controlled through the machinery of the Staple. Yet here, as in the cloth trade, the official policy came to grief through the reluctance and inability of the merchants to carry it out. The so-called Ordinance of Partition of Wool of 1430, which introduced a rigid system of control over the transactions of individual merchants, provided that payments for wool should be made in hand, and the bullion be brought without delay to the mint at Calais.[19] The Ordinance could hardly have been obeyed to the letter; still it was effective enough to provide the merchants with a grievance.[20] In 1442 it was enacted upon a petition of the Commons that the Staplers should bring to the mint only one-third of the bullion,[21] which virtually legalized the " lending " of the remaining two-thirds of the cost of wool. But even this milder regulation was found to be unenforceable, and when in October of the same year the

---

[17] G. Desmarez, *Lettres des Foires*, no. 157.

[18] L. Gilliodts van Severen, *Le Cotton Manuscrit Galba B.*1 (Brussels, 1896), no. 101. See also *ibid.* nos. 127, 133, 135, 168.

[19] 8 Hen. VI, c. 17, 18. (Re-enacted for another three years in 1433, 11 Hen. VI, c. 13.) *Rotuli Parliamentorum*, IV, 358-9.

[20] *Ibid.* IV, 490, 509.  [21] *Ibid.* V, 64; 20 Hen. VI, c. 12.

Crown approached the Company of the Staple for a loan, it was confronted by the demand that the " merchants English mygt selle their wolles withoute that they shold to be arted to take the thirde part in bullion ".  The question came up for discussion before the Council and the conditions of the Staplers were vigorously opposed by Cardinal Beaufort on the ground that their acceptance would be equivalent to a Flemish victory on this issue, as " yif they could feele that the kyng for necessitee sholde thus dispense with the statute of bringing in of bullion . . . he shulde never hereafter by constreint make hem bringe in any bullion "  The Cardinal on this occasion was less of a business man than usual.  He failed to recognize that the law could not be executed. When the Council met a few days later it had before it the statement of the mayor of the Staple to the effect that it was impossible to bring in the third part in bullion, and that the Staple had " of ther owne auctoritee . . . dispensed " with the Act of 1442.[22]  Thus ended the endeavour of the Lancastrian Government to restrict the credit in the wool sales,[23] in the interests of its bullionist policy.  An attempt to revive the policy was made under Edward IV in 1463, when it was enacted that no merchant of the Staple should sell wool at Calais without that he " take ready payment ", of which one-half he must bring in bullion or English coin to England within three months following the sale.  This Act sounded more formidable than it actually was, for in spite of its general prohibition of credit sales merchants could allow the buyer three months' credit on one-half of the price and unlimited credit on the rest.[24]  But whatever the provisions of the law meant, they could not be of great importance, since the Staplers continued to sell as they thought best: the contemporary business of wool sales in Calais abounds with references to sales on credit; and in 1473 the legal restrictions of credit were swept away.[25]

So much for the foreign end of the trade.  The issue becomes somewhat more complicated as we pass to the trade on this side of the Channel.  What is striking about the sale credits in the English wool trade abroad is not only their frequency, but also their uniform " direction ".  As in other branches of trade, it was commonly the seller who gave credit: goods were sold for deferred payments, and the " flow " of credit was from the seller to the buyer.  The practice was not quite so regular and uniform in the wool trade at home.  The sales on credit were at least as common as in the foreign wool marts, only the direction of credit was not invariably the same.  In the transactions between the exporters and the merchants who supplied them with wool deferred payments apparently formed the rule;[26] so much so that the very fact

[22] *Proceedings of the Privy Councils*, V, 216-19.
[23] For a fruitless attempt to revive the policy, see *Rotuli Parliamentorum*, VI, 256-76.
[24] 3 Edw. IV, c. 1.                    [25] *Rotuli Parliamentorum*, VI, 60.
[26] Letter Books A and B, and Recognizance Rolls 1-3, *passim*; *Calendar of the Plea and Memoranda Rolls*, 9, 262 ; P.M. Rolls, A 23 m. 6 dorso, A 84 m. 5, etc. ; E.Ch.Pr. 26/395, etc.

that the Italians paid *au comptant* more frequently than the English
was regarded as an unfair advantage over the native merchant.[27]   This
rule, however, does not seem to have applied to every wool sale in
England irrespective of who were the contracting parties.   Mr Bond
and Mr Whitwell have shown that in the thirteenth century the Italians,
in their dealings with the monasteries, commonly paid for the wool
before it was shorn or collected.[28]   They advanced to the monasteries
sums of money as payment, full or partial, for wool to be delivered in
the course of one or several " seasons " next following.   Transactions of
this type were even older than the thirteenth century.   The unique roll
of debts to William Cade, a twelfth-century financier, records several
advance payments for wool.   " Monaci de Parco de Luda debent 70
marcas quas receperunt de lana sua quam Willelmus debuit habere 6
anni post mortem Teobaldi archiepiscopi. . . ."[29]   The curia regis rolls
report what seems to be a similar transaction for the closing years of the
twelfth century between William, son of Robert, and the Prior of Swine.[30]
References of this kind become very common in the thirteenth century.
The accounts of Flemish merchants whose goods and debts were arrested
by Edward I teem with entries of sums owed to them on account of
advances made to monasteries and others for wool of future growth.
But it was the great Italian houses of the thirteenth and fourteenth centuries—the Ricardi, the Peruzzi, the Bardi, and others—which made a
common practice of these transactions.   The exact terms varied with
each contract.   Sometimes only the next year's wool was sold, sometimes
the sale was made for four, six, and even twelve years ahead.   Sometimes the advance payment formed only a part of the price, and the
transaction was then commonly described as one of wool sale.   Sometimes the payment represented the full value of the wool, or occasionally
even exceeded it, and then the transaction could be described as a loan
repayable wholly or partly in wool.   But whatever were the forms in
which these contracts were expressed, they all represented one and the
same type of commercial transaction.   They were credit deals in which
it was not the seller but the buyer who gave credit.[31]   This variation in
the direction of credit is a fact of considerable interest for the study of
medieval economy, but it does not affect the conclusion that, whether

[27] *Rotuli Parliamentorum* V, 334 (1455) ; a complaint against the Italians, who obtain
their wool cheaper than the English because they pay for it in ready money, but wool
sales to Italians on credit were frequent (*infra*, 83).
[28] *Archaeologica*, XXVIII, 221-2; V.S.W.G. (1913).
[29] Jenkinson, " William Cade " in *English Historical Review* (1913), 209 *et seq.*
[30] *Calendar of the Curia Regis Rolls*, I, 144; III, 27, 177.
[31] A.V., Foreign Merchants, 127/3, etc.   G. Espinas, John Boine Broke in V.S.W.G.
(1904), 95, 221 *et seq.*   Espinas, *La vie urbaine de Douai*, III, no. 860.   For the deals of
Italian merchants, see the Recognizances on the L.T.R. and K.R. Memoranda Rolls,
Rose Graham, *The Finance of Malton Priory, 1247-1257* (Trans. Royal Hist. Soc., 1904),
148 *et seq.*

the seller or buyer figured as debtor, sale credits entered into every stage of the wool trade.

## LOANS AND INVESTMENTS

Sale credits by no means exhaust the forms of mercantile credit. Short-time loans and investments are at the present likely to be regarded as equally common, if not the commoner, forms of alliance between trade and credit; and no description of a system of mercantile credit is complete which leaves them out of account.

The ordinary short-time loan had for its object to satisfy immediate want of cash. Sudden liabilities which could not be met from the regular resources of the business, payments impending before the corresponding receipts fell due, promptitude of creditors and procrastination of debtors—in short, all the maladjustments of the regular system of sale credits—would create a demand for short loans. In a sense these maladjustments could be described as emergencies, but in so far as selling and buying was generally based on credit, they were both frequent and inevitable, and the "emergencies" were therefore part of the ordinary commercial routine. The Celys borrowed and lent money for terms of two, three and six months whenever they were either short of ready money or had a surplus, and they were regularly short of money on the eve of the payments to the woolmen, just as they always had a surplus of cash immediately after the payment at the great Brabant fairs. These loans were probably even more numerous, and certainly less uniform, than direct reference in our records to the *mutuum*, or loan, would lead us to think. Apart from the fact that a great many mercantile debts remained unrecorded, they often appeared in such forms as would leave no traces, or else very misleading ones, in the records of debts. A very obvious instance of this are the "loans by sale". Loans of money between merchant and merchant were sometimes disguised in the shape of ordinary sale. This was often done to conceal the charging of interest, as in those cases of "false chevisance" which came before the city tribunals of the fifteenth century. On 26 June 1421, one John Sadiller, vintner, was attached to answer in several prosecutions for "feigned sale". It was alleged that to one, Richard Trogonold, he had sold on credit Spanish iron for £25 4s., and then repurchased it for £23 10s. in ready money; and that to John Lawney, John Bernard, Robert Haxton, and even to Sigismund, the King of the Romans, he had lent money in a similar way.[32] If a fictitious sale of this kind could easily be distinguished from a legitimate commercial bargain, it had to be but slightly modified to become absolutely indistinguishable from a genuine

[32] P.M. Rolls, A 49 mm. 8-10; other cases, *ibid.* A 63 m. 7 *et seq.* Thomas, *Calendar of the Plea and Memoranda Rolls* (1364), 279-80, etc.

sale. How could anybody detect the real nature of similar transactions when they were carried out by three parties instead of two, when goods were bought on credit from one man and sold for cash to another?[33] The raising of funds by means of a three-cornered sale was common both in this country and abroad. It was employed by Bruges, Leiden and other continental towns, and by English kings, notably Edward III, in their transactions with wool.[34] There are on the whole surprisingly few references in English records to this method of raising loans; but the fact that these transactions were seldom recorded is less a sign of rarity than of identity with ordinary buying and selling. For every merchant who had bought goods on credit, and then, when in need of money, sold them possibly at a lower price than he had stipulated to pay for them, would be raising a loan " by means of a sale ".

Arguing from the very few instances that are to be found in the records, it would seem as if the concealment of interest was not always the only motive for the employment of this type of loan. Quite often goods were " chevised " because they happened to be more readily available than money. This was certainly the reason why the English Crown and the foreign municipalities had recourse to this type of transaction, and this was the avowed motive of a number of private " chevisances by sale ". Thus, apart from their employment for the disguising of interest, they also had a legitimate and independent economic function, which distinguished them from ordinary money loans.

The " loan by sale " has been described at length, not so much for the intrinsic importance of the transaction, but for its interest as a characteristic example. Other types of medieval loan, like " chevisances by sale ", often remained unrecorded or " misrecorded " among the ordinary entries of debts. Most of these different types of loan were therefore even commoner than the numerous references to them would suggest. Then, what is still more important, every one of them, just as the " loan by sale ", or even more so, had a distinct economic function of its own to fulfil in medieval trade. This will become clear from even a cursory review of the main types of loan.

A type of loan very common in foreign trade, especially in the fourteenth and fifteenth centuries, was the so-called " loan on exchange ". The London members of the Cely family, when short of money, " took up " from London merchants certain sums in pounds sterling and undertook to repay them, in several months, abroad in a foreign currency at an agreed rate of exchange. Similarly, the man who represented them abroad—George or William Cely—would periodically " give out " to

---

[33] In 1390 a City ordinance made such sales punishable when they were carried out by two partners, one selling and the other buying: *Liber Albus*, III, 162.

[34] I am indebted to Dr Power for material throwing light upon Edward's transactions with wool merchants. For chevisances of wool by Henry VI's government, see *Proceedings of the Privy Council*, IV, 291-3.

other English merchants sums he had received from his customers to be repaid in England in pounds sterling.[35] Transactions of this type seem to have been a part of the business routine of Staplers and English importers notably the mercers of London, and references to them are very abundant.[36] Now these exchanges were essentially credit transactions, and would probably be classified by medieval legists as "fictitious exchange". We must not, however, take this description at its face value. It is true that the carrying out of an exchange was seldom the sole object of a transaction of this type. Nevertheless, it was not a "fictitious exchange" in the sense of ordinary loans disguised as exchanges; it was more often a genuine exchange transaction employed for the purpose of credit. The difference is certainly only one of emphasis, but it is worth noting. The Celys and their other contemporaries did not adopt this method of borrowing money merely in order to disguise interest charges; and this was certainly not the only form of short loan which they employed. Over and over again we find them contracting ordinary loans repayable in this country, which they describe as "lones", "prestes" or "chevisances". It was only when the repayment of the loan really involved a transfer of money from one place to another, or manipulations with several currencies, that the loan was contracted in the form of exchanges. The only type of exchange loan which in all justice could be described as a "feigned exchange" (*cambio fittizio*)[37] was the "dry" exchange—a contract of loan which stipulated repayment in the same place and in the same currency in which it was contracted. The references to these "dry" exchanges, however, are very few; they were apparently infrequent in medieval England, and the bulk of the exchange loans mentioned in the English records belong to the same type of transaction as those described in the Cely papers. The whole class of transaction as it figures in the medieval practice in this country was specially adapted to, and used in connection with, financial dealings between merchants in different countries.[38]

No financial transaction has attracted so much attention as the so-called sale of rent. Rents were sold commonly either for life or for

---

[35] Cely Papers and Accounts, *passim*.

[36] E.Ch.Pr. 58/291, 64/614, 29/161, etc. Gilliodts van Severen, *Cartulaire*, II, 6, 12, 712. P.M. Rolls, A 74, m. 2 and 4; A 43, m. 70; A 61, m. 3; A 57, m. 6; A 41, m. 76; A 54, m. 1, etc.

[37] For the medieval classification of "cambio" and the meaning of "cambio fittizio", see Tawney, *Discourse*, 72-8; Frendt, *Wechselrecht*, I, 1-5.

[38] Closely allied to the exchange loans were the so-called "sea loans" (*fœnus nauticum, Seedarlehn*). (E.Ch.Pr. 26/193, 11/38, Cely Accounts, Chancery Miscellanea, bundle 37, file 13, f. 31; Year Book, 21 Edw. IV, Pasch., plate 23.) This was a loan to a merchant or a master of a ship proceeding to another port. The loan was commonly repayable in the place of the boat's destination and in the coin current there; it was therefore very similar in function to the exchange loans (J. Goldschmidt, *Universalgeschichte des Handelsrechts*, 354, 413 *et seq.*). But in so far as the risk was borne by the lender, it often served the purposes of maritime insurance. We shall also see that it was sometimes merely a modified type of an ordinary investment.

a certain number of years in every country and all through the Middle Ages; in some of the continental towns they formed the basis of municipal finance. It is generally held that the buying and selling of rents was common, for the simple reason that it was a convenient method of disguising the interest on loans. Here, again, we have a case of misplaced emphasis. It is probably true that the selling and buying of rents was stimulated by anti-usury legislation. It would, however, be entirely wrong to ascribe the constancy with which the rents circulated in the Middle Ages entirely and chiefly to the evasion of the usury laws. The real significance of the rent sales and the explanation of their popularity in the Middle Ages lies in the fact that they had a place to fill in medieval economy which was very important and, in a sense, entirely their own. Their function was related not to the ordinary borrowing and lending, but to the mobilization and demobilization of capital, and was fulfilled by a group of transactions, all of which were connected with real property.

Recent investigators have been struck by the frequency with which medieval merchants bought and sold land. Whether mercantile capital in the Middle Ages originated in the profits of agriculture and the accumulated ground rent of urban landlords, which is Sombart's view, or whether it was drawn from various sources, including trade, which is the view of most historians, the fact remains that every merchant of substance was also a landlord. John of Northampton, the famous Mayor of London, possessed in 1384—the year of his disgrace—over ninety tenements in the city to the annual value of over £150. William Eynsham, a wealthy wool exporter and cloth merchant of Edward III's reign, owned in London over seventy tenements to the annual value of c. £110. Stephen of Cornhill, one of the rulers of the City of London, a draper and an important exporter of wool, possessed at his death in 1295 some twenty-five rents in London to the annual value of £36 4s., and lands in various places outside London; and he had sold, shortly before his death, a number of messuages and rents in the city to the annual value of £33 18s. 8d.[39]

All these men were, of course, magnates of the city; but their possessions differed from those of the other wealthy merchants in quantity rather than in kind. There was hardly a merchant of substance in the city who would not possess a certain amount of real property, including leases and rents, and there was certainly no merchant of substance who would not, from time to time, engage in transactions with real property, be it buying, selling, pledging, or letting it. There was a constant movement of mercantile capital out of and into real property; the pace of the movement may have changed from generation to generation, but it never ceased, and always claimed the attention of the municipal administrator.

[39] Northampton, Parliamentary and Council Proceedings, Roll 15; Eynsham, P.R.O. Rentals and Surveys, Portfolio 1/12; Cornhill, *ibid*. Roll 797.

The motives which prompted the flow of investments into real property were many and various. Rural estates were often bought for no other purpose than social advancement. More than one city family of the fourteenth and fifteenth centuries ended in this way its connections with the city and entered the coveted circle of country gentry. The bulk of the investments, however, had a purely economic end in view, and served the same purposes to which investments into " safe " and regular sources of income are now put: annuities for widows and orphans, dowries, endowments for charitable or religious purposes. And just as non-speculative securities are nowadays employed by merchants as one of the methods of holding reserves or temporarily unemployed capital, so also in the Middle Ages the investment in landed property and rents was often merely a way of holding unemployed capital in readiness for needs to come.[40] Now, if the buying of lands or rents meant locking up for a time a certain amount of liquid capital, the selling or pledging of rents, like the selling and pledging of the land itself, was one of the ways in which capital, immobilized by investment into real property, could be released. It is therefore wrong to lump the " rent sale " with all the different forms of loan and describe it as one of the many methods of disguising interest. There were several varieties of rent sale, and only one of them could, with some stretching, be classified as a loan—namely, the sale of a newly constituted rent  A German or Flemish municipality could raise a loan repayable by annual instalments, and these instalments would often represent, not the rent levied upon property before the loan had been contracted, but entirely new charges upon it. The moment, however, the " new " rent was sold and entered into the market of the town, its future sales were merely successive mobilizations and immobilizations of capital. In public borrowing today it is only the issuing of the stock, and not the subsequent sales of shares by one holder to another, that constitute a loan; so also in the Middle Ages every sale of an "old " rent, be it municipal or private, was not a loan, but a transformation of capital from a smaller to a greater liquidity.[41] In other words, the sale of rents had a function of its own in the economic life of the Middle Ages, and from the point of

---

[40] R. Davidsohn has shown that the landed property of the great houses of Florence was in their hands merely one form of their mercantile capital: *Forschungen zur Geschichte von Florenz*, IV, 272-3. The same can be demonstrated for at least a dozen English merchants of the thirteenth, fourteenth and fifteenth centuries.

[41] Even this distinction must not be carried too far. From the point of view of the economic process embodied in it, the constitution and the sale of a " new " rent, representing a real profit of the land, and not a mere promise to make certain annual payments, was as much a " liquefaction " of capital as the sale of an old rent. Then, as Desmarez and Génestal point out, even when sales of rents were employed for purposes of loan they differed from ordinary loans in that they did not entail the return of the principal, and were often contracted for a long or an indefinite term: R. Génestal, *Le rôle des monastères comme établissements de crédit*, p. x; G. Desmarez, *Etude sur la propriété foncière*, 339. But the difference was not so clearly marked as Desmarez thinks.

view of this function it resembled other transactions with real property and not loans. If it had any relation at all to the financing of trade, it meant the financing of a merchant's trade out of his own resources. It is the financing of trade out of the capital resources of other persons that constitutes a commercial loan.

Next to the rent sales the type of financial transaction in the Middle Ages most popular with the historian is the *societas*. Partnerships loom large in the records of medieval trade, and there is no wonder that they have attracted so much attention. Their abundance, however, called for explanation, and attempts have been made to find causes sufficiently medieval to account for the popularity of the partnership in the Middle Ages. Hence the view of the *societas* as one of the methods adopted by medieval merchants in order to circumvent the prohibition of interest. It has, however, been pointed out by both Ashley and Cunningham[42] that medieval partnerships were not merely devices for the concealment of loans on interest; they had a function of their own to play in medieval trade, for it was by means of partnerships that capital was commonly invested in commercial undertakings. With this conclusion every student of medieval finance will concur. The medieval partnerships, or, to be more exact, the institutions which were regarded as such in the Middle Ages, had a double function to perform. One was related to the financing of medieval trade, the other to its organization. Like every association, the medieval partnership had its *raison d'être* in carrying out such tasks as were beyond the powers of a single person. A commercial undertaking would require greater capital than one person was able or willing to bestow upon it, or would require an amount or a type of personal service which he himself could not give. Partnerships would therefore be employed to overcome either or both of these difficulties. A person possessing the capital, but unable to conduct the trade or do it alone, could associate with a partner who would contribute his services. A person able to do the work, but not to contribute the capital, or at least the whole of it, could associate with others ready to make the required investment. Thus theoretically it is possible to distinguish three types of partnership: (1) one in which the capitalist hired the services of a trader; (2) another in which the trader hired capital (the "financial partnership" proper); (3) the "complete" or "real" partnership (*vera societas*), in which all the members contributed both capital and services, and which in its pure form was nothing else but a "joint business", or a union of several undertakings.[43]

The distinctions are not easy to apply. The question as to who hires whom—whether the merchant hires his capital, or capital hires its

---

[42] Ashley, *English Economic History*, ii, 42; Cunningham, 364 *et seq.*
[43] In some cases the finance partnership bore a strong resemblance to the "complete" one, since investors often could, and sometimes did, engage in management of the business.

merchant—cannot be decided by any general rule, and no single principle of classification would enable us to group finance partnerships separately from the rest.[44] The whole combination of circumstances must be taken into account whenever we try to discover the economic nature of a partnership. When a merchant received a " stock " in goods or money " to merchandise withal ", and the stock was obviously too small to constitute in itself a complete business undertaking, or where we know that it merely formed a part of the capital employed, we may safely assume that we have before us, not the contract of service, but one of investment. We can assume the same in most partnerships in which the user of the capital is known to have been an important merchant, and the owner of the capital was a widow, an orphan, or a person otherwise prevented from engaging in trade—a prince, a lord, an ecclesiastic.

Financial partnerships so identified will probably be found in every class of *societas* recorded in the English sources. They were apparently quite numerous among the commonest and simplest type of English partnership—namely, in the occasional partnerships of " joint purchase and sale ", where two or more merchants associated to carry out an isolated transaction. John Croche, a petitioner in the Chancery, was asked by one John Ellys, who had bargained with one Richard, a mercer of London, for £24 worth of merchandise, to be partners with him in the same, and " to be bounde jointly with hym to the same Richard ", and he became Ellys's partner in this bargain.[45] In this particular case it is clear that the arrangement was purely financial : Ellys wanted someone to shoulder a part of the financial responsibility involved in the transaction. But in the majority of the occasional partnerships our information is too scanty for the purely financial arrangements to be singled out, and it is difficult to say how far this practice of investment in the form of separate transactions was general.

[44] The classification to which most historians adhere is that which the Italian and the German writers have borrowed from the history of the Italian *societas*. Ashley, *English Economic History*, ii, 411-16, and Mitchell, *An Essay on the Early History of the Law Merchant* (1904), 126, 138, contain the best accounts of this classification. Attempts have been made to treat the various classes of *societas* as "labour" partnerships and "capital" partnerships respectively (*cf.* Lastig in *Zeitschr. f. d. ges. Handelsr.*, XXXIV, and his *Accomendatio* (1909), Introduction and 41 *et seq.*; also A. Lattes, *Diritto Commerciale* (1884), 154). These attempts, however, were bound to end in failure. The principle by which partnerships are classified in the medieval sources is not that of "economic function"; therefore partnerships fulfilling either the function of organization or that of finance, or both, will be found in each of the traditional classes of *societas*: Silberschmidt, *Teilhaberschaft und Beteilung*, 12-13; also his *Kommenda*, 103 *et seq.*). In England neither the law nor the terminology made any of the distinctions we see in Italy, so that the Italian classification into *commenda*, *collegantia*, and *compagna* not only fails to provide the key for the separation of the financial partnerships from the others, but is altogether inapplicable.

[45] E.Ch.Pr. 48/154.

The distinction becomes more marked when we pass to partnerships of a more continuous nature, founded on a more or less permanent "joint stock", or where one partner delivered to the other a certain sum in money or goods to be employed in his business.    Financial partnerships of this type were common in medieval Europe from the earliest days, and references to them abound in the earliest collections of commercial laws and records.[46]    In this country William Cade, the first financier to figure in English official records, apparently was in the habit of investing different sums in the undertakings of merchants.[47]    This practice, known to Cade in the twelfth century, was apparently common throughout the Middle Ages.    There were *societas*-like investments of varying magnitudes and types; and investors could be drawn from every class and station.    On occasions they were orphans, widows, princes, ecclesiastics, nobles; while foreigners figured both among investors and recipients of investments.    But most of the financial partnerships on record represent transactions of English merchants with each other.    A fifteenth-century case in the Chancery describes a partnership between Nicholas Mylle and Richard West, both tailors of London, by which West invested in Mylle's business £400 and £900.[48]    The counterpetitions, rejoinders and replications in this case make it one of the most complete records of financial partnership in existence, but similar transactions more scantily reported occur in the English records over and over again.

There is nothing surprising in the fact that investments were so commonly made through the medium of partnerships.    Investment, connecting as it does the interest of the lender with the fortunes of the business, is by its very nature not a loan, but a specific form of association.    It was always regarded as such, and it constantly found a congenial embodiment in the contract of partnership.    As Ashley correctly observed,[49] modern investments in industry and trade also take, as a rule, the form, not of loans for fixed interest, but that of shares in joint-stock companies.    Of course, the identification of investments with partnerships must not be carried too far; not every partnership represented an investment, and not every investment took the form of partnership.    Yet there is little doubt that the bulk of investments were embodied in *societas*-like arrangements; and even investments which were treated as loans were often, probably, nothing else than partnerships miscalled or modified.    The type of *societas*-like investment corresponding to the Italian *commenda* or *implicita*, where the investor "entrusted" a stock to a merchant for a specified length of time, was often hard to distinguish from an ordinary loan.    Whatever distinction existed was

---

[46] The "continuous" partnership was sometimes, though not very often, merely a series of occasional ones—e.g. E.Ch.Pr. 46/238.

[47] *English Historical Review* (1913), 730.                    [48] E.Ch.Pr. 59/160-65.

[49] *English Economic History*, i, 435-7.

subtle enough to permit of conflicting interpretations of the same arrangements by the very people concerned in them.[50]  Hence we find instances of investments, described as ordinary loans, which in reality were *commenda*-like contracts.  To take an instance.  A friar, John Woderowe, warden of the house of Deptford, sought to recover " certain moneys lent to John Chynle, mercer, and his partner Ralph Knylton, who had traded and profited by the money ".[51]  Can we really be certain that this was an ordinary loan, and not a financial *societas?*

It was chiefly by the method of remuneration that the financial partnership was commonly distinguished from an ordinary loan.  It was therefore sufficient for the contract of partnership to adopt a fixed rate of profit to become almost completely indistinguishable from ordinary loans, and it was not unusual for the medieval *commenda* to adopt these conventional rates of interest instead of fluctuating shares in profits. Weber has shown that the *foenus nauticus,* with fixed rates of interest, was nothing else than a modification of the ordinary *commenda* resulting from the greater certainty of trade in the Western Mediterranean and the possibility of calculating the average rate of profits.[52]  Sometimes this conventional rate of profits was the result of official action, as in the case of the rate fixed in the investments of wards' funds in London, which in all other respects preserved traces of their *commenda*-like nature and origin.

The investment of wards' funds was a practice frequent and important enough to deserve special consideration.  If there was in the Middle Ages any fund that could claim to be the source from which the mercantile community drew its investment credits, it was the orphans' funds, and especially those administered by the municipalities.  In most of the towns of Northern Europe the funds left to orphans were employed by the municipal authorities either as public loans or given out on long terms to private merchants.  The London practice in the Middle Ages did not differ much from that of continental towns.  The City of London claimed a number of rights with regard to the administration of the goods of orphans, especially when their parents died intestate. Guardians were appointed by the Mayor and Chamberlains of the city, and were accountable to them for the discharge of their duty to the orphans.  A child could be committed to a guardian with or without its goods, but usually the former was the case, so that the acceptance of a ward became a financial transaction, the funds being handled like ordinary investments.  The goods, and sometimes even the charge of the orphan's " body ", could change hands several times during the period of minority; on a number of occasions the goods were from the outset committed for a period obviously related, not to the duration of

[50] Several such cases are recorded in the early Chancery Proceedings—*e.g.* 46/306.
[51] P.M. Rolls, A 13, m. 1, 1367.  *Cf.* Year Books, 12 Hen. VI, Pasch. f. 3.
[52] M. Weber, *Zur Geschichte der Handelsgesellschaften,* 109-10.

the child's minority, but to the financial exigencies of the borrower's business.[53]

Sir William Ashley has pointed out that these investments were a variety of *commenda*-like agreements.[54] It was very usual in Western Europe throughout the Middle Ages to " commend " dowries and patrimonies to merchants for employment in trade,[55] and of this *commenda* the investments of wards' funds described above were merely a variant. In one respect, however, these transactions did differ from the ordinary *societas*—namely, in the fixed rate of profits. The distribution of profits was regulated by a reputedly old custom, according to which the average " mesne " profits were estimated at a flat rate of four shillings per pound per year, of which the guardian had one-half and the ward the other half, minus the cost of his maintenance and education.[56] Thus, in spite of the fact that the fixed rate of profits had converted it into ordinary annual interest of 10 per cent, the fiction of division of profits was still maintained to bear witness to the origin and economic essence of the transaction.[57]

To conclude: the use of partnership in medieval finance was determined by the same principles as governed all the other forms of loan discussed here. The choice of the appropriate form was in every case determined not by mere whim, fortuitous chance, or an incorrigible desire to cheat, but by the economic essence of the contemplated deal. Loans on exchange, rent sales, sea loans, partnerships, were not various devices indiscriminately employed by the medieval merchant in order to disguise his ordinary loans. Each of them embodied a type of financial transaction distinct from others both in purpose and method; each of them had an economic function of its own to perform.

## CREDIT AND CASH

What has been said as to the ubiquity and variety of medieval credit does not yet solve the purely quantitative aspect of the problem—that is,

[53] The chief source of evidence is the Guildhall Letter Books. A few isolated entries of orphans' goods committed to merchants occur in the first two letter books among the miscellaneous recognizances (L.B.A., 177, 188; L.B.B., 38); in letter books G and H, belonging to the second half of the fourteenth century, they become common; in letter books I, K, and L, belonging to the fifteenth century, they fill more than two-thirds of the contents. [54] *English Economic History*, ii, 417-18.

[55] For an early Italian instance, see Lastig, *Accomendatio*, 72. For English instances, see *Testamenta Eboracensia* (Surtees Soc.), IV, 207-10; Sharpe, *Calendar of Wills*, 393; E.Ch.Pr. 65/149.

[56] Riley, *Memorials of the City of London*, 378, 446; P.M. Rolls, A 19, m. 8 dorso; Letter Book G (MS.), 132, 169, 323, etc. Occasionally funds were entrusted *sine proficuo*. In the second half of the fifteenth century the references to profits in the entries become less frequent.

[57] There was much in common between the commitment of the wards' funds to guardians and the financial transactions accompanying the contract of apprenticeship. See G. Desmarez, " L'apprentisage à Ypres " in *Revue du Nord* (1911), 41 *et seq.*; also Espinas and Pirenne, *Documents*, etc., III, nos. 854, 855, 857, 864, 870; II, nos. 470, 482. *Cf.* also the employment of funds of gilds for the purposes of investment.

the question as to the relative importance of credit transactions in the total volume of medieval trade, or in the turnover of individual merchants. For an inquiry of this kind we are singularly ill-equipped, as the surviving evidence consists chiefly of records of debts. Nevertheless, in several isolated instances the evidence of debts supplemented by other sources can be made to yield not merely a vague impression of abundance, but also something approaching a quantitative statement. For some individual merchants the records of debts are, or can be, so grouped as to throw a great deal of light on the relative importance of credit in their transactions. For some merchants we are given or are able to compile something like inventories of their debts, which can then be compared with what we know or can guess of the total volume of their trade. These instances, of course, are few, but their importance is heightened by the fact that they all tell the same tale. The Celys, who were apparently an average fifteenth-century Staplers' firm, sold wool on credit in eleven out of every twelve transactions recorded in their letters and accounts. Some of George Cely's notes about his financial transactions at the fairs of Antwerp and Bergen-op-Zoom show that he never had much ready money on his hands, and most of the firm's capital consisted of wool not yet fully paid for, and of debts owing to them. The state of George's account in winter, 1482, was as follows: £50 in cash, £200 in goods, £663 in debts maturing in May, and £234 8s. 3d. in more recent debts.[58] In this state of account there was nothing extraordinary or exceptional. In 1424 the executors of William Lynn, a wealthy Stapler, submitted to the city authorities an account of his moveables. The total amount left was £4,842 7s. 2d., of which about £965 was in coin, about £811 in merchandise, and about £39 in plate and utensils. The rest, about £3,027, was in debts owing to him from various persons in England and abroad. In his turn, he owed various men £1,637 1s. 4d.—that is, about as much as he had in cash and merchandise.[59] A day book of John Thorp, a London scrivener (1458-60), supplies somewhat similar information about the credit transactions of a number of English wholesale clothiers and pewterers.[60] Thomas Dounton, a cloth merchant of London, figures in the book twenty-six times between September 1458 and May 1460 as creditor of various German merchants for cloth bought from him. The total amount of debts is £1,359 4s. 5d., while the value of cloth was apparently in the vicinity of £1,700.[61] It would, therefore, seem that these credit sales

[58] Cely Papers and Accounts, *passim*, and Chancery Miscellanea, bundle 37, file 12, ff. 38-9.
[59] Guildhall Letter Book K (MS.), f. 16. The account shows the relation of credit to Lynn's turnover and not to his capital. As will be shown in another place, Lynn's real property, or most of it, would have to be included in his business capital.
[60] A.V. 128/37. I am indebted to Mr Hilary Jenkinson for the identification of Thorp.
[61] This statement is based on the assumption that an instalment, commonly one-quarter or one-third of the price, was as a rule paid at the time of the purchase.

represented the bulk of Dounton's business, as he was not a city magnate and his annual turnover could not very much exceed £1,000.

Instances of this kind are not confined to the fifteenth century, and certainly not to Englishmen alone. The transactions of foreign importers trading to England are well illustrated by the inventories of their debts made on several occasions during the later thirteenth century in connection with the arrests of their goods by the Crown. At the time of the royal confiscation, the firm of Burnettus, Johann Vanne and partners, merchants of Lombardy and dealers in mercery, had a sum of over £1,100 owing to them for goods sold on credit to various English merchants. The other possessions of the firms in England (" bona et mercimonia ") were estimated by the assessors at £1,400.[62] A similar use of credit would probably be revealed by an analysis of the transactions of the better-known merchants of the thirteenth and early fourteenth centuries, English and foreign alike, such as Gregory de Rokesle, William Servat, Philip Tailor, William Trente, John of Burford, William of Donecastre. Richard of Resham, William Hauteyn, John Boine Broke,[63] Wautier Pied d'Argent, the several Betoins, Basings, Blunds, etc., not to mention the de la Poles and other commercial magnates associated with Edward III's transactions.

These individual instances, however, must not be misunderstood. Significant as they are, they do not prove the absence or the rarity of transactions for ready money, as merchants often paid for their goods "on the spot" or even in advance, and there were also persons who seldom sold on credit. All they prove is that the medieval merchant displayed no preference for any particular financial method. His choice between purchase on credit or for ready money was not determined by any "medieval" dislike or ignorance of credit, as Bücher suggests, nor by any special liking for it, as a hasty deduction from the evidence here presented might suggest, but by a very obvious economic factor which is as little medieval as it is modern. This factor was the amount of available capital. It was the relative abundance or scarcity of capital at the disposal of an individual merchant that determined the employment of credit in selling and buying. An ordinary medieval merchant, a vintner like William Barache, or a Stapler like Richard Cely, obtained his goods on credit, and could therefore afford to wait for payment from his own customer. In its ideal form this type of trade needed very little capital. But the shorter and smaller the credit which the merchant received relative to the length and amount of credit he himself allowed, the greater had to be the capital engaged in trade, and the greater the

[62] A.V. 126/6.

[63] Accounts of Boine Broke's and Servat's activities are contained in the articles of G. Espinas in V.S.W.G., 1904; F. Arens, ibid. 1904; and Edmond Albe, Bull. de la Société des Etudes du Dép. du Cot, 1908 (according to the latter there were two William Servats at the end of the thirteenth century).

capital at the disposal of the merchant, the more he was able—given the same turnover—to dispense with credit in buying, or even to pay for his goods in advance. Similarly, a wealthy seller was able to allow credit to his customers, while a needy one would require full payment or even pre-payment.

The sales of wool for future delivery described above[64] are a case in point. In seeking to explain why sale credit changed its usual direction in these particular transactions we may easily be led astray by the fact that they took place mainly in the late thirteenth and early fourteenth centuries; and that the debtors were chiefly monasteries and the creditors Italians. The temptation thus arises to explain everything by what we know of the financial domination of the Italians in the thirteenth century, their advanced commercial methods, and their pioneering work in the English wool trade; or else by the peculiarities of manorial economy which made it easier to collect monastic debts and papal dues in kind. Either explanation contains a grain of truth: neither contains the whole of it. That the advance sales of wool were not peculiar to the thirteenth century is shown by the Statute of 1465 enacting that " come per subtile bargains faitz en achater des laines devaunt que les berbizes, que ceo portent soient tondrez ", none except spinners and cloth-makers shall be allowed for the next two years to buy " unshorn " wools in the eighteen principal wool-growing counties.[65] Nor, again, can the transaction be described as exclusively Italian. While Italians often bought wool for advance payment or ready money, they were not the only merchants to do so. We find Flemings, like Boine Broke and others, buying wool from monasteries in the same fashion; and there is no doubt that some of the English merchants followed a similar practice.[66] Still less can this type of transaction be regarded as a peculiarity of monastic trade. First of all, there are numerous instances of similar advances made to laymen,[67] secondly, there was hardly a wool-growing monastery in England which would not at one time or another sell its wool for deferred payments. Frequently, monasteries combined both methods of payment, receiving a part of the price in advance and the rest some time after the delivery of the wool.[68] The real explanation lies in the buyer's abundance of capital or the seller's shortage of it. If the Italians made the widest use of the method of advance payment, this was merely because in the later thirteenth and early fourteenth centuries they were

---

[64] *Supra*, 67 *et seq*  [65] 4 Edw. IV, c. 4.

[66] *Chron. de Melsa*, Rolls Series, III, 84-7, 144. Rec. Roll, 1, m. 1 (Basing), etc.

[67] Rec. Roll, 1, m. 1 (Ricardi); A.V. 126/28, m. 2 dorso; Northumberland Pleas, 310 (1271); M. R. 52 (6 Edw. I), m. 11, 60 (15 Edw. I), m. 19 dorso and 20 (Holm aad Tattershall), etc.

[68] The fifteenth-century views of hosts show a number of abbeys in the West of England selling their wool to Italians, obviously for ready money or deferred payments: A.V. 128/30 and 128/31; Whittaker, Craven, 449 *et seq.*; *Chron. de Melsa*, III, 233, etc.

better provided with capital than most other wool exporters, while the monasteries at this period frequently found themselves in financial difficulties.[69]   In other words, in a trade where demand was always keen, and supplies were more or less fixed, buyers who were powerful capitalists came into contact with sellers who were poor.   Advance payments came as naturally, both before and after the thirteenth century, between lay sellers and non-Italian buyers, whenever the same conditions were re-enacted.

Thus far only are we justified in accepting the assertion that advance payments for goods constituted the rule in commercial dealings between agricultural producers and urban capitalists.  As a statement of fact the assertion is more or less correct, for in the sales of agricultural produce advance payments were indeed very common, especially on the Continent.   But as a scientific generalization or an attempt at an explanation it is misleading.  In the example already described, that of advance sales of wool, the wool growers frequently allowed credit to monastic buyers; nor were the recipients of advances always wool growers—there were numerous contracts for future delivery of wool between merchant and merchant.[70]   But what is still more important is that even wool growers, lay and monastic, often sold not their own wool, but wool bought from others.  We find monasteries selling for future delivery quantities of wool out of all proportion to the size of their flocks, and employing the advances received from merchants in buying wool on the local markets. The Cistercian and Sempringham orders attempted to suppress this practice, as did also on one occasion the Crown, but for a long time their attempts apparently produced no immediate effects.[71]  The monasteries continued to buy wool to fulfil their contracts with merchants; and the contracts frequently gave them the right or even made it their duty to supply wool not of their own growth.[72]   It is therefore not as producers of wool that monasteries demanded or accepted advances.  If agricultural producers and not merchant buyers accepted credit, this was because the latter were, as a rule, well supplied with capital, while the former were commonly short of funds.   When these conditions were absent, when the trader was not an important capitalist, and the producer was not impoverished, the credit, if given, was likely to flow in the

[69] R. Snape, *English Monastic Finances in the Later Middle Ages*, 120 et seq.; R. Graham, *St. Gilbert*, 136 et seq.

[70] At Leicester and Northampton it was at one time usual for strangers to entrust money to local merchants, who bought wool on their behalf in the surrounding counties: *Records of Leicester*, I, 88, 91, 93, 186-7, 201-2, etc.; *Records of Northampton*, I, 230-1, cap. xlix. Most of these transactions represented *commenda*-like partnerships, but it was only a short step from them to ordinary advances from big wool merchants to smaller traders who collected wool from the growers: A.V. 126/128 (Bonaventura); M.R. 60; 15 Edw. I, m. 15 (Guidicione); and many other references in the M.R.

[71] Rose Graham in *Transactions Royal Historical Society* (1904), 148; Whitewell, *op. cit.* 8-10.

[72] M.R. 60, 15 Edw. I, m. 16 d. (Rievaulx), m. 20 (Toteshale), etc.

opposite direction—from the seller to the buyer. The occurrence of cash deals does not, then, constitute an exception to the practice of credit sales. The advances, the deferred payments, and the cash payments did not each represent a different financial principle in medieval trade: they were all various manifestations of one and the same elementary maxim that " the rich lend, the poor borrow ".

There is yet another reason why " cash sales ", however frequent, cannot be contrasted with the employment of credit—namely, the connection between the different forms of sale credits on the one hand and investments on the other. We have said that the greater the capital at the disposal of the merchant the more credit could he allow in his sales and the less he would need in his purchases. Now, if we remember that the trading capital of medieval firms often belonged to other people, we shall also understand the connection which sometimes existed between investments and sale credits. The *Grosse Ravensburger Gesellschaft*, a great South German trading organization, sold goods on credit, but, as a rule, bought them for ready money,[73] since it possessed a greater capital than was usual in the fifteenth century, its capital being made up of deposits, investments and special loans received from numerous persons. Thus its cash purchases, credit sales and investments were all parts of the same commercial policy: it preferred to owe money to its partners and depositors rather than to sellers of goods; but—given the same turnover—it would have needed a much smaller capital, and owed much less on account of investments, if it had bought goods on credit. Similarly, if it is true that the Medici, Spinelli, Strozzi, Contarini and the other Italian merchants of the fifteenth century paid for their wool in cash more frequently than did English merchants, this was the result of, and a testimony to, their possessing larger capitals than the native wool merchants. And in so far as the trading capital of these firms was largely made up of other people's investments, their use of credit was not so very different from that of ordinary wool merchants. They merely borrowed from, and paid interest to, a different set of people. The same applies also to the Italian houses of the thirteenth century, which so commonly paid for the wool in advance.[74] Apart from what is known of the system of investment and deposits which these houses practised in Italy itself, there is also evidence of Italians accepting investments from people in this country. Matthew Paris, writing about the behaviour of the Italian usurers in England, alleges that even after their expulsion by Henry III a large number of them remained in England under the protection of the magnates who had invested their money with them " after the

[73] A. Schulte, *Geschichte d. Grossen Ravensburger Handelgesellschaft* (1923), I, 123, 301, 458, *et seq.*, 472; III, *passim*.

[74] R. Davidson, *Geschichte von Florenz*, IV, 202-8; Giovanni Villani, *Cronica*, III (ed. 1844-5), libro xi, cap. lxxxviii, describing the loans of Italian banks to Edward III, says: " E nota, che i detti danari erono la maggior parte di gente che gli aveano dati loro in acomandigia e in deposito, e de più cittadini e forestieri ".

example of the Roman Curia ".[75] That these investments--at any rate in the late thirteenth and fourteenth centuries—were not unconnected with the wool transactions of the great Italian houses, and may have formed part of those large capitals which enabled them to pay for their wool in advance, is shown by an interesting thirteenth-century case relating to a sum delivered on deposit (*tradite fuissent*) by William Servat and another Anglo-French merchant of London to the Riccardi of Lucca, a firm most commonly mentioned as paying in advance for its wool.[76]

It is not always that the connection between investments and sale credits can be established. Theoretically, in most medieval trades, and especially in those in which the turnover of the individual business was more elastic than it seems to have been in the wool trade, the obvious connection was not between investments and sale credits, but between investments and the volume of trade, since the additional capital was more likely to be used for the extension of the business than for the modification of the methods of payment. It is therefore impossible to speak of anything in the nature of a general and necessary connection between investments and sale credits. For our present purpose, however, no such general rule is required. It is sufficient to observe that very often a connection of this kind did exist; that the elimination, complete or partial, of credit in buying and selling was likely to be offset by borrowings in other directions; and that consequently " cash deals ", in some of those instances in which they were frequent, signified, not the merchant's dislike or disuse of credit, but merely a different choice between its various forms.

Several aspects of medieval trade have been neglected in this article. To begin with, of Dr Cunningham's binomial formula—" dealing for credit was little developed, and dealing in credit was unknown "—only the first element—*i.e.* the " dealing for credit "—has been analyzed here; the " dealing in credit "—*i.e.* the selling and buying of credit and of financial instruments—still awaits examination. Secondly, there is the problem of chronology: the antiquity of medieval credit and its evolution from century to century. Thirdly, there is the question of interest, and of the public attitude towards credit and interest. Finally, no study of medieval credit is complete which does not describe the organization of credit, the professional standing of financial agents, and the social standing of the owners of capital. And this in its turn demands a preliminary study of the " origin " of loanable capital. To these problems the present article provides merely an introduction. Its purpose

---

[75] " Quia magnatum quorundam, quorum, ut dicebatur, pecuniam ad multiplicandum seminabant, exemplo Romanæ curiæ, favore defendebantur " (*Cron. Maj.*, V, 245).

[76] *Rotuli Parliamentorum*, I, 43.

has been to show how the economists, and through them also the historians, have underestimated the volume of medieval credit, and consequently misunderstood its nature. Sale credits, of which the existence has been generally denied, in reality formed the financial basis of medieval trade. As to the other forms of credit their existence was never doubted, but their function was wrongly interpreted. Because of its ubiquity, medieval credit displayed greater variety than is commonly supposed; and of this variety the multiplicity of form was merely an outward expression.

# THE PROGRESS OF TECHNOLOGY AND THE GROWTH OF LARGE-SCALE INDUSTRY IN GREAT BRITAIN, 1540-1640

## J. U. NEF

SINCE Arnold Toynbee gave his famous lectures at Oxford, fifty years ago, closer study has taken from the concept of the "Industrial Revolution" much of its revolutionary character.[1] Nowhere, perhaps, has the revision of earlier notions concerning the period from 1760 to 1832 been more drastic than with respect to the nature and magnitude of the changes in industrial technique and organization. The industrial plant owned by private capitalists, who employed in it dozens and sometimes scores or even hundreds of workmen, was not the novelty it was once believed to be. Evidence has been piling up to prove that large-scale industry, in this sense, was common in mining and many branches of manufacture long before the middle of the eighteenth century. At the same time, more detailed studies of nineteenth-century economic history, especially the quantitative survey of Professor Clapham, have shown that earlier writers, with their eyes focused upon cotton and iron and upon the most advanced industrial areas, have exaggerated the place of the steam-engine and of large-scale industry in the economy of the eighteen-thirties.

But it is still common to regard the sixties and seventies of the eighteenth century as an important historical boundary, in the sense that there began at this time the first great speeding up of industrial development. If Toynbee had lived to reply to some of the criticisms of the phrase "Industrial Revolution", he might have defended his position by referring to the passage in Macaulay's celebrated third chapter —which may possibly have influenced him during his short life—where Macaulay says that about the middle of the eighteenth century economic progress became for the first time "portentously rapid".[2] But was this the first period of English history in which a remarkable speeding up of industrial development occurred? The opinion is gaining strength that there was at least one earlier period during which the rate of change was scarcely less striking. This period begins at about the time of the dis-

[1] *Cf.* H. L. Beales, "Historical Revisions: The Industrial Revolution" in *History*, XIV, especially 126-8.

[2] T. B. Macaulay, *History of England* (1866 edn.), I, 220. According to the late Professor Ashley, Toynbee used the term "revolution" in the sense of a speeding up of evolution (Henry Hamilton, *The English Brass and Copper Industries to 1800* (1926), p. ix).

solution of the monasteries, and the industrial development becomes most rapid during the latter half of Elizabeth's reign and the reign of James I. The forces of rapid change then set in motion continue throughout the seventeenth and early eighteenth centuries, but it is not until the second half of the eighteenth century that the pace again becomes as fast as it had been during Shakespeare's lifetime.

Support for this view of industrial history is to be found in the excellent book of Mr Wadsworth and Miss Mann on the cotton textile industry. It is there suggested that the growth of an elaborate network of middlemen, who supplied the materials upon which thousands of domestic workpeople laboured at their spinning-wheels and looms, was so remarkable in the late sixteenth and early seventeenth centuries that the changes in the face of industrial Lancashire were scarcely less important than between 1760 and 1832, when the county was the classic home of the "revolution" in cotton manufacture.[3] Evidence of an enormous expansion, beginning about the middle of the sixteenth century, in the output of coal, salt, glass and ships, and of a great increase in the production of many other industrial commodities, such as alum, soap, gunpowder, metal goods and accessories, will be found in my book on the coal industry.[4] The growth in the importance of mining and manufacturing in the national economy was, it seems, scarcely less rapid between the middle of the sixteenth century and the Civil War than between the middle of the eighteenth century and the first Reform Act. Some other results of recent research[5] seem to indicate that the rapid

[3] A. P. Wadsworth and J. de L. Mann, *The Cotton Trade and Industrial Lancashire* (1931), 11.

[4] J. U. Nef, *The Rise of the British Coal Industry* (1932), I, 19 et seq., 123-4, 165-89.

[5] For books and articles dealing with the industrial history of the sixteenth and seventeenth centuries, the reader is referred to Professor R. H. Tawney's "Studies in Bibliography: Modern Capitalism", *The Economic History Review*, IV, 336-53; and to the economic history section of Professor Conyers Read's *Bibliography of British History, Tudor Period, 1485-1603* (1933). A knowledge of the following books is indispensable for an understanding of industrial development during the two centuries preceding the "Industrial Revolution": T. S. Ashton and J. Sykes, *The Coal Industry of the Eighteenth Century* (1929); T. S. Ashton, *Iron and Steel in the Industrial Revolution* (1924); J. W. Gough, *The Mines of Mendip* (1930); Hamilton, *op. cit.*; Herbert Heaton, *The Yorkshire Woollen and Worsted Industries* (1920); A. K. H. Jenkin, *The Cornish Miner* (1927); G. R. Lewis, *The Stannaries* (1908); E. Lipson, *The Economic History of England* (1931), II and III; G. I. H. Lloyd, *The Cutlery Trades* (1913); W. H. Price, *The English Patents of Monopoly* (1906); W. R. Scott, *The Constitution and Finance of Joint Stock Companies*, 3 vols. (1910-12); Ernest Straker, *Wealden Iron* (1931); George Unwin, *Industrial Organization in the Sixteenth and Seventeenth Centuries* (1904); Wadsworth and Mann, *op. cit.* In the present article, I have made free use of these works, without specific acknowledgment. Where I have drawn on other material for important statements of fact, I have generally given references. Only a close study of manuscript sources, especially those relating to industries like soap and pottery-making, printing, paper-making, saltpetre, gunpowder, alum and salt manufacture, and building, which have been hitherto neglected by economic historians, can give us an adequate account of the industrial progress between 1540 and 1640. The survey here attempted makes no pretence at completeness. I have omitted altogether some industries in which the factory form of enterprise was common in the sixteenth and seventeenth centuries,

7

growth of industry, and the striking increase in the importance and complexity of the domestic system, which began in the Elizabethan Age, were accompanied by equally remarkable changes in industrial technique and scale of enterprise.

Three kinds of technical development helped the growth of large-scale industry between 1540 and 1640. The first was the introduction of a series of capitalistic industries which had hardly gained a foothold in Great Britain before the Reformation. The second was the application to old industries of various technical processes known before, especially in some districts on the Continent, but hitherto very little used in Great Britain. The third was the discovery and application of new technical methods. It is necessary to consider each of these before turning to other factors which also stimulated the growth of large-scale industry.

### (i) *The Introduction of "New" Industries*

During the last sixty years of the sixteenth century the first paper and gunpowder mills,[6] the first cannon foundries, the first alum and copperas factories, the first sugar refineries, and the first considerable saltpetre works were all introduced into the country from abroad. The discovery of calamine, the ore of zinc, in Somerset and elsewhere, together with the first really effective attempts to mine copper ore, made possible the establishment of brass-making and battery works for hammering brass and copper ingots into plates. Not all the commodities turned out by these manufactures were being produced in England for the first time. If English-made sugar and brass were new, some paper and alum, probably some saltpetre and gunpowder, and perhaps some copperas had been obtained from native workshops before the sixteenth century. But the quantities had been insignificant, the plant for producing them primitive. The important thing about the "new" Elizabethan industries was that in all of them plant was set up involving investments far beyond the sums which groups of master-craftsmen

---

because I had not the knowledge or the space to deal with them adequately. Printing, for example, has been entirely neglected, though specially built houses with expensive equipment in presses and type were the rule from the start (*cf.* Henri Hauser, *Ouvriers du temps passé*, xve-xvie *siècles* (1899), *passim;* Joseph Moxon, *Meckanick Exercises* (1683) (reprint, New York, 1896), 9 *et seq.*). A still more serious omission, because of the larger number of workmen engaged, is the building industry. And I have no doubt that many valuable references in secondary works to large-scale enterprises in the industries actually treated have escaped my notice.

[6] A paper mill of the type successfully introduced into England in Elizabeth's reign had been set up at Hertford, probably about 1500, but it had a short life of not more than ten years. Apparently no further attempt was made to erect a large paper mill until 1557. This, too, was a failure; but paper-making by water-driven mills was established before the end of the sixteenth century (Rhys Jenkins, "Early Attempts at Paper-making in England, 1495-1680", *Library Association Record*, II, ii, 481-5; G. H. Overend, "Notes upon the Earlier History of the Manufacture of Paper in England", Huguenot Society of London, *Proceedings*, VIII, 177-80). For the introduction of gunpowder-making in the fifties, see *V.C.H. Surrey*, II, 246.

could muster, even if these artisans were men of some small substance. While in London, Sheffield, or any provincial town, the typical workshop of the smith, the cutler, or the weaver could be equipped with its forge or grinding wheel or loom and other necessary tools for a few pounds, the establishments erected in these new industries cost hundreds, and in many cases thousands, of pounds. A further heavy outlay had to be made on materials and labour, because the process of production frequently required a long time, and it was many months before any return could be expected from sales.

In the reign of James I, the alum houses near Whitby, on the Yorkshire coast, were great wooden structures. Each contained large brick furnaces and cisterns, piles of alumstone, coal and wood fuel, and about ten metal pans for boiling the ingredients. Many thousands of pounds had been spent on each of them, and the annual expense of the materials consumed in the manufacture exceeded £1,000. As George Lowe, one of the farmers of these houses, wrote in 1619, alum making was " a distracted worke in severall places and of sundry partes not possible to bee performed by anie one man nor by a fewe. But by a multitude of the baser sort, of whom the most part are idle, careless and false in their labour."[7] Actually, about sixty workmen were regularly employed at a single house, and, in addition, there was the casual labour of coopers, smiths and carpenters to keep the building and equipment in repair. Eighteen drivers with their carts were needed for each house, to bring alumstone, coal and wood, and to carry away the finished product.[8] In the reign of Charles I, the copperas house at Queenborough in Kent, with its great wooden troughs, leaden pipes and cisterns, was built on a similar scale.[9] In 1613 John Browne, later Crown commissioner for making ordnance and shot, and official gunmaker to the Parliament in the Civil War, employed 200 men in his cannon foundry at Brenchley in Kent.[10] At Dartford, in the same county, a paper mill had been set up by a John Spilman, a naturalized German, about the middle of Elizabeth's reign. According to Thomas Churchyard, who wrote a long poem about it,

> " The mill itself is sure right rare to see,
> The framing is so queint and finely done,
> Built all of wood, and hollowe trunkes of tree
> That makes the streames at point device to runne,
> Nowe up, nowe downe, nowe sideward by a sleight,
> Nowe forward fast, then spouting up on height,
>
>       *    *    *
>
> The hammers thump and make as lowde a noyse,
> As fuller doth that beates his wollen cloth."

[7] Lansdowne MSS. 152, f. 57.    [8] *Ibid.* 152, no. 6 ; S.P.D. James I, LXXIV, no. 20.
[9] Sir William Brereton, *Travels in Holland, the United Provinces, England, Scotland and Ireland* (Chetham Soc. Publications, I, 2-3).
[10] S.P.D. James I, CV, no. 92 (as cited Straker, *op. cit.* 163).

The building in which the paper was produced seemed to Churchyard " a house of some estate ". The enterprise certainly employed scores of hands, though the poet probably exaggerated when he spoke of 600 workmen.[11] One of the two great water-wheels which drove the hammers for beating the cloth and the stamping machinery had formerly been used to drive the bellows of a blast-furnace on the same site, and the cost of converting it to its new purpose is said to have been between £1,400 and £1,500. Powder mills, introduced in Surrey just after the middle of the sixteenth century, were also driven by water-power, and the machinery was perhaps no less costly than at the paper mills. In addition, there were at least two other elaborately equipped buildings at a powder factory—the corning house and the stove, a separate establishment about twenty feet square in which the powder was dried, the whole room being heated to the proper temperature by an iron fireplace. The battery works introduced from Germany in Elizabeth's reign, with their furnaces and numerous great hammers, some of which weighed 500 pounds, probably cost as much to build as the larger powder and paper mills. The hammers were driven by water-power at a heavy cost. As in all the rising English industries, the overshot wheel was generally used rather than the much less expensive undershot wheel. To turn the former a stream had to be diverted from its course, and a dam built to store up the water against a drought.

Among other industries introduced into England during the last sixty years of the sixteenth century, sugar-refining, brass-making by the process of cementation, and the manufacture of saltpetre apparently required a rather less extensive outlay in buildings, furnaces, boilers, machinery, tools, and materials than was frequently needed in those we have been considering. But all three manufactures were carried on in small factories. Sugar makers had to invest scores and sometimes hundreds of pounds in lead pipes, cisterns, copper kettles and iron rollers for grinding the cane. Brass makers had to provide expensive metal pots, in which the copper was mixed with prepared calamine, and one or more large ovens in which eight or more of the pots were placed for heating. The " saltpetre men " had a comparable investment to make, for the preparation of saltpetre involved the mixing of ingredients in a number of large tubs, followed by two long boilings of the liquid in copper kettles, heated by a big furnace of brickwork.

The introduction of all these manufactures into England during the last sixty years of the sixteenth century opened an entirely fresh field for the growth of industrial capitalism. It is important to form a rough impression of the number of enterprises, and of the influence upon industrial organization in Great Britain of the new manufactures. While all of them gained a firm foothold in England before the Civil War, they

[11] Thomas Churchyard, A Description and playne Discourse of Paper (1588) (reprinted in John Nichols, The Progresses of Queen Elizabeth (1788), II).

had an earlier history in Europe, and some of them were carried on much more extensively abroad than in England. This was the case with paper-making and sugar-refining. Although ten or more paper mills are known to have been at work in England in the thirties of the seventeenth century, the great new demand for paper, brought about by the growing importance of the printing press, continued to be met largely by imports, especially from France.[12] Most of the sugar consumed in Great Britain was brought in refined from the West Indies. The other manufactures with which we have been dealing had made more headway in capturing the domestic market. England was becoming much less dependent upon imports for its supplies of alum, copperas, brass and copper than for its supplies of paper and sugar, and the output of saltpetre and gunpowder were perhaps more than sufficient to meet native demands. English-made cannons proved so excellent in quality and so cheap in price that, before the end of Elizabeth's reign, they were in demand all over the Continent. Yet in each of these manufactures, the market could be supplied by a rather small number of factories. There were probably not more than a dozen, or at the most a score, of large alum houses in the reign of Charles I, and neither the brass and battery works nor the powder mills and cannon foundries could have been much more numerous. Sussex, perhaps the principal seat of the cannon manufacture, apparently had only four foundries for casting cannons in 1613.[13] Wars were still won with what seems to us an infinitesimal expenditure of metal and gunpowder. Yet it is clear that the number of considerable establishments at work in all these new manufactures, taken together, had reached several scores before the Civil War. And the introduction of such establishments, with their elaborate water-driven machinery, their large furnaces and acccessories, must have had an influence upon the growth of industrial capitalism in England beyond that which can be measured in terms of the output or the number of workpeople engaged in them. Mechanics and inventors could study the new machinery, furnaces and boilers with a view to adapting them to suit other processes of manufacture. Landlords and merchants, with capital to invest in other industries, were stimulated by example to set up works on a larger scale than they might otherwise have done.

(ii) *The Progress of Advanced Technical Methods in Old Industries*

A far greater number of workpeople and a far larger amount of capital were drawn into large-scale enterprise by the extensive changes in old industries than by the introduction of these " new " manufactures. The very rapid growth of markets for coal and ore was making it imperative to adopt less primitive methods in mining and the production

[12] Jenkins, *op. cit.* 581-6; Edward Heawood, "Paper Used in England after 1600", *The Library*, 4th ser., XI, 292 *et seq.*
[13] Straker, *op. cit.* 163.

of metals. As a result of the application of improved technical methods known before the middle of the sixteenth century, at least on the Continent, but not extensively used, conditions in these industries were largely transformed during the century following the dissolution of the monasteries.

Before the sixteenth century, in Great Britain, the expensive adit or long tunnel for draining mines was rare,[14] machinery driven by water or horse power for pumping out water or raising minerals was almost unknown. The problems for prospecting for coal and ore, of sinking through rocky strata, and of ventilating the pits to force out noxious gases, hardly tried the ingenuity of the miner, for the depths of the workings seldom exceeded a few fathoms. Except at silver mines,[15] which were scarce in Great Britain, and at a very few tin and coal mines, mining seldom required the investment of much capital. Ore and coal were normally dug by independent partnerships of working miners.

Between 1540 and 1640, when copper ore was first sought after with sufficient zest to make the rights of the landowner to property in this mineral an important subject of judicial controversy before the Court of Exchequer, and when the output of coal probably increased at least eightfold, and the output of iron and lead ore several times over, it became necessary to sink to depths of twenty, thirty, and even forty or fifty fathoms. In many parts of England, Scotland and Wales, the miners were threatened by water which drowned out their workings, and by gas explosions which killed scores. Though the output of tin, unlike that of other metallic ores, was not increasing, even in tin mining technical problems assumed an entirely new importance, because the more easily accessible supplies of ore had been largely exhausted in the Middle Ages. During the reigns of Elizabeth and her two Stuart successors, money was poured out lavishly in the construction of hundreds of adits and ventilation shafts, and of hundreds of drainage engines driven by water and more often by horse power, at tin, copper and lead mines and, above all, at collieries. As the digging and lining of an adit often cost thousands of pounds, and as the expense of operating a horse-driven pump sometimes amounted to about £2,000 a year, the new mining enterprises had to be conducted on a scale which would have seemed incredible to an Englishman of the time of Sir Thomas More. While the annual output of a coal mine before the middle of the sixteenth century had rarely exceeded a few hundred tons, and much of the mining had been done casually by manorial tenants who worked part of the year as husbandmen, collieries producing from 10,000 to

---

[14] I am aware, of course, that we find references to adits comparatively early in the Middle Ages (Jenkin, *op. cit.* 83-4; L. F. Salzman, *English Industries of the Middle Ages* (2nd edn. (1923), 53-4). *Cf.* Nef, *op. cit.* I, 354, especially n. 2.

[15] Stephen Atkinson, *The Discoverie and Historie of the Gold Mynes in Scotland, 1619* (Bannatyne Club, 1825, 51). *Cf.* Lewis, *op. cit.* 194.

25,000 tons of coal, representing an investment of many thousands of pounds, and employing scores and sometimes hundreds of miners, became common before 1640 in the north of England, in Scotland, and even in the Midlands. By that time large enterprises were the rule in the mining of copper, as well as in the much less extensive mining of silver; they were common in the mining of tin and were not unknown in the mining of lead.[16]

In the conversion of metallic ores into metals, and the preparation of these metals for the smiths, nailers and other craftsmen who fashioned them into finished articles, large-scale enterprise made no less striking progress than in mining. The blast-furnace for producing cast iron was probably introduced from the Continent towards the end of the fifteenth century.[17] But it was little used even in Sussex, the centre of the English iron industry, and apparently not at all elsewhere, until after 1540.[18] Before that time, most English wrought iron had been obtained directly from the ore, by the so-called "bloomery" process, at small forges, which cost little to build, rarely produced more than twenty tons a year, required few tools and appliances, no buildings beyond the forge itself, and seldom employed more than half a dozen or so manorial tenants. Between 1540 and 1640, the process of iron-making assumed a new and highly capitalistic form, and the changes were second in importance only to those which revolutionized the industry during and after the seventies of the eighteenth century. The ore came to be generally smelted in blast furnaces,[19] first in Sussex, then in Glamorganshire, Monmouthshire, the Midlands, the Forest of Dean and Scotland.[20] These furnaces were vast structures compared with the earlier forges. They often rose to a height of thirty feet and were usually more than twenty feet square at the bottom, with walls five or six feet thick of brick and stone to withstand the great heat necessary to obtain molten iron. That heat itself was generated with the help of a large leathern bellows about twenty feet long, usually driven by an overshot wheel almost as high as the furnace itself. To obtain the power, the water from a dam was carried high above the ground along a wooden trough, often seventy-five yards or more in length, to a point above the

[16] Cf. V.C.H. Derbyshire, II, 332.

[17] Water-power was occasionally used for driving the bellows or the hammers at more primitive iron works in the Middle Ages.

[18] Beck believed that, even on the Continent, the use of large furnaces and water-power in the manufacture of iron did not become extensive until the middle of the sixteenth century (Ludwig Beck, Die Geschichte des Eisen (2nd edn., 1891), I, 781.

[19] I do not mean, of course, that all the primitive bloomery forges had disappeared by the time of the Civil War, or even by the beginning of the eighteenth century.

[20] Straker, op. cit.; W. Llewellin, "Sussex Ironmasters in Glamorganshire", Archaeologia Cambrensis, 3rd ser., IX, 83-111; V.C.H. Derbyshire, II, 358-9; Rhys Jenkins, "Iron-making in the Forest of Dean", Transactions of the Newcomen Society, VI, 42-65; Ivison MacAdam, "Notes on the Ancient Iron Industry of Scotland", Proceedings of the Society of Antiquarians, Scotland, XXI, 89, 109, 112-13.

wheel. A large additional outlay in buildings was required—a furnace house of stone and timber, a bridge house to protect the water-wheel, several smaller houses and cabins for the workmen, stables for the horses used in hauling ore, timber and coal, and dry storage space for the ore and the charcoal which had to be obtained in greater quantities as the scale of enterprise increased, and at higher prices as the cost of wood rose more rapidly than that of other commodities. These new iron works involved an original outlay which normally exceeded £1,000; they often employed scores of workmen to bring the materials, to convert wood to charcoal, to operate the machinery, and to handle the cast iron, and they were capable of producing from 100 to 500 tons and even more in a year. They were sometimes combined with, sometimes separate from, the finery and chafery, at which cast iron was made into wrought iron. The latter process was, in any case, scarcely less capitalistic than the former, for before the Civil War water-power came to be generally employed both to fan the flames at the hearths and to drive the great hammers which forged the metal into bars. As early as 1607, Camden had commented upon the sound of the water-driven hammers throughout Sussex, which filled " the neighbourhood . . . night and day with continual noise ".[21] Whether the forges were situated near the furnace or at a distance, they were often owned by the same entrepreneur or partnership, so that many ironmasters in calculating their outlay had to add the cost of the forge to that of the furnace.

Other branches of the metallurgical industry, besides the making of iron, were changing their form under the stimulus of technical improvements introduced from abroad. With the help of skilled workmen from Germany, copper-smelting was combined with copper-mining in the gigantic financial enterprise of the Society of Mines Royal. According to a writer who had known the works of the Society at Keswick before the Civil War practically put a stop to their operations, " the smelting houses were so many that they looked like a little town ".[22] Other metals were usually produced in less elaborate plants than iron and copper, and sometimes without the aid of machinery. But mills driven by water-power came to be extensively used in the last half of the sixteenth century for breaking lead ore[23] and for smelting and stamping tin. As a result, the process of smelting tin ore passed from the hands of small craftsmen to those of capitalist employers.

These changes of industrial organization in connection with the conversion of ores into metals were accompanied by similar changes in all the processes which supplied the craftsmen with standardized metal goods, in the form of ingots, sheets, rods and wire. Steel had been made in England in small quantities throughout the Middle Ages,

[21] William Camden, *Britannia* (Gough edn., 1753), I, 195.
[22] Quoted Hamilton, *op. cit.* 55.
[23] Salzman, *op. cit.* 55·6.

but the country had been mainly dependent for its supplies upon Germany. The first attempts to introduce a manufacture on a large scale occurred early in Elizabeth's reign in Sussex, Kent and Glamorganshire, with the help of skilled Dutch technicians. Thirty foreign workmen were employed in a steel-works at Robertsbridge in Sussex, started in 1565,[24] and the buildings included two large coal houses and a dwelling house, besides the work house and several forges. A partnership, which included Sir Henry Sidney and Jone Knight, the widow of an important London merchant, spent £1,960 in 1565-6 in setting up a steel-making plant in Kent.[25] From that time on, the industry was undertaken increasingly under factory conditions. In James I's reign, cutting mills were set up in or near London for producing iron rods to be used by nailers, smiths and shipwrights.[26] The drawing of metal wire, which had been carried on exclusively by hand labour until the sixties of the sixteenth century, changed its character during the next few decades. Water-driven machinery was adopted both for hammering the metal bars into the proper form and for the actual drawing of the wire from the metal. The new processes involved an extensive outlay in buildings and machinery, for there were two mills, one for the small and another for the large wire, besides the furnaces in which the metal was annealed. The celebrated wire works at Tintern apparently employed about 100 hands as early as 1581. So, except in the finishing processes, the considerable plant, consisting usually of a group of small buildings, and based on water-driven machinery and large furnaces, made its way into one branch of the metallurgical industry after another, and established itself firmly before the Civil War.

Large-scale industry was thus becoming the normal form of enterprise both in mining and in metallurgy. The adoption of new machinery and large furnaces was accompanied, as we saw, by a phenomenal expansion in the output of coal, and a somewhat less striking growth in the output of metal. The demand for workpeople was increasing nearly as rapidly as the output; for while the introduction of machinery reduced somewhat the labour costs of producing metal from the ore, the advantages provided by labour-saving devices in mining were offset by the increasing difficulties of extracting coal and ore from greater depths. During the century preceding the Civil War, a great many thousands of men and some women, whose ancestors had laboured on the land or as small craftsmen in their own homes in medieval towns and villages, were drawn into large-scale enterprise in mining and in converting ore into a form of metal suitable for craftsmen to fashion into anchors, tools, machine parts, wool combs and cards, axle-trees, bits and spurs, grates,

[24] Rhys Jenkins, " Notes on the Early History of Steel Making in England ", *Transactions of the Newcomen Society*, III, 17-18, 33-40.      [25] Straker, *op. cit.* 313-14.
[26] John Nicholl, *Some Account of the Company of Ironmongers* (2nd edn., 1866), 164-9.

nails, locks and keys, ploughshares, kettles, pots and pans, and hundreds of other metal articles, which were wanted in much larger quantities than ever before as a result of the increase in population, the general expansion of industry, and the spread of comfort among the upper and middle classes.

While the progress of large-scale industry in mining and metallurgy from 1540 to 1640 was stimulated by the application of technical processes introduced with the help of skilled foreign artisans, it is probable that before the middle of the seventeenth century these processes were being more extensively used than in foreign nations. Great Britain was not only catching up with continental countries; she had already begun to forge ahead of them. There was no growth in the output of coal abroad at all comparable to that in Great Britain, and, on the eve of the Civil War, three or four times as much coal was probably produced in Great Britain as in the whole of continental Europe. Britain had gained no comparable lead in the extraction of ores, but as coal mining already required the investment of more capital and the employment of more labour than all other kinds of British mining combined, it may be presumed that mining already occupied a more prominent place in the national economy than in any foreign country. Only the failure to solve the problem of smelting ores with coal had prevented Great Britain from capturing a place of equal pre-eminence in metallurgy.

With the critical shortage of timber that accompanied the industrial expansion of the Elizabethan Age, manufacturers spendthrift of fuel were heavily handicapped unless they could substitute coal, which was abundant and cheap, for firewood and charcoal, which were increasingly scarce and dear. Nowhere were the effects of rising timber prices felt more keenly than in smelting. The high cost of fuel began to check the expansion in the output of iron before the end of Elizabeth's reign; it brought this expansion to a standstill before the Civil War, and had begun to interfere with the production of lead, copper and tin, all of which could be smelted with less fuel than iron. But the effects of the failure to solve the technical problem of substituting coal for wood in the process of converting ores to metals was somewhat less serious for the metallurgical industry as a whole than has been sometimes assumed. During the reigns of Elizabeth, James I and Charles I, coal was successfully substituted for wood fuel in calcining the ores prior to their smelting, in remelting lead after it had been smelted, in extracting silver from lead, in converting iron into steel, in battery and wire work, and in nearly all the finishing processes. While Great Britain stood at a disadvantage in smelting ores as compared with continental countries,[27]

[27] It is a mistake to suppose that in the ordinary process of producing wrought iron, no coal at all was used prior to the successful introduction of coke in the blast furnace by the elder Derby about 1709. Some coal was commonly employed along with charcoal during the seventeenth century, at least in the Forest of Dean and the Midlands,

where the timber shortage became critical somewhat later, she had already obtained an advantage in the other metallurgical processes through the greater abundance and accessibility of her coal supplies. She had begun to supplement her domestic stock of metals by more substantial imports of iron from Flanders and Scandinavia.

### (iii) *The Discovery and Application of New Technical Methods*

The substitution of coal for wood frequently involved technical problems of considerable magnitude in other processes than smelting and in other industries than metallurgy. By the successful solution of a number of these problems early in the seventeenth century, the British were already making a positive contribution of their own to industrial technology. Owing to the critical shortage of timber, fuel economy became a much more vital matter in the Elizabethan Age in England than on the Continent, and English " inventors " spent much of their time experimenting with new kinds of heating apparatus, which, it was hoped, would either reduce the consumption of wood[28] or make possible the use of coal. As a coal fire damaged the quality of the raw materials with which it came in contact, it was necessary either to devise more elaborate and expensive furnaces than had hitherto been used, in order to separate the materials from the sulphurous flames and fumes of the new fuel, or to attempt to purify the coal itself. About the middle of the seventeenth century, the second kind of attack on the problem led to the discovery of coke, which was first used in drying malt. Already during the reigns of James I and Charles I, the introduction of new kinds of furnaces, suited to the use of raw coal, had begun to increase the capitals and alter the nature of the work in a number of manufactures.

The calcining of ore prior to smelting it had always been accomplished in an open-air fire before the seventeenth century. It was almost certainly in order to make possible the substitution of coal for charcoal that the process came to be carried on in brick kilns in the Midlands and the Forest of Dean before the Civil War. Bricks had occasionally been baked in coal fires on the Continent in the sixteenth century, but the adoption of a more elaborate kiln heated by several small furnaces was apparently a device worked out in England in the reign of James I. This facilitated the use of coal and greatly increased the importance of the production of bricks, which were coming into general use for the first time in building, paving, and in the construction of cisterns, furnaces and kilns of all kinds. Shortly before 1612, glass-making was

---

at the forges where pig-iron was made into bars. Such a use was not limited to the finery, as my book suggests (Nef, *op. cit.* I, 250), but extended to the chafery (Jenkins, " Iron-making in the Forest of Dean ", 60).

[28] *Cf.* Lansdowne MSS. 105, no. 44.

transformed by the discovery of the method of closing the clay crucibles in which the potash and sand were melted down, in order to make possible the substitution of a coal for a wood fire.[29] It has been suggested[30] that the invention of the closed crucibles for making glass may have inspired William Ellyott and Mathias Meysey, in 1614, only a few years later, in their important invention of the cementation process for steel manufacture. The enclosing of bar iron and charcoal in crucibles, similar to those invented for melting glass, was an essential feature of the process.

The newly awakened interest in mechanical improvements, which spread among all classes in England from the nobility to the humblest artisan, and sent those who could afford it travelling in foreign countries for instruction, was not limited to the problem of saving firewood. In an age that Jevons and other nineteenth-century writers believed to be virtually barren of practical inventive achievement, England was actually becoming a busy hive of experiments designed to reduce labour. Shortly before the end of Elizabeth's reign, boring rods for finding out the nature of underground strata, and railed ways with large horse-drawn wagons for carrying coal, were devised by the ingenuity of some inventors who remain anonymous, apparently in southern Nottinghamshire, where at about the same time, in 1589, William Lee gave the world his celebrated stocking-knitting frame.

It is impossible to determine to what extent workmen were drawn into large-scale industry before 1640 as a result of English inventions. In some cases, the technical discoveries had little, if any, effect upon the form of industrial enterprise. Framework knitting remained a domestic manufacture until the nineteenth century, for Lee's invention did not cause a sufficiently great increase in the capital required to draw it into the factory.[31] Boring rods added something, but not much, to the costs of mining. Railed ways involved a far heavier outlay, especially where collieries were worked at some distance from navigable water and where the terrain between was full of hills and ravines. Their installation eliminated the independent local carter, who plied his horse and cart for hire, and changed the carriage of coal into a capitalistic industry. But neither railed ways nor boring rods made any great headway in connection with mining until the end of the seventeenth century.

The introduction of new furnaces, making possible the burning of coal, was of greater immediate importance. Calcining kilns added to

---

[29] There can be no doubt that this was a British invention, for it was introduced later at various places on the Continent. Cf. F. Pholien, *La verrerie et ses artistes au pays de Liége* (1899), 57, 77.

[30] By Mr E. W. Hulme. See Jenkins, " Notes on the Early History of Steel Making ", 28-9.

[31] See J. D. Chambers, *Nottinghamshire in the Eighteenth Century*, chap. v.

the cost of iron works. Glass-making had been done by the foreign artisans, who introduced extensive commercial glass work into England after the middle of the sixteenth century, in specially built houses, with oblong furnaces about six feet long, before the invention of the closed pots;[32] so it would be inaccurate to say that this invention converted a domestic into a factory industry. But it furthered the concentration of capital, and had far reaching consequences for the progress of the British glass manufacture. It was not only that the new houses for producing sheet glass were larger structures, costing more to build and equip and employing more hands than those for producing fine goblets and mirrors which they partly superseded; the labour done at the new houses was of a different nature. Glass-making as carried on at Altare and Venice in the late fifteenth and sixteenth centuries, and as taught by the Italians to the French, the Dutch, and the English, was an art, and the persons who practised it in Italy enjoyed a prestige and dignity similar to that attaching to the goldsmith, or even the sculptor and painter. An Italian glass goblet of the early sixteenth century can be appropriately set beside Benvenuto Cellini's saltcellar or a fine canvas by Carpaccio. But the new glass furnaces in seventeenth-century England came to be largely staffed with stokers and other unskilled labourers, whose social status resembled that of the workers at alum houses. It was the coarsest glass—especially such as was used for windows and bottles—which consumed the largest quantities of coal, and was made in the biggest houses; and the English especially excelled in the manufacture of this cheap glass,[33] wanted much more generally now that the use of glass windows and vessels was becoming common, and that luxuries were spreading from the highest to the middle orders.

Wherever coal was substituted for wood in manufactures, it tended not only to increase the cost of the installation, but also to cheapen the quality of the product and reduce the prestige attaching to manual work. By cheapening the quality of the product it widened the market for it, and thus further increased the advantages of large-scale production. Quite apart from the direct influence of the substitution of coal for wood in encouraging large-scale manufacture, it is clear that the inventions making this substitution possible enabled several capitalistic industries, which would otherwise have withered, to flourish as they could not in foreign countries lacking cheap and easily accessible coal supplies. The progress during the seventeenth century of brick-making and commercial glass-making, both of which had been of little importance before Elizabeth's reign, would have been impossible but for the technical changes in the processes.

[32] For the description of a glass house erected by some Frenchmen at Buckholt, near Salisbury, probably about 1576, see E. W. Hulme, " English Glass-Making in the Sixteenth and Seventeenth Centuries ", *The Antiquary*, XXX, 214.
[33] Cf. *The Mischief of the Five Shillings Tax Upon Coal* (1699), 22.

## (iv) *Other Factors Causing the Concentration of Industrial Capital*

The adoption of mechanical methods, little used in Great Britain before the Reformation or discovered during the following century, clearly played an important role in the rapid growth of large-scale industry between 1540 and 1640. But there were manufactures in which the factory form of enterprise made remarkable headway without any fundamental change in the technique of production. Two principal factors were making large-scale industry more economical, even without the introduction of labour-saving machinery or new types of furnaces. One was the growth in the size of markets; the other was the shift from wood to coal fuel in a great many branches of industry, where the substitution involved no technical problem. As coal supplies were localized and the costs of transporting so bulky a commodity extremely high, the substitution encouraged industrial concentration. Under the influence of these factors, the size of the enterprise in a number of industries increased greatly.

In no industry perhaps was the increase in the scale of manufacture more impressive than in the making of salt by the evaporation of sea-water. Although the manufacture of salt at the brine springs in Cheshire had been carried on at least as early as the thirteenth century in small salt houses, normally furnished with from six to twelve tiny lead pans,[34] sea-salt had been generally produced on a smaller scale without special houses at points scattered all along the coasts of Great Britain. The growth of population in London and other towns during and after Elizabeth's reign caused a great increase in the demand for salt to be used in preserving fish and meat; and the advantages offered by abundant supplies of an inferior grade of coal, which would have gone to waste at the mine but for the salt works, drew the growing industry to the colliery districts. During the last two decades of the sixteenth century and the first three of the seventeenth, most of the sea-salt manufacture in Great Britain came to be concentrated at the mouth of the Tyne and Wear and along the coasts of the Firth of Forth. The old casual workings of local peasants were superseded by great iron pans twenty feet or more square, and five or six feet deep, in which sea-water was evaporated by the heat of a great furnace. This whole structure was set in a wooden house, which also served as a storing place for the supplies of coal and often as a dwelling place for the workmen recruited into this labour. Many scores of pounds were required to set up such a plant, and although only four workmen were needed to keep a single pan in operation, the principal salt works were composed of many pans, clustered together. As early as 1589, one capitalist claimed to employ 300 men at salt works on the Wear in which he had invested

[34] H. J. Hewitt, *Medieval Cheshire* (1929), 109 *et seq.*

£4,000. The works at South Shields, which came into the hands of the State at the time of the Civil War, employed about 1,000 men, and represented an original investment of many thousands of pounds.[35]

Changes in the supplies of fuel and raw materials and a growth in the market for the products also combined to bring about a similar increase in the scale of enterprise in soap-boiling, and a slower increase in the scale of enterprise in lime-burning and brewing. Before the dissolution of monasteries, all three had been almost entirely household manufactures;[36] lime-burning and brewing perhaps remained predominantly so at the time of the Civil War. But in the meantime a number of considerable enterprises had crept in. From the large orders that some London brewers placed with coal dealers about the middle of the seventeenth century, it appears in a few cases that the small domestic manufacturer, with a brewing equipment worth £25 or so installed in a part of his house,[37] was being superseded by the brewer who set up a small factory. One London brewery in the reign of James I had a capital of £10,000.[38] Large lime-kilns made of brick, in which the fire was not extinguished from one end of the year to the other,[39] were appearing not only in and near the capital, but in provincial towns like Newcastle-on-Tyne, where large quantities of lime were constantly needed by builders, who purchased it from the owners of the kilns.[40] Before the end of Elizabeth's reign, the soap-boiling industry of London, which supplied most of the Kingdom, was already being carried on mainly in factories, with an outlay in vats of brick and boilers of metal which was in some cases almost as expensive as the equipment at the Yorkshire alum houses built in James I's reign.

Two other important industries remain to be considered: ship-building and textiles. The former had long been organized in large-scale units, for while smiths and carpenters, sail and rope makers might prepare the materials in their own households, the shipyards where these materials were assembled were large and costly establishments in which many workers laboured for wages. Those in seventeenth-century Holland were fitted with wind-driven sawmills and large cranes for moving heavy timbers;[41] and it seems probable that similar machinery was set up in English yards before the Civil War. In the century

[35] Lansdowne MSS. 59, no. 69; *Calendar S.P.D.* (1655), 36.

[36] Although special lime kilns were erected to supply solder for the great medieval buildings, these works were abandoned as soon as the building had been completed. There were probably no large lime-works in the towns comparable to those set up in the seventeenth century for supplying the general market.

[37] " Inventory of Goods found in the Tenements and Ale-brewhouse of James Barre " (1598) (Sloane MSS. 2177, ff. 23-4).

[38] For this information I am indebted to Mr F. J. Fisher.

[39] *Cf.* Brereton, *op. cit.* 1-2.

[40] *Cf.* Sir Balthazar Gerbier, *Counsel and Advice to all Builders* (1663), 55.

[41] Violet Barbour, "Dutch and English Shipping in the Seventeenth Century", *The Economic History Review*, II, 274. See *infra*, 239.

following the dissolution of the monasteries, the importance of English
shipping increased greatly, as a result of the rapid growth of the Royal
Navy, the progress in all branches of foreign trade and in the fishing
trade, and the phenomenal expansion in the coastwise trade, above all
in the coastwise trade in coal, which increased from less than 30,000
tons per annum to upwards of 500,000 tons.  While the bulk of the
English fishing trade and of foreign commerce was in the hands of Dutch
shipowners during the seventeenth century, and while a good many
mercantile vessels which flew the English flag had been built in Dutch
shipyards, where they could be produced more cheaply,[42] shipbuilding
in England became a very much more important industry than it had
ever been before, both in state-owned and in private yards, like those at
the principal ports of East Anglia and at London, Bristol and Newcastle-
on-Tyne.[43]  It is probable that the number of persons employed in
shipyards owned by private individuals or by partnerships multiplied
several times over.  As the size of the ships was increasing, there was
doubtless a corresponding increase in the cost of the materials and the
yards in which they were built.

   In the textile industry, with its endless ramifications, the domestic
workshop remained the rule.  But semi-factory conditions in connection with the finishing processes—dyeing, fulling and calendering—
were much less exceptional even in medieval times than was once
believed.  It is not possible to estimate the extent to which such conditions existed in England before the Reformation.  But a number of
developments during the next century encouraged their spread.  The
growth in the demand for cloth of all kinds, and especially for worsteds,
cottons and linens, which were being extensively produced in England
for the first time, was accompanied by a notable increase in the proportion of all cloth dyed and dressed at home.  It was the finishing
processes, most readily suited to semi-factory conditions, that expanded
most rapidly in importance.  With the very great increase in the market
for cloth in London, which resulted both from the rapid growth in
population, and from the increase in the quantity of clothing, bedding,
and hangings used by the rising middle class and by domestic servants,
the advantages of large-scale production grew.  Before the middle of
the seventeenth century, some London dyers were buying coal in as
large quantities as the chief brewers and soap boilers.  This they could
hardly have done unless their equipment in furnaces and metal boilers
had been equally extensive.  Hat-makers, too, were sometimes large

   [42] Violet Barbour, " Dutch and English Shipping in the Seventeenth Century ", *The
Economic History Review*, II, 265-6, 274-7, 288-90 ; (*infra*, 230-1, 239-42, 251-3).  *The
Mischief of the Five Shillings Tax on Coal*, 18.  The proportion of English mercantile
tonnage which was foreign built is quite uncertain, but Professor Barbour does not
think that it exceeded one-third or one-fourth after the three Dutch wars, and, as these
wars brought the English many captured Dutch ships, the proportion before the Civil
War may have been even smaller.  England was building her own warships.
   [43] *Cf.* Defoe, *Tour* (ed. Cole), I, 40, 42 ; Nef, *op cit.* I, 174 ; II, 25-8.

buyers of coal, and this suggests that the introduction of felt-hat making in the Elizabethan Age may also have furthered the growth of the factory form of enterprise.

### (v) *Conclusion*

Without a thorough investigation of many industries hitherto neglected by economic historians, no quantitative estimate can be made of the total number of labourers employed in capitalistically owned mines and manufacturing establishments on the eve of the Civil War. No doubt the great majority of all the workpeople engaged in industry laboured in their homes, in town cellars or garrets, or in village cottages. But that majority was by no means so overwhelming as has been supposed. During the previous century it had been greatly reduced. Tens of thousands of workpeople had been swept from the country dwellings and town shops of their forefathers, or from a ragged existence of vagabondage, into hundreds of new, capitalistically-owned enterprises. The introduction of new industries and of new machinery, tools and furnaces in old industries, had brought about technical changes in the methods of mining and manufacturing only less momentous than those associated with the great inventions of the late eighteenth and early nineteenth centuries.

It must not be supposed that the developments we have attempted to sketch came to an end at the time of the Civil War. While workpeople were probably drawn into large-scale industry at a somewhat less rapid rate in the century following than in the century preceding 1640, the striking changes in technique and the striking concentration of capital which began in the Elizabethan Age led directly to the rapid industrial progress of the late eighteenth and nineteenth centuries. The rise of industrialism in Great Britain can be more properly regarded as a long process stretching back to the middle of the sixteenth century and coming down to the final triumph of the industrial state towards the end of the nineteenth, than as a sudden phenomenon associated with the late eighteenth and early nineteenth centuries. It is no longer possible to find a full explanation of "the great inventions" and the new factories of the late eighteenth century in a preceding commercial revolution which increased the size of markets. The commercial revolution, if that is the proper term to apply to a rapid growth in foreign and domestic trade during a period of two centuries, had a continuous influence reaching back to the Reformation upon industrial technology and the scale of mining and manufacturing. But so, in turn, the progress of industry had continually stimulated in a variety of ways the progress of commerce. The former progress was quite as " revolutionary " as the latter, and quite as directly responsible for the " Industrial Revolution ".

8

There are reasons for believing that the progress of technology and the concentration of industrial capital were more rapid in Great Britain than in any foreign country between the middle of the sixteenth and the middle of the eighteenth centuries. Before the dissolution of the monasteries, Great Britain was, industrially, in a backwater compared with Italy, Spain, the Low Countries, the South-German states, and even France. Englishmen had almost nothing to teach foreigners in the way of practical mechanical knowledge, except in connection with the production of tin and the manufacture of pewter. By the end of the seventeenth century, the position was reversed. "Our artisans", wrote a certain James Puckle in 1697, "[are] universally allow'd the best upon Earth for Improvements."[44] His remark is typical of the opinion of most men of his age, and it was more than a patriotic boast. Foreigners spoke soon after no less emphatically in the same sense. In the letters which he wrote during the thirties and forties of the eighteenth century, Voltaire's admiration for the skill of the English mechanics and the solidity of the products of English manufactures was second only to his admiration for the minds of Newton and other English scientists, whose own exploits were to some extent a reflection of the need for solving the mechanical problems raised by the rapid growth of mining and manufacturing.[45] If, as seems probable, the English were as far ahead of foreigners in their knowledge and application of technological skill in the early eighteenth century as they had been behind before the middle of the sixteenth, it is plain that during the intervening period progress must have been far more rapid in England than in any foreign country.

The concentration of industrial capital in Great Britain during the period from 1540 to 1640 and after was caused to a considerable extent, as we have seen, by the progress of technology. If this progress was more rapid in England than elsewhere, that in itself suggests that large-scale industry made more rapid headway in England than on the Continent. Other considerations point to the same conclusion. Another very important cause for the concentration of industrial capital in Great Britain was the general change from a wood-burning to a coal-burning economy. Except for the Catholic Low Countries, there was no other area in the world besides Great Britain in which any extensive use was made of coal before the forties of the eighteenth century, and the development of the coal industry in the Low Countries between 1540 and 1740 was very much slower than in Great Britain. The growth in the size of markets, which also promoted industrial concentration, was due partly to the facilities for cheap water transport, which Great Britain,

---

[44] *A New Dialogue between a Burgermaster and an English Gentleman* (1697), 20.
[45] *Cf.* B. Hessen, "The Social and Economic Roots of Newton's 'Principia'" in *Science at the Cross Roads* (papers presented to the International Congress of the History of Science and Technology by the Delegates of the U.S.S.R., London, 1931), 151-212; and Nef, *op. cit.* I, 240-56.

by virtue of her insular position and good harbours, enjoyed to a greater degree than any foreign country except Holland.   The cost of the plant in many British industries was increased by the use of water-power.   As England possessed fewer dependable rapid-flowing streams than did most continental countries, it was necessary to resort much more frequently to the overshot wheel.   It followed that the use of water-driven machinery was costly, and that the discovery of an alternative to water-power was an urgent necessity.   The British climate was partly responsible for the heavy investment in salt works.   Along the Mediterranean and the Bay of Biscay it was possible to produce salt without artificial heat.   Sea-salt manufacture in Great Britain became capitalistic while the equally important manufacture of France remained the work of peasants.   While no definite comparison of large-scale enterprise in England and on the Continent after 1540 can be made until we have many more studies of special industries, such evidence as is now available suggests that the concentration of capital in mining and manufacturing was more striking in England than in any other area of equal size.

It was probably not, as has been supposed, during the late eighteenth and early nineteenth centuries that the contrast between industrial progress in England and in continental countries was most striking, but in the two centuries preceding the "Industrial Revolution".   As the continuous rapid progress of industrial capitalism appears to cover the longest period of time in England, the concept of an "Industrial Revolution" would seem to be especially inappropriate as an explanation of the triumph of industrial civilization in Great Britain.   It gives the impression that the process was especially sudden, when it was in all probability more continuous than in any other country.

# PRICES AND INDUSTRIAL CAPITALISM IN FRANCE AND ENGLAND, 1540-1640 [1]

## J. U. NEF

THROUGHOUT Western Europe during the second half of the sixteenth century, peasants, craftsmen and shopkeepers, as well as princes and bishops, all shared one novel experience of some importance for their daily lives. In each decade they found that any standard coin, even if it contained precisely the same quantity of precious metal as in the previous decade, would buy less of almost any commodity bought and sold.

This "price revolution", as it has come to be called, was caused mainly by the abundant supplies of precious metals which poured into Europe from South and Central America. Prices—measured in silver—rose in the various European countries, we are told, from two- to more than three-fold between 1520 and 1650.[2] The prices which people actually paid rose much more, because princes everywhere were debasing the currency.

For some time historians and economists have been disposed to regard the price revolution as an important cause for the rise of modern capitalism. But, until recently, no one attempted to show concretely how the inflow of American treasure promoted the development of large-scale enterprise in industry, commerce and finance. In 1929 Professor E. J. Hamilton, to whom we owe our exact knowledge of the price revolution in Spain, suggested that the rapid increase in prices stimulated the growth of capitalism mainly by cheapening labour costs, and thus making possible exceptionally large profits during a period of many decades.[3] These profits brought about an unprecedented accumulation of wealth in the hands of enterprising merchants and other rich men, who could afford to invest in large-scale enterprises, and who were tempted to do so by the prospect of abnormally large returns. Later,

---

[1] The substance of a paper read in July 1936 at the Economic History Section of the Anglo-American Historical Conference in London.

[2] Georg Wiebe, *Zur Geschichte der Preisrevolution des 16 und 17 Jahrhunderts* (Leipzig, 1895), 376-7, 379, 382; Earl J. Hamilton, *American Treasure and the Price Revolution in Spain* (Cambridge, Mass., 1934), 205-10, 403. *Cf.* François Simiand, *Recherches anciennes et nouvelles sur le movement général des prix du XVI⁰ au XIX⁰ siècle* (Paris, 1932), 167-8.

[3] Hamilton, "American Treasure and the Rise of Capitalism" in *Economica*, XXVII (1929), 338-57.

in his *Treatise on Money*, Mr Keynes used his great authority to support and interpret Dr Hamilton's thesis.[4]

Dr Hamilton observed that the effect of the price revolution upon the material welfare of the wage earner was not the same in all countries. In Spain, he found, rising wages did not lag behind rising prices anything like as much as they apparently did in England.[5] He concluded that the differences between the course of wages in the two countries provided a very important explanation for the greater progress made by capitalist enterprise in England than in Spain, especially during the first two or three decades of the seventeenth century. At that time wages caught up with prices in Spain, and the Spanish wage workers regained all they had lost in earning power during the previous eight decades.[6] But in England wages apparently lagged farther than ever behind prices, and the wage workers were able to buy only about half as much with the money they received as at the beginning of the sixteenth century.[7] The greater fall in the standard of living of the English labourer was a part of the cost the country had to pay for great national progress.[8] Without the price revolution, an extensive and prolonged decline in real wages could hardly have occurred. Therefore, according to this theory, the price revolution was the principal driving force behind large-scale enterprise during the late sixteenth and early seventeenth centuries.[9]

### (i) *The progress of large-scale industry during the price revolution*

A comparison of French with English industrial history during the century from 1540 to 1640 suggests that there is a danger of exaggerating the rôle played by the price revolution, and the decline of real wages that it made possible, in stimulating the progress of capitalist enterprise in industry.[10] When Dr Hamilton wrote it was assumed that large-scale industry was developing rapidly in France as well as in

[4] J. M. Keynes, *A Treatise on Money* (New York, 1930), II, 152-63.

[5] Dr Hamilton's calculations concering the course of real wages in Spain, as announced tentatively in his article in *Economica* (*loc. cit.* 253-4), were borne out by his further researches (*American Treasure and the Price Revolution in Spain*, 273).

[6] *Ibid.* 273, 279-82.

[7] Hamilton, " American Treasure and the Rise of Capitalism ", 350-2.

[8] *Cf.* Keynes, *op. cit.* II, 163.

[9] Hamilton, " American Treasure and the Rise of Capitalism ", 338, 344, 349. *Cf.* Keynes, *op. cit.* II, 159. Dr Hamilton's argument about the influence of the discoveries in promoting capitalism was not concerned exclusively with the rôle played by the price revolution in reducing the cost of labour. He also wrote of the phenomenal profits made by merchants in the East India trade, and of the probable decline in the real cost of renting land, as further factors which increased the accumulation of capital and encouraged investments in large-scale enterprise (" American Treasure and the Rise of Capitalism ", 347-50). But it was to the fall in real wages that he attached the most importance (*Ibid.* 349, 355-6), and it was to this aspect that Mr Keynes drew attention.

[10] In this article we are not concerned, as Dr Hamilton was, with the influence of the price revolution upon commercial and financial, as well as industrial, organisation.

England.[11]  But it now seems that there were important differences. In England the rate of industrial change from 1540 to 1640 was much more rapid than in any other period before the late eighteenth century. But in France it was probably slower between the death of Francis I and the accession of Louis XIV than during the previous hundred years, when the inflow of treasure from America had hardly begun.  There was no growth in the output of coal, glass, salt, alum, building materials, metal wares and ships comparable in rapidity to that which raised England from an industrial backwater to the foremost industrial country in the world.  Technical changes in the methods of mining and manufacturing which greatly increased the amounts of capital needed to set up in industry were less widely introduced.  The number of new, large-scale industrial enterprises started must have been much smaller, relative to population, than in England.[12]  What we have to explain in the case of France is not, as in that of England, why industrial capitalism made so much progress in the age of the price revolution, but why it made so little.

The explanations arrived at for France have a special interest, because the case of France was more representative of European countries generally than the case of England.  In Italy, southern Germany, and the Spanish Netherlands, the age of the price revolution was, as compared with the age of the Renaissance, a period of slow industrial development.  Only in Holland, and perhaps in Sweden and the Principality of Liége, was there a speeding-up in the rate of industrial development resembling to some extent that which occurred in England.

Were there any differences between the course of wages in England and France from 1540 to 1640 which help to account for the great differences in the progress of industrial capitalism?  The only index numbers of wages and commodity prices in the two countries available when Professor Hamilton wrote his article in 1929, were those compiled in 1895 by Georg Wiebe, who used the voluminous records of wages and prices, collected by Thorold Rogers[13] and the Vicomte d'Avenel,[14] as a basis for the first comprehensive inquiry into the price revolution.[15] Dr Hamilton reprinted these index numbers in order to compare the course of real wages in Andalusia and in England and France.[16]  Mr Keynes derived from them tables of what he called " profit inflation ". These tables give for successive periods during the sixteenth and seventeenth centuries the ratio of commodity prices to costs of production, on

[11] Hamilton, " American Treasure and the Rise of Capitalism ", 338, 356.
[12] J. U. Nef, " A Comparison of Industrial Growth in France and England from 1540 to 1640 " in *Journal of Political Economy*, XLIV (1936), 289-317, 505-33, 643-66.
[13] *A History of Agriculture and Prices in England*, 7 vols. (Oxford, 1866-1902).
[14] *Histoire économique de la propriété, des salaires, des denrées et de tous les prix*, 7 vols. (Paris, 1894).                           [15] Wiebe, *op. cit*, 374-9.
[16] Hamilton, " American Treasure and the Rise of Capitalism ", 352-4.

the assumption that in both England and France money wages accounted for half the costs of production, and that the other half rose exactly as commodity prices.[17]  For the convenience of the reader in following our argument, Mr Keynes' tables are reproduced below.

### MR KEYNES' TABLES[18]

| England | | France | |
|---|---|---|---|
| Period | Price/Costs Ratio | Period | Price/Costs Ratio |
| 1500–50 . . . . 100 | | 1500–25 . . . . 100 | |
| | | 1525–50 . . . . 103 | |
| 1550–60 . . . . 116 | | | |
| 1560–70 . . . . 112 | | 1550–75 . . . . 110 | |
| 1570–80 . . . . 116 | | | |
| 1580–90 . . . . 120 | | 1575–1600 . . . 139 | |
| 1590–1600 . . . 137 | | | |
| 1600–10 . . . . 139 | | 1600–25 . . . . 118 | |
| 1610–20 . . . . 135 | | | |
| 1620–30 . . . . 141 | | | |
| 1630–40 . . . . 134 | | 1625–50 . . . . 128 | |
| 1640–50 . . . . 133 | | | |

His results suggest that the behaviour of real wages in the two countries was similar.  The standard of living among labourers apparently fell in France nearly, if not quite, as much as in England.[19]  On Wiebe's showing, there were at least two generations of French workers whose wages would buy only about half the quantity of commodities that the wages of their ancestors in the late fifteenth century would have bought.[20]  While France belongs, like Spain, to the group of countries where industrial capitalism made comparatively slow progress from 1540 to 1640, it seems to belong, as England does, to a group of countries where the fall in real wages was much greater and more prolonged than in Spain.

As can be seen from Mr Keynes' tables, Wiebe's index numbers were worked out by decades for England and by twenty-five year periods for France.  If we are to study the relations between price changes and industrial development, it is important to know not only that industrial capitalism made much slower progress in France than in England during

[17] Keynes, *op. cit.* 159-60.          [18] Taken from Keynes, *op. cit.* II, 159-60.
[19] Wiebe compiled two sets of index numbers for commodity prices in England, based on different methods of weighting the commodities (*op cit.* 374-6, 383).  If Dr Hamilton had reprinted not the first but the second set, which shows prices rising a good deal more slowly, it would have appeared that the workers' standard of living fell more in France than in England.
[20] Hamilton, " American Treasure and the Rise of Capitalism ", 353.

the century from 1540 to 1640 as a whole, but also to know in which portions of the century the contrasts were greatest.

For the purpose of comparing the growth of industrial capitalism in the two countries, the century can be divided into four fairly well-defined periods.[21] The first ran from 1540 into the sixties of the sixteenth century. In France this period was probably marked by some slight slowing down in the rate of industrial growth, which had been rather rapid since the end of the Hundred Years War. In England it was marked by a speeding-up in the rate of growth. The rapid increase in the output of cloth, which had begun in the reign of Henry VII, was accompanied, after the dissolution of the monasteries in 1536 and 1539, by a rapid increase in the output of other industrial commodities, such as beer, coal and iron. Blast furnaces, costing with their water-driven bellows and hammers thousands of pounds, multiplied in Sussex, and large foundries for casting iron cannons were introduced from the Continent. The amount of capital invested in new mines and small factories was probably much larger—relative to population—than in France.

The differences between development in the two countries during this first period were slight compared with those during the next, which began in the sixties and ran into the nineties of the sixteenth century. During the seventies and eighties in England many new industries, like the manufacture of brass, paper, sugar, alum and copperas, were introduced, and the output of older industries, like mining, smelting, shipbuilding, salt and glass making, grew at a more rapid rate than during the forties and fifties. The phenomenal growth in industrial output, together with the widespread adoption of costly horse and water mills, hitherto little employed except in parts of southern Germany and the Low Countries, produced an unprecedented demand for industrial capital. Hundreds of new mines and small factories were started. But in France the seventies and eighties were decades of religious warfare and civil strife. While the effects of the wars upon economic life have been represented by contemporary writers and even by modern historians as more disastrous than they were, they did hold back investments in new enterprises. Much less capital was probably invested in large-scale industry during the seventies and eighties than during the forties and fifties. This was the period when the contrasts between industrial progress in the two countries were greatest.

The third period began in the nineties of the sixteenth century and lasted until about 1620. In England it may be regarded from the point of view of industrial history as a continuation of the previous period. The rate of growth in industrial output after 1604 was possibly even

[21] What follows is derived mainly from the material referred to in my article, " A Comparison of Industrial Growth in France and England " (loc. cit.). It is intended to be a tentative statement, which I hope to correct and amplify with the help of a study of further documents.

greater than during the seventies and eighties of the sixteenth century. New inventions cheapened the products and increased the scale of enterprise in industries like glass and steel making. Horse- and water-driven engines and large furnaces and kilns, which had been adopted in many ventures during Elizabeth's reign, replaced the older more primitive tools and ovens even more extensively, both in manufacturing and mining, in centres of population like London and centres of industry like the Tyne valley. Except in Sussex, Surrey and Kent, where the exhaustion of the forests stopped the progress of the iron and glass manufactures, more capital found investment than during the previous period in new mines and small factories and in the expansion of old ones. But, unlike the seventies and eighties, this was also in France a period of expanding industrial output and of marked technical development. A large number of new enterprises were started in many French provinces, especially after the publication of the Edict of Nantes in 1598 had brought to an end the most destructive phases of the religious wars. In comparison with the twenty-five years from 1570 to 1595, those from 1595 to 1620 were a bright period for the progress of manufactures in France. Though progress was slow compared to that in England, the contrasts were much less remarkable than during the religious wars.

The fourth period, from about 1620 until the outbreak of the English Civil War and the death of Louis XIII, was marked in both countries by a pronounced slowing down in the rate of industrial development. In England the rapid growth in the output of iron, which had begun with the dissolution of the monasteries, finally came to an end.[22] As is well known, the cloth manufacture underwent, especially during the early twenties, one of the most serious depressions in its history. Coal-mining in Durham and Northumberland suffered after 1652 from an over-supply of capital.[23]

In France the depression in the Levant trade, which began about 1620, proved a serious blow for industry at Marseilles and elsewhere in the south. Throughout Provence and Languedoc many enterprises in such manufactures as soap-boiling, shipbuilding, iron and glassmaking shut down for lack of markets. Nor was the depression confined to the south. Manufacturing was on the decline in Poitou, and, at least in so far as the building of merchant ships and the production of iron was concerned in Brittany and Champagne.

The depression of the twenties was not followed in France, as it was to some extent in England, by a substantial recovery during the early thirties. We can find nothing in France to rival the rapid expansion which occurred at that time in English merchant shipbuilding, in the manufacture of alum in Yorkshire and Durham, and in the building

---

[22] Nef, " Note on the Progress of Iron Production in England " in *Journal of Political Economy*, XLIV (1936), 402-3.
[23] Nef, *The Rise of the British Coal Industry* (London, 1932), II, 75-6.

trades of London. The depression in the French Levant commerce, which began in the twenties, was followed by a collapse in the thirties. While the output of iron in England did not increase after the twenties, new and larger furnaces were built during the thirties in the Midlands and the Forest of Dean to replace the older ones in south-eastern England. It was not until the reign of Louis XIV that a similar development of great new blast furnaces and forges occurred in central and western France to offset the decline of the iron manufacture in Champagne and the Cévennes. The picture painted by Voltaire of the deplorable condition of French industry and trade at the great King's accession, while overdrawn, contains much truth.[24] Notwithstanding the depression which beset the English textile and iron-making industries in the two decades preceding the Civil War, England's lead over France with respect to the investment of new capital in large-scale industry may have been greater than during the previous period of booming trade and industry.

When we consider the progress of large-scale industry in England and France during these four periods in relation to the course of profit-inflation as shown in Mr Keynes' tables, what do we find? While there is nothing in the tables to account for the depression which came in England at the end of James I's reign, there is certainly a remarkable coincidence between profit-inflation, which reflects the fall in real wages, and the growth of industrial capitalism in England during the first three of the four periods. Conditions appear to have been increasingly favourable for exceptional profits between 1550[25] and 1620. Except for two decades, 1560-70 and 1610-20, the openings for profits were greater in every decade than they had been in the previous one. With these figures before us, there is a temptation to regard the price revolution as the principal explanation of the early English industrial revolution. There is a temptation to believe that the new shipyards, the hundreds of new mines, smelting furnaces and forges, the numerous soap, starch and sugar houses, the glass furnaces, breweries, brick and lime kilns, and the alum and copperas factories, were built, equipped, supplied with raw materials and staffed by workmen, largely because the exceptional profits obtained by the wealthy as real wages fell had created great new reservoirs of capital awaiting investment, and because the cheapness of labour made investments exceptionally attractive.

[24] Voltaire, Le siècle de Louis XIV, chap. ii.

[25] Mr Keynes' tables give the impression that in England prices began to rise more rapidly than wages only after 1550. But Wiebe's index numbers show that the fall in real wages began much earlier, as soon as prices started upward. Prices actually began to rise in the second decade of the sixteenth century, and the rise became rather rapid during the forties. The real situation has been obscured because Wiebe's index numbers, which give prices in terms of their silver values, make it appear that prices fell during the forties (Wiebe, op. cit. 70, 376-7; cf. below, 174). This point was called to my attention by Mr John Saltmarsh.

But in France, after 1550, according to the tables, labour was hardly less cheap than in England; yet no industrial revolution occurred. It is true that from 1550 to 1575, according to the table, profit-inflation was slightly less in France than in England. But from 1575 to 1600 profit-inflation reached its zenith in France, and was even greater than in England. Theoretically this was the period in France when conditions seem to have been most favourable for investments in new enterprises; it was a period when they were more favourable in France than in England. But, in fact, this was of all four periods (with the possible exception of the last), the one during which the least new capital flowed into large-scale industry in France. It was the period during which English development was in most striking contrast to French.

According to the tables, real wages in France were a good deal higher in the first quarter of the seventeenth century than in the last quarter of the sixteenth. Theoretically this should not have been as good a time for industrial progress as either the preceding or the succeeding period. But, in fact, it proved to be a much better time.

Some years ago Monsieur André Liautey, now the Under-Secretary of State for Agriculture, wrote in his study of the price revolution in France, that a rise in prices " is . . . compatible with the most dissimilar economic conditions ".[26] The same thing seems to be true of a fall in real wages. Periods of profit-inflation coincided with periods of in-dustrial expansion; they also coincided with periods of industrial depression.

(ii) *The cost of industrial labour during the price revolution*

Since Wiebe compiled his index numbers, several sets of price and wage records, not contained in the volumes of Rogers and d'Avenel which he used, have been published. A brief examination of these records and of new data collected by the International Scientific Committee on Price History,[27] together with the old data on which Wiebe's work was based, suggests that the decline in the material welfare of the English workers from 1500 to 1642 was much less than Wiebe's index numbers suggested. Before the studies of Thorold Rogers were published, some writers claimed that the mechanic could get more wheat for a day's work on the eve of the Civil War than at the beginning of Elizabeth's reign.[28] Rogers' transcription of thousands of price and

[26] *La hausse des prix et la lutte contre la cherté en France au XVI⁰ siècle* (Paris, 1921), 337.

[27] Made possible through the generosity of Sir William Beveridge, the Chairman of the English Price Committee. My work was greatly facilitated by the kind help of Miss M. E. Rayner, the Secretary of the Committee, who not only found for me the relevant material, but made some calculations of the price averages for timber purchased by the Royal Navy. I am much indebted to both of them.

[28] E.g. William Playfair, *A Letter on our Agricultural Distresses* (London, 1821), charts facing 50 and 44, and also 48, 29. I am grateful to my colleague, Professor Jacob Viner, for calling my attention to this tract.

wage records made that position untenable. But he and some other scholars who used his volumes seem to have exaggerated the losses which the workers suffered from rapidly rising prices almost as much as ill-informed persons, who had no reliable statistics to establish their case, once exaggerated the gains which the same workers obtained from increases in wages.

To begin with, wage-rates apparently rose appreciably more than Rogers' data indicated. His data do not concern the wages of mechanics like smiths or cutlers, or the wages of spinners and weavers, or those of miners, smelters and workers in other rising manufactures. They relate entirely to the wages of labourers in the building trades, such as masons, carpenters, tilers and bricklayers. According to the averages worked out from Rogers' tables by Wiebe and others, wage-rates rose a shade less than two-and-a-half-fold between the first decade of the sixteenth century and the decade preceding the Civil War.[29]

We now have a number of new, rather complete series for the money wages paid to the same kinds of workmen in connection with building enterprises at several places in southern England. Three are for London.[30] The others are for Eton, Winchester, Dover, Canterbury, Cambridge and Exeter.[31] The new data indicate that—on the average —wage-rates rose nearly, if not quite, threefold between 1510 and 1640, or something like 20 per cent more than Wiebe's tables show. It is mainly for the sixty years from 1580 to 1640, the period during which, according to Wiebe's index numbers, the building workers suffered most from rising prices, that his figures understate the increase in their money wages. According to these figures, wage-rates rose about 39 per cent between the period 1571-82 and the decade 1633-42.[32] The new data suggest that they rose more than 50 per cent.[33]

[29] If we take the average wages in the decade 1501-10 as 100, then, according to Wiebe, the average in the decade 1633-42 (not in silver, but in English money) was 248 (Wiebe, op. cit. 377, 70). According to Steffen, the average was 237 (Gustaf F. Steffen, *Studien zur Geschichte der Englischen Lohnarbeiter* (Stuttgart, 1901), I). Professor Knoop and Mr Jones have worked out from Rogers' data separate averages for Oxford and Cambridge. The result for the decade 1633-42 is 200 for Oxford and 266 for Cambridge (Douglas Knoop and G. P. Jones, *The Medieval Mason* (Manchester, 1933), 236).

[30] From one of these—the London Bridge series—averages have been derived and published (Knoop and Jones, op. cit. 236). The other two—for the Royal Works and for Westminster College and Abbey—are among the manuscripts of the Price Committee at the Institute of Historical Research.

[31] Manuscripts of the Price Committee at the Institute of Historical Research. The Committee has not yet worked out index numbers from these records.

[32] Wiebe, loc. cit. According to Steffen's averages, also obtained from Rogers, wages rose only about 27 per cent (Knoop and Jones, loc. cit.).

[33] According to the averages worked out by Knoop and Jones, the wages paid for building work at London Bridge increased between the decades 1501-10 and 1633-42 practically three-fold—from 8d. to about 23d. a day. Between 1571-82 and 1633-42 wages increased from about 14d. to about 23d. (Knoop and Jones, op. cit. 236). My examination of the new records collected by the Price Committee indicates that these averages are more typical than those worked out by Thorold Rogers and used by Wiebe and Steffen (Rogers, op. cit. IV, 518-23 ; V, 664-7).

If we are to estimate the effects of the price revolution upon the labourers' standard of living, we ought to know whether unemployment among the building workers increased or diminished. We ought to know exactly what the workers bought with their wages. We ought also to know whether they made their purchases from the same kinds of tradesmen and on the same terms as did the Crown and the municipalities, and the colleges, hospitals, and other institutions, since practically all the price records that have been collected have been taken from the account books of such authorities and establishments. No satisfactory answer can be given to these questions. But, in dealing with them, certain rather misleading assumptions have been made by nearly all the authorities who have discussed the standard of living among wage workers during the period of the price revolution. It has been assumed that money wages were all that workmen received for their labour, and that these wages were spent almost exclusively on the purchase of certain foodstuffs and foods.

First of all, we have to consider whether the foodstuffs and foods have been selected in such a way as to give a true picture of the rise in the cost of diet among the labouring classes. Englishmen early in the seventeenth century were fond of saying that bread, and after bread, ale or beer, were the chief " stay " of the poor. But cereal products were not by any means the only nourishment of working people, as has been often assumed in attempting to determine the standard of living. Since Rogers' time authorities who have tried to estimate the rise in the price of food during the sixteenth and seventeenth centuries have never been able to include in their computations the prices of either bread or beer. They have got around this difficulty by substituting the prices paid in towns for the various grains from which bread and beer were produced. But in the principal towns at the beginning of the seventeenth century home-brewing had largely disappeared, and even home-baking was of less importance than it had been before the Reformation.[34]

Can we assume that the prices of drink, bread and meal were rising as much during the price revolution as the prices of the grains from which they were produced? The matter is of importance, because the prices of grains, grain products, and grasses rose almost twice as much between the first decade of the sixteenth century and the decade preceding the Civil War as the prices of most foods. Wheat increased about six-and-a-half-fold in price, oats and malt between seven- and eight-fold, hay and straw more than eight-fold.[35] Meanwhile peas increased about five-fold in price, butter about four-and-a-third-fold, hens and eggs a shade under four-and-a-third-fold, and pigeons about

[34] Cf. Sylvia Thrupp, A Short History of the Worshipful Company of Bakers (London, 1933), 74-5, 79.
[35] These figures are taken from Sir William Beveridge's manuscript, " Provisional Index Numbers of Food and Fuel—1500-1800 " (1932), Institute of Historical Research.

three-and-a-third-fold.[36] There was at least one food—herrings—which apparently increased in price somewhat less rapidly than the wages of building craftsmen rose. It is possible that, with the enactment of laws to encourage fish-eating, herrings came to occupy an even more important place in the diet of the common people than before the Reformation. We have not as yet any index numbers for the prices of meat until the reign of Elizabeth. But between the decades 1580-9 and 1630-9, when the price of grain almost doubled, the price of beef and mutton rose less than 50 per cent,[37] hardly more than the wages of carpenters.[38] During this half-century the price of foods, other than cereal products, appears to have risen only about as rapidly as wage-rates in the building trades.

The prices of bread and drink were determined by the cost of making them as well as by the prices of the grains and grain products from which they were made. When it is assumed that bread and drink rose in price as rapidly as wheat, oats, rye, barley, malt and hops, it is also assumed that the price of labour and the price of materials other than grain employed in milling, baking, malting, and brewing increased as rapidly as the price of grain, and that there was no reduction in the quantity of either labour or grain used in these processes. It seems to me that none of these assumptions is warranted.

To judge from conditions in the building trades, wage-rates rose only about three-fold between the first decade of the sixteenth century and the decade preceding the Civil War.[39] The cost of labour in baking and brewing probably increased somewhat more than these figures indicate, because the workmen were frequently supplied with food in addition to their wages,[40] but it could not have been increased anything like as rapidly as the price of grain.

Firewood alone among the materials needed in making bread or beer rose in price more than grain.[41] But in brewing, coal, which was cheap, was widely substituted for wood fuel during the reigns of Elizabeth and her two successors, so that by 1637 only one of the five brewhouses in Westminster had a log-burning furnace.[42] In baking, coal was still little used,[43] but even as late as 1619, when logs and faggots were extremely dear, wood accounted for only about one-tenth of the costs of the baker in London.[44] It is unlikely that any of the other costs increased as rapidly as the price of grain.

Nor can we assume that the quantity of labour or of grain which went into making a loaf of bread or a gallon of drink remained constant

[36] As Sir William does not have index numbers for these foods covering the whole period from 1500 to 1640, I have used Steffen's ten-yearly average prices (op. cit. I, 254-5, 365-6).
[37] Manuscript " Provisional Index Numbers ", loc. cit. Cf. Steffen, op. cit. I, 255, 366.
[38] As these are shown in the records of the Price Committee at the Institute of Historical Research.          [39] See 116.          [40] See 121.          [41] See 130.
[42] Nef, Rise of the Coal Industry, I, 213-14; Calendar S.P.D., 1636-1637, 415.
[43] Nef, op. cit. I, 216; Thrupp, op. cit. 17, 115.          [44] Ibid. 17.

during the sixteenth and early seventeenth centuries. Although the equipment and the staff of the London baker, with his small oven and his three or four journeymen, did not alter much between the reigns of Henry VII and Charles I,[45] the equipment of the miller improved. More efficient mills for grinding corn were introduced throughout the country, especially towards the end of the sixteenth century,[46] and a new class of capitalist millers, upon whom the bakers were coming to depend for their meal and even for their flour, arose in the neighbourhood of London.[47] The growing use of better machinery and the increase in the scale of operations undoubtedly reduced the labour required in milling. The price of bread probably rose appreciably less rapidly than the price of wheat.[48]

If the course of grain prices was an imperfect guide to the course of bread prices during the sixteenth and early seventeenth centuries, it was no guide at all to the course of drink prices. Technical changes in methods of production affected the costs much more in brewing than in bread making. As a result of the introduction of hop cultivation in Henry VIII's reign and the discovery of improved methods of drying malt, small beer replaced ale during the sixteenth century as the common beverage of the English people.[49] In Elizabeth's reign, for the first time, Englishmen could take pride in their native beer. It had come to rival in quality the best continental brews.[50] The quantity obtained from a given amount of grain had increased, for small beer was not so strong as medieval ale had been, and the use of hops was a great economy in malt.[51] Costs of brewing had been further reduced by the growth in the scale of enterprise, and the substitution of coal for wood fuel. Some large breweries, with expensive copper boilers, brass siphons and new coal-burning furnaces, were built in London at a cost of many hundreds of pounds.[52]

[45] Thrupp, op. cit. 98-9.
[46] This is an impression I have derived from the calendars and indexes of the Exchequer Special Commissions, the Exchequer Depositions by Commission, the Chancery and Star Chamber Proceedings.                [47] Thrupp, op. cit. 27.
[48] In 1619-20, when wheat was selling in London for between 25s. and 28s. a quarter (Rogers, op. cit. VI, 32), the expenses of converting this quantity into bread—including apparently the miller's charge—was estimated at 13s. (Thrupp, op. cit. 17). We may perhaps infer that the expense of milling and baking accounted for nearly, if not quite, a third of the price of white bread on the eve of the Civil War. If, as seems possible, the expense of making meal and bread did not increase more than four-fold between the first decade of the sixteenth century and the decade preceding the Civil War, then the price of bread would not have increased, like the price of wheat, six-and-a-half-fold, but only about five-and-a-half-fold. In the conversion of inferior grains into bread, milling and baking doubtless accounted for a larger proportion of the cost. Bread made from rye or maslin probably rose in price slightly less rapidly than bread made from wheat.
[49] Cf. Nef, "A Comparison of Industrial Growth in France and England", 647-8.
[50] Michael Combrune, The Theory and Practice of Brewing (London, 1762), p. x.
[51] Cf. Rogers, op. cit. IV, 550.
[52] Nef, "The Progress of Technology", Supra, 103; cf. Rogers, op. cit. V, 705-6.

These changes in manufacturing methods prevented the price of the cheapest brews from rising anything like as rapidly as the price of malt between 1500 and 1640. In every town and in many large villages by the beginning of the seventeenth century poor workmen obtained a part of the daily nourishment for themselves and their families by purchase of small beer from brewers, inn-keepers and victuallers.[53] They probably drank much more beer than their descendants in the age of Dickens and Thackeray. This they could hardly have done if it had been expensive, and they appear to have seldom paid more than 3d. a gallon for small beer before the Civil War.[54] As the cheapest ale had rarely cost less than a penny a gallon in the last half of the fifteenth century,[55] the rise in wage-rates during the price revolution seems to have covered the increase in the price of drink.

If bread was rising in price appreciably less rapidly than wheat, and drink hardly as rapidly as the wages of masons and carpenters, it is misleading to work out costs of living mainly or even partly on the basis of grain prices. By doing so, all authorities since Rogers' time have exaggerated the rise in the price of subsistence during the sixteenth and early seventeenth centuries. Men did not eat hay or straw, or even oats or wheat. In the towns seven or eight times as much money may have been required to feed a horse in the reign of Charles I as in the reign of Henry VII. But it would be surprising if even five or four and a half times as much was needed to nourish a man.[56] Except for green vegetables, which were probably little eaten by town labourers, and bread, there was apparently not a single article in the poor man's diet which rose in price as much as four-and-a-half-fold. As the price of bread apparently increased more than that of other foods, it is possible that the poor replaced bread, cakes and porridge to some extent by other kinds of nourishment, such as herrings, beef, mutton, eggs, cheese and small beer, which, unlike bread, could be had for much less money in Shakespeare's time than today.[57] While there was a marked decline in the purchasing power of the building craftsman's wages in terms of food until the sixties of the sixteenth century, it is by no means certain that this decline continued thereafter.

[53] Cf. Calendar S.P.D., 1637-1638, 580-1.

[54] The indications are that small beer usually cost about 2d. a gallon during Elizabeth's reign, and that under her two successors the normal price was 2d. or 2½d. (Sir George Shuckburgh Evelyn, in Philosophical Transactions, LXXXVIII (1798), 176—a reference for which I am indebted to my colleague, Professor Jacob Viner—and M. Combrune, An Inquiry into the Prices of Wheat, Malt . . . etc. (London, 1768), 107). Sixteen inhabitants of the villages of St Neots and Eynesbury, west of Cambridge, claimed in 1638 that they had been accustomed to buy small beer from local innkeepers and victuallers at a penny a gallon and a farthing a quart (Calendar S.P.D., 1637-1638, 580-1).

[55] W. Fleetwood, Chronicon Preciosum (London, 1745), 88-9, 92; Rogers, op. cit. III, 249.          [56] Cf. Knoop and Jones, op. cit. 213.

[57] A. V. Judges, " A Note on Prices in Shakespeare's Time " in A Companion to Shakespeare Studies (ed. H. Granville-Barker and G. B. Harrison) (Cambridge, 1934), 384.

But the decline in the English labourer's standard of living would still be exaggerated by comparing the course of wage-rates with the course of town food prices, even if we were able to substitute the prices of bread and beer for the prices of grain, and to determine what changes took place in the diet of the workers.   In the first place, the practice of feeding workers was common in the sixteenth and seventeenth centuries.   Journeymen bakers in London were provided by their masters with their meat and drink in addition to their money wages.[58]   Coal miners also frequently had an allowance for food and drink.[59]   We cannot be sure that money was all the reward received by the building artisans.[60]   Professor Knoop and Mr Jones think it conceivable that the practice of providing these craftsmen with some nourishment in addition to their money wages became more common in the sixteenth century than it had been before.[61]   In so far as an employer supplied his workmen with food, the rise in the price of diet bore down on him.   His costs of production increased more than we should infer from a study of wage-rates.

Nor is it probable that wage workers engaged in industrial occupations, particularly in rural districts, had to buy all their food, even when their employers did not provide it for them.   Men lived closer to the earth in the sixteenth century than today.   Most labourers—particularly the multitudes who spun or wove or forged metal wares in their cottages under the putting-out system, and even many of those who found work in the new mines and metallurgical plants—held a plot of land capable of furnishing them with a part of what they needed to live.[62]

The prices of such foodstuffs and foods as the village labourer had to buy could hardly have risen as fast as the prices of the same articles in the towns.   Town prices were forced up partly by the need which arose during the Elizabethan Age to draw on the supplies of distant farms.   London was growing from a large town of some 50,000 or 60,000 people to a metropolis of more than 300,000.[63]   Its inhabitants, nourished before the Reformation almost entirely by the produce of the home counties, became increasingly dependent on grain, meat, milk, butter, cheese and salt brought by wagon, packhorse and small ship from more remote parts of the realm.[64]   The increase in prices in the capital and

---

[58] Thrupp, *op. cit.* 17-18.          [59] Nef, *Rise of the Coal Industry*, II, 187.

[60] *Cf.* Rogers, *op. cit.* IV, 501; V, 637-8.

[61] Knoop and Jones, *op. cit.* 212.

[62] *Cf.* R. H. Tawney, "The Assessment of Wages in England by the Justices of the Peace", *Vierteljahrschrift für Sozial- und Wirtschaftsgeschichte*, XI (1913), 535-7. Knoop and Jones tell us that some of the masons must have had agricultural holdings (*op. cit.* 214).

[63] N. S. B. Gras, *The Evolution of the English Corn Market* (Cambridge, Mass., 1915), 75.

[64] F. J. Fisher, "The Development of the London Food Market, 1540-1640", *The Economic History Review*, V (1935), *infra*, 135-140.

9

in some other growing towns must be attributed partly to the cost of driving livestock and carrying foodstuffs and foods greater distances, and also to the multiplication of the profit-making middleman through whose hands the commodities passed on their way from the husbandman to the consumer. On the whole the industrial labourer in rural areas escaped paying many of the new charges which fell heavily upon some items in the diet of his fellow in the larger towns.[65]

Three main points emerge from this discussion of food prices. In the first place, the index numbers hitherto compiled exaggerate the increase in the cost of subsistence during the price revolution. Secondly, the increase in the cost of the workmen's diet was borne to some extent not by them but by their employers. Thirdly, many workmen held small plots of land from which they obtained some of their necessary supplies. It follows that they were probably able to spend a more than negligible portion of the money wage they received on commodities other than food.

Were the prices of these commodities rising faster than wage-rates? After food, fuel was the most costly item in common housekeeping. But not all workers had to buy their fuel. The practice of granting fire coal to coal miners was universal, and the number of regularly employed coal miners increased many-fold between 1540 and 1640.[66] It is impossible to determine whether the majority of the workers who had to buy their own fuel were worse off on the eve of the Civil War than industrial workers had been on the eve of the Reformation, because coal replaced logs and charcoal in the housekeeping of a great number—perhaps the majority—of Englishmen during the reigns of Elizabeth and James I.[67] The change was brought about chiefly by the pheno-menal rise in the price of firewood.[68] Up to the time when a workman installed an iron grate in his home and adopted a coal-burning fire, the price of his fuel undoubtedly rose much more rapidly than his wages. But once he had made the change, the price of his fuel rose more slowly than his wages. According to some provisional index numbers worked out by the Price Committee, coal in the south of England was not appreciably dearer in the decade 1620-9 than in the decade 1570-9, and was only about 15 per cent dearer in the decade before the Civil War.[69] Wage-rates in the building trades had risen during these sixty years 50 per cent or more. This is just the period when it has been assumed, from comparisons between the course of grain prices and wage-rates, that the workers' standard of living fell precipitately.

[65] Cf. A. P. Usher, "The General Course of Wheat Prices in France, 1350-1788", Review of Economic Statistics, XII (1930), 165.

[66] Nef, Rise of the Coal Industry, II, 187, 136-40.          [67] Nef, op. cit. I, 196-8.

[68] See 130.

[69] Manuscript "Provisional Index Numbers of Food and Fuel Prices in England", at the Institute of Historical Research.

We know nothing about the costs of lodging. But it is by no means certain that industrial workmen had to spend a larger proportion of their wages on housing in the reign of Charles I than in that of Henry VII. Employers in the new capitalistic industries often built cottages for their workmen, many of whom had migrated from distant counties.[70] The costs of building must have risen very rapidly during the price revolution because of the phenomenal increase in timber prices.[71] But in the Elizabethan Age, all observers were struck by the widespread substitution of brick and stone for wood as building materials. To judge from conditions in the building trades, wage-rates rose during the reigns of Elizabeth and her two Stuart successors at least as rapidly as the prices of bricks and lime.[72] If grain prices are not a satisfactory guide to the cost of subsistence during the price revolution, neither are timber prices a satisfactory guide to the cost of housing.

What was happening to the cost of such manufactured commodities as workers and their families were likely to need? While the price of candles rose more rapidly than wage-rates in the building trades between 1540 and 1640,[73] the price of ordinary textile wares, nails and paper rose much less rapidly,[74] the price of some kinds of glass apparently did not rise at all[75] and the price of smokers' pipes fell a great deal, at least after 1601.[76] While wage-rates increased less rapidly than the prices of most foods, they increased more rapidly than the prices of most industrial products. If a workman was able to spend as large a proportion of his wages upon manufactured commodities on the eve of the Civil War as on the eve of the Reformation, he could in all probability have bought substantially larger quantities.

Without more knowledge concerning yearly earnings as distinct from wage-rates, and concerning the items which money wages covered, prices in rural districts and wages in other industries than building, we cannot hope to make an accurate comparison between the standard of living among industrial workmen at the beginning of the sixteenth century and on the eve of the Civil War. No doubt their real earnings fell with each rapid rise in prices. But there was also a persistent tendency throughout the period for earnings to overtake prices during the intervals between these rapid rises. The indications are that this tendency was especially marked after the accession of Elizabeth. Starting with the second decade of the sixteenth century, the general trend of the wage workers' standard of living was certainly downward until at least the sixties, and the fall in their real earnings was probably most rapid during

---

[70] Cf. Nef, op. cit. II, 187.                    [71] See 130.

[72] Manuscripts of the Price Committee: "Chairman's Report on English Naval Stores" (September, 1933). Cf. Wiebe, op. cit. 375.

[73] Manuscript "Provisional Index Numbers of Food and Fuel Prices in England"

[74] Wiebe, op. cit. 375-7, 383.

[75] Manuscript "Chairman's Report on English Naval Stores".

[76] Hist. MSS. Comm., Report on the MSS. of the Duke of Rutland, IV, 437, 526, 542.

the forties and fifties.  But it is doubtful whether, as has been generally believed, the downward trend in their standard of living persisted during the four or five decades of most rapid industrial expansion from about 1575 to 1620.  Changes were introduced both by the Statute of Artificers of 1563 and by a later Statute of 1603, in the principles and the methods used by local authorities in assessing wages.  The new legislation, and the policy followed until the Civil War by the Privy Council in enforcing it, made the raising of wages by law, especially in the textile industry, more easily possible than it had been.  And when, as was often the case, the regulations under the Statutes were evaded, the market rate of wages was usually above the legal rate.[77]  Partly perhaps as a result of the new Government policy, wage workers seem to have been at least as well off materially in the reign of Charles I as on the eve of the Armada.  During the half-century preceding the Civil War, their wages had probably risen on the average less rapidly than the price of bread, but about as rapidly as the prices of other foods and drink, and more rapidly than the prices of coal and the products of manufactures.  The contrasts between the movements of real wages in England and Spain throughout the period of the price revolution were much less striking than Wiebe's index numbers suggested.

In considering the influence of labour costs upon the progress of industrial capitalism, we are more interested in the wages paid to work-men in mines, at smelting furnaces and forges, and in other small factories than in those paid to masons, carpenters and other workmen in the building trades.[78]  And we are more interested in the prices obtained for the products of these mines and factories than in the prices paid for grains, grasses, livestock and foods, commodities which were given heavy weight in Wiebe's index numbers.  The fact that wage-rates in the building trades rose more slowly than the town prices of foodstuffs and foods, did not offer any special inducement to draw an enterprising country landlord to sink shafts to his coal seams or a wealthy city mer-chant to enter a partnership for smelting iron ore or manufacturing glass or paper.

Wage-rates could hardly have risen much less in the new industries than in the building trades.  It is even possible that special bait in the form of good pay had to be sometimes offered to induce men to enter novel and disagreeable occupations like coal mining and sheet-glass manufacturing.[79]  As wage-rates in the building trades rose much more rapidly between 1560 and 1640 than the prices of coal, ordinary textile wares, and most manufactured articles, wage-rates in other industries probably also rose more rapidly.  But if wage-rates were rising in most industries more rapidly than the prices of the products, how could

[77] Tawney, op. cit. 311, 321, 534-5, 542-52, 561-4.          [78] Cf. Wiebe, op. cit. 240.
[79] Cf. Nef, op. cit. II, 192, 194.

industrial ventures have been exceptionally profitable during the reigns
of Elizabeth and James I?

When, more than forty years ago, Wiebe advanced our knowledge
of the price revolution by publishing his book, he warned us against
assuming that the cheapness of manufactured goods could be explained
entirely, or even primarily, by the slow rise in wages. Further investigation, he believed, might show that mechanical improvements were a
more important factor than cheap labour.[80] We now know that labour
was dearer in England than his calculations suggested, and that the
improvements in industrial technology were more sweeping than he
suspected.[81] The openings for profits arose mainly because costs of
production were reduced by the widespread adoption of better machinery
and improved kilns and furnaces, by the increase in the scale of industrial enterprise, and by the discovery and use of new supplies of raw
materials, such as calamine, alum stone and, above all, coal.


Labour in France, as well as in England, was no doubt dearer than
Wiebe's index numbers indicate. These index numbers were worked
out in terms of silver in order to show the effects of the inflow of treasure
upon prices. But during the century from 1540 to 1640, the *livre tour-
nois* lost about half, and the shilling between a third and a fourth, of
its silver content.[82] Prices rose rather more in France than in England,
not less as might be supposed from a glance at Wiebe's tables. If, in
these tables, we substitute prices and wages actually paid for prices and
wages in terms of silver, the absolute spread between prices and wages
which occurs as we proceed through the sixteenth and early seventeenth
centuries is increased considerably more in the case of France than in that
of England, but the ratio between the two remains the same. In the case
of England, as we have seen, that ratio greatly exaggerates the decline
in the real earnings of the wage worker during the sixteenth and early
seventeenth centuries. Is this equally true in the case of France?

The most important work done on French wages and prices since
Wiebe wrote is the study of Poitou by the late Monsieur Raveau.[83]
Comparisons are difficult between his results and those which Wiebe
obtained from d'Avenel's data, partly because the periods selected by
Raveau are not the same as those selected by Wiebe, and partly because
Raveau's averages are computed from wage records for a single province,

[80] Wiebe, *op. cit.* 239-43.     [81] *Cf.* Nef, "The Progress of Technology", *loc. cit.*

[82] A. Dieudonné, *Manuel de numismatique française* (Paris, 1916), II, 314, 351; H.
Hauser, Introduction to *La réponse de Jean Bodin à M. de Malestroit* (Paris, 1932), pp.
xxvii *et seq.*; Wiebe, *op. cit.* 30 n., 70. (*Cf.* A. E. Feaveryear, *The Pound Sterling*
(Oxford, 1931), especially 56-65, 78-9.)

[83] P. Raveau, "La crise des prix au XVI⁰ siècle en Poitou" in *Revue historique.*
CLXII (1929), 16-24. *Cf.* his *L'agriculture et les classes paysannes dans le haut Poitou*
(Paris, 1926), p. xxxii.

while Wiebe's are computed from a miscellaneous mixture of sparse records for several provinces.[84]    But the two results do not differ widely. Both show that although money wages rose rapidly, their purchasing power in terms of food, fuel and some other commodities fell continually from the accession of Francis I, in 1515, down to the passage of the Edict of Nantes, in 1598, when they were worth hardly half as much as at the beginning of the sixteenth century.    Both suggest that real wages rose at the beginning of the seventeenth century.    They rose in Poitou more than they are represented by Wiebe's index numbers as rising, but even in Poitou the wage workers were still much worse off in the reign of Louis XIII than their ancestors had been in the reign of Louis XII.

The results obtained by the Commandant Quenedey for Rouen suggest that workmen in the building trades fared better there than in Poitou throughout the period of the price revolution.[85]    While food prices apparently rose less in Normandy than in Poitou during the sixteenth century,[86] wage-rates rose more.    In Poitou, masons were apparently earning about twice as much money in 1578 as during the last half of the fifteenth century; at Rouen they were apparently earning appreciably more than twice as much.[87]    After the Edict of Nantes, the workmen in Poitou gained on their fellows at Rouen.    In both cases money wages continued to rise.    But food prices were apparently rising in Normandy more than in Poitou,[88] where there was a sharp fall in the price of grain and wine at the end of the sixteenth century.[89]    In spite of the gain made by labourers in Poitou during the second half of Henri IV's reign, they were probably still somewhat worse off under Louis XIII than those at Rouen.

The new wage data collected by the Price Committee for the Ile-de-France are too scanty to serve as a basis for generalisation.    So far as they go, they suggest that during the sixteenth century the course of real wages in the neighbourhood of Paris differed from that at Rouen as well as from that in Poitou.    Workmen appear to have suffered nearly if not quite as much as in Poitou, but the fall in the purchasing power of their wages seems to have been more pronounced during the first half of the century and less pronounced during the second.[90]

[84] Wiebe, op. cit. 378-9, 417-19.    Cf. d'Avenel, op. cit. III, 491 et seq.

[85] R. Quenedey, Les prix des matériaux et de la main d'œuvre à Rouen (offprint from Bulletin de la Société du commerce et de l'industrie de la Seine-Inférieure) (Rouen, 1927), 23-5.

[86] For Normandy: Quenedey, op. cit. 26; Wiebe, op. cit. 378; R. Jouanne, " Report on Prices at Caen ", among the manuscripts of the Price Committee at the Institute of Historical Research.    For Poitou: Raveau, L'agriculture et les classes paysannes, p. xxxii, passim.        [87] Raveau, " La crise des prix ", 17, 20-21 ; Quenedey, op. cit, 24.

[88] Jouanne, loc. cit., Wiebe, op. cit. 378; Quenedey, op. cit. 26.

[89] Raveau, L'agriculture et les classes paysannes, p. xxxii.

[90] Reports by Yvonne Bézard and Jean Mallon among the manuscripts of the Price Committee at the Institute of Historical Research.

It is even more difficult to generalise concerning the material welfare of wage workers in France than in England, not only because we have much less data, but because conditions apparently varied more from region to region.[91]   This is not surprising in view of the economic self-sufficiency that persisted in French provinces during the sixteenth and early seventeenth centuries, when it was breaking down in England.[92] What little we know suggests that Wiebe's index numbers exaggerate the decline in the material welfare of the wage workers in most French provinces, as well as in England, but probably not quite as much.

As in England, wage-rates in the building trades appear to have risen nearly everywhere between 1540 and 1640 appreciably more than has been supposed.   As in England, they rose more slowly than the prices of foodstuffs and food.   We have no means of knowing whether employers provided their workmen with food and drink, in addition to wages, less frequently in France than in England.   The French workman who had to support himself and his family mainly out of his wages seems to have suffered more from rising prices than the English workman, in at least two respects.   Technical improvements designed to reduce the costs of manufacturing were less widespread in France than in England during the century from 1540 to 1640.   It is therefore probable that the costs of milling were not reduced as much to offset the great rise in grain prices common to both countries.   When it came to drink, the French workmen, except to some extent in northern France, continued to depend on wine as their ancestors had done from time immemorial.   And the price of wine, like that of food, but unlike that of the Englishman's common drink, was rising in some provinces substantially more rapidly than wage-rates.[93]

That was also true of the price of logs and faggots, which remained almost the only fuels burned in hearths and stoves throughout France. Until the period of the religious wars the French workman had an advantage over his English fellow, because firewood was rising in price more slowly in most parts of France than in England.[94]   But after the English workman had substituted coal for logs and faggots, the advantage lay with him, because the price of coal in England increased much more slowly than the price of wood in France.   It is not possible to say in which country the workman had to spend a larger proportion of his wages on fuel at the eve of the English Civil War, but for at least half a century in England the proportion had been diminishing.

In France as in England, manufactured articles, such as plain cloth, were rising in price more slowly than wage-rates in the building trades. If the French workman in the reign of Louis XIII had as large a portion of his wages as the English workman to spend in buying these wares,

[91] Cf. Usher, op. cit. 165.
[92] Cf. Nef, " A Comparison of Industrial Growth in France and England ", 313.
[93] Raveau, L'agriculture et les classes paysannes, p. xxxii.          [94] See 132.

he could have got almost as much for his money.[95]   But we know that
the output of mines and manufactures was increasing between 1540 and
1640 at a much more rapid rate in England than in France, and it is
probable that on the eve of the Civil War the volume of cloth, metal
wares, tobacco pipes and perhaps even window panes produced was
greater, relative to population, in England.[96]  The English manufacturer
excelled in the making of plain cloth and other homely wares, which
found some sale even among the poorer subjects.  This suggests that
the purchases of the workmen may have increased more in England
than in France, and that by the reign of Charles I the Englishman may
have been able to lay out a larger part of his wages than the Frenchman
upon the products of the rising industries.

The effects of the price revolution upon the poor man's standard of
life were similar in the two countries.  Such differences as we have
found seem to have been mostly unfavourable to the French workmen.
Their real earnings had almost certainly fallen more than those of
English workmen by the last quarter of the sixteenth century, as Wiebe's
own figures indicated.[97]   During the next twenty years their position
improved somewhat in many provinces.  But it no longer seems likely
that the English workmen lost ground in the half-century preceding
the Civil War.

Wiebe's index numbers did not indicate that the fall in real wages
favoured the English much more than the French employer of labour.[98]
The new evidence collected since Wiebe's time suggests that the cost of
hiring workmen may have decreased more, not less, in France than in
England.  If cheaper labour had been the principal driving force
behind the flow of capital into large-scale enterprise, the pace of industrial change should not have been very much slower in France than in
England; it should have been as fast or even faster.

(iii) *The cost of timber during the price revolution*

Money wages, Mr Keynes rightly pointed out, formed only a part of
the expenses of carrying on an enterprise in the sixteenth and seventeenth centuries.   In constructing his tables of profit-inflation in France
and England, he assumed that money wages accounted for half the
expenses of production.  He further assumed that in both countries all
other expenses rose just as rapidly as, according to Wiebe's index num-

[95] It might be supposed that the cost of manufactured goods would have risen more
in France than in England, as technical improvements which reduced the quantity of
labour needed in manufacturing were less widespread.  But the advantage which the
English employer enjoyed in this respect was offset by the fact that the prices of the
lumber and firewood (and possibly the price of the labour) needed in industry were
rising more in England than in France (see 132).

[96] Nef, " A Comparison of Industrial Growth ", 661-3.        [97] See 115.

[98] See 111.

bers, general commodity prices rose. Is this second assumption justified? Did the materials needed in mining and manufacturing rise in price no more and no less rapidly than the average price of all commodities? Were the costs of materials rising equally rapidly in France and in England, or were there differences in the behaviour of these costs which help to explain why more capital should have been invested in large-scale industrial enterprises in England than in France?

After wages, the chief expenses borne by the owners of mines and small factories in the sixteenth century were the sums spent on timber, firewood and charcoal. In the development of large-scale industry at this time, wood largely took the place occupied during the nineteenth century by both iron and coal. Metal was used only for the cutting or striking face of tools, for the gears and axles of machinery, and for the cauldrons and boilers in which various raw materials were heated. Stone and brick were commonly used only for the furnaces and kilns. In spite of the poor resistance wood afforded to the frequent fires, the rest of the plant was nearly all of timber.[99] And, in many industries, the plant was extensive. The clusters of alum and salt houses and the metallurgical works often formed so impressive a phalanx of buildings that contemporaries compared them to villages and even to small towns. At the larger mines, the houses and barns were no less numerous than at the alum works, and hundreds of pounds were often spent to obtain the additional deal boards and oaken bars required to timber the shafts. By the middle of the seventeenth century, and possibly even earlier, payments for lumber and planks of various sizes accounted for more than half the cost of building and launching a ship.[100]

Logs, faggots and charcoal were almost the only fuels used in manufacturing in France throughout the period of the price revolution. In England they were the principal fuels until at least the reign of James I, for it was not much before the end of the sixteenth century that coal began to replace wood extensively in processes other than forging of crude metal wares and the calcining of limestones, for which it had served to some extent even in the Middle Ages. The cost of fuel was considerable in most manufactures; in some, such as glass-making and the smelting of ores, it greatly exceeded the cost of lumber for construction work. Scores of acres of woods were consumed every year in supplying one of the large blast furnaces. Farmers of iron works in the Forest of Dean were legally entitled in 1639 to an annual wood supply of 13,500 cords,[101] and they probably used a much larger quantity.

In some industries, therefore, more was spent for lumber, charcoal and firewood than for labour at the plant. In very few industries did

[99] Cf. W. Sombart, Der Moderne Kapitalismus (1916), II, 1138-40; Néf, Rise of the Coal Industry, I, 191.

[100] R. G. Albion, Forests and Sea Power (Cambridge, Mass., 1926), 94.

[101] Calendar S.P.D., 1638-1639, 557.

the cost of obtaining wood form a negligible proportion of the costs of production. If we are to discover whether price conditions were more favourable for the development of large-scale industry in England than in France, we must consider the course of timber prices as well as the course of wages.

Everywhere in England the manufacturer was concerned during the reigns of Elizabeth and the first two Stuarts over the phenomenal rise in the price of firewood and lumber. In county after county trees were felled in such profusion to feed the rising industries, that lands once thick with forests could be converted into runs for sheep and cattle, or broken by the plough to supply the new demands for grains. Lumber, logs and faggots, once available in abundance just beyond the town gates, had to be hauled or carried by waggon and packhorse for miles over rough ground and along miserable pathways full of ruts, or brought in ships from the Baltic countries. Between the decade following the dissolution of the monasteries and the decade preceding the Civil War, while the price of grains increased little more than four-fold and the price of textile wares and various other manufactured goods much less than doubled, the price of firewood increased almost seven times over. Before the second decade of Elizabeth's reign had ended, firewood was already more than twice as dear as it had been in the last decade of her father's reign. By the second decade of Charles I's reign, it was nearly three times again as dear. About eleven pounds were needed at this time to buy as many logs and faggots as had sold for a pound in the first decade of the sixteenth century.[102]

The rise in the price of some kinds of lumber was no less startling, as is revealed by the accounts of the Admiralty for the purchase of naval stores. Continuous records of these purchases do not go back beyond the first decade of Elizabeth's reign. But between this time and the outbreak of the Civil War, planks and timber, mainly of oak, were growing dearer as rapidly as firewood. Four-inch planks cost the Navy more than four times as much in 1632 as in 1567, and timber more than three times as much. In 1637 timber was almost five times, and in 1641 four times as dear as in 1567.[103] Meanwhile the prices of ordinary textile wares and some manufactured goods remained practically stationary,[104] and the price of coal increased only about 20 per cent.[105] Scattered figures covering a longer period[106] suggest that the Navy paid at least fifteen times as much for oak in Charles I's reign as at the accession of

---

[102] Wiebe, op. cit. 70, 375.

[103] The data on which these statements are based was kindly supplied by Miss Rayner, who worked out for me, from the Admiralty Accounts (Treasurers' Ledgers), five-year samples of the average price paid for timber and planks from 1567 to the Civil War.

[104] Wiebe, op. cit. 383, 375.

[105] Manuscript " Chairman's Report on Naval Stores ", cited above.

[106] Collected by Professor Albion, op. cit. 91.

Henry VIII. Meanwhile the general price level, according to Wiebe, had not risen much more than four-fold.[107]  In spite of these rising costs of the basic material used in shipbuilding, the shipyards grew in number and importance. The tonnage of the Royal Navy doubled and that of the merchant marine nearly quintupled.[108]  A great many other conditions, besides cheap labour, favourable to the progress of industry must have been present to produce an expansion in shipbuilding under such unfavourable price conditions.

With firewood and timber mounting in price much more rapidly than any other commodities, it is natural to suppose that charcoal followed suit. But, in fact, charcoal prices do not seem to have increased more rapidly than the average prices for all commodities. Charcoal was scarcely four times as dear on the eve of the Civil War as at the beginning of the sixteenth century.[109]  At first sight this is very puzzling. The price of charring wood was of course an important element in the price of charcoal. It is certain that the price of charring wood rose very much more slowly than the price of timber, probable that, as a result of technical improvements in the process, it rose less than four-fold. But this can hardly provide an adequate explanation of the great differences between the course of charcoal and timber prices. A more important one is possibly to be found in the fact that charcoal was cheaper to transport than logs. Our prices for both firewood and charcoal are town prices. The rise in timber prices in the towns was undoubtedly caused more by the necessity for hauling wood from greater and greater distances than by the rise in the prices paid where the trees were felled. Costs of transportation were of less, costs of production of more, importance in determining the price of charcoal than in determining the price of logs.

But charcoal was not widely used for fuel by any manufacturer save the smelter, and the prices he paid were not town prices. He bought or leased large tracts of woodlands and hired colliers to char his logs. His blast furnaces and forges exhausted the neighbouring supplies of timber, and the local price of charcoal rose nearly as fast as the local price of firewood.[110]  The inevitable result was to force the smelter eventually to move to another wooded site at a greater distance from the chief markets for metal and metal wares. While this kept the price of his fuel from rising rapidly, it made it necessary for him to invest large sums in new furnaces and forges and in water-driven machinery to operate the bellows and the hammers. The rise in charcoal prices in the towns

---

[107] Almost exactly four-fold if we take Wiebe's second set of index numbers rather than his first (see above, 111 n. 19).

[108] Nef, " A Comparison of Industrial Growth ", 308-9.

[109] Wiebe, *op. cit.* 70, 375.

[110] *Cf. e.g. Hist. MSS. Comm., Report on the MSS. of the Marquis of Salisbury*, XII, 20-3.

is a poor guide to the rise in the costs of producing metal caused by the exhaustion of the forests.

In the Age of Elizabeth, England was faced with a timber crisis, brought about partly by the increase in population but mainly by the remarkable growth of industry. This crisis increased the expenses of mining and manufacturing so much that the average rise of commodity prices is no index to the rise in the costs of industrial materials.

The course of wood prices, like that of grain prices and wages, varied more from region to region in France than in England. But except in few regions, such as the densely populated Ile-de-France,[111] firewood did not become conspicuously dearer than other commodities during the price revolution. Wiebe's index numbers for France, which were compiled from data collected by d'Avenel for several provinces, show no very great deviation between the trend of firewood and general commodity prices.[112] Raveau's more recent and more detailed work shows that in Poitou between 1515 and 1598 the price of firewood rose less than the price of grain and about as much as that of wine.[113] We have a new series of prices from 1558 to 1640 for logs and faggots bought at Château-Gontier, on the Mayenne.[114] While faggots were about three and a half times as dear in the last decade of Louis XIII's reign as in the decade preceding the religious wars, logs were rather less than two and a half times as dear. They had not risen in price more than such commodities as beans, butter, salt and red wine. In most French provinces, the rise in the price of wood is explained almost entirely by the increase in the supply of silver and the debasement of the currency.

The costs of fuel and doubtless also of lumber, the principal materials needed in mining and manufacturing, were rising in England much more than in France until at least the beginning of the seventeenth century. After that coal replaced firewood and charcoal in many English industries so extensively that most English manufacturers, except the smelters, began to have an advantage in the costs of fuel. Their disadvantage probably increased when it came to the purchase of lumber.

If industrial enterprise proved less profitable in France than in England during the price revolution, this cannot be explained on the ground that wood or labour were dearer. In fact wood, and probably

[111] Reports of Yvonne Bézard and Jean Mallon among the manuscripts of the Price Committee at the Institute of Historical Research.

[112] Wiebe took 100 as the price of all commodities during the last half of the fifteenth century. With this base, his index numbers for the first half of the seventeenth century —which express prices in terms of silver—show firewood at 212·5, general commodity prices at 216 in France. For England, they show firewood at 554 and general commodities at 282, or 245 if Wiebe's second, differently-weighted table is the basis of comparison (Wiebe, op. cit. 278-9, 375, 377, 383).

[113] L'agriculture et les classes paysannes, p. xxxii.

[114] Report of René Gauchet among the manuscripts of the Price Committee at the Institute of Historical Research.

also labour, were cheaper.   The immediate explanation seems to be that in France technical changes which reduced the quantity of labour required in mining and manufacturing were less frequently made than in England, that there was no such growth in the scale of enterprise, and no such exploitation of new supplies of raw materials, like calamine, alum and coal, the widespread use of which cheapened production in many industries.

*Neither the sweeping changes in technique and in the scale of industrial enterprise, nor the exploitation of new raw materials, were an inevitable result of the inflow of American silver, or of the decline in real wages that accompanied it.   If they had been, an early industrial revolution would have occurred in France to match the one in England.


(iv) *Conclusion*

A comparison of prices and industrial capitalism in France and England from 1540 to 1640 does not prove that the price revolution failed to stimulate industrial development.   It shows that the influence of price changes was complex rather than simple, and it warns us against the tempting assumption that the remarkably long period of rising prices, common to all European countries, was of compelling importance for the rise of industrialism.

By raising prices, the inflow of treasure from America helped to keep down the costs of the labour and the land[115] needed for mining and manufacturing, and thus encouraged the investment of capital in large-scale enterprise, as Professor Hamilton and Mr Keynes pointed out. But the decline in the real earnings of wage workers was nothing like as great as has been supposed since the time of Rogers and d'Avenel.   Had the standard of living among the English working people really fallen by anything approaching half, the advantages which employers derived from hiring labour cheaply might have been offset by the reduction in the amount workmen could have spent on manufactured goods.   The expansion of the mining, metallurgical, the glass and the textile industries in Elizabethan England was brought about to some extent by the growth of home markets among the common people.   If the earnings

---

[115] As I remarked above (see 109 n. 9), Professor Hamilton suggested that cheap land as well as cheap labour probably stimulated investments in industrial enterprises.   We do not know whether land rents rose more slowly than did the prices paid to mine owners and manufacturers for their products.   In any case, the price revolution probably kept the costs of rent lower in every country than they would have been but for the inflow of American treasure.   But the dissolution of the monasteries, which occurred on the eve of the early English industrial revolution, was probably of as great importance in England as the inflow of silver and the debasement of the coinage in making it possible for adventurers to acquire land for mining and manufacturing on favourable terms (*cf.* Nef, *Rise of the Coal Industry*, I, 133-56).   Unlike the price revolution, the dissolution of the monasteries helps to explain why industrial development in England should have been more rapid than in France.

of nearly all wage workers had been cut to the bare minimum required for subsistence according to medieval standards, the demand for grates, window panes, cloth, bedding, tobacco and crude table ware could hardly have grown as rapidly as it did.

The moderate fall in real wages that occurred in England with every rapid rise in prices tended to increase profits, to promote the accumulation of wealth and to encourage the investment of funds in mining and manufacturing, especially during the forties and fifties of the sixteenth century, the only period of considerable duration in which wage-rates may have risen more slowly than the prices of manufactured products. But the discoveries had little to do with the rise in prices which made possible the decline in real wages before the accession of Elizabeth. The rise in prices during the first half of the sixteenth century was caused by debasement of the coinage, and more commodities could be bought with the same quantity of silver when Edward VI became King, in 1547, than in the reign of his grandfather, Henry VII.

The rapid rise in the real costs of the indispensable supplies of timber provided a stimulus of a different kind from the fall in real wages. It helped to bring about improvements in industrial technique, which might have been less widespread had the need for them been less urgent. Without these improvements, the increasing costs of materials must have checked the growth of English industries, no matter how cheaply labour could have been hired.

French history shows that a prolonged decline in the real wages of labour, while undoubtedly an incentive to enterprise, was not by itself a sufficiently powerful influence to cause an industrial expansion, or even to prevent an industrial depression. It is possible that during the last quarter of the sixteenth century the fall in the workmen's standard of living in France was so great as to stop the growth of the demand for some industrial products and that the misery of the poor hindered more than it helped the progress of manufactures during the religious wars.

Industry was responding in different ways in the various European countries to the strains and the stimuli provided by the inflow of American treasure and the debasement of the coinage. Whether or not the response took the form of greatly increased activity in sinking mining shafts and setting up new manufacturing enterprises, depended mainly on conditions independent of the price revolution. Further comparisons between French and English history will help to reveal these conditions.

# THE DEVELOPMENT OF THE LONDON FOOD MARKET, 1540-1640

## F. J. FISHER

O F the factors that mark the transition from the medieval to the modern economic system, three are, by general consent, outstanding—the aggregation of capital, the improvement of technique, and the increase in the size of the market. The last number of *The Economic History Review* contained an illuminating article by Dr Nef on the operation of the first and second in English industry during the century preceding the Civil War.[1] The purpose of this more modest essay is to consider the development of one particular market—the London food market—in the same period. By the seventeenth century, and even earlier, there were in England a number of commercial and industrial centres of sufficient size and concentration to have a considerable influence, as markets, upon both agriculture and the trade in agricultural produce. London and the larger provincial towns, the embryonic Black Country, the Tyneside mining area, the textile districts of Yorkshire, East Anglia, and the west must all have been important in this respect. Each meant a considerable body of consumers relying upon purchases for the majority of their victuals. Yet the study of their influence has been curiously uneven. On the one hand, the repercussions of their demand for wool have been the subject of lengthy, if somewhat barren, discussions. On the other, the repercussions of their demand for food have been almost entirely neglected. The course of history, nevertheless, has not been entirely unaffected by the fact that men, as well as looms, need food; agrarian history is rapidly approaching the point where further advance must wait upon the study of the reactions to these growing markets.

Essentially, of course, this must be a problem for the agrarian specialist, when he can free himself from his peculiar obsession with the more recondite niceties of land tenure. But in the case of London—the most populous, the most rapidly growing, the wealthiest, and the most compact of all these centres of consumption—the reactions were so clearly marked that their trend is apparent even to the more general historian. A mass of evidence, not specifically agrarian in character, shows the direction in which things were moving. Complete statistics

[1] J. U. Nef, "The Progress of Technology and the Growth of Large Scale Industry in Great Britain, 1540-1640", *The Economic History Review* (1934), V, 3-24. *Supra* 88-107.

of food imported coastwise into London exist for only six of the hundred years in question and are therefore too few to be in themselves conclusive. Yet their story is sufficiently corroborated by the customs records of the outports and by other more miscellaneous material to be substantially beyond question. The perpetual concern of the authorities for the city's food supplies casts, by inference, considerable light upon the agricultural system whence those supplies were drawn. And, under the early Stuarts, comments on the problem began to creep into contemporary agricultural literature. Consequently, a student of London history may perhaps be excused of presumption in writing of a subject of admittedly more than municipal significance.

In the first place, it is quite clear from Tables I and II that the area from which the city obtained its food was growing, and that by 1640 it

TABLE I

COASTWISE CEREAL IMPORTS INTO LONDON (QUARTERS)

| From | 1579–80[1] | 1585–6[2] | 1587–8[3] | 1615[4] | 1624[5] | 1638[6] |
|---|---|---|---|---|---|---|
| N.E. coast | 345 | 914 | 25 | 33 | 672 | 4,840 |
| Lincolnshire | 293 | 1,238 | | | 757 | |
| Norfolk | 550 | 12,439 | 390 | 7,670 | 10,873 | 19,550 |
| Suffolk | 807 | 2,696 | 458 | 258 | 2,127 | 1,843 |
| Essex | 1,797 | 2,732 | 4,463 | 10,368 | 12,765 | 5,532 |
| Kent | 13,546 | 28,004 | 12,080 | 41,823 | 27,957 | 57,187 |
| Sussex | 2 | 258 | 100 | 7,604 | 5,722 | 3,807 |
| Hants | 40 | | 250 | 670 | 464 | 208 |
| S.W. coast | | 120 | 10 | 170 | 312 | 2,747 |
| Totals | 17,380 | 48,401 | 17,776 | 68,596 | 61,649 | 95,714 |

NOTES TO TABLES

[1] Exchequer K.R., Port Books, bundle 6, no. 8.
[2] Ibid. bundle 7, no. 6.
[3] Exchequer, K.R., Miscellanea, bundle 15, no. 5.
[4] Exchequer K.R., Port Books, bundle 18, no. 1.
[5] Ibid. bundle 28, no. 5. The returns for July and August are missing from this volume. The totals for the remaining ten months have therefore been increased by 20 per cent to provide an estimate of the trade of the whole year.
[6] Ibid. bundle 41, no. 6.

was large. For obvious geographical reasons, the home counties were, no doubt, always the chief source of supplies. At the very end of the sixteenth century, London was said still to be fed "principallie . . . from some fewe shires neare adioyninge",[2] and as late as 1632 it was argued that the assize of bread should be regulated by the price of wheat in the neighbouring markets of Uxbridge, Brentford, Kingston, Hampstead, Watford, St. Albans, Hertford, Croydon and Dartford.[3] But as the years pass it is possible to watch the city's tentacles spreading over

[2] S.P.D., Elizabeth, CCLIV, no. 10.　　　　　　　[3] Ibid. Charles I, CCXXIV, no. 64.

## TABLE II

### COASTWISE DAIRY IMPORTS INTO LONDON (Unit for butter: barrel. Unit for cheese: wey)

| From | 1579-80[1] | | 1585-6[2] | | 1587-8[3] | | 1615[4] | | 1624[5] | | 1638[6] | |
|---|---|---|---|---|---|---|---|---|---|---|---|---|
| | Butter | Cheese | Butter | Cheese | Butter | Cheese | Butter | Cheese | Butter | Cheese | Butter | Cheese |
| N.E. coast | 6 | | 11 | | 2 | | 102 | | 1,394 | 26 tons | 4,132 | 20 tons |
| Lincolnshire | 16 | 83 | 11 | | 29 | | 65 | | 547 | | 500 | |
| Norfolk | 68 | 30 | 218 | 2 | 235 | 1 | 152 | 4 | | | 459 | |
| Suffolk | 1,457 (21 loads) | 2,317 / 756 wey | 4,179 (10 loads) | 3,768 / 925 wey | 2,984 (12 loads) | 2,629 / 663 wey | 1,563 (7 loads) | 1,545 | 1,739 (38 loads) | 1,580 | 1,656 (128 loads) | 2,303 |
| Essex | 6 | 352 / 742 wey | 41 | 188 / 2,194 wey | | 2,190 wey | 1 (438 loads) | 70 / 460 wey | (352 loads) | 76 / 188 wey | 6 (580 loads) | 92 / 498 wey |

## TABLE III

### Cereal Imports into London (Unit : 100 quarters)

| From | 1579-80[1] | | | 1585-6[2] | | | 1587-8[3] | | | 1615[4] | | | 1624[5] | | | 1638[6] | | |
|---|---|---|---|---|---|---|---|---|---|---|---|---|---|---|---|---|---|---|
| | Wheat | Malt | Oats | Wheat | Malt | Oats | Wheat | Malt | Oats | Wheat | Malt | Oats | Wheat | Malt | Oats | Wheat | Malt | Oats |
| N.E. coast | 3·5 | 2·8 | | 2·8 | 6·1 | | 0·3 | | | 0·3 | | | 0·2 | | 4·8 | 11·3 | 5·3 | 31·2 |
| Lincolnshire | 0·3 | 1·4 | | 0·4 | 5·8 | 0·3 | | 1·4 | 1 | | | | 1 | 0·7 | 5·9 | 13·1 | 172·1 | 9·8 |
| Norfolk | | 7·4 | 3·5 | 9·7 | 46·4 | | 1·5 | 3·5 | | 0·5 | 71·2 | 3·9 | 31·6 | 50 | 23·6 | 2·7 | 6 | 4·6 |
| Suffolk | 1·5 | 1 | 0·6 | 3·5 | 22·8 | 0·6 | 0·8 | 2·9 | 1 | 0·3 | 0·7 | 1·6 | 11·5 | 3·3 | 6·3 | 2·7 | 4·8 | 32·2 |
| Essex | 129·4 | 12 | 7·6 | 4·8 | 0·3 | 22·1 | 5 | | 34·5 | 21·6 | | 79·9 | 26·2 | 0·4 | 96·6 | 18·1 | 4·8 | 32·2 |
| Kent | | | 4·8 | 240·6 | 38·4 | | 99·5 | 16·5 | 39·2 | 105·6 | 279·4 | 32·4 | 46·5 | 151 | 80·7 | 331·7 | 190·9 | 48·5 |
| Sussex | 2·6 | | | 2·6 | | | 0·5 | 0·5 | | 44·7 | 16·4 | 4·8 | 41·3 | 6·3 | 5·2 | 32 | 4·6 | 1·6 |
| Hants | | 0·4 | | | | | 1·7 | 0·8 | | 4·5 | 2·2 | | 2·4 | 1·6 | 0·4 | 0·4 | 4·6 | 1·7 |
| S.W. coast | | | | | 1·2 | | 0·1 | | | | | 1·7 | 2·9 | | | | 7·6 | 19·8 |
| Total | 134·7 | 25 | 16·5 | 264·4 | 121 | 23 | 109·4 | 25·6 | 74·7 | 177·5 | 369·9 | 124·3 | 163·6 | 213·3 | 223·5 | 409·3 | 391·3 | 149·4 |

the provinces until by the middle of the seventeenth century they reached to Berwick, Cornwall and Wales.

As one would expect, the evidence is most abundant, and the process of expansion most easily traced, in the corn trade. By the middle of Elizabeth's reign, the city was already drawing to a considerable degree upon the south Midlands.[4] The growth of the down-river trade from Berkshire and Oxfordshire was reflected in the increasing importance of Queenhithe as a meal and grain market.[5] But, save in years of scarcity, both coastwise and foreign imports were comparatively slight.[6] In 1573, the Lord Mayor and aldermen could speak of foreign imports as negligible save in times of dearth, and of heavy demands upon the maritime counties as something exceptional, due to the fact that " the contrey about them doth not bringe corne to the markett there in such plentie as they were wonte and as will suffice the Citie ".[7] Of the three years 1580, 1586 and 1588, it was only the scarcity year of 1586 that showed considerable coastwise supplies. In the more normal years, the total was well below 20,000 quarters, of which Kent alone supplied nearly 75 per cent. The next half-century saw a striking change. Imports continued to fluctuate with prices. Foreign, and the more distant provincial, sources were still drawn upon more heavily when harvests were bad. But by now the mean around which the coast trade fluctuated was much higher. Neither 1615, nor 1624, nor 1658 was a year of scarcity; yet each saw coastwise imports around 60,000 quarters, well above the famine level of 1586.[8] Under the early Stuarts, north-east Kent was a vast granary for the city's service. Both Norfolk and Essex were sources of regular, as well as of exceptional, supplies. The Sussex grain trade rose from insignificance into some prominence. In times of dearth, both the north-east and the south-west coasts made substantial contributions.

Except that foreign imports were always slight, the story of the dairy trade is very similar. Milk and fresh butter, no doubt, always came from the neighbouring countryside;[9] yet already by the sixteenth century there was a well-developed trade in cheese and salt butter from Essex and Suffolk. In the seventeenth, the city's feelers crept steadily northwards up the coast to Norfolk, Lincolnshire, Yorkshire, Durham and Northumberland.[10] Some of the city's eggs and poultry came from Bedfordshire and Northamptonshire.[11] Above all, the city's meat trade was organised upon a national basis. Sheep were brought in from as

[4] N. S. B. Gras, *The Evolution of the English Corn Market* (1915), 109, and see below, 148.
[5] City Repertories, XVI, ff. 10, 133, 147.
[6] Table I; Gras, *op. cit.* 275.                    [7] Gras, *op. cit.* 105.
[8] For statistics of foreign imports, see Gras, *op. cit.* 275; for those of coastwise imports, see *ibid.* 319, and Table I above.
[9] See below, 143.                    [10] See Table II.
[11] Lansdowne MSS., XLVI, f. 207; *Hist. MSS. Comm., Var. Coll.*, III, 93.

far away as Gloucestershire and Northampton.[12]   Many of its cattle
were bred in Wales, or the north or west of England, and fattened in
the Midlands, East Anglia or the home counties before being sold to
the city butchers.[13]   In 1724, Defoe was to write of the "general dependence of the whole country upon the city of London—for the consumption
of its produce ".[14]   The situation which obtained a century earlier
differed from that described by him in degree rather than in kind.

In the second place, it seems highly probable that the growth of the
London market gave a definite stimulus to English agriculture.   Its
increased demands for food were, quite clearly, not met to any noteworthy degree by larger supplies from abroad.   Small quantities of
foreign cheese trickled in,[15] but otherwise imports of meat, poultry and
dairy produce were negligible.   The trade in foreign fruit and vegetables, which had shown signs of decay even under Elizabeth,[16] rapidly
dwindled under the early Stuarts.[17]   Save in years of scarcity, the consumption of foreign corn was not heavy and showed no tendency to
grow.[18]   Merchants in the Netherlands, Germany and the Baltic, carefully watched the London grain market,[19] and their shipments helped
to steady prices.[20]   But under anything approaching normal conditions,
foreign grain went in serious danger of finding no purchaser.   Freights
were high, the risk of deterioration was great, and even in the years of
dearth promises of free re-export were sometimes necessary to attract
substantial imports.[21]   Nor is there any evidence that the city's demands
were met to any considerable extent by the diversion of supplies previously exported.   It is possible that there was some slight falling off in
the exports of English corn during this period.   But the evidence is
doubtful, and, even on the most liberal interpretation, suggests no
decline comparable to the city's increased consumption.[22]   The conclusion, therefore, seems inevitable that there was an important net
increase in the output of English agriculture.

[12] A. J. and R. H. Tawney, " An Occupational Census of the Seventeenth Century ",
*The Economic History Review*, V (1934), 27, n. 2 ; J. Gutch, *Collectanea Curiosa*, I (1781),
222.

[13] See C. J. Skeel, " The Cattle Trade between Wales and England from the Fifteenth
to the Nineteenth Century ", *Transactions Royal Historical Society*, IX (1926), 4th ser.,
135-58; Cotton MSS., Faustus, C. ii, f. 164.

[14] *A Tour through England and Wales* (Everyman edn., 1928), I, 3.

[15] Court of Request, Proceedings, bundle 64, no. 80; Exchequer K.R., Port Books,
bundle 40, no. 2; Letter Books, FF, f. 81 b.

[16] In 1582 the fruitmeters complained that " nowe there cometh verie small stoare of
fruite from beionde the seas ", Letter Books, EE, f, 106.

[17] *Samuel Hartlib, His Legacy* (1652), 9; Hops and onions, however, continued to
come in (Exchequer K.R., Port Books, bundle 40, no. 2).

[18] Gras, *op. cit.* 275; *Calendar of S.P. Venetian, 1607-1610*, 146.

[19] Cranfield MSS., no. 2020; I am indebted to Professor R. H. Tawney for this reference.

[20] S.P.D., Charles I, CCCCL, no. 14.

[21] S. P. Docquet, 25 March 1608; *Calendar S.P.D., 1611-1618*, 261.

[22] Gras, *op cit.* Appendix C.

In certain commodities this increase is beyond all doubt. In many places within easy reach of the city, the production of fruit, hops and vegetables rose from the position of insignificant and neglected branches of general farming almost to the status of independent industries. " Gardening ", wrote Fuller in 1660, " was first brought into England for profit about seventy years ago; before which we fetched most of our cherries from Holland, apples from France, and had hardly a mass of rath ripe peas but from Holland which were dainties for ladies, they came so far and cost so dear. Since gardening hath crept out of Holland to Sandwich, Kent, and thence to Surrey where, though they have given 6*l.* an acre and upwards they have made their rent, lived comfortably, and set many people on work. . . . 'Tis incredible how many poor people in London live thereon, so that in some seasons the gardens feed more people than the field." [23] The testimony of Hartlib was the same: " Market-gardening ", he wrote in 1652, " is but of few years standing in England, and therefore not deeply rooted. About 50 years ago, about which time Ingenuities first began to flourish in England, This Art of Gardening began to creep into England, into Sandwich and Surrey, Fulham and other places. Some old men in Surrey, where it flourisheth very much at present, report that they knew the first Gardiners that came into those parts to plant Cabages, Colleflowers, and to sowe Turneps, Carrets and Parsnips, to sowe Raithe (or early ripe) Rape, Pease, all which at that time were great rarities, we having few, or none, in England, but what came from Holland and Flaunders. These Gardiners with much ado procured a plot of good ground, and gave no lesse than 8 pound per acre; yet the Gentleman was not content, fearing they would spoil his ground, because they did use to dig it. So ignorant were we of Gardening in those dayes. . . . In Queen Elizabeth's time we had not onely our Gardiners ware from Holland, but also Cherries from Flaunders; Apples from France; Saffron, Licorish from Spain; Hopps from the Low-Countreys: . . . wheras now . . . the Licorish, Saffron, Cherries, Apples, Peares, Hopps, Cabages of England are the best in the world." [24]

Probably both, as historians are wont, exaggerated the novelty of what they described. Small quantities of English fruit and vegetables had for many years been trickling into the city from the orchards and gardens of the neighbouring gentry; [25] quite early in Elizabeth's reign that trickle became a stream of some proportions.[26] The fruit and hop industries of Essex and Kent seem to have begun earlier and to have developed more slowly than either Fuller or Hartlib suggests. Essex hops were commented upon by Harrison in 1587 and were being grown around Colchester at least sixteen years earlier. Kentish fruit was praised by Lambarde in 1576, and some orchards dated back to the times

[23] Quoted by D. Lysons, *The Environs of London* (1792), I, 28.    [24] *Op. cit.* 8-9.
[25] H. T. Riley, *Memorials of London and London Life* (1868), 228.
[26] Letter Books, Y, f. 251.

of Henry VIII.[27]  But their main argument stands.  It was in the early seventeenth century that the orchards of Kent and the hop-grounds of Kent, Essex, Suffolk, Sussex and Surrey, became really prosperous.  And that they were called into being primarily to serve the London market is scarcely open to doubt.  To all of them, a temporary closing of that market meant " such a dampe in the trade as will be in short tyme the undoing of many Farmers and other labouring men . . . and a greate losse to the lords and owners of the lands in their rents and revenues ".[28]  Equally, it was in the early seventeenth century that the suburban market-gardeners first rose to prominence.  In 1605 they obtained a royal charter of incorporation with jurisdiction over all gardening within six miles of London, a charter of which the city disapproved and which was to be questioned as a grievance in Parliament.[29]  Already by 1617 they claimed to be employing " thowsandes of poore people, ould menn, women and children in sellinge of their Commodities, in weedinge, in gatheringe of stone, etc."; in the middle of the century they estimated their labour force more specifically at 1,500 men, women and children, and 400 apprentices.  By that time they had contrived a minor revolution in the ordinary citizen's diet and their gardens clustered thickly in the suburbs.[30]

To a degree that makes some criticisms of open-field farming read strangely, this increased production of fruit and vegetables was fitted into the common-field routine of the neighbouring villages.  An aldermanic report of 1635, on the agriculture of Chelsea, Fulham and Kensington, relates of the husbandmen there that " they sowe seedes for parsnipps, turnopps, carriotts and the like in their Comon feildes whereof most of them they plough upp and others they digge upp with the spade according to the nature and ritchness of their grounds.  And ye same feilds sometymes sowe with corne whereby the grounds are the more fruitfull And . . . by this manner of Husbandry and ymployment of their groundes the Cittys of London and Westminster and places adiacent are furnished with above fower and twenty Thousand loades yearely of Rootes as is credibly affirmed. . . . whereby as well the poore as the ritch have plenty of that victuall at reasonable prices and . . . some of them have belonging to their houses one two or three acres of ground in

[27] V.C.H., Essex, II, 366-7; Kent, III, 420-1; J. F. Bense, Anglo-Dutch Relations (1925), 114.

[28] S.P.D., Addenda, XLII, no. 63.  Cf. Ibid. nos. 64-5; and The Essex Review (1908), 173-4.  Since most of these commodities came into the city by land, adequate statistics are unobtainable.  But the coast trade figures at least show the direction in which things were moving.  In the 1580s London imports of English fruit and hops were negligible; by 1638 the former amounted to 621 baskets and the latter to 1,594 bags.  (Exchequer K.R., Port Books, bundle 41, no. 6.)

[29] Proceedings and Debates of the House of Commons in 1620 and 1621 (1766), edited by T. Tyrwhitt, I, 132-3.

[30] C. Welch, History of the Gardeners Co. (1900), 28; W. T. Crosweller, The Gardeners Co. (1908), 15.

orchards and gardens which they ymploy and husband in setting forth and planting of Roses, Raspesses, strawberries, gooseberries, herbes for foode and Phisick which besides their owne necessary use they bring to the Marketts both of this Citty, the Citty of Westminster and other places adiacent."[31]

But the significant developments which struck the imagination of contemporaries were the work, not so much of open-field farmers, as of specialists working enclosed holdings by intensive methods, often borrowed from abroad, and by the heavy expenditure of both capital and labour.

Individual market-gardens in Bermondsey, Battersea, Stepney, Lambeth, and the other suburbs, do not seem to have been large; the Gardeners Co. established a maximum of ten acres.[32] Some members, however, held other gardens elsewhere in the home counties; one, with a plot in St Martins-in-the-Fields, had others as far apart as Wandsworth, Woking and Dunmow (Essex).[33] And the suburban gardens were obviously highly cultivated. Two hundred pounds, for example, were estimated to have been sunk in improving a four-acre holding in Stepney.[34] The labour employed upon them was great.[35] Dressings of the city's street soil were regularly applied.[36] Despite high rents, it was estimated that an able man could keep a family and even employ outside labour on a holding of three acres or even less.[37] And save that their holdings were probably larger, the hop-masters and fruit-growers were working along the same lines. Their grounds were enclosed. They depended on wage labour. They paid rents that only intensive farming could make possible.[38]

The benefits of the London market, moreover, were not confined to the growers of fruit and vegetables. The city diffused throughout Middlesex a prosperity that could be shared by all willing and able to provide the "small acchates" that it needed. "Such as live . . . in body or hart of the Shire, as also in the borders of the same ", wrote Norden, " for the most part are men of husbandrye, and they wholly dedicate themselves to the manuringe of their lande. And theis comonlye are so furnished with kyne that the wife or twice or thrice a weeke conveyeth to London mylke, butter, cheese, apples peares, frumentye, hens, chyckens, egges, baken, and a thousand other country drugges, which good huswifes can frame and find to gett a pennye. And this yeldeth them a lardge comfort and releefe. Besyds the husbande castinge the quantetie of his corne, and proporcioninge the same with the expens of

[31] Repertories, XLIX, f. 262.    [32] Crosweller, op. cit. 16.
[33] Ibid. 13.
[34] Chancery Proceedings, ser. i, Charles I, bundle B. 14, no. 6. This prosperity was naturally reflected in the rents paid, and in 1621 the copyholders of Stepney and Hackney took a private bill to Parliament to confirm their customary rights of sub-letting (House of Lords MSS.).    [35] See above, 142.
[36] Welch, op. cit. 28; Norden, Surveyors Dialogue (1618 edn.), 226.
[37] Hartlib, op. cit. 8.    [38] Ibid. 15.

his howse, of the overplus he maketh monie to mayntayn his family and to pay his rent.

"Another sort of husbandmen or yeomen rather ther are, and that not a few in this Shire, who wade in the weedes of gentlemen; theis only oversee their husbandrye, and give direction unto their servauntes, seldome or not at all settinge their hand unto the plowgh, who havinge great feedinges for cattle and goode breede for younge, often use Smyth-felde and other lyke places with fatt cattle, wher also they store them-selves with leane. And thus they often exchaunge, not without great gayne, wherby and by their daylye increase at home they comonly become very riche."[39]

The glimpses that we catch of their economy suggest that the same description would fit quite well the nearer parts of Hertfordshire, Essex, Kent and Surrey.[40]

Outside of this area concentrating on the production of butter, milk, poultry, eggs, fruit, vegetables, pork, bacon and other "country drugges", for the London market, the influence of the capital can only be suggested with diffidence. Diffused over too large an area to be spectacular, it was too entangled with other factors to be easily discern-ible. One conclusion, however, seems justified. London's demands on the more distant sources of supply were selective rather than indiscrimi-nate. It drew on each district, not so much for food in general, as for those victuals in particular which the district was best fitted to produce. Its stimulus, that is to say, was not merely in the direction of increased production but also in that of specialisation; and in that direction lay agricultural progress.

The coast books show that the corn and dairy regions were distinct. Suffolk, the chief source of cheese and butter, was negligible as a supplier of grain. Sussex and the great granary of Kent sent almost no dairy produce at all. Norfolk and the north-east coast sent both, but from different parts. Corn came chiefly from Berwick, Hull, Wells and Yarmouth; butter from Stockton, Whitby, Boston and Lynn. Within the cereal areas themselves further specialisation tended to appear. Sussex was primarily a source of wheat, Essex of oats, Norfolk of malt. Kent supplied all three, but shipped most of its malt through Sandwich, most of its wheat and oats through Faversham and Milton. Under the prevailing system of farming the raising of cattle was widespread, but its relative importance varied from place to place. Fattening was a major industry in the south Midlands,[41] parts of East Anglia[42] and on

[39] *Descriptions of Essex*, ed. Ellis (Camden Soc., 1840), p. xii. In his introduction Ellis prints a description by Norden of "The meanes most usuall how the people of Myddlesex doe live" to be found in manuscript in Harleian MSS. 570 but not included in the printed description of Middlesex.

[40] Norden, *Surveyors Dialogue* (1618 edn.), 215; Lansdowne MSS., XLVI, f. 193; LXXXI, f. 145.

[41] Privy Council Register, XL, 356.      [42] S.P.D., Charles I, CCLVII, no. 121 (i).

the marshes which fringed the coast from Romsey to Lincoln and where it was the annual practice for men to lay out money " uppon Heiffors and such other young ware, emptying their purses of Crownes to cram the Fens with Cattell." [43]   Breeding was more practised in Wales, the north and the west. [44]

Specialisation along such lines was, of course, inherent in local soil conditions; its explanation must be framed primarily in terms of economic geography.   But inherent specialisation becomes actual only when there is at hand some market to act, in the words of Burleigh, as " an encouragement to the husbandmen to apply and follow their tillage with confort of gayn." [45]   And it was becoming more and more the lot of the capital to supply that encouragement and thereby to promote, in some degree, agricultural specialisation and the most profitable use of the soil.   It would, of course, be absurd to exaggerate the importance of London in this respect.   In some districts, such as Norfolk, it was only one among several alternative markets; in others, its influence was too slight to be of much effect.   Nevertheless, in some regions, and those not the least highly specialised, its influence was paramount.   The corn-growers of Cambridgeshire, [46] south-east Essex, [47] and north-east Kent, [48] the dairy farmers of Suffolk, [49] the graziers of the south Midlands, [50] all looked to the London market as the hub of their economic universe.

With these developments in agriculture there went, of necessity, others in the organisation of the trade in foodstuffs.   Like all townsmen, the Londoner purchased many of his victuals in the common market places in the city; and as the population grew, so there was an increase in the volume of this market trade.   The growth of the river and coastal traffic necessitated the development of Queenhithe to handle the overflow from Billingsgate. [51]   The growth of the meal trade led to the extension of the markets at Newgate and Leadenhall, and the opening of new ones at Bishopsgate and Queenhithe. [52]   In 1615, the creation of a common market place in Smithfield was almost agreed upon " by reason that Newgate Market, Cheapside, Leadenhall and Gracechurch Street were unmeasurably pestred with the unimaginable increase and

[43] *A True Report of certain wonderful Overflowings of Waters in Somerset, Norfolk and other parts of England* (reprinted 1884), 26.

[44] G. Markham, *Cheap and Good Husbandry* (1631), 88 ; *Hist. MSS. Comm., Rep. iii*, 6; *Calendar of Wynn Papers*, nos. 627, 1228, 1406.

[45] S.P.D., Elizabeth, XXXVI, no. 69.

[46] *Ibid.*                                    [47] *Ibid.* Charles I, CLXXXII, no. 67.

[48] *Ibid.* James I, CXII, no. xii (i) ; In the reign of Charles I London was taking two-thirds of the cereal exports from Sandwich (Gras, *op. cit.* 311), and over 90 per cent of those from Milton and Faversham (Exchequer K.R., Port Books, bundle 659, nos. 2 and 4).

[49] *Ibid.* bundle 474, nos. 10 and 20 ; bundle 604, no. 15.

[50] Privy Council Register, XL, 356.              [51] Letter Books, V, f. 57 ; CC, ff. 161-2.

[52] Repertories, XVI, ff. 10, 133, 147; XXII, ff. 315b, 364b; XXXI, ff. 175, 178; XXXVIII, f. 188.

multiplicity of market-folkes ".[53]   Yet all this evidence of growth is, in a sense, misleading.   It suggests that the city was fed by a simple expansion of the orthodox medieval marketing system; in actual fact, London had long passed and was rapidly leaving behind the stage when its needs could be even approximately satisfied in any such way.

A comparison between the city's food trade and that of the ordinary provincial town, in which the medieval system continued almost unchanged, reveals two important differences.   In the first place, the London markets relied to a far greater degree upon middlemen for their supplies.   Their corn was handled almost entirely by country mealmen.[54]   Much of their meat was brought in by suburban butchers who competed with the free butchers in the purchase of cattle and probably sold indifferently in Leadenhall or the suburban shambles.[55]   Even the trade in poultry, eggs and dairy products, the traditional sphere of the country wives, was shared by a swarm of petty higglers.   In the second place, a large and increasing proportion of the capital's food passed, not through the common market places, but through the hands of the free retailers.   Every town, of course, had its bakers, brewers and butchers; craftsmen processing the wares which they sold rather than simply dealers.   But no other town could show a body of retailers comparable to the fishmongers, fruiterers, poulterers, chandlers and cheesemongers of London.   The common market places formed a bottleneck through which the trade from the provinces and abroad, as distinct from that of the nearer parts of the home counties, could not easily be squeezed; as more distinct sources were drawn upon for food, so the influence of the city retailers grew.   And this growth, reacting as it did on the organisation of the food trade, was during this period the most important feature of London's alimentary system.

Most significant was their development of channels of supply other than those which fed the common market places.   The often lamented forestalling in city inns and suburban lanes seems, for the most part, to have been the work of hucksters and other small fry.   More substantial men were primarily concerned with supplies of more distant origin, which they normally obtained by one or other of two methods.   Much was simply purchased in the city from producers and middlemen, who, for various reasons, were tacitly and sometimes explicitly, excused from selling by retail.   Butchers bought heavily in Smithfield, and as late as 1612 it was thought that an additional market day there would enable them to obtain all the cattle they needed " without further travell or expence ".[56]   The growth of waterborne traffic was reflected in the development along the riverside of a flourishing wholesale trade in fish,

[53] Stowe, *Survey of London*, ed. Howes (1631), 1023.          [54] See below, 148.
[55] Letter Book, EE, ff. 88, 179.   There were shambles at Temple Bar, Holborn Bars, Smithfield Bars, Whitecross Street, Bishopsgate Bars, Aldgate Bars, East Smithfield, and St Katherines (Harleian MSS., 6363, f. 22).          [56] Letter Books, EE, f. 179b.

fruit and grain.   The brewers obtained nearly all, and the bakers a large part, of their corn from provincial dealers.

These purchases were made from a variety of sellers.   Imports from abroad were brought in by alien merchants; save in years of scarcity English merchants do not seem to have taken any considerable interest in the provision trade.[57]   Cattle were sold either by graziers or by drovers who " leavinge their accustomed order to buy leane ware in the remote partes where Cattell are better cheape and to bringe the same tc places nearer to serve the grasiers and feaders of Cattell . . . do now bothe buy of the grasiers in places and marketts neare the Cittie and also do buy fatt cattell to sell the same againe ".[58]   As Professor Gras discovered, the coastal corn trade was for the most part in the hands of men who confined their interests to occasional and rather speculative shipments.   In 1638 prices were high and therefore favourable to regular trading.   Yet of the 481 men who brought corn from the coast to London, only 80 brought more than two, only 25 brought more than five, and only 10 brought more than eight consignments.   Prior to the Civil War, the growth of the coastwise trade in corn was not accompanied by the rise of a class of grain merchants.[59]

The overland trade in corn, however, was organised on rather different lines, dictated, to a considerable degree, by the fact that it was more convenient to process grain before, rather than after, it came to the city.

[57] Exchequer K.R., Port Books, bundle 15, no. 5; bundle 18, nos. 3 and 6; bundle 40, nos. 2 and 6; Lansdowne MSS., LXXXI, ff. 88, 119b.
[58] Cotton MSS., Faustus, C ii, f. 164; Letter Books, EE, f. 179b.
[59] Some idea of the relative importance of large and small traders can be obtained from the following analysis of coastwise imports for the years 1580, 1586, 1615 and 1638.

| Quarters imported per merchant | 1580 | | 1586 | | 1615 | | 1638 | |
|---|---|---|---|---|---|---|---|---|
| | No. of mch'ts | Imports | No. of mch'ts | Imports | No. of mch'ts | Imports | No. of mch'ts | Imports |
| 1–100 . . | 72 | 3,473 | 145 | 6,701 | 228 | 10,137 | 212 | 11,840 |
| 101–200 . . | 14 | 1,942 | 64 | 9,330 | 91 | 13,476 | 136 | 20,328 |
| 201–300 . . | 4 | 920 | 21 | 5,282 | 56 | 13,857 | 52 | 12,884 |
| 301–400 . . | 1 | 340 | 6 | 2,199 | 13 | 4,419 | 32 | 11,299 |
| 401–500 . . | 1 | 500 | 11 | 5,003 | 9 | 3,971 | 16 | 7,116 |
| 501–1,000 . . | 2 | 1,380 | 11 | 8,029 | 18 | 11,962 | 27 | 17,342 |
| Over 1,000 . . | 5 | 8,654 | 5 | 11,694 | 5 | 7,540 | 6 | 12,538 |

It will be noticed that the group of big men bringing in over 1,000 quarters each a year showed no marked tendency to grow.   Those handling between 500 and 1,000 quarters increased considerably; but the proportion of total imports handled by these two upper groups declined.   It was 58 per cent in 1580, 41 per cent in 1586, only about 30 per cent in the early seventeenth century.   The expansion of the corn trade was primarily the work of smaller men.   (These figures are taken from the same port books as those in Table I.   The slight discrepancies between the totals for the various years arise from imperfections in the manuscripts, whereby some consignments can be ascribed to a shipper, but not to a port, others to a port but not to a shipper.)

Not merely were transport costs thereby reduced; London had no facilities for malting, and, in the absence of adequate running water, few for milling. Consequently, a number of country towns found their major employment in the processing of the city's corn, and their inhabitants a regular occupation as middlemen. To the north, Enfield was famous for its mealmen and maltmen.[60] Hertford was a flourishing milling centre.[61] Hatfield, Hitchin, St Albans, Hexton, Cheshunt, Aldenham, Elstree, Luton, Shefford and Dunstable collected the surplus grain of Bedfordshire, Buckinghamshire and Northamptonshire and "were onely upholden and maynteyned by the trade of making of Maults and of the cariage therof up to London by horse and carts".[62] By the time of Charles I, the more distant Royston was buying "a very great parte of the Corne in Cambridgeshire" and sending 180 great malt waggons to the city every week.[63] To the west, Henley,[64] High Wycombe[65] and Brentford seem to have been important entrepôts. Kingston, Croydon and Reigate, played the same role in Surrey. And the river Wandle supplied the power for a highly prosperous milling industry. Its twenty-four mills returned gross annual earnings of £5,252 and ground, not only for the Surrey mealmen, but also for those of Brentford and for many city bakers.[66] The mere carriage of cereals enabled many inhabitants of Middlesex "to live verye gaynfully".[67]

There seems to have been considerable variation in both the status and methods of these town middlemen. Some maltmen were obviously wealthy, engrossing "into their handes out of manye of the best maultinge townes verie greate quantities of Malte—wch they sent to London daylie, eyther out of their howses or els from their private shopps in market townes",[68] and giving credit to brewers up to as much as £1,500.[69] At the other extreme were the petty and would-be independent carriers who "used to take up money and graine of maltsters and other corne men upon trust".[70] Most seem to have sold to brewers under a contract for weekly deliveries over a period of months, or even years.[71] Mealmen purchased not meal but grain, which they either

---

[60] Norden, *Description of Essex*, p. xii.
[61] *Calendar S.P.D., 1595-1597,* 126, 336.     [62] S.P.D., Elizabeth, CLXXVII, no. 8.
[63] *Ibid.* Charles I. I, no. 70 ; CXCIII, no. 3.     [64] Gras, *op. cit.* 105-6.
[65] S.P.D., Charles I, CLXXVII, no. 50. In 1699 the trade of Wycombe was said to consist chiefly in buying of corn and sending the same to London. (*Commons Journals,* XII, 615.)
[66] M. Giuseppi, "The River Wandle in 1610", *Surrey Archaeological Collections,* XXI (1908), 170-91.
[67] Norden, *Description of Essex*, p. xii.     [68] Lansdowne MSS., XLVIII, f. 116.
[69] *Ibid.* XXXII, f. 104.     [70] *Ibid.* XXXVIII, f. 84.
[71] In 1574 nearly all the alebrewers of London were obtaining malt in this manner from Cambridgeshire, Hertfordshire and Bedfordshire (Cotton MSS., Faustus, C ii, ff. 162-3). For specimen contracts, see Court of Requests, Proceedings, bundle 60, no. 88; bundle 63, no. 99 ; bundle 65, no. 62 ; bundle 116, no. 31 ; bundle 119, no. 25 ; bundle 168, no. 61 ; bundle 488, Jellyman *v.* Hamond ; Chancery Proceedings, ser. i, Charles I, bundle C. 13, no. 35.

milled themselves or had milled for them, and sold not only to bakers but also directly to consumers in the open city markets.[72]

Wholesale purchases within the city, however, did not solve all the problems of the retailers. Allowed by the authorities to the butchers, brewers and bakers, they were less acceptable when made by the non-craftsmen victuallers, who on occasion had to submit to arbitrary interference in the interests of the consumers. And whether craftsmen or not, the man who waited to buy in the city must face the risk of being disappointed. Consequently there was a steady permeation of the countryside by London retailers purchasing for resale in their shops. The poulterers' ordinances forbade them to buy rabbits except from breeders under annual contract; their other poultry had to be obtained from chapmen who were little more than their servants.[73] Fish was obtained directly both on the coast and from the ponds of country gentlemen.[74] Fruit, hops, butter and cheese, were all bought up in the country;[75] the coast trade in dairy produce, in striking contrast to that in corn, was dominated by a handful of London dealers.[76] In their anxiety to obtain supplies, the butchers not only established direct contact with the graziers on their farms,[77] but, in the early seventeenth century, transferred an increasing portion of their market trade from Smithfield to Barnet.[78] Bakers, chandlers and brewers, all bought in the provinces.[79] And except in the case of grain and cattle, few of these purchases seem to have been made in the open markets.

The process of permeation, moreover, did not stop with direct buying on the part of retailers. There grew up a body of London wholesalers who resold at least part of their country purchases to the smaller city shopkeepers. They were not welcomed by the authorities, but glimpses of them can be caught in the meat, fish, fruit, dairy, poultry and hop trades.[80] Another aspect of the matter is disclosed by the

---

[72] Lansdowne MSS., XLVIII, f. 139; *Calendar S.P.D., 1595-1597*, 126; S.P.D., Charles I, CCXXIV, no. 64; Giuseppi, *loc. cit.*

[73] Letter Books, Z, f. 207; AB, f. 300; Repertories, X, f. 331; for specimen contracts, see Court of Requests, Proceedings, bundle 38, no. 3; bundle 181, no. 61.

[74] *Losely MSS.*, 276-7; Norden, *Surveyors Dialogue* (1618 edn.), 226; Lansdowne MSS., XXXIV, f. 58. For a description of a London fishmonger going to Yarmouth " to buy fish uppon the coast to make his provisions for the whole yeare ", see Court of Requests, Proceedings, bundle 487, Gense *v.* Heron; and *cf.* bundle 192, no. 19; Chancery Proceedings, Early, bundle 1008, no. 13.

[75] Court of Requests, Proceedings, bundle 58, no. 22; bundle 61, no. 39; S.P.D., Addenda, XLII, nos. 63-5; Repertories, X, f. 319b; Letter Books, Q, f. 86b; X, f. 48.

[76] Exchequer K.R., Port Books, bundle 18, no. 1; bundle 41, no. 6.

[77] Court of Requests, Proceedings, bundle 12, no. 56; bundle 27, no. 156; bundle 61, no. 55; bundle 127, no. 53; Chancery Proceedings, Early, bundle 940, no. 17; bundle 986, no. 32.   [78] Letter Books, EE, f. 88.

[79] S.P.D., Charles I, CLXXXII, nos. 7 and 81; CLXXXIII, no. 37; CLXXXIX, no. 79; CXC, nos. 44 (v) and 66. For sample transactions, see Court of Requests, Proceedings, bundle 29, no. 42; bundle 491, Beasley *v.* Harding.

[80] Repertories, XV, ff. 289, 293; Chancery Proceedings, Early, bundle 1004, no. 64; Letter Books, AB, f. 301; *Acts of the Privy Council, 1615-1616*, 524; S.P.D., Addenda, XLII, nos. 63-5.

complaint of the Hertfordshire magistrates that "wheras diverse of our Countrye Inhabitants (being by trade Badgers and Loaders) dyd usuallye goe from markett to markett and ther dydd buye Corne and grayne, wch they weekly carryed to the Citye of London for the provision thereof: whereby many of them grewe to be men of good wealthe and abilitye, and dyd set verye many poore men a worke—Now thos Bakers and Brewers of London, not content to receive thos comodities from thes Loaders as heretofore they have donne, doe dailye come downe into the countrye and verye greadely doe buye great quantities of corne and grayne and doe offerr such deare and high prices for the same . . . that . . . they have utterly overthrowne the former trade of the Loaders and getting the gayne from them doe make the loaders their servauntes and carriers."[81]

Direct buying meant, in fact, a tendency to depress formerly independent rural middlemen into the employees of London dealers.[82] And in some cases the process of penetration culminated in the Londoners obtaining an interest in the actual production of food. Poulterers made loans to warreners and themselves bred poultry.[83] Fruiterers helped to establish orchards and leased them when established.[84] Butchers themselves became graziers.[85]

Naturally, there were obstacles. Particularly in the sixteenth century, the city authorities objected both to the rise of the city wholesalers and to direct purchase of certain victuals in the country.[86] They found it difficult to distinguish between harmless direct buying and forestalling. County justices occasionally made themselves a nuisance by their efforts to protect rural consumers.[87] At different times the trade in grain, hops and dairy produce was seriously embarrassed by the statutes against middlemen.[88] The growing coast trade was vulnerable both to the weather and to foreign enemies.[89] And the rural vested interests

[81] S.P.D., Elizabeth, CCLIV, no. 10. *Cf.* the complaints from Kent (Lansdowne MSS., LXXVIII, f. 153), High Wycombe (S.P.D., Charles I, CLXXVII, no. 50), and Kingston (*Ibid.* CLXXXII, no. 7).

[82] Every London poulterer, for example, had to undertake not to buy from another's chapman; the chapmen were allowed to change their customers only once a year (Letter Books, AB, f. 300).

[83] Repertories, XV, f. 223; XXIII, f. 512; Letter Books, Z, f. 207.

[84] Add. MSS., 33,924, f. 32; Court of Requests, Proceedings, bundle 34, no. 38.

[85] *Ibid.* bundle 12, no. 56; Privy Council Register, XL, 356.

[86] Repertories, XIII, f. 341; Letter Books, Q, f. 86b; X, f. 48; AB, f. 301; S.P.D., Charles I, CCXXIV, no. 64.

[87] Lansdowne MSS., XLIX, no. 5; LI, f. 97; S.P.D., Charles I, V. no. 2; LX, no. 49.

[88] *Ibid.* James I, CXII, no. 12 (i); Addenda, XLII, nos. 63-5; Repertories, XXXII, f. 271b; *Acts of the Privy Council, 1615-1616*, 524.

[89] S.P.D., Charles I, CLXII, no. 41. Curiously enough, the difficulties of land carriage do not seem to have impressed contemporaries. They were simply accepted to a degree which historians, debauched by the standards of a pampered age, are apt to forget. The normal way of bringing fish from the Cinque ports to London, for example, was not by river, but by packhorse. The road was divided into stages of fifteen miles, and one set of carriers worked from the coast to Chepstead, another set from Chepstead to the city. (Court of Requests, Proceedings, bundle 74, no. 4.)

disturbed by the changes periodically caused trouble. The rise of the Barnet cattle market brought loud protests from Leighton Buzzard and Smithfield; its desertion meant complaints from the Barnet men themselves.[90] The butchers' experiments in fattening their own cattle brought them, at the suit of the outraged graziers of the south Midlands, before Parliament, Council and the Star Chamber.[91] When the bakers bought from mealmen they offended the suburban millers; when they bought in the country they aroused the opposition of the rural middlemen.[92] The famous struggle over the navigation of the river Lea was only in part a clash between rival transport interests; in part it was a struggle between a group of London brewers and the middlemen of Enfield for control of part of the trade in Midland grain.[93] Yet none of these things could stop development along the lines sketched above. London had to be fed, and no practical alternatives were ever suggested. Vested interests could only delay what they could not prevent. City, county and national authorities all learned in time to tolerate what they had previously damned.

It is, of course, impossible to measure and easy to exaggerate the novelty, rapidity and efficacy of these various responses to the growing London market. Medieval research will, no doubt, reveal in embryo much of what has been described above. By the early seventeenth century, there was a general feeling that the city's appetite was developing more quickly than the country's ability to satisfy it. Imports from abroad, it is true, do not appear to have risen. But the complaints of the rural justices show that the trade to London was placing an increasing strain on local resources; the high profits of landlords and farmers were obtained in part by pinching the bellies of the local poor. Under the early Stuarts, the theory that the city was too large became generally accepted, partly because of this difficulty of obtaining food, and it became usual to fight unduly high prices by limiting the city population. But when all reservations have been made, the fact of these repercussions remains beyond dispute. The city retailers won a new importance and an increasing control over the trade in agricultural produce. Suburban farming was revolutionised. Prosperity was diffused through the nearer parts of the home counties and south Midlands. And a powerful impetus was given to the forces that were working for the commercialisation of agriculture in England at large.

[90] *Hist. MSS. Comm., Rep. iii, Appendix*, 7; Letter Books, EE, f. 88; Privy Council Register, XL, 356.
[91] *Hist. MSS. Comm., Rep. iii, Appendix*, 31 ; Privy Council Register, XL, 356 ; XLI, 37-8; A. Pearce, *The History of the Butchers' Company*, 95.
[92] Letter Books, X, f. 378 ; and see 150 above.
[93] Lansdowne MSS., XXXII, ff. 91-2, 104-10; XXXVIII, ff. 84, 88-90; XLI, f. 188. For a similar struggle between the bakers, brewers, and victuallers of Bristol and the merchants of Gloucester for the control of the corn trade to Bristol, see MSS. Records of the Corporation of Gloucester, 1450, f. 93.

# COMMERCIAL TRENDS AND POLICY IN SIXTEENTH-CENTURY ENGLAND

### F. J. FISHER

B Y now it is almost an axiom of historiography that each generation must re-interpret the past in terms of its own experience, and in accordance with that principle much has recently been done to transform the accepted views of Tudor history. To men brought up in a world of liberalism and *laissez-faire* it was possible to endow sixteenth-century policy with an impressive consistency of both theory and practice; to think of Tudor despotism and mercantilism as coherent entities; and to imagine the pattern of English life as being slowly moulded from above in accordance with some preconceived plan. During the last fifty years, however, historians have been given abundant opportunities to learn at first hand of the piecemeal methods by which the mosaic of official ideas and actions is, in fact, built up, and in the light of that knowledge the earlier views of sixteenth-century states-manship have undergone a gradual change. More than twenty years ago Unwin questioned the right of mercantilism to be considered a "system", and Marshall reduced it from "a body of definite doctrines which arose suddenly, quickly overcame all minds, and after a time was wholly discarded" to a "tendency of thought and sentiment which had its roots in the past; which never, even at the height of its power, com-pletely dominated all minds; and which has not yet completely dis-appeared".[1] More recently, Professor Allen has shown that the sixteenth century was characterised less by any positive theory of the state than by a naïve belief in "the ability of centralised government to realise its ends. . . . Emergence, or even partial emergence, from the anarchic conditions of the fifteenth century brought with it an accession of faith and hope in the shaping power of government. Whatever men in large numbers desired, whether mere peace and order, or wealth, or justice, or true religion or even happiness, they tended to look to the Prince to supply it. . . . Reformers tended to think that everything was possible to this strange thing, a government able to enforce obedience."[2] By now it is a common-place of undergraduate essays that the Tudor state was more forced than forceful, and that the origins of its actions are to be found less in any theories held by its rulers than in the pressure

---

[1] A. Marshall, *Industry and Trade*, 719-20.
[2] J. W. Allen, *English Political Thought, 1603-1660*, I, 59-60.

to which it was subjected from vested interests and urgent social and financial problems. The twentieth century, in short, is busily recreating the sixteenth in its own image and the purpose of this article is to suggest that any such process should logically include some enquiry into the possible connection between state policy and the fluctuations in foreign trade. For no one who has studied the great depression of the eighteen-seventies and 'eighties and lived through that of the nineteen-thirties can doubt the influence of commercial crisis to influence policy; in sixteenth-century England foreign trade was already important; and the correlation that can be established between trade fluctuations and the various phases of government policy is close enough at least to be suggestive.

Tudor trade statistics are notoriously imperfect and misleading; but a reasonable guide to the main commercial trends of the time is to be found in the figures of shortcloths exported from London, for throughout the sixteenth century cloth was by far the most important commodity exported and by far the greater proportion of English cloth went out through London.

TRIENNIAL AVERAGES OF SHORTCLOTHS EXPORTED FROM LONDON[3]

*(The figures in italics relate to single years)*

| | | | | | | | |
|---|---|---|---|---|---|---|---|
| 1500–2 | 49,214 | 1536–8 | 87,231 | 1568–70 | 93,681 | | |
| 1503–5 | 43,884 | 1539–41 | 102,660 | 1571–3 | 73,204 | | |
| 1506–8 | 50,373 | 1542–4 | 99,362 | 1574–6 | 100,024 | | |
| 1509–11 | 58,447 | 1545–7 | 118,642 | 1577–9 | 97,728 | | |
| 1512–14 | 60,644 | *1550* | *132,767* | 1580–2 | 98,002 | | |
| 1515–17 | 60,524 | *1551* | *112,710* | 1583–5 | 101,214 | | |
| 1518–20 | 66,159 | *1552* | *84,968* | 1586–8 | 95,087 | | |
| 1521–3 | 53,660 | | | 1589–91 | 98,806 | | |
| 1524–6 | 72,910 | 1559–61 | 93,812 | 1592–4 | 101,678 | | |
| 1527–9 | 75,431 | 1562–4 | 61,188 | | | | |
| 1530–2 | 66,049 | 1565–7 | 95,128 | 1598–1600 | 103,032 | | |
| 1533–5 | 83,043 | | | | | | |

And a glance at the cloth figures is sufficient to show that English overseas trade in the sixteenth century passed through three clearly defined phases. As can be seen from the above table, the first half of the century was marked by a meteoric rise in the number of shortcloths exported. That rise, it is true, was not unbroken. With an almost cyclical regularity war, or the danger of war, produced a depression at the beginning of every decade save one. But as against the general trend these politically-induced setbacks were of no significance; the vital fact was that in fifty years the cloth trade grew in volume by 150 per

[3] The statistics for 1550-2 have been taken from the Exchequer Miscellaneous Customs Accounts, bundle 166, nos. 1 and 8, and bundle 167, no. 1. The remaining figures are from the enrolled accounts of which those for the reigns of Henry VII and Henry VIII have been printed in Schanz, *Englische Handelspolitik gegen Ende des Mittelalters*, II, 86-7.

11

cent.[4]  By contrast, the third quarter of the century saw not only a contraction of some 25 per cent in exports, but also two catastrophic slumps in which those exports were halved.  Finally, the Tudor age ended with three decades of comparative stability in which London cloth exports remained fairly steadily at a level some 20 per cent below that reached at the peak of the boom.  To analyse those changes and the reaction of the business and political worlds to them is to suggest a clue, albeit a minor one, to the development of Tudor economic policy.

Of the expansion which took place in the first half of the century by far the most significant feature was the change which gradually came over it after the middle of the 'twenties.  Until then its story was simple enough and there is no difficulty in enumerating the more important factors of which it was the result.  Something, no doubt, was due to the peace which the Henrys were able to maintain.  Something, also, must be attributed to that process whereby the lines of the international division of labour were being redrawn, and the manufacture of certain types of cloth was migrating from the Netherlands to this country.[5]  But the major impetus came from another source.  It was a commonplace of the age that English commerce was overwhelmingly dependent upon the Low Countries and that economically London was a satellite of Antwerp.  It was upon the looms of Flanders that most of the exported wool was woven; it was through Antwerp that English cloth reached its consumers not only in the Netherlands themselves, but also in Germany, eastern Europe, Italy and the Levant; it was from Antwerp that nearly all imports came.  "If English men's fathers were hanged at Andwarpes gates", ran a contemporary Flemish proverb, "their children to come into that towne would creepe betwixt their legges."[6]  Therefore, it is hardly fanciful to see a connection between the growth of London trade and the fact that it was during these years that Antwerp was climbing to the zenith of its power as the commercial and financial centre of the western world.  As the moon of Antwerp waxed the laws of nature dictated that the tide of London trade should rise, and as English cloths were among the major commodities handled in the Flemish city it is not surprising that the export of them increased as the business of that city grew.

Nor are the results of that expansion much more difficult to discover than its causes.  On the one hand, there was a marked diversion of national resources into new channels.  Arable land was converted to pasture; the textile industry spread over the countryside; the ranks of

[4] Neither the figures of provincial exports nor those of goods other than cloth sent out from London rose at anything like that pace, so that the London cloth statistics rather exaggerate the general growth in trade.

[5] It would not, however, be strictly true to say that during these years England was abandoning the trade in wool for that in cloth for the wool figures remained fairly stable.

[6] S.P.D., Elizabeth, XXXVI, no. 34.

the merchants were swollen with new entrants. On the other, the growth of exports brought with it a corresponding growth of imports. For the latter no complete set of statistics appears to exist, but some light is thrown on their behaviour by at least three sets of figures. There are the official values of the goods paying subsidy; and although the Henrician accounts do not always distinguish between exports and imports, they are useful because the contribution of the former to their total was comparatively small. There are, in the second place, the official values of the goods brought in by Hanseatic and other foreign merchants; and although the aliens' share in London trade was by no means a constant proportion of the whole, the records of exports suggest that its variation was not great enough to rob these values of all significance for this purpose. Finally, there are the statistics of wine imports. No two of these groups, it is true, moved in exactly the same manner but, until the late 'twenties, all three rose at a pace in some degree comparable to that of the soaring exports.[7] And their story can be confirmed from other sources. Foreign imports were among the grievances of the rioting apprentices in 1517,[8] and one of Armstrong's bitterest complaints was that England " is in such maner alwey stuffid, storid and pesterid so full of straunge merchaundise. . . . It is over long to describe the myschief that merchaunts werkth thorowt the reame by bryngyng such quantite of straunge merchaundise and artificiall fantasies." If Armstrong is any criterion, contemporaries found little cause for rejoicing in the direction which the country's economic life was taking.[9] To a less righteous and possibly more enlightened age, however, it is clear that there was another aspect to the matter. In the same words in which they prophesied disaster contemporaries unconsciously bore witness to a rise in their standard of living, a rise that was emphasised by the sumptuary legislation designed to check its most obvious manifestations. And there seems little doubt that the first quarter of the sixteenth century must be regarded as essentially a period of commercial prosperity.

The influence of Antwerp upon London trade continued to operate until the 'sixties, but in the 'twenties it was joined, and in the 'forties it was overshadowed, by a far less healthy stimulus—that of exchange depreciation. By now, the story of that depreciation is well known. The fall of sterling began with the French war of 1522, and its first stage was crystallised by the reduction of the weight of coins in 1526, by which time the value of the pound had dropped from 32s. Flemish to 26s. 8d. During the 'thirties the exchanges probably weakened still further, and

---

[7] Schanz, *op. cit.* II, 62, 63, 146-8.
[8] Tawney and Power, *Tudor Economic Documents*, III, 83.
[9] *Ibid.* 90-114. The whole of Armstrong's *Treatise Concerning the Staple* is the description of a commercial boom by one who disliked everything which that boom implied.

with the successive debasements of the 'forties they finally collapsed until, in the early months of 1551, the pound was worth only 13s. 4d. Flemish.[10] Nor were the effects of that decline completely nullified by the accompanying rise in the internal price level. The fall in the external value of the pound began before inflation,[11] and always kept ahead of it.[12] The result was inevitable. During the second quarter of the sixteenth century, and particularly during the 'forties, silver prices slowly fell in England while they rose on the Continent[13] and, as English goods thereby became relatively cheap, there was a natural increase in their sales abroad. The relevant statistics are too imperfect and the intrusion of other factors is too great for any exact correlation to be possible, but the connection between the fall of the exchanges and the rise of exports is reasonably obvious. The depreciation of the early 'twenties was followed by a distinct jump in the cloth figures; that of the 'forties was accompanied not only by a boom in textiles, but also by a recovery in wool shipments; and it is perhaps of some significance that when the revaluation of the currency restored its silver content to approximately that of the early 'forties the cloth figures gradually stabilised themselves at a level not far removed from that which obtained in those years.[14]

As the expansion of exports grew to depend more and more upon exchange depreciation, so its economic significance gradually changed. An immediate result of the new impetus to trade was to accelerate the diversion of national resources into the exporting industries. The conversion of arable land to pasture was already an established phenomenon, but in the 'thirties and 'forties it took on a new magnitude, and the Tudor Government was driven to vastly more energetic attempts to handle the problem.[15] The growth of the textile industry was not new, but it was the 'thirties and 'forties that produced an embryo factory system under men such as William Stumpe. And as the pace of economic change grew, so the strain which it put upon the comparatively rigid structure of Tudor England grew with it. In the earlier years of the century that strain had been tolerable, although the enclosure agitation and apprentice riots of 1517 must in part be laid to its charge. But as, under the stimulus of exchange depreciation, cloth exports reached new high levels and even the trade in wool revived, the pains of adaptation became increasingly acute. It would, of course, be foolish to attribute all or even most of the troubles of those times to the developments in foreign trade. Far more important, no doubt, was the rise in the internal price level. But the connection between exchange depreci-

[10] Feavearyear, The Pound Sterling, 64.　　　[11] Ibid. 47.
[12] Ricardo, Principles of Political Economy (Everyman Ed.), 239. I am indebted to my colleague, Mr J. K. Horsefield, for this reference.
[13] Wiebe, Zur Geschichte der Preisrevolution des xvi und xvii Jahrhunderts, Appendix A.　　　[14] See the statistical table on p. 153.
[15] Tawney, The Agrarian Problem in the Sixteenth Century, 358.

ation and the agrarian problem was obvious even to an age not usually gifted with economic insight. As Lane once wrote to Cecil:

> "The fall of the exchange within thys iiii dayse hathe cawsyd and wyll cause to be boughte clothes at lvi *li.* the packe wyche before wold not have byn bowghte for lii *li.* the packe; so that yow may perseve that the exchange doth ingender dere clothe, and dere clothe doth engendar dere wolle, and dere wolle doth ingendar many scheppe, and many scheppe doth ingendar myche pastor and dere, and myche pastor ys the dekaye of tyllage, and owte of the dekaye of tyllage spryngythe ii evylls, skarsyte of korne and the pepull unwroghte, and consequently the darthe of all thynges." [16]

And it was by no mere chance that Starkey, Latimer, Hales, Crowley and the "commonwealth party" were most vocal when overseas commerce was booming or that Norfolk rose in rebellion when London exports were greater in physical volume than they had ever been before or were to be again for more than half a century.

Moreover, as exports became more costly in terms of the social changes needed to produce them, so they tended to become less lucrative in terms of the foreign wares which they purchased. Contemporary complaints against the excessive volume of imports still continued, yet the customs figures already mentioned as throwing some light on the subject all suggest that, for most of the 'thirties and 'forties, that volume was either stable or declining. Certainly the volume of imports did not grow as rapidly as that of exports, and its failure to do so seems to admit of only three explanations, all of which were probably in some measure operative and none of which was conducive to general prosperity. That failure may have been due in part to a net increase in the inflow of bullion although, despite the raising of the Mint price, the tendency to smuggle abroad all the better coins must have prevented that ever becoming great and the writers of the time were not aware of any such increase. It was undoubtedly due in part to the growth of invisible imports such as the alien shipping services against which the navigation laws of 1532 and 1540 were directed, the interest on the royal debt abroad, and the expenses of the French wars in the early 'forties. Finally, the natural result of the depreciation of sterling was to alter the terms of trade in a direction unfavourable to this country. Contemporaries were aware of the extraordinary dearness of foreign goods even to the point of attributing to it the rise in the domestic price level; Wiebe has shown that there was in fact a marked divergence between silver prices here and abroad; and it is not difficult to believe that as the exchanges declined an ever larger volume of exports was needed to purchase a

---

[16] Tawney and Power, *op. cit.* II, 184.

given quantity of foreign wares. Because of that change in the terms of trade, together with the increasing strain which the provision of exports placed upon the whole economic structure, it is not, perhaps, too fanciful to argue that by the 'forties commercial expansion had changed from a force making for general economic progress into one of the causes of that distress and discontent which were such outstanding features of those years.

Yet, although the first two quarters of the sixteenth century were rather less alike than the export figures at first sight suggest, they had one major characteristic in common. Together they formed, especially in contrast with the years which followed, one of the great free trade periods of modern English history. They were preceded by the famous statute of 1497 which temporarily curtailed the power of the Merchant Adventurers;[17] they were marked by the collapse of the usury laws,[18] the relaxation of the restrictions upon the export of unfinished cloth,[19] and by the virtual cessation of the attacks upon the Hanseatic merchants;[20] there was a period in the 'thirties and 'forties when the differential duties imposed on aliens were abolished;[21] and none of the spasmodic efforts of the Government to interfere in commercial affairs seems to have been more than half-hearted. For that comparative liberalism the reasons were doubtless several. Something must be attributed to the worldly wisdom of the early Tudors. Certainly Henry VIII, than whom no man was more adept in the art of cloaking private ends in the decent robes of public sentiments, had no illusions about "the inordinate desire of gaynes . . . naturally given to merchaunts". As he once explained to the Emperor, he made it his policy "to give no further credit unto them in their sutes, clamours and complaynts thenne is convenient".[22] More important, no doubt, was the delicate international situation which made it dangerous in any way to antagonise the Emperor upon whose subjects the brunt of any trade restrictions must inevitably fall. Of still greater moment was the fact that England was in no good position for economic warfare. The only foreign merchants worth penalising were those of the Hanse towns and Flanders. Medieval experience suggested that to interfere with the privileges of the former was to enter into a struggle which was sure to be long and likely to be unsuccessful. To molest the latter was to cross swords with the Emperor, whose economic armoury included weapons deadlier than any that Henry could command. He could close the Antwerp market to English goods and he could extend the conflict by penalising English traders in Spain. Yet later sovereigns as astute as the Henrys and in no better position to risk offending their neighbours were soon to reverse

[17] 12 Hen. VII, c. 6.          [18] 37 Hen. VIII, c. 9.          [19] 27 Hen. VIII, c. 13.
[20] J. A. Williamson, *Maritime Enterprise, 1485-1558*, chap. 7.
[21] *L. and P. Henry VIII*, XVI, no. 13.
[22] Brit. Mus. Add. MSS., 25, 114, f. 122b.

their policy of free trade, and the ultimate explanation for that policy must be sought elsewhere. It is to be found in the simple fact that at no time during the first half of the century was strong and consistent pressure brought to bear on the Government drastically to interfere in commercial affairs. On the one hand those, and they were many, who thought it the duty of the State to promote English mercantile interests had little cause for action when trade was so continuously growing. In every minor slump they clamoured for and obtained legislation but the enforcement of that legislation was probably as transitory as the depressions which produced it. On the other hand those, and they were also many, who thought it the duty of the State to keep commercial expansion within reasonable bounds found, as Americans were to rediscover in the nineteen-twenties, that stables are seldom locked until their horses have been stolen and that booms, like floods, can seldom be controlled until the waters have begun to subside of their own accord. They obtained some largely ineffectual legislation against enclosures, but for more drastic measures they had to wait. They did not have to wait for ever.

In so far as the later stages of the export boom had been based upon currency devaluation they had been inherently unstable. As internal prices rose the advantages of exchange depreciation were bound to dwindle and already in 1550 there were complaints of overproduction.[23] Unless the process of debasement was continued indefinitely the physical volume of exports was in time certain to fall, and there was a point beyond which debasement could not be taken without endangering the whole economic and social system. But although some decline in exports was inevitable, its pace and severity depended largely upon whether internal and external prices were left to adjust themselves or whether that adjustment was hastened by a change in currency policy. The merchants, eager to reap the benefits of devaluation for as long as possible, were all for allowing matters to take their own course. To the Government, however, the matter appeared differently. Faced with the necessity of checking the rise in domestic prices and of repaying its heavy debts abroad, it saw a bitter truth in the dictum that " the exchainge is the thing that eatts ought all princes to the wholl destruction of their commonweal ". Therefore, despite mercantile opposition, the currency was called down in 1551, the exchanges shot up, and there was a drastic fall in the sterling equivalent of the prices reigning upon the Antwerp market. " The exchange in King Edward's time ", wrote Gresham, " was but 16s. Dyd I not raise it to 23s.? . . . Whereby wool fell in price from 26s. 8d. to 16s. and cloths from lx li. to xl li. and xxxvi li. a packe."[24] Unfortunately, as the merchants pointed out, English internal prices fell neither as rapidly nor as far, and there followed a painful and protracted struggle until a new equilibrium could be

[23] Acts of the Privy Council, 1550-1552, 20.
[24] J. W. Burgon, Life of Sir Thomas Gresham, I, 261.

reached.  At first the physical volume of exports shrank quickly; the number of shortcloths sent out from London fell from 132,767 in 1550 to 112,710 in 1551, and to 84,969 in 1552.  Then, as costs were slowly adjusted, as the international bickerings of the early 'fifties died down, and as the exchanges once more collapsed, exports shot up once more to reach a new record in 1554.[25]  But in the following year there was an epidemic of bankruptcies in the city;[26] in 1556 all shipments to the Netherlands had to be stayed for four months in order to ease the glut there;[27] and the opening years of Elizabeth's reign found the cloth trade at a level some 30 per cent below the peak of the boom, a level which was not to be substantially exceeded until the next century.  The great expansion of trade was over.

To see in that change any great national catastrophe would, no doubt, be absurd.  The appreciation of the exchanges meant a change in the terms of trade in favour of this country.  The value of exports must have fallen less than their volume.  It is conceivable that imports and the national income were scarcely diminished.  But the mere falling-off in the physical volume of exports meant that in trade, in the textile industry, and in shipping there was left a body of unemployed resources that had in some way to be liquidated or relieved.  And in attempting to solve the problems thus created men at first succeeded only in damaging commerce still further.  In the early 'sixties and again in the early 'seventies, partly because of the measures taken in the 'fifties, Antwerp was closed to English goods, the major prop of London trade was knocked away, and exports fell to levels which they had not known for a generation.[28]  Followed as they were by those even greater setbacks, the maladjustments of the 'fifties opened a new chapter in English economic history.  It is a platitude that periods of intense or repeated depression are fertile in changes in both economic thought and economic practice, for it is when men's established expectations are not fulfilled that they become most critical of the system under which they live and are most readily led to experiment.  The depressions of the early nineteenth century were a potent factor in the development of classical theory and laissez-faire practice; those of the 'seventies and 'eighties had their fruit in economic imperialism, tariff reform and the rise of collectivism; those of the nineteen-thirties have stimulated changes of which the effects are bound to be immense; and those of the third quarter of the sixteenth century had repercussions which make that period comparable to any of the other three in its significance.  On the one hand, it saw an outburst of economic discussion which, although it drew

[25] See statistical table on p. 153 and Exchequer Miscellaneous Customs Accounts, bundle 175, no. 4.                [26] Hist. MSS. Comm., Report III, 37.
[27] Acts of the Privy Council, 1554-1556, 295.
[28] For a discussion of these later depressions, see Unwin's lectures on the Merchant Adventurers in his Studies in Economic History.

heavily on the past for its ideas, was carried on in a different language and with a different emphasis from those of the 'thirties and 'forties. Then the important thinkers had been preachers and social reformers but now they were merchants and statesmen; then the characteristic vehicle of expression had been the sermon and the treatise but now it was the more technical memorandum; then the criterion by which contemporary life was tested had been that of social justice but now it was that of economic expediency; then the great topic of discussion had been agriculture but now it was trade and industry. Faced with the problem of recurrent depressions the men of the 'fifties, 'sixties and 'seventies fused the ideas and prejudices of the Middle Ages into a loosely coordinated body of doctrine, and in applying that doctrine they imposed upon the economic system a set of regulations that were substantially to affect its working for the next two generations.

Some measure of adjustment to the new circumstances took place without any major interference on the part of the Government and without any radical departure from established habits. Land that had been converted from tillage to pasture could easily enough be reconverted to tillage.[29] It is possible that some mercantile funds went into the privateering which grew into such evil prominence under Mary. Certainly, to judge by the outcry against them, both merchants and clothiers transferred some of their capital to land and, willingly or otherwise, many of the former invested in Government loans. More spectacular were the attempts of the Government to bring under control the foreign exchanges which, in a sense, had been the original cause of all the difficulty. As Professor Tawney has shown, the third quarter of the sixteenth century was marked by almost ceaseless discussions about the international money market, and every falling-off in trade produced some scheme for reducing that market to order. However loudly Gresham might repeat his father's axiom that " merchants can no more be without exchanges and rechanges than ships at sea without water ", the demand for exchange control appeared in every slump with the automatic regularity of a reflex action. It was part of the revaluation policy of the early 'fifties, when private exchange business was banned as from June 1551. It re-appeared in the commercial crisis at the end of the decade and in 1559 private exchange business was suspended once more. The depression of the early 'sixties led to the Royal Commission of 1564; that of the early 'seventies led to the ban of 1576.[30] Save as a nuisance, however, exchange control probably exercised little influence

---

[29] Miss Bradley (*The Enclosures in England*) has suggested that the reconversions after 1550 were due to the recuperation of soil which had been put down to grass because of its exhaustion. They may equally well be attributed to the fall in the demand for wool.

[30] See R. H. Tawney's introduction to Thomas Wilson's *Discourse on Usury*, 145-50. It is significant that usury was once more prohibited in 1552.

on trade and the more important results of the depression have to be sought elsewhere.

An obvious measure was to seek new markets for English cloth and in the 'fifties, when the problem was essentially one of a shrinkage in the effective European demand, those markets were of necessity sought further afield. The immediate result of the slump induced by the over-production of the 'forties and the revaluation of 1551 was, in fact, to launch England on the quest for Eastern and African trade. Previously, despite the country's favourable geographical position and the activity of a few enthusiasts, English interest in the search for and the exploita-tion of new lands had been of the slightest. On the one hand, the fear of Spanish hostility made the Government cautious. On the other, the profits to be earned at Antwerp left merchants content to be tied to Europe and reluctant to face the retaliation that any infringement of the Spanish and Portuguese monopolies might bring. During the first half of the century it had been only in periods of slack trade that projects for more daring ventures could hope for the attention of business men, and with every check to commercial expansion such projects had appeared. In the early 'twenties Henry VIII had proposed to the Londoners that they should finance a company to trade to Newfound-land and beyond;[31] in the early 'thirties Thorne and Barlow had joined forces to work out their scheme for a north-west passage; in the early 'forties Barlow had revived that scheme and a pilot had actually been brought from Seville in the hope of discovering a way between Iceland and Greenland.[32] But all those depressions had been too brief for the merchants' interest to be seriously captured and it was not until the 'fifties, when men saw quite clearly that under the impetus of exchange depreciation the cloth trade had reached dimensions which could not be maintained upon the basis of purely European markets, that effective action was taken. Then, in 1551, a ship was sent to Morocco; in 1553 others went to Guinea; and in the latter year Chancellor and Willoughby sailed in search of a north-east passage and thereby opened up trade with Russia. The later depressions served only to intensify the movement. To see more than a coincidence in the fact that the traffic in slaves to the West Indies began when cloth exports were once more falling would, no doubt, be dangerous. But the overtrading of which men were complaining in Africa by 1567 may well have been due to the closing of Antwerp in 1562 and the following years;[33] and the same crisis almost certainly encouraged the Russian merchants in their efforts to establish an overland trade with Persia, for those efforts were more and more directed to obtaining the spices which previously Antwerp had

[31] Williamson, *Maritime Enterprise, 1485-1558*, 245-6.
[32] *Ibid*. 265. For a full account of the Thorne-Barlow project see Professor Taylor's introduction to Barlow's *Brief Summe of Geographie*.
[33] S.P.D., Elizabeth, XLII, no. 49.

supplied. Finally, the slump of the 'seventies had the most important result of all, for it led to the reopening of direct trade with the Levant.[34] England was at last launched upon the pursuit of world commerce. Nor was such enterprise peculiar to trade. The textile industry, unable for technological reasons to meet depression by drastically reducing its costs, met it in some measure by diversifying its products. For it was these years that saw the beginning of the " new draperies " in England; and although those draperies owed much to Protestant refugees from abroad there is no reason either to believe that all the new cloths were introduced by foreigners or to doubt that the welcome which those foreigners were given was in some part due to the employment which they could create. The depressions of the third quarter of the sixteenth century, in short, resembled those of the last quarter of the nineteenth in turning the eyes of English merchants to more distant markets and the hands of English manufacturers to new commodities.

The immediate relief to be expected from such developments was, however, but slight and for the most part men pinned their faith on other and more dubious remedies. The most obvious characteristics of the 'fifties were an outburst of economic nationalism aimed at maximising the Englishmen's share of such trade as there was and a crop of restrictions designed to protect certain vested interests from the necessity of contraction, to bolster up prices, and to make impossible any repetition of the feverish expansion of the preceding decades. Neither of those phenomena was, of course, by any means new. But during the first half of the century, although they had not lacked occasional expression in either words or action, they had been generally held in check by the prevailing prosperity. When trade is booming the sting of economic inequality is magically softened and the interests threatened by restrictions and xenophobia are too powerful to be lightly ignored; the danger comes with depression. When, for other reasons, markets are shrinking, the fear that they will be closed in retaliation for nationalistic measures obviously loses some of its potency; when sales and prices are falling the compulsory restriction of output and the bridling of competition acquire a specious rationality which it is difficult to resist; and as profits dwindle the former champions of liberty lose both their convictions and their influence. Therefore it is not surprising that the 'fifties opened a period which saw, if not a complete reversal, at least a drastic refashioning of economic policy.

The revival of economic nationalism was, of course, by no means confined to merchants and in 1563 a general prohibition was placed upon all that foreign haberdashery against which pamphleteers had been railing for a generation.[35] But the great protagonist of economic nationalism was still the merchant rather than the manufacturer.

---

[34] Cotton MSS., Nero B. xi, f. 292.    [35] 5 Eliz., c. 7.

Imports were still complementary to rather than competitive with the products of England, and the really urgent problem was not whether they should be admitted but who should bring them in and carry out exports in exchange. Whereas in the twentieth century the aim of economic nationalism has been to limit international co-operation, in the sixteenth it was rather to decide upon the agents by whom that co-operation should be carried on. And inevitably the major enemy in that struggle were the Hanseatic merchants, for by virtue of their tariff privileges those merchants were more important than all the other foreigners engaged in English trade and by virtue of their opposition to the growing English penetration of the Baltic it was against them that most bitterness was felt. One of the first results, therefore, of the depression of the early 'fifties was a recrudescence of that anti-Hanseatic feeling which had been smouldering ever since the great eruptions of the fifteenth century but which the early Tudors had never permitted to come to a head. As in the fifteenth century, the opposition to the Hanse turned partly on the question of parity of treatment for English merchants in the Baltic; but now there was added a new element. For the centripetal tendency which had drawn the Londoners towards Antwerp had also been felt by the Hanse merchants, so that the Low Countries which had earlier been a refuge from their competition now became its very centre.[36] Armstrong had drawn a sharp distinction between the Prussian merchants trading "owt of the cold contreys in the este parties" and those of western Germany who carried on their trade through Flanders,[37] and when the storm broke in the 'fifties it was upon the latter that its greatest violence fell. That development, which contemporaries dated from the 'twenties, was important because it ranged against them not only the Baltic traders but also the much more powerful Merchant Adventurers just at the time when the Adventurers were rendering important financial services to the Government and were therefore in a position to press for favours. To that situation there could be but one outcome; the special privileges of the Hansards were at last curtailed. In 1552 they were abolished entirely; but that was no more than the opening to a wearisome series of negotiations during which those privileges were restored, modified and again cancelled before, in 1560, a settlement was reached on the basis of a new tariff that left the Hansards more favourably placed than other aliens but with no advantages over native merchants. In their business with their own towns they were to pay as Englishmen, but in that with Antwerp they were to be taxed at a rate only slightly below that for other foreigners.[38] Those other foreigners had fewer privileges to lose but, even so, their position

[36] For the tendency of Hanseatic exclusiveness to divert English trade to the Netherlands, see Power and Postan, *English Trade in the Fifteenth Century*, 150-3.
[37] Tawney and Power, *op. cit.* III, 108-9.
[38] Williamson, *op. cit.* chap. 7.

was steadily undermined. The early 'fifties were full of complaints from Low Country merchants about their ill-treatment in England;[39] Italian, Ragusan and French merchants were forced to enter bond not to sell English cloth in Antwerp or elsewhere save in their own countries and beyond;[40] the petty obstacles in the way of aliens were multiplied; and the policy reached its climax in the new tariff and the navigation act of 1558. "The natives here", reported the Venetian ambassador, "have laid a plot to ruin the trade of all foreign merchants",[41] and in the next twenty years there were repeated attempts to hamper those merchants by enforcing the statutes of employment, by making them host with Englishmen and employ English brokers, by excluding them from retail trade and by limiting the types of goods which they might export.[42]

Even more spectacular than this outburst of economic nationalism was the wave of restrictionism which accompanied it. In great crises the cost of industrial and commercial expansion seems disproportionately large and, in the spirit of caution which those crises bring with them, it seems the epitome of wisdom to control production and to avoid the curse of plenty. Thus the great depression of the twentieth century has produced its restrictive planning to act as a brake upon progress; that of the late nineteenth produced its cartels and its trusts; and that of the sixteenth proved a worthy forerunner of them both by inspiring a similar flight from competition towards organisation. As the boom of the first half of the century had been largely confined to the textiles, it is not surprising that the policy of restraint was first elaborated in the cloth industry. Attacks upon the rapid expansion of that industry were not new. It had created, and threatened to create in the future, problems to which men could not remain blind. and all the arguments now used in favour of restriction had, in fact, been heard in the days of prosperity. But although they had been heard they had not been seriously heeded, for Tudor governments seldom met their difficulties before they became acute. While the industry was flourishing and profits were easy the diversion of resources into it imposed a serious strain only upon agriculture and the Government contented itself with trying to check the conversion of arable land into pasture. It was only in the depression, when those resources had to be rediverted, that attention was seriously turned to industry itself. That "experience hath taught that overmuche draperie, besides divers other inconveniences, hath destroyed more necessarie Artificers than it hath bred" became a bitter platitude

---

[39] *Calendar S.P. Spanish, 1550-1552, passim.* For the general wave of anti-foreign feeling which, based on hatred of the Spaniards, swept over the country, see *Calendar S.P. Venice, 1555-1556,* 1056 and 1066; *1557-1558,* 1544.

[40] *Calendar S.P.D., 1547-1565,* 518; Baschet Transcripts, bundle 23, letter of 8 January, 1557.     [41] *Calendar S.P. Venice, 1556-1557,* 1011.

[42] *Calendar S.P. Foreign, 1560-1561,* 91-2; *Calendar S.P.D., 1547-1565,* 531-2; *Acts of the Privy Council, 1577-1578,* 281, 379, 401; S.P.D., Elizabeth, LXXX, no. 61; LXXXIII, nos. 35-6; CVI, nos. 27-8; CXXX, no. 25; Harleian MSS.. XXXVI, ff. 81 *et seq.*

of which the truth became ever more obvious with each successive collapse in trade. And as the long term costs of rapid industrialisation became more apparent men began to devise means for making such industrialisation impossible.

The arguments for restriction came mainly from three sources. There were, in the first place, those conservatives to whom all change was necessarily suspect and to whom the rise of a new class of industrialists implied a threat to the whole well-ordering of society. Complaints about the contemporary confusion of social classes were many, and to some the greatest of all offenders was the clothier " whoe doth most harme of all other degres in this land by purchasing lande or leses, or by maynteyning in his sonne in the Ynes of Cort like a gentleman or by byeng offices for him ".[43] To the progressive landlord deriving much of his income from the sale of wool those views may have seemed extreme; but there were plenty of men in the Commons to whom they appealed and the restrictions on the cloth trade were voted partly in the spirit in which the Tory squires of the nineteenth century were to fasten the Factory Acts upon the cotton lords.

There was, in the second place, the approach of the statesman concerned for the preservation of law and order and for the maintenance of those conditions which made law and order possible. Their views were expressed by Cecil:

> " It is to be thought that the diminution of clothyng in this realme were proffitable to the same for manny causes: first, for that therby the tilladg of the realm is notoriously decayed, which is yerly manifest in that, contrary to former tymes, the realme is dryven to be furnished with forrayn corne, and specially the Citee of London. Secondly, for that the people depend uppon makyng of cloth ar worss condition to be quyetly governed than the husband men. Thyrdly by convertyng of so many people to clothyng the realme lacketh not only artificers, which were wont to inhabitt all corporat townes, but also labours for all comon workes."[44]

Experience showed that such fears were by no means imaginary. The dependence of London upon French corn was an important factor in Anglo-French relations during the 'fifties;[45] the repeated danger that Philip might bring England to heel by the use of economic sanctions illustrated the political inexpediency of industrialisation;[46] and the

---

[43] Rawlinson MSS., D., CXXXIII, f. 13.　　　　[44] Tawney and Power, op. cit. II, 45.
[45] Baschet Transcripts, bundle 23, ff. 279, 281, 290.
[46] In the early 'sixties the policy of sanctions found a powerful advocate in Cardinal Granvelle, the virtual ruler of the Netherlands and the man most responsible for the embargoes placed upon English cloth in 1562 and 1563 (Rich, The Ordinance Book of the Merchants of the Staple, 45-51). In the later 'sixties and early 'seventies Norfolk, Arundel and Ridoli all wanted a similar ban in support of their conspiracies (Calendar S.P. Spanish, 1568-1579, 136; Calendar S.P. Rome, 1558-1571, 338). For the influence of trade depression on the rising of 1569, see Calendar S.P. Venice, 1558-1580, 437.

results of unemployment in the textile industry were, to say the least, disconcerting. It was found that whenever trade fell off:

" infinite nombers of Spynners, Carders, Pickers of woll are turned to begging with no smale store of pore children, who driven with necessitie (that hath no lawe) both come idelie abowt to begg to the oppression of the poore husbandmen, And robbe their hedges of Lynnen, stele pig, gose, and capon, and leave not a drie hedg within dyvers myles compas of the townes wher they dwell to the great destruction of all mannor of grayen sowen and to the spoile of mens meadowes and pastures, And spoile all springes, steale fruit and corne in the harvest tyme, and robb barnes in the winter tyme, and cawse pore maydes and servantes to purloyne and robbe their masters, which the foresyd spynners etc. receve Besides many other myscheifes falling owt the Weavers, Walkers, Tukkers, Shermen, Dyers and suche being tall lusty men and extreame pore streyght being forced by povertie stele fish, conies, dere, and such like, and their streight murmur and rayse comocions as late experience in Suffolke shewed."[47]

On occasion, as in 1563, the Government might meet such a position by purchasing cloth with public funds;[48] but the temptation to avoid the problem by checking the growth of the industry was irresistible.

Finally, there was the pressure of those vested interests who could make restriction serve their purpose and increase their profits. The established manufacturers had never looked kindly upon newcomers and, when contraction became inevitable, they immediately demanded that it should be so regulated as to fall entirely upon those whom the boom had drawn into production. When examined by the Privy Council in 1550 they immediately explained the glutting of the Antwerp market and consequent collapse in prices by " finding great fault with the moltitude of clothiers lately encreased in the realme ".[49] And the Staplers could be relied upon to welcome any scheme that, by diminishing the home consumption of wool, would leave more for export.

When Parliament met in 1551 the depression was already upon the country and during the next twelve years the policy of restriction was slowly given legislative form. On the one hand, the pressure upon landlords to reconvert their pasture land to tillage became stronger.[50] On the other, the textile industry itself was subjected to stricter control. The first suggestion was to limit the industry by confining it to towns.[51] For some reason, however, that device was abandoned. Instead, after consultation with clothiers, merchant tailors and representatives of the finishing trades, two other bills were preferred and passed. The first

[47] Rawlinson MSS., D., 133, f. 4b.
[48] Calendar S.P. Spanish, 1568-1579, 113.
[49] Tawney and Power, op. cit. I, 184.
[50] Tawney, op. cit. 354.
[51] Commons Journal, I, 16.

established a detailed code of regulations for the maintenance of the quality of English woollens, for as prices fell manufacturers had as usual resorted to the debasement of their workmanship in an effort to reduce their costs.[52]   The second allowed broadcloths to be woven only by such persons as had either served an apprenticeship or followed the trade for seven years, for in that way the most recent recruits to the industry could be weeded out.[53]   Unfortunately, however, the problem of enforcing that contraction was complicated by the desire of the Government to preserve urban interests from loss and to make the burden fall entirely upon their rural competitors.   For that purpose the statute of 1552 was too general, for it created unemployment in town as well as country and within three years it had to be twice modified.   In 1553 towns and cities were exempted from its operation.[54]   And in 1555, when the Antwerp market was again glutted, the policy of discrimination and restraint was carried a stage further by limiting the number of apprentices and looms that even a qualified rural manufacturer might employ.[55]   Finally, when the slump of the early 'sixties made all existing restrictions seem inadequate and all arguments against industrialisation appear unanswerable, the sphere of State action was widened and, in place of the further regulation of textiles as such, there appeared the famous Statute of Apprentices applying to trade, industry and agriculture alike.[56]   Like all great measures of social reconstruction that statute had many roots and, in the absence of the debates upon it, it is impossible to trace all the causes to which it was due.   But among its results was one so obvious that it could not have been unpremeditated.   By insisting upon apprenticeship in trade and industry, by defining the classes from which apprentices might be taken, by fixing wages, and by prohibiting the sudden termination of contracts between employer and employed, it made illegal that mobility of labour without which rapid industrialisation and spectacular commercial expansion are impossible.   Had the Statute of Apprentices been in effective operation in the 'thirties and 'forties the boom of those years could not have taken place; in view of the economic opinions which prevailed in the 'fifties and 'sixties it is, perhaps, not unreasonable to see in that fact one of the motives which inspired it; and to that extent it stands as a classic example of the restrictive legislation which great depressions tend to produce.

But although the policy of restriction found its most obvious manifestations in industry it by no means left commerce free.   An immediate result of the crisis had been to strengthen among merchants not only their hostility to foreigners but also their insistence that the quintessence of economic wisdom lay in raising prices by controlling sales.   The

[52] 5 and 6 Ed. VI, c. 6.          [53] 5 and 6 Ed. VI, c. 8.
[54] Mary, sessio tertia, c. 7.          [55] 2 and 3 Ph. and Mary, c. 11.
[56] 5 Eliz., c. 4.

attraction of that device has always varied inversely with the prosperity of trade. While the boom kept prices buoyant and profits high it had languished. Now, as those conditions passed, that idea became the basis of commercial policy and its acceptance as such, although owing much to the financial services which its champions were at this time affording to the Government, was made infinitely easier by the attempts to deflate the cloth industry itself. In the first place, the textile legislation provided an obvious instrument whereby the volume of cloth coming on to the market could be controlled at its source.[57] What was even more important, that legislation answered the most obvious objection to the merchants' programme. To allow them to control sales meant, as contemporary critics did not fail to point out, the sacrifice of the manufacturers to them. It was, therefore, highly convenient for them that the revival of their policy of restriction coincided with a public opinion temporarily biased against the manufacturer and inclined to see the limitation of production rather as a blessing than otherwise. Finally, the same school of thought that advocated a reduction in the number of textile workers welcomed the attempts of the merchants to reduce their own.

During the boom years new capital and labour had flowed into commerce as into industry, and the increase in merchants had been as conspicuous and as unpopular as the multiplication of clothiers. It presented a similar challenge to the established order of society; it aroused a similar opposition among both the established traders and the gentry; and with the advent of the depression that opposition flared up into a general attack upon the newcomers. Upon their misdemeanours there was no disagreement. By their competition they raised the prices of imports and lowered those of exports; by their purchases of land they undermined the social hierarchy of the countryside; in so far as they were young men without capital they were forced to trade with borrowed money and thereby weakened the exchanges; coming as many of them did from the ranks of the artisans and retailers they complicated the problems of those among the gentry who looked to commerce for the employment of their younger sons. Nor was there much doubt about the remedies. Trade should be restricted to those who had served an apprenticeship; apprenticeship should be restricted to the sons of the well-to-do; and for each branch of trade there should be established a company to enforce those restrictions and to regulate the conduct of such merchants as were admitted to it. One of the major results, therefore, of the depressions in the third quarter of the sixteenth century was to fasten upon English commerce a framework of companies which were to dominate its history for the next half-century.

[57] For a discussion of the attitude of London merchants to this textile legislation, see Miss Cay's article on "Aspects of Elizabethan Apprenticeship" in *Facts and Factors in Economic History*, 134-63.

Of the growth of those companies the story is too well known to need repeating in any detail.[58]   For the most part it marched in step with the fluctuations in trade and each successive slump added its quota of restrictions.   Ever since 1497 the Merchant Adventurers had been divided into the " Old Hanse " of old-established firms and the " New Hanse " of those admitted under the statute of that year.   Theoretically, the status of the two groups was the same.   But the former had always contrived to determine the company's bylaws and to dominate its court of assistants, and with the depressions of the 'fifties they used their power to cramp the activities of the others, to multiply the obstacles to the admission of new members, and to punish any who should appeal to the royal courts against their policy of discrimination and restraint. The particulars of the resulting struggle are confused, but from the recrimination to which it gave rise it is clear the restrictions were aimed primarily at those whom the boom had drawn into trade.   To the objections of the New Hanse it was replied, no doubt with some truth, that

"some of the parties that do complayne have not bene in the said company passing iiii or v yeares, and many of them not passing thre or two yeares, and some of them not passing one yere. . . . The chief of the same complaynants were clothe-workers and of other handy crafts and so brought up."

And it was taken as an axiom that old-established ought of right to be protected from the competition of newcomers who combined retail with overseas trade and, in their thirst for business, sank to bartering their wares and paying illegal taxes.   It was a contest in which the Old Hanse held all the winning cards.   There was growing a general sentiment in favour of restriction; the financial services which they were rendering the Government assured them of official support against the English as well as their foreign competitors; and the elimination of the new traders formed an integral part of Gresham's policy for raising the exchanges. Against such an array of forces the opposition could no nothing; its leaders were either imprisoned or expelled from the company; and with each succeeding depression the system of control was carried a step further.[59]   During that of the early 'sixties the Russia Company was able to obtain a ban on the trade of non-members to Narva; the shifting of the cloth staple from Antwerp to Emden was favoured partly because it would eliminate the weaker merchants whose existence depended upon the quick returns which could be had from the Netherlands;[60] both the Adventurers and Staplers obtained new charters; the latter, if not the former, immediately used their new powers to tighten their control over

[58] Most of the facts mentioned here have been taken from Unwin's lecture, already referred to, on the Merchant Adventurers.

[59] Rawlinson MSS., c. 394, 121 st seq., Burgon, *Life of Gresham*, I, 463.

[60] S.P.D., Elizabeth, XXXV, no. 33.

trade;[61] and an unsuccessful attempt was made to incorporate the merchants trading to Barbary[62] The slump of the 'seventies in turn produced a Spanish and an Eastland Company; for although the former was not set up until 1577 it was suggested as early as 1574 to check the influx of new merchants when Philip removed his embargo and that trade was reopened;[63] and although the latter was not created until 1579 it had as one of its objects the exclusion from the Baltic of those who had begun trading there after the closing of the Spanish market after 1568.[64] Nor were these developments confined to London, for many of the companies also covered the outports and during these years the merchants of Chester, Exeter, Bristol and York all acquired chartered corporations of their own.

To complete that story one thing more was necessary. As entry to trade and industry was made progressively more difficult there disappeared the hope that unemployment would speedily be cured, and it is no mere coincidence that it was during these years that the system of poor relief was revolutionised by the introduction of a compulsory poor rate and a system of public relief works. Thus the depressions of the third quarter of the sixteenth century were a not unimportant episode in English economic history, for they saw an erratic attempt to mould the economic system according to something like a pattern. And the details of that pattern . . . economic nationalism, the opening of distant markets and the organisation of those already in existence, the encouragement of new industries and the control of production in the old, the regulation of the whole pace of economic change and the public provision for the unemployed . . . give it familiar appearance. It is, in many respects, the pattern of the mercantilism of the textbooks and of the economic policy of more than one country since 1929. What, finally, was the result of it all? To answer that question would require an article in itself but perhaps three broad generalisations might be hazarded. In the seventeenth century, although not before, the new extra-European markets and the new draperies were to be of great importance to this country, and in that way the depressions may be said to have given a stimulus to economic progress. By the end of the sixteenth century the London export trade was almost entirely in the hands of English merchants and in that fact may perhaps be seen one of the fruits of economic nationalism. During the last quarter of the century the general trend of the cloth trade showed a remarkable stability.[65] Partly, no doubt, that was due to the war with Spain. But it may also

[61] Rich, op. cit. 30-1, 87 et. seq.  [62] S.P.D., Elizabeth, XLII, no. 49.
[63] Ibid. XCIX, nos. 8 and 9.
[64] Deardorff, English Trade to the Baltic during the Reign of Elizabeth, 258.
[65] Scott (English Joint Stock Companies to 1720, I, chap. v) argues that the period 1587-1603 was one of depression. In the export trade, however, that depression showed itself in the form not of a downward trend but of wider fluctuations around a fairly stable average.

be attributed in part to the regulations which had been expressly
designed to preserve stability and to prevent rapid growth.  Certainly
that was the explanation favoured by contemporaries, for as the years
passed and commerce failed to expand there arose a free trade agitation
which reached its climax in the May of 1604 when the Commons passed
two bills for greater freedom of trade.[66]  That vote did not mean that
men had changed their views on economic causation, for the relation
between freedom and commercial expansion was a truism to the Tudors.
What had changed had been men's scale of values.  By the end of the
sixteenth century the stability that had seemed so desirable a generation
earlier had been found irksome; as conditions for trade expansion once
more came into being the feeling against such expansion declined; and
the uprooting of those vested interests that had grown behind the
restrictions of the great depression became one of the major tasks of
the seventeenth century.

[66] *Commons Journal*, I, 218.

# THE RISE OF THE GENTRY, 1558-1640 [1]

## R. H. TAWNEY

THE first French translator[2] of Locke's *Thoughts on Education* introduced it with the remark that foreign readers, in order to appreciate it, must remember the audience to whom it was addressed. It was composed, he explained, for the edification of an element in society to which the Continent offered no exact analogy, but which had become in the last century the dominant force in English life. To M. Coste, in 1695, the triumphant ascent of the English gentry —neither a *noblesse*, nor a bureaucracy, but mere *bons bourgeois*— seemed proof of an insular dynamic of which France, with the aid of his translation, would do well to learn the secret. His compatriots, a century-and-a-half later, hailed the effortless survival of the same class in an age which had seen *seigneurs* in flight from their castles, and even *junkers* cajoled into some semblance of concessions, as an example of social stability as eccentric as it was admirable, and marvelled at the depth to which the tree had struck its roots. De Tocqueville in the 'forties, de Lavergne in the 'fifties, Taine in the 'sixties and 'seventies, wrote in a mood of reaction; but they had some excuse for opening their eyes.[3] In spite of the influx in the interval of Scots, Nabobs, some merchants, a few bankers, and an occasional industrialist, not less than one in every eight of the members sitting for English and Welsh seats in the last un-reformed House of Commons, and one in five of the House of Lords, belonged to families which, two centuries before, had given representatives to the House of Commons in the Long Parliament.[4] Ten English counties had been blessed in 1640 with some sixty-two leading landowners, masters of six or more manors apiece. Of

---

[1] The omission of some references, which should have been inserted, and the incompleteness of some others, require an apology. They are due to circumstances which, since the article was written, have made it difficult to consult some of the sources used.

[2] Pierre Coste, *De l'éducation des enfants* (1695).

[3] de Tocqueville, *L'ancien régime* (trans. by H. Reeves), 15, 72, 77, 85; L. de Lavergne, *The Rural Economy of England, Scotland and Ireland* (trans. 1855), chaps. ix and x; H. Taine, *Notes sur l'Angleterre* (1872).

[4] *Official Return of Members of the House of Commons* (1878). Mr J. R. McCormack has called my attention to the remarks to the same effect made by a well-known author in the 'sixties of the last century. In an article entitled " The Long Parliament and the Reformed Parliament of 1869 " (*Notes and Queries*, 4th ser., III (27 Feb., 1869), 189-90), Samuel Smiles commented on the " hereditary influence of the English gentry in the present Parliament ", and printed by way of illustration a list of fifty members of the House of Commons of 1869, " being, as far as can be ascertained, direct lineal descendants of those who sat in the Long Parliament in 1640 ".

those in the whole ten one-half, of those in five just under two-thirds, had descendants or kin who owned 3,000 acres or upwards in 1874.[5]

## I

The political rôle of this tenacious class has not lacked its eulogists. It has itself, however, a history, which is not only political, but also economic; and the decisive period of that history is the two generations before the Civil War. " Could humanity ever attain happiness," wrote Hume of that momentous half-century, " the condition of the English gentry at this period might merit that appellation." Contemporary opinion, if more conscious of the casualties of progress, would have been disposed, nevertheless, to endorse his verdict. Observers became conscious, in the later years of Elizabeth, of an alteration in the balance of social forces, and a stream of comment began which continued to swell, until, towards the close of the next century, a new equilibrium was seen to have been reached. Its theme was the changing composition, at once erosion and reconstruction, of the upper strata of the social pyramid. It was, in particular, since their preponderance was not yet axiomatic, the increase in the wealth and influence of certain intermediate groups, compared with the nobility, the Crown and the mass of small landholders. Of those groups the most important, " situated ", as one of its most brilliant members wrote, " neither in the lowest grounds . . . nor in the highest mountains . . . but in the valleys between both ",[6] was the squirearchy and its connections.

Holding a position determined, not by legal distinctions, but by common estimation; kept few[7] and tough by the ruthlessness of the English family system, which sacrificed the individual to the institution, and, if it did not drown all the kittens but one, threw all but one into the water; pouring the martyrs of that prudent egotism, their younger sons, not only into the learned professions, but into armies, English and foreign, exploration and colonisation, and every branch of business enterprise; barred themselves by no rule as to *dérogeance* from supplementing their incomes from whatever source they pleased, yet never, as

---

[5] The counties concerned are Hertfordshire, Bedfordshire, Buckinghamshire, Surrey, Hampshire, North Riding of Yorkshire, Worcestershire, Gloucestershire, Warwickshire, Northamptonshire. The facts for the first seven in 1640 are taken from the lists of manors and their owners given in the *V.C.H.*, and for the last three from Sir R. Atkyns, *The ancient and present state of Gloucestershire;* Dugdale, *Antiquities of Warwickshire;* J. Bridges, *History and Antiquities of Northamptonshire.* Those for 1874 are taken from John Bateman, *The Acreocracy of England, a list of all owners of three thousand acres and upwards . . . from the Modern Domesday Book.*

[6] Sir W. Raleigh, *Concerning the Causes of the Magnificency and Opulency of Cities.*

[7] Thomas Wilson, *The State of England Anno Dom. 1600* (ed. F. J. Fisher, Camden Miscellanea, XVI, 1936), 23, put the number of gentlemen at " 16,000 or thereabouts ", plus some 500 knights. For the purpose of this article, no distinction is drawn between knights and gentry.

in Holland, wholly severed from their rural roots, the English gentry combined the local and popular attachments essential for a representative rôle with the aristocratic aroma of *nobiles minores,* and played each card in turn with tactful, but remorseless, realism. Satirists [8] made merry with the homely dialect, strong liquor and horse-coping of the provincial squire; but, in spite of the Slenders and Shallows, the mere bumpkins of the class, for whom the French invented a special name, were not too distressingly conspicuous. Its failures, instead of, as on the Continent, hanging around its neck and helping to sink it, discreetly disappeared with the disappearance of their incomes. Its successes supplied the materials for a new nobility. They provided more than one.

Inconsistencies were inevitable in speaking of a class freely recruited from below, in a society where the lines of social stratification were drawn, not, as in most parts of the Continent, by birth and legal privilege, but by gradations of wealth. The elasticity which such peculiarities conferred has often been applauded, but they were not favourable to precise classifications; nor was precision in demand. There were moments, it is true, when it was convenient to stand on an hereditary dignity, authentic or assumed; did not the arch-leveller of the age, freeborn John himself, win one of the earliest of his famous collection of judicial scalps by refusing to plead to an indictment drawn against " John Lilburne, yeoman "? [9] There were voices from the past which, when the crash came, hailed the fall of the monarchy as the inevitable nemesis of a general downward slide towards the abyss of social " parity ", and reproached the professional custodians of traditional proprieties with opening to fees doors which a prudent rigour would have locked. [10] But agricultural, commercial and industrial interests were, in most parts of the country, inextricably intertwined. Mere caste had few admirers—fewer probably among the gentry militant of the early seventeenth century than among the gentry triumphant of the early eighteenth—and that note was rarely heard. Common sense endorsed the remark that " gentility is nothing but ancient riches ", [11] adding under his breath that they need not be very ancient. Sir Thomas Smith had said that a gentleman is a man who spends his money like a gentleman. [12] Of the

[8] Samuel Butler, *Characters and Passages from Notebooks,* ed. A. R. Waller, and J. Earle, *Micro-Cosmographie* (1628). See G. Davies, *The Early Stuarts, 1603-1660,* 264-272.

[9] *The Examination and Confession of Captain Lilbourne* (Brit. Mus. E.130/33). I owe this reference to Miss P. Gregg.

[10] See, for the tendency towards a " parity ", Sir Edward Walker, *Historical Discourses upon Several Occasions* (1705), and, for the laxity of heralds, the same writer's *Observations upon the Inconveniences that have attended the frequent Promotions to Titles of Honour and Dignity since King James came to the Crown of England* (1653).

[11] *Hist. MSS. Comm., MSS. of the Duke of Portland,* IX, 5.

[12] *De Republica Anglorum* (ed. L. Alston, 1906), 39-40, " and, to be shorte who can live idly and without manuall labour, and will bear the port, charge and countenance of a gentleman, he shall be . . . taken for a gentleman ".

theorists rash enough to attempt a definition, few succeeded in improving on that wise tautology.

In spite, nevertheless, of ambiguities, the group concerned was not difficult to identify. Its members varied widely in wealth;[13] but, though ragged at its edges, it had a solid core. That core consisted of the landed proprietors, above the yeomanry, and below the peerage, together with a growing body of well-to-do farmers, sometimes tenants of their relatives, who had succeeded the humble peasants of the past as lessees of demesne farms; professional men, also rapidly increasing in number, such as the more eminent lawyers, divines, and an occasional medical practitioner; and the wealthier merchants, who, if not, as many were, themselves sons of landed families, had received a similar education, moved in the same circles, and in England, unlike France, were commonly recognised to be socially indistinguishable from them. It was this upper layer of commoners, heterogeneous, but compact, whose rapid rise in wealth and power most impressed contemporaries. Literature celebrated its triumphs. Travelled intellectuals sought to polish its crudities. Manuals[14] written for its edification laid the foundations of a flattering legend. Education, the professions, the arts, above all, architecture, reflected its influence. Nor were there wanting observers who discerned in a changing social order the herald of a new state.

Interpretations of the political breakdown of the age, of a kind which today would be called sociological, have commonly received short shrift from historians. The tougher breed which experienced it has some right to an opinion. It was disposed to take them seriously. Once thought has been stirred by a crisis, the attempt to pierce behind controversial externals to the hidden springs of the movement is in all periods common form. The influence in the second half of the century of doctrines which sought one of the dynamics of revolution in antecedent economic change is not, therefore, surprising. But the disturbance of the social equilibrium had excited the curiosity of a generation which could only guess at its political repercussions. Theories canvassed in the 'fifties in the Rota Club had faint fragmentary anticipations before Harrington had started on his travels, and when Neville was still a schoolboy.

The facts were plain enough. The ruin of famous families by personal extravagance and political ineptitude; the decline in the position of the yeomanry towards the turn of the century, when long

[13] Thomas Wilson, op. cit. 23-4, gives £650-£1,000 a year as the income of a gentleman in London and the home counties, and £300-£400 as the figure for the remoter provinces. He describes knights as men of £1,000-£2,000 a year, but cites some with incomes of £5,000-£7,000.

[14] E.g. H. Peacham, The Complete Gentleman (1622); R. Braithwaite, The English Gentleman (1633).

leases fell in; the loss, not only of revenue, but of authority, by the monarchy, as Crown lands melted; the mounting fortunes of the residuary legatee, a gentry whose aggregate income was put even in 1600 at some three times that of peers, bishops, deans and chapters, and richer yeomen together, and who steadily gathered into their hands estates slipping from the grasp of peasant, nobility, Church and Crown alike—such movements and their consequences were visible to all. Not only a precocious economist like Thomas Wilson the younger, the nephew of Elizabeth's Secretary of State, but men of greater eminence; Bacon; Cranfield; Selden; the shifty, but not unintelligent, Goodman; those artists in crying stinking fish, the Venetian embassy in London; Coke, most amiable and most futile of secretaries of state, who begs Buckingham, of all people, to save Crown lands from the spoiler—wrote footnotes on the same theme.[15]

The man who saw deepest into the moral of it all was primarily neither a theorist nor a politician, though he had the gifts of both. He was a great man of action, perhaps the greatest of his age. The doctrine that political stability depends on the maintenance of that Balance of Property, which was later to become a term of art, was not, in essence, novel. It was implicit in the conception of society as an organism, requiring the maintenance of a due proportion between its different members, which was part of the medieval legacy. But it is one thing to repeat a formula, another to apply it. Raleigh's dialogue, composed, it seems, in 1615, just after the central crisis of James' reign, was the first attempt to state the relevance of that conception to the changing circumstances of his day, and to deduce from it the need, not for mere conservatism, but for reform. The argument with which his country gentlemen confutes the noble parasite is no abstract disquisition on constitutional formalities. It is a deduction from social history. The centre of social gravity has shifted; political power is shifting with it. The Earl who could once put a thousand horse into the field cannot now put twenty-five; if the greatest lord lifts a finger, he will be locked up by the next constable. The commons today command most of the wealth, and all the weapons. It is they, not the heirs of the feudal past, who hold the keys of the future. It is with them; with their natural leaders, the gentry; with the House of Commons, which is their organ, that the monarchy, if it is wise, will hasten to make its peace.[16]

[15] Thomas Wilson, *op. cit.* 18-24; Bacon, " Certain Observations upon a libel published this present year 1592 " in *Works* (Bohn edn.), I, 385; Dr G. Goodman, *The Court of King James I*, ed. J. Brewer, I, 311, 290-1, 322-3; Selden, *Table Talk*, under " Land " (see also under " Knight Service "); *Calendar S.P., Venice, 1603-1607*, no. 729, *1617-1619*, no. 658, *1621-1623*, no. 603, *1629-1632*, no. 374; *Hist. MSS. Comm., MSS. of the Earl of Cowper*, I, 129.

[16] *The Works of Sir Walter Raleigh, Knt.*, ed. by Thomas Birch (1751), I, 9 (where the metaphor of a scales is used) and 206-7.

## II

These hints of political deductions from the fact of social change must not now detain us. In considering the character of that change itself, the right point of departure is that which Raleigh suggests. To speak of the transition from a feudal to a bourgeois society is to decline upon a *cliché*. But a process difficult to epitomise in less hackneyed terms has left deep marks on the social systems of most parts of Europe. What a contemporary described in 1600 as the conversion of "a gentry addicted to war" into "good husbands", who "know as well how to improve their lands to the uttermost as the farmer or countryman",[17] may reasonably be regarded as an insular species of the same genus.

It was a precocious species, which later, when its survival was assured, was to be the admiration of foreigners, but which for long found few imitators; nor was it accomplished without anguish. The movement passed through the three familiar stages of breakdown, reconstruction and stabilisation. If one aspect of the first phase consisted in the political and legal reforms[18] by which the Tudor State consolidated its power, another aspect was economic. Jolted sharply by the great depreciation; then squeezed by its masters to find the means for new styles in fashion and display; then pulled by expanding markets, when expedients adopted to stave off catastrophe were discovered, once systematised, to pay dividends beyond hope, agrarian society was everywhere under strain. The ability of nature to cause confusion with her silver is greatly inferior, we now know, to that of human art; and, in view of the dimensions of the movement, the lamentations provoked by it seem today overdone. But, in judging the effects of this most unrevolutionary of monetary revolutions, three truisms must be remembered. It broke on a world which had known within living memory something like a currency famine. The society which experienced it was crossed by lines of petrification, which make modern rigidities seem elastic. Except for brief intervals, the movement was continuous, on the Continent for some three generations, in England for nearly four. The wave of rising prices struck the dyke of customary obligations, static burdens, customary dues; rebounded; struck again; and then either broke it, or carved new channels which turned its flank.

More than one country had known a dreadful interlude, when anarchy was not remote. In most it was discovered, when the worst was over, that the land system which came out of the crisis was not that which had gone into it. The key, as usual, was finance. The items comprising the landowner's revenue change their relative importance.

---

[17] Thomas Wilson, *op. cit.* 18.
[18] See the admirable article by Miss Helen M. Cam, "The Decline and Fall of English Feudalism" in *History*, XXV (Dec. 1940), and *Transactions of the Royal Historical Society* (N.S.), XX, R. R. Reid, "The Rebellion in the North, 1569".

The value of all customary and non-commercial payments tumbles down;[19] that of the more elastic sources of income increases. Some groups can adapt themselves to the new tensions and opportunities; others cannot. The former rise; the latter sink. Examples of both are to be found in every stratum of society. There are grounds, nevertheless, for thinking that what Professor Bloch has called *la crise des fortunes seigneuriales*[20] was felt more acutely, and surmounted with greater difficulty, by the heirs of ancient wealth, with its complex and dispersed interests, and large public responsibilities, than by men of humbler position or more recent eminence. Contemporaries noted the turn of the wheel in their superb prose. " How many noble families have there been whose memory is utterly abolished! How many flourishing houses have we seen which oblivion hath now obfuscated . . . ! Time doth diminish and consume all."[21] But time was not the chief destroyer.

Such a family, inheriting great estates, often inherited trouble. Its standards of expenditure were those of one age, its income that of another. " Port "—the display becoming in a great position—was a point of honour; who would wish to be thought, like Lord Dencourt, to " live like a hog "?[22]   " What by reason ", wrote a close observer, " of their magnificence and waste in expense, and what by reason of a desire to advance and make great their own families ",[23] the life of a considerable part of the aristocracy was apt to offer an example of what a modern economist has called " conspicuous waste ". Other regalities might have gone; what remained, and, indeed, increased, was a regal ostentation. The overheads of the noble landowner—a great establishment, and often more than one; troops of servants and retainers; stables fit for a regiment of cavalry; endless hospitality to neighbours and national notabilities; visits to court, at once ruinous and unavoidable; litigation descending, like an heirloom, from generation to generation —had always been enormous. Now, on the top of these traditional liabilities, came the demands of a new world of luxury and fashion.

---

[19] For the fall in the value of one item, profits of Courts, see *Cottoni Posthuma* (1651 edn.), 180, where it is stated that on Crown estates " the casual profits of courts never paid to the present officers their fees and expenses ", and that in 44 Eliz. the costs of collection exceeded the receipts by £8,000. For a similar condition on a private property, see *Bedford MSS.*, " Answere to my L. Treasurer's demands, and what may growe to the payment of my late lordes debts ", 20 April 1586, " the profyttes of Courtes will not be much moare than to answer the stuerdes and officers' fees, and in some places the same will not be discharged with their profyttes ". I am indebted to Miss G. Scott Thomson for a transcript of this document.

[20] M. Bloch, *Les Caractères Originaux de l'histoire rurale française*, 117, 127 *et seq.*

[21] *Harleian Miscellany*, II, 515 *et seq.*, " The Mirror of Worldly Fame ", 1603, chap iii.

[22] Clarendon, *History of the Rebellion*, VI, 58.

[23] Bacon, " Of the True Greatness of the Kingdom of Britain ", in *Works* (Bohn edn.), I, 507.

With the fortunes resulting from inflation and booming trade all stand-ards are rising. London, rapidly advancing in financial and commer-cial importance, with a Court that under James is a lottery of unearned fortunes, exercises a stronger pull. Town houses increase in number; visits to the capital are spun out; residential quarters are developed; to the delight of dressmakers, something like a season begins to emerge. Culture has demands to which homage must be paid. New and more costly styles of building; the maintenance of a troop of needy scholars and poets; collections of pictures; here and there—an extreme case—the avenues of posturing nudities which Bacon saluted at Arundel with ironical dismay—"the resurrection of the dead!"[24]—all have their votaries. Public duties, in some cases, complete what private prodigality has begun. They yielded some pickings; but, under Elizabeth and her two successors, more than one bearer of a famous name was brought near to ruin by the crowning catastrophe of a useful career.

So towering a superstructure required broad foundations. Too often they were lacking. The wealth of some of the nobility, and especially of the older families, was not infrequently more spectacular than sub-stantial. It was locked up in frozen assets—immobilised in sumptuous appurtenances, at once splendid and unrealisable. More important, the whole structure and organisation of their estates was often of a kind, which, once a pillar of the social system, was now obsolescent. Side by side with more lucrative possessions, their properties included majestic, but unremunerative, franchises—hundreds, boroughs, fairs and markets; a multitude of knights' fees, all honour and no profit; free-holds created in an age when falling, not rising, prices had been the great landowners' problem, and fixed rents were an insurance; hundreds of prickly copy-holds, whose occupants pocketed an unearned increment while the real income of their landlord fell. What was the use, a disconsolate peer expostulated with the Queen, of pretending to relieve his necessities by the gift of a manor whose tenants were protected by law against an increase in rents, and by custom against an increase in fines?[25] That cheerless condition was to be expected in properties which Elizabeth thought suitable for presents; but it was not, unfortunately, confined to them. The administrative machine which controlled a great estate had some of the vices of a miniature state department. It was cumbrous, conservative, difficult to divert from its traditional routine to new and speculative enterprises. The very magnitude and wide dispersion of the interests concerned—property of a dozen different kinds in a dozen different counties—made drastic reconstruction a formidable business, which it needed an exceptional personality to force through. It is not

[24] L. Aikin, *Memoirs of Court of King James I*, 300.
[25] *Bedford MSS.*, " Reasons to move her Mat gracious consideration towards the Erle of Bedf.", February 1579. I am indebted to Miss G. Scott Thomson for a trans-cript of this document.

surprising that inherited opulence should sometimes have lacked the initiative to launch it.

Such difficulties confronted all conservative landowners, both peers and commoners, in proportion to the magnitude of their commitments and the rigidity of their incomes.  The most that can be said is that the former usually carried more sail than the latter, and found it, when the wind changed, more difficult to tack.  Mere majestic inertia, however, was an expensive luxury.  As the tension tightened, something had to go.  What went first was an aspect of life once of the first importance, but to which justice today is not easily done.  The words "hospitality" or "house-keeping", its ordinary designation, were the description, not of a personal trait or a private habit, but of a semi-public institution, whose political dangers, once a menace to the State, were a thing of the past, but whose social significance had survived little abated.  As the centre of a system of relations offering employment, succour, a humble, but recognised, niche to men helpless in isolation, the great household had performed somewhat the same rôle as was played, till yesterday, by the informal communism of the family system in China, and its break-up was attended by the same symptoms of disintegration as have followed in the Far East the shattering of ancient social *cadres* by western industrialism.  The stream of lamentations voiced by popular opinion, conservative moralists, and the Government itself, all strike the same note.  Their burden is that, as expenses are cut down, staffs reduced, and household economy put on a business footing, a cell of the social organism is ceasing to function.  The plight of younger brothers, put off, like Orlando "with the stalling of an ox", or compelled—to the public advantage, but to their own exasperation—to take "to letters or to arms",[26] is a footnote to the same story; it is not a chance that attacks on primogeniture become more vocal at the moment when once prosperous families are feeling the pinch.  The social dislocation, if exaggerated, was not a trifle; but the relief to the landowner was not proportionate to it.  Since his real income, in default of other measures, continued to decline, it was, at best, only a respite.

The materials for generalisation have hardly yet been put together; but to say that many noble families—though not they alone—encountered, in the two generations before the Civil War, a financial crisis is probably not an over-statement.  The fate of the conservative aristocrat was, in fact, an unhappy one.  Reduced to living "like a rich beggar, in perpetual want",[27] he sees his influence, popularity and property all melt together.  Some, like Lord Howard of Effingham and the Earl of Sussex, part with their estates to their creditors, or sell out-lying portions to save the remainder.  Some resort to half-obsolete claims on their tenants, with which, as a Lancashire landlord remarked,

[26] Thomas Wilson, *op. cit.* 24.
[27] *Hist. MSS. Comm., MSS. of Duke of Portland,* IX, 5.

the victims comply, "if not for love, then for fear"[28] claims resembling, in their pedantic and exasperating legality, those most criticised
in the Crown, but which—so merciful is history to the victors—are
commonly ignored in the case of private landlords. Some, like the
Berkeleys, do both. The sixth Earl,[29] for whom his admiring biographer
—a lover of honorific titles—could find no more appropriate name than
Lord Henry the Harmless, combined with the style and establishment
of a medieval potentate the sporting tastes of a country gentleman;
periodical plunges into the world of fashion in London; the maintenance
of a *salon* as a concession to culture; and an heirloom in the shape of a
lawsuit, which, when he inherited it, had already lasted a century, and
which, in 1609, four years before his death, he steered at last, with cries
of self-congratulation, to a disastrous victory. While continuing to
manage his Gloucestershire estates with a conservatism as agreeable to
his tenants as it was fatal to himself, he sinks ever deeper into debt to
tradesmen, to scriveners, to merchant-bankers; sells land outside the
county to the value of £60,000; and ends his life in a maze of financial
expedients, charged with a slightly exotic odour, as of the Seine rather
than the Severn—collecting an aid from his free-holders to knight his
eldest son, releasing his customary tenants from irksome obligations that
had elsewhere long vanished, and raising a benevolence to pay for the
ruinous results of his triumphs as a litigant. Other landowners again
—Lord Compton, Lord Noel, Lord Willoughby, the Earl of Holderness
—restore their fortunes by marrying City money.[30] Others, with a pull
in the right quarter, plant themselves on the preposterous pension list
of the Crown, angle—an odious business—for "concealed lands", or
intrigue, with a kind of amateurish greed, for patents and monopolies.

Whether their embarrassments were increasing it is impossible to
say; some debts, it is fair to remember, represented reproductive expenditure on development and improvements. But soundings, wherever
taken, show much water in the hold. The correspondence of Burleigh,[31]
in the last decade of Elizabeth, reads like the report of a receiver in
bankruptcy to the nobility and gentry. A few years later, when, with

---

[28] *Chetham Miscellany,* III, 6-7, "Some Instructions given by William Booth to his
stewards . . .".

[29] John Smyth, *Lives of the Berkeleys,* II, 265-417, and Smyth Papers in the Gloucester Public Libary.

[30] Lord Compton married the daughter of Sir John Spencer, Lord Mayor in 1594, who
died worth £300,000 (some said £800,000), Goodman, *op. cit.* II, 127-32; Lord Noel a
daughter of Sir Baptist Hicks, mercer, *Court and Times of Charles I,* II, 355; Lord
Willoughby a daughter of Alderman Cockayne, "who brought him £10,000 in money
. . . £1,000 a year pension out of the Exchequer, and a house very richly furnished",
*ibid.* II, 220; the Earl of Holderness another daughter of Cockayne, with £10,000 as
portion, *Calendar S.P.D., James I,* 1623-1625, CLXX, 54.

[31] See *Hist. MSS. Comm., MSS of the Marquis of Salisbury, passim.* Some references
to the indebtedness of the nobility will be found in Thomas Wilson, *A Discourse Upon
Usury,* Introduction, 31-42.

the opening of the great boom which began in 1606, things should have been better, Cranfield, no financial leviathan, had a score of them in his books, while, to judge by stray references, Hicks the silk-man and banker—later Lord Campden—and Herriott, the goldsmith, may well have had more. Rubens, no stranger to the costly futilities of courts, still retained sufficient naïveté to lift his eyebrows at the orgy of extravagance and peculation—"business, public and private, sold cash down, over the counter "[32]—which distinguished that of James. Clarendon's[33] account of the notabilities of his day is a catalogue of splendid spendthrifts. When, in 1642, all went into the melting-pot, the debts owed to the City by Royalists alone were put, in a financial memorandum, at not less than £2,000,000.[34] Of the commercial magnates who, a few years later, scrambled for confiscated estates, not a few, as Dr Chesney[35] has shown, were creditors entering on properties long mortgaged to them. It was discovered, not for the last time, that as a method of foreclosure war was cheaper than litigation.

## III

For, if the new world had its victims, it had also its conquerors. That "the wanton bringing up and ignorance of the nobility force the prince to advance new men that can serve, which . . . subvert the noble houses to have their rooms themselves ",[36] had been noted with uneasiness in the early years of Elizabeth, when suggestions were considered for redressing the balance. Half a century later, the consequences of the movement were visible to all, and there could be no question of reversing it. "The age was one ", writes Miss Wake in her account of Northamptonshire under James, "which had recently seen the rise of the solid middle class of lesser landowning gentry on the ruins of the ancient aristocracy. The families were few which . . . managed to survive the turbulent end of the middle ages. . . . Many of the knights and squires belonging to families of local and extraneous origin who had made money early in the previous century by the law, trade, or sheepfarming."[37] That picture is true of more counties than one. The conditions which depressed some incomes inflated others; and, while one group of landowners bumped heavily along the bottom, another, which was quicker to catch the tide when it turned, was floated to

---

[32] Max Roose et Ch. Ruelens, *Correspondence de Rubens et Documents Epistolaires,* V. 116, ". . . molti altri, signori e ministri . . . sono sforzati a buscarsi la vita come possono, e per cio qui si vendono gli negoci publici e privati a dinari contanti ".
[33] E.g. *History of the Rebellion,* I, 131-6, 115-26, 131, 167, 170; III, 27, 93, 95, 283.
[34] S.P.D., Charles I, CCCCXCVII, no. 59, March 1642-3.
[35] H. E. Chesney, " The transference of lands in England, 1640-60 " in *Transactions of the Royal Historical Society,* 4th ser., XV, 181-210.
[36] *Hist. MSS. Comm., MSS of the Marquis of Salisbury,* I, 162-5.
[37] *The Montagu Musters Book, 1602-1623,* ed. by Joan Wake (VII of the Publications of the Northamptonshire Record Soc.), Introduction, pp. xiv-xv.

fortune. The process of readjustment was complex; but two broad movements can be observed, affecting respectively the technique of land-management and the ownership of landed property.

While the crisis of depreciation was not confined to one country, the English response to it had a character of its own. Partly for economic reasons, partly owing to the political and military conditions of a frontier region, parts of eastern Europe had met the emergency by a servile reaction which gave villeinage a new life. In East Prussia, in particular, the great estate, half farm, half fortress, swollen by the holdings of evicted peasants, and worked by its owner with the aid of *corvées*, became the dominant institution, against which the reforming monarchy, when it took the matter up—not to mention its successors—would for long struggle in vain. France had felt the same tightening of the screw, but the French escape from the *impasse*—if it was an escape—took the opposite direction. Precluded by law from evicting the *censitaires*—the customary tenants—French landowners had been thrown back on the policy of a more remorseless exaction of customary dues, of which the last desperate gamble, when the clock had almost struck, was to be denounced under the name of the feudal reaction, but which in fact, other avenues being blocked, had gone on piecemeal for centuries. In England, as elsewhere, it was necessary for landlords, if ruin was to be averted, to play to the score; but the tune called by English conditions was neither the despotism of the *Junker* nor the half-abdication of the *Seigneur*. English agriculture had as its setting a commercial, increasingly individualistic society, in process of an industrialisation that was more than merely local. Landowners learned—when they did learn—from their environment, and cured their wounds with a hair of the dog that bit them. Fixed incomes falling, and profits rising, who could question that the way of salvation was to contract interests as a *rentier*, and expand them as an entrepreneur? The experts, at any rate, felt no doubts on the subject. Business is booming. They cry with one accord, " Go into business and prosper ".

Business methods and modernisation, the fashionable specific, have different meanings in different ages. The stage at which matters stood under the early Stuarts was that, not of crops and rotations, but of marketing, management, tenures, the arrangement of holdings, and reclamation. If modern analogies are sought, they are to be found in the sphere, not of cultivation and breeding, but of rationalising the administration of estates and improving their lay-out. The problem was, in the first place, a financial one. Certain sources of income were drying up; a substitute must be found for them. Several lines of attack were possible, but the most characteristic were four. First, customary payments dwindling, the landlord could revise the terms on which his property was held, get rid of the unprofitable copyholders when lives ran out, buy out small freeholders, and throw the land so secured into larger farms to be let on lease. Rent at this period is an ambiguous category; but leasehold rents were certainly rising—on the view of Thorold Rogers[38] six-fold in half a century, on the estimate of a contemporary[39] five-fold in rather less, on the evidence of some estate documents about three- to four-fold. Second, instead of, or in addition to, letting, he could expand his own business activities, run his home-farm, not to supply his household, but as a commercial concern, enlarge his demesnes, and enclose for the purpose of carrying more stock or increasing his output of grain. Third, if he had the means, he could invest capital in bringing new land into cultivation, clearing woodlands, breaking up waste, draining marshes. Finally, he could supplement his agricultural income by other types of enterprise, going into the timber trade, exploiting coal, iron and lead, speculating in urban ground-rents. Naturally, none of these departures was without abundant precedents. Naturally, again, the particular policy, or combination of policies, adopted depended both on local circumstances and on individual resources. But the tendency of all was the same. In each case, whatever the particular expedient used, the emphasis of the up-to-date landowner is increasingly thrown on the business side of land-management. He relies for his income on the rents or profits derived from it.

The situation confronting the landed classes in the half-century before the Civil War resembled in miniature that of 1850-70. Not only were prices rising, but, with the progress of internal unification, the development of specialised semi-industrial areas, and the growth of urban markets, demand was expanding. The advice to put estate management on a business footing was, in such circumstances, sound; but not everyone could take it, and not all who could would. Then, as now, rationalisation might look easy on paper but was, in fact, no simple matter. Then, as now, therefore, what appeared at first sight a mere pedestrian improvement in methods of administration set in motion, as it developed, subtle social changes. It was to be expected that men with the resources and ambition to play the part of pioneers should gain at the expense of groups, whether below them or above, less qualified by means and traditions to adapt themselves to a new climate. The well-to-do yeoman, the *kulak* of the day, might maintain, or even improve, his position; but the extension of demesne farms, the upward movement of rents and fines, and encroachments on commons, combined in parts of the country to tilt the scales against the humbler peasants. To that chapter of the story, whose local diversities still remain to be worked out, but of which the outlines are known, must be added another, of which historians have said less, but by which contemporaries were impressed. There was a struggle for survival, not only between large landowners and small, but between different categories among the former.

[38] Thomas Rogers, *A History of Agriculture and Prices*, V, 812.
[39] *Harleian Miscellany*, III, 552 *et seq.*, "The present state of England" by Walter Carey, 1627.

It was primarily a struggle between economies of different types, which corresponded more closely with regional peculiarities than with social divisions. There are plenty of gentry who stagnate or go down hill. It would be easy to find noble landowners who move with the times, and make the most of their properties; the sheep-farming of Lord Spencer; the enclosures of Lords Brudenell, Huntingdon and Saye and Sele; the coal-mines of the Earl of Northumberland and the Earl of Wemyss; above all the grandiose reconstruction carried through by the Russells, are cases in point. The smaller the part, nevertheless, played by passive property, as compared with active enterprise, the larger the opportunities of rising; and the increased rewards to be reaped by the improving landlord favoured classes still ascending the ladder compared with those already at the summit. The charms of established wealth might be represented by an Earl of Newcastle, with a rent-roll of £22,000, or an Earl of Pembroke, with the ninety-three manors, four boroughs and estates scattered over ten counties from Middlesex to Yorkshire, which gave him, at his death in 1630, the reputation of one of the richest peers in England.[40] But, when experiment and innovation were the order of the day, the cards were in other hands. They were all on the side of the enterprising country gentleman.

Professor Kosminsky has described the owners of "small and medium-sized estates" in the thirteenth century as "all people less intimately involved in the economic system of feudalism, and early subject to capitalist transformation".[41] It is the representatives of much the same indeterminate middle class, with interests large enough to offer a secure base for manoeuvre, but not so large as to be top-heavy, who, three centuries later, are quickest, when the wind shifts, to trim their sails. Such a man was not tempted by great possessions into the somnolence of the *rentier*; was less loaded than most noble landowners with heavy overhead charges in the shape of great establishments; did his work for himself, instead of relying on a cumbrous machine to do it for him; owned, in short, his property, instead of being owned by it. Usually, unless one of the minority of active administrators, he was freer from public duties in his county, and more immune to the blandishments of London. The problem confronting him, if he undertook reconstruction or development, was of manageable dimensions. It demanded practical experience of farming, common sense, attention to detail, not the rarer gifts of the business strategist.

Under the pressure of an environment in motion, several types emerge. Some strike no roots; others survive and become fixed. There

---

[40] Marg. Duchess of Newcastle, *Life of the Duke of Newcastle* (Everyman edn.), 98-100; *Abstract of Wilts Inquis. p/m.*, 97-101; Clarendon, *History of the Rebellion*, I, 120-6.

[41] E. A. Kosminsky, "Services and Money Rents in the Thirteenth Century" in *The Economic History Review*, V, no. 2, April 1935.

is the gentleman farmer, leasing land, till he makes money, without owning it, and not infrequently—since the thing is his profession—running several farms at once. There is the man who works his land as a commercial undertaking—a John Toke in Kent, buying Welsh and Scottish runts to finish on Romney marsh for the London market; a Robert Loder in Berkshire, all piety and profits; a Sir Thomas Tresham in Northamptonshire, selling everything, from rabbits supplied on contract to a poulterer in Gracechurch Street to wool to the value of £1,000 a year, whose dual rôle as a leader of the Catholic cause in England and the most hated encloser in his much disturbed county is a point on the side of those who dismiss as a mare's nest the alleged affinities of economic and religious radicalism; a Sir John Wynn in North Wales, cattle breeder, tribal chieftain, land-grabber, scholar, and prospector for minerals unknown to science, with the vanity of a savage and the credulity of his beloved alchemists, whose dealings with his tenants were too much for his own class, and cost him his seat on the Council of Wales. There are families like the Pelhams and Twysdens, living mainly on rents, but doing on the side a useful trade in grain, hops, wool and iron in local markets and in London.[42]    Each type has its own idiosyncrasies, but none is in land for its health.    All watch markets closely; buy and sell in bulk; compare the costs and yields of different crops; charge the rent, when custom allows, which a farm will stand; keep careful accounts. Mr Fussell's[43] description of one of them—" before all things a business man "—is true of all.

It was agricultural capitalists of this type who were making the pace, and to whom the future belonged.    Nor, if land supplied the base from which they started, were their interests confined to it.    The lament that " it is impossible for the mere country gentleman ever to grow rich or raise his house, he must have some other profession ",[44] was uttered at a moment when pessimism was pardonable, and was too pessimistic.    It is true, however, that many of the class, whether of necessity or by choice, were up to the eyes in other branches of business.    Naturally, they turned first to the industries native to their own districts—iron in Sussex and the Forest of Dean; tin in Cornwall; lead in Derbyshire and North Wales; coal in Nottinghamshire, Durham and Northumberland; textiles in a dozen counties.    But their business connections were not merely local.    The habit of investment was spreading rapidly among the upper

    [42] The Account-book of a Kentish Estate, 1616-1704, ed. by Eleanor C. Lodge (1927); Robert Loder's Farm-Accounts, ed. G. E. Fussell (Camden Soc.); Brit. Mus. Add. MSS., 39836, and Hist. MSS. Comm., Report on MSS. in Various Collections, III, 1904 (Tresham papers); Wynn Papers in National Library of Wales, Aberystwyth, and published Calendar of Wynn Papers; Brit. Mus. Add. MSS., 33142 (agricultural accounts of the Pelhams) and 33154 (accounts relating to iron); Brit. Mus. Add. MSS., 34167-77 (Twysden papers).          [43] Robert Loder's Farm-Accounts, Introduction.
    [44] A Royalist's Note-book, the Commonplace Book of Sir John Oglander of Nunwell, 1622-1652, ed. Francis Bamford, 75.

classes, and the starry host of notabilities, who lent lustre to the Virginia and East India Companies, contributed less to its development than did the web woven by the humbler ventures of hundreds of obscure squires. Some of them, too, held shares in those much advertised undertakings. More had relations in the City, and sent their sons into business. An increasing number—for the current did not run only one way—had been in business themselves.

"See", wrote Cobden to Bright, "how every successful trader buys an estate!"[45] The remark might have been made with equal truth under James I. The movement from trade into land had long been an old story. Each successive generation made its bow to the proprieties by affecting surprise at it. It was not so long, indeed, since a statesman, alarmed at the crumbling of the social pyramid, had proposed to shore it up by fixing a legal maximum to the real property which vulgar persons, like mere merchants, might buy.[46] Thirty years later that pose had worn thin. The Government of the first two Stuarts continued, on a more majestic scale, the Elizabethan policy of turning Crown estates into cash. So far from deprecating the acquisition of land by the business world, it threw land at its head. It was not surprising that a successful merchant, who had made his pile in trade, should prefer to the risks of commerce the decorous stability of what was regarded as a gilt-edged investment. By the middle years of James, if not, indeed, earlier, it is difficult to find a prominent London capitalist who is not also a substantial landowner; even such dubious cosmopolitans as Van Lore and Burlamachi, like Pallavicino before them, feel obliged to astonish the natives by setting up as country gentlemen. Fortunes made in law went the same way. Whether it is true or not, as was alleged, that leading barristers[47] were making, in the later years of Elizabeth, £20,000 to £30,000 a year, there was general agreement that their emoluments were not trifling. Their profession had taught them what, properly handled, land could be made to yield; naturally, they used their knowledge. Popham, who speculated heavily in Crown lands; Ellesmere, who left his son £12,000 a year; the odious, but indispensable, Coke, were all substantial landowners; the last, indeed, with his fifty odd manors, was well up in the first flight. In the 'twenties, the inroads of the London plutocracy on the home counties gave rise to complaints; and what was true of the neighbourhood of London was hardly less true of the environs of other growing cities, for example, Bristol.[48] In such

<hr/>

[45] Quoted by O. F. Christie, *The Transition to Democracy*, 147-8.

[46] *Hist. MSS. Comm., MSS. of the Marquis of Salisbury*, I, 162-3, "Considerations delivered to the Parliament, 1559". See for earlier complaints, King Edward VI's *Remains*, "Discourse Concerning the Reformation of many Abuses", and F. J. Fisher, "Commercial Trends and Policy in Sixteenth-Century England" in *The Economic History Review*, X, no. 2, 110.  [47] Thomas Wilson, *op. cit.* 25.

[48] S.P.D., James I, XXII, no. 63, contains complaints of the purchase of Suffolk manors by Londoners. For Bristol, see *S.P.D., Charles I*, XXXV, no. 43, 8 September, 1626, and W. B. Willcox, *Gloucestershire, 1590-1640*, 105.

conditions, the social categories used to distinguish the landed and trading classes, which in France and Germany remained terms with a legal significance, lost in England any claim to precision which they may once have possessed.   The landowner living on the profits and rents of commercial farming, and the merchant or banker who was also a land-owner, represented, not two classes, but one.   Patrician and *parvenu* both owed their ascent to causes of the same order.   Judged by the source of their incomes, both were equally *bourgeois*.

## IV

The advance of the classes representing a more business-like agricul-ture was accompanied by a second movement, which at once reflected its influence and consolidated its results.   That movement was the heightened rapidity with which land was changing hands.   The land-market deals in a form of capital, and, in many societies, the most important form.   The article which it handles is not merely a com-modity, but an instrument of social prestige and political power.   It is most active, therefore, when a rise in incomes swells the surplus for investment, and when wealth, in addition to increasing, is passing into new hands.   Commercial expansion, industrial progress, discovery and invention, but also financial recklessness, revolution and war, have all at different times set the wheel spinning with heightened speed.   In the age of Elizabeth and her two successors, economic and political con-ditions combined to mobilise real property, while the hostility of the courts to entails gave both forces free play.[49]   The former, apart from occasional severe depressions, acted continuously, and with increasing force, to augment the demand for it.   The latter, by periodically bring-ing fresh blocks of land into the market, supplied recurrent opportunities for profitable speculation.

The economic causes which lent property wings need no lengthy explanation.   By depreciating fixed incomes, and inflating profits, rising prices sapped the reluctance of conservative owners to sell, and heightened both the eagerness and the ability of the business classes, whether agriculturists or merchants, to buy.   The very customary arrangements —fixed freehold and copyhold rents, and, sometimes fixed fines—which, if maintained, threatened ruin, could be turned by a bold policy of innovation from a liability to an asset.   Involving, as they did, the existence of a wide margin between the actual receipts from a property and its potential yield, they offered, like an old-fashioned company which has survived into a boom, a golden opportunity for a remunerative reconstruction.   Given a knowledge of the ropes, manors could be

[49] The attitude of the Courts is well summarised in Mr H. J. Habakkuk's article, "English Landownership 1680-1740" in *The Economic History Review*, X, no. 1, February 1940.

refloated as easily as mills, with results as agreeable to those who got in on the ground floor, and equally unpleasant to everyone else. To the purchaser with the capital and capacity to undertake it, modernisation was as profitable as it was unpopular with his tenants. If himself a farmer, he sold his produce in a rising market. If he dealt in land as a speculation, he could count on reselling at a profit. If he bought to hold, he could feel a reasonable confidence that he would leave to his heirs an estate appreciating in value. In the event, many bought for a committee of enemies at Goldsmiths Hall. But none foresaw the war.

Our first formal accounts of the land-market seem to be subsequent to the Restoration.[50] The picture then drawn is of a stream of mortgages and sales in London, which, owing to its financial resources, had the bulk of the business, even from the remotest counties, in its hands. Before the end of the previous century, however, it had been realised that the increased volume of transactions raised some awkward problems. The later 'seventies and early 'eighties appear to have been a period of exceptional activity. There were complaints of malpractices, and legislation was passed to check them. An Act of 1585 voided fraudulent conveyances, imposed heavy penalties on the guilty parties, and required all mortgages to be entered with the clerks of recognisances, who were to keep a record, which intending purchasers could inspect on payment of a small fee.[51] The last provision appears to have remained a dead letter, but the issue raised did not die down. The unorganised condition of the market was thought to depress prices, and a patent was granted in 1611 for the establishment of a public office, which was to have as part of its business the provision of facilities for dealing in real property and the recording of transactions. Copyholds —it was an advantage to set against their inconveniences—were transferred publicly in the court of the manor, so that encumbrances on them could not be concealed. It was natural that it should be asked whether the purchaser of a freehold could not be given similar security. Registration of title, advocated and opposed on the same grounds as today, was being urged from the left by the 'forties, and found later a place in the abortive programmes of land reform prepared during the Interregnum [52]

Long before that date, a second unpleasant symptom of the increased

---

[50] *Harleian Miscellany*, VII, 488-93, " Reasons and Proposals for a Registry . . . of all Deeds and Incumbrances of Real Estate " etc., by Nicholas Philpott, 1671; *ibid.* 493-501, "A Treatise concerning Registers . . . of Estates, Bonds, Bills, etc., with Reasons against such Registers ", by William Pierrepoint.

[51] 27 Eliz. c. 4. An earlier Act requiring the enrolment of sales of land had been passed in 1536. For an example of enrolments under it in one county, see Somerset Record Society, LI, " Somerset Enrolled Deeds ", by Sophia W. B. Harbin.

[52] *Harleian Miscellany*, VI, 72, " A word for the Army and two words for the Kingdom ", by Hugh Peters, 1647; *ibid.* VII, 25-35, " A Rod for the Lawyers ", by William Cole, 1659.

scale of the business had attracted general comment. Lawyers were not beloved by laymen; " Peace and law ", wrote an indignant country gentleman, who had seen much of the tribe, " hath beggared us all." [53] The portentous inflation of the legal profession—the figures of men called to the bar at Gray's Inn and Lincoln's Inn rose [54] by almost two-thirds between 1591-1600 and 1631-40—was ascribed largely to the new opportunities open to the conveyancer. Nor, perhaps, is it without significance that it was in 1612, towards the end of the greatest orgy of speculation seen since the Reformation, that another body of practitioners which handled the same business, the growing trade of scriveners, applied for a charter of incorporation. [55] " Sell not thy land; . . . rather feed on bread and water than be the confusion of thy house ", [56] might be the motto of parents. Things were in the saddle and rode their sons. The earliest version of " clogs to clogs in three generations " was applied, not to Lancashire mills, but to Lancashire land. [57] The rapid absorption by absentee aliens of estates in Northamptonshire and Nottinghamshire was noted with disfavour under James I, and much the same statement as to properties in Berkshire was made half a century later by Fuller; while nearly two-thirds of the gentry owning land in Bedfordshire in 1620 were said to have sold it and left the county by 1668. The oft-quoted remark that half the properties in conservative Staffordshire had changed hands in sixty years does not, in the light of such evidence, appear too unplausible. [58] The passing of familiar names, the break-up of patriarchal households, the unpleasantness of the *parvenus* who rose on their ruins, provided dramatists with materials for satire and moralists for sermons. If Sir Petronel Flash and Sir Giles Overreach were successful as parodies, it was that the nauseous reality was not too grossly caricatured.

Lamentations that the oaks are shedding their leaves are a piece of sentimental common form, too fashionable in all ages to throw much light on any one of them. Rising classes, like crowned heads, have always known how to grab and weep at once; nor, once in possession of the title-deeds, are they at a loss for a pedigree. In reality, the Bladesovers of England, repeatedly submerged beneath a flood of new wealth, have been refloated not less often, with undiminished buoyancy, as wealth has found a way to make novelty venerable. The statistical

[53] *A Royalist's Note-book*, etc., 14. An earlier complaint on the same subject is contained in Thomas Wilson, *op. cit.* 24-5.
[54] For Gray's Inn, see Harleian MSS., 1912, no. 16, f. 207b, and for Lincoln's Inn, *Records of Lincoln's Inn*, " The Black Books ", II.
[55] *Calendar S.P.D., Charles I*, CXCIV, 87, 20 June 1631.
[56] *A Royalist's Note-book*, 212.
[57] *The Dr. Farmer Chetham MSS.* (Chetham Soc., 1873), 122-3.
[58] *Hist. MSS. Comm.*, MSS. of Duke of Buccleuch, III, 182 (Northants); J. D. Chambers, *Nottinghamshire in the Eighteenth Century*, 6-7; Thomas Fuller, *The History of the Worthies of England* (1840 edn.), 140; *Harleian Society Publication*, XIX (1884), 206-8 (Beds); Sir Simon Degge in Erdswick's *Survey of Staffordshire*.

evidence of the dimensions of the movement has not yet been put together, nor is it often in the form most instructive to posterity.  Contemporaries commonly thought in terms, not of acreage, but of manors; they spoke of a man owning manors, or selling them, much as today he might be said to hold, or to dispose of, large investments, in order to convey an impression, not to record precise facts.  The category, needless to say, is a highly ambiguous one, embracing estates varying widely in magnitude, value and organisation.  At best, it covers only one species of real property, and that not the most marketable.  In the two generations before the Long Parliament such property seems, nevertheless, for what the fact is worth, to have changed hands with fair rapidity.  Of 2,500 odd manors in seven counties, whose owners can be traced, just under one in three were sold once in the forty years between 1561 and 1600 and rather more than one in three between 1601 and 1640.  In the case of the six hundred odd in Hertfordshire and Surrey, which felt the wash of the London whirlpool, the figure in the second period was over 40 per cent.[59]

The only continuous register of sales of smaller parcels of land, which naturally came into the market more often, seems to be that supplied by the records of the Office of Alienations.[60]  The land which it handled, being subject to awkward financial obligations to the Crown, was not attractive to purchasers.  But the average sales per decade described a rising curve, in rough correspondence with the movement of foreign trade, which helped to determine the surplus available for investment. In the expansion of the 'seventies and early 'eighties the figure bounded up; declined with the slump which began on the eve of the Armada; rose again with the beginning of recovery at the turn of the century; reached the highest point yet attained in the boom of 1606-14; and fell sharply with the depression of the early 'twenties.  It ended at a level which, from 1630 to 1639, stood well above twice that at which it had started.  It is not, perhaps, an exaggeration to say that for two generations there was an intermittent real estate boom.  Naturally, land values bounded up.  An observer who stated in the later years of Elizabeth that they had risen ten-fold[61] within living memory over-stated his case; but there was general agreement that the rise had been impressive. Not much weight can be attached to the fact that under James I some Crown land was sold at the fantastic price of forty-five[62] years purchase,

[59] The counties concerned are Surrey, Hertfordshire, Bedfordshire, Buckinghamshire, Hampshire, Worcestershire and North Riding of Yorkshire.  The figures, which I owe to the kindness of Mr F. J. Fisher, are taken from the lists of manors and their owners given in the *V.C.H.*  They exclude transfers of leases, and transfers due to marriage, gift, inheritance, forefeiture, or other non-commercial transactions.

[60] Exchequer Accounts, Alienations Office, *Entries of Licenses and Pardons for Alienations.*          [61] Cotton MSS., Otho E x., no. 10, ff. 64-78 (c. 1590).

[62] Lansdowne MSS., 169, art. 51, f. 110, Contract made with Sir Baptist Hicks and others, 19 December, 18 James I (by which land with an annual value of £1,000 was sold for £45,000).

for such land—it was one of its attractions—was notoriously under-rented. Twenty-eight[63] years purchase, however, was quoted in the later 'twenties as the price at which some estates were then changing hands.

This mobilisation of property, the result of commercial expansion and inflation combined, was not peculiar to England. As Professor Bloch and M. Raveau have shown, a similar reshuffling of possessions was occurring at the same time in France.[64] But in England the results of an accelerated economic tempo were heightened by adventitious causes. The State threw its weight into the scales, and permanently depressed them. Intending to buttress its own foundations, it released currents which, in the end, carried them and it away.

Periodical redistributions of land by acts of public policy, to the gain or loss now of this class, now of that, are not the astonishing departure from pre-established harmonies which they appear to their victims. In one form or another, they are a recurrent feature of European history, whose repeated appearance lends colour to the view which sees in them, not an accident, but the prelude to a new era. The decorous story of England is no exception to that rule. In the century and a half between the Reformation and Restoration, such a redistribution took place on a scale not seen since the Conquest. There were two immense confiscations, the result of revolution and civil war, and a steady alienation, under financial duress, of estates formerly used to provide a revenue for public purposes.

The opening act of the drama is not here in place. But the story which had begun with the Dissolution had not ended with it. Like taxation, the fruits of confiscation do not always rest where they first light. It is an error to suppose that, when James skipped happily on to his throne of thorns, the results of that great transaction were already ancient history. Property producing a gross income equal to about half the then yield of the customs had been cut adrift from its moorings, and added to the acreage available for acquisition by influence or enterprise. When the first fever of speculation was over, it had continued to float from hand to hand in the ordinary way of business, coming at intervals to anchor, only again to resume its exciting voyages. Nor had the Crown's interest in the matter ceased with the mere act of confiscation and the sales which followed it. For one thing, though it had disposed within a decade of the greater part of the spoils, those which it retained remained substantial. For another, part of the land with which it parted had not been sold outright, but had been leased for terms of

[63] S.P.D., Charles I, CIX, 44, quoted by W. R. Scott, *English Joint Stock Companies*, I, 192. As Professor Scott points out, the price of land reflected not only the annual rent, but casualties, such as fines.

[64] Marc Bloch, *op. cit.* 140-5; Paul Raveau, *L'Agriculture et les Classes Paysannes dans le Haut-Poitou au xvi* siècle*, especially chap. ii.

years, and ultimately returned to it.  In the third place, part of that
which it sold came back to it later through escheats and confiscations.  Two generations later, therefore, it still owned, as a result of the
Dissolution, a great mass of property, which could be leased, mortgaged
or sold, and which, when the Court of Augmentations was wound up in
1554, had continued to be administered by the Augmentations office of
the Exchequer.  A vast deal in Chantry lands brought temporary relief
to the financial embarrassments of the early years of James.  His son was
disposing of monastic estates within a decade of the Long Parliament.

    The continued redistribution of monastic property in the century
following the Reformation was as momentous, therefore, as that which
accompanied it.  The transference to lay hands of part of the land
owned by bishops and by deans and chapters—" their wings . . . well
clipt of late by courtiers and noblemen, and some quite cut away "[65]—
has been studied in detail only during the Interregnum, but the statements of contemporaries suggest that the scale on which it took place
under Elizabeth was not inconsiderable.  Nor was it only ecclesiastical
property which came into the market in large blocks.  Few rulers have
acted more remorselessly than the early Tudors on the maxim that the
foundations of political authority are economic.  They had made the
augmentation of the royal demesnes one of the key-stones of their
policy.[66]  They had enjoyed, as a consequence, not only a large revenue
from land, but the extensive economic patronage which great estates
conferred, and had been powerful as kings partly because unrivalled as
landowners.  A shrewd foreigner remarked, as he watched in the next century the headlong plunge downhill of the Crown finances, that the Stuarts
were on the way to be overshadowed in wealth by their subjects before
they were overthrown by them.[67]  There was some substance in the
view, hinted more than once under James, that the New Monarchy was
undermined by reversing for three generations the financial policy which
had helped to establish it.  Each of the three great crises of Elizabeth's
reign carried its own block of Crown estates away; she sold in her forty-
five years land to the value, in all, of some £817,000.  Her two successors
inherited the nemesis of living on capital, as well as of rising prices and
of their own characters.  They sold in thirty years nearly twice as much.
In spite of half-hearted attempts to tie his hands, alienations of property
under James reached about £775,000, and those of Charles I, in the first
decade of his reign, over £650,000.[68]  The estates remaining to the

[65] Thomas Wilson, op. cit. 22-3.
[66] F. C. Dietz, English Government Finance, 1485-1558.
[67] Calendar S.P., Venice, 1603-1607, no. 709; 1617-1619, no. 658; 1621-1623, no. 603;
1629-1632, no. 374.
[68] For sales of Crown land under Elizabeth, see S.P.D., James I, XLVII, nos. 99, 100.
101, and S. J. Madge, The Domesday of Crown Lands, 41-2; under James, Lansdowne
MSS., 169, art. 51; under Charles I, Brit. Mus. Add. MSS. 18705, ff. 2-22, and S.P.D.,
Charles I, CXXIV, 51; and under the last two, and 1649-56, Madge, op. cit. 47-64.

Crown when the Long Parliament met, were still, of course, substantial; but how ruinously they had been dilapidated can be shown by
a comparison. Between 1558 and 1635 Crown lands to the value of some
£2,240,000 had been thrown on the market. When, in the crisis of the
Civil War, the remains were swept together and put up to auction, the
sum realised, it seems, was under £2,000,000.[69]

V

What, if any, were the social consequences of these portentous land-
slides? Did they, while changing, or reflecting a change in, the fortunes
of individuals, leave unaltered the distribution of property between
different groups? Or was the set of social forces such that some classes
gained, while others lost? Is there truth in the suggestion of a later
political theorist that " two parts in ten of all those vast estates " of the
nobility, " by the luxury and folly of their owners, have . . . been purchased by the lesser gentry and commons ", and that " the crown-lands,
that is the public patrimony, are come to make up the interest of the
commons "?[70]

As to the tendency of private transactions, little can at present be
said. Some great estates can be seen disintegrating, and others being
formed. A comparison of the distribution at different dates of certain
categories of property reveals the results. But the threads in the intricate
skein leading from the first stage to the last can rarely be unravelled.[71]
The dealings in monastic and Crown lands left a trail which is easier to
follow. Much is still obscure; but enough is known to suggest certain
provisional conclusions.

The natural starting-point, in considering the former, is the classification of grantees made, some thirty years ago, by Dr Savine.[72] His
figures suggest that the lion's share of the spoils had passed, in the first
instance, to two categories of persons. The first, the peers, received the
largest individual grants; the second, the gentry and their connections,
the largest aggregate share. What is known of the subsequent history
of the land in question suggests that the second of these groups had the
greater survival value. Properties dispersed, like the acquisitions of some
noble grantees, over half-a-dozen different counties, were more readily

<hr />

[69] Madge, *op. cit.* 256.

[70] Henry Neville, *Plato Redivivus* (1763 edn.), 39.

[71] One example may be given. John Smythe (*Lives of the Berkeleys*, II, 356-61)
gives particulars of property sold by Lord Henry Berkeley between 1561 and 1613 to the
value of approximately £42,000. Sales of 25 manors and of the lease of one manor,
realising £39,279 odd, were made to 13 persons (7 knights or baronets, 5 esquires and
the trustees of a peer), the remainder, to the value of £2,789, going to 25 other persons
of unspecified condition. Thus (i) 38 owners succeeded one; (ii) over nine-tenths of the
property sold was acquired by purchasers relatively high in the social scale.

[72] Dr Savine's figures are printed in H. A. L. Fisher's *The Political History of
England, 1485-1547*, App. ii, 497-9.

sold than smaller and more compact estates, to which their owners were bound by strong local attachments. The squirearchy was less exposed to the vicissitudes which ruined some aristocratic families; while keen farmers and business men as many of them were, they were in a better position to reap the fruits of commercial progress and improved methods of agriculture. Hence while, as a class, they had gained most by the Dissolution, they not only succeeded in retaining their acquisions, but continued to add to them in the course of the next century.

"As the Gibeonites", wrote Fuller, " though by their mouldy bread and clouted shoes pretending to a long peregrination, were but of the vicinage; so most of those gentry [sc., in the later years of Henry VIII], notwithstanding their specious claims to antiquity, will be found to be . . . low enough in themselves did they not stand on the vantage ground heightened on the rubbish of the ruins of monasteries."[73]   The settlement of monastic estates into the hands of the most progressive element in rural society may be illustrated by the course of events in one small corner of the country. In Gloucestershire, Northamptonshire and Warwickshire about 317 manors, together with a mass of miscellaneous property—tithes, rectories and land in different places—appear to have changed hands at the Dissolution.[74]   Of the manors, which are more easily traced than the smaller acquisitions, between 250 and 260 passed into the ownership of individuals, the remainder being obtained by bishops, deans and chapters, colleges and other corporations. The nobility had done fairly, though not immoderately, well; twenty-six[75] peers had acquired monastic property of some kind, and seventeen had secured just over forty manors. Crown officials, like Sadler and Kingston, the two largest grantees of Gloucestershire estates; big business, in the persons of Gresham, Sharington and Stump; and an ubiquitous group of professional speculators, had all got their share; while a number of smaller men picked up crumbs from the cake. The bulk of the property had gone, however, not to influential aliens, but to well-known local families. In Gloucestershire the beneficiaries had included Chamberlains, Poynzs, Thynnes, Throckmortons, Tracies, Dennises, Porters, Comptons and Botelers; in Northamptonshire Montagues, Knightleys, Kirkhams, Cecils and Fermors; in Warwickshire Knightleys, Aglionbys and Throckmortons. Precision is impossible; but it is probably not an exaggeration to say that from one-half to two-thirds of the

[73] Thomas Fuller, op. cit. I, 60.

[74] The following account of the fate of monastic property in three counties does not pretend to complete accuracy. It is based mainly on Sir Robert Atkyns, The Ancient and Present State of Gloucestershire, and Men and Armour in Gloucestershire in 1608 (London, 1902, no editor stated), a list compiled by John Smythe from the Musters roll of 1608; J. Bridges, History and Antiquities of Northamptonshire; and Dugdale, Antiquities of Warwickshire.

[75] I.e. eliminating duplication arising from the fact that several peers acquired monastic property in more than one of the three counties in question.

property acquired by individuals had passed to men of this type and to humbler members of the same class. In so far as there had been competition between national notabilities and tenacious local interests, local interests had won.

Their victory became steadily more decisive in the course of the next century. Compared with the adventurers who dealt in properties that they had never seen, the local gentry were a settled population confronting mere marauders. As the revolution receded, and its first turmoil died down, their strategic advantage—the advantage of a settled base—asserted itself with ever-increasing force. Political convulsions shook down the estates of one group of absentees; financial embarrassments sapped the staying-power of another. As each over-rigged vessel went on the rocks, the patient watchers on the shore brought home fresh flotsam from the wreck. Long after the last monk had died they were adding to their abbey lands, and, if not admitted on the ground floor, became shareholders at one remove. In Gloucestershire the estates of Cromwell, Northumberland and the Seymours drifted, some quickly, some gradually, into the hands of the Duttons, Winstons, Dorringtons and Chamberlains. The property of the Earl of Pembroke, who browsed juicier pastures elsewhere, passed, soon after its acquisition, to the Dennises and Comptons. The lands of Sir Thomas Gresham came by marriage to the Thynnes, and those of Lord Clinton and Sir Robert Tyrwitt to the Heydons; while, of the eight manors secured by Sir Anthony Kingston, more than half had passed by 1608 to other families, in particular the Baynhams and Sandys. Sir Ralph Sadler's descendants continued to be considerable landowners in the county; but the property acquired by him from the Abbey of Winchcombe, and four of the six manors taken from the college of Westbury-on-Trim, had left them by that date, some passing to the Actons and Bridges, others to less well-known families. In Northamptonshire, of the property acquired by peers at the Dissolution, some, by the beginning of the next century, had returned to the Crown; most of it had come to Kirkhams, Hattons, Spencers, Andrews, Stanhopes, Cradocks, Griffins and Ishams. In Warwickshire, the families who gained most by later re-shuffles were the Leighs, Dilkes, Throckmortons and Spencers. The general result in these counties, in spite of the reputation of Northamptonshire as the Dukeries of the age, was that, of the forty odd manors which had gone to peers at the Reformation, those remaining to them two generations later numbered only six, while the remainder swelled the fortunes of rising middle-class families. Something between two-thirds and three-quarters of the manors secured by private persons had gone originally to the squirearchy. By the early years of the next century, the proportion in their hands was over nine-tenths. Thus the ultimate consequences of the Dissolution, if similar in kind to its immediate effects, were different in degree. In this part of England, at any rate, it did not so much endow an existing nobility, as lay the foundations of a new nobility to arise in the next century.

"It is owing", writes Dr Chambers in his study of Nottinghamshire, " to the elimination of these factors, the monasteries, the copyholders, the Crown and the Church, as rivals to the gentry, that Thoroton is enabled to place them on the pedestal of unchallenged local supremacy."[76] The full effects of the dismemberment of Crown estates before the Civil War still remain to be worked out; but enough is known to suggest that it is not of one county alone that his statement is true. The individuals into whose hands the land in question passed fell, between 1600 and 1640, into three main categories. Part of it was acquired by the peasants on Crown estates; part, in the first instance, by syndicates of speculators, who bought land in large blocks, subdivided, and resold it; part by well-to-do landowners and business men. The Government's dealings with the first class in parts of Lancashire and Yorkshire have been described by Dr Tupling.[77] Their social effects were not without interest; but, as a solution of the financial problem, that method of disposing of Crown property was of worse than dubious value. It involved prolonged higgling with obstinate copyholders; years of surveying, hearings before commissions, and litigation; the extraction from thousands of petty transactions of sums which, in the end, were liable to be unimpressive. What the Government wanted was to get large tracts of land taken off its hands for prompt and substantial payments. If it was to secure that result, it must clearly look elsewhere than to the cautious avidity of inpecunious peasants.

These reasons caused the best markets for Crown property to be found, not among the smaller cultivators, but in the classes who could afford to deal on a large scale. Many well-to-do families had been interested in particular estates long before they came to be offered for sale. Among the lessees of Crown lands in the first decade of Elizabeth appear, side by side with humble members of the Royal Household, distinguished civil servants and statesmen, like Smith and Cecil, judges and law officers of the Crown, and leading country gentlemen.[78] Down to, and after, the beginning of the century, much of the property in question was notoriously under-rented.[79] As a consequence, a would-be purchaser

[76] J. D. Chambers, op. cit. 4.

[77] G. H. Tupling, The Economic History of Rossendale (Chetham Soc., N.S., LXXXVI, 1927).

[78] The source of this statement is a list of lessees of Crown land 1-12 Eliz., contained (I think) in S.P.D., Elizabeth, CLXVI, but the reference has been mislaid. The list includes among others, Sir William Cecil, Sir Thomas Smith, Anthony Brown (Justice of the Common Pleas), David Lewis (Judge of the Court of Admiralty), Sir Francis Knollys, Sir Maurice Berkeley, Sir Henry Jernigan, Sir Walter Mildmay, Sir Gervase Clifton, Richard Hampden, etc.

[79] Bacon, "Discourse in the Praise of his Sovereign" in Works (Bohn edn.), I, 371. For statistical evidence of under-renting, see S. J. Madge, The Domesday of Crown Lands, 55-6.

could offer a figure which appeared on paper impressive, but which, in fact, especially if he bought to reconstruct, was money in his pocket. In such circumstances, it was natural that prosperous landowners, who already held Crown land on lease, should welcome the prospects of acquiring the freehold. The Irish war had brought one great opportunity. The accession of James was the occasion of a second. The great deals in Crown property were financed largely on credit;[80] one leading speculator professed to have raised £80,000 in the City, and to have burned his fingers. The boom in trade, which began with the peace of 1605, meant easy money. With a debt which by Michaelmas, 1606, was over £550,000, and showed signs of mounting, fresh spoils were in the offing. As usual, it was complained that Scots got more than their fair share; but there is no sign that the higher civilisation was backward in the scramble. " At court ", wrote a future secretary of state, shocked—not for the last time—by the magnitude of the depredations, "every man findeth way for his own ends."[81] Coke was not alone in thinking that the thing threatened to become a ramp.

The dimensions of the business, and the anxiety of the Government to realise without delay, prompted the adoption of a technique which, if not new in principle, was now practised on a novel scale. The traditional expedient of sale through Special Commissions brought in, between 1603 and 1614, just over £180,000. What was done, in addition, was to use the financial machinery of the City. The procedure was somewhat analogous to the underwriting of a Government loan today by a group of issuing houses, except that what was involved was an actual transference of property. Instead of itself dealing with prospective purchasers, the Crown disposed of land wholesale to financial syndicates, who paid cash down, retained as much as they wanted for themselves, and peddled the remainder over a period of years. One group, for example, took over in 1605-6, and again in 1611, a mass of tithes, priory lands and chantry lands; a second just over 400 Crown mills, with the land attached to them; several others different blocks of property. The " contractors ", as they were called, included, in addition to certain guineapigs in the shape of courtiers and officials, the leading business magnates of the day, such as Garway and Jones, two farmers of the Customs; Hicks, the silk merchant and banker; the masters and prominent members of certain city companies; and—the man who plunged most heavily, being engaged in seven separate deals to the value of £137,055—Arthur Ingram, the controller of the customs. The separate bargains made with these syndicates between 1605 and 1614

[80] This was so, e.g. in the case of Lionel Cranfield's speculation of 1609. His ledger shows that he and his partners borrowed £529 from Sir John Spencer, £427 from Lady Slanye, and £209 from Thomas Mun. I am indebted to Lord Sackville and Professor A. P. Newton for permission to examine the Cranfield papers.

[81] Hist. MSS. Comm., MSS. of the Earl of Cowper, I, 50.

numbered seventeen, and the total sum thus obtained—apart from sales direct to individuals—amounted to just under half a million.[82]

The capitalists concerned bought primarily, of course, not to hold, but as a speculation, unloading partly on subsidiary rings of middlemen, whose names also are known, partly on the public, at the best price they could get. It was complained in the House in 1614 that they made 100 per cent and skinned purchasers alive.[83] The procedure adopted masked the personalities of the ultimate beneficiaries; but, wherever the latter can be traced, while part of the land goes in small lots to obscure peasants or craftsmen in Devonshire, the Isle of Wight and elsewhere, the bulk of it is seen passing, as would be expected, to people of substance, such as leading lawyers, country gentlemen and business men.[84] The same tendency can be traced in greater detail in the transactions of the next reign. The most imposing deals were two. In the first place, a Commission[85] was set to work, which, between 1625 and 1634, disposed of property to the value of £247,597. In the second place, with a view to settling outstanding debts and to raising a further loan, the Crown transferred to the City Corporation land valued at £349,897.[86] The City marketed it gradually during the next twelve years, using the proceeds to pay the Crown's creditors.

The purchasers concerned in the first of these transactions numbered 218, and the value of the land which can be traced £234,437. The comment of a foreigner—that most of the property went to courtiers who had secured promises for it in advance—exaggerated the part played by influence, as distinct from money; but, in emphasising that the sales of Crown land under Charles, when the financial system of the monarchy was tottering to its fall, were, to an even greater extent than under his predecessors, a deal between the Crown, big business and the richer country gentry, he put his finger on a vital point. For obvious reasons of speed and economy, the policy of the Commission was to sell in large blocks. Lots of £1,000 and upwards, accounting for four-fifths of the land sold, went to less than one-third of the purchasers. The scale of the transactions naturally narrowed the market. Five merchants got one-tenth of the total; twenty-seven peers between one-quarter and one-third; a group of 133 knights, esquires and gentlemen rather more than

[82] A summary of these transaction, with the names of the principal contractors, is contained in Lansdowne MSS., 169, art. 51, f. 110. S.P.D., James I, XL to LXXV, contain many references to the subject.
[83] C.J., 1614, 18 April, speech of Mr Hoskyns.
[84] I take these particulars from the Cranfield MSS. For the deal in which he was specially engaged, see S.P.D., James I, XLV, no. 159 (articles between the Commissioners for the sale and demise of Crown Lands and John Eldred and others, contractors for purchase of the same).          [85] Brit. Mus. Add. MSS., 18795, ff. 2-22.
[86] Calendar S.P.D., Charles I, 1628-1629, CXXIV, 51. The sale of land to the City was the result of a contract made in 1628 with Edward Ditchfield and other trustees acting on behalf of the Corporation. Particulars as to the subsequent sale by the City of the properties concerned are contained in the Royal Contract Deeds in the Guildhall.

half.  The second and larger deal, in which the City was the auctioneer,
differed from the first only in the fact that the business world had a
larger hand in it, and the nobility a smaller, the latter acquiring about
one-tenth of the land and the former one-quarter.  But the bulk of it
went in the same direction as before.  Among the 350 odd purchasers
the squirearchy and its dependants formed the largest group, and
acquired well over half the total.  It is not an exaggeration, in fact, to
say that, apart from purchases affected through other channels, these
two transactions alone had the effect that, in the course of something
over fifteen years, several hundred families of country gentry added to
their possessions land to the value of £350,000 to £400,000.  Nor is that
the whole story.  Much of the property was sold as undeveloped land
to men who, when the time came, would seize the chance to develop it.
If an exasperated official, who put the difference in value between the
two at twenty-fold,[87] over-stated his case, we know from other sources—
for example, the margin between old rents and improved rents on private
estates—that the difference sometimes ran into hundreds per cent.  It
was this margin—not merely the price at which Crown land was transferred, but the prospective increment of rack-rents, enclosure, exploitation of timber and minerals—which must be considered in estimating
the gains accruing to its purchasers.

To complete the picture of property passing from the Crown to its
wealthier subjects, it would be necessary, in the first place, to take
account of further less obtrusive changes, which went on side by side
with these grandiose deals.  The process of piecemeal disintegration
associated with the dubious business of " concealed lands ", and with
gifts and grants, such as the concessions of " drowned lands " to persons
willing to reclaim them, still awaits its historian.  Even the famous
matter of the forests made little noise till near the end, when it made too
much.  The *de facto* transference of possessions involved in the absorption by neighbouring landowners of the last alone would seem not to
have been a trifle.  " The King loseth daily by intrusion and encroachments "; " wholly converted to the private benefit of the officers and
private men "; " [private] claims do swallow up the whole forest, not
allowing his Majesty the breadth of one foot "[88]—such lamentations,
though uttered before the question entered politics, may sound like the
voice of official pessimism; but the routine returns of encroachments
contained in the records of some forest courts make them appear not

[87] *Calendar S.P.D., James I*, CXI, no. 80, 15 December 1619.  Sir T. Wilson to Master
of Rolls.  " The King was greatly deceived in the Chantry lands which he granted to
discharge that debt, for he passed the lands with £5,000 or £6,000 a year at the old
rents, which are now worth 20 times as much. . . . The whole affair was a cozenage."
[88] Cranfield MSS., 8236, 1622, Selwood forest; *ibid.* 8328, 1622, Crown forests in
generai, parts of Whittlewood, Barnwood and Sherwood being specially mentioned;
S.P.D., James I, LXXXIV, no. 46, Norden's Survey of Kingswood Forest.

unplausible. It would be necessary, in the second place, for the purpose of obtaining a comprehensive view, to compare the course of events in England with the history of those parts of the Continent where matters went a different way. Leaving these further questions, however, on one side, what significance, if any, it may be asked, is to be attached to the movement of which the dull transactions described above are specimens?

## VI

Its financial consequences are obvious; they were those which led Hobbes to make his comment on the futility of attempting to support a State by endowing it with property subject to alienation.[89] The effect on the peasants of recurrent orgies of land speculation, if less conspicuous, is equally certain. In the third place, such figures as we possess suggest that the tendency of an active land-market was, on the whole, to increase the number of medium-sized properties, while diminishing that of the largest.[90] Mr Habakkuk has shown in a striking article[91] that " the general drift of property in the sixty years after 1690 was in favour of the large estate and the great lord ", and has explained the causes of that movement. During the preceding century and a half the current, as he points out, appears to have flowed in the opposite direction, with the result that, as the number of great properties was levelled down, and that of properties of moderate size levelled up, the upper ranges of English society came to resemble less a chain of high peaks than an undulating table-land. Is it too incautious, in the fourth place, to regard as one symptom of the change in the distribution of wealth the acquisition of new dignities by members of the class which gained most from it? Of 135 peers in the House of Lords in 1642, over half had obtained their titles since 1603. They included some lawyers and merchants, but

[89] *Leviathan*, chap. xxiv.

[90] The following figures, which I owe to the kindness of Mr F. J. Fisher, are based on the lists of manors and their owners contained in the *V.C.H.* They relate to manors whose ownership is known at all the four dates given below in the seven counties of Hertfordshire, Bedfordshire, Buckinghamshire, Surrey, Worcestershire, Hampshire and the North Riding of Yorkshire.

| | 1561 | per cent | 1601 | per cent | 1640 | per cent | 1680 | per cent |
|---|---|---|---|---|---|---|---|---|
| Total | 2547 | | 2547 | | 2547 | | 2547 | |
| Belonging to owners with 4 manors and under | 1445 | 56·7 | 1457 | 57·2 | 1638 | 64·3 | 1684 | 66·1 |
| Belonging to owners with 5 manors and under 10 | 490 | 19·2 | 544 | 21·3 | 488 | 19·1 | 556 | 21·8 |
| Belonging to owners with 10 manors or more | 612 | 24·0 | 546 | 21·4 | 421 | 16·5 | 547 | 13·6 |

[91] H. J. Habakkuk, " English Landownership, 1680-1740 " in *The Economic History Review* X, no. 1 (Feb. 1940), 2.

the majority of them were well-to-do country gentlemen. The creation by the Stuarts of a *parvenu* nobility, like the sale of baronetcies to knights and esquires with an income from land of £1,000 a year, if politically a blunder, showed some insight into economic realities. It owed such fiscal utility as it possessed to the existence of a social situation which such expedients could exploit.

Nor, finally, were political attitudes unaffected by the same influences. With the growth of speculative dealings in land, the depreciation of the capital value of certain categories of real property by the antiquated form of land-taxation known as the feudal incidents became doubly intolerable. The more intimately an industry—agriculture or any other—depends on the market, the more closely is it affected by the policy of governments, and the more determined do those engaged in it become to control policy. The fact that *entrepreneur* predominated over *rentier* interests in the House of Commons was, therefore, a point of some importance. The revolt against the regulation by authority of the internal trade in agricultural produce, like the demand for the prohibition of Irish cattle imports and a stiffer tariff on grain, was natural when farming was so thoroughly commercialised that it could be said that the fall in wool prices alone in the depression of 1621 had reduced rents by over £800,000 a year. The freezing reception given by the Long Parliament to petitions from the peasants for the redress of agrarian grievances is hardly surprising, when it is remembered that one in every two of the members returned, up to the end of 1640, for the five Midland Counties which were the disturbed area of the day, either themselves had been recently fined for depopulation or belonging to families which had been.[92] The economic reality behind the famous battle over the forests was the struggle between more extensive and more intensive methods of land utilisation, to which the increased profitableness of capitalist farming lent a new ferocity. Most of the attitudes and measures, in fact, which were to triumph at the Restoration can be seen taking shape between the death of Elizabeth and the opening of the Civil War.

To attempt an answer which went beyond these commonplaces would, perhaps, be rash. But it is not presumptuous to address the question to contemporaries; and some of them have left us in little doubt as to their opinion. Mr Russell Smith,[93] in his interesting study of Harrington, has suggested that the thesis as to the political repercussion of changes in the distribution of landed property, which is the central doctrine of the *Oceana*, if partly inspired by a study of Roman history,

[92] *Chancery Petty Bag, Miscellaneous Rolls*, no. 20, gives the names of persons fined for depopulation 1635-8. The five counties in question are Leicestershire, Northamptonshire, Nottinghamshire, Huntingdonshire and Lincolnshire, which accounted for 560 out of 589 individuals fined and for £39,208 out of £44,054 collected. The names of M.P.s are taken from the *Official Returns of Members of the House of Commons* (1878).

[93] H. F. Russell Smith, *Harrington and his Oceana*, chap. iii.

derived its actuality from the English confiscations in Ireland under the
Act of 1642 and the Diggers' movement in England. In reality, it was
needless for Harrington to look so far afield as the first, or in spheres so
humble as the second. In so far as he was in debt to previous writers,
his master was Machiavelli; but the process from which he generalised
had been taking place beneath his eyes. His own relatives had been
engaged in it.[94]

Had he shared the modern taste for figures, he would have found
little difficulty in supporting his doctrine by some casual scraps of
statistical evidence.[95] He would have observed, for example, had he
taken as a sample some 3,300 manors in ten counties, that out of 730
held by the Crown and the peerage in 1561, some 430 had left them (if
new creations are ignored) by 1640, while an additional 400 had been
acquired by the gentry. He would have discovered that, as a consequence, the Crown, which in 1561 owned just one-tenth (9 per cent) of
the total, owned in 1640 one-fiftieth (2 per cent); that the peers held one-
eighth (12·6 per cent) at the first date, and (ignoring new creations)
one-sixteenth (6·7 per cent) at the second; and that the share of the
gentry had risen from two-thirds (67 per cent), when the period began,
to four-fifths (80 per cent) at the end of it. His remarks on the social
changes which caused the House of Commons " to raise that head which
since hath been so high and formidable unto their princes that they have
looked pale upon those assemblies ", and his celebrated paradox,
" Wherefore the dissolution of this Government caused the war, not the
war the dissolution of this Government ",[96] were based on his argument
as to the significance of a " balance " of property; and that argument
took its point from his belief that in his own day the balance had been
altered. To the sceptic who questioned its historical foundations, he
would probably have replied—for he was an obstinate person—by inviting him either to submit rebutting evidence, or to agree that there was
some *prima-facie* reason, at least, for supposing that, in the counties in
question, the landed property of the Crown had diminished under
Parthenia, Morpheus and his successor by three-quarters (76 per cent),
and that of the older nobility by approximately half (47·1 per cent),
while that of the gentry had increased by not much less than one-fifth
(17·8 per cent).[97]

[94] J. Wright, *History and Antiquities of Rutland* (1684), 135; E. J. Benger, *Memoirs
of Elizabeth Stuart, Queen of Bohemia* (1825), 68, 285; Grove, *Alienated Tithes*, under
Leicestershire, parishes of Bitteswell, Laund, Loddington, Melbourne and Owston; Brit.
Mus. MSS., 18795, 2-22, which shows Sir William Harrington and a partner buying Crown
lands between December 1626 and February 1627.

[95] See on the figures here given the remarks in the Postscript at the end of this essay.

[96] *Oceana*, ed. S. B. Liljegren, 49-50.

[97] The figures in this paragraph relate to the counties of Hertfordshire, Bedfordshire,
Buckinghamshire, Surrey, Hampshire, Worcestershire, North Riding of Yorkshire,
Gloucestershire, Warwickshire, Northamptonshire. For those of the first seven counties
I am indebted, as before, to Mr F. J. Fisher.

In reality, however, as far as this side of his doctrines were concerned, there were few sceptics to challenge him.  To regard Harrington as an isolated doctrinaire is an error.  In spite of its thin dress of fancy, his work was not a Utopia, but partly a social history, partly a programme based upon it.  Contemporaries who abhorred the second were not indisposed to agree with the first, for it accorded with their own experience. The political effect of the transference of property appeared as obvious to authors on the right, like Sir Edward Walker, whose book appeared three years before the *Oceana,* as to Ludlow, to that formidable bluestocking, Mrs Hutchison, and to Neville, on the left.[98]  If, in 1600, it could be said [99] that the richer gentry had the incomes of an Earl, and in 1628 that the House of Commons could buy the House of Lords three times over,[100] the argument advanced in some quarters in 1659 that, since the Peers, who once held two-thirds of the land, now held less than one-twelfth, the day for a House of Lords was passed, was not perhaps surprising.[101]  It overstated its case; but a case existed.

The next generation, while repudiating Harrington's conclusions, rarely disputed his premises.  Dryden was not the only person to see political significance in the fact that

> The power for property allowed
> Is mischievously seated in the crowd.

Thorndike complained that " so great a part of the gentry as have shared with the Crown in the spoils of the monasteries think it in their interest to hold up that which . . . would justify their title in point of conscience "; that the result had been " a sort of mongrel clergy of lecturers "; and that " it is visibile that the late war hath had its rise here ".  Temple defended the plutocratic composition of his proposed new Council with the remark that " authority is observed much to follow land ".  Burnet wrote that the Crown had never recovered from the sales of land by James I, not merely for the reason of their effect on the revenue, but because they snapped the links which had kept the tenants of the Crown " in a dependence " upon it; Sidney that the nobility, having sacrificed " the command of men " to the appetite for money, retained " neither the interest nor the estates " necessary to political leadership, and that, as a consequence, " all things have been brought into the hands of the Crown and the commons ", with " nothing left to

---

[98] Sir Edward Walker, *Observations upon the Inconveniences,* etc. (1653), especially his remarks on the effect of granting monastic lands to " mean families "; E. Ludlow, (1750 edn.), 311-13 ; *Somers Tracts,* XIII, 679, Richard Harley, " Faults on both sides " ; C. Davenant, *A Discourse upon Grants and Resumptions.*  See also P. Larkin, *Property in the Eighteenth Century* (1930), 33-57.

[99] Thomas Wilson, *op. cit.* 23.          [100] *Court and Times of Charles I,* I, 331.

[101] Burton's *Diary,* III, 408.  See on the whole subject, Firth, *The House of Lords during the Civil War,* 21-32.

cement them and to maintain their union "; an author—possibly Defoe —with the *nom-de-plume* of Richard Harley, that the " second and less observed cause " of the troubles of his youth was " the passage of land from its former possessors into the hands of a numerous gentry and commonalty "; Davenant that the case for a resumption, at any rate of recent grants, was overwhelming, though it would be prudent to try it, in the first place, in Ireland.[102]

The moral for governments desirous of stability was drawn by a writer[103] who borrowed Burnet's name, and whose father—if the ordinary ascription is correct—had had much to say half a century before on the effects of the transference of land in his own county of Gloucestershire. He condemned the book of Harrington—" calculated wholly for the meridian of a Commonwealth"—but quoted its doctrines, and propounded a policy, which, but for his Republicanism, Harrington himself might have endorsed. The cause of all the trouble, he wrote, had been the reckless alienation of the estates of the Crown and nobility. Salvation was to be found by reversing the process. The Crown should by purchase gradually build up a new demesne, which should remain inalienable; and—"since a monarchy cannot subsist without a nobility" —should confine new peerages to persons with estates worth at least £6,000 a year and entailed on their heirs. Of these proposals, the first had long been impracticable, the second was superfluous.

## Postscript—July, 1954

THE article reprinted above has, I understand, occasioned some discussion. The latest contribution to the debate is contained in Mr Trevor-Roper's interesting *Supplement* to *The Economic History Review* for April 1953. Whether the scope and tenor of my essay are accurately indicated by his reference to "Professor Tawney's searchlight seeking only to illuminate prosperity among the gentry and aristocratic decline" its readers are better qualified than its author to judge; nor does space permit me to pursue his speculations on the rôle of the Independents in the revolution and of the "mere", "lesser" or "declining" gentry among the Independents. One of his criticisms, however, raises issues possibly of some interest to future workers in the same field, and

---

[102] Dryden, *Absolom and Architophel*, i, 777 ; H. Thorndike, *Theological Works*, V, 440-2, 337-9, 371-3; Sir W. Temple, *Miscellaneous Writings*, iii, 16; Burnet, *History of his own Times* (1815 edn.), I, 12; Algernon Sidney, *Discourses Concerning Government* (1750 edn.), 311-13 ; *Somers Tracts*, XII, 679, Richard Harley, " Faults on both Sides " ; C. Davenant, *A Discourse upon Grants and Resumptions.* See also P. Larkin, *Property in the Eighteenth Century* (1930), 33-57.

[103] *A Memorial Offered to Her Royal Highness the Princess Sophia (1815).* Foxcroft (*Life of Gilbert Burnet*, II, App. II, 556) ascribes the work to George Smythe of North Nibley.

sufficiently specific to be discussed at not excessive length.  This note is confined to it.

I take seriously the not uncommon contemporary opinion, to which Mr Trevor-Roper gives short shrift, that the two generations before the Civil War saw an advance in the fortunes of the class described as the gentry.  The criticism in question relates to part of the statistical evidence adduced in my article as offering some corroboration of that view. The relevant figures are those contained in the Table in footnote 90 on p. 202 above, and those appearing on p. 204.  The former shows the direction of the changes taking place in the relative importance of estates of different sizes in terms—a point touched on below—of manors owned. The latter illustrate the opinion expressed by Harrington and others as to the simultaneous alteration, which they believed to have occurred, in the distribution of land between different categories of owners.

It is unfortunate, I think, that Mr Trevor-Roper, in his preoccupation with the fate of the aristocracy, concentrated his whole attention on the second set of figures, and, unless I have overlooked some passage, ignored the first.  In reality, of course, it was precisely the growth, depicted in the first, of middle-sized estates as compared with large which prompted contemporary comments on the change in the " balance " of property, and to which reference has recently been made from different angles by writers entitled to respect, including Professor Campbell, Dr Hoskins and Mr Stone.  On a few of the causes of that movement I endeavoured, in touching on the effects of the Dissolution, of the sale of royal domains and of the progress, such as it was, of a more business-like agriculture, to throw a little light.  The Table on p. 202 above shows it at work. It does so without raising the problems of definition and classification which, not unnaturally, perplex Mr Trevor-Roper, and which cause him to dismiss as a mare's-nest, not only my own very inadequate contribution, but the conclusions of intelligent observers who knew the facts at first hand.

Obviously, as I emphasised in my article, the movement in question was accompanied by changes in the opposite direction.  To call attention to its significance no more implies a denial of the existence of imposing fortunes, whether territorial or derived from commerce and finance, at the upper end of the scale than would a similar reference by a historian of Victorian England to the rising incomes and influence of manufacturers and mine-owners.  But one cannot disprove the reality of a trend merely by producing a handful of specimens which do not reflect it; and, as a criticism on the argument of my article, Mr Trevor-Roper's useful little catalogue of noble plutocrats is, it seems to me, beside the point.  In order to refute my by no means novel thesis that, in the period concerned, economic and political tides were running in favour of medium-sized estates and the social groups based upon them, Mr Trevor-Roper should have produced equally comprehensive figures

showing that no discernible trend affecting the size of estates occurred,
or that, if one did occur, its direction was contrary to that suggested in
my Table. Such new evidence would have been a welcome addition to
our knowledge of a difficult subject, of which, I should be the first to
agree, I touched only the fringe. Unfortunately, apart from interesting
individual instances, Mr Trevor-Roper does not attempt to supply it.

A contribution which treats so lightly the central issue is necessarily
something of an *ignoratio elenchi*; but it may, nevertheless, contain
suggestive observations on other points. One such point rightly raised
by Mr Trevor-Roper is the question of the relative gains made and losses
sustained, in respect of landed property, by the peers as compared with
the gentry. On his strictures on my use, in that connection, of the
category, manor, I need not dwell. My comments on the ambiguities
of the term were more emphatic than his own. The fact remains that,
in employing manors as a rough index of property owned, I followed, as
most students of agrarian documents and literature will, I think, agree,
the prevalent practice of the day. To sweep aside, as a mere will-of-
the-wisp, that whole mass of contemporary usage, on the ground that a
manor was "a definition of rights, not a unit of wealth",[1] is not—to
speak with moderation—according to light. The main burden, however, of Mr Trevor-Roper's censures on this part of my article rests, as I
understand him, elsewhere. As I explained, I classified as manors
owned by gentry in 1640 those owned by families so described in 1561,
even if those families had in the interval been ennobled. The result,
he remarks, is to compare the properties of a growing body of gentry
with those of a stationary or diminishing group of peers. "No wonder
the gentry, thus calculated, appear to 'rise' at the expense of the
peerage."

This objection to the classification used in my article did not escape
my notice when, after some hesitation, I decided to adopt it. An
obvious alternative to it, and one not open to the same criticism, would
have been an arrangement which included in the manors owned in 1640
by peers, and excluded from the manors owned at that date by gentry,
all those in the ownership of families ennobled since 1561. I considered that course and rejected it. I did so, I hope—though one never
knows—not as one of the criminal crew of "advocates of theories who

---

[1] Mr Trevor-Roper's description of a manor is correct enough, as far as it goes; but
it omits too much to be of more than limited use. Since—to mention nothing else—
the rights concerned derived their value from the actual and prospective income yielded
by them, his sharp contrast between a "definition of rights" and "a unit of wealth"
is a false antithesis. It can hardly be suggested that surveyors, in recording such rights,
were uninterested in their economic aspects, or that, in stating the revenue from a manor
and indicating methods by which it could be increased, they did not regard the property
in question as a "unit of wealth". What possibly Mr Trevor-Roper means is that a
manor was not a uniform or standardised unit. If so, his statement is, not only true,
but a truism.

have looked for the evidence which they want only in the field in which, if found, it would fit those theories ", but for a more pedestrian reason. It seemed—and seems—to me unrealistic to credit to the peerage properties many or most of which had been acquired by gentry before they were ennobled, and the successful accumulation of which, as Mr Godfrey Davies reminds us, had been among the attributes mentioned in 1629 by the Lords as qualifying their possessors to blossom into peers. Indeed, in view of the mass additions[2] to the peerage which, when allowance is made for peerages extinguished, more than doubled between 1603 and 1639 the lay membership of the House of Lords, and which, of course, converted by a stroke of the pen properties owned by gentry into properties owned by peers, the adjective "unrealistic" strikes me, on second thoughts, as too weak a word. If only James and Charles had manufactured, not a miserable handful of ninety or so peers, but a full-blooded three hundred, how dizzy the heights to which, on the procedure which I am rebuked for rejecting, aristocratic landed fortunes would have been seen to soar, and how tragic the stagnation or decline of those of the gentry!

A classification, whether employed by Mr Trevor-Roper or by myself, which permits a change in the nomenclature of property-owners to be confused with a shift in the ownership of property clearly will not do. I am not at all concerned, however, to defend as beyond reproach the basis of calculation adopted in my article. It had, in my opinion, the advantage of throwing light on the dynamic tendencies at work, but I should agree that it was more useful for that purpose than as a precise statement of the situation obtaining in the year 1640. The gravamen of Mr Trevor-Roper's indictment is, I understand, that, in crediting to the gentry, instead of to the peers, the manors owned by families ennobled between 1561 and 1640, I artificially limited the aristocracy to "a diminishing group of families which happened to be noble at the beginning and still noble at the end of the period ". If such was my sin, I am happy to earn an easy absolution by substituting, against my better judgement, the second for the first of the two methods of classification mentioned above. The change, needless to say, makes some difference to the figures on p. 204 of the present volume. The important question is how great that difference is.

An attempt to offer a provisional answer to that question is made in the Table printed below. In the case of 2,547 manors in seven counties the number of manors owned in 1640 by families ennobled since 1561

[2] The lay membership of the House of Lords appears to have been 59 at the death of Elizabeth. She had created in the course of her reign 8 new peers. Those created by James numbered about 60, and those created by Charles in the first fifteen years of his reign, exclusive of 8 eldest sons of peers called up, about 30. (G. Davies, *The Early Stuarts, 1603-1660*, 264.) The number of peerages extinguished between 1560 and 1640 is given by Mr Trevor-Roper (*Supplement*, 5) as 20. The net addition to the peerage made between 1603 and 1639 would appear, therefore, to have been in the region of 70.

is at my disposal.[3]  The figure appears to have been approximately 186. Lines 2(a) and 2(b) of the Table set out the distribution of manors in 1640 between different categories of owners on two assumptions: (a) that the 186 manors concerned should be credited, as in my article, to the gentry, (b) that, as I understand Mr Trevor-Roper to hold, they should be credited to the peers.  Thus the reader has before him the results of two alternative methods of classifying the figures for 1640.  Comparing them with each other, and both with the figures for 1561 which appear in line (1) of the Table, he can reach his own conclusions for himself. One further point should, perhaps, be mentioned.  Mr Trevor-Roper reproves me for failing to take account of "the yeomen and merchants who throughout the period were buying manors", and whose property, he suggests, I improperly included in that of the gentry.  Whatever significance that criticism may have possessed for the figures printed in my article (p. 204 above), it has no application to those in line 2(b) of the Table given here.  The latter assign to the gentry the manors of yeomen and merchants gentilised between 1561 and 1640 in precisely the same manner as they assign to the peers the manors of gentry ennobled between those dates.  Thus the majestic goddess, Parity of Reasoning, to whom Mr Trevor-Roper rightly makes his bow, has received her due.

THE OWNERSHIP OF 2,547 MANORS IN SEVEN COUNTIES IN 1561 AND 1640

(1) 1561

| Total | Crown | Peers | Gentry | Ecclesiastical | Colleges, Hospitals and Schools | Other |
|---|---|---|---|---|---|---|
| 2,547 | 242 | 335 | 1,709 | 185 | 67 | 9 |
|  | (9·5 p. cent) | (13·1 p. cent) | (67·1 p. cent) | (7·2 p. cent) | (2·6 p. cent) |  |

(2) 1640

(a)

Assigning to gentry manors owned by families ennobled 1561–1640

| Total | Crown | Peers | Gentry | Ecclesiastical | Colleges, Hospitals and Schools | Other |
|---|---|---|---|---|---|---|
| 2,547 | 53 | 157 | 2,051 | 179 | 76 | 31 |
|  | (2·0 p. cent.) | (6·1 p. cent) | (80·5 p. cent) | (7·0 p. cent) | (3·0 p. cent) |  |

(b)

Assigning to peers manors owned by families ennobled 1561–1640

| Total | Crown | Peers | Gentry | Ecclesisatical | Colleges, Hospitals and Schools | Other |
|---|---|---|---|---|---|---|
| 2,547 | 53 | 343 | 1,865 | 179 | 76 | 31 |
|  | (2·0 p. cent) | (13·4 p. cent) | (73·3 p. cent) | (7·0 p. cent) | (3·0 p. cent) |  |

The points in this Table which first deserve notice are, perhaps, two.

In the first place, a comparison of 2(a) and 2(b) shows that, as would have been expected, the difference made by crediting to the peers, instead of to the gentry, the 186 manors owned by families ennobled

[3] The seven counties in question are Hertfordshire, Bedfordshire, Buckinghamshire, Surrey, Worcestershire, Hampshire and the North Riding of Yorkshire.  Those represented in the figures on p. 204 above, but not included here, are Gloucestershire, Warwickshire and Northamptonshire, for which the number of families ennobled 1561-1640 is not at the moment to hand.

between 1561 and 1640 is substantial.   The effect is more than to double
both the number and the percentage of the manors owned in 1640 by
peers, and to reduce the proportion then owned by gentry from 80 to 73
per cent or by over one-eighth.   On my original basis of calculation,
which corresponded with that of 2(a), peers owned in 1640 just over one-
sixteenth, and gentry four-fifths, of the manors concerned: on that used
in 2(b) the former then owned something between one-seventh and one-
eighth, and the latter slightly less than three-quarters.   On the second
method of classification, the gentry still owned more than five times as
many manors as the peers, but the change produced by the substitution
of it for the first, though not revolutionary, is evidently marked.

In the second place, it is necessary to return to the object with which
the figures were originally compiled, and to compare the distribution of
manors in 1561 and 1640.   For the reasons stated above, I do not accept
the view that the correct course is to assign to the peers all the manors
owned at the second of those dates by families ennobled since the first.
If, however, that issue be waived, and a comparison made between (1)
and 2(b), the following points emerge.

First, in spite of the transference of the 186 manors in question from
gentry to peers, those owned by the latter have increased between 1561
and 1640 by only 8, or between 2 and 3 per cent.   Their property, in
short, has been virtually static.   The manors owned by the former have
increased, again in spite of the same transference, by 156, or by approximately one-tenth.

Second, the proportion of manors in the ownership of the peers is at
both dates almost exactly the same, 13 per cent of the total.   That in
the ownership of the gentry has risen from slightly more than two-thirds
to just under three-quarters.

In view of these facts, it cannot plausibly be argued, as far as the
seven counties in question are concerned, either that the landed wealth
of the nobility was on the ascent between 1561 and 1640 or that that
of the gentry was stationary or in decline.   The movement, in short,
was in the opposite direction from that which, unless I misunderstand
him, is suggested by Mr Trevor-Roper.[4]

It is proper that emphasis should be laid on the differing results
of the alternative bases of calculation in 2(a) and 2(b).   I am grateful
to Mr Trevor-Roper for inciting me to ascertain the dimensions of
the difference in question.   It does not seem to me, however, that
the employment of the second method greatly alters the picture of the
upper strata of rural society suggested by the first.   Whether the gentry

---

[4] "The rise of the aristocracy under the Stuarts is far more significant than any
decline they may have experienced under Elizabeth, and . . . the decline of the declining
gentry in the early seventeenth century is at least as significant as the rise of the rising
gentry" (Supplement, 32).   See also the reference to the " decline of the gentry " in
Mr Trevor-Roper's article "The Elizabethan Aristocracy: an Anatomy Anatomised " in
The Economic History Review, 2nd ser., III (1951), 294-5, note 5.

owned in 1640 four-fifths of the manors or just under three-quarters is, no doubt, an interesting question, but it is not one of the first importance. In either case they remained, as owners of that species of property, overwhelmingly the predominant group, and one whose lead had in the two preceding generations increased. Partly because, in the cease-less re-shuffling of property between well-to-do landowners, they gained, in these counties, during the eighty years in question, more from the peers than the peers gained from them, but principally because it was the gentry, not the nobility, who acquired the lion's share of the estates sold by the Crown, their preponderance was more marked in 1640 than in 1561.[5]

An apology is due for inflicting on the reader this tedious re-examination of the figures contained in my article. If I have ventured to trespass on his patience, the reason has not been a proprietary attach-ment to a thesis which, when published, thirteen years ago, in *The Economic History Review*, had no pretensions to originality, and which since then, corrected, supplemented, elaborated, refuted, and on occa-sion, perhaps, partially confirmed, has floated upwards into intellectual spheres beyond its author's worm's eye view. It has been merely a desire to review my admittedly crude conclusions in the light of the latest criticisms on them. Mr Trevor-Roper's *Supplement* contains a variety of observations, some questionable, some instructive, on topics of interest not touched on in my article. While welcoming his strictures on the latter, I remain, save on points of detail, unconvinced by them. On some important subjects, which space forbids me to discuss, for example—to mention only one—the course of landed incomes—his comments do not seem to me to be confirmed by such additional evi-dence as recent work has brought to light; nor, though agreeing that grants by the Crown deserve a heavier emphasis than I gave them, do I regard them as possessing in this connection the preponderant signifi-cance ascribed them by Mr Trevor-Roper. For the rest, apart from a faint distrust of his occasional orderly-room manner with those bold,

---

[5] I note with interest that, on the point of the landed property of peers, Mr Stone has arrived, by a much more thorough and comprehensive investigation than mine, at conclusions similar in kind to those suggested by me. In his admirable article, "The Elizabethan Aristocracy—a Restatement" (*The Economic History Review*, IV, (1952), no. 3), he has shown that, between 1558 and 1602, the net sales of manors by peers created before 1602 amounted to 28 per cent of the manors owned, inherited and granted 1558-1602, and, between 1603 and 1642, to 16 per cent of those owned, inherited, and granted 1603-1642. In the twelve and a half years represented in his article, "all the peerage, old and new taken together in 1642, held slightly fewer manors than did the Elizabethan peers in 1558. The peerage had more than doubled its numbers, but its landed property had failed to increase." Mr Stone's contrast between the rates at which noble disinvestmen. was taking place in the periods before and after 1603 is a great improvement on my treatment of the subject. He does not discuss the question of the purchasers of the 337 manors (net) disposed by the peers over the whole period. If the properties in question went the same way as in the counties covered by my figures, a large proportion of them were absorbed by the gentry.

bad men, the seventeenth-century deviationists[6] who fail to keep in step, my principal grounds of dissent from those of his criticisms to which I have here confined myself are two.

The first, to which I have already referred, is his failure to rebut, or indeed, to examine, the evidence indicating a growth of what, for lack of a better phrase, I have called medium-sized estates, as compared with the relative decline of large. I regard that change, which has parallels in other departments of economic life, as among the most important movements of the day. The Table on p. 202 illustrating it is probably, on a broad view, of greater significance than the statistics relating to the distribution of manors between different categories of proprietor; but pointing, as they do, in the same direction, the two sets of figures reinforce each other. If the movement revealed by the first is a mere figment, it should surely have been possible for Mr Trevor-Roper to produce some evidence to that effect. As far as I can see, apart from some interesting biographical matter, he produces none.

In the second place, he greatly exaggerates, it seems to me, the effect of my assignment to the gentry, instead of to the peers, of the manors owned in 1640 by families ennobled since 1561. The choice of statistical methods is partly a matter of judgement, and my judgement on

---

[6] See *e.g. Supplement*, 44-7. I must confess to finding the argument of these pages slightly obscure. Statements by Bacon, Raleigh and Selden are dismissed, partly, if I rightly understand Mr Trevor-Roper, because they relate to a past too remote to be relevant, partly because they refer to political factors with which, he appears to imply, I have no concern. Statements by later writers and speakers are rejected, partly on the opposite ground that they relate, not to "a historical process" of some length, but to "the violent change of the last decade", partly because their evidence, "being evidence of confiscation not voluntary sale, is quite irrelevant to Professor Tawney's thesis".

I stated in my article that, at the period in question, "economic and political conditions combined to mobilise real property". I am somewhat surprised, therefore, that Mr Trevor-Roper should seem to suppose that I was concerned solely with the former, and that political factors were outside my purview. I also dwelt at some length on the gains accruing to the gentry as a result of the Dissolution, gains in which both confiscation and "voluntary sale" played a part. I am not less surprised, therefore, to be told that my business was with the latter alone. If it was proper, as obviously it was, to refer to the changes in the distribution of property caused by the greatest confiscation of the sixteenth century, I find it difficult to grasp why it is "quite irrelevant" to refer to the analogous changes produced by the greatest confiscation of the seventeenth, and to cite contemporary opinions on them.

I have not elsewhere thought it necessary to notice Mr Trevor-Roper's minor misinterpretations of my views, such, for example, as his ascription to me of the opinion —which I expressly disclaimed—"that it was only the gentry who took trouble over their estates"; but one of them, since it relates to Harrington, ought, perhaps, to be corrected. After referring to a passage in which I correctly stated that Harrington's relatives had obtained ecclesiastical and royal property, and that the author of the *Oceana* had, therefore, an instance of such a transfer beneath his eyes, he continues, "In other words" [*sic*] "the Harringtons themselves were"—according to me—"a family of 'rising' gentry". I made no such statement. To assert that many gentry found in the acquisition of such property a means of rising is not to suggest that all who acquired it were rising gentry. Mr Trevor-Roper's admonitory disquisition on the history of the Harringtons, therefore, is off the mark.

the point in question remains what it was.  Since, however, Mr Trevor-Roper's opinion differs from mine, I have been happy to give a trial to a method of calculation which I understand him to regard as not open to the same objections as that used in my article.  The results, as given above, do not, it seems to me, go far to confirm his suggestion that the rise of the gentry is an optical illusion which the procedure preferred by him would be sufficient to dispel.  *E pur si muove.*  Even when submitted to Doctor Trevor-Roper's lowering treatment, the incorrigible patient continues to swell.

An erring colleague is not an Amalekite to be smitten hip and thigh. My correction of some of Mr Trevor-Roper's misconceptions has, I trust, been free from the needless and unpleasing asperity into which criticism, to the injury of its cause, is liable on occasion to lapse.  Let me conclude by referring to a topic of, I hope, a non-controversial kind.  A comment which I am disposed to make, not only on his contribution and my own, but on much other work in the same and adjacent fields, relates to the ambiguities of the terminology employed.  "Nobility" is, perhaps, an exception; but the groups described by the words "aristocracy" and "gentry" melt at their edges into each other, and the terms themselves contain an element of opinion as well as of fact.  There are indications that "yeoman" carried different shades of meaning in different regions. "Merchant", as used by contemporaries, commonly embraced, not only the wholesale exporters who asserted in vain their exclusive title to the name, but financiers of several different types, as well as, in spite of protests, shopkeepers who might ship a parcel or two, but whose stand-by was retail trade.  On the disastrous twilight shed by the worst offender of all, a very prince of darkness, "the middle-classes"—a phrase then, in a slightly different form, coming into use—it is needless to dwell.

Categories so general are not useless, and cannot be discarded. Apart from their serviceableness as missiles in the mutual bombardments of historians, they have the virtue of suggesting problems, if at times they increase the difficulty of solving them.  It would obviously be an advantage, however, if the composite social entities described by these comprehensive terms could be broken up, and the crude classifications in vogue today supplemented by an analysis sufficiently refined to bring to light the variety of species, economic, regional and cultural, within the groups concerned, which our conventional phraseology tempts us to overlook.  How such a more discriminating procedure can most hopefully be attempted, and what lines it should pursue, cannot here be discussed.  It seems to me, however, that the problem is sufficiently important to deserve that part of the attention of economic and social historians should be devoted to it.

# THE DECLINE OF SPAIN

## EARL J. HAMILTON

THE union of Castile and Aragon, the overthrow of the Moslem kingdom of Granada, the discovery of America, the conquest of Naples, and the annexation of Navarre under the Catholic Kings; the acquisition of Burgundy, Flanders, the Low Countries, Franche-Comté, and Milan under Charles V; and the addition of Portugal, with its vast oriental possessions, under Philip II, gave Spain the political hegemony of Europe and an Empire far greater than any other nation had ever controlled. Even the boldest proponents of an economic interpretation of history would probably hesitate to explain the rise of the Spanish Empire in materialistic terms; but, despite unsatisfactory knowledge of almost every phase of Spanish economic history, it seems safe to say that agriculture, industry and commerce moved forward throughout most of the sixteenth century, and that the economic support of the Empire under Charles V and Philip II was not drawn solely from Flanders, Italy and America.

The navigation Acts of Ferdinand and Isabella, subsidies for the construction and operation of ships meeting royal specifications by the Catholic Kings and Charles V, and the maritime problems entailed by world dominions gave Spain at least the second largest merchant marine in Europe during the reign of Philip II. In fact, with the Portuguese fleets included, in 1585, the Spanish merchant marine rivalled, if it did not outrank, the Dutch, doubled the German and trebled the English and French.[1]

Inasmuch as the lag of wages behind prices, the chief cause of industrial progress in all countries during the price revolution precipitated by the influx of Mexican and Peruvian silver, was considerably less than in England and France,[2] Spanish manufacturers advanced less rapidly than the English and French in the sixteenth century;[3] but the phenomenal

---

[1] A. P. Usher, "Spanish Ships and Shipping in the Sixteenth and Seventeenth Centuries", Facts and Factors in Economic History (Cambridge, Mass., 1932), 202-13; Earl J. Hamilton, "Spanish Mercantilism before 1700", ibid. 214-39; Archivo General de Indias, Contratación, 42-6-5/9 to 42-6-13/17.

[2] See Earl J. Hamilton, "American Treasure and the Rise of Modern Capitalism", Economica (Nov. 1929), 338-57.

[3] In a forthcoming article on "Prices, Wages, and the Industrial Revolution" I demonstrate that the increase in the supply of capital and enhanced business incentive resulting from a sharp advance of commodity prices and a notable lag of money wages in the last half of the eighteenth century rank as a major cause, hitherto unnoticed, of the Industrial Revolution. See Pennsylvania University, Bicentennial Conference. Studies in Economics and Industrial Relations. (Philadelphia 1941) 99-112.

growth of all industrial cities, with the virtual doubling of the population of such centres as Burgos, Segovia and Toledo between the censuses of 1530 and 1594, attests the industrial progress of the kingdom in the *siglo de oro*. It is true that Spain remained, as always, primarily a producer of raw materials, exporting wine, olive oil and wool in return for foreign wares; but, although satisfactory data on the development of manufactures are not available,[4] it seems that the silk, wool, glove, leather and cutlery industries not only supplied a large part of the domestic market but furnished considerable exports to the Indies.[5] The increase of population in peninsular Spain, exclusive of Portugal, by approximately 15 per cent (in spite of emigration to the New World, the garrisoning of fortresses in Italy, Flanders and Africa, and heavy losses in continuous wars) reflected substantial economic progress in the sixteenth century.[6]

Obviously it is impossible to date with precision the beginning of economic decline. Some of the causes extended back into the Middle Ages, and there is evidence that decadence was incipient late in the reign of Philip II; but catastrophic changes did not occur before 1598. In broad terms one can say that it took Spain only a century (from the union of Castile and Aragon, in 1479, to the annexation of Portugal, in 1580) to attain political pre-eminence and only a century (from the death of Philip II, in 1598, to that of Charles II, in 1700) to fall into the rank of a second-rate power. Economics and politics were clearly interrelated, but a loss of economic strength appears to have been more largely a cause than a result of the political decline.

Strong biases, pulling in the same direction, have infused into econo-mico-historical literature an exaggeration of Spanish economic decadence in the seventeenth century. The Germans have tended to magnify the extent of the collapse in order to glorify the Emperor Charles V through contrast; the French in order to exalt the economic policy of the first Bourbons; and the liberals of all countries in order to place absolutism,

---

[4] *Cf.* Julius Klein, *The Mesta* (Cambridge, Mass., 1920), 62; Manuel Colmeiro, *Historia de la Economía Política de España* (Madrid, 1863), II, 15.

[5] Maurice Ansiaux, " Histoire Économique de la Prospérité et de la Décadence de l'Espagne au XVIe et au XVIIe Siècles ", *Revue d'Economie Politique*, VII, 544-5, 550; Manuel Colmeiro, *op. cit.* II, 185.

[6] *Cf.* Ignacio de Asso, " *Historia de la Economía Política de Aragón* (Saragossa, 1798), 307-8, 331-2, 337-40; Konrad Häbler, *Die wirtschaftliche Blüte Spaniens im 16 Jahrhundert* (Berlin, 1888), 144-59; Tomás González, *Censo de Población de la Corona de Castilla en el Siglo XVI* (Madrid, 1829), 126-57, 160-70, 312, 390-4.

Largely through comparisons of the glaringly inaccurate guess at the Castilian population by Alonso de Quintanilla in 1482 with the subsequent censuses published by Tomás González, Albert Girard (" Le Chiffre de la Population dans les Temps Modernes ", *Revue d'Histoire Moderne* (Novembre-Décembre 1928), 425-6, 430; Janvier-Février (1929), 3-5), Bernard Moses (" The Economic Condition of Spain in the Sixteenth Century ", *Journal of Political Economy*, I, 514), and Manuel Colmeiro (*op. cit.* I, 238-9; II, 11-13) concluded that the population of Spain stood lower at the end than at the beginning of the sixteenth century. For a refutation of this thesis, see Earl J. Hamilton, *American Treasure and the Price Revolution in Spain, 1501-1610* (Cambridge, Mass., 1934), 298-9.

the Inquisition, the persecution of minorities and the Moorish expulsion in a more unfavourable light. But no reasonable allowance for over-estimation by economic historians can invalidate the abundant evidence that agriculture, industry and commerce declined sharply in the seven-teenth century. Contemporary economic literature and the proceedings of the Cortes complain of economic retrogression, and the inductive evidence available corroborates the jeremiads of authors and statesmen.[7]

From the last quarter of the sixteenth century to the last quarter of the seventeenth the tonnage of the ships plying between Spain and the Indies fell by approximately 75 per cent,[8] and in the latter period the trade had virtually passed into the hands of foreigners who supplied " five-sixths of the cargoes of the outbound fleets ".[9] It has been said that by the middle of the seventeenth century enough fishermen could not be found to equip a fleet.[10] Despite the attempts of Philip IV and Charles II to stimulate maritime revival, shipbuilding in Spain virtually ceased; and, with the naval losses in Europe and America, the Spanish flag almost disappeared from the seas.[11]

Dr Julius Klein has shown that the number of sheep in the flocks of the Mesta, or guild of migratory herders, diminished after 1560 and fell precipitately in the seventeenth century; but it seems that gains in sedentary grazing partially compensated for this loss.[12] In 1619 it was reported that the livestock in the bishopric of Salamanca had declined by 60 per cent since 1600, and in the same year the Council of Castile complained that villages were falling into ruins and fields becoming deserts.[13] The lag of agricultural behind non-agricultural prices in the second quarter of the seventeenth century[14] indicates that in this period agricultural was less severe than industrial decadence, but the complaints of rural depopulation and agricultural distress continued throughout the century. In fact, at the end of the century agriculture remained rudi-mentary;[15] and the country was on the verge of famine.[16]

The increasing dependence on foreign markets for masts, tar, hemp, sail-cloth and other naval supplies after 1600[17] reflected industrial

[7] Earl J. Hamilton, " The Mercantilism of Gerónimo de Uztáriz: A Re-examination ", *Economics, Sociology, and the Modern World* (Cambridge, Mass., 1935), 111.

[8] A. P. Usher, *op. cit.* 202-13 ; Archivo General de Indias, *Contratación*, 42-6-9/13 to 42-6-13/17.

[9] C. H. Haring, *Trade and Navigation between Spain and the Indies in the Time of the Hapsburgs* (Cambridge, Mass., 1918), 113, 122, 213-15.

[10] Maurice Ansiaux, *op. cit.* 1049. In the first half of the seventeenth century fish prices rose a great deal more than the general price level in Andalusia and Valencia but less in Old Castile, which Dutch and French vessels supplied as the Spanish fisheries decayed (Earl J. Hamilton, *American Treasure and the Price Revolution*, 230).

[11] C. H. Haring, *op. cit.* 243, 270.

[12] *Op. cit.* 28, 337, 342-3, 352.                    [13] Manuel Colmeiro, *op cit.* II, 82.

[14] Earl J. Hamilton, *American Treasure and the Price Revolution in Spain*, 261.

[15] Albert Girard, " L'Espagne à la Fin du XVII Siècle ", *Revue de Synthèse Histo-rique*, XXVI, 104.

[16] Maurice Ansiaux, *op. cit.* 1057-8.                    [17] A. P. Usher, *op. cit.* 203.

15

decadence. By 1619 industrial stagnation had proceeded far enough to evoke a *consulta* from the Council of Castile, and the following year Philip III formed a *junta* to consider remedies for languishing industry. Complaints of impoverishment from such important manufacturing cities as Toledo, Cordova, Seville, Granada and Valencia received the attention of the Crown in 1655.[18] In the same year Francisco Martínez Mata noted the disappearance of numerous craft guilds, including workers in iron, steel, copper, tin, sulphur and alum; and the once flourishing glove industry was almost dead.[19] According to contemporary complaints, Burgos was in ruins and Segovia was a desert.[20] The number of woollen manufacturers in Toledo declined about three-fourths in the first two-thirds of the seventeenth century;[21] and the manufacture of arms, the one industry that should have flourished under the stimulus of perpetual wars, reached such a low ebb that the Cortes petitioned the Crown to import artisans to revive it.[22] In 1674 the Aragonese established a *junta* to formulate remedies for industrial ruin.[23] Almost all manufacturing cities suffered a catastrophic decline in population between the censuses of 1594 and 1694; Valladolid, Toledo and Segovia, for example, lost more than half of their inhabitants. The decrease of the Spanish population by approximately 25 per cent in the seventeenth century leaves little doubt that, unlike the Italian city states in the sixteenth century, Spain suffered an absolute as well as a relative economic decline.

With almost complete unanimity, previous writers since the seventeenth century have regarded the Moorish expulsion of 1609-14[24] as the overshadowing cause of Spanish economic decadence.[25] There has been common agreement that the Moors were the most industrious, intelligent, persevering and thrifty inhabitants of Spain, "the flower of her artisans", the cream of her agriculturists, and almost the only subjects who did not disdain manual labour, routine operations and prosaic toil.[26] We are told that the expulsion of the Moriscos utterly ruined the rice fields of Valencia, the sugar industry of Granada, and the vineyards

[18] Manuel Colmeiro, *op. cit.* II, 202.
[19] Raymond Bona, *Essai sur le Problème Mercantiliste en Espagne* (Bordeaux, 1911), 66; Maurice Ansiaux, *op cit.* 1049. [20] *Ibid.* 1049-50.
[21] Sarah E. Simons, "Social Decadence", *Annals of the American Academy of Political and Social Science*, XVIII, 264.
[22] Raymond Bona, *op. cit.* 65. [23] Manuel Colmeiro, *op. cit.* II, 204.
[24] The Moors were expelled from Valencia, Castile proper, Extremadura, and la Mancha in 1609; from Granada, Andalusia, and Aragon in 1610; from Catalonia in 1611; and from Murcia in 1614.
[25] Henry Charles Lea, "The Decadence of Spain", *Atlantic Monthly*, LXXXII, 37; "The Arabs in Spain", *The Eclectic Magazine* (Aug. 1858), 555; Maurice Ansiaux, *op. cit.* II, 69-70, 85; *Quarterly Review*, CLXXXIX, 218.
[26] Henry Charles Lea, *The Moriscos of Spain: Their Conversion and Expulsion* (London, 1901), 383, 400; Richard H. Titherington, "The Rise and Fall of Spain", *Munsey's Magazine*, XIX, 728; Francis Wharton, "The Commercial Decline of Spain", *Hunt's Merchants' Magazine*, VII, 502; Raymond Bona, *op. cit.* 40; Bernard Moses, *op. cit.* 520-1; Maurice Ansiaux, *op. cit.* 1036; Manuel Colmeiro, *op. cit.* II, 71, 85.

of Spain; that irrigation channels immediately fell into hopeless disrepair; and that artisans were lacking and unskilled labourers scarce.[27]

Facts are not in accord with the accepted thesis concerning the
economic consequences of the Moorish expulsion. It is difficult to see
how a race largely denied educational opportunities, social privileges,
civil liberties and equality before the law[28] could have been the most
enlightened portion of the Spanish nation. If the Moors were strikingly
superior and if great numbers were expelled, why did they not develop
the geographically similar Barbary States into which most of them
passed?[29]

The price stability of most of the commodities formerly produced by
the Moriscos in the decade following their expulsion affords strong
evidence that this despicable act of religious intolerance was not a major
cause of economic decadence. The Moors were outstanding producers
of wine, and the Koran deterred them from consuming alcoholic bever-
ages; yet the movement of wine prices in 1610-20 fails to reflect a notable
decrease in supply with little, or no, countervailing drop in demand.
The downward trend of rice quotations (against the current of general
prices) in the decade following the expulsion indicates that the loss of
Morisco labour from the Valencian fields, which largely supplied Spain,
had no significant effect upon production.[30] The continuation of sugar
purchases from Granada by the Hospital dels Inocents at Valencia on
the usual scale after 1609 (despite increasing competition with low-cost
producers in America) and the approval by the Cortes in 1617 of an
excise tax on sugar produced in Granada, as one means of relieving a
bankrupt treasury,[31] demonstrate that the Moorish expulsion did not
wreck this industry. "Although a considerable part of the Moriscos
were peddlers, traders and mendicants, by far the greater number were
peasant agriculturists."[32] Agricultural prices actually dropped in the
two years following the great expulsion of 1609, when most of the deportation took place; failed to rise faster than non-agricultural in
1612-25; and lagged far behind the non-agricultural series in the second

---

[27] André Mounier, *Les Faits et la Doctrine Économique sous Philippe V* (Bordeaux,
1919), 10; Leon Androoni, "Commerce and Industry in Spain during Ancient and
Mediaeval Times", *Journal of Political Economy*, XXI, 436; "The Arabs in Spain",
*The Eclectic Magazine* (Aug. 1855), 563; "Spain under Charles II", *Littell's Living Age*,
C, 452; Bernard Moses, *op. cit.* 521; Maurice Ansiaux, *op. cit.* 1038-9; Manuel Colmeiro,
*op. cit.* II, 95.

[28] Francisco García, *Tratado Utilissimo de Todos los Contratos* (Valencia, 1583), 11;
Henry Charles Lea, *The Moriscos of Spain*, 178 *et seq.*

It seems that the status of the Moors at the time of the expulsion was somewhat
similar to that of the Negroes in the lower South of the United States today.

[29] Cf. Louis Bertrand, "L'Espagne Musulmane", *Revue des Deux Mondes* (15 Jan-
vier 1932), 320.

[30] Earl J. Hamilton, *American Treasure and the Price Revolution*, 221, 304-5.

[31] *Actas de las Cortes de Castilla*, XXXIX (Madrid, 1916), 85-6.

[32] Julius Klein, *op. cit.* 338.

quarter of the seventeenth century.[33]    The expulsion obviously did not ruin agriculture.

The complete failure of the Moorish expulsion to raise either wages in general or the remuneration of any particular class of workers affords the strongest evidence available that the exodus of the Moriscos was not the chief cause of the decadence of Spain.[34]    That wage movements were not too sluggish to reflect the loss of a large percentage of the workers is shown by the rise of wages by nearly 30 per cent throughout the country in the three years following the severe pestilence of 1599-1600[35] and by an even higher percentage in Andalusia after the great plague of 1648-50.[36]

The Inquisition certainly would have prevented strong condemnation of the Moorish expulsion by the economists who witnessed it, but the Church could hardly have compelled the unqualified approval which pervades the economic literature of the first half of the seventeenth century.[37]    In the famous *consulta* of 1619 the Council of Castile did not list the Moorish expulsion among the numerous causes of economic distress;[38] and the debates in the Cortes in the following four decades, which were by no means devoid of opposition to the Church, failed to register denunciations of this act of intolerance.    The literary and artistic talents of Velásquez, Cervantes and Lope de Vega eulogised the expulsion; and, in fact, "all Spain regarded the expulsion of the Moors as the most glorious event in the reign of Philip III ".[39]

The failure of wages and prices to reflect the expulsion strongly suggests that few Moors were expelled.    The figure of 101,694, exclusive of nursing infants, compiled by the royal commissioners in charge of deportation[40] was apparently much more complete than economic historians have believed.    On 13 July, 1626, a deputy from Granada complained in the Cortes that there was a great number of Moors in Andalusia, " none of whom are willing to work in the fields or to take care of cattle, for which there is a notable lack of hands ".[41]    The strong traces of Moorish blood in Andalusia and Valencia at present suggest that many Moors remained in Spain.    Perhaps the resistance of the nobility and large landowners, which the Crown envisaged and attempted

---

[33] Earl J. Hamilton, *American Treasure and the Price Revolution*, 260-1.
[34] *Ibid.* 306.                    [35] *Ibid.* 271-3.
[36] See my book on *Money, Prices, and Wages in Spain, 1651-1800*, now in preparation.
[37] See, for example, Sancho de Moncada, *Restauración Política de España* (Madrid, 1619), f. 29.                    [38] Henry Charles Lea, *The Moriscos of Spain*, 384.
[39] " The Arabs in Spain ", *Eclectic Magazine* (Aug. 1855), 555.
While recognising a great intellectual debt to medieval Cordova, Claudio Sánchez Albornoz (" L'Espagne et Islam ", *Revue Historique*, CLXIX, 327-39) and Louis Bertrand (*op. cit.* 164-5) attribute such subsequent economic and political ills as particularism, neglect of industry and internal improvements, imperialism, and vagabondage to the Moorish invasion, domination, and reconquest.
[40] Tomás González, *op. cit.* 110.
[41] *Actas de las Cortes de Castilla*, XLV (Madrid, 1926), 222-3.

to placate by promising them the immobile property of deported tenants, took the form of shielding the Moors (more docile and easily exploited than Christians) against expulsion.

There has been general agreement among scholars [42] that one of the salient causes of Spanish economic decadence was the progressive decline in the character of the rulers from Philip II until the advent of the Bourbons.[43] Through their absolutism and tireless energy Charles V and Philip II greatly extended the centralisation of authority in the Crown begun by the Catholic Kings. Owing to their devotion to duty and their amazing capacity for work, Charles V and Philip II were able to govern the Empire almost single-handed. But the mediocrity of Philip III and the dissolute character of Philip IV led them to abandon the affairs of State to court favourites. During the reign of Philip III economic progress was stifled by the unscrupulousness and insatiable avarice of the Duke of Lerma.[44] Under the guidance of his imperialistic favourite, the Count of Olivares, Philip IV played a pitiable and ridiculous rôle while trying to emulate Philip II. Unmindful of the nation's weakness, he pitted Spain against France in 1635 and England in 1655. On several occasions a tottering Spain attempted to stand alone against the combined might of Europe. The Thirty Years' War was for Spain a thirty-nine years' war; and while it was in progress internal weakness permitted a revolt of the Catalans, which lasted twelve years and exhausted the economic life of that region to such a point that a hundred years was required for recovery. There were also serious uprisings in Andalusia, Biscaya, Sicily and Naples; and, frightened by the prospect of complete absorption under the imperialistic Olivares, Portugal waged a successful war for independence.

Although dependent upon favourites, Philip III and Philip IV were able to provide political stability by keeping their Prime Ministers in power for long periods. Diseased in mind and body from infancy, and constantly preoccupied with his health and eternal salvation, Charles II was incapable not only of governing personally but of either selecting his ministers or maintaining them in power. From the assumption of the regency by the Queen Mother, Mary Anne of Austria (too young, too ignorant of politics, and too servile to the pleasures of the court to

[42] Francis Wharton, "The Commercial Decline of Spain", *Hunt's Merchants' Magazine*, VII, 511; Henry Charles Lea, "The Decadence of Spain", *The Atlantic Monthly*, LXXXII, 41; David Hannay, "A King and a Wise Woman", *Blackwood's Magazine*, CCXXVIII, 605; "Edifying Letters", *ibid.* CCXXVII, 366-82; Albert Girard, *op. cit.* 101; Richard H. Titherington, "The Rise and Fall of Spain", *Munsey's Magazine*, XIX, 731; Maurice Ansiaux, *op. cit.* 1026, 1044-8; Review of W. Coxe's "Kings of Spain of the House of Bourbon", *Edinburgh Review*, XXI, 179; Bernard Moses, *op. cit.* 532-3.

[43] "It has been said that Charles V was a warrior and a king, Philip II only a king, Philip III and Philip IV not even kings, and Charles II not even a man" ("Spain under Charles II", *Littell's Living Age*, C, 467).

[44] Maurice Ansiaux, *op. cit.* 1033, 1040.

govern wisely), to the death of Charles II not one of the many individuals who rose to power displayed genuine ability.[45]  For years the King was expected to die at any moment, and his impotence early became evident. Consequently the whole reign of this imbecile creature, aptly characterised as "royal anarchy", was a protracted plot for the succession.[46] Spain was spared the internal revolts of the previous reign; but, taking advantage of her weakness, Louis XIV dismembered the European Empire.  In more than half of the thirty-five years' reign of Charles II Spain was at war against the powerful forces of the Sun King.

Great military conflicts (precipitated by imperialism, religious fanaticism and lavish expenditures) had increased the State debt and the burden of taxation under Charles V and Philip II; but when the rulers were able and the Spanish infantry was the terror of Europe, the results of these policies were less disastrous than under the weak kings of the seventeenth century, when Spanish arms were no longer invincible.

All economists recognise the evil effects of misgovernment even under *laissez-faire*; but, with the State intervention and paternalism prevailing in Spain, the economic consequences of progressively inferior administration were catastrophic.[47]

It was the crushing burden of taxation resulting from costly wars, the extravagance of the royal household, the inefficiency of tax farmers and collectors, and the avidity of court favourites rather than the expulsion of the Moriscos that ruined the sugar industry of Granada.  As taxes rose, the number of taxpayers fell with the decline in population and the increase in the ranks of the clergy and the nobility.  The unbearable burden of taxation at the end of the sixteenth century and throughout the seventeenth was an important factor in the decline of Spain.[48]

During the century of decline the Church seems to have been the only institution that grew.  Long before the close of the Middle Ages the extension of mortmain and the increase in the number of convents were condemned in the Cortes and in the writings of moral philosophers; but throughout the sixteenth century the Church gained ground, and in the seventeenth it marched forward at a phenomenal pace.  In 1619 the Council of Castile reported that the excessive number of ecclesiastics

[45] Albert Girard, *op. cit.* 111-14.

[46] Charles E. Chapman, *A History of Spain* (New York, 1930), 268-9.

[47] "It was no mere coincidence that the greatest triumphs of the sheep owners' gild should synchronise with the golden age of the Spanish empire under Charles V and Philip II.  The prestige of both crown and Mesta was dependent upon the supremacy of the same powers of centralisation.

"Similarly the collapse of the Mesta was inevitable with the decline of the monarchy, which had begun before the end of the sixteenth century " (Julius Klein, *The Mesta*, 356).

[48] Maurice Ansiaux, *op. cit.* 561, 1044-5; Henry Charles Lea, "The Decadence of Spain", *The Atlantic Monthly*, LXXXII, 41-2; Albert Girard, *op. cit.* 102.

and ecclesiastical institutions was ruining Spain, and the Spanish economists of the seventeenth century almost unanimously concurred in this
judgement.[49] There is reason to believe that the combined number of
priests, monks and nuns approximately doubled in the seventeenth century and constituted at the end of the period almost 180,000 out of a
total population of less than 6,000,000. The celibacy of the ecclesiastics
contributed to depopulation, and the indiscriminate distribution of alms
aggravated the grave problem of vagrancy and vagabondage. Although
the incompetence of the Church as a landowner has generally been
exaggerated, the increase in mortmain accompanying ecclesiastical expansion was probably a factor in the decline of agriculture. In every
European country during the seventeenth century religious censorship
of the press and speech undoubtedly stifled the intellectual progress
upon which economic advancement has always largely depended; but,
owing to the heavy hand of the Inquisition, the interference of the
Church with learning was at its worst in Spain.[50]

Dr Julius Klein has shown that the migratory sheep herds of the
Mesta contributed in various ways to deforestation and deterred the
development of arable agriculture. During the semi-annual migrations
the shepherds enjoyed the privilege of cutting enough branches from
trees to make corrals, fences, cabins, tanbark, fuel and dairy implements.
Futhermore, they were entitled to trim or even to fell trees in time of
drought, during the winter, and whenever for any other reason pasturage
was scarce. Far more serious was the practice (by migratory and
sedentary herders alike) of burning the trees in autumn to provide better
spring pasturage. Erosion was increased by the damage done to tender
shoots and moisture-retaining turf by the sheep themselves. The right
to pasture on waste lands, crown lands and even on town commons was
conferred by the *Fuero Juzgo*, or Visigothic Code. Profiting by the
growing power of the Crown, its ally, in the sixteenth century, the Mesta
prevented the enclosure of commons for arable. Throughout the two
centuries of Hapsburg rule continuous legislation provided for the return
to pasture of land converted into arable; but under the weak rulers of
the seventeenth century the laws were not enforced. The suppression of
competitive bidding for pastures by the Mesta organisation lowered the
incomes of the owners, and during the sixteenth century the judicial
authority vested in Mesta officials prevented adequate indemnities for

[49] In 1624 Fray Angel Manrique deplored the fact that there was not a town in which
the number of convents had not trebled in the last fifty years (Henry Charles Lea, *The
Moriscos of Spain*, 381).

[50] G. Desdevises du Dezert, *L'Espagne sous l'Ancien Régime*, 47-8; Henry Charles
Lea, "The Decadence of Spain", *The Atlantic Monthly*, LXXXII, 37, 40; Manuel
Colmeiro, *op. cit*, II, 51-2, 54; Sarah E. Simons, *op. cit*. 74, 257, 260-2; Bernard Moses,
*op. cit*. 524-5, 533; Raymond Bona, *op. cit*. 23-39, 52; André Mounier, *op. cit*. 18-21;
Albert Girard, *op. cit*. 102, 109; Maurice Ansiaux, *op. cit*. 511-13, 1028-29, 1052-3;
"Spain under Charles II", *Littell's Living Age*, C, 452.

the depredations of the migratory herds. But, with the decline of royal authority in the seventeenth century, the Mesta itself suffered through arbitrary levies by the local officials. The Mesta began to lose ground early in the reign of Philip II and became but a shadow of its former self in the seventeenth century, when, according to writers prior to Dr Klein,[51] its flocks crowded out other forms of agriculture. By the end of the reign of Charles II wool growing was absorbing the attention of nearly every Castilian peasant. Arable agriculture had given way to sheep raising in a large part of Spain, but it was to the sedentary pastoral industry in no way connected with the Mesta.[52]

The growth of *latifundia* through primogeniture, entailed estates and mortmain apparently gave grazing an advantage over arable agriculture. In the last quarter of the sixteenth century and the first half of the seventeenth grain prices in Andalusia and New Castile forged considerably ahead of the general price level, while the prices of animal products were moving harmoniously with those of general commodities.[53] The growth of large estates, the crushing burden of taxes[54] and the decline in consumer demand following the decimation of the population by the great plagues of 1599-1600 and 1648-50 [55] were the major causes of agricultural decadence. The sharp rise in the prices of forest products in the first half of the seventeenth century [56] suggests sufficiently rapid deforestation to aggravate the dearth of rainfall. The legal maximum grain prices were not a factor in the decline of agriculture, as has been alleged,[57] is evident from their complete lack of control over market quotations.[58]

Though by no means generally effective, to some extent the mercantilist obstructions to the outflow of specie impounded in Spain a part of the great influx of Mexican and Peruvian silver. Before the end of the century this process had raised prices and costs above the level in other European countries and thus handicapped export industries, naval construction and navigation. The illusion of prosperity created by American gold and silver in the age of mercantilism were partially responsible for the aggressive foreign policy, contempt for manual arts, vagrancy, vagabondage, luxury and extravagance, which led to the economic decadence of the seventeenth century. After 1600 the imports of American treasure fell precipitately, and by 1660 shrank to a small

---

[51] Miguel Caxa de Leruela was an exception. His *Restauración de la Abundancia de España* (Naples, 1631) was written to prove that the decadence of Spain was due to interference with the privileges of the Mesta.

[52] *The Mesta*, 28, 46, 86, 93-4, 105, 190, 301, 306-7, 320, 328-9, 337, 342-3, 351-2.

[53] Earl J. Hamilton, *American Treasure and the Price Revolution*, 228-9, 241-2.

[54] "Spain under Charles II", *Littell's Living Age*, C, 445-56; Maurice Ansiaux, *op. cit.* 521, 535, 555, 1053; Manuel Colmeiro, *op. cit.* II, 94; Julius Klein, *The Mesta*, 337.

[55] Earl J. Hamilton, *American Treasure and the Price Revolution*, 220, 273, 306.

[56] *Ibid.* 225.            [57] See, for example, Albert Girard, *op. cit.* 104.

[58] Earl J. Hamilton, *American Treasure and the Price Revolution*, 258-9.

fraction of their volume in the reign of Philip II.[59]   Since Spanish industry and commerce were geared to this steady and increasing stream of treasure, the sharp drop in the returns from the American mines was a severe shock to the economic life of the nation.

The industrial and commercial progress stimulated by the lag of wages behind prices during the first eight decades of the sixteenth century,[60] while technology was advancing, was checked by the parallel movement at the close of the century.   In the first half of the seventeenth century the index numbers of wages on a 1571-80 base were considerably above those of prices in all except five years.   Without technological progress to reduce costs correspondingly, business profits were eliminated; and under capitalism a ruinous decline of industry and commerce inevitably resulted.[61]

The golden age in literature and the fine arts and the silver age in money (during the sixteenth century) were succeeded by a bronze age in the seventeenth century.   While universally envied because of her monopoly of the American gold and silver mines, Spain saw the precious metals driven completely out of circulation by a cumbersome medium of exchange.   Like almost all monetary derangement from medieval debasement of the coinage to the inflation of currency and central bank credit of modern times, the unbridled alteration of the coinage in Spain, which began near the end of the reign of Philip II and gained momentum as the seventeenth century progressed, was largely due to a chronically unbalanced budget.   At frequent intervals in the last three-quarters of the seventeenth century the evils of inflation called forth corrective deflation, with sharp declines in the commodity price level and severe commercial crises as inevitable consequences.   The deflationary decree of 1628 brought prices downward by 9 per cent. From March 1641 to August 1642 wholesale prices at Seville rose by 93 per cent; and in a few days following the deflation of 15 September 1642 they dropped about 87 per cent.[62]   In 1680-2 commodity prices fell by 45·43 per cent as a result of deflation in 1680.[63]   From September 1929 to February 1933 wholesale commodity prices in the United States fell only 37·86 per cent, and the drop in the annual index from 1929 to 1933 was but 30·9 per cent.

While many beneficial effects flowed from the constant, and therefore dependable and predictable, rise in prices in the sixteenth century, it was not so with the sudden inflation and deflation in the seventeenth.

[59] Earl J. Hamilton, *American Treasure and the Price Revolution*, 34-5.

[60] Earl J. Hamilton, "American Treasure and the Rise of Modern Capitalism", *Economica* (Nov. 1929), 338-57; "Wages and Subsistence on Spanish Treasure Ships ", *Journal of Political Economy*, XXXVII, 430-50.

[61] Earl J. Hamilton, *American Treasure and the Price Revolution*, 273.

[62] Earl J. Hamilton, "Monetary Inflation in Castile ", *Economic History*, II, 177-212.

[63] See my book on *Money, Prices, and Wages in Spain, 1651-1800*, in preparation.

The numerous and sharp fluctuations in prices upset calculations, stifled initiative, impeded the vigorous conduct of business enterprise, and wreaked havoc upon the economic life of Spain.[64]

In a grave national emergency economists were right, for once, in their diagnoses and prescriptions. With prophetic vision, the Spanish economists of the seventeenth century (Sancho de Moncada, Pedro Fernández Navarrete, Gerónimo de Cevallos, José Pellicer de Ossau, Diego Saavedra Fajardo, Francisco Martínez Mata, Miguel Alvarez Osorio y Redín, and many others) denounced most of the evils leading Spain to ruin—such as primogeniture, mortmain, vagabondage, deforestation, redundance of ecclesiastics, contempt for manual labour and arts, indiscriminate alms, monetary chaos and oppressive taxation. Their reform programme comprised technological education, immigration of artisans, monetary stability, extensión of irrigation and improvement of internal waterways. History records few instances of either such able diagnosis of fatal social ills by any group of moral philosophers or of such utter disregard by statesmen of sound advice.[65]

[64] Earl J. Hamilton, *American Treasure and the Price Revolution*, 7, 103, 212.
[65] Earl J. Hamilton, "Spanish Mercantilism before 1700", *Facts and Factors in Economic History*, 237.

# DUTCH AND ENGLISH MERCHANT SHIPPING IN THE SEVENTEENTH CENTURY

## VIOLET BARBOUR

IN the early years of the seventeenth century the distinction between men-of-war and merchantmen was not clean-cut and exclusive. That a ship—any ship—must fight on occasion was almost as axiomatic as that she must float. Governments omitted nothing of encouragement or prescription to induce merchants to build stout ships and to arm and man them well, with the double purpose of securing the national trade and maintaining a supply of large ships from which a navy could be improvised when need should arise. But the seventeenth century saw the rise of highly professional navies, prolonged campaigns at sea, and an altered technique of fighting, in which boarding and hand-to-hand combat yielded slowly—but not entirely—to reliance on guns. With the recognition of ordnance as the major factor in naval victory came certain structural alterations in the fighting ships to accommodate more and bigger guns. Before the middle of the century the English navy, which was in advance of Continental navies in this adaptation, had developed distinctive fighting types: the great ship and the frigate.[1]

This evolution worked to the exclusion of armed merchantmen from the line of battle, and gradually reduced them to humble employment as victuallers, convoyers, or fireships. But the change in the naval status of merchantmen did not release the merchant service from the obligation of self-defence which would have enabled it to develop

---

[1] The great ship was well described by the Venetian Secretary in London in a letter to the Doge dated 12 November (N.S.), 1655: "There has lately been invented, a build of enormous ships, carrying as many as 120 brass guns, & which without exaggeration may be termed moving fortresses, and floating garrisons, for there are from 7 to 8 hundred men on board of each, nor would one of these vessels single handed be afraid of 200 light gallies": Venetian Transcripts (P.R.O.) 37, No. 19. Broad and high, heavy and slow, they were difficult to manoeuvre and too topheavy for safety, but once in action: "The great ships are the ships do the business," declares Pepys, "They quite deadened the enemy": Diary, 16 June 1665. The frigate, by contrast, was swift, nimble, unencumbered, effectively but not ponderously armed. Not being intended for boarding the enemy, she was built lower to the water than the great ship, with decks more nearly flush. Originally a Dunkirk type, she was adopted into the navy of Charles I, and developed effectiveness in the Interregnum. For the history of the frigate, see J. S. Corbett, *England in the Mediterranean* (1904), I, 181 et seq.; M. Oppenheim, "The Navy of the Commonwealth" in *English Historical Review* (1896), 50.

usefully along its own lines. Historic tradition and national pride forbade such specialization. Strong ships and many of them were taken as implied by England's insular position, her titular sovereignty of the seas, the consideration of her trade, the reputation of Elizabethan captains, the stalwartness of Elizabethan seamen, the stoutness of English oak. There is often a hint of robust contempt in English allusions of this time to "weak ships", to convoy, even to insurance.[2] Dangers should be defied. To reinforce these sentiments there were practical considerations: the King's fleet might be destroyed, in which case the duty of defending the kingdom would revert to the merchantmen; privateering was perennial in European waters, and to the southward the Barbary pirates were numerous and audacious; financial difficulties which beset all English Governments in this century forbade adequate organization of convoy even in time of war.

In devotion to the principle of armed merchantmen there was little to choose between the successive Governments of seventeenth-century England. By Navigation Acts, giving preferences or monopolies to English shipping, by bonuses to the builders of ships of force, by remissions of customs duties, by prohibitions to sell ships of fighting capacity, by penalties to such masters as should surrender their ships without fighting, and finally by much reiteration, English subjects were reminded of their patriotic duty to build large and defensible ships. They did not always act upon this reminder. Indeed, the greater part of the merchant marine consisted of vessels of less than a hundred tons burthen.[3] But

[2] For this point of view, see Thomas Mun, *England's Treasure by Forraign Trade* (1928, reprint of the edn. of 1664), 78; Samuel Lambe, *Seasonable Observations humbly Offered to his Highness the Lord Protector* (1657, Brit. Mus. 712, m. 1, 26), 3 *et seq.*; Sir William Monson, *Naval Tracts*, V, 39 *et seq.*; "A Discourse of the Navy, 1660", by Sir Robert Slyngesbie (ed. J. R. Tanner), *Navy Records Soc. Pub.*, VII, 354-5.

[3] Of the numerous English craft fetching wine and brandy from Bordeaux in 1664, "les trois quarts des Navires Anglois sont des petits navires et Catches": State Papers, Foreign (P.R.O.), France, 118, ff. 264-5 [Arguments for a consulate at Bordeaux]. From a memorandum of the English ships that cleared for France between 29 September 1699 and 29 September 1670 we learn that 106 ships, averaging 54·2 tons, cleared from London (omitting those in ballast); while from the outports 802 ships (including those in ballast) averaged 36·5 tons: Shaftesbury Papers, Supplementary (P.R.O.), bundle vii, no. 602. In the same year, 1669, Sir John Finch, Resident in Tuscany, declared that the forbearance of the Algerines was being severely tried by the practice of English merchants "loading with rich commodities inconsiderable small ships": Bodleian Library, Rawlinson MSS., A 478, f. 1, 8 March 1668-9, to Lord Arlington (copy). The Bristol Port Books for the year 1670-1 show that the average burthen of 124 English-built ships clearing from that port was 47·8 tons; the average burthen of the 160 English-built ships entering the port of Bristol was 43·1 tons: Bristol Port Books (P.R.O.), 1137/2-3. In 1676, a year when English trade was prospering finely, a correspondent at Deal informed Secretary Williamson that "'tis observed that within the last three years more small craft of between 60 and 120 tons have been built, than were in 20 years and above before": *Calendar of S.P.D.*, 1676-1677, 300, 28 August 1676, Richard Watts to Williamson. In 1675-8, C. C. Rumpf, the Dutch Resident at Stockholm, characterized the English shipping trading to Sweden with the diminutive "scheepjens"—*e.g.* in his letter of 4 May (N.S.) 1675 to the Greffier, Arch. Staten-Generaal (Algemeen Rijksarchief, Den Haag), Lias Sweden 6541; and that to the States General

ships of greater tonnage were frequently built for the ocean-borne and Mediterranean trades, and in these the results of tradition, conservatism and government suasion were embodied, for they were in general reduced versions of men-of-war. This meant that the greatest width of the ship came not at or near the water-line, but some 3 to 5 ft. higher at the gundeck, which narrowed the hold considerably, the more so as to improve sailing quality the lines of the sides tapered to the keel somewhat sharply, renouncing the nearly flat bottom, which Dutch builders found roomy and steadying. The rake fore and aft and the square tuck still further reduced stowage. The heavy timbers, high superstructure and elaborate rigging of the man-of-war were all reproduced.

In the navy of Charles II the most powerful ships, third to first rates, ranged from 900 to 1,400 tons, and thus greatly excelled in size the largest merchantmen, which might have a capacity of from 400 to 800 tons.[4] But between the King's fourth- and fifth-rates and these large merchantmen there was little difference in architectural plan, in dimensions, or in the size of timbers used. The man-of-war, if she were not flying the King's jack, might be identified not by her shape, her rigging, or the number of her ports, but by the decoration lavished upon her.[5]

This approximation of the English trading ship to the English fighting ship was recognized abroad as at home,[6] but while foreign kings

---

of 16 May (N.S.) 1678, Lias Sweden 6542. At the close of the eighteenth century the average tonnage of English merchantmen was only 100 tons: R. G. Albion, *Forests and Sea Power* (1926), 116.

[4] A few merchant ships of greater burthen than I have mentioned may have been built, as, for instance, the ill-fated *Trades Increase* in the reign of James I, but they were very rare, and the preference of the time was for vessels " of the middle Rank ", as being not only ton for ton less costly, but also more seaworthy: see Nathaniel Boteler, *Six Dialogues about Sea-Services* (1685), 312. The thirty-eight ships in which Sir Henry Johnston, a shipbuilder in Blackwall in the latter part of the century, had acquired an interest were for the most part engaged in the trades requiring ships of size *i.e.* the East India, Virginia, Barbados and Guinea trades. They range from 150 to 800 tons, the average being 432·9 tons: Add. MSS. 22,184, f. 151, "A List of S$^r$ Henry Johnsons Writeing of M$^{er}$ chantmen Tunnes Gunns and men ".

[5] L. G. Carr Laughton, *Old Ship Figure-heads and Sterns* (1925), 22. Men-of-war sometimes attempted to disguise themselves as merchantmen by spreading tarpaulins over their decorations, and the *Kingfisher*, built in 1676, had a detachable figure-head to facilitate deception of the enemy (*ibid.*). In 1672 Capt. Knevet of the *Algier* disarmed the suspicions of a Dutch privateer by housing his guns, showing no colours, striking even his flagstaff " and working his ship with much apparent awkwardness ": *The Diary of Henry Teonge* (1825), 5, n. 5. Two other Dutch privateers were taken in the course of this same war through mistaken identifications of this kind: one tried to board the *Resolution*, believing her to be a merchant, and another bore up to the *Portsmouth* with similar intent in the conviction that she was a collier: *Calendar of S.P.D.*, *1672-1673*, 85, 26 October 1672, Silas Taylor to Williamson ; S.P.D. (P.R.O.), Car. II, 332, f. 318, 26 January 1673, Philip Lanyon to James Hickes.

[6] In 1629 certain merchants of Amsterdam who were attempting to organize an insurance company referred to the high figure of English freights as due to the fact that " zij als ten oorloghe gemonteert varen ": P. J. Blok, " Koopmansadviezen aangaande het Plan tot Oprichting eener Compagnie van Assurantie (1629-35)", *Bijdragen en Mededeelingen van het historisch Genootschap te Utrecht* (1900), 67.

and their admirals looked with favour on great ships and frigates, foreign merchants and factors held English-built carriers in low esteem, finding Dutch flyboats cheaper and more convenient, in which opinion English merchants concurred. Sir George Downing, who represented England at The Hague both before and after the Restoration, observed the superiority of Dutch shipping and came to the conclusion that the historic policy of encouraging private owners to build warships was no longer practicable in view of Dutch competition with unarmed (or but lightly armed) vessels built especially for merchandizing.

> And for our English ships they are rather tubs than ships, made to look like a man of warre, and yett not of strength to defend themselves against a single chaloupe by reason of their shortness and of their fore castles and steerages they are so little in hold and so bigg above water, that there is noe good to be done with them. . . . In a word I doe not know of anything more worthy his Maj[ty] & the Duke of Yorke in point of Trade then to force those that trade from London to Norway & the Baltique to employ our owne shipping. & to putt them upon the building (though it were but one or two) merely for bulk without any Guns Steerage or Roundhouse, whereby she may carry a greate deale & be sailed with a few men. I confess it were good that all our ships were fitt to make Men of Warre if it were possible; But the Question here is whether it is not better to have ships of our owne, though without Guns, & your owne Seamen employed your owne Victualls Spent in the victualling of them, the Money paid for freight & Wages kept at home, then to have foreigne ships and Seamen Employed, their Victualls Spent, & So much Money carried out of the Kingdome as is yearely for freight & Wages. The East India, Turky & other rich Trades, will beare the employing of Ships with Guns, but the Norway and Eastland Trade can by noe means beare it.[7]

In this last observation Sir George touched upon a distinction often made in the seventeenth century. With regard to shipping, the area of the world's trade could be divided into two fields. First the regions exporting bulky commodities on which freights ran high in comparison to costs, which required many ships and could best be served by vessels of from two to five hundred tons, cheaply built and cheaply operated, built for stowage and carrying no guns. Roughly speaking, this field embraced northern and eastern Europe from the mouth of the Garonne to Archangel, from which were exported great quantities of wine, salt, fish, grain, timber of all kinds and other weighty naval supplies, as pitch, tar, hemp, flax; also lead, tin, iron and copper. The second field comprised southern Europe from Biscay to the Levantine ports of the Mediterranean, the Canaries, Madeira, Guinea and the East Indies.

---

[7] S.P., Foreign, Holland, 168, ff. 219-20, 25 December (O.S.) 1663, to Sir Henry Bennet.

These regions nourished what Downing had called the "rich trades". Though they produced some bulky wares, their exports were for the most part of small size and weight in proportion to their value. In a commerce of this nature, the figure of freights would not have the supreme importance that it possessed for the northern field. In general the rich trades were also the dangerous trades into which unarmed ships could venture only at great risk.[8] Dutch Directors of the Levant Trade and the Dutch East and West India Companies were no less convinced advocates of armed ships than were King, Council and Parliament in England. It is true that unarmed vessels, both Dutch and English, traded to the Mediterranean in defiance of laws, regulations and risks, but many of them were lost in so doing, and merchants were chary of trusting their goods to weak carriers in spite of the enticement of low freights.

In the sphere of the rich trades, then, English-built shipping was able to compete with Dutch carriers which, for the sake of defence, were obliged to renounce some of the excellences and economies used in the northern field of trade. In this latter, English merchantmen made but a poor figure and Dutch flyboats were everywhere. "The lost trades", as English writers fondly and mournfully called them, included Norway, Muscovy, the entire region of the Baltic and most of Germany. The commerce of Flanders, Ireland and Scotland was little better than lost, as were the "Greenland" or Spitzbergen whale-fishery and the North Sea fisheries for herring and cod. The port-to-port trade throughout Europe north of the Straits was almost a monopoly of Dutch shipping. Dutch and other foreign bottoms shared extensively in the export trade from England, especially in weighty commodities, as lead, coal, tin, corn and alum.[9]

It was the intention of the Navigation Act of 1660 and of the Act of Frauds of 1662 to exclude the Hollanders and other foreigners from the import trade of England, except as carriers of their own native commodities and of such as were of trifling consumption in England. The Levant trade, like all extra-European trade, was limited to ships

[8] In agreement with Downing both Roger Coke and James Houblon suggested that the requirement of English-built ships for the Northern and Eastland trades be abandoned: Coke in *England's Improvements* (1675), 92, and Houblon in his "Discourse touching the Grounds of the Decay of the English Navigation", Bodleian Library, Rawlinson MSS., A 171, f. 283 v. Nicolaes Witsen also differentiates between the two areas of trade: "Schepen die van hier om de Noort en Oost vaeren, met weinigh Schepelingen zijn bemant, om de West met veel; waer van hier de vrede, en daer den oorlogh oorzaeck zy." *Aeloude en Hedendaegsche Scheeps-Bouw en Bestier* (1671), 160.

[9] On the "lost trades", see especially Roger Coke, *A Discourse of Trade* (1670), and *Britannia Languens* (1680), reprinted in J. R. McCulloch's *Select Collection of Early English Tracts on Commerce* (1856), no. 6. In no. 4 of this collection, *England's Interest and Improvement* (1673), by Samuel Fortrey, the export trade is discussed, 243. Houblon's "Discourse", referred to in the previous note, is interesting in regard to the carrying trade, f. 283.

of English build (and to such as were foreign-built but of English ownership and made free). With this exception, English-owned ships (that is to say, foreign-built and not made free) were entitled—on paper at least—to import European commodities from their places of origin on payment of aliens' duties.[10]  But this last stipulation was in effect prohibitive for the trade in bulky commodities.  The unlooked-for result of the Acts was a rapid increase of the navigation of the Scandinavian kingdoms, whose nationals bought Dutch ships and easily eclipsed the clumsy merchant-man-of-war which Englishmen were expected to employ.  Hamburg also profited by the Navigation Acts.  Though the Muscovites did not go to sea, and thus were unable to avail themselves of their opportunities, English participation in that important trade threatened in the middle of the century to disappear entirely.[11]  Even more complete was English withdrawal from the whale fishery.  The whales, as Roger Coke observed, had no ships at all,[12] therefore whale products were of necessity imported from Holland.

All this was sincerely deplored in England, for it was recognized that the heavy commodities in which the lost trades abounded gave employment to far more ships than piece goods and fine wares.  The Dutch sent 700 to 800 ships a year to the Baltic.[13]  Popular estimates affirmed that the number of their craft engaged in the herring fishery alone was no less than a thousand sail.[14]  In the second place, the operation of the Navigation Acts just described placed England at the mercy of foreign shipping in the very tender point of naval supplies.  Prices for timber, deals, plank, hemp, flax, pitch and tar were far higher in England than in Holland.  These high prices were reflected in the cost of shipbuilding, and the cost of shipbuilding was reflected in freight rates.  The English merchant could not build cheaply because he could not import timber

[10] 12 Car. II, c. 18; 14 Car. II, c. 11.

[11] The expulsion of English merchants from Russia in 1649, preceded by the loss of the Muscovy Company's privileges, had given a severe shock to the trade, from which it did not recover until the opening of the eighteenth century.  There were but two English merchants in Moscow in the summer of 1669: S.P., Foreign (P.R.O.), Russia 3, f. 172 v, 7 July 1669, Robert Yard to Williamson.  The Dutch were at this time sending twenty to thirty ships to Archangel yearly: H. C. Diferee, *De Geschiedenis van den nederlandschen Handel* (1905), 375.

[12] Coke, *Discourse*, 30.  The Dutch whale fishery in 1680, or a little later, was employing 200 to 250 ships, of 200 to 300 tons: see the "Mémoire touchant le Négoce et la Navigation des Hollandois" [1699], by Izaak Loysen, ed. P. J. Blok in *Bijd. en Meded. v. h. historisch Genootschap de Utrecht* (1903), 251.

[13] *Ibid.* 247.  Of a total of 1,035 ships which passed the Sound between 19 June and 16 November 1645 all but 49 were Dutch.  Between 26 June and 14 November 794 ships left the Baltic, of which all but 99 were Dutch: G. W. Kernkamp, *De Sleutels van de Sont* (1890), Bijlage, I, 279-80.

[14] Tobias Gentleman put it at 1,000 sail, of which 600 were great busses: *England's Way to Win Wealth* (1614) in *Harleian Miscellany* (1809), III, 398.  John Keymor is more fantastic in his figures in his *Observations touching Trade and Commerce with the Hollander* [1620], reprinted (and attributed to Sir Walter Raleigh) by J. R. McCulloch in *A Select Collection of Scarce and Valuable Tracts on Commerce* (1859), no. 1, 21 *et seq.*

and other materials cheaply, and he could not import cheaply because he could not build cheaply.

The resistance of English merchants who were not themselves ship-owners to restrictions which limited them to ships of English build began when navigation laws began, but the seventeenth-century chapter of this resistance opens with the proclamation of 17 April 1615, which enjoined the King's subjects to freight English ships in preference to foreign bottoms. Trinity House, which sponsored the policy, found itself in constant altercation with Yarmouth merchants, Hull merchants, London merchants and others, who persisted in using Dutch ships.[15] After the Civil War the Navigation Act of 1651 met with similar pro-tests, and these were continued upon the re-enactment and sharpening of the Act after the Restoration: English-built shipping was too dear; it stowed too little; it was inconvenient. The agreement on these points by persons whose interest was in the trade in bulky commodities leaves no room for doubt.[16]

If these criticisms came to the notice of shipwrights, as they un-questionably did, why were they not spurred to experiment with the more capacious and cheaply worked type of which there was no lack of patterns, Dutch-built and English-owned? Roger Coke inclined to divide the responsibility between the Navigation Act and the ship-wrights.[17] Sir George Downing blamed the conservatism of builders.[18]

[15] See MSS. of the Corporation of the Trinity House, *passim*, in *Hist. MSS. Comm.*, Report VIII.

[16] For criticisms of English shipping in comparison (expressed or implied) with Dutch, see Keymor's *Observations, op. cit.* 6; Sir William Monson, *Naval Tracts*, V, 265; *Calendar of S.P.D., 1666-1667*, 337-8, 11 December 1666, Sir John Hebden to the Navy Commissioners; *ibid. 1672*, 231, 15 June 1672, Josiah Child, T. Papillon and B. Gauden to the Navy Commissioners; Carew Reynel, *The True English Interest* (1674), 14; Coke, *England's Improvements* (1675), 93: Houblon, *op. cit.* f. 283 v. Typical of many objections put forward by merchants trading to Norway or the Baltic is the peti-tion of William Harrington, importer of Prussian plank for the Navy, who, after delivering two ships' ladings, "to his great losse findeth by experience that English Shipps are very unfitt for the Stowage of that Comodity, not being capable to take in above halfe their Loading. . . . But besides the excessive Rates, & inconveniency of Stowage in English Bottoms, the Peter. now findeth . . . he cannot be served by Shipping either from Dantzick or Koningsberg, which being but a few in Number are all Ingaged in the service of their Owners": Privy Council Records (P.R.O.), 2/62, 185, 13 May 1670.

[17] "It will be necessary", he stated, "to permit all forrein Ship-wrights to inhabit, and have equal freedom to exercise their Professions in all convenient places in England for building Ships; for no man is born an Artificer, but it comes to pass by Education, Labour, and Experience: the English are unacquainted in building Busses for the Fish-ing Trade, and in building ships for the Norway or Greenland Trades, and many others. The Dutch build ships for all Trades according to the best convenience: we only know how to build Men of War; and our ships for other Trades are of like figure, whether it be convenient or not": *England's Improvements*, 97. He had already grumbled about this in his *Discourse*: "Notwithstanding we yet continue our old way of building Ships . . . for the English know no other; and if the English Merchant will not build as the English Carpenter pleases, and his way, he must not Trade at all" (p. 59).

[18] "And what a doe was there at first to bring England into the way of building ffrygotts": S.P., Foreign, Holland, 168 ff. 219-20, 25 December 1663. To Sir Henry Bennet.

16

But Nicolaes Witsen, whose great treatise on shipping was published at Amsterdam in 1671, realized the difficulties of innovation in this industry. "It is surprising", he wrote, "that foreigners, though they may have studied economical building in the dockyards of this country, can never practise it in their own land. . . . And this in my opinion proceeds from the fact that they are then working in an alien environment and with alien artisans. From which it follows that even if a foreigner had all the building rules in his head, they would not serve him, unless he had learned everything here in this country by experience, and still that would not help him, unless he should find a way to inculcate in his workmen the thrifty and neat disposition of the Hollander, which is impossible." [19]

Granting the commonsense of these observations, and granting too that English shipwrights preferred to build as they had always built, it is nevertheless certain that they were not incapable of learning from foreign builders, as the frigate, the yacht, and certain improvements adapted from French men-of-war bear witness.[20] Only very rarely did they try the flyboat, the whaler, the dogger, or the herring-buss, for they were not commissoned to build them. Many English owners of Dutch ships petitioned to have them made free on the ground that they would serve as models. But they were never modelled after. These vessels offered an excellent investment when Dutch-built, because they could be had cheap, but they could not be built cheaply in England because of the high prices of imported ships' supplies.

There was a popular superstition in England, which the Navigation Acts probably encouraged, that English ships were built of English oak. So far was this from being the case that in respect to such prime essentials as masts, deals and plank, England enjoyed no substantial advantage in native growth over the Dutch, and was worse off for sail-cloth, cables and cordage.[21] In 1686 nine shipwrights consulted by the Navy Com-

[19] "Te verwonderen is't dat alle uytlanders, schoon zy op Timmer-werven hier te lant de zuynigheyt bevlijtigen, in haer eygen lant gekomen, nimmer zulks na konnen volegn. . . . En dit komt mijns bedunkens oock daer by, dat zy buyten's lants met buyten-lantsche mannen arbeyden. Waer uyt volgt, schoon een vreemdelingh alle de Bouw-regelen in zijn hooft hadde, zy hem echter niet dienen konnen, ten ware hem alles in deze landen by ondervindinge wiert getoont, en dan noch niet, 't en waer hy kans zag den aerd zijns volks, waer mede hy arbeyden moet, den zuyning en zindelijken hollantschen inborst gelijck te maken, 't geen niet doenlijck": Witsen, op.cit. "Aen den Leser".

[20] These improvements in naval shipbuilding, however, were rather the result of royal interest in the efficiency of the Navy than of initiative on the part of the shipwrights. With the single exception of his protégé, Sir Anthony Deane, Pepys held a low opinion of the builders, both royal and private, with whom he came in contact. The Company of Shipwrights of London, chartered in 1605, was, like most organizations of its kind, more intent on augmenting its privileges than its craftsmanship. Shipbuilding at this time was still a handicraft, and training for it was practical and manual, rather than theoretical and technical.

[21] For the situation in England with regard to ships' timber, see Albion, op. cit. chap. iii. The provenance of English naval supplies was noted by the Marquis de Seignelay,

missioners admitted that in the outports as in London one hundred loads of foreign plank were used to every twenty tons of English growth.[22]   Four-fifths of the canvas expended for sails came from abroad, chiefly from Brittany.[23]   If there was never an absolute famine in ships' materials in England, there was frequent dearth, and little to spare ordinarily between demand and supply.  Swedes, Danes and Norwegians were able to transport bulky wares at lower freights than the English, limited to shipping of their own build, could do, but far from as cheaply as the Dutch managed to carry them.  Though Englishmen were fain to blame this on the profiteering appetite of the Scandinavians, it was more probably due to the mercantile experience of the Hollanders and to the capitalistic organization of their trade.

The nine shipwrights above mentioned explained to the Navy Commissioners that for vessels of 80 tons or less, English plank was more durable and more suitable, but for ships of greater burthen, and especially for those of 300 tons and up, Prussian or Bohemian was better and more economical.[24]   English plank of sufficient length (without tapering) and free from " waniness " for these large ships was difficult to find near the sea, or near navigable rivers.  Transport by land was both dear and troublesome.  This is probably the explanation of the small average tonnage of English shipping in this century.  Vessels of 100 tons or less could be built economically with a minimum of imported supplies; larger ships, whose construction leaned more heavily on such supplies, could be afforded only by the privileged or by the monopolized trades, or by those in which freight rates were not an important consideration, or by those so highly dangerous that the armed merchantman was an appropriate carrier—namely, the Straits, Levant, Guinea and East India trades; less completely and exclusively the American trade.

In comparing the capital investment that two ships of the same tonnage might represent if one were built in Amsterdam and the other in London, one must not overlook the differing rates of interest prevailing in these two cities.  In England the legal rate was 6 per cent, but heavy borrowing by the Crown at 10 per cent or higher naturally forced up the rate to merchants and shipowners in spite of the law.  In Holland there was no legal rate, but capital was abundant; the Province of Holland could borrow on better terms than any Government in Europe, and mercantile credit was far more active and expansive than in England.  Naturally the rate at which a Dutch merchant could borrow

---

on his visit to England in 1671: "Mémoire concernant la Marine d'Angleterre" in Lettres, Instructions, et Mémoires de Colbert, ed. P. Clément (1861-82), III, ii, 322 et seq.
    [22] Pepys' Memoires of the Royal Navy, 1679-1688, ed. J. R. Tanner (1906), 38 et seq.
    [23] Anchitell Grey, Debates of the House of Commons (1769), III, 408, 3 November 1675.
    [24] Pepys' Memoires, 40 et seq.

varied with the circumstances and the risks, but 3½ to 4 per cent was customary.[25] How importantly this difference in the interest rate affected investment in the two countries may readily be imagined. " And what encouragement is there ", cried Charles Davenant in 1699, " for men to think of Foreign Traffic (whose returns for those commodities that enrich England must bring no great profit to the private adventurers) when they can sit at home, and, without any care or hazard, get from the state by dealing with the exchequer, 15 and sometimes 20, 30, 40, and 50 per cent? . . . Where interest is high, the merchants care not to deal in any but rich commodities, whose freight is easy, and whose vent is certain in corrupted countries. . . . It is the bulky goods, whose returns are not of so great profit, that breed most seamen, and that are most nationally gainful; but such goods cannot be very much dealt in where interest is high."[26]

Davenant was right in his contention that the carriage of bulky wares was not profitable to English shipowners—not profitable to them even in Dutch-built ships, several hundred of which were naturalized in the reign of Charles II. To clear a profit on the timber and grain trades it was necessary not merely to own cheap and serviceable shipping but to operate it as cheaply as the Danes or the Dutch could do; necessary also to organize buying and marketing in the most economical way possible. These were trades for large-scale methods, the net gain per piece or per measure being trifling. The English merchants and shipowners were unable to keep down costs as such commerce required. The rate of interest was an important item in costs, though it was not the whole story. All the Dutch prizes that came into English possession in the three naval wars, all the naturalizations of Dutch bottoms purchased by English merchants, and all the pretended naturalizations by which more flyboats slipped inconspicuously into the privileges of the Acts of Navigation, and the sixty permissible ships made free for the Norway trade in 1669 —all these availed nothing to the recovery of the lost trades, nor did the

---

[25] " It is a great Advantage for the Traffick of Holland that Mony may be taken up by Merchants at 3½ per Cent. for a Year, without Pawn or Pledg ": John De Witt [Pieter de la Court], *The True Interest and Political Maxims of the Republic of Holland and West Friesland* (1702), 33. At a later date J. P. Ricard wrote that it was possible to borrow on the security of merchandise at 4 per cent, or 6 per cent when money was high, but in order to evade the law against usury, it was necessary to call this last rate ½ per cent per month: *Le Négoce d'Amsterdam* (1723), 111 *et seq*.

[26] " An Essay upon the Probable Methods of making a People Gainers in the Balance of Trade " in *The Political and Commercial Works . . . of Charles Davenant*, ed. Sir Charles Whitworth (1771), II, 294-5. " And for Shipping which is the strength and safety of this Land; I have heard divers Merchants of good Credit say, that if they would build a Ship, and let it to any other to employ, they cannot make of their Money that way counting all charges, tear and wear, above ten or twelve in the Hundred, which can be no gainful Trade, Money it self going at ten in the Hundred. But in the Low-Countries, where Money goeth at six, the building of Ships, and Hiring them to others, is a gainful Trade ": [Sir Thomas Culpeper], *A Small Treatise against Usury*, included in the pamphlet with Sir Josiah Child's *A New Discourse of Trade* (1698), 239.

acquisition of Dutch fishing craft in the same ways enable the English to take over the fisheries. The Eastland merchants were among the most persistent employers of foreign shipping after the Restoration. "Aske them", wrote Downing, " why they doe not employ the Dutch shipping that doe belong to England."[27] It was because as fast as the *fluits* accrued to English owners they were turned into the more profitable trades, especially, I believe, the Plantations trade, for which mounted ships were not so necessary as for the other rich trades. In 1675 a London merchant, who for twenty years had carried on a trade to Trondhyem in Norway, complained that the previous autumn he had been unable to find a single ship in the whole port of London willing to make that voyage.[28]

The number and excellence of the merchant ships belonging at this time to the maritime provinces of the Netherlands were marvellous in the eyes of all Europeans, astonishing even to the Dutch themselves, says Witsen.[29] Foreigners commented on the curious perversity of the Lowlanders in going to sea when Nature had pent them behind sandbars in shallow waters that were frozen three months of the year, and the prevailing wind dead against their getting to sea at all. Their ports were singularly unfavoured, and the small area of meadow, dune and heath that constituted the Republic bore no trees fit for ships' timbers; nor did it yield iron or any other materials used in the building and equipment of ships except hemp and flax, and not enough of either. It was, an Englishman observed, " such a Spott, as if God had reserved it as a place onely to digg Turf out of ".[30] Yet this was the land that by popular count launched a thousand ships a year and sent them out on giants' errands through all the seas of the world.

The story of the brilliant rise of Dutch shipping from medieval beginnings to its supreme attainment in the seventeenth century cannot be told here. In the second half of this century the pre-eminence of the Dutch merchant service was the product of many factors: the geographical position of the provinces between two great complementary regions of European trade, and at the place where several great river highways reached the sea; the supremacy of Amsterdam as the money market of Europe and the *entrepôt* for the exchange of commodities from all over the world; the colonial empire wrested from Spain and Portugal; the commercial diplomacy of the States General abroad, and the political importance of mercantile oligarchies in the more considerable towns at home. These are the setting and circumstance of Dutch trade as a whole, but we shall consider here the Dutch fleet as an achievement in the building and navigation of ships.

[27] S.P., Foreign, Holland, 168 ff. 219-20, 25 December 1663. To Sir Henry Bennet.
[28] S.P.D., Car. II, 382, f. 282. Petition of John Hammond, read 5 July 1675.
[29] Witsen, *op. cit.* " Aen den Leser ".
[30] [Charles Molloy], *De Jure Maritimo et Navali* (1676), 4.

The desiderata for merchantmen were cheap but seaworthy construction, good burthen with convenience of stowage suited to the cargo, simplicity of rigging so that a small crew would suffice, a low wage for seamen, cheap victualling.

Cheap construction depended on accessibility to foreign sources of materials, and the cost of these materials when delivered in the Netherlands, thus including freight and customs; it depended also on the wage scale for carpenters and other artisans, and the organization of the industry. Of these conditions, that of low customs was assured by State action: the tariff bore lightly on timber or other supplies used by shipwrights. The chief producing regions were Norway, Germany, the Baltic countries and Russia. For all naval commodities the Dutch were far and away the best customers Their merchants made large purchases at the season when prices were lowest, paid punctually in goods, in rix-dollars, or in bills of exchange on Amsterdam, and allowed generous credit in their dealings with native merchants. It was a principle with the Dutch to avoid middlemen and buy " out of the first hand ". Not seldom their investments abroad, or partnerships formed with compatriots who had acquired burgher rights in foreign centres of trade, enabled them to buy on far better terms than strangers were legally entitled to do. Thus the Hollanders were actually able to supply their shipwrights with Norwegian masts and timber at prices lower than those which were paid by shipwrights in Norway.[31] In 1669 Doctor Benjamin Worsley, who was soon to become secretary to the English Council of Trade, estimated that in shipbuilding the cost of materials came to eight times the cost of labour.[32] The Dutch by cheap purchasing, low freights and low duties were able to reduce greatly the more formidable item.

In the matter of labour the Hollanders were in some respects better and in some respects worse off than their English competitors. Wages were notoriously high in the United Provinces, where heavy excise taxes burdened all articles of general consumption, and high rents raised further the cost of living. This was somewhat offset by certainty of employment for artisans engaged in shipbuilding, who therefore worked for less than if employment had been seasonal.[33] Another mitigation

[31] Coke, Discourse, 58 et seq.; John Cary, An Essay on the State of England in Relation to its Trade (1695), 123-4. At the end of the century the English Government was informed that " near half the ships belonging to Denmark are of Hollands built, being that is cheaper than the Danish, though the materials come from these countries ": G. N. Clark, The Dutch Alliance and the War against French Trade (1923), 136.

[32] S.P.D., Car. II, 258, f. 154, 2 April 1669. [Notes by Williamson, " As to the buying of Foreigne Shipping ", an argument by Doctor Worsley against licensing sixty foreign-built ships for the Norway trade.]

[33] The Sieur Arnoul, visiting Dutch yards in 1670, in the interest of the French marine, reported that carpenters' pay is higher in Holland than in France; he mentions the regularity of pay and employment. " Remarques Faictes par le Sieur Arnoul sur la Marine d'Hollande et d'Angleterre " in H. T. Colenbrander, Bescheiden uit vreemde

which drew the admiration of foreigners was the use of labour-saving machinery, especially the saw-mill wind-driven, and the great cranes which lifted and moved heavy timbers, and masted ships.[34]   It was perhaps appreciation of these machines that influenced certain Dutch carpenters to decline a pressing invitation from Colbert to remove to France and work in the royal dockyards at greatly improved wages. The work, they said, would be too hard.[35]

The industry, economy and neatness of Dutch artisans were widely esteemed.  Colbert, who with a scratch of the pen ordered forty carpenters from Holland for the King's service, was hopeful that these virtues would prove contagious.   " Surtout ", he wrote, " meslez des François avec eux, afin que vous puissiez introduire doucement dans leurs esprits l'économie du bois et l'application continuelle au travail que les Hollandois ont et que les François n'ont pas."[36]   It was the opinion of the Marquis de Seignelay that they sometimes carried economy too far, even to the point of considering cost of construction more than the durability of the ship.  In their effort to use their wood to the last fragment they sometimes worked in poor pieces.[37]  They economized also by using pine and fir for their merchantmen,[38] employing the dearer oak sparingly except for men-of-war and ships that must make long voyages.  Iron nails were spared too, in favour of wooden pins or rivets which were both cheaper and lighter.  Small relatively short masts, less costly than the great ones, were made to serve, and single sails where the English were wont to use double.[39]

The result of all these economies and advantages was that for ships of equivalent burthen, building was cheaper in Holland by a third or

---

*Archieven omtrent de Groote Nederlandsche Zeeoorlogen* (1919), II, 15.  In 1692 ships' carpenters were receiving in Amsterdam 24 to 36 stuyvers a day according to the season, the summer wage being one-third higher than the winter: O. Pringsheim, *Beiträge zur wirtschaftlichen Entwicklungsgeschichte der vereinigten Niederlande* (1890), 50.

[34] All three Colbertian emissaries, Hubac in 1669, Arnoul in 1670, and Seignelay in 1671, mention the *crocs de fer*, by which one man could move weights that otherwise would require three or four men to lift: *Lettres, Instructions, et Mémoires de Colbert*, III, i, 199; *ibid.* ii, 305; Colenbrander, *op. cit.* II, 15.

[35] " Il n'y a pas grand mal que les charpentiers hollandois ne veuillent pas venir en France, de crainte d'y trop travailler ", 6 December (N.S.) 1669.  To the younger Hubac: *Lettres . . . Colbert*, III, i, 199.

[36] *Ibid.* III, i, 133, 6 June (N.S.) 1669.  To Colbert de Terron.

[37] " Mémoire concernant la Marine de Hollande ", *ibid.* III, ii, 305.

[38] Witsen, *op. cit.* 178-80.

[39] See the " Remarques " of Arnoul (Colenbrander, *op. cit.* II, 11 *et seq.*) and the " Mémoire " of Seignelay (*Lettres . . . Colbert*, III, ii, 305 *et seq.*;  also the letter of Colbert to Colbert de Terron, 19 February (N.S.) 1671, *ibid.* III, i, 337).  Sir William Petty refers to the practice of the Hollanders " undermasting and sailing such of their Shipping, as carry cheap and gross Goods, and whose Sale doth not depend much upon Season ": " Political Arithmetick " in *The Economic Writings of Sir William Petty*, ed. C. H. Hull (1899), I, 261.  Roger Coke, speaking of fishing craft, said that those built of heavy English timber required a third more sail and cordage than the Dutch used: *England's Improvements*, 82.

a half than it was in England.[40]  In 1669 a flute could be built in
Holland for £800 that in England would cost £1,300.[41]  A larger ship
might cost £1,400 in Holland, but £2,400 in England.[42]  In 1676 the
building of an English merchantman of 250 tons would cost £7 2s. 6d.
per ton.[43]  In that same year a London merchant purchased a 200-ton
flute at Saardam for 9,050 guilders, or about £4 10s. per ton.[44]  In
England building was cheaper in the outports than in London, but in
very few of the outports could materials be found for building large
ships.[45]

The seaworthiness of Dutch shipping was a matter of controversy.
Seignelay criticized the carpenters for failing to dry wood adequately
before using it, thus turning out vessels whose seams opened dangerously
after a few months of service, a defect which could never be entirely
remedied by caulking.  The timbers of Dutch ships were slighter than
French shipwrights were accustomed to use.[46]  Pine and fir were fragile
to resist cannon-shot or heavy seas.  Witsen admitted that even
Bohemian or Westphalian oak was not as strong as Biscay or English.[47]
It was an English ship that he mentioned as an example of longevity—
one that made her voyage year upon year for seventy years.[48]  Elsewhere he observed that Dutch ships were durable by reason of the care
and cleanliness with which they were kept.[49]  English ships were far
more heavily timbered, and their strength and sailing qualities were
proudly asserted by Englishmen from Monson to Defoe.[50]  Even Roger

[40] Coke put the Dutch advantage at ½ for merchantmen (*Discourse*, 56), and at ⅔
for fishing vessels (*England's Improvements*, 82).  A tract of 1668 called *Inconveniences
to the British Nation which have ensued the Act of Navigation* (Brit. Mus. 816, m. 11,
108) affirmed that " a foreign ship may be built for half the price ".  One-half is also
the estimate of the author of *Britannia Languens* in McCulloch's *Select Collection of
Early English Tracts on Commerce*, 318.  Houblon wrote: "Their [Dutch] ships are
built for ⅔ if not ½ the cost of ours ", *op cit.* f. 281.  At the close of the century other
nations with cheap labour and native materials were closing the gap between the figure
of their building costs and that of the Dutch.  See the pamphlet by T. T., Merchant,
*General Considerations relating to our Trade* (1698), Brit. Mus. 8244, c. 31, 4; and
Defoe's, *A Plan of the English Commerce* in McCulloch's *Select Collection of Scarce and
Valuable Tracts on Commerce*, no. 3, 129.
[41] S.P.D., Car. II, 258, f. 154.  [Notes by Joseph Williamson " As to the buying of
Foreigne Shipping ".]                                   [42] *Ibid.*
[43] J. R. Tanner, *A Descriptive Catalogue of the Naval Manuscripts in the Pepysian
Library at Magdalene College, Cambridge* (1903), I, 230.
[44] S.P.D., Car. II, 382, f. 284, 3 June 1676: Affidavit of John Hammond.
[45] See Pepys' remarks about the difficulties attending the building of the *Edgar* at
Bristol: Grey, *Debates*, III, 389, 3 November 1675.
[46] Seignelay's Mémoire in *Lettres . . . Colbert*, III, ii, 305.
[47] Witsen, *op. cit.* 179-80.                          [48] *Ibid.* 157.
[49] " Ons ingebooren zindelijkheyt, die de schepen langdurend maeckt ", *ibid.*  " Aen
den Leser ".
[50] " The English ships will double a lee-shore when the others will be forced in foul
weather upon the rocks; the cables and anchors of the English will hold when the others
will be forced to come home and break.  The English will be able to put out sail at
sea when the others will take in sail.  The English go deep in water which makes them
wholesome in the sea and carry the merchants' goods with little loss; the Hollanders

Coke, who had little kindness for the English merchantman, granted the stoutness of English build.[51]

But though the Dutch *fluit* was not built either to fight or to be mishandled, the very "floatiness and buoyancy" with which she was reproached contributed to make her seaworthy. The Norwayman and the buss built of fir could weather a storm with less distress than the ponderous Dutch man-of-war.[52] The broad, flat bottom checked rolling, the roundish bows lessened the tendency to pitch. She was compact of long seafaring experience. Scraps of evidence point to the trustworthiness of other Dutch types. An English Postmaster-General preferred a Dutch packet-boat to any English craft for carrying the mails across the choppy Irish Sea.[53] A renegade Dutch captain in English service, Van Heemskerck, declared that Dutch fishing doggers could bear the seas better than the King's ships.[54] The ambassador of the States General at Paris enjoyed discreetly the fact that Colbert de Terron, Intendant of Rochefort and cousin of the Minister of Marine, when returning from Lisbon did not entrust his preciousness to his "Françoish fregatje", but hired a Hollands ship.[55] Riding out a storm on the high seas, however, was not so dangerous as riding it out in the Channel or on any lee shore. In a great storm in the Baltic in the autumn of 1675 seven Dutch merchantmen were lost in the road of Dantzig, and eleven others coming from Königsberg were stranded. "The people are most saved", reported the Deputy of the English Eastland Company, "and some part of the ladeings: but the shipps being weake built are like to be all lost."[56] Herein lay the vulnerability of Dutch ships. If forced ashore

---

are laboursome and dangerous in a storm, which causes great leakage in oil, wine and such commodities, to the great annoyance of the merchant; yea, oftentimes, more than the difference of the freight": Monson, *Naval Tracts*, V, 248-9. "It is evident the Dutch and French, Swedes and Danes, build cheaper; but the English build stronger and firmer; and an English ship will always endure more severity, load heavier, and reign (as the seamen call it) longer than any foreign built ship whatever": Defoe, *op. cit.* in McCulloch's *Select Collection of Scarce and Valuable Tracts on Commerce*, 129.

[51] *England's Improvements*, 93.          [52] *Ibid.* 99.

[53] "That in regard the Sea between England and Ireland is so subject to Stormes & so broken, that the Vessells built on those shoares not being able to endure the same at all Seasons, it happens that the due course of his Ma[ts]: Mailes is often interrupted, And the Pet[r]: having had experience of the ffitness of Dutch Bottomes for such Service, and having made provision of two fit and proper Boates built in Holland to transport his Ma[ts]. mailes between the Kingdomes of England and Ireland", would like to have them naturalized: Privy Council Records, 2/26, 219, 13 July 1670. Lord Arlington had already secured the naturalization of three Holland packets for the Harwich-Holland service: *Calendar of S.P.D.*, 1668-1669, 448, 12 August 1669.

[54] *Ibid.* 1666-1667, 496, Harwich, 5 February 1666/7: Silas Taylor to Williamson.

[55] *Brieven geschreven ende gewisselt tusschen den Herr Johan de Witt . . . ende de gevolmaghtigden van den Staedt* (1723-5), I, 667, 23 July (N.S.) 1663: W. Boreel to De Witt.

[56] S.P., Foreign, Poland, 14, f. 102, 23 November, 1675: Francis Sanderson to Sir Joseph Williamson.

they were apt to break up, when an Englishman, more staunchly timbered, might survive the disaster and be got safely off.

Something must be said of the organization of shipbuilding in Holland, where it was a key industry. The standardization of type made it possible for the builders to turn out the simpler, more commonly used craft with what for that day was astonishing speed. The reserves of timber were so great that carpenters were able to assemble their materials without loss of time. In Saardam alone wood sufficient for the building of four or five thousand ships was stored with a neatness and order for which Colbert, faced with the disorder of his costly arsenals, sighed in vain.[57]   In the great State arsenal at Amsterdam an English visitor noted the precision with which all things necessary to rig a ship were arranged; cables here, anchors there, sails, yards, cordage, so that—the hull once built—a ship could be made ready for the sea in a few hours.[58]   It is probable that the private yards excelled the Admiralty in these dispositions, as they unquestionably did in honesty of management and cheapness of production.   During the second war with England, the shipwrights of Saardam engaged to turn out a ship a day, provided they were allowed two or three months in which to assemble supplies and organize construction.[59]   Normally Saardam confined production to the thirty or forty ships of all types which could be accommodated on the available stocks at one time.[60]   But Saardam was only one of many shipbuilding towns, though the industry was greatest there. It flourished mightily in Amsterdam, as also in the other Admiralty towns—Rotterdam, Middelburg, Harlingen and Hoorn—all building merchantmen as well as men-of-war.   The smaller ports supplied their own needs, and even the fishing villages built their busses, doggers and pinks.   Some of them, says Witsen, would build as many vessels in a year as the year has days.[61]

In Holland shipping was commonly regarded as a good investment.

[57] *Lettres . . . Colbert*, III, i, 216, n. 1, 30 February (N.S.) 1670: To Léger, Controleur Général de l'Arsenal à Toulon.

[58] S.P., Foreign, Holland, 188, f. 76 *et seq.*, 2 February 1671/2: J. Vernon to Williamson.

[59] "Mémoire sur tout ce qui doit s'observer pour former les magasins des arsenaux de marine du Roi," *Lettres . . . Colbert*, III, i, 295; also Seignelay's journal, 26 July 1671, *ibid*. III, ii, 299.  This story of Saardam must have been in the minds of Sir George Downing and Henry Coventry when in a Commons debate of 21 February 1675/6 the former remarked: "A proposition was made to the States of Holland to build them a frigate in 6 weeks, and so on; but the planks were all found, laid dry, and prepared. . . . Mr. Secretary Coventry.  They [the Dutch] have materials ready for ships to a pin, as Venice had for galleys, when they made and launched one while Henry III of France was at dinner": Grey, *Debates*, IV, 125-6.

[60] This number were building when Seignelay passed through Saardam: *Lettres . . . Colbert*, III, ii, 299.  In 1675 Pepys estimated the facilities for building men-of-war of the yards royal and private in and around London at twenty-seven docks, slips and launches: Grey, *Debates*, III, 328-9, 22 October 1675.

[61] Witsen, *op. cit.* "Aen den Leser".

The owning and operation of ships was becoming more and more distinct from merchandizing, and the practice of persons having neither seafaring nor trading experience putting their savings in ships' shares was surprisingly widespread. It was not uncommon, wrote J. P. Ricard in his *Négoce d'Amsterdam*, for merchant capitalists to equip two, three or four Greenlanders for the whale fishery, and offer them to such as would adventure in shares of $\frac{1}{48}$, $\frac{1}{3}$, $\frac{1}{16}$, or greater, and they found it not difficult to interest the public in acquiring these shares.[62] The herring fishery was another field for co-operative investment in shipping, and property in merchantmen was similarly partitioned. In what other country did peasants buy shares in ships?[63] We hear of a trading vessel built in 1666 for the Shoemakers' Company of Amsterdam—somehow an incongruous adventure.[64] An English merchant living in Rotterdam had a quarter interest in a ship in which $\frac{1}{8}$ belonged to a Dutch baker, $\frac{1}{16}$ to a brewster, the rest appertaining to several Scots of Rotterdam.[65] In England this division into shares was familiar, being especially used by the London merchants for the large, costly ships in which they traded,[66] but persons not interested in the trade were not likely to acquire an interest in the ships. The small craft which constituted the greater part of the merchant service were frequently the property of a single owner, or the shares were held by a few persons. In the outports the reproach that Colbert hurled at the Marseillais might have reached its mark: " Messieurs de Marseille ne veulent que des barques afin que chacun eut la sienne."[67]

The importance attached by Dutch builders to the capacity of their ships and to convenience for the stowage of goods was another condition of their success. For the carriage of massive yet cheap commodities of common consumption in most European countries, vessels must be constructed to hold a great deal and yet be navigable by a small number of men. Experience in adapting craft to function had come to the shipwrights through solving the problems of construction for inland navigation, and for shallow waters. "Purpose, in which there is infinite variation, compels the builders to diverge from measurements and rules."[68] Witsen, whose dictum this is, enumerates no fewer than

---

[62] *Op. cit.* 424-5.

[63] The promoters of a marine insurance company in Amsterdam in 1628-9—a time when shipping was suffering heavily from the depredations of the Dunkirkers—declared that no intelligent person would then invest in ships—only the peasants, who knew nothing better to do with their money: Blok " Koopmansadviezen ", *op cit.* 48.

[64] *Calendar of S.P.D., 1666-1667*, 347, 15 December 1666: Silas Taylor to Williamson.

[65] S.P., Foreign, Holland, 188, f. 166, 4/14 April 1672: Rotterdam [S. Tucker to Williamson].

[66] Sir Henry Johnson, shipbuilder and shipowner of London in the last quarter of the century, owned shares in thirty-eight ships, amounting in all to $\frac{24}{32}$ and $\frac{1}{56}$ of ships: Add. MSS. 22,184, f. 151.

[67] E. Levasseur, *Histoire du Commerce de la France* (1911), I, 382.

[68] " Het gebruik, 't welk van oneindelijke veranderingh is, dwingt bouw meesters, maet en wetten te kreuken," *op. cit.* 53.

thirty-nine types of *binnenlants-vaerders*—river and canal boats.[69]  The catalogue of fishing craft is bewildering for the specialization and complexity implied.

Among the merchantmen the crowning triumph of Dutch craftsmanship was the *fluitschip,* which the English called flute or flyboat, a type designed for the northern and Eastland trades, though in slightly variant forms it found its way into all seas.  A *fluit* was a light, slight, but practicable shell employed to contain and float a ponderous and clumsy cargo.  She had commonly one deck, but otherwise she was as nearly a closed hold and nothing more as a ship under sail could be. Her distinguishing feature was inordinate length (for a ship of her day), which is to say four to six times her width.  Her bows were rounded without beak or figurehead, and her stern was even rounder with broadspreading buttocks.  Though her burthen was great, she was insignificant above the water-line owing to the "tumble-in" or converging lines of her sides, which greatly reduced her upper proportions.  The virtues of this structure were that the restriction of surface made the ships easier to work with few men, and that small bulk above the waterline lessened resistance to the wind, and improved sailing quality.  For this last reason she was given a precipitous forward rake.  She carried three masts, short rather than tall, had no forecastle, no roundhouse, no guns (or only a few light ones), and no decoration except the identifying picture on her tafferel.  In tonnage the *fluit* might have a burthen of from 100 to 900 tons, but the most workable sizes seem to have been those between 200 and 500 tons.  One could not expect a heavily laden ship of this kind to be a greyhound of the sea, and that she was not, but the buoyancy of her construction, her slight draught and small superstructure made her far less sluggish a traveller than her appearance suggested.  Indeed, her improved sailing quality as compared with vessels previously used for the Baltic trade was so considerable that masters could add an extra voyage to their season's calendar.[70]

The flute made her *début* in the last decade of the sixteenth century with a success shattering to the old navigation.  Soon these vessels were being launched in great numbers, especially during the Twelve Years' Truce, when the Dunkirkers ceased from troubling—almost—and an

[69] Witsen, *op. cit.,* 165, 169-71.  On the variety of Dutch ships, see Sir William Petty, *Political Arithmetic (op. cit.* I, 260-1).

[70] The *fluit* is fully described by Bernhard Hagedorn, *Die Entwicklung der wichtigsten Schiffstypen bis ins 19. Jahrhundert* (1914), 102 *et seq.*  Witsen describes the type also, *op cit.* 159-60, giving dimensions and illustrative plates (nos. lx, lxi).  He gives the measurements of an ordinary *fluit,* perhaps of 500 tons, as 130 ft. long over all, 26½ ft. wide, and 13 ft. 5 in. deep ; an Oostvaerder of 300 tons might be 115 ft. long, 23 ft. 6 in. wide, the depth not given, but probably 11 or 12 ft.  There are contemporary models of the *fluit* in the Ned. Hist. Scheepvaart Museum at Amsterdam, to whose Director, Mr W. Voorbeÿtel Cannenburg, I am much indebted for information in regard to the type, and for the privilege of obtaining photographs of models.

unarmed ship was reasonably safe in northern waters. In 1612 the shipowners of Lubeck complained that they could get no return freights from Spain, because the Dutch were underbidding them.[71]   In England a navigation bill which passed the Lords in the spring of 1614 attributed the decay of navigation to the competition of foreign ships built solely for carrying merchandize and requiring few men to work them.[72]   The bill was lost in the Commons, but the following year a royal proclamation called for the observance of existing navigation laws in favour of English shipping.[73]   In 1620 John Keymor's *Observations* described the "great long ships" of impressive burthen and low freights, whose competition was everywhere worsting English trade.[74]   Even in the Mediterranean Sea, where the flute should not have ventured, being about as warlike as a coal-scuttle, she enjoyed precarious successes.[75]   In the Baltic the Sound Registers recorded the overwhelming predominance of the new type.[76]   The Admirals of Holland and Zealand protested against such flimsy, ill-manned shipping as discouraging by impossibly low freights the building of stronger vessels.[77]   The States General laid down stipulations as to men and guns.[78]   There was a setback in the 'twenties, due to the resumption of war with Spain, discriminatory legislation by Denmark, and perhaps also to overproduction of shipping during the Truce.   But the flute had come to stay.   To make the seas safe for her, her owners demanded adequate convoy, and after a long struggle the State found itself compelled to extend its responsibilities for the protection of trade, though never to the entire satisfaction of merchants and masters.[79]

[71] Hagedorn, *op. cit.* 109.

[72] *Hist. MSS. Comm.*, Report IV (Cal. House of Lords MSS.), 119, 6 May 1614.

[73] *Ibid.* Report VIII (MSS. of the Corporation of the Trinity House), 246.   Proclamation of 17 April 1615.

[74] *Observations touching Trade and Commerce with the Hollander, and Other Nations* in McCulloch's *Select Collection of Scarce and Valuable Tracts on Commerce,* 13.

[75] Hagedorn, *op. cit.* 109-10.   To protect the Dutch Mediterranean trade, the Directie van den Levantschen Handel had been organized in 1625.   It enforced strictly regulations for the arming of ships employed in this trade, and exacted a tax, in return for which it provided convoy.   But besides the heavily armed Straatsvearder, which was practically a man-of-war, "Il y va jusqu'a des flutes, qui sont sans deffence, ce qui fait tort aux navires armés parce qu'ils peuvent faire meilleur marché de fret": Loysen, *Mémoire, op. cit.* 275.

[76] Hagedorn, *op. cit.* 111-12.          [77] *Ibid.* 112.

[78] *Ibid.* 113.   The placaat underwent occasional revision.   Witsen gives a summary of the regulations in effect when he published his work in 1671 (*op. cit.* 425-6), and Pringsheim summarizes those of the placaat of 1663 for the Levant trade (*op. cit.* 26).

[79] Sir George Downing, like many of his countrymen, considered that convoy was the real secret of Dutch success with cheap, unarmed ships: "If theire Merchant men have constant Convoy and the English Merchant men must be both Merchant and man of warr, he cannot sayle at so easy a rate as a Hollander, and consequently all the Trade must still dayly more and more fall to the Hollanders and give mee leave to tell your LoDD: that in this very thinge is the mystery of this State and by this meanes doe they gayne all theire wealth, and whereas it is comonly sayd that the English cannot sayle soe cheape because they will fare better, and because they goe with more men in a

With accumulating experience the carpenters tried further adaptation. The Noortsvaerder that carried timber from Bergen could stand 2 ft. more of depth than an Oostvaerder of the same length bound for Dantzig to fetch corn. The hull of the former was nearly rectangular, while the shape of the Oostvaerder was roundish.[80]   Then there was the East India version, much more staunchly built, with extra breadth at the stern to allow for a roomy cabin.[81]   But the most curious adaptation of the flute was evoked by a treaty with the King of Denmark in 1647, which permitted Dutch traders to Norway to pay the export duty on timber according to official measurement of the capacity of their ships. Now the treaty stipulated that the burthen should be calculated from the figures for length, width and depth, and the width was to be taken at the midship beam, where presumably she was broadest. Great was the vexation of the Danes when the Dutch shipwrights devised an hourglass shape, narrow at the waist and swelling fore and aft, which, measured according to the treaty, came to far less than the actual capacity of the ship. It required another treaty to extricate the Danes from this extraordinary monster. The type did not survive its privileges.[82]

The economical operation of Dutch ships was affirmed by more than a century of testimony. This was a matter determined by the number of seamen carried, the figure of their wages, and the cost of victualling. The simple rigging of the flute and the absence of guns made possible her navigation by a small crew. "For example", explained Keymor in 1620, "though an English Ship of two hundred tun, and a Holland Ship, . . . of the same burthen be at Danske, or any other place beyond the Seas, or in England, they do serve the Merchant better cheap by one hundred pounds in his freight than we can, by reason he hath but nine or ten Marriners, and we near thirty; thus he saveth twenty mens meat and wages in a voyage."[83]   Very similar is an admission by Sir William Monson in the reign of Charles I;[84] a merchants' petition printed in 1659 is of the same tenor;[85] so also Roger Coke in 1670;[86] so also the author of *Britannia Languens* in 1680.[87]   From French *Observations sur le commerce du Nord* of the year 1769 we learn that a Dutch

---

shipp and because theire Shipps have another kinde of make, give me leave to say that if convoy were given they would build other kinds of shipps and consequently sayle with ffewer men": Bodleian Library, Clarendon MSS., 104, f. 253 v, 26 August (N.S.) 1661, to the Earl of Clarendon.

[80] Witsen, *op. cit.* 160.          [81] *Ibid.* 159.          [82] *Ibid.* 160.
[83] *Op. cit.* 6.
[84] "You must understand that the Hollanders' ships go with fewer men than ours, occasioned by the slight building and tackling of their ships in comparison of us. And as there is twenty to forty men difference in the sailing of them, the like difference there is in the strength of them": *Naval Tracts,* V, 248.
[85] *The Marchants Humble Petition and Remonstrance to his late Highness* (Brit. Mus. 712, m. 1, 4), 15.
[86] *Discourse,* 59.          [87] *Op. cit.* 317.

galliot of 200 tons could navigate with seven or eight men; one of 300 to 400 tons with sixteen to eighteen men, while French ships of these burthens would carry double the number.[88]

The Navigation Act of 1660 had increased the difficulties of English masters by requiring that English-built ships should be navigated by English seamen to the extent of three-fourths of their crews in order to enjoy their privileges under the Act. This made the merchant service something of a " closed shop ", the masters being legally debarred from reducing expenses as the Dutch did by employing large numbers of foreigners of a lower standard of living than the native-born.[89] Naturally the English tar made the most of this opportunity to improve his hard lot. Wages went up,[90] and though they seem to have been not greatly higher than those given in Holland in this period, perhaps not always as high, it was impossible for English masters to redress the balance with their rivals by substantial saving on this item. Sir George Downing maintained patriotically that nine Englishmen could do the work of ten Dutchmen, but the conviction was abroad in Europe that Dutch seamen were the best in the world.[91] Certainly they believed that they were, and looked down on English mariners as having, in Witsen's dry phrase, more stomach for the mess table than for hard work.[92] Pepys, drinking mum and discussing sails and cables with some Dutch seamen at a tavern in Limehouse, was not spared this disparagement: " But to see how despicably they speak of us for our using so many hands more to do anything than they do, they closing a cable with 20, that we use 60 men upon." [93]

As to victuals, even Sir George Downing admitted " the betterness of the English Seaman's Dyett beyound the Dutchmans ", yet supposed

[88] J. Hayem, *Mémoires et Documents pour servir à l'Histoire du Commerce et de l'Industrie en France* (1912-22), 4ème Série, 254.

[89] In 1665 Downing had reported concerning the seamen who then manned the Dutch fleet: " The halfe of them at least are forreigners of severall Nations & of those forreigners most Danes & Norweighers ": S.P., Foreign, Holland, 174, f 144, 28 February 1664/5, to Sir Henry Bennet. See also Sir William Temple, *Observations upon the United Provinces of the Netherlands* (1692), 183.

[90] " As this Law [Navigation Act] makes a few Merchants Masters of all the Trade of England: so it makes Mariners the Merchants Masters ; for being but few, and the Merchant being restrained to them, if he gives not them what wages they please, he must not trade at all ": Coke, *Discourse*, 29. *Cf.* Defoe on "the intolerable oppression upon trade from the exorbitance of wages and insolence of mariners": " Essay on Projects " in *The Earlier Life and the Chief Earlier Works of Daniel Defoe*, ed. Henry Morley (1889), 159. The Navigation Act was not entirely to blame, as wages were generally rising, and both trade and the Navy were using more men than ever before. At the time of the Third Dutch War seamen were receiving 40s. to 45s. per month ; Houblon, *op. cit.* f. 279 v.

[91] On Dutch seamen, see A. de Montchrétien, *Traité de l'Œconomie Politique*, ed. Th. Funck-Brentano (1889), 183; *The Dutch Drawn to the Life* (1664), 112-13; and the " Remarques faictes per le Sieur Arnoul sur la marine d'Hollande ", Colenbrander, *op. cit.* II, 22.

[92] *Op. cit.* 207.         [93] *Diary*, 13 February 1664/5.

that it might be more than offset by the low prices of food prevailing in England.[94] But the fare of Dutch fishermen was only bread, fish and " grutt ", which is defined by Downing as " a sad kinde of meale of broken Corne ". On the merchantmen victuals were somewhat less depressing, but here the astute Hollanders scored again by victualling with Irish beef and butter, both very cheap after the English Parliament had prohibited the importation of Irish cattle.[95]

That the Dutch were not too sparing with their seamen as compared with the English merchant service is sufficiently demonstrated by the fact that they drew large numbers or mariners from both England and Scotland.[96] Some of these had crossed over at the Restoration in discontent over impending political and religious changes. In Rotterdam English and Scottish seamen had their own quarter of the town.[97] It cannot be said that the treatment of seamen by either nation was conspicuously humane, but the Dutch out of a wider commercial experience were somewhat more lenient, as in allowing their men to do a little trading.

In a long *Discourse* on the decay of trade, addressed to Pepys and written not long after the accession of James II, James Houblon, member of a distinguished mercantile family, included English masters with English seamen in a sweeping condemnation for debauchery and prodigality, and praised the Dutch *schippers* for sobriety and frugality[98]— antithesis of a kind that English writers on trade were even fonder of at this time that the facts warranted. As to sobriety, it was not a seagoing virtue, but the Dutch masters enjoyed a reputation for honesty and reliability. They had, said Bishop Huet, " une grande fidelité & exactitude a rendre bon compte de tout ce qu'on leur confie ".[99] In the Norway trade they served as merchants or factors in the sale of cargo and the purchase of timber, which materially reduced costs in that important commerce.[100] Their skill in navigation was prodigious. In 1667, after destroying the English fleet at Chatham, the Dutch carried off the *Royal Charles*. Their seamanship in working a mounted great ship of foreign build down an unknown channel stirred the admiration

---

[94] S.P., Foreign, Holland, 168 ff., 219-20, 25 December, 1663. To Sir Henry Bennet.

[95] On the victualling trade in Ireland, see *Calendar of S.P.D., 1673-1675*, 166 [February?], 1673/[4]. Reasons offered to the consideration of Parliament for remitting the prohibition of the importation of Irish cattle: *Britannia Languens* (*op. cit.* 318); Houblon, *op. cit.* f. 281 v.

[96] In 1667 there were reported to be 3,000 English and Scottish seamen serving in the Dutch fleet: *Calendar of S.P.D., 1667*, 207, 18 June 1667, Col. Titus to Lord Arlington. In 1673, out of 600 men on De Ruyter's flagship, 200 were the enemy's nationals: *Catalogue of the ... Manuscripts in the Pepysian Library*, II, 32, 21 August 1673, Pepys to Sir Thomas Allin.

[97] *Calendar of S.P.D., 1671-1672*, 362, 22 April 1672, Richard Bower to Williamson.

[98] *Op. cit.* f. 281.           [99] *Mémoires sur le Commerce des Hollandois* (1717), 41.

[100] " Ce commerce s'y fait par les maistres de navire mesme, sans que l'on employe personne ": Loysen, *Mémoire, op. cit.* 246.

of the Secretary of the Navy: "I find it true that the Dutch did heele 'The Charles' to get her down, and yet run aground twice or thrice, and yet got her safe away, and have her, with a great many good guns in her, which none of our pilots would ever have undertaken."[101]   The cleanliness maintained on Dutch ships was no less proverbial than the cleanliness of Dutch houses, contributing unquestionably to the good condition of the lading, the health of the crew and the life of the ship.[102] When Pepys became part-owner of a Dutch prize, he and his associates made a jolly party to test the wines she was carrying when taken.  " But it did grate my heart to see the poor master come on board, and look about in every corner, and find fault that she was not so clean as she used to be, though methought she was very clean; and to see his new masters come in, that had nothing to do with her, did trouble me to see him."[103]

The advantages gained by cheap and adaptable shipbuilding, and cheap and careful navigation, were summed up in the lowest freight rates in Europe, and the most extensive and efficient merchant marine.   In years when both England and the Republic were at peace, Dutch rates would be ⅓ to ½ lower than English for the same voyage.[104]   In the last two decades of the century the Scandinavian nations in the northern sphere of trade, and France in the Mediterranean were competing with the Hollanders through cheap navigation, but their captains were neither so reliable nor so experienced as the Dutch *schippers*, their ships were not sufficiently numerous, nor their commerce sufficiently organized to displace the Netherlanders in the carrying trade.   Merchants in reckoning the cost of importing wares often stipulated carriage in Dutch vessels.[105]   It was always easy to find a ship bound for Amsterdam, and

[101] *Diary*, 30 June 1667; see also 22 June of that year.

[102] " La propriété que les Hollandois observent dans leurs vaisseaux est fort grande ; ils les balayent et nettoyent très souvent par dedans lorsqu'ils sont dans le port, les grattent et goudronnent par dehors deux ou trois fois par an et ne manquent jamais de les calfater à la fin de l'esté parce que la chaleur de cette saison fait toujours entr'ouvrir le bois.   Quand le vaisseau est en mer, encore qu'ils le balayent tous les jours à l'ordinaire, ils font oster deux fois la semaine tous les coffres des matelots et tout l'embarras du vaisseau afin de nettoyer toutes choses.   Ils lavent aussy quelquefois entre deux ponts avec de l'eau et du vinaigre ": Seignelay's *Mémoire, op. cit.* III, ii, 314.

[103] *Diary*, 28 March 1667.

[104] In 1634 Dutch merchants stated that freights asked by Netherlands shipping were ⅓ to ½ less than those demanded by the English, Scots or French: Blok, " Koopmansadviezen ", *op. cit.* 72.   In 1651 the author of a tract on trade called *Advocate* (1651) in Brit. Mus. 712, m. 1, 1, p. 4, asserted the same difference between English and Dutch rates.   In 1676, when many Dutch merchantmen were concealing their identity behind English passes, one of Secretary Williamson's informants complained that the King's subjects in their small ships had no chance against these interlopers, which were great ships and flyboats able to sail ⅓ per ton cheaper than the English could do: *Calendar of S.P.D., 1676-1677*, 130, 26 May 1676, Richard Watts to Williamson.

[105] *E.g.* the cost of the marble for the monument to Lady Verney was estimated with the proviso of transport from Italy to England in a Dutch ship: *Memoirs of the Verney Family during the Seventeenth Century*, ed. F. P. and M. M. Verney (1907), I, 530.

17

from thence to ship goods to any part of the world. Usually this was the cheapest procedure, though in miles it might be the longest way round.[106]

"It is evident", wrote Pieter de la Court, "that Shipwrights work in Holland must not be considered as a mere Consumption, but as a very considerable Manufacture and Merchandise, seeing almost all great Ships for Strangers are built by the Hollanders."[107] The ships sold abroad from the Provinces were of all types, from men-of-war with guns nosing out of their portholes, through all varieties of merchantmen, small carriers and fishing vessels, to pleasure yachts gay and gilt for kings. The Dutch supplied the French East India Company with ships of force to compete for the Oriental trade, England with flutes and herring-busses to lower freights and to essay the Great Fishery, Spain with shipping for her colonial trade, Hamburg and Ostend with carriers according to their needs. Denmark made such extensive use of Dutch bottoms that her King requested a dispensation from the Navigation Acts to enable his subjects to trade to England in "foreign-built" ships.[108] He explained that the Danes could not build their own vessels because they had no oak. Neither—he might have recollected—had the Hollanders. In the last decade of the century it was estimated that approximately half of the shipping of both Denmark and Sweden was Dutch-built.[109]

That the seas burgeoned with ships of Holland built but owned by nationals of other states was not unproductive of curious results. The Dutch-owned merchantman, when the Republic was at war, could masquerade as an innocent Lubecker or a strictly neutral Genoese—at least until boarded. "It is inferred", wrote Sir Richard Fanshaw from Madrid on the eve of the second Anglo-Dutch war, "that all Hollanders whom we shall take, will make themselves Flemings; and all Flemings, that shall take us, themselves Hollanders."[110] One reason alleged for denying the Scots admission to the Plantations trade was their use of Dutch-built shipping. Obstruction on this score to the Scottish coasting

[106] " So that the English and Flemish Merchants do ofttimes know no better way to transport their goods to such Foreign Parts as they designe, than to carry them first to Amsterdam, and from thence to other places ": De Witt [Pieter de la Court], op. cit. 38. " You will find that any ship at Barbadoes which comes seek freight . . . will go for Amster. or Rott. for the same fraight they will for London (except a winter be coming on) for if they do well in their home Voyage, 'tis 10-1 but they meet with further employ back again ": Samuel Hayne, An Abstract of all the Statutes made concerning Aliens trading in England (1685), Brit. Mus. 8245, b. 41, p. 12.

[107] Op. cit. 35.     [108] Privy Council Records, 2/55, 284, 3 July 1661.

[109] Clark, op. cit. 136. Dutch ships penetrated even the Spanish colonial trade: " De vlooten, die uyt Spagniën naer de Spaensche Indien toegaen voor een seer groote gedeelte door coopluyden in Hollandt ende Zeelandt wonende, werden verbodemt ende uytgerust ": J. G. Van Dillen, Bronnen tot de Geschiedenis der Wisselsbanken (1925), I, 218, Memorial from the Masters General of the Mint to the States General, 29 November (N.S.) 1683.

[110] S.P., Foreign, Spain, 46, f. 60, 18/28 May 1664. To Secretary Bennet.

trade went so far that the Scots complained in 1662 that they were being debarred from all trade.[111]  The Scottish salt-makers admitted that the entire shipping of the kingdom was of "outlandish" build.[112]  In 1672 the tables were momentarily turned when certain Scots privateers, cruising against the Dutch, chanced upon some twenty Dutch-built but English-owned timber-ships, homeward bound from Norway, and bagged them all for prize.  Naturally they had to release them when the wrath of the English Council was made known,[113] but without doubt there was pleasure in the doing.  More amusing from an English point of view was the adventure of a galliot hoy, Dutch-built, but in 1666 the property of the English Navy.  She was detailed to spy out the Dutch fleet, and happened somewhat suddenly on four or five of the States General's men-of-war.  As she was flying no colours, she managed to pretend she was one of theirs, and got safely away.[114]

Of all patrons of Dutch shipping the English were the most persevering.  In the last years of the Dutch War of Independence there was a ship-market at Dunkirk which was kept supplied with Dutch prizes by corsairs in the service of Spain.  Hither came the English, Danes, Norwegians, Lubeckers, Dantzigers and other mercantile folk to drive good bargains.  On 4 June 1642 the Dutch Resident at Elsinore in the Sound reported to the States General: "The English used always to pass this place in ships of English build, now most of them come in Netherlands ships bought at Dunkirk.  In the course of this spring fully eighty to ninety such ships sailed by the English have passed here, to the great regret of many good patriots."[115]

The acquisition of foreign ships by English owners was discouraged by the Navigation Act of 1660 and supplementary legislation intended to promote native shipbuilding.[116]  But how persistently the round sterns and broad bottoms found English owners and received their freedom, the Acts notwithstanding!  In 1674 an attempt to put a stop to naturalizations was justified by the Council on the grounds "that there

[111] Privy Council Records 2/56, 145, 24 September 1662.
[112] Add. MSS. 23,122, f. 335, Lauderdale Papers [1668].
[113] Privy Council Records 2/63, 290, 24 July 1672.
[114] *Calendar of S.P.D., 1665-1666*, 480, 30 June 1666, Silas Taylor to Williamson.
[115] " De Engelschen hierdoor plachten altijt te voeren scheepen in Engelandt gemaeckt, nu voeren se meest al Nederlantsche scheepen tot Duijnkercken gecoft.  In dit voorjaar heeft men hier sien passeeren wel 80 a 90 soodaenige scheepen bij de Engelschen gevoert tot groot leetweesen van veele goede patriotten ": Kernkamp, *op. cit.* 13.
[116] The Act of 1660, 12 Car. II, c. 18, was supplemented by an Act for preventing Frauds and regulating Abuses in his Majesties Customes (14 Car. II, c. 11); an Act for the Encouragement of Trade (15 Car. II, c. 7); an Act to prevent the delivering up of Merchants Shipps (16 Car. II, c. 6, renewed by 22-3 Car. II, c. 11); an Act for the encouragement of the Greenland and Eastland trades, and for the better securing the plantation-trade (25 Car. II, c. 7).  Subsequent reigns brought further additions and modifications to the policy of the Navigation Acts, but the essentials of the programme were laid down in the Acts above-mentioned.

are at present in his Ma^ts: Dominions Ships sufficient both for number and quality to carry on the Trade of the Kingdome if it were greater then it is, and that it hath been experimentally found, That fforrain Built Ships are of little use to his Ma. at such times as the Kingdome hath most occasion for them."[117]   But the merchants thought otherwise,[118] and the process by which the English merchant marine was being quietly but profitably expanded continued until the general peace of 1678, after which there was a long depression, the Dutch and other belligerents turned their attention once more to trade.   But even in the decade between the Peace of Nymwegen and the War of the League of Augsburg the ingress of foreign bottoms could not be arrested.   That they penetrated even the sacrosanct coastwise trade in coal is sadly admitted by an Act of 1685.   This statute found the principal cause of the decay of shipbuilding in the outports, "the freedom which foreign ships and vessels, bought and brought into this kingdom, have enjoyed in the coal and other inland trade equal to that of English built ships."[119]

How many foreign-built ships—and of these, how many Dutch-built —came into English ownership in the forty years following the Navigation Act of 1660, cannot be determined with accuracy.   Records were kept only of ships officially made free, and these are incomplete.   On 11 July 1676 Sir John Shaw, Surveyor under the Act, affirmed that the prizes taken in the first two Dutch wars, and made free by Act of Parliament, amounted to 463; of these 341 belonged to the Port of London and 122 to the outports.   Those naturalized between 1 September 1667 and 11 July 1676 came to 328, 306 being London-owned.[120]   The sum of these totals is 791.   Taking into consideration the probable fallibility

---

[117] Privy Council Records 2/64, 317, 25 November, 1674.

[118] Certain London merchants protested that they had been encouraged "to buy severall fforeign built Ships in Order to the making them free to which end yo^r Pet^rs. have bought Sev^ll. of the afores^d. freedoms, for w^ch. they bona fide p^d. severall consideable sums of Mony.   That yo^r. Pet^rs expecting to have the benefit of them as others have had, doe contrary wise find that there is a Stop put to the passing of them as was usuall, which is very much to the detrim^t. of yo^r Pet^rs, their respective Ships lying on Demurrage ": C.O. (P.R.O.), 389/11, 60-1 (copy), July 1676.   Especially in the Mediterranean the number of foreign-built ships under the English flag increased so greatly that the Commissioners of Customs proposed to withhold passes from such ships even if English-owned unless they could prove naturalization.   But a brief experience demonstrated that the Barbary pirates could not digest the distinctions of the Navigation Acts, nor could they understand why, if a ship were not sufficiently English to have a pass, she should yet be too English for them to take: Calendar of S.P.D., 1677-1678, 470-2, 27 November 1677: S. Pepys to William Blathwayt.   Many of these ships to which exception was taken were actually foreign-owned, "coloured" as English and protecting themselves by English passes: see Williamson's notes about the misdeeds of the brothers Houblon in employing Dutch ships and procuring English passes for them: Ibid. 693 [1677?].

[119] An Act to encourage the building of ships in England, 1 Jac. II, c. 18.

[120] Calendar of S.P.D., 1676-1677, 218, 11 July 1676.   From other lists presented by Sir John Shaw (S.P.D., Car. II, 383 ff., 278-82) it would appear that between August 1667, the end of the second Dutch War, and July 1676, 375 vessels had received naturalization.

ot these lists, and the numbers of foreign-built ships in English owner-ship not made free, one may guess without pretending accuracy that there may have been some 1,200 foreign bottoms in the English mer-chant marine just prior to the Peace of Nymwegen, when navigation under the English flag had reached its greatest extent in this century. Of these foreign ships the great majority had been built in the Nether-lands.   With still more hesitation one may advance the supposition that a third or a fourth of England's mercantile tonnage at this time may have been of foreign build,[121] the fraction being higher for London than for the outports.   The depression of trade in the 'eighties and England's participation in the war against France made shipping a less attractive investment in the last two decades of the century than it had been in the period 1660-1680.   A great deal of English trade was then carried by neutral ships, and it is therefore unlikely that the acquisition of foreign-built ships continued with the same enthusiasm, though they increased, as we have noted, in the coastwise trade, possibly also in the export and Plantation trades.

If foreign bottoms had a larger share in the prosperous period of English trade than the framers of the Navigation Acts had contemplated, English shipwrightry likewise enjoyed brisk employment, and did not dwindle and die as some of its critics thought it deserved to do.   It is possible to attribute this survival to the protection accorded by the Acts. To the writer it seems that the more decisive factors were the new trades inviting and the old trades opening new opportunities, the development of England's colonies, and the long peace—five years of war in the twenty-nine years before the War of the League of Augsburg.   It was the common error of both English and Dutch in this century to suppose that the trade of either people could prosper only at the expense of the other: " If England ", said Sir George Downing, " were once brought to a Navigation as cheap as this Country, good night Amsterdam."[122] But the night of Amsterdam was then far off, though the day of English commerce was bright in the sky.

[121] The Port Books of Bristol for the year 1670-1 (Port Books, P.R.O., 1137/2-3) show that 160 English-built ships and 43 foreign-built entered the port; 124 English-built and 41 foreign-built cleared, second voyages of the same ships not counted.   A register of ships' passes (Adm. 7/630) issued between June 1662 and April 1668 indicates that passes were granted to 807 ships, of which 465 were presumably of English build, 268 of foreign build, 87 uncertain.   I have counted those described as "doggers", or as having round sterns, as foreign.   For these lists and those of the Bristol Port Books I am indebted to Mr Lawrence A. Harper of Oakland, California, as also for much valuable counsel on the working of the Navigation Acts.

[122] S.P., Foreign, Holland, 169, f. 98, 12/22 February 1663/4, to Sir Henry Bennet.

# THE ECONOMIC DECLINE OF
# THE NETHERLANDS

## C. H. WILSON

## I

DUTCH and English observers have commonly conspired to antedate the commercial decline of the Netherlands by attaching it to what appeared obvious or catastrophic—the British Navigation Acts or the Anglo-Dutch wars. Thus it was widely held that the peak of Dutch prosperity was reached about 1648 and that the British Navigation Acts spelt the beginning of economic decadence. The recent work of Dutch historians—Dr van Dillen and Dr van der Kooy in particular—has made it necessary to discard this theory, and has done a good deal to clarify the stages in the real decline of Holland by analysing the subtler changes in her economic structure. It is now safe to assume that the practical monopoly of European transport and commerce which the Dutch established in the early seventeenth century by reason of their geographical position, their superior commercial organisation and technique, and the economic backwardness of their neighbours, stood intact until about 1730. Premature attacks on the Dutch world market by England and France in the second half of the seventeenth century most certainly failed to penetrate that monopoly. The English Navigation Acts were riddled by exemptions on licence, as well as by the clauses in the Treaty of Breda which nominated the Rhineland as Holland's rightful hinterland, whose goods counted as her own. The French tariffs of 1664 and 1667 may be construed as a parallel attempt by Colbert to eliminate the Dutch from their function as intermediaries between France and Northern Europe.[1] By the Treaty of Nimeguen, however, the Dutch obtained a substantial rebate on these duties: in 1688 fresh concessions were obtained, and the researches of M. Sagnac indicate that the carrying trade between France and Northern Europe from 1697 to 1713 was entirely in the hands of the Dutch—a position which was confirmed in 1713.[2]

There was, of course, no lack of gloomy prophecies, and as competent an observer as Sir William Temple forecasted in 1672 that the trade of the Dutch had "past its Meridian"[3]—a judgement which was received

---

[1] J. B. Manger, *Recherches sur les Relations Économiques entre la France et la Hollande pendant la Révolution Française*, 1.

[2] Manger, *op. cit.* 2.      [3] Temple, *Observations upon the United Provinces*, 214.

with some relief in England, where it has since often been accepted as reliable and even final. In actual fact, what Temple took for permanent decay was merely a temporary depression due to the war of 1672, which had quite lifted by 1680, and Temple was specifically contradicted in 1714 by the Anglo-Dutch writer Mandeville, who wrote that Holland was a land of prosperity and even luxury, though it was true that in 1671 and 1672, when Temple had made his observations upon their manners and government, they had been in great straits.[4]

Pamphleteers are notoriously risky guides, but Mandeville's statement is borne out by the figures for convoy and licence duties, which show that in 1698 and 1699 Dutch trading reached an unprecedented volume, and pretty well maintained this level until 1715.[5] The Bank of Amsterdam also triumphantly survived the crisis year 1672.[6] During the first half of the eighteenth century, foreign observers contrived to set before the eyes of their less advanced compatriots this example of a flourishing community, confident in its leadership of world commerce. Foremost amongst French writers was Archbishop Huet of Avranches, whose *Memoirs of the Dutch Trade* appeared in 1700; in Spain Don Geronymo de Uztariz wrote his *Theory and Practice of Commerce and Maritime Affairs* to contrast Dutch freedom and prosperity with the restrictions of his own country (1742). In England, Defoe, writing in 1728, described the Dutch as " the Carryers of the World, the middle Persons in Trade, the Factors and Brokers of Europe . . . they *buy* to *sell* again, *take* in to *send* out: and the Greatest Part of their vast Commerce consists in being supply'd from all parts of the World, that they may supply all the World again ".[7]

Until 1730, at any rate, French and English attempts to throw off their dependence on the Dutch intermediary trade failed. The Netherlands remained Europe's chief *entrepôt*, to which came merchandise from north Europe to be transferred to the south. For long in the eighteenth century Amsterdam remained the granary from which the Mediterranean was supplied with Baltic grain. In return went wine and fruits. From France and Germany came wine and textiles, silks from Italy, cotton from the Levant, metal from Sweden and Austria, specie and colonial goods from the Far East. Trade with England consisted mainly with the importation of English cloth from London and from the west country ports, Exeter and Topsham, and the re-export of British colonial goods. In the reverse direction went German linens bleached at Haarlem. In addition, Amsterdam was the centre of the trade in

---

[4] Mandeville, *Fable of the Bees* (1795 edn.), 110-11.
[5] H. E. Becht, *Statistische Gegevens betreffende den Handelsomzet van de Republiek der Vereenigde Nederlanden, 1579-1715*, Appendix Tables No. 1 and No. 3.
[6] J. G. van Dillen, *Jaarboekje 1928 Departement Amsterdam der Nederlandsche Maatschappij voor Nijverheid en Handel*, 63. *History of Principal Public Banks*, 117-23.     [7] Defoe, *A Plan of the English Commerce*, 192.

precious metals—gold from Guinea and silver from Spanish America, and in 1700, English traders were reflecting ruefully that their attempts to intrude into the bullion trade at Cadiz had failed miserably.[8]

Dutch industry was of two kinds—independent industries like the textile industry at Leiden, which was already in decline in 1700, and the finishing industries (" trafieken "), which were dependent on the staple market: these were primarily malting, brewing and distilling (depending on the grain trade), tobacco cutting, tanning, sugar boiling, cotton printing, dyeing and bleaching,[9] and they were still flourishing in 1730.

These are a few of the economic activities in the Netherlands in the first quarter of the eighteenth century, and it is necessary to emphasise that the natural changes in this economy were not catastrophic. They may be summed up as follows: first, Holland lost her intermediary position in world trade as other European countries developed their own shipping and port facilities, and direct trading routes were established between nations which had previously used Dutch shipping and trading agents. Secondly, this decline in the stapling organisation was not counterbalanced by any industrial development, such development being hindered by the high level of wages and the conflict of interests between the powerful free-trading staplers and the protectionist industrialists.[10] Thirdly, there was a gradual shift of interest from trade to finance—to insurance and credit banking, and, because of the low rate of interest in Holland, to foreign loan business and speculation. This did not necessarily indicate economic decline, but the recurrent crises due to an overdevelopment of speculation sapped confidence in Amsterdam, and indirectly strengthened the position of London.

As has been remarked, no startling decline is revealed by trade statistics. The fact was rather that while the total volume of world trade was rapidly increasing, Holland's share remained about the same. Figures for the trade with England show this clearly.

|  | 1696-7 | 1772-3 |
| --- | --- | --- |
| *Imports* to England | £3,483,000 | £11,407,000 |
| Of this from Holland came | £507,000 | £412,000 |
| *Exports* from England | £3,526,000 | £14,763,000 |
| Of this to Holland went | £1,462,000 | £1,874,000 |

In other words, Holland's share sank from 14·6 per cent to 3·6 per cent in imports, and from 41·5 per cent to 12·7 per cent in exports.[11] In maintaining this position from 1730 to 1780, Holland was considerably assisted by the incessant wars between France and England—the countries whose rapid industrial development made them the most dangerous advocates of direct trading. Holland had abandoned power

[8] van Dillen, *Jaarboekje*, 63.
[9] T. P. van der Kooy, *Hollands Stapelmarkt en Haar Verval*, 8-9.
[10] *Ibid.* 53.          [11] Manger, *op. cit.* 8.

politics in 1713: from 1713 she pursued a policy of neutrality, which enabled her to take over in war time those trading functions which in peace time were done directly. In 1739, for example, when Holland's commercial treaty with France was renewed, a considerable part of France's trade to the Levant, previously carried on by the Dutch, was in French hands.[12] But from 1739 to 1740, 1743 to 1748 and 1756 to 1763, shipping largely reverted to the Dutch neutrals. These temporary war booms actually had the effect of shelving attempts at tariff reforms.

The change in European trade routes is seen clearly in the case of Anglo-Dutch trade, which consisted largely in exports of English cloth to Dutch commission agents in Rotterdam and Amsterdam, and exports of German linens bleached at Haarlem to England. In the heyday of this trade, say 1700, English cloths were actually warehoused and sometimes dyed at Amsterdam. By 1750, they were ceasing to go to Holland at all. It is true that Dutch merchants were still concerned in the trade, but their function was restricted to buying cloths on sample for German and Spanish buyers. The goods themselves were exported from Topsham and Exeter and London directly to Hamburg, Bilbao, Cadiz and Leghorn. In the reverse direction, west country and London merchants were ceasing to buy their German linens in Holland, and going to Hamburg, Bremen and Altona for them. Bleacheries grew up in Westphalia and Silesia, and Hamburg linens were appreciably cheaper than those bleached at Haarlem. The correspondence between English merchants in Exeter, Tiverton and London and their Dutch agents (preserved in the Archief Brants in the Gemeente Archief, Amsterdam) makes it abundantly clear that the extra shipping and commission charges of this indirect trade in Holland, made such business unprofitable when the goods could be obtained directly. But the most severe blow to the Dutch bleaching industry and the export trade which went with it came from the competition of the protected and subsidised linen industry in Ireland and Scotland, the products of which gradually ousted Dutch-bleached linens from the British market. London merchants wrote in the 'forties and 'fifties to their Dutch agents grumbling about the quality of the Dutch linens compared with the superior lawns and cambrics which were being manufactured in Scotland and Ireland.[13] The verdict of the latest historian of the Dutch bleaching industry is that it was this British competition which delivered the final blow to one of the most flourishing Dutch industries.[14]

From the middle of the eighteenth century, other "trafieken" suffered from foreign competition. The dyeing industry at Amsterdam

[12] van der Kooy, op. cit. 25-36.
[13] Archief Brants 372 and 373. Correspondence of J. I. de Neufville with Badcock, Dochsey, Bowles, Danby and Grenville and others.
[14] S. C. Regtdoorzee Greup-Roldanus, Geschiedenis der Haarlemmer Bleekerijen, 329.

declined,[15] saw mills and oil mills moved to the Baltic and gin distilleries to the Elbe. As early as 1738, the products of the French sugar refineries were entering Holland in large quantities,[16] and by the end of the century this competition had completely undermined the Rotterdam sugar market. All these developments stimulated direct trading relations between London and Cadiz, Bordeaux, Rouen, Ostend, Bremen, Altona and Hamburg—this last growing rapidly in wealth and importance and possessing fiscal duties which stood in the proportion of 1 : 5 to those of Holland.[17] Hamburg merchants who had previously bought American, French and Spanish goods through Dutch agents were, by 1750, placing their orders with agents living in the ports of those countries.[18]

Not the least important aspect of British trade policy in the eighteenth century is that of a drive to throw off the shackles of the Dutch monopoly. The Act of 1736 requiring every British ship to have at least one set of sails made in England was a direct hit at the Dutch sail cloth industry. Similarly the prohibition on foreign cambrics of 1750 was directed against Dutch importers. British pottery from Staffordshire was ousting Delft ware which was so popular previously, and imports of gin were restricted by the Gin Acts and the gradual decline of dram drinking in England.

Perhaps the most vigorous, but not the most successful, drive was for the fisheries—the Dutch "Gold Mine" as it was called. Some progress was made, but on the whole the Dutch remained supreme, and Goldsmith remarked laconically, "We have picked up very little gold that I can learn; nor do we furnish the world with herrings as was expected".[19] Even in 1805, Jepson Oddy was urging Britain to capture the Dutch fishing as she had captured her other trades.[20] The herring fishery remained to the last one of Holland's most valuable possessions.

In the Baltic, Dutch shipping remained supreme, but the richest branch of the northern trade—the Russia trade—from which the Dutch had ousted the English in the seventeenth century was a different story. In 1766, 167 British vessels arrived at St Petersburg, as against 67 Dutch, and it was estimated that well over half the trade now belonged to British merchants.[21]

Trade with the Americas and the colonies was, by 1750, proving more difficult, though here again there was no obvious or startling decline. The loss of the sugar trade with Brazil in the seventeenth century had been counterbalanced by the growth of a large sugar trade with Surinam and the West Indian islands, particularly Essequibo and Demerara,[22]

[15] van der Kooy, 44.                                              [16] Manger, op. cit. 9.
[17] Sérionne, Le Commerce de la Hollande 1778, II, 75.      [18] Ibid. 165.
[19] Quoted by A. M. Samuel, The Herring, 132.
[20] J. Jepson Oddy, European Commerce, 522.
[21] Macpherson, Annals of Commerce, III, 454. Also Sérionne, op. cit. II, 57-61.
[22] Candid and Important Considerations on the Nature of the Sugar Trade, 1763.
(Cambridge University, Marshall Library, Pryme Collection.)

and in spite of the Asiento Treaty, the Dutch remained the most important slavers in West Africa. The Methuen Treaty had had the effect of diverting the gold trade with Brazil to London, though large quantities still went to Amsterdam until 1780.[23] In the East Indies, things were going less well: Clive expelled the Dutch from Bengal in 1760 and their trade there was ruined. Both East and West Indian Companies were hopelessly corrupt, though it would be inaccurate to equate corruption with economic decadence. The East India Company (like its English equivalent) was no longer primarily a trading company; it was a source of influence, and membership was acquired by those who wanted not large profits but patronage in the East Indian establishments or influence in Europe.[24]

The stagnation of Dutch trade became painfully clear in the slump which followed the Treaty of Aix-la-Chapelle, and many of the tendencies described above are reflected in the "Propositie" of 1751.[25] This extremely competent survey of Dutch trade was compiled by de Larrey from evidence collected from a number of Dutch commercial houses, and presented to the States General on 27 August 1751.[26] The position was that for a period of twenty-five years, the trade of the Republic was "remarkably diminished and in many branches lost". This was ascribed mainly to "the adopting of our political maxims in trade by foreign powers"—particularly by England. The intermediary trade between Northern Europe and France, Spain, Portugal and Italy had been lost, and Germany was ordering directly from those countries through Hamburg. Out of the total exports of sugar, indigo and coffee from Bordeaux and Nantes, three-quarters now went to Hamburg and only a quarter to Amsterdam. Hemp and flax from the north was going to the Mediterranean in boats belonging to Spanish, Portuguese and French merchants, there were no longer any Dutch trading houses in Spain, and the Levant trade was declining. The trouble was believed to lie partly with the high duties on trade which had multiplied rapidly during the seventeenth century and compared badly with those of Hamburg, though they were still low compared with those of England or France. A general reduction of duties on goods imported and exported appealed to the staple merchants, but on the one hand the revenue of the College of Admiralty had to be maintained, and on the other hand there were the claims of Dutch manufacturers to be considered.[27] It was suggested that the goods which ought to be freed from taxation were

[23] van Dillen, *Jaarboekje*, 72-3. *Principal Public Banks*, 104.
[24] Brougham, *An Enquiry into the Colonial Policy of the European Powers*, 332.
[25] An English translation (under the title of "Amending the Trade of the Republick") is printed in J. R. McCulloch's *Select Tracts on Commerce* (1859).
[26] P. J. Blok, *Geschiedenis van het Nederlandsche Volk*, VI, 249-50.
[27] The only protection afforded to them at the time was a duty on imported blankets and a prohibition on the export of rags in the interest of the paper industry (van der Kooy, *op. cit.* 53).

those chiefly imported and re-exported; raw materials necessary to manufacture should also be freed, but goods consumed in Holland should be taxed, and competitive manufactures should be most heavily taxed. This proposal for a " limited free port " seemed on paper to resolve most of the problems, but it proved more difficult to agree on practical details. Although the powerful merchant, " free trade " element got its own way in stating that if sacrifices were to be made, industry must be sacrificed to commerce,[28] it is recorded that " in the contriving of the Plan . . . a variety of jarring interests did frequently occur ".

The " Propositie " came to nothing: it was killed by the death of the moving spirit, William IV, and the revival of trade which followed naturally from the Seven Years' War. But its failure indicates the obstinate refusal of the Dutch traders to admit the inevitability of the changes which were overtaking European trade, and their equally obstinate refusal to consider any new economic activities besides the stapling and commission business.

The first possibility of economic compensation for the loss of the intermediary trade lay in industry. There was a natural affinity between the world market and the " trafieken " which depended on it, but there was an equal hostility between the free market and, say, the textile industries. It is true that Holland was poor in raw materials and that the transfer of the world market to England, with its industrial advantages and growing population, was inevitable, but more might have been done to save the Dutch textile industries from extinction in the face of British competition. So long as the world market was in any degree retained, however, the merchant view predominated, the industrialists were unable to carry their claims, and Dutch exporters of finished goods had to meet the increasing competition of subsidised and protected goods from England and elsewhere.[29] At the same time, industry had to face the drain of high wages. The price of labour rose as the successive increases in duties, charges and imposts made the necessities of life dearer, and the cost of manufactured goods followed a parallel upward trend in the cost of raw materials.[30] In the cotton printing industry, workmen were earning 9 to 10 guilders per week, and there were signs of embryonic trade-union action amongst the operatives[31] to keep wages up to the level of the constantly rising cost of living. Certainly in the linen bleaching, high working expenses, due chiefly to the high price of labour, were an important contributory factor in the decline of the industry.[32]

Another possible compensation for this decline in the intermediary trade lay in the development of the transit trade through Holland:

[28] McCulloch, *op. cit* 466.　　　　　[29] van der Kooy, *op. cit.* 53-6.
[30] Sérionne, *op. cit.* 50.
[31] van Dillen, *Het Economische Leven in de Republiek der Zeven Provincien*, 3634.
[32] S. C. Regtdoorzee Greup-Roldanus, *op. cit.* 329.

this, however, the older staple merchants were unwilling to encourage because they believed it tended to diminish still further the intermediary trade proper and the " trafieken ".   The aim of Dutch staple policy was to obstruct as far as it could the growth of any active industrial enter-prise in the Rhineland,[33] and transit policy was thus a powerful weapon against foreign merchants.   The Plakaat of 1725 made no provision for transit rates: goods passing through Holland paid the full import and export duties.[34]   The Propositions suggested that a special transit rate should be allowed, but the supporters of the staple trade indignantly vetoed the suggestion, declaring that such a policy would only encourage direct trading.   While the Dutch traders were systematically discour-aging the transit trade (by this time inevitable), the Austrian Govern-ment was undertaking a mercantilist policy for the benefit of Ostend, with the express purpose of attracting the transit trade from the Rhineland; as a result, Holland had to face the growth of the so-called " Vlaemsche Vaert " and the increasing competition of Ostend.[35]

## II

The organisation of commerce in Holland in the eighteenth century made the transition from trading to banking and finance peculiarly easy. Traders were divided roughly into three categories—overseas traders, who had their factors and supercargoes all over the world, second-hand merchants, who bought from the former to sell on their own account, and commission traders.[36]   The development of Amsterdam into the intermediary market for the world made this last class increasingly important,[37] particularly at Amsterdam and Rotterdam.

The peculiar strength and weakness of the commission trade was its flexibility.   On the one hand, it suffered most from the shifting of international trading connections; on the other hand, the transition from the commission business to acceptance credit banking was smooth and natural.   It was quite general, for example, for commission agents to make a forward advance of capital to the foreign owner of goods which were awaiting sale at Amsterdam before those goods were actually sold. In the Franco-Dutch trade, the Dutch commission trader selling French textiles to the West Indies often paid three-quarters of an agreed price to the French manufacturers in advance,[38] and received interest on this advance.   He then attempted to get a higher price for the consignment than he had fixed with the owner, pocketed the difference, and also got his commission fee.   This, it is clear, was already a credit-giving

[33] van der Kooy, op. cit. 58.
[34] Exception was made for trade to Brabant and Flanders which paid only a single rate (i.e. import or export according to which was higher), van der Kooy, op. cit. 58.
[35] van der Kooy, op. cit. 63.
[36] Ibid. chap. 2.
[37] van Dillen, Jaarboekje, 72-3.
[38] Manger, op. cit. 45 n.

function. The next stage came when the Dutch "Commissionaire" abandoned the actual trading function and merely lent money to foreign commission traders which they advanced to merchants.[39] The most natural transition from trade to finance was effected in the case of "accept-crediet" banking. The commission trader who was already used to acting as acceptant for overseas suppliers was usually pretty willing to put his capital at the foreigner's disposal (in the form of acceptance credit) when his services were no longer required in the actual trading operation. It was, in fact, only a short step from the stage in the commission trade where the Amsterdam commission trader made a forward advance of capital to his client before sale, to the stage where he acted as acceptant for bills drawn on the buyer by the owner.[40]

In this way, Dutch houses came to act as paymasters, transferring capital from one part of Europe to another. Particularly between countries where trade was not reciprocal, this drawing credit service was indispensable, and the older contacts of the commission trade formed a convenient framework within which the bill business could be conducted. Not all commission trade changed into financial operations, of course, and some commission business lasted into the nineteenth century. Old-fashioned merchants denounced the new tendencies as being an indication of idleness and inertia, and as tending further to encourage the "voorbijland vaerders" who traded directly and cut out the Dutch entrepreneurs. The development was inevitable, however; the bill business was necessary for the Dutch traders themselves, and as they met increasing difficulties which restricted trade within old limits, they naturally took advantage of the opportunities for profits offered by banking developments.[41] To acceptance business was added insurance, discounting in trade and finance bills, mortgages, and foreign loan business.[42]

All this did not necessarily diminish the prosperity of Holland: it produced, in fact, increasing wealth. But at two points there was danger: First, there was the risk of a credit inflation through an overgrowth of finance bills; secondly, there was the danger of overspeculation in foreign securities, particularly British securities. The Amsterdam Bank was, it should be noted, concerned solely with exchange and specie business, and took no part in credit banking apart from a sort of clandestine overdraft which it allowed to the East India Company. This, on one or two occasions, and noticeably between 1742 and 1749, reached

[39] Manger, op. cit. 48-51. Also Sérionne, op. cit. II, 101 and 193.

[40] Ricard, Traité Général, I, 205.

[41] Sérionne (op. cit. 168) wrote in 1778 "on peut estimer à plusieurs milliards le montant de papiers monnoyés que les négociants produisent dans le commerce de l'Europe— . . . —de sorte que si les négociants Hollandois tirent ou acceptent pour compte des étrangers pour deux cents millions circulant toute l'année, leur provision d'un demi pour cent monte à la fin de l'année à six millions."

[42] Ricard, op. cit. 204.

dangerous proportions, but was successfully redeemed. The Bank survived the crises of 1763 and 1773, and was sound until 1781.[43] Credit banking was outside its sphere, however, and the Bank could not, by its very nature, exercise any stabilising influence on private speculation as the Bank of England could by its control of credit and discounting—a deficiency which proved extremely serious in 1763 and 1773. These financial developments, then, while they brought large short-term profits, did render the whole structure of economic life something less stable, and more liable to fluctuation, panic and fraud than it had been previously. Simultaneously, Holland was becoming a defenceless neutral power in a world increasingly dominated by power politics.

It would be wrong to attribute these financial developments entirely to the decline of trade. Time bargains in securities, for example, were known at the time of the building of the Bourse in 1609,[44] and in 1688 Joseph de la Vega described the fully-developed speculative market at Amsterdam in the *Confusion de Confusiones*. Participants in speculation included great capitalists looking for permanent investments, merchants who risked a little of their capital in moderate flutters, and the out-and-out gamblers. A class of brokers worked for the first and second classes. The increasing speculative activity on the Amsterdam Bourse is one of the most remarkable features of the eighteenth century in Holland. It coincided with, and was largely due to, the increasing importance of the Portuguese Jews on the Bourse. A Settlement Day regulation for 1764 was signed by forty-one members of the Bourse, out of whom thirty-six or thirty-seven were Portuguese Jews.[45] Speculation went on in all kinds of securities, but British Annuities. and the shares of the Bank of England, the South Sea Company, and the East India Company were the most popular and the most exciting. They were at once safe, yet subject, by reason of the continual political upheavals after 1739, to fluctuations which were sufficient to make gambling in them exciting and profitable, and the whole technique of time bargains, prolongations and premium bargains, which had grown up first in the grain and herring trades, then in Dutch East Indian securities, came into play in the foreign security market. Special price lists of English shares were published, and this list grew longer and longer.[46] The permanent stimulus to foreign investment was the low rate of interest in Holland. In the seventeenth century it had fallen from $6\frac{1}{4}$ per cent to $3\frac{1}{2}$ per cent, and in the eighteenth century it was 3 to $2\frac{1}{2}$ per cent.[47] Abroad, Dutch capitalists were still able to command 6 per cent in Bank of

[43] van Dillen, *Principal Public Banks* (" The Bank of Amsterdam "), 113, *passim*.

[44] van Dillen, " Isaac le Maire et le Commerce des Actions " (*Révue d'Histoire Moderne*, 1935), *passim*.

[45] Dr M. F. J. Smith, *Tijd Affaires in Effecten*, 143.

[46] van Dillen, " Effectenkoersen aan de Amsterdamsche Beurs 1723-94 " (*Econ. Hist. Jaarboek*, 1931). [47] van Dillen, *Het Economische Leven*, 3633.

England Stock, 5 per cent in annuities (until the conversion of 1749) and 5 per cent in colonial mortgages. Many took advantage of the offer of 5 per cent in the West Indies Estates Bill passed by Parliament for the benefit of the West Indian sugar planters in 1773. Many other European loans offered 6 or 5 per cent, and Dutch lenders figured on subscribers' lists for almost every country in Europe. Particular houses specialised in particular loans. The Trips and de Geers were traditionally agents for Swedish loans, and in the eighteenth century they were joined by Hopes & Horneca Fizeaux. Daniel Hogguer worked with John Law and secured a permanent option on French loans. Fizeaux Grand lent to Sweden and Poland, the Pels (perhaps the biggest of all) to Prussia, Hamburg and other German states, de Petersens to Denmark. Hopes also lent to Denmark, Bavaria, Prussia, Nassau-Saarbrück, the King of Poland, Spain and France, and in 1788, Henry Hope took over from de Smeths the great Russian loan of 9 million guilders. Deutz were agents for the Emperor, and Cliffords lent to Danzig and Denmark.[48] In London, the chief Dutch agents were Joshua van Neck & Co., the biggest underwriters for the Duke of Newcastle.[49] These firms and many others were responsible for a continuous flow of Dutch money into European and colonial loans from the middle of the eighteenth century onwards.

The first great crisis which shook European confidence in Amsterdam came in 1763, and followed the peace which ended seven years of war and four years of intensive Dutch investment in British war loans. The war had brought increased profits to some trades and some districts in Holland: whether it brought general prosperity is more doubtful.[50] What was clear was the enormous extension of the money trade which sprang from the war necessities of Prussia and England; England especially took advantage of the services of Dutch bankers to send large sums in bills and specie to support Prussia and pay her own troops in Hanover. These bills were usually payable in Holland or Hamburg. The opportunity to expand the volume of drawing credit tempted many dealers to grant credits without security in the form of a parallel commodity relationship. Unlike the official bill brokers, who took care to keep substantial reserves at the Bank of Amsterdam, financial parvenus like Gebroeders Neufville rarely had more than a thousand or two to fall back on.[51] When the peace was signed, then, there was an unprecedented inflation of credit in the form of unsecured finance bills. Bankers and merchants who had borrowed from one another by chains of bills found themselves unable to meet their obligations, the chain of

[48] E. Baasch, Holländische Wirtschaftgeschichte, 195. Elias, De Vroedschap van Amsterdam, 874, 875, 950, 1054-62.

[49] L. B. Namier, The Structure of Politics at the Accession of George III, I, 69.

[50] Dr E. E. de Jong-Keesing, De Economische Crisis van 1763 te Amsterdam (1939), 19-24.          [51] Ibid. chap. 2, passim, and 216.

credit snapped and a crop of bankruptcies followed in Amsterdam and Hamburg.

The biggest bankruptcy in Amsterdam was that of Gebroeders Neufville, a firm of twelve years' standing, with relations in Europe, India and the Levant who failed for 9½ million guilders. Investigations showed that a good part of its dealings had been extremely shady and a general panic ensued in August, when many of Neufville's business colleagues collapsed.[52]   English bankers, and particularly the Bank of England, came to the rescue and lent heavily to their Dutch correspondents.[53]   The Bank of England also generously suspended the payments of its own bills to tide matters over.[54]   The worst of the crisis was over by November, but the goods trade took longer to recover fully, and in the meantime, British shipping and trade were getting surer footholds.

Certain things were clear as a result of the crisis.   First, the situation was the result of an overdevelopment of credit by a group of financial novices,[55] aggravated by the heavy outflow of Dutch capital into the British Funds from 1759 to 1763.   Secondly, the crisis encouraged other countries to seek direct commercial contacts, so that, for the first time, a rate of exchange was established between England and Russia, and subsequent payments between those countries were made directly instead of through Amsterdam.[56]   Thirdly, London had given proof of its growing importance and stability in crisis conditions.

The big bill-broking bankers—the Hopes, Cliffords and Pels—were not involved in the crisis and continued to expand their operations, specialising more and more in finance as their share in the goods trade became smaller.   Hope's turnover of bills increased between 1756 and 1777 from 800 to 2,159, while the number of chartering contracts dwindled from 89 to 22.[57]   This development is important in considering the second great crisis which followed exactly ten years later and was due, not so much to *wisselruiterij*, like that of 1763, as to the failure of an attempt on the part of Cliffords and other bill-broking bankers to corner the market in British East India shares and to raise their price by heavy purchases.   To get to the root of the crisis it is necessary to go back to 1766, when the popularity of annuities was overshadowed by a revival of interest in East Indian shares.   These became the object of wild speculative dealings and a good many fortunes were made, among them that of a plausible scoundrel from Aberdeen named Alexander Fordyce.   Further speculations by Fordyce in 1772 failed, however, and

[52] de Jong-Keesing, *op. cit.* 217.
[53] W. P. Sautijn Kluit, *De Amsterdamsche Beurs in 1763 en 1773*, 10-23, *passim*.
[54] Macpherson, *Annals*, III, 372.          [55] de Jong-Keesing, *op. cit.* 216.
[56] van Dillen, " De Beurscrisis te Amsterdam in 1763 " (*Tijdschrift voor Geschiedenis* 1922), 253.
[57] de Jong-Keesing, *op. cit.* 216.

he bankrupted, carrying with him the Ayr Bank of Scotland (Douglas, Heron & Company) which had been in close correspondence with him and with his correspondents in Amsterdam, as well as a number of London banks. The crisis in London was over by September, but there then followed a second wave of speculation, this time by a group of Dutch houses. Clifford & Sons, Herman Johan van Seppenwolde, Willem Clifford & Chevalier, and Abraham Ter Borch were the leading conspirators in this attempt to raise the price of British East India shares, which had shown a consistent tendency to fall since early in 1772. The attempt failed in face of news from India that the Company was meeting fresh reverses from Hyder Ali. *De Koopman*, the weekly merchants' paper in Amsterdam, wrote in December 1772:

" The dreadful year 1763 has returned—but the causes are different from those of 1763 and take root in England: the East India Company is the cause . . . our diseased credit is dead, discounting has gone wholly out of fashion, a loan cannot be had except on double security."[58]

Just as in 1763, it was found that there was a complete absence of cash to meet obligations, and *De Koopman* stated that not a merchant in Amsterdam could raise 50,000 guilders in cash.[59] Houses stood 700,000 to 800,000 guilders in debt. The whole system of trade was temporarily paralysed. Again the Bank of England came to the rescue by allowing specie to be sent to Dutch correspondents (van Neck is reputed to have sent half a million sterling[60]) and by refusing to discount any doubtful paper.

In the summer of 1773 conditions were still bad, and the goods trade was still at a standstill. It picked up gradually, but even in March 1774 the French Consul at Amsterdam wrote gloomily of the effects of the crisis. The bankruptcies had, he said, caused anxiety and lack of confidence, but even more serious was the fact that five or six of the biggest trading houses were going out of business, amongst them André Pels and Son.[61]

The effects of the crisis (though not obvious from trade figures) were profound and far-reaching: Amsterdam was again shown up as the headquarters of dubious speculation, and older merchants grumbled about the speculative monopoly of the Portuguese Jews whom they accused of discouraging real trade in favour of the *windhandel* (inflated speculations).[62] The danger was more serious in Amsterdam than in London, owing to the complete and traditional decentralisation of credit banking, which was entirely in the hands of the private bankers and merchants. Most of these were themselves involved in speculation in foreign securities, as well as in *wisselruiterij*, and the fall of one house

[58] Translated from *De Koopman*, IV, 295-6.
[59] *Ibid.* IV, 301.
[61] van Dillen, *Jaarboekje*, 1928, 89 n.
[60] *De Koopman*, IV, 423.
[62] *De Koopman*, V, 254.

involved the ruin of dozens of others.[63]   In London, on the other hand, there was a fairly clear line of demarcation between the speculators of Change Alley and the respectable bankers, and credit policy was, finally, in the charge of the responsible directorate of the Bank of England.

Such figures for trade as are available indicate that the crisis of 1773 did not affect seriously what remained of the Dutch carrying trade. Exports from England to the Dutch market continued to fall, but imports from Holland to England show an increase between 1773 and 1779.   Holland took her usual profits out of the war with the American colonies, and St Eustatius particularly became the centre of a flourishing smuggling trade.   To sum up the economic position of the Netherlands when the catastrophe of war fell in 1780, we may say that though she had lost her monopoly of the carrying trade, she still had a bigger share of it than any other nation.   She still carried on a flourishing colonial trade, particularly with Surinam and the West Indies, in sugar, coffee, cotton, cocoa, tobacco and indigo and this trade showed a marked improvement between 1777 and 1779.[64]   In Europe she still dominated the fisheries, and Amsterdam was still the granary for German, Russian and Polish wheat.   The Bank had come through the crises unscathed, though credit had received a severe shock, and London was gradually replacing Amsterdam as the world's banking centre.   It is probably true that with her rapidly increasing volume of industrial exports, England was bound to replace Holland as the world market *par excellence,* but the change came more suddenly than anyone anticipated.   It proceeded from the inability of the Dutch to maintain their precarious neutrality in a world of power politics.   In the war of 1780 to 1783, the Dutch were hopelessly beaten, their commerce was reduced to nothing, the Bank of Amsterdam ruined, and Dutch capital lured away by French propaganda from the safest investments in Europe.

The war with England followed several years' political and financial indecision in the Netherlands.   All the Dutch financial ties were, until about 1779, with England.   Dutch money had seen the British Government through several difficult periods.   But after Britain was worsted by America, Dutch confidence weakened, and Dutch investors began to listen to those Francophile advisers who were recommending them to sell out their British holdings while they could.   A new British loan in 1780 only took £100,000 out of Holland, while Necker's loans were beginning to attract substantial sums.[65]   Meanwhile, the United States were trying hard to attract Dutch capital there, and John Adams was sent as financial representative to the Hague to woo the stubborn Dutch capitalists with plausible comparisons of the histories of the two Republics and the offer of unusually favourable terms to Dutch lenders.[66]   In

[63] *De Koopman,* IV, 356.

[64] Ricard, *op. cit.* I, statistics, 148.

[65] Manger, *op. cit.* 16-18.

[66] J. C. Westerman, *The Netherlands and the United States.   Their Relations in the Beginning of the 19th Century,* 2-10.

1780, Holland had to make up her mind which way she was going to jump: France and England each wanted exclusive use of Dutch transport facilities, and each put the screw on her to ensure that Holland did not extend her favours to the other.[67] Ultimately, Britain made up her mind for her by declaring war. There is no doubt, however, that the whole tendency of Dutch policy had, under the economic pressure and effective propaganda of France, become Francophile. France, too, hoped, by persuading Dutch investors to sell out their British holdings, to cause a panic on the London Exchange. This abandonment of her traditional neutrality was the real ruin of Holland. The Dutch coast was blockaded, and the Dutch fleet decimated, while in the West Indies Rodney seized Dutch colonial possessions. The Bank of Amsterdam failed in 1781, and there was, wrote the French Ambassador, " une véritable inaction dans toutes les branches de commerce ".[68] In the opinion of Dr van Dillen, the war of 1780 to 1783 was fatal to the Republic.[69] Holland became a pawn in the game between France and England, and what was left of the trade in 1783 was destroyed by the war of 1795. In 1805, the Prussian Ambassador wrote that half the population of Amsterdam was on the poor rate.[70]

In the new economic world which emerged in 1815, Holland was a second-class power. She had the good fortune to regain her colonies, but in a world of iron and steel, she necessarily took a second place. Since 1713, her policy had been directed by a clique of merchant regents, and her neutrality had deprived her of the stimulating unifying influence which Britain's war policy had had, first on British finance, secondly on British industry. That very coincidence of the interests of trade and government which was often held to account for Holland's seventeenth-century prosperity, relegated her inevitably in the eighteenth century to the status of a second-class power. Dutch capital continued to be important, and holdings of some millions stayed in France, England and America, where Dutch speculators were prominent in the wild land speculations in Pennsylvania and New York.[71]

The merchant class refused obstinately to recognise that a new economic order had come into being, superseding the era when the Dutch had been carriers and paymasters for an economically undeveloped Europe. As late as 1824 a Dutch writer remarked that Holland's trade rested on surer foundations than England's because it depended only to a small extent on industrial products, while 70 per cent of

[67] Manger, op. cit. 14-15.
[68] Ibid. 18-19.
[69] van Dillen, Het Economische Leven, 3634.
[70] The Economist, 15 February 1913, " The Early History of Dutch Foreign Investment ".
[71] P. D. Evans, The Holland Land Company, passim.

English exports came from factories.[72]  It remained for King Willem I to bring the Netherlands into line with contemporary economic ideas, refounding the Netherlands Bank as a bank of issue, cherishing the colonial trade, protecting the textile and metal industries, and making what could be made of the previously despised transit trade.

[72] van der Kooy, *op. cit.* 67-8.

# THE SMALL LANDOWNER, 1780-1832, IN THE LIGHT OF THE LAND TAX ASSESSMENTS [1]

## E. DAVIES

THERE is a wide divergence of opinion among economic historians on the question of the disappearance of the yeoman farmer, using the term here in the sense of small occupying owner. As an illustration may be compared the views of Rae and Gonner. The former held that, in the eighteenth century, " no really serious breach had yet been made in the ranks of the yeomanry, if indeed their strength had not positively risen ".[2]   The latter asserted that " there is little room for doubt at the steady and widespread disappearance . . . of the small owner cultivating his own little farm.  The fact is beyond all doubt . . . from all sides rose the cry that the very valuable order of small yeomen farmers was vanishing." [3]   The views of contemporaries were equally divided.  A contributor to the *Annals of Agriculture* in 1803 expressed the opinion that " the possession of great capital acquired frequently or increased by trade has thrown the landed property into large allotments . . . every field upon sale too often passes into the hands of the rich land-owner of adjacent lands ".[4]   But another writer (1797) declared that the influx of trade and commerce had " tended to the division of property and the increase of the number of small freeholders in many parts of the kingdom.  Lords of manors . . . found they could make more of it by parcelling it out in small lots than by selling it in entire manors." [5] Girdler maintained that " on the enclosure of the common fields they were sure to pass into the hands of the lord of the manor, the squire or the parson ";[6] while Marshall asserted that after the Vale of Pickering had undergone enclosure, " no county of equal extent can boast of so numerous a body of yeomanry as the Vale under survey ".[7]

[1] No exhaustive treatment of the so-called " Agrarian Revolution " is intended in this article, but the new evidence of the land tax assessments is brought forward as a fresh and little-worked source of information, of which all future discussion of the question must take account.  The investigation is confined mainly to one section of the agricultural population only—the small occupying owners.
[2] Rae, *Contemporary Review* (October 1883), 551.
[3] Gonner, *Common Land and Enclosure*, 369, 370.
[4] *Annals of Agriculture*, XL, 54, 55.          [5] Davis, *Report on Wiltshire*, 12.
[6] Girdler, *Observations on Forestalling, Regrating and Engrossing* (1800), 40-1.
[7] Marshall, *Rural Economy of Yorkshire*, 258.

There are several sources of evidence of which little use has been made: the enclosure awards; the poll books; the returns of the poor rate; the land tax returns; and, possibly, the returns to the property tax. The awards embrace a single year; they fail to distinguish between owners and occupying owners; they frequently deal only with a fraction of the parish; they are restricted to parishes enclosed by Act of Parliament; and they furnish no indication as to whether the land was retained in ownership or disposed of. The poll books exclude copyholders as well as those owning land to the value of less than 40s. a year; they make no distinction between occupying and non-occupying owners; they take no account of freeholders who absented themselves from the poll;[8] and, finally, the land conferring the qualification was often remote from the parish where the voters resided and on whose lists they were included.[9] The returns to the poor rate are confined to occupiers alone; they include tenants and occupying owners; and, though they provide useful information concerning the consolidation of farms, they yield no evidence as to the fate of the small landowner. The land tax returns also have their limitations; but they are the only documents that distinguish between proprietor and occupier, and they include all grades of landowners. They appear, therefore, to be the sole source from which reliable evidence can be gleaned concerning the yeomanry during the period 1780-1832.

The land tax was based on an assessment made in 1692, and was originally intended as a tax on personalty, offices and other incomes, as well as on income from land. By 1733, with the exception of a few isolated and easily detected taxes on offices, it had become a pure land tax. Quotas were allotted to counties, and within the counties to hundreds and parishes, and remained fixed. County quotas bore no relationship to acreage, but within the counties they were equitably distributed.[10] The most serious effects of the assessments lay not in the nature, character and application of the tax, but in the incomplete and defective compilation of the returns made by the assessor. With insignificant exceptions, no attempt was made before 1780 to distinguish between proprietors and occupiers. A single list of names was given, with the sum due from each. It was impossible to ascertain whether the sum was paid in respect of land, office, or tithe; and, when it was paid on land, whether the owner occupied or leased to a tenant. Further, unaccountable and sudden fluctuations in the numbers of proprietors are to be noticed about 1780. Those who are proprietors in the early assessments sometimes appear as tenants in the later assessments, though no

---

[8] Nicholls, *History of Leicester*, II, i, 19.
[9] *Ibid.* 106-8.
[10] Dowell, *History of Taxation*, II, 4, 5, 33, 50, 51. *Letter to a Freeholder on the Late Reduction of the Land Tax* (1731-2), 7. *Annals of Agriculture*, V, 70. *Report of the Select Committee on Agriculture, 1836*, Qs. 9056-9112.

change of ownership has occurred in the meantime.[11]   The explanation appears to be that the tenant was responsible for the payment of the tax; and that this had greatly influenced the mode of compilation previous to 1780,[12] the assessor having adopted the practice of inserting the name of the payee, whether landlord or tenant, in the one column of the assessment.

From 1780 onwards, however, greater care and precision were shown in drawing up the parish lists.   Printed forms were issued by the commissioners, with columns for proprietors, occupiers, and amount assessed, and—in some cases—for rental and description of property. This change was due, not to an accidental coincidence, but to the Act of 1780.   Enacted primarily for the removal of " certain difficulties relative to voters at county elections ",[13] it changed the assessments from incomplete and inaccurate parochial records into documents of supreme value to the economic historian.   Commissioners, after appointing assessors. were to " cause to be delivered to each of the said assessors a printed form of an assessment as set forth in the schedule hereunto annexed [14] . . . a fair copy thereof to be stuck upon one of the doors of the church or chapel of the parish . . . and if any person or persons shall rent, hold or occupy messuages, lands or tenements belonging to different owners or occupiers, the same shall be distinctly rated . . . that the proportion of land tax to be paid by each separate owner or proprietor respectively may be known and ascertained ".   It was not until 1786 that all assessors distinguished between owners and occupiers.

Henceforth it was no longer possible to confuse owners with tenants, but the difficulty of determining the exact title of the " proprietors " to their land still remained.   Descriptions of tenure are often given; and, in addition to " freeholders " and " copyholders ", the term " freehold leaseholder " occurs frequently, particularly in the Cheshire assessments. Take, for example, the return for the parish of Marston, in Oxfordshire. There is no indication that any of the land in this parish was held on life leasehold; yet Corpus Christi, Magdalen and Brasenose Colleges—the principal landowners in the parish—do not appear in the assessment, since they leased their land, and the lessees appear in the " proprietor " column.   This inclusion of the leaseholder for life or lives has an important bearing on the term " yeoman farmer " or " occupying owner " as employed in the tables below, since it was necessary to apply the term not only to the freeholders and copyholders but also to the life leaseholders.   Another difficult problem is the status of two other classes

[11] For a good example, see Assessments for Little Addington, Northamptonshire.
[12] 38 Geo. III, c. 5, 1797-8, clauses 17 and 35. *Report of the Select Committee on Agriculture, 1836*, Qs. 9071, 9087. Eden, *State of the Poor*, I, 40. *Letter to a Freeholder, op. cit.* 46.          [13] 20 Geo. III, c. 17, Preamble.
[14] *Ibid.* clause 3. The schedule annexed was a specimen assessment form with columns for proprietors, occupiers, and amount assessed.

prior to enclosure—the squatters and owners of cottages to which rights of common were attached. The former in many cases had been in possession of their encroachments for so long a period that it is difficult to differentiate between them and other landowners; and Arthur Young gives an example of one who contributed to the land tax before enclosure.[15] But how many years' occupation was necessary to convert an encroacher into a landowner who paid the land tax? Again, according to Marshall, owners of cottages to which rights of common were attached appeared to have paid the land tax in the Vale of Pickering, where the land, when it was enclosed, was allotted on the basis of the land tax paid.[16] But, judging from the sudden increase in the number of taxpayers contributing less than 10s. in the post-enclosure assessments, squatters and owners of cottages to which rights of common were attached, as a rule, only became contributors when they obtained legally recognized allotments.

Another serious defect in compilation was the inconsistent use of the word " do." or " ditto " in the occupier column, despite the injunctions laid down in the Act of 1780, that " himself " or the name of the tenant should be inserted. The abbreviation refers quite as frequently to the person in the parallel proprietor column as to the person immediately above. This is a point of vital importance, since in the first instance it means that the proprietor occupied the holding himself, and in the second that he leased it to a tenant. Another stumbling-block appeared in 1798, when the tax was made a perpetual rent charge of 4s. in the pound, with the option of redeeming it at fifteen years' purchase. In some instances the tax was redeemed and the land immediately disappeared from the returns. Generally speaking, however, all land was included, though in the case of exonerated land the assessors became indifferent as to who occupied the holdings, since the tenants, who previously—when they paid the tax—were of importance in the eyes of the assessors, no longer concerned them. With increasing frequency from 1798 onwards the tenants' names disappeared: with the result that it is no longer possible in many instances to distinguish between the occupying owners and proprietors generally.

Despite these defects, the majority of the assessments from 1780 onwards are complete, and are of immense value to the economic historian. With their help the consolidation and dispersal of estates can be traced. The exact year of the exit of the old landed families, and of the entry of the parvenus of commerce, can be ascertained. After a study of them, it is no longer a matter of conjecture who was sacrificed to provide the Peels, the Arkwrights and the Strutts with landed properties. An unfortunate evening at White's or Brooks's or a calamitous day on the Epsom Downs saw a mysterious " ——, Esq., of London " replacing

---

[15] *Annals, XXXVI*, 580.          [16] Marshall, *Rural Economy of Yorkshire*, 96, 97.

a well-known eighteenth-century sportsman in the subsequent assessment for Middleton Parva. It is possible to trace the immense transfer of landed property which occurred during the years 1780-1815. Land-owners and tenants in parishes undergoing enclosure can be traced for years previous to and after enclosure, and the exact effect of the latter ascertained. A comparison can be made between parishes in the open field, parishes already enclosed by Act, and those of "ancient enclosure". It is possible to determine the effect of the financial debacle of 1814-25, and of the collapse of the country banks, on the unfortunate mortgagee, by tracing the newly created farming proprietors through the assessments of 1815-26. Indeed, the usefulness of these documents to the economic, family and social historian is unquestionable, and it is hoped that the plea of Mr Johnson for their preservation and publication will receive sympathetic consideration.

The assessments previous to 1832, where they exist, are in the custody of the Clerks of the Peace. As far as we have been able to ascertain, they exist in the county muniment rooms as follows:

| County | Year | County | Year |
|---|---|---|---|
| Bedford | 1750,[17] 1799, 1801–32 | Middlesex | 1767, 1780–1830 |
| Berkshire | None before 1832. | Norfolk | 1767–1832 |
| Buckingham- | | Northampton | 1746–1832 [19] |
| shire | None before 1832. | Northumberland | 1748–81, 1791, 1805–31 |
| Cambridge | 1829–32. | Nottingham | 1780–1832 [20] |
| Cheshire | 1780–1832 | Oxford | Some 1760–85; all 1785–1832 |
| Cornwall | 1770–1832 | | |
| Cumberland | None before 1832 | Shropshire | Borough of Wenlock only, 1799 |
| Derby | 1778–1832 | | |
| Devon | 1747, 1751, 1780–1832 | Somerset | 1766–1831 [21] |
| Dorset | 1780–1830 | Stafford | 1766–1835 [22] |
| Durham | 1783–1828 | Suffolk: East | None before 1832 |
| Essex | 1781–1832 | West | None before 1832 |
| Gloucester | 1775–1832 | Surrey | 1780–1832 |
| Hampshire | 1798–1832 | Sussex: East | 1780–1832 |
| Herefordshire | 1777, 1802–32 | West | 1780–1832 [23] |
| Kent | 1682, 1760–1832 | Warwick | 1774–1832 |
| Lancashire | 1677, 1740, 1780–1832 | Westmorland | 1790–1832 |
| Leicestershire | 1773–1832 | Wiltshire | 1773–4, 1780–1831, 1833[24] |
| Lincoln | | Wight, Isle of | None before 1832 |
| Lindsey | 1780–1832 | Yorkshire: | |
| Holland | None before 1832 | North Riding | 1769–1832 [25] |
| Kesteven | 1789–1835 | West Riding | Few before 1832 [26] |
| Monmouthshire | None before 1832 [18] | East Riding | 1782–1832 |

We have received no replies from the Clerks of the Peace for Hertford, Rutland and Worcester.

[17] For the hundred of Manstead only—deposited with the County Records Committee. [18] Some may be deposited amongst some old papers at Usk Session House.
[19] Many of those for the years 1746-80 are missing.
[20] Many for the years 1780-90 missing.
[21] In custody of the Records Officer to the County Council, Taunton Castle.
[22] Some years missing and the returns for many of the years incomplete.
[23] These are in the custody of the Clerk of the Peace, East Sussex.
[24] Those for 1783 missing.
[25] The returns for 1771, 1775, 1777, 1779, 1780 are missing, and those for 1770, 1772, 1773, 1776, 1778 and 1808 are incomplete.     [26] These have not been scheduled.

Many of the early assessments, having been at one time indifferently preserved, proved to be indecipherable, or crumbled when handled. They have occasionally emerged from the gloom of the muniment room into the twilight of the law-courts to substantiate title to land, but seldom into the full light of popular knowledge through the medium of the historian.   They have been partially used by the Rev. A. H. Johnson and Professor H. L. Gray.[27]   Basing his observations on the returns of 500 parishes, Mr Johnson concluded that there was a remarkable consolidation of estates, and a corresponding diminution of small owners, some time between the end of the seventeenth century and 1785; that between the years 1785 and 1802, with the exception of Lancashire, there was no shrinkage of owner occupiers, but rather a slight increase; while between the years 1802-32 there was a decrease all round, but not serious enough to justify attributing a general disappearance to this period; and that since 1832 no great fluctuation has occurred in their numbers. Mr Gray came to similar conclusions, but indicated further that parishes destitute of occupying owners were old enclosures, and that occupying owners in parishes undergoing parliamentary enclosure experienced the same modification in number as in the remaining parishes.   The most serious critic of these two writers has been Dr Levy.[28]   He maintained that both restricted their researches to a limited area, and consequently were not justified in drawing general conclusions; and that, even on this narrow basis, a distinction between the size of the holdings was made only in the case of 94 parishes analyzed by Mr Johnson: hence it was possible that, while the totals remained constant, the small owner disappeared and large occupying owners came into being by purchase during the corn-growing boom.   Finally there was the fact that other occupying owners—for example, the squire and the parson—were included, and so swelled the total number of yeoman occupying owners.

In the table below every effort has been made to meet these criticisms. The returns of approximately 2,000 parishes have been analyzed: these were the parishes for which complete assessments were forthcoming in Cheshire, Derbyshire, Leicestershire, Lindsey (Lincoln), Northamptonshire, Nottinghamshire, Oxfordshire and Warwickshire.   All but the first of these counties were selected on the ground that they were among the chief agricultural counties of England, that enclosure in them during the latter half of the eighteenth century had been heavy, and that some were rapidly becoming manufacturing counties during the period under review, while some were seats of thriving domestic industries.   Cheshire was selected for the purpose of comparison, since in the county there were few, if any, enclosures during the latter half of the eighteenth

[27] A. H. Johnson, *The Disappearance of the Small Landowner*, 1910.  Gray, " Yeoman Farming in Oxfordshire ", in *Quarterly Journal of Economics*, February 1910.
[28] Hermann Levy, *Large and Small Holdings in England*, chaps. i and ii.

century. The landowners have been divided into three main classes, and these have been subdivided according to the amount of land tax paid on their properties. The first class is that of the yeoman farmer or small occupying owner. This class is subdivided into those paying less than 4s., 4s. and under 10s., 10s. and under £1, £1 and under £2, £2 and under £3, £3 and under £4, £4 and under £5, £5 and under £8, £8 and under £10, £10 and under £20, and £20 and over.[29] The second class is that of the small landowners paying less than £20 in land tax, who did not occupy their holdings. This class has been subdivided on the same basis as the first. The third class is that of the large landowners, who contributed £20 and over to the land tax, and who were frequently in occupation of a moiety of their property. This latter classification involved considerable labour; in Leicestershire alone there were approximately 400 potential large landowners, each of whom has to be traced through 762 different assessments.

Our study has been confined to the periods 1780-1802 and 1802-32; and our object in this article is to present a summary of the main conclusions as to the distribution of landed property in the eight counties mentioned. While it is possible that the real turning-point in the history of agriculture was 1815-16, the fact that the last two decades of the eighteenth century are said to have witnessed "the agony of the yeomanry"[30] justifies the fixing of the dividing point at 1802. Table I, Section A, enumerates the total number of occupying owners or yeoman farmers, classified according to the land tax paid on their holdings, in 1,706 parishes in the seven counties of Cheshire, Derby, Leicester, Lindsey, Northampton, Nottingham and Warwick for the years 1780-6[31] and 1802. Section B affords the same information for 1,395 parishes in the six counties of Derby, Leicester, Lindsey, Northampton, Nottingham and Warwick for the years 1780-6, 1802 and 1832. Section C gives the unclassified total of the 1,706 parishes mentioned above together with those for 237 Oxfordshire parishes for the years 1780-6 and 1802-4.[32] Section D furnishes the total for the six counties, together with Oxfordshire, for the years 1780, 1802-4 and 1832.

Table II gives the combined totals of the small non-occupying owners (i.e. those contributing less than £20 to the land tax) and large landowners (i.e. those contributing £20 and over to the land tax), subdivided according to the extent of their estates.

[29] Since the assessors were meticulous in their use of titles such as Esqs., Revs., etc., the occupying owners not so described have been included with the occupying owners of the yeoman class, despite the fact that they contributed over £20.

[30] Mantoux, La Révolution Industrielle, 129.

[31] Since in many of the counties various assessments for the years 1780-6 were either defective or indecipherable, the earliest complete assessments were always analyzed. The majority were complete in 1782, but in some cases, particularly in the hundred of Kington in Warwickshire, and in Cheshire, those for 1786 were taken.

[32] For Oxfordshire the assessments for 1804 were analyzed.

## TABLE I (OCCUPYING OWNERS)

### SECTION A

OCCUPYING OWNERS IN 1,706 PARISHES SITUATED IN CHESHIRE, DERBYSHIRE, LEICESTERSHIRE, LINDSEY, NORTHAMPTONSHIRE, NOTTINGHAMSHIRE AND WARWICKSHIRE FOR THE YEARS 1780-6 AND 1802.

| | Land tax under— | | | | | | | | | Land tax over £20 | Total | Total paying 4s. and over | Total paying 10s. and over |
|---|---|---|---|---|---|---|---|---|---|---|---|---|---|
| | 4s. | 10s. | £1 | £2 | £4 | £5 | £8 | £10 | £20 | | | | |
| 1780–6 . | 2,766 | 3,061 | 1,696 | 1,555 | 1,106 | 287 | 359 | 171 | 138 | 24 | 11,163 | 8,397 | 5,336 |
| 1802 . | 3,542 | 3,173 | 2,067 | 1,813 | 1,344 | 306 | 480 | 225 | 225 | 40 | 13,215 | 9,673 | 6,500 |
| Increase | 776 | 112 | 371 | 258 | 238 | 19 | 121 | 54 | 87 | 16 | 2,052 | 1,276 | 1,164 |
| Decrease . | — | — | — | — | — | — | — | — | — | — | — | — | — |

### SECTION B

OCCUPYING OWNERS IN 1,395 PARISHES SITUATED IN DERBYSHIRE, LEICESTERSHIRE, LINDSEY, NORTHAMPTONSHIRE, NOTTINGHAMSHIRE AND WARWICKSHIRE FOR THE YEARS 1780-2, 1802, 1832.

| | Land tax under— | | | | | | | | | Land tax over £20 | Total | Total paying 4s. and over | Total paying 10s. and over |
|---|---|---|---|---|---|---|---|---|---|---|---|---|---|
| | 4s. | 10s. | £1 | £2 | £4 | £5 | £8 | £10 | £20 | | | | |
| 1780–6 . | 2,289 | 2,655 | 1,391 | 1,180 | 861 | 244 | 359 | 124 | 130 | 23 | 9,256 | 6,967 | 4,312 |
| 1802 . | 3,074 | 2,738 | 1,776 | 1,488 | 1,129 | 266 | 480 | 168 | 215 | 40 | 11,374 | 8,300 | 5,562 |
| 1832 . | 4,303 | 2,660 | 1,700 | 1,299 | 978 | 262 | 409 | 156 | 231 | 45 | 12,043 | 7,740 | 5,080 |
| Increase 1780–6 to 1832 | 2,014 | 5 | 309 | 119 | 117 | 18 | 50 | 32 | 101 | 22 | 2,787 | 773 | 678 |
| Decrease 1780–6 to 1832 | — | — | — | — | — | — | — | — | — | — | — | — | — |

### SECTION C

GRAND TOTAL OF ALL GRADES OF OCCUPYING OWNERS IN 1,943 PARISHES (NAMELY, 1,706 PARISHES IN THE SEVEN COUNTIES OF SECTION A, PLUS 237 OXFORDSHIRE PARISHES) FOR THE YEARS 1780-6 to 1802-4.

| | |
|---|---|
| 1780–6 . . . . . . . | 12,319 |
| 1802–4 . . . . . . . | 14,465 |
| Increase . . . . . . . | 2,146 |
| Decrease . . . . . . . | nil |

### SECTION D

GRAND TOTAL OF OCCUPYING OWNERS IN 1,632 PARISHES (NAMELY, 1,395 PARISHES IN THE SIX COUNTIES OF SECTION B, PLUS 237 OXFORDSHIRE PARISHES) FOR THE YEARS 1780-6, 1802-4, AND 1832.

| | |
|---|---|
| 1780–6 . . . . . . . | 10,412 |
| 1802–4 . . . . . . . | 12,616 |
| 1832 . . . . . . . | 13,107 |
| Increase 1780–6 to 1832 . . . . | 2,695 |

# TABLE II (NON-OCCUPYING OWNERS)

## SECTION A

Non-occupying owners in 1,706 parishes situated in Cheshire, Derbyshire, Leicestershire, Lindsey, Northamptonshire, Nottinghamshire and Warwickshire for the years 1780-6 and 1802

| | Land tax under— | | | | | | | | | | | | | | | | Total | Total paying 10s. and over |
|---|---|---|---|---|---|---|---|---|---|---|---|---|---|---|---|---|---|---|
| | 10s. | £2 | £5 | £20 | £40 | £80 | £100 | £300 | £600 | £800 | £1,000 | £1,100 | £1,200 | £1,300 | £1,400 | £1,500 | | |
| 1780-6 | 5,643 | 5,468 | 3,010 | 2,158 | 381 | 264 | 88 | 216 | 29 | 3 | 5 | 1 | — | 1 | — | — | 17,267 | 11,624 |
| 1802 | 5,251 | 4,374 | 2,393 | 1,920 | 381 | 280 | 78 | 199 | 31 | 2 | 7 | 1 | — | — | 1 | — | 14,918 | 9,667 |
| Increase . | — | — | — | — | — | 16 | — | — | 2 | — | 2 | — | — | — | 1 | — | — | — |
| Decrease . | 392 | 1,094 | 617 | 238 | — | — | 10 | 17 | — | 1 | — | — | — | 1 | — | — | 2,349 | 1,957 |

## SECTION B

Non-occupying owners in 1,395 parishes situated in Derbyshire, Leicestershire, Lindsey, Northamptonshire, Nottinghamshire and Warwickshire for the years 1780-6, 1802 and 1832

| | Land tax under— | | | | | | | | | | | | | | | | Total | Total paying 10s. and over |
|---|---|---|---|---|---|---|---|---|---|---|---|---|---|---|---|---|---|---|
| | 10s. | £2 | £5 | £20 | £40 | £80 | £100 | £300 | £600 | £800 | £1,000 | £1,100 | £1,200 | £1,300 | £1,400 | £1,500 | | |
| 1780-6 | 4,593 | 4,141 | 2,320 | 1,837 | 344 | 233 | 79 | 202 | 26 | 3 | 5 | 1 | — | 1 | — | — | 13,785 | 9,192 |
| 1802 | 4,152 | 3,365 | 1,886 | 1,641 | 339 | 252 | 69 | 183 | 24 | 2 | 7 | 1 | — | — | 1 | — | 11,923 | 7,771 |
| 1832 | 5,699 | 3,549 | 1,736 | 1,670 | 340 | 232 | 66 | 198 | 28 | 5 | 4 | 1 | — | — | — | — | 13,530 | 7,831 |
| Increase 1780-6 to 1832 | 1,106 | — | — | — | — | — | — | — | 2 | 2 | — | — | — | — | — | — | — | — |
| Decrease 1780-6 to 1832 | — | 592 | 584 | 167 | 4 | 1 | 13 | 4 | — | — | 1 | — | — | 1 | — | — | 255 | 1,361 |

Section A gives the totals for the years 1780-6, and 1802 for the same parishes as in Table I, Section A.

Section B gives the totals for the years 1780-6, 1802 and 1832 for the same parishes as in Table I, Section B.

Table III gives the amounts of the land tax paid by the large landowners (contributing £20 and over), by all small owners (contributing less than £20), and by occupying owners (contributing less than £20). Section A gives the amounts contributed by the large landowners in 1,706 parishes for the years 1780-6 and 1802; and Section B the respective sums of the three groups in 1,395 parishes for the years 1780-6, 1802 and 1832.

## TABLE III

### SECTION A

LAND TAX OF LARGE LANDOWNERS (*i.e.* THOSE CONTRIBUTING £20 AND OVER ANNUALLY) IN 1,706 PARISHES SITUATED IN CHESHIRE, DERBYSHIRE, LEICESTERSHIRE, LINDSEY, NORTHAMPTONSHIRE, NOTTINGHAMSHIRE AND WARWICKSHIRE FOR THE YEARS 1780-6 AND 1802.

| Year | | | | | | | Land tax of large landowners |
|---|---|---|---|---|---|---|---|
| | | | | | | | £ s. d. |
| 1780-6 | . | . | . | . | . | . | 91,694 15 3 |
| 1802 | . | . | . | . | . | . | 92,085 2 10 |
| Increase | . | . | . | . | . | . | 390 7 7 |
| Decrease | . | . | . | . | . | . | nil |

### SECTION B

LAND TAX OF LARGE LANDOWNERS, OF ALL SMALL OWNERS * AND OCCUPYING OWNERS * IN 1,395 PARISHES SITUATED IN DERBYSHIRE, LEICESTERSHIRE, LINDSEY, NORTHAMPTONSHIRE, NOTTINGHAMSHIRE AND WARWICKSHIRE FOR THE YEARS 1780-6, 1802 AND 1832

| Year | Land tax of large landowners | Land tax of all small owners (occupying and non-occupying) | Land tax of occupying owners |
|---|---|---|---|
| | £ s. d. | £ s. d. | £ s. d. |
| 1780-6 . . . . | 84,366 5 10 | 47,236 1 5 | 13,755 6 0 |
| 1802 . . . . | 83,571 1 11 | 48,031 5 4 | 18,490 2 0 |
| 1832 . . . . | 84,316 14 1 | 47,285 13 2 | 17,595 9 0 |
| Increase 1780-6 to 1832 . | — | 49 11 9 | 3,840 3 0 |
| Decrease 1780-6 to 1832 . | 49 11 9 | — | — |

* Those who contributed less than £20.

Table IV classifies the parishes into those owned by one large landowner, those owned by more than one large landowner, those with no occupying owners, and those with less than six occupying owners. Section A gives the figures for 1,706 parishes in 1780-6 and 1802, and Section B for 1,395 parishes in 1780-6, 1802 and 1832.

If we take Table I, Section A, it will be seen that all grades of occupying owners exhibited a marked increase during the period 1780-6 to 1802. Though there were marked diminutions of those contributing 4s. to 10s. in Leicester and Northampton, the increases in Lincoln and

Derby more than preserved the balance. Relatively the smallest augmentation occurred in this grade of landowners—the owners of 4 to 15 acres of land. If the contributors of less than 4s. be included, the 1802 total exceeded the 1780-6 total by 2,052; if these be excluded, by 1,276; and if contributions of less than 10s. be excluded, by 1,164. Such increases amongst the contributors of 10s. and over were only possible

## TABLE IV

### SECTION A

DISTRIBUTION OF OCCUPYING OWNERS IN 1,706 PARISHES IN 1780-6 AND 1802

| Year | Number of parishes owned by one large landowner | Parishes owned by more than one large landowner | Parishes with no occupying owners | Parishes with less than six occupying owners |
|---|---|---|---|---|
| 1780-6 . | 203 | 106 | 547 | 514 |
| 1802 . | 183 | 107 | 452 | 503 |
| Increase . | — | 1 | — | — |
| Decrease . | 20 | — | 95 | 11 |

### SECTION B

DISTRIBUTION OF OCCUPYING OWNERS IN 1,395 PARISHES IN 1780-6, 1802 AND 1832.

| Year | Number of parishes owned by one large landowner | Parishes owned by more than one large landowner | Parishes with no occupying owners | Parishes with less than six occupying owners |
|---|---|---|---|---|
| 1780-6 . . . | 174 | 98 | 470 | 400 |
| 1802 . . . | 150 | 93 | 380 | 392 |
| 1832 . . . | 148 | 88 | 377 | 372 |
| Increase 1780-6 to 1832 . . . | — | — | — | — |
| Decrease 1780-6 to 1832 . . . | 26 | 10 | 93 | 28 |

through numerous sitting tenants purchasing their holdings.[33] If we take Table I, Section B, we find that augmentations occurred in all grades during the years 1780-6 to 1802; it was relatively more pronounced

[33] Other contemporary evidence confirmed the evidence of the assessments. See J. Tucker, *The Causes of the Dearness of Provisions Assigned*, 21, 22; Young, *Six Weeks' Tour*, 22, 23, 30 86; Young, *Report Essex*, 39, 40; Marshall, *Rural Economy Midland Counties*, I, 15, 16; Marshall, *Rural Economy of Yorkshire*, 30; Tuke, *Report North Riding*, 30; Griggs, *Report Essex*, 22; Billingsley, *Report Somerset*, 204; Vancouver's *Report Cambridge*, 168; Davis, *Report Wiltshire*, 8; Plymley, *Report Shropshire*, 91; Stevenson, *Report Surrey*, 73; Mavor, *Report Berkshire*, 50, 51; *Annals of Agriculture*, XVI, 547; XXIV, 362; XXIX, 522; XXXIII, 35; XXXVII, 351, 352; *Report Agricultural State of the Kingdom*, 1816, I, 147, 148; II, 24, 148; *Report Select Committee on Agriculture*, 1822, 212, 213, 214, 242; *Report Select Committee*, 1833, Qs. 1246, 1266, 1704, 2197, 2534, 3105, 3106, 5820, 5825, 6715; *Observations on the State of the Country since the Peace* (1817), 10.

than in Table I, Section A, since Cheshire, where a diminution occurred, is excluded. During 1802-32 all except contributors of less than 4s., and of £10 and over, diminished. The marked diminution amongst the contributors of £1 to £10 was due to the selling of their holdings by the sitting tenants who had bought at boom prices.[34] The great increase in number contributing less than 4s. was only to be expected when population expanded and vast areas of the common and waste were enclosed. Occupying owners contributing £10 and over were more numerous than in 1802, and those paying £8 to £10 had only declined slightly; a fact which indicated that the occupying owners in possession of large holdings had weathered the post-war storm better than those in occupation of smaller holdings. Yet, compared with 1780-6, all grades were more numerous in 1832. Despite the fact, therefore, that marked diminutions occurred during the years 1802-32, the yeomanry of England did not "fall at Waterloo" as Rae would have us believe:[35] in the 1,632 parishes of Table I, Section D, the occupying owners totalled 2,695 more in 1832 than in 1780-6.

The most surprising feature of Table II is the large number of small landowners not in occupation of their holdings in 1780-6. The existence of this large class of small landlords illustrates, incidentally, the futility of endeavouring to ascertain from manorial rolls, enclosure awards, the poll books or the figures given by King, Defoe and Horner, the existence or otherwise of a numerous yeomanry. These little landlords greatly outnumbered the occupying owners, and, if they existed in King's day, would be included in the " 140,000 freeholders of the lesser sort ". It would be difficult for Defoe to distinguish between the " grey coats " who let, and those who occupied, their holdings.[36] Horner's argument, that " there is scarce any county in which the number of freeholders does not turn out upon an election poll much more considerable than formerly ",[37] was no proof of the survival of a large body of occupying proprietors. During the last two decades of the eighteenth century there occurred in the 1,706 parishes of Table II, Section A, a pronounced diminution of non-occupying owners. Compared with a total of 17,267

---

[34] See also Glover, " Observations on the Present State of Pauperism in England ", *Pamphleteer*, X, 385; Preston, *Review of the Present Condition of the Landed and Agricultural Interest*, 2, 3; *Report 1816*, II, 241; I, 75, 76, 85; *Observations on the State of the Country since the Peace*, 9, 10; Cobbett, *Rural Rides*, 100; *Report Select Committee, 1833*, IX, X, Qs. 1267, 1693, 1697-1701, 1703, 1704, 2346-8, 2533, 3103-7, 3601-14, 4862-4, 4866, 5816, 5818, 5821, 6701, 6704, 6711, 6712, 6715, 6718, 8474, 8480, 8572, 8579, 8580, 8583, 8587, 9197, 9200, 12,216, 12,219, 12,523-30.

[35] *Contemporary Review* (October 1883), 553. Rae's contention that the occupying owners increased during the years 1780-1815 receives confirmation from the assessments. His assumption, however, that the decline which began about 1815 was the first great encroachment upon the ranks of the yeomanry, was disproved by the land tax returns. From the majority of the parishes studied they had almost completely disappeared before 1780.          [36] Defoe, *Tour*, I, letter ii, 38.

[37] Horner, *An Essay on the Nature and Method of Enclosing our Open Fields* (1766), 15.

19

in 1780-6, there were only 14,918 in 1802. The decline had been confined almost exclusively to the non-occupying owners contributing less
than £20 to the land tax, of whom there were 2,341 less in 1802. Though
in the case of large landowners there were sixteen additional contributors of £40 to £80, twenty-seven landowners paying £80 to £300 had
disappeared; thus large as well as small owners disposed of their properties. Considerable acquisitions were made by a few: forty-two
contributed £300 to £1,400 as compared with thirty-nine at the commencement of the period. In the 1,395 parishes of Table II, Section B,
similar augmentations and diminutions occurred, and collectively there
was a decrease of 1,862 during the period 1780-6 to 1802. In the thirty
years ending in 1832, on the other hand, there was a marked increase of
non-occupying owners; and, compared with 1780-6, the total in 1832 was
only 255 less; this was due to the inclusion of non-occupying contributors
of less than 4s. If these are excluded, there was a diminution of 1,361
during the fifty years from 1780-6 to 1832. The non-occupying owners
who disposed of their properties in considerable numbers were those
contributing 10s. to £20, of whom 1,343 disappeared.

Table III may now be studied. According to Section A, the land
tax contributed by the large landowners (i.e. those who paid £20 and
over to the land tax) in 1,706 parishes increased from £91,694 15s. 3d.
in 1780-6 to £92,085 2s. 10d. in 1802. This augmentation of £390 7s. 7d.
is, however, insignificant; though a few individuals added to their
acreages, the large landowner class as a whole made few acquisitions,
and these were made almost solely in Cheshire.[38]  In the 1,395 parishes
of Section B (from which the Cheshire parishes have been excluded)
89·6 per cent of the land in 1780-6 was owned by those who rented their
land to the tenantry.   Although we have included occupying copyholders and lessees for lives in the term "occupying owner", 10·4 per
cent only, or little more than a tenth, of the land remained the property
of those who combined ownership with occupation in 1780-6.   The large
landowners contributed £795 3s. 11d. less in 1802 than in 1780-6.  The
land represented by this sum, together with a considerably greater acreage which had been purchased either directly from the small non-
occupying owners, or from the large landowners—who had in their
turn purchased from the small—had passed over to the occupying
owners, who contributed £18,490 2s. in 1802, as compared with
£13,755 6s. in 1780-6.  During 1802-32 the land tax of the large landowners increased slightly; but, despite this, their total contributions in
1780-6 exceeded that of 1832 by £49 11s. 9d.  During the years 1802-32
the land tax of the occupying owners as a class diminished from

---

[38] And in Cheshire it was largely due to a refusal to renew life leases.  For typical
examples, see the assessments for the parishes of Audlem, Dodcott and Walgherton in
the hundred of Nantwich; Bunbury and Spurston in the hundred of Eddisbury; and
Over Alderley in the hundred of Macclesfield.

£18,490 2s. to £17,595 9s., but in 1832 it exceeded the 1780-6 total by £3,840 3s. Of the three classes of landowners, therefore, the small occupying owners alone owned a greater acreage in 1832 than in 1780-6.

Of the 1,706 parishes in Table IV, Section A, 203 were in 1780-6 the exclusive property of one large landowner, 106 were owned by more than one large landowner, 547 were without any occupying owners, and 514 contained less than 6 occupying owners. The occupying owners, therefore, were comparatively numerous in 645 only of the 1,706 parishes. During the period 1780-6 to 1832 the number of parishes in the exclusive ownership of large landowners diminished from 203 to 183, and occupying owners appeared in 95 of the 547 yeomanless parishes of 1780-6. Altogether the number of parishes which contained 6 or more occupying owners increased from 645 to 751. Of the 1,395 parishes in Table IV, Section B, 174 were in 1780-6 the sole property of one large landowner, 98 were the property of more than one large landowner, 470 were destitute of occupying owners, and 400 contained less than 6. Thus the occupying owners were numerous in 525 only of the 1,395 parishes. By 1832, 36 of the parishes exclusively owned by large landowners had been considerably subdivided, and there had been a marked augmentation of occupying owners in 121 of the parishes in which there were none, or few, in 1780-6. Not only, then, did the occupying owners increase in numerical strength during the years 1780-6 to 1832, but they appeared even in those parishes where land was in the possession of the few in 1780-6.

In Table V an attempt has been made to study the effect of enclosure on the distribution of land as it prevailed in 1780-6, and on the changes that occurred during the period 1780-6 to 1832. For this purpose the 1,395 parishes situated in Derbyshire, Leicestershire, Lindsey, Northamptonshire, Nottinghamshire and Warwickshire have been divided in Sections A and B into three divisions—those of "ancient enclosure" (i.e. parishes enclosed by other than parliamentary means before 1780); parishes which had already undergone parliamentary enclosure by 1780; and parishes which were in open field at that date. In Section A the parishes of these three groups have been further subdivided into those owned by one large landowner, those owned by more than one large landowner, those with no occupying owners, and those with less than 6 occupying owners. In Section B are given the number of occupying owners contributing less than 10s., 10s. and less than £10, £10 and over, the total number of occupying owners, together with the average number per parish in each case for each of the three divisions.

Of the 1,395 parishes 737 have undergone enclosure by other means than by Act of Parliament, and have been considered as of "ancient enclosure" in the table on p. 284; 315 parishes, almost all of which were in open arable before enclosure, had already by 1780-6 undergone enclosure by Act; 343 parishes were still open or partly open in 1780-6. In many

# TABLE V

One thousand three hundred and ninety-five parishes situated in Derbyshire, Leicestershire, Lindsey, Northamptonshire, Nottinghamshire and Warwickshire, distinguishing between old enclosed parishes, parishes enclosed by Acts before 1780–6, and open field parishes

## SECTION A

### The Distribution of Land

| Parish | Number of parishes owned by one large landowner | Parishes owned by more than one large landowner | Parishes with no occupying owners | Parishes with less than six occupying owners | Parishes with either no occupying owners or with less than six |
|---|---|---|---|---|---|
| 737 old enclosed parishes | 166 | 78 | 374 | 231 | 605 |
| 315 parishes enclosed by Act before 1780–6 . | 3 | 11 | 36 | 58 | 94 |
| 343 parishes in open field or partly open, 1780–6 . . | 5 | 9 | 60 | 111 | 171 |

## SECTION B

### Occupying Owners

| Parishes | Occupying owners paying less than 10s. in land tax | Average of these per parish | Occupying owners paying 10s.–£10 in land tax | Average of these per parish | Occupying owners paying £10 and over in land tax | Average of these per parish | Total no. of occupying owners | Average per parish |
|---|---|---|---|---|---|---|---|---|
| 737 old enclosed parishes | 952 | 1·3 | 1,200 | 1·6 | 64 | 0·09 | 2,216 | 3·0 |
| 315 enclosed by Act before 1780–6 | 2,140 | 6·8 | 1,641 | 5·2 | 59 | 0·18 | 3,840 | 12·2 |
| 343 parishes in open field or partly open field, 1780–6 . | 1,852 | 5·4 | 1,318 | 3·8 | 30 | 0·09 | 3,200 | 9·3 |

of these, however, the enclosure only affected the common pasture or waste, since the arable had already undergone enclosure, either by agreement or by some other means than Act. Of the 737 parishes of "ancient enclosure" 166 were owned by one large landowner, 78 by more than one large landowner, 374 were totally destitute of occupying owners, and 231 contained less than 6 of the latter. Occupying owners were comparatively numerous in 132 only of these 737 parishes. Of the 315 parishes which had undergone enclosure by Act previous to 1780-6, 3 only were the exclusive property of one large landowner, 11 of more than one large landowner, 36 were without occupying owners, and 58 contained less than 6 occupying owners. Occupying owners were therefore numerous in 221 of the 315 parishes. Of the 343 parishes still to undergo enclosure by Act, 5 were in the possession of one large landowner, 9 of more than one large landowner, 60 were destitute of occupying owners, and in another 111 their numbers never exceeded 5. In 172 of the 343 parishes there were 6 or more occupying owners. Again, according to Table V, Section B, the occupying owners who contributed less than 10s. averaged only 1·3 per parish in the 737 parishes of "ancient enclosure", as compared with 6·8 in the parishes already enclosed by Act, and 5·4 in the open field; those contributing 10s. to £10 averaged 1·6, as compared with 5·2 and 3·8; and the total number of occupying owners averaged 3 in the old enclosed parishes, 12·2 in the parishes already enclosed by parliamentary means, and 9·3 in those yet to undergo enclosure by Act. From the above tables, therefore, it may be concluded that the occupying owners had almost ceased to exist in the old enclosed parishes, and that they were more widely distributed and numerous in parishes already enclosed by Act than in those yet wholly or partly open.

Table VI states the number of occupying owners, classified according to the amount of land tax paid, before and after enclosure in the parishes that underwent parliamentary enclosure during the period 1780-6 to 1832. Section A gives the figures for the parishes enclosed 1780-6 to 1802, and Section B for those enclosed 1802 to 1832.[39]

In both the 149 parishes enclosed from 1780-6 to 1802, and the 158 enclosed from 1802 to 1832, the occupying owners were more numerous after the parishes had been enclosed than when they were wholly or partly open. If we exclude contributors of less than 4s., there was a net increase of 154 during 1780-6 to 1802, and of 183 during 1802 to 1832. The great increase of contributors of less than 4s. was due to the conversion of squatters, and owners of cottages to which rights of common were attached, into landowners and consequently land tax contributors,

[39] These parishes are included in the 343 parishes described as open or partly open in Table V. One hundred and forty-nine were enclosing during 1780-6 to 1802, and 158 during 1802 to 1832. The remaining 36 were enclosed after 1832.

and the selling of tracts of the waste to resident farmers in order to defray enclosure expenses.

In view of Tables V and VI, it is difficult to associate any decline of occupying owners in these 1,395 parishes of Derbyshire, Leicestershire, Lindsey, Northamptonshire, Nottinghamshire and Warwickshire with parliamentary enclosure either previous to 1780-6 or since. Squatters, or owners of cottages to which rights of common were attached, who were otherwise landless, may have disappeared; but those who owned and occupied land and contributed to the land tax—the

## TABLE VI (OCCUPYING OWNERS BEFORE AND AFTER THE ENCLOSURES)

### SECTION A

ONE HUNDRED AND FORTY-NINE PARISHES ENCLOSED BY ACT FROM 1780-6 TO 1802

| | Land tax under— | | | | | | | | | Land tax over £20 | Total | Total paying 4s. and over | Total paying 10s. and over |
|---|---|---|---|---|---|---|---|---|---|---|---|---|---|
| | 4s. | 10s. | £1 | £2 | £4 | £5 | £8 | £10 | £20 | | | | |
| 1780-6 | 378 | 503 | 256 | 164 | 131 | 40 | 49 | 12 | 12 | 1 | 1,546 | 1,168 | 665 |
| 1802 | 633 | 514 | 302 | 212 | 155 | 43 | 45 | 26 | 19 | 6 | 1,955 | 1,322 | 808 |
| Increase | 255 | 11 | 46 | 48 | 24 | 3 | — | 14 | 7 | 5 | 409 | 154 | 143 |
| Decrease | — | — | — | — | — | — | 4 | — | — | — | — | — | — |

### SECTION B

ONE HUNDRED AND FIFTY-EIGHT PARISHES ENCLOSED BY ACT FROM 1802 TO 1832

| | Land tax under— | | | | | | | | | Land tax over £20 | Total | Total paying 4s. and over | Total paying 10s. and over |
|---|---|---|---|---|---|---|---|---|---|---|---|---|---|
| | 4s. | 10s. | £1 | £2 | £4 | £5 | £8 | £10 | £20 | | | | |
| 1802 | 417 | 408 | 244 | 200 | 151 | 31 | 52 | 17 | 34 | 31 | 1,585 | 1,168 | 760 |
| 1830 | 772 | 485 | 292 | 244 | 155 | 42 | 47 | 22 | 34 | 30 | 2,123 | 1,351 | 866 |
| Increase | 355 | 77 | 48 | 44 | 4 | 11 | — | 5 | — | — | 538 | 183 | 106 |
| Decrease | — | — | | — | — | — | 5 | — | — | 1 | — | — | — |

traditional election "grey coats"—were more numerous after the enclosures than when their parishes were open. Similarly they were more widely distributed and numerous, in 1780-6, in those parishes which had already undergone parliamentary enclosure than in those still open, or in old enclosed parishes ("ancient enclosure"). On the other hand, in 605 of the 737 old enclosed parishes occupying owners could hardly be said to exist. From over 82 per cent, therefore, of the parishes of "ancient enclosure" the occupying owners had almost completely disappeared. In this respect the assessments confirmed contemporary opinion which, whenever expressed regarding old enclosed parishes, always dwelt on the fact that farms were large and property in the hands of a few.[40]

## THE COUNTIES

In the individual counties the following changes occurred in the number of occupying owners and in the land tax contributed by the class as a whole. The estimated acreage of the holdings is also given.[41]

### A. LEICESTER
(Number of parishes studied, 254)
OCCUPYING OWNERS IN 1780-2, 1802 AND 1832

|  | Land tax under— | | | | | | | | | Land tax over £20 | Total | Total paying 4s. and over | Total paying 10s. and over |
|---|---|---|---|---|---|---|---|---|---|---|---|---|---|
|  | 4s. | 10s. | £1 | £2 | £4 | £5 | £8 | £10 | £20 | £20 |  |  |  |
| Estimated acreage | 3 | 7½ | 15 | 30 | 60 | 75 | 120 | 150 | 300 | 600 | — | — | — |
| 1780–2 | 647 | 667 | 344 | 288 | 183 | 58 | 96 | 24 | 27 | 4 | 2,338 | 1,691 | 1,024 |
| 1802 | 815 | 596 | 374 | 332 | 275 | 68 | 112 | 46 | 49 | 8 | 2,675 | 1,860 | 1,264 |
| 1832 | 1,013 | 498 | 374 | 294 | 229 | 47 | 93 | 40 | 59 | 8 | 2,655 | 1,642 | 1,144 |

LAND TAX PAID AND ESTIMATED ACREAGE OF OCCUPYING OWNERS

| Year | Land tax £ s. d. | Estimated acreage |
|---|---|---|
| 1780–2 | 3,162 16 0 | 47,445 |
| 1802 | 4,316 7 0 | 64,745 |
| 1832 | 3,984 11 0 | 59,760 |

### B. WARWICK
(Number of parishes studied, 207)
OCCUPYING OWNERS IN 1780-6, 1802 AND 1832

|  | Land tax under— | | | | | | | | | Land tax over £20 | Total | Total paying 4s. and over | Total paying 10s. and over |
|---|---|---|---|---|---|---|---|---|---|---|---|---|---|
|  | 4s. | 10s. | £1 | £2 | £4 | £5 | £8 | £10 | £20 | £20 |  |  |  |
| Estimated acreage | 3 | 7½ | 15 | 30 | 60 | 75 | 120 | 150 | 300 | 600 | — | — | — |
| 1780–6 | 167 | 340 | 198 | 192 | 182 | 42 | 71 | 24 | 44 | 10 | 1,270 | 1,103 | 763 |
| 1802 | 226 | 380 | 250 | 223 | 188 | 58 | 111 | 36 | 57 | 12 | 1,541 | 1,315 | 935 |
| 1832 | 301 | 396 | 220 | 198 | 193 | 52 | 99 | 42 | 62 | 15 | 1,578 | 1,277 | 881 |

[40] Among others, see *The True Interest of the Landowners of Great Britain or The Husbandman's Essay* (1734), 37-9; Maxwell, *Report Huntingdon*, quoted *Annals*, XXI, 154; Pitt, *Report Leicester*, 22, 23; J. Nicholls, *History of Leicester* (1795), II, i, 160, 196, 228, 278, 283, 285; John Throsby, *A Series of Excursions* (1790), 30, 48, 59, 61, 65.

[41] Since quotas for the counties varied, this difference had to be taken into consideration in estimating the acreage. The " acre equivalent ", or the sum due per acre, has been based on the relationship of the total acreage of the county to the assigned quota. In numerous assessments, the acreage of the holdings was given together with the tax due. Invariably, when such was the case, the amount of land tax per acre corresponded to the acre equivalent as given in the above table.

LAND TAX PAID AND ESTIMATED ACREAGE OF OCCUPYING OWNERS

| Year | Land tax £ s. d. | Estimated acreage |
|---|---|---|
| 1780–6 . . . . | 2,957 9 0 | 44,362 |
| 1802 . . . . | 3,767 17 0 | 56,518 |
| 1832 . . . . | 3,849 19 0 | 57,749 |

## C. NORTHAMPTON
(Number of parishes studied, 243)

OCCUPYING OWNERS IN 1780–2, 1802 AND 1832

| | Land tax under— | | | | | | | | | | | Total | Total paying 4s. and over | Total paying 10s. and over |
|---|---|---|---|---|---|---|---|---|---|---|---|---|---|---|
| | 4s. | 10s. | £1 | £2 | £4 | £5 | £8 | £10 | £20 | £40 | £60 | | | |
| Estimated acreage | 2¾ | 6¾ | 13 | 27 | 53 | 67 | 104 | 133 | 267 | 534 | 801 | — | — | — |
| 1780–2 . | 491 | 601 | 326 | 288 | 213 | 63 | 99 | 35 | 36 | — | — | 2,152 | 1,661 | 1,060 |
| 1802 . | 489 | 500 | 319 | 295 | 249 | 61 | 114 | 44 | 54 | 5 | — | 2,130 | 1,641 | 1,141 |
| 1832 . | 579 | 425 | 282 | 254 | 205 | 67 | 92 | 41 | 50 | 6 | 2 | 2,003 | 1,424 | 999 |

LAND TAX PAID AND ESTIMATED ACREAGE OF OCCUPYING OWNERS

| Year | Land tax £ s. d. | Estimated acreage |
|---|---|---|
| 1780–2 . . . . | 3,357 19 0 | 46,062 |
| 1802 . . . . | 4,023 13 0 | 55,194 |
| 1832 . . . . | 3,712 13 0 | 50,928 |

## D. NOTTINGHAM
(Number of parishes studied, 158)

OCCUPYING OWNERS 1780–2, 1802 AND 1832

| | Land tax under— | | | | | | | | | Land tax over £20 | Total | Total paying 4s. and over | Total paying 10s. and over |
|---|---|---|---|---|---|---|---|---|---|---|---|---|---|
| | 4s. | 10s. | £1 | £2 | £4 | £5 | £8 | £10 | £20 | | | | |
| Estimated acreage | 4 | 10 | 20 | 40 | 80 | 100 | 160 | 200 | 400 | 400 | — | — | — |
| 1780–2 . | 219 | 308 | 154 | 116 | 70 | 18 | 22 | 10 | 10 | 3 | 930 | 711 | 403 |
| 1802 . | 344 | 362 | 228 | 154 | 104 | 20 | 31 | 13 | 15 | 3 | 1,274 | 930 | 568 |
| 1832 . | 410 | 352 | 222 | 132 | 94 | 18 | 33 | 9 | 18 | 6 | 1,294 | 884 | 532 |

LAND TAX PAID AND ESTIMATED ACREAGE OF OCCUPYING OWNERS

| Year | Land tax £ s. d. | Estimated acreage |
|---|---|---|
| 1780–2 . . . . | 1,183 4 0 | 23,664 |
| 1802 . . . . | 1,614 0 0 | 32,280 |
| 1832 . . . . | 1,636 10 0 | 32,730 |

## E. DERBY
### (Number of parishes studied, 213)
OCCUPYING OWNERS IN 1780-2, 1802 AND 1832

| | Land tax under— | | | | | | | | | Land tax over £20 | Total | Total paying 4s. and over | Total paying 10s. and over |
|---|---|---|---|---|---|---|---|---|---|---|---|---|---|
| | 4s. | 10s. | £1 | £2 | £4 | £5 | £8 | £10 | £20 | | | | |
| Estimated acreage . | 5 | 13 | 26 | 53 | 106 | 130 | 212 | 265 | 530 | 530 | — | — | — |
| 1780–2 . | 599 | 429 | 201 | 160 | 99 | 33 | 32 | 6 | 3 | — | 1,562 | 963 | 534 |
| 1802 . | 891 | 472 | 297 | 199 | 112 | 21 | 41 | 7 | 7 | 1 | 2,048 | 1,157 | 685 |
| 1832 . | 1,344 | 594 | 331 | 233 | 125 | 35 | 37 | 9 | 16 | 3 | 2,727 | 1,383 | 789 |

LAND TAX PAID AND ESTIMATED ACREAGE OF OCCUPYING OWNERS

| Year | Land tax £ s. d. | Estimated acreage |
|---|---|---|
| 1780–2 . . . . | 1,353 6 0 | 35,862 |
| 1802 . . . . | 1,670 11 0 | 44,269 |
| 1832 . . . . | 2,049 14 0 | 54,316 |

## F. LINDSEY
### (Number of parishes studied, 320)
OCCUPYING OWNERS IN 1780–2, 1802 AND 1832

| | Land tax under— | | | | | | | | | Land tax over £20 | Total | Total paying 4s. and over | Total paying 10s. and over |
|---|---|---|---|---|---|---|---|---|---|---|---|---|---|
| | 4s. | 10s. | £1 | £2 | £4 | £5 | £8 | £10 | £20 | | | | |
| Estimated acreage . | 4 | 10 | 20 | 40 | 80 | 100 | 160 | 200 | 400 | 400 | — | — | — |
| 1780–2 . | 166 | 310 | 168 | 136 | 114 | 30 | 39 | 25 | 10 | 6 | 1,004 | 838 | 528 |
| 1802 . | 309 | 428 | 308 | 285 | 201 | 38 | 71 | 22 | 33 | 11 | 1,706 | 1,397 | 969 |
| 1832 . | 656 | 395 | 271 | 188 | 132 | 43 | 55 | 15 | 26 | 5 | 1,786 | 1,130 | 735 |

LAND TAX PAID AND ESTIMATED ACREAGE OF OCCUPYING OWNERS

| Year | Land tax £ s. d. | Estimated acreage |
|---|---|---|
| 1780–2 . . . . | 1,740 12 0 | 34,812 |
| 1802 . . . . | 3,097 14 0 | 61,954 |
| 1832 . . . . | 2,362 ? 0 | 47,242 |

## G. CHESHIRE
### (Number of parishes studied, 311)
OCCUPYING OWNERS IN 1780–6 AND 1798–1802

| | Land tax under— | | | | | | | | Land tax over £20 | Total | Total paying 4s. and over | Total paying 10s. and over |
|---|---|---|---|---|---|---|---|---|---|---|---|---|
| | 4s. | 10s. | £1 | £2 | £4 | £5 | £10 | £20 | | | | |
| Estimated acreage | 5 | 12 | 24 | 48 | 96 | 120 | 240 | 480 | 480 | — | — | — |
| 1780–6 . | 477 | 406 | 305 | 375 | 245 | 43 | 47 | 8 | 1 | 1,907 | 1,430 | 1,024 |
| 1798–1802 | 468 | 435 | 291 | 325 | 215 | 40 | 57 | 10 | — | 1,841 | 1,373 | 938 |

In all the counties, with the exception of Cheshire and Northampton-shire, there was a marked increase of almost all grades of occupying owners and in the acreage owned by occupying owners as a whole during the years 1780-6 to 1802. The decline in these two counties was slight: it was the more pronounced in Cheshire; and if contributors of less than 10s. be excluded, there was even an increase in Northampton-shire. During the years 1802 to 1832, on the other hand, there occurred a slump in the number of occupying owners in Leicestershire, Lindsey, Northamptonshire and Warwickshire, but not in Derbyshire, where the increase persisted as late as 1832. The occupying owners of Nottingham-shire, including contributors of less than 4s., increased also; but if these be excluded, there occurred a diminution. The actual acreage owned by the occupying proprietors was increased during the years 1802-32 in Derbyshire, Nottinghamshire and Warwickshire, but in the other three it declined. The increase, where it occurred, was due to a growth in the number of those in possession of large farms. Two features need to be emphasized. In the counties of Leicester and Northampton there was a marked diminution of small owners contributing 4s. to 10s.—the owners of approximately 3 to 7½ acres of land—during the whole fifty years. The other feature was the phenomenal growth in the number of small occupying owners in possession of less than 13 acres in Derby-shire. This increase occurred mainly in the High Peak Hundred.[42]

As previously stated, Cheshire was selected for the purpose of com-parison. It was an old enclosed county, and a comparison with the other counties should indicate whether counties, where individual control as opposed to communal had prevailed longest, were favourable or other-wise to the continued existence of a numerous peasant proprietary.[43] Below are given the average number of occupying owners per 100 parishes, classified according to the extent of their properties for the years 1780-6.

[42] Many of these were in existence as late as 1881. Mr Druce, in his evidence before the Royal Commission of that year, stated: " I did find a few proprietors quite up in the hills in the High Peak district, but they were men who had made their money in lead-mining and had bought a few acres of land " (*Report of the Commission on Agriculture, 1881*, Q. 29704).

[43] Gonner and Slater estimate the percentage of the county areas that underwent enclosure by Act of Parliament as follows. Gonner's estimate is from 1700 to 1870, and Slater's from 1700 to recent times.

| County | Cheshire | Derby-shire | Leicester-shire | Lincoln-shire | Northampton-shire | Nottingham-shire | Warwick-shire |
|---|---|---|---|---|---|---|---|
| Gonner | 3·4 | 21·3 | 47·9 | 37·1 | 54·3 | 32·0 | 25·2 |
| Slater | 0·5 | 15·9 | 38·2 | 29·3 | 51·5 | 32·5 | 25·0 |

Curtler, *The Enclosure and Redistribution of our Land*, 188, 194, 204, 205, 206, 208, 209.

## TABLE VII

AVERAGE NUMBER OF OCCUPYING OWNERS PER ONE HUNDRED PARISHES IN 1780–6

| | Acre equiva-lent [44] | Land tax under— | | | | | | | | Land tax over £20 | Total | Total pay-ing 4s. and over |
|---|---|---|---|---|---|---|---|---|---|---|---|---|
| | | 4s. | 10s. | £1 | £2 | £4 | £5 | £10 | £20 | | | |
| Cheshire . | 10d. | 153 | 130 | 98 | 121 | 79 | 14 | 15 | 3 | 0·3 | 613 | 460 |
| Derbyshire . | 9d. | 281 | 201 | 94 | 75 | 46 | 16 | 19 | 1·4 | — | 733 | 452 |
| Leicestershire | 1/4 | 255 | 262 | 135 | 113 | 72 | 23 | 47 | 11 | 1·5 | 920 | 665 |
| Lindsey : Lincolnshire . | 1/– | 52 | 97 | 52 | 42 | 36 | 9 | 20 | 3 | 1·9 | 313 | 261 |
| Northampton-shire . | 1/5½ | 202 | 247 | 134 | 118 | 88 | 26 | 55 | 15 | — | 885 | 683 |
| Nottingham-shire . | 1/– | 139 | 195 | 97 | 74 | 44 | 11 | 20 | 6 | 1·9 | 588 | 449 |
| Warwickshire | 1/4 | 81 | 164 | 95 | 93 | 88 | 20 | 46 | 21 | 4·8 | 613 | 532 |

It is difficult to draw any definite conclusions from the evidence supplied by the above Table without making an illegitimate use of the figures. Generally speaking, however, Lindsey in Lincolnshire falls far below Cheshire; there is a greater preponderance of occupying owners, particularly those contributing less than 10s., in Leicester and Northampton; the smaller owners also predominate in Derby, but otherwise there is a close resemblance between Cheshire, Nottinghamshire and Warwickshire. Cheshire thus compares quite favourably with all the other counties. On the other hand, open fields in the other counties [45] appear to have preserved the smaller occupying owners—those who contributed less than £1. Parliamentary enclosure was mainly effective in Derby after 1780, and almost 50 per cent of Leicester and Northampton underwent enclosure by Act after 1750. In the two latter counties, which had preserved almost half their open fields until the middle of the eighteenth century, the occupying owners were 40 to 50 per cent more numerous than in an old enclosed county like Cheshire. Incidentally Cheshire, like the other counties, contained its formidable quota of yeomanless parishes. This suggests that the absence of occupying owners from all the counties was due to economic forces rather than directly to "ancient enclosure". The hedges of the copyholders and freeholders of Cheshire in the fifteenth and sixteenth centuries failed to protect them from the avarice of the lord of the manor, intent on participating in the profits of the wool boom. The early enclosure in the open field counties had been mainly incidental—the result of the

[44] See n. [41] on p. 287.
[45] In Lindsey, Lincolnshire, they were mainly concentrated in the open field parishes of the Isle of Axholme and Barton-upon-Humber, and in the few parishes that remained open in the "middle marsh", a narrow belt of land stretching from Boston to the Humber, a little distance from the sea.

consolidation of estates and engrossing of farms, which had prevailed alike in the open field counties and those enclosed from time immemorial. On the other hand, the fate of the occupying owners in Cheshire during the years 1780-1802 illustrates the futility of associating the disappearance of the occupying owners or yeoman farmers with parliamentary enclosure. Though it escaped enclosure by Act, it was the one county where the yeoman not only decreased appreciably in number, but also lost territory.

As far as the limited area surveyed in this article is concerned, the main conclusions appeared to be the following. By 1780 the occupying owners, including the freeholders, copyholders and lessees for lives, had ceased to be an outstanding feature of English rural economy. In 1,395 parishes situated in Derbyshire, Leicestershire, Lindsey, Northamptonshire, Nottinghamshire and Warwickshire, they contributed only 10·4 per cent of the land tax, so that already nearly 90 per cent of the land was in the occupation of tenant farmers. One in five of the parishes was the exclusive property of the large landowners; and those contributing £20 and over owned 64 per cent of the land. The remaining 36 per cent was considerably subdivided, but was mainly in the possession of non-occupying owners. In 1,706 parishes situated in Cheshire, Derbyshire, Leicestershire, Lindsey, Northamptonshire, Nottinghamshire and Warwickshire the non-occupying owners numbered 17,267, as compared with 11,163 who combined occupation with ownership. An all-round increase of occupying owners occurred during the period 1780-6 to 1802,[46] and the percentage owned by the class increased from 10·4 to 14. All grades contributing 4s. to £10 diminished during 1802-32,[47] but compared with 1780 they were more numerous and owned a greater acreage. No large estates were formed during these fifty years at the expense of the occupying owners. Some very large estates increased in size, but there was partial compensation in the subdivision of other estates which came into the market. The assessments indicated that a new race of landowners produced by the industrial revolution and the war appeared on the countryside; but these acquired not the isolated holdings of the yeomen, but the land of the old eighteenth-century landed gentry.[48]

[46] *I.e.* taking the counties collectively. In Cheshire and Northamptonshire there occurred a slight diminution.

[47] Excluding Derbyshire.

[48] In the 213 Derbyshire parishes, of the seventy-six large landowners contributing £20 to £200 in 1832, forty-seven only of the names appeared in the 1802 assessments, so that twenty-nine were men who had purchased their estates since 1802. Of five new contributors of £200 to £300 one, Sir Richard Arkwright, paid £35 19s. 8d. in 1780, another £148 19s., a third £189 14s. 9d., a fourth £199 15s. 11d., and a fifth £189 3s. The four last were members of the peerage. Altogether thirty-six large estates came into the market. Approximately 10,000 acres became the property of the sitting tenants, but the remainder was bought by the wealthier of the old landowners and by men who had gained their riches in commerce. The two latter phenomena have been generally

Enclosure, in its effect on the distribution of land, has to be divided into two parts: enclosure by Act of Parliament, and non-parliamentary enclosure previous to 1750. After 1780 the former led to an increase of all grades of occupying owners; and before 1780 it is doubtful whether they were affected adversely, since they were present in greater numerical strength in parishes which had undergone such enclosure than in those still in open field. In parishes enclosed by other than parliamentary means previous to 1780 the occupying owners had almost ceased to exist. The comparative quiescence of the rural community in the eighteenth century, compared with the loud outcries and bitter lamentations of the sixteenth and seventeenth centuries, appears natural in the light of the evidence of the land tax assessments. Maxwell's remark that " the old enclosed part therefore is, generally speaking, in the hands of large proprietors, but property in the new enclosures is pretty much diffused ",[49] seems to have a wider application than to the county of Huntingdon only.

The direct effect of the industrial changes on the fate of the occupying owners before 1832 appears to have been greatly exaggerated. Their disappearance was largely accomplished by 1780-6, since nearly 90 per cent of the land was in the occupation of tenants-at-will or tenants on short lease. If industrial changes had been a potent factor in bringing about this result, then they must have been in operation prior to 1780. But it is difficult to believe that the industrial revolution had gathered sufficient momentum before 1780 to cause such far-reaching changes. From 1780-1815 the movement appeared to have favoured rather than harmed the occupying owner, since it provided him with a growing and lucrative market. His old markets also remained, as there was no evidence to indicate that domestic industries in the counties studied were in any way adversely affected previous to 1814; indeed, most of them flourished as late as 1832.[50]

---

associated with the decline of occupying owners, but it actually occurred during 1780-1832, mainly at the expense of those owning above 500 acres, and who were not in occupation.

The evidence of the assessments is confirmed by the witness from Derbyshire before the Select Committee of 1833: " There have been nev purchasers, the manufacturers have purchased immensely: three or four of them have purchased to the extent of a million, but not in one district . . . the Marquis of Ormond's estate, for instance, has been bought by one of these gentlemen." (*Report of Select Committee on Agriculture, 1833*, Qs. 12528, 12530. See also Qs. 12523-8.)

[49] *Annals*, XXI, 154.

[50] See *Report on the Framework Knitters* (1819), 3, 7, 13, 14, 17, 22, 27. Lipson, *History of the Woollen and Worsted Industries*, 184. *Report Lords Committee Framework Knitters* (1837), Q. 1773. W. Smith, *History of Warwick* (1830), 12, 102, 210, 367, 371, 372-3, 374. West, *History of Warwick* (1830), 491, 506-7 539-46, 552, 561-4, 576-8, 582-4, 605, 669-78, 697-9, 735-6. J. R. McCulloch, *Dictionary of Commerce and Commercial Navigation* (1832), 697-9. J. Hunter, *Hallamshire*, 173, 211. Glover, *History of Derby* (1832), 232, 233, 240, 254; *A Description of the High Peak of Derbyshire together with an Account of Poole's Hole*. Gough, Derby, 17, Bodleian Library, p. 5.

The Revolutionary and Napoleonic wars appear to have been very similar to the recent war in their effect on the distribution of land. Currency inflation and soaring prices forced land into the market, which led numerous sitting tenants to purchase their holdings.  Many of these who contributed 4s. to £10 in land tax succumbed during the depression of 1815-32; and, had the assessments of 1815 been analyzed, the returns would doubtless have revealed a far greater diminution.[51]  This was not, however, the first great encroachment upon the ranks of the yeomanry, since those that were mainly affected were the unfortunate mortgagees, who were foreclosed upon before the final debacle of the country banks. The heavy demands of the poor rate and the national charges did not affect the occupying owners before 1815, since during a period of national prosperity they were able to transfer the burden from the producer to the consumer.   After 1815, when this was no longer possible, additional taxation was one of the many factors that contributed to their partial decline.

We are to look, therefore, to some era prior to 1780 for the great disappearance of the occupying owners, whether freeholders, copyholders or lessees for life.   Their concentration mainly in 38 per cent of the parishes studied enforces the conclusion that the occupying owners of 1780-6 were merely survivals of a once numerous class.[52]   The Tudors failed to give the peasant a title to his land, with the result that nearly all the old enclosed parishes in 1780 were found destitute of occupying owners.   In those parishes that had remained open till 1750—the commencement of parliamentary enclosure on a large scale—the occupying owners, with few exceptions, were comparatively numerous, and enclosure by Act safeguarded the interests of those owning land.   These few received additions during the years 1780-1815, and then a decline set in which, according to subsequent contemporary evidence, proved continuous until 1918.   But this was not the first great disappearance of the yeomen of England.   It was the dwindling of the few survivors of a class that had once, before the early agrarian revolution, been large.

[51] If we judge by a cursory examination of the assessments of 1802-15, there is every reason for believing that the buying by sitting tenants continued until 1815.  Consequently, the numbers in 1815 would have been far more numerous than in 1802.

[52] The prevalent belief that the freeholders, as distinct from the other two classes of occupying owners, survived until the latter half of the eighteenth century does not receive confirmation from the assessments. The almost total absence of occupying owners from 62 per cent of the parishes studied (1780-6) suggests that in most of the parishes they had undergone the same modification in number as the copyholders and life leaseholders.

# THE OLD POOR LAW, 1662-1795

## DOROTHY MARSHALL

THE prominence given in late years to the problems of unemployment and destitution has been responsible for an increased interest
in the Old Poor Law. Until the beginning of this century, except
for the period covered by the reports of the Poor Law Commissioners of
1834, its history had been little studied. Such accounts as were available,
of which Sir George Nicholls' three-volume *History of the English Poor
Law* was typical, were narrative in treatment and provided hardly more
than a series of extracts from the relevant statutes. There was no
attempt to find out how far the law was enforced or what the results of
that enforcement were. Such treatment implied that the Poor Law
sprang full fledged from the wisdom of Parliament and was administered
on a national scale long before this was in fact the case. Miss Leonard,
in her *Early History of English Poor Relief,* showed how fallacious such
assumptions were for the period before 1640. It was not, however, until
after the war that similar research on the period dominated by the law
of Settlement and Removal (1662-1795) was undertaken. The aim of
this article is to summarise the contributions that have been made to the
subject since then.

To understand the old Poor Law it is necessary to concentrate on
administration rather than on legislation. This has meant viewing the
problem from a different angle, and as a result the importance of regional
studies has been increasingly emphasised. Miss Leonard showed how
much national legislation owed to local experiment. This debt did not
cease with the first framing of a national code in 1597; examples of the
evolution of a law of settlement, the use of certificates, the development
of an allowance system, the employment of paid overseers and the expedient of uniting parishes for the provision of workhouses, are all to be
found in local records before their adoption at Westminster. Secondly,
and perhaps of even greater importance for an understanding of the
period, such studies bring out the great diversity that existed in different
parts of the country. The influence exercised by the law over the practice
of the parishes was often very slight. Mr and Mrs Sidney Webb have
come to the conclusion that: "Between the statute book and the actual
administration of the parish officers there was, in the eighteenth century,
normally only a casual connection."[1] This is a fact of considerable

[1] S. and B. Webb, *English Poor Law History,* I, 149.

295

importance, for it means that even as late as the close of that century a national, uniform Poor Law only existed on paper. As an example of the lag between the passing of an Act and its general enforcement, Miss Hampson points out that the parish of Sawston in Cambridgeshire levied no regular poor rates until 1658, nearly a hundred years after such a rate had become compulsory.[2] This means that all generalisations must be regarded with more than ordinary caution. The main outlines of eighteenth-century Poor Law have been traced in *The English Poor in the Eighteenth Century*,[3] and in the more recent and longer *English Poor Law History*, I,[4] but the full picture can only be completed gradually by a series of detailed local studies. The importance of such work has already been realised, and the latest contributions to the subject have been of this type. With the help of such monographs it is becoming possible to examine and correct the generalisations that have been accepted in the past.

Many of these concern the law of Settlement and Removal (1662), which enabled parish officers, with the consent of two justices of the peace, to remove any person within forty days of their coming to the parish if they had not rented a tenement worth £10 a year and appeared likely to become chargeable. Sir George Nicholls writes as if this Act introduced a new principle into the administration of the law, but it is now clear that " The Act of 1662 marked a change in the legal rather than in the actual position of the labourer ".[5] Local records show many instances of removals prior to 1662 and several attempts were made by Parliament in the first half of the seventeenth century to provide some statutory definition of the practice. The importance of the Act lay, therefore, in the conditions it imposed rather than in any new ideas which it contained. Together with the subsequent modifications and additions made between 1686 and 1723, it has been described as " the flywheel " round which administration revolved, and an understanding of its working is vital to any comprehension of eighteenth-century Poor Law. Until recently unproved assumptions have been the extent of our knowledge. Adam Smith condemned the settlement laws wholeheartedly on the ground of their interference with the mobility of labour. Actually this seems to have been one of the least of their evil consequences. Such evidence as is now available suggests that the number of persons moved was not large enough to have much effect on the mobility of labour. The number of removal orders obtained and enforced never seems to have exceeded a few tens of thousands per year for the whole 15,000 parishes and townships involved.[6] Moreover,

---

[2] E. M. Hampson, *The Treatment of Poverty in Cambridgeshire, 1597-1834*, 45.
[3] D. Marshall, *The English Poor in the Eighteenth Century*.
[4] S. and B. Webb, *English Poor Law History*, I.
[5] J. D. Chambers, *Nottinghamshire in the Eighteenth Century*, 260.
[6] S. and B. Webb, *op. cit.* 334.

many of the persons affected, by reason of age or infirmity, could add little to the working strength of the country.

There were many loopholes which might prevent the law being enforced in its entirety, and research has shown that they were constantly used.   Some of them were legal, others were due to the common sense of officers administering the law.   The evolution of the certificate illustrates both these points and also provides a further instance of the way in which the legislature was content to borrow its ideas from local practice, since the device was first improvised by individual parishes and later given legal sanction by the Act of 1697.   These certificates were, in effect, a promise entered into by the parish to take back without demur the person whom the certificate named, should he or she become chargeable at any time.   These certificates are to be found in considerable numbers in most collections of parish papers, which certainly suggests that they were freely used.   They have not yet, however, been studied in sufficient numbers for it to be clear to what extent they modified the working of the law.   In attempting to assess their influence on the mobility of labour, it should be remembered that they were usually given for one definite parish and were not general passes to wander and settle at will. They were, therefore, more likely to affect local than long-distance migration.   In Cambridgeshire the majority of them were exchanged by parishes within the county [7] and an examination of the certificate papers of a parish such as Bleasby (Notts) also shows that most of them came from within a radius of ten miles.[8]   Their numbers were also limited by the fact that they were granted at the discretion of the parish officers.   As there was less chance of a certificated person gaining a settlement elsewhere some parishes never granted them, while others, after pursuing a more generous policy, gradually curtailed their issue. It is not safe, therefore, to assume that such relief as they afforded was equally available at all times.   In Cambridgeshire, for example, certificates were apparently most numerous between 1740 and 1780.[9]

It is probable that most of the people who moved did so without any safeguard.   After the 1 Jac. II, c. 17 declared that the forty days necessary to gain a settlement dated from the presentation of a notice in writing, few persons on coming into a parish risked ejection by presenting such a notice and, if industrious, healthy unmarried men were rarely removed until they became chargeable.   For example, at Tysoe men, who had spent most of their working life in London or Birmingham, were only moved back when their health failed and they were forced to ask for assistance.[10]   Moreover, as, until 1814, the overseer was legally obliged to escort the persons to be removed back to their place of

[7] E. M. Hampson, *op cit.* 147.                    [8] J. D. Chambers, *op. cit.* 270.
[9] E. M. Hampson, *op. cit.* 147.
[10] W. Ashby, *A Hundred Years of Poor Law in a Warwickshire Village* (Oxford Studies in Social and Legal History, III, 66).

settlement, he was anxious that removals should not be too numerous. Accordingly some rough principles of selection appear to have been adopted. In the rural county of Cambridgeshire, out of 532 persons moved between 1699 and 1732 and 1736-49 inclusive, 224 were married people, 165 widows and single women, 77 children, and only 66 single men. In Middlesex, where urban conditions predominated, the selection was rather different. From 1690-8, out of 212 persons moved there were 49 single women, 9 widows, 47 women with children, 56 children, 40 married persons and 11 single men.[11] In every case the woman, whether burdened with children or not, was at a disadvantage, but the married couple, though suspect in the country, where the labourer's resources were in general inadequate for the maintenance of a family, was more welcome in the town. The number of removals was probably lessened also by the fact that though they may have been rashly undertaken while the provisions of the Act were still unfamiliar, the parish officers grew more cautious with time. Miss Hampson points out that the generalisation made by Mr and Mrs Webb to the effect that a warrant was " usually issued as a matter of course " upon complaint by the parish officers, is too sweeping. She shows that paupers were often carefully examined by the magistrates before an order was signed and, particularly after 1750, parish officers frequently engaged in considerable correspondence to ascertain the facts before a removal was carried out.[12] Nor was such an investigation always followed by removal, even when there was clear legal ground for it. To meet a temporary emergency or to avoid the expense of bringing back a distant family, parishes sometimes paid pensions to non-resident paupers. For instance, " All the town parishes of Cambridge paid considerable sums annually by the late eighteenth century, on account of non-residents, and were on the other hand repaid for their own expenditure on paupers legally settled elsewhere ".[13]

If the interference with the mobility of labour was less than has often been supposed, the other evils resultant on the law of Settlement and Removal have been more fully substantiated. Though the number of those removed may have been comparatively small, the amount of suffering which was inflicted was disproportionately great; it is not difficult to find instances in which not only destitution but death followed forced and brutal removals.[14] Where a question of settlement was concerned, decency and morality were frequently disregarded. Marriage was deliberately discouraged by the knowledge that a married man, who was not a settled parishioner, would probably be moved on with his wife as soon as the ceremony was over. Hence the great growth of immorality. Parishes safeguarded themselves as much as they could from the conse-

---

[11] D. Marshall, op. cit. 165.          [12] E. M. Hampson, op. cit. 134.
[13] E. M. Hampson, op. cit. 149.          [14] Ibid. 134-6.

quences which their own actions had produced.  Single women who were known to be with child by a stranger were promptly and forcibly married, sometimes the bridegroom having to be brought to church in chains. Such pressure was not in the interests of morality but to " save the parish harmless ", since by this means it freed itself from the responsibility for both the mother and the unborn child.  Where it was impossible to shift the burden by a forced marriage, the woman, by bribes or threats, was often driven from the parish.  This deliberate harrying of pregnant women, which led not infrequently to loss of life, was inspired by the determination that the bastard should not be born in the parish, since previous to the Act of 1744 a bastard was settled where born.[15]

The pauper child was also frequently a victim of the settlement laws. The provision that a settlement should be gained by apprenticeship twisted the Elizabethan laws from being an attempt to provide suitable maintenance and training for children to a device to save the parish rates.  Undoubtedly the temptation to bind children out in other parishes, without consideration as to the suitability of master or mistress, and then abandon them to their fate, was great.  How far the law was abused in this way is not clear.  There is plenty of evidence to show that such a course of action was often taken, but a study of local records indicates that this was by no means always the case.  Mr Emmison states that for Eaton Socon " there is no scrap of evidence pointing to abuse of the system; while many entries seem to denote efficiency ".[16] Here between 1693 and 1731 only sixteen out of seventy-two children apprenticed were sent to masters living in other parishes.  Against this, however, must be ranged the fact that in the parish of Maulden in the same county, out of sixty-six apprentices placed out between 1658 and 1788, forty-five were bound to masters living in other parishes.  That the law was not everywhere misapplied is true also of Cambridgeshire, where the evils, though serious enough, pressed less hardly on the pauper apprentices there than they were reputed to do in other counties.[17]  As little detailed work has yet been done in the majority of counties, it may be that continued investigation will show a further lightening of the picture.  Perhaps what emerges most clearly at the moment is the diversity of local custom and the possibility of misuse rather than the certainty of it.  It seems likely that in rural parishes, where the numbers were small and the children known personally to the majority of the parishioners, no great abuse took place and that it was only in the crowded and impersonal town parishes that its full evils were to be found.

Apart from the law of Settlement and Removal the most important branch of the Poor Law administration that has been explored is that

[15] D. Marshall, op. cit. 212.
[16] F. G. Emmison, The Relief of the Poor at Eaton Socon, 1706-1832 (Bedford Historical Record Soc., XV, 63).
[17] E. M. Hampson, op. cit. 164.

which deals with the attempts to employ the poor. Though apparently in some counties "the parish stock far from having fallen into complete disuse in the eighteenth century continued to form part of the ordinary Poor Law administration of many country parishes ",[18] employment was largely provided by the establishment of workhouses. Recent research has emphasised the fact that though great differences existed between them these workhouses fell into two groups, the one composed of incorporated bodies which owed their existence to private Acts of Parliament, the other comprising the ordinary parish workhouses. Because of their greater resources and continuity of policy the incorporated bodies were, from the point of view of their influence on the development of the Poor Law, the more important. The numerous benefits which their promoters hoped to secure have been described as a " complete medley which it is difficult to analyse or classify ".[19]  The pamphlet literature of the latter part of the seventeenth century, with its elaborate schemes, such as those put forward by Bellars, for increasing the national wealth by setting up joint stock companies to employ the poor, reveal how strongly the delusion was held that the labours of the poor could be so organised as to enrich the community as well as to make them self-supporting. It was with this hope that many of the private Acts were obtained. Later, when experience proved the improbability of this result being attained, the expectations of workhouse promoters changed. It was now thought that even though workhouses failed to produce a profit they might at least keep down the rates by discouraging people from seeking relief when that relief was given in a workhouse. It was to facilitate the application of this principle of deterrence rather than to employ the poor that the Workhouse Test Act of 1723 was passed. Though these were the two main reasons for establishing workhouses other motives played their part. The idea that the poor could be maintained with decency and without disorder in well-regulated workhouses was widely held. The promoters of the scheme for Carlford and Colneis declared their aims to be " a proper comfort and assistance to the sick, infirm and aged ", their children were to be made " useful to society " and they hoped " to ease the respective parishes in their rates ".[20]  There was generally some mixture of motive. It is not uncommon to find attempts to combine the profitable employment of the poor with the use of the workhouse both as an asylum and a deterrent. Where this happened confusion of policy was inevitable.

The desire to make the poor self-supporting if not profitable gave rise to some very interesting experiments in the provision and running of workhouses. Little could be done while there was no statutory authorisation permitting parishes to unite together and while overseers retired

[18] J. D. Chambers, *op. cit.* 234.                    [19] S. and B. Webb, *op. cit.* 144.
[20] S. and B. Webb, *op. cit.* 120, 128.

at the end of their year of office and so made continuity of policy impossible. This difficulty was met by obtaining private Acts, which authorised the union of parishes to support a common workhouse and which incorporated the ratepayers of the united parishes for the purpose of managing the poor. The usual procedure was to vest control in the hands of local authorities known as Guardians, Trustees, Governors, Directors, or Corporations of the Poor, who were composed of all holders of property above a certain amount. For example, at Shrewsbury it was necessary to possess freehold or copyhold property worth £10 a year or to be the inhabitant occupier of premises rated at £15 per annum. These Guardians were responsible for the election of directors to supervise the administration and appoint salaried officials such as a governor, steward, matron, chaplain to do the actual work. The obtaining of such an Act did not, in theory, exempt the area concerned from the ordinary operation of the Poor Law. The overseers, under the direction of the Guardians, still managed the business of poor relief, but the actual running of the workhouse was taken out of their hands and the control of policy was vested in the permanent body. The earliest of these statutory authorities was the Corporation of the Poor of the City of London, but the most famous was the Corporation of the Poor of the City of Bristol, established by the 7 & 8 W. III, c. 32. This body provided a model and inspiration which had by 1712 been followed by fourteen other towns. The earlier experiments were all urban, where the small parishes of a single town offered an obvious inducement to union. It was not until 1756 that an enthusiastic attempt was made to apply the same principles to the rural districts. In that year the Hundreds of Carlford and Colneis in Suffolk got an Act setting up a local body empowered to build a workhouse and take over the administration of the poor. At first the experiment seemed to promise well and inspired other neighbouring hundreds to adopt the same methods, with the result that by 1785 fourteen such bodies had been incorporated.

Though the most notable attempts were made by these special statutory authorities, many parishes, without obtaining any other powers than those conferred by the Act of 1723, rented or built small workhouses, either with the hope of employing the poor or with the aim of keeping down the rates by using the workhouse as a deterrent. These establishments were of very varied types. Some of them were set up as a result of the encouragement afforded by the Act of 1723, but many of them were of earlier date. Some of them were fairly large and moderately well run, others were little more than poorhouses which provided common lodging places for a handful of impotent, aged or infant poor. Both their distribution and their character were governed to a large extent by geographical considerations. Most large and crowded urban parishes possessed workhouses, but in the rural districts the scantiness of the population made an adequate workhouse impossible and bad

roads and scattered parishes prevented unions.   In Cambridgeshire " It
was the poor house rather than the workhouse which was typical "[21] of
the rural districts where, even as late as 1776, six out of the fourteen
hundreds were without workhouses.   Even in a comparatively thickly
populated and compact rural parish like Eaton Socon the problem of
management proved almost insurmountable to the local, untrained
administrators.   In 1719, before the passing of the general Act, Eaton
Socon made its first experiment with a workhouse.   The parish officers
managed it themselves, the overseers buying the food and a minimum
of supervision being provided by a caretaker.   Only a little lace-making
was carried on.   From 1728-30 the parish reverted to outdoor relief, but
returned to the use of a workhouse, this time under stricter control, from
1731-44.   In that year rising rates led to a contract, which, however, only
remained in force from 1745-9, though after a few months of direct
management it was again revived from 1749-62.   During this period it
was held by several small contractors, often for no more than a year each.
From 1762-88 the accounts are missing.   In the latter year the workhouse
seems to be under direct management but between 1789-91 a contractor
was once more in evidence.   In 1791 there was a further change; direct
control was again resumed until 1799, when the first contract on a *per
caput* basis was signed.[22]   It is likely that a detailed examination of the
history of other parish workhouses will reveal similar experiences.   In
Cambridgeshire, for example, there is the same hesitancy and swinging
backwards and forwards between some system of contracting and direct
parochial management.

    The traditional picture of the internal economy of the workhouse is
one of misery and depravity.   In many places this may be an overstate-
ment which the detailed study of particular workhouses will refute.
For example, though as a workhouse the Eaton Socon establishment was
not a success, since little work seems to have been done there, the parish
papers show many signs of consideration for its inmates.   Except for the
perhaps too considerable drop in expenses from nearly £400 in 1744 to
hardly £200 in 1745, when the house was given over to a contractor, there
is little to hint at really unsatisfactory conditions.   Until many more
parishes have been studied in equal detail it is impossible to know
whether the care which Eaton Socon displayed in the management of its
poor characterised many rural parishes.   Such evidence as we have for
Cambridgeshire suggests that the workhouses in the Isle of Ely were
more competently run than those in the other rural districts of the
county.[23]   With regard to the profitable employment of the poor greater
knowledge has only confirmed the impression of failure.   The reasons
for this lack of success have been exhaustively analysed in *English Poor*

[21] E. M. Hampson, *op. cit.* 93.               [22] F. G. Emmison, *op. cit.* 9-10.
[23] E. M. Hampson, *op. cit.* 264.

*Law History* and are too complicated and numerous to be adequately summarised here.[24] Outstanding among them was the administrative difficulty of securing honest management from ill-paid and slackly supervised officials or continuous industry from inefficient labour. Raw materials were bought at uneconomic prices, while the finished articles were marketed at a loss. In many workhouses their sale did not even pay for the purchase of new raw material. The difficulty of finding a suitable manufacture, which could be carried on profitably in these conditions, became almost insurmountable. In spite, however, of their failure to attain the results hoped for by their promoters these experiments had a very considerable influence on the subsequent development of the English Poor Law. In the case of the statutory authorities, their "Principle of combining an elective controlling power with a paid executive"[25] made an important contribution to English local government. Secondly, every type of workhouse combined to demonstrate by their failure the impossibility of employing the poor at a profit. Thirdly, the promoters of workhouses "stumbled" on the idea of the workhouse test, which was to play so large a part in nineteenth-century Poor Law policy.

The difficulty of managing the workhouse, either by the direct control of the overseers or by means of their salaried servants, led to the adoption of an administrative device which was increasingly used in the eighteenth century. This was the system of contracts. The importance of these contracts has only been revealed gradually as the focus of attention has been shifted from legislation to administration. Contracts for the management of the parish workhouse were sanctioned by the Act of 1723, and where rising rates seemed to call for drastic remedies they were often employed, especially in the second half of the century. In Cambridgeshire contracts were rarely made before 1750, but the 'sixties and the 'seventies saw them adopted widely.[26] Sometimes the contract was only for the workhouse poor and covered little besides their clothes and board, sometimes the contractor took over the entire liabilities of the parish, including the payment of outdoor relief. Where this was done it was to his interests to run the workhouse with such harshness as to exclude all but the desperate and to force most paupers to take inadequate payments to remain outside the house. Later in the century payments on a *caput* basis were more common and here the pauper may be supposed to have suffered less than when the contractor received a fixed sum to cover all contingencies. The possibilities of abuse were certainly great, particularly when the farmer of the poor was a professional who removed the paupers to his own central workhouse, far

---

[24] S. and B. Webb, *op. cit.* 134 *et seq.*, 223 *et seq.*

[25] Chapman's "Report on Statutory Authorities" in Appendix A of the *First Report of the Poor Law Inquiry Commissioners, 1834,* 522 (Quoted Webb, *op. cit.* 148.)

[26] E. M. Hampson, *op. cit.* 265.

distant from the supervision of the responsible overseers and justices. How far the evils of the system were modified in practice only the investigation of local records can show.   Mr and Mrs Webb were of the opinion that contracts farming out not only the workhouse but the payment of outdoor relief could be found in all parts of England, but Miss Hampson expressly states that she discovered no such comprehensive contracts in Cambridgeshire.[27]   Moreover, where the contractor was a local man, using the local workhouse, as was the case in the earlier contracts at Eaton Socon, some of the evils may have been mitigated.   The hesitancy with which parishes adopted the expedient of a contract and the frequent changes of policy which they made certainly suggest that the officials were not completely satisfied as to the desirability of this method of managing the poor, even though it saved trouble and tended to reduce the rates.   Contracts, either for a lump sum or on a *caput* basis, were not confined to the maintenance of the poor.   In most parishes special arrangements were made for medical attendance, and where this was not covered by the contractor, or where the poor were directly managed by the parish officers, contracts, usually of a very cheese-paring nature, were made with local doctors.   In addition, the very complicated business of moving vagrants back to their place of settlement was organised by an elaborate network of county contractors.

So far the study of the administration of ordinary parochial outdoor relief has revealed few new features.   There appears to be little deviation from the Elizabethan methods of looking after the aged and impotent poor.   Parochial papers, from parishes as far apart as Westbury-on-Trym,[28] Eaton Socon and Tysoe all record the same provision of small pensions, occasional doles, house room, fuel, food and clothing.   They also show that outdoor relief was managed with some real attention to individual wants.   In spite of this impression of kindliness given by many of the parish papers, the pensions paid to the poor " in the book " are strikingly small.   This suggests that they were never intended to cover their complete maintenance but were supplementary to low and inadequate wages. If this is so then the allowance in aid of wages, once thought so characteristic of the break-up of the old Poor Law, had in reality a much longer history.   Nor were these early allowances in aid of wages given only to the aged and infirm.   Definite instances occur of allowances made to men whose families were too large to be supported by their wages.   The comments of pamphleteers at the close of the seventeenth century show that the practice was well established even then.[29]

The result of concentrating on administration rather than on legislation has been to emphasise the lack of all central control and policy. As late as the end of the eighteenth century there was no uniformity

[27] E. M. Hampson, *The Treatment of Poverty in Cambridgeshire, 1597-1834.*
[28] H. J. Wilkins, *The Poor Book of Westbury-on-Trym.*
[29] D. Marshall, *op. cit.* 105.

and the attitude and practice, not only of neighbouring counties, but even of neighbouring parishes, might be diametrically opposed. That the main premises now laid down will be radically altered by further investigation is perhaps unlikely. The general influence exercised by the law of Settlement and Removal is now comparatively clear, as is the main outline of the history of the workhouse movement, but the accumulative evidence of much local study will certainly be necessary before the complete picture can be painted. The main features have been sketched in, but the light and shade has been no more than suggested. Along these lines there is still much to do.

# THE POPULATION PROBLEM DURING THE INDUSTRIAL REVOLUTION

## A NOTE ON THE PRESENT STATE OF THE CONTROVERSY

### T. H. MARSHALL

THE problem of the English population a century ago has recently attracted several independent—too independent—investigators. It is naturally tempting to economic historians, since it offers them an opportunity for the exercise of the now popular quantitative method in a field in which they have not been seriously anticipated by the statisticians. They should remember, however, that they owe the privilege of priority chiefly to the absence of statistics, and that, consequently, the appeal from logic to mathematics is here particularly dangerous. Mr Griffith's book on *Population Problems of the Age of Malthus* made an immediate impression, as, indeed, it deserved to, but his estimates have been too readily accepted and his conclusions too hastily grasped as a cudgel with which to belabour a certain school of historians and theorists. Even when the facts have been ascertained, their interpretation is a matter of great delicacy. And the facts can, for the most part, only be guessed. In these circumstances the results of statistical research have no more title to respect—probably less—than the views of well-informed contemporaries and the reasoned expectations of the modern historian and economist.

One point, at least, is clear. However great may be the margin of error in Mr Griffith's calculations, it cannot wipe out the great dip in the death-rate curve during the Industrial Revolution. This can be accepted as fact. The statistical evidence is convincing, and it does not conflict with evidence of other kinds. There is a logical explanation in the advance in medical science, affecting in particular infant mortality, and there is corroboration from contemporary sources. All the investigations into local and particular death-rates made at the time pointed that way,[1] and the belief that mortality was declining in England as a whole was shared, not only by Rickman and McCulloch,[2] but also by Malthus himself. The second edition of the Essay, written shortly after the first Census, contains the following passage: " It would appear, by the present proportion of marriages, that the more rapid increase of population, supposed to have taken place since the year 1780, has arisen

---

[1] See M. C. Buer, *Health, Wealth and Population*, 270-1.     [2] See Griffith, 40-1.

more from the diminution of deaths than the increase of the births." [3]
The point was reiterated in the Report on the 1851 Census, and the
main causes of the decline of mortality since the seventeenth century
were sketched.[4]

These facts should by now be well known.  Mr Griffith admits that
Malthus's second thoughts differed little from his own theories, but he
does not acquit him on that account.  Malthus has laid himself open to
a new charge, that of either missing or deliberately suppressing the
logical implications of his knowledge.  He should, it is suggested, have
considered the falling death-rate as proof that the population was not
too large.  But he was looking to the future, and in twenty years the
death-rate was rising again.  If he still insisted that a check was desirable, " he might have been tempted to advocate measures which, instead
of checking the birth- and marriage-rates, should check the decline in
the death-rate.  The obvious impossibility of advocating such measures
is probably one reason why it was not done." [5]  This is a cruel libel on
a man whose one object in desiring to reduce the birth-rate was to keep
down the death-rate, to substitute " preventive " for " positive " checks.
He could not have been tempted for a moment, and his reasons are perfectly obvious.  It is a fallacy to suppose that, in this matter, the nature
of the cause is an index to the nature of the remedy.  It is perfectly
logical to hold that population pressure induced by a falling death-rate
should be alleviated by reducing the birth-rate.  In fact no other course
is possible.  As Sir William Beveridge has neatly said, " the idea that
mankind . . . can control death by art and leave birth to Nature is
biologically absurd ".[6]

It is, indeed, fatally easy to distort the picture.  The obvious temptation is to assert that the death-rate was not only the variable, but also
the determining, factor in the increase of population, and that, to understand the causes of this increase, we should study the deaths rather than
the births.  But, clearly, a horizontal line on a graph may be as dynamic
as a diagonal; the forces that prevent a birth-rate from falling may be as
significant as those that make it rise.  This is elementary.  The next
stage along the road of error is travelled, I think, under the influence of
a sense of symmetry, which demands that the new theory should be the
exact reverse of the old.  Tradition said that the increase of population
during the Industrial Revolution was accompanied by a high death-rate
but a still higher birth-rate.  The truth is that the birth-rate was low
and the death-rate lower.  We know why the death-rate fell: we must
look for the forces which pulled the birth-rate down, as Malthus
looked for those that were pushing it up.  The most recent writers on

---

[3] Second edn. (1803), 311.
[4] " The first evident cause of the increase of the population is a diminution of their
mortality ", I, ii, p. lii.
[5] Op. cit. 99.                              [6] The Economic Journal (December 1923), 473.

the subject, J. S. Blackmore and F. C. Mellonie,[7] are so ingenious as to force symmetry one step further by selecting the same cause as Malthus, the Speenhamland Poor Law policy, and attributing to it opposite effects. Their article is in many ways remarkable. They very diffidently submit the, to them, new theory that the death-rate was falling, in apparent ignorance, not only of the authorities cited above, but also of the recent writings of Dr Brownlee and Mr Griffith, and they show a touching faith in the sanctity of even the shadiest figures. Arguments, they say, are "empty theorising", unless supported by a study of "objective facts". But it is folly to suppose that any facts obtainable about the allowance system of those days could hold their own for a moment against the theories of modern economists, based, as they are, on far more accurate observations of human action. I shall return to their figures.[8]

Undoubtedly many contemporaries believed that the birth-rate was rising, and grossly under-estimated, or even denied, the fall in the death-rate. It has been proved that they were wrong. But the essence of what we may call the "Malthusian" position was this. First, the population was increasing faster than was desirable. Secondly, the birth-rate should be checked. Thirdly, the birth-rate was being stimulated by certain economic forces which could be removed by proper political action, notably the Poor Laws and the demand for child labour. I wish to suggest that the best modern estimates of the births and deaths for England and Wales as a whole most certainly do not prove this view to have been false. Rather, they appear to confirm it, or, as I prefer to say, in view of the highly speculative nature of the statistics, they are consistent with it. The result is purely negative. It is only by a comparative study of local figures that there is any hope of proving the last, and most important, point of the three either true or false. That I have not attempted.[9]

We may approach the problem from various angles. We may speak of a law of population. If we do we shall be in good company. It is not necessary for this argument to believe that the law of growth is capable of exact expression nor to subscribe to the theory of Professor Raymond Pearl that all growth follows the logistic. We may say, for example, that population growth is determined by births and deaths, emigration and immigration, and that these are related to the socio-

<hr />

[7] "Family Endowment and the Birth-Rate", *The Economic Journal*, Historical Supplement, no. 2, May 1927.

[8] In a second article, *The Economic Journal* (Supplement), January 1928, these authors have abandoned their theory. They find no evidence of a relation, positive or negative, between Family allowances and the birth-rate.

[9] For the difficulties involved in local estimates, see Barbara Hammond, "Urban Death-Rates in the Early Nineteenth Century", *The Economic Journal* (Supplement), January 1928. As they arise largely from "the bewildering tangle of English local divisions", they are greatly reduced when a national average is taken.

economic environment of the people in ways that can be analysed and, to some extent, foreseen. But we must go a step further to avoid confusion. More fundamental is the relation between the total population of a country and its socio-economic organisation, the relation on which is based the theory of the optimum. The total is, of course, regulated by the ratio between births and deaths—if we ignore migration as irrelevant to our particular problem—but both the birth-rate and the death-rate vary independently under the influence of forces which do not affect the conditions which determine the optimum. If population growth and economic progress are to keep step together, a balance must be maintained between births and deaths, but that balance is bound to be frequently disturbed by the action of forces which have nothing whatever to do with social and economic progress, measured by its capacity to sustain population. If there is any truth in the conception of a law of population, we should expect to find that, when the balance is disturbed in this way, it tends to rediscover itself, probably at a new level. For example, a victory of medicine over disease will lower the death-rate and increase the pace of population growth without providing sustenance, employment or the rudiments of comfort for a single extra person. If no corresponding economic progress takes place, we should, on this hypothesis, expect to see the birth- and death-rate curves, which have diverged, converge again, though, very possibly, without exactly recovering their previous relation; we should, at least, assume a pressure or pull in favour of a *rapprochement*. A similar state of affairs may arise if an economic revolution stimulates a rapid increase of population, and the population gathers a momentum which carries it further than is required. We have, then, a path sketched out for the population curve by the conditions of ecconomic progress, and oscillation about that path caused by the disturbance and readjustment of the balance between births and deaths. This path is, of course, not necessarily that of the optimum. This view is consistent with the fact to which Mr Yule has drawn attention, that, although short-period percentage increases of population give an incoherent succession of ups and downs, when long-period figures are taken, for fifty years in the case of England and Wales, these oscillations disappear, and a smooth and clearly directed movement is revealed.[10] It is as though Nature were trying to hit the mark by a system of trial and error, each error setting up a pull in the contrary direction.

A further symptom that should appear if there is a law, in this very general sense, in operation, is an associated movement of birth- and death-rates. The law, by prescribing limits within which the balance should fall, links the two together. Mr Yule has examined this point

---

[10] " The growth of population and the factors which control it." *Journal of the Royal Statistical Society*, LXXXVIII, 12.

also, with some interesting results.  His first assertion is that, among nations of about the same state of economic development, or, as supporters of a more precise law would say, at about the same point in the cycle of growth, the higher the death-rate the higher the birth-rate, and *vice versa*.  This is sustained by a correlation of + 0·81 between the figures for 1901-10 for twenty-two western European States.  This does not merely mean that where the rate of growth is the same, the excess of births over deaths must be the same also, except for a relatively small allowance to be made for migration.  That is axiomatic.  Nor does it merely mean, though this is important, that since western Europe became an economic unit, the rate of population growth in the parts selected— and it should be noted that they do not include France—has been of the same order of magnitude.  Its significance is this.  It suggests that the more fundamental forces controlling the aggregate population of an area, and therefore the rate of increase, are stronger than the particular forces working directly on the births and deaths, and that over an area of this kind, in normal times, variations in birth- and death-rates are greater than variations in the rate of population growth.  Consequently, when we find, as we do in England at the end of the eighteenth century, an unprecedented fall in the death-rate, caused, for the most part, by non-economic forces, we should not expect the whole of this to be passed on, unmodified, into the rate of population growth.  We should assume a pull set up, tending to drag the birth-rate down, and if the birth-rate did not fall, we should conclude that exceptionally strong forces were at work holding it up.

Mr Yule goes on to show the " consilience between the movements of the birth-rate and the death-rate ", illustrating it with two tables. The first covers fifteen countries between 1841-50 and 1871-80, the second nineteen countries between 1871-80 and 1901-10.  The former is the more important for our purpose, as it deals with a period when deliberate control of births played about the same part as in the England of the Industrial Revolution.  The correlation here is + 0·70.  In nine cases a falling death-rate is associated with a rising birth-rate.  What is the interpretation?  The table clearly covers a period when conditions in western Europe were favourable to a high rate of natural increase and a rising birth-rate.  In only two cases, Sweden and Belgium, did it fall. Of these, Sweden heads the list on the death-rate side with the biggest fall recorded, namely, 2·3 points per 1,000.  Belgium comes third.  The correlation suggests, therefore, that the more the death-rate fell, the less the birth-rate rose, and that a falling death-rate is a limiting check on a rising birth-rate.  We observe, too, that when the fall exceeded 2 per 1,000, the rise was negatived.  As the fall in our case was, at the least, nearly 9 points we may say that this statistical evidence fits in with the view that, in such circumstances, a stationary, or slightly falling, birth-rate must be taken as indicative of phenomenally high fertility.  Mr

Yule concludes with the important confession, which should be carefully weighed by students of the population problem of this period, that " my neglect of the death-rate as a factor in the movements of the birth-rate in former papers was a serious mistake ".[11]

But, even if the birth-rate was surprisingly high, it does not follow that it was undesirably high. The downward pull might have been counteracted by the rapidity of economic progress, and the truth may be that the Industrial Revolution called into being no more people than it required and could sustain, so that the balance between births and deaths was not upset by the doctors, but simply adjusted to the needs of the new situation. So neat a harmony between unrelated forces would be very startling. Nature does not, as a rule, imitate the ballet dancer, who springs accurately through the air and lands in perfect equilibrium. She is more likely, under the influence of a severe shock, to oscillate like a drunkard steering for a lamp-post. And there are special reasons for expecting this in our case. For even if it cannot be proved that the population ever became excessive, yet it can be urged that the peculiar character of its growth brought pressure to bear locally on those responsible for bearing and rearing the new generation, which might have been expected to depress the birth-rate even if such a depression were not imperatively demanded by the economic circumstances. We know that the chief feature of the falling death-rate was a rapid decline in infant mortality. It was a question of saving lives in the first few hours, days or weeks after birth. Imagine the effect on parents. It may be possible to bring ten children into the world, if you only have to rear five, and, while one is " on the way ", the last is in the grave, not in the nursery. But if the doctor preserves seven or eight of the ten, and other things remain equal, the burden may become intolerable. In so far, therefore, as there was, at this time, any conscious or unconscious control of the birth-rate in the interests of economic welfare or physical comfort, the decline in infant mortality must have acted as a strong incentive to restriction. The point appears more substantial if it is treated nationally rather than individually. The economic historian is interested in the rate of increase of a population in relation to the social and economic conditions of its country. The birth-rate is a factor in that rate of increase. With respect to its economic consequences—and they become, in turn, economic causes—a decline in infant mortality is almost exactly equivalent to an increase of births. It is true that new persons arrive without new confinements, but the economic significance of a confinement is small compared with that of the labour of suckling, nursing and rearing, the cost of feeding and clothing, the pressure on house-room, which follow. We might, in fact, speak of the number of children reaching the age of six months or one year as giving the " net birth-rate ", which is more vital than the " gross birth-rate " to the population

[11] *Loc. cit.* 33.

problem as it presents itself to the economic historian. In the early part
of our period a stationary, or slightly declining, " gross birth-rate " implies a rising " net birth-rate ". It is, therefore, misleading to contrast a
falling death-rate with a rising birth-rate as causes of population growth,
without pointing out that death may come at any age, but birth usually
occurs about the end of the ninth month. If the lives saved had been
those of septuagenarians, the contrast would be real. Actually, it is
false.[12]

In the foregoing discussion I have avoided using the phrase " over-
population ". I did not want to queer the pitch. In the exact sense to
which modern theory would confine it, it is of so little service to the
discussion of actuality that even the most reputable writers on practical
problems use it to denote something less tenuous and equally entitled to
the name. Still nearer to the heart of life we find the frank misuse by
the journalist, which defeats all clear thinking. Consequently, the word
is, to any argument in which it appears—if I may be allowed to mix my
metaphors—a loophole through which every critic can draw a red
herring. In its exact sense it is a term of static economics denoting a
state of affairs such that a reduction in the numbers of the occupants of
the area under consideration, while all other circumstances, including
the age distribution, remained the same, would be followed by an
increase in returns per head. Writers on practical issues use it in a
dynamic sense to indicate the presence within the area of more persons
than can be supported without a fall in the standard of life, or, perhaps,
without retarding the rise in the standard, within a reasonable time and
assuming a normal adaptability of economic structure to changing conditions. This view is implicit in Sir William Beveridge's address on
Population and Unemployment, where, arguing that unemployment in
1879 was not a sign of over-population, he remarks that anyone who
" had argued that the existing population of the United Kingdom was all
that the country could support without lowering its standards would have
been lamentably discredited at once ".[13] The country had received a
shock, it had been disturbed by the emergence of new economic factors,
but, by adapting itself to the changes, it swiftly recovered and resumed
its progress, and this recovery required only a reasonable time—three
or four years perhaps—and demanded, not a revolution, but simply the

[12] On this point compare M. Rubin and H. Westergaard, *Statistik der Ehen*, 109.
They produce statistical evidence to show that infant mortality rises in proportion to
the number of children in the family. This is partly due, they say, to the increased
difficulty of caring for the children. They then add: "Uebrigens wird man auch mit
einigem Rechte behaupten können, dass nicht die vielen Kinder die aussergewöhnliche
Sterblichkeit hervorrufen, sondern ungekehrt die grosse Sterblichkeit die vielen Kinder,
insofern der Kinderverlust physiologisch und psykologisch die weitere Kindererzeugung
ermöglicht und dazu anspornt." If high infant mortality is an incentive to births, then
low infant mortality must be a deterrent.
[13] *The Economic Journal* (December 1923), 448.

amount of vitality normal in a healthy economic society.   That is the picture suggested.

I shall not try to prove that the England of, say, 1820 was over-populated in either of these senses.   Conditions were in such a state of flux that an application of the first test is hardly possible.   Miss Buer, in her recent essay on the Malthusian controversy,[14] leaves us in some doubt whether she intends to apply it or not.   " Strictly speaking," she writes, " over-population was impossible according to Malthus's theory. He, however, was not a clear thinker."   This certainly suggests the pure classical conception.   But when she proceeds to argue that in fact England was not over-populated at this time, she permits herself the following sentence :  " From the point of view of food supply there seems little historical basis for the statement that England in 1815 was over-populated as compared with earlier periods," which suggests no concep-tion at all.   Malthus's retort is a simple *tu quoque*.   Her exact meaning, however, is unimportant, as she does not get within measurable distance of a proof.   Two arguments are put forward.   One is that food imports did not increase with the population, a point that only carries weight if it can be shown that the people continued to eat the same quantity of food per head.   The history of Ireland shows that a country may export food while living on the brink of famine.   The other is the familiar assertion that the distress is fully accounted for by the effects of war, based on a false analogy with 1918.   Careless comparison of these two epochs has done much harm to the cause of historic truth.   A subsidiary argument, derived from the age-constitution of the people, is interesting, and I shall revert to it later.   Over-population in the second sense cer-tainly did not exist, for it is demonstrable that, within a reasonable time, the country supported an even larger population at a definitely higher standard of life, and a sudden cessation of population growth at that moment might have shot economic progress dead in its tracks.

There are, however, peculiar features in the history of the early nineteenth century which suggest two things.   First, that economic con-ditions created a force calculated to check the rate of population growth in the immediate future.   Secondly, that this force was consequent on the pace and character of population growth in the immediate past.   In other words, even if there were not over-population, there was popula-tion pressure, resulting from a failure of economic progress and the increase of numbers to keep step together.   A pressure of this short-period dynamic kind, being not that of a moving body impinging on a stationary one, but of two moving bodies in frictional contact, will be remedied, not by an absolute reduction in the size of the population, but

---

[14] " The Historical Setting of the Malthusian Controversy " in *London Essays in Economics*, see 138 and 141.

by an adjustment of the rate of growth. But before we can appreciate this we must have certain figures before us.

Take first the annual rate of increase of the total population, including army, navy and merchant seamen, as given in the Census Report for 1861. The figures are:[15]

TABLE I

| | |
|---|---|
| 1801–11 . . . . . . . . . | 1·307 |
| 1811–21 . . . . . . . . . | 1·533 |
| 1821–31 . . . . . . . . . | 1·446 |
| 1831–41 . . . . . . . . . | 1·326 |
| 1841–51 . . . . . . . . . | 1·216 |
| 1851–61 . . . . . . . . . | 1·141 |

The rate of increase, as is well known, reached its maximum in the second decade of the century. Although we expect some lag in the response of population growth to economic conditions, it is rather surprising to find the lag so great. The first years of this decade saw acute food shortage, amounting almost to famine, and we should have expected this to reduce the rate for the decade. But in this same period the death-rate reached its minimum, a fact which the mere cessation of hostilities must have contributed to produce. The decline in the rate which begins after 1821 lasts till 1861. In the following decade the rate was 1·23. Here again there is a slight lag, since, without doubt, the period 1851-61 was more prosperous than the period 1841-51, though the change was gradual. But the correspondence between population growth and economic prosperity is clear. and can be traced on into the twentieth century.

The next point is to determine the share of the birth-rate and death-rate respectively in producing this response to the pressure of economic distress. The most recent, and best known, estimates of these rates are those in Mr Griffith's book, but they do not stand examination. On the birth-rate side the problem is to discover by what factor to multiply recorded baptisms in order to arrive at the probable number of actual births, it being well known that a considerable proportion of births were not registered among the baptisms. Mr Griffith uses a constant factor of 1·15. He found that this, applied to the figures for 1825, 1830 and 1835, obliterated the jump which occurs when civil registration became effective, about 1841. This is all he tells us. The calculation is suspect from the first. Civil registration was far from effective in 1841. Farr estimated the number of births unregistered annually between 1841 and 1850 at over 38,000, and believed that, taking the period 1838-76 as a whole, 5 per cent of the births remained unrecorded.[16] Secondly, it is certain that the ratio of births to baptisms was not constant. Mr Griffith made the mistake of ignoring the work of Farr. The name does not even appear in his index. And yet his contribution to the

[15] General Report, I, 81.        [16] Vital Statistics, ed. N. A. Humphreys, 523 and 89.

subject is more important even than that óf Rickman. Rickman spent infinite pains collecting and sorting the material, but Farr was its first fully competent interpreter.

In Table 61 in the Appendix to the General Report on the Census of 1871 appears a calculation—presumably the work of Farr—of the births in each decade from 1741 to 1850. The purpose of the Table is to show the age constitution of the people, and the births seem to have been estimated by working down through the age groups from a recorded figure, using Farr's Life Table, 1838-54, with an allowance for migration based on the three Censuses of 1841, 1851 and 1861. These factors are treated as constant. The results are checked by comparing the calculated and enumerated totals in the nineteenth century, and the biggest error is one of 35,000 in 1801. If we set beside these the registered baptisms and the resulting ratios we get:

TABLE II

|  | Registered Baptisms (000) | Estimated Births (000) | Ratio |
|---|---|---|---|
| 1781–90 . . . . . | 2,397 | 2,641 | 1·102 |
| 1791–1800 . . . . . | 2,618 | 2,988 | 1·142 |
| 1801–10 . . . . . | 2,879 | 3,675 | 1·276 |
| 1811–20 . . . . . | 3,255 | 4,425 | 1·359 |
| 1821–30 . . . . . | 3,753 | 4,798 | 1·278 |
| 1831–40 . . . . . | 3,966 | 5,289 | 1·334 |

The result differs profoundly from Mr Griffith's constant of 1·15. The fact that the latter almost agrees with Farr for the decade 1791-1800 will not inspire us with confidence, since Farr's figure is there certainly wrong. By not allowing for the rapid decline in infant mortality about the year 1800 he has seriously underestimated the births needed to sustain the later age groups at their known level. This decline in infant mortality is attested by contemporary evidence and confirmed by modern research. Its effect is seen in the age statistics of the Censuses for 1821 and 1841. As has been pointed out in an article by the late Dr Brownlee, to which I shall refer more fully in a moment, the high rate of increase of the age-group 20-40 between these two dates as compared with that of other groups indicates that those born in the early nineteenth century had a much better chance of survival than those born at the end of the eighteenth. Further examination of the figures shows that the decline in infant mortality became effective about 1780, reached its climax about 1800 and expired during the first decade of the nineteenth century.[17]

It follows that Farr's estimate of births for 1780-1800 must be too low, but that he is probably approximately correct for the period 1800-40. Mr Griffith bases his whole calculation on an estimate of the ratio of

[17] "The History of the Birth- and Death-Rates in England and Wales taken as a whole from 1570 to the present time", Public Health (June and July 1916), 219.

births to baptisms in the years immediately before the introduction of civil registration. His estimate is 1·15, Farr's 1·334. The difference is vital, and Farr's method is, at this point, undoubtedly superior. Mr Griffith's whole scale must therefore be abandoned. If it is correct for earlier periods it can only be so by accident.

Farr's figures must be our starting-point, but they need correction. Fortunately for historians they have been corrected by an eminent statistician. Brownlee's work on the history of the English birth- and death-rates deserves more attention than it has received.[18] His calculations are far too elaborate for summary and should be studied at first hand. He starts with the assumption that the known ratio of deaths to burials for 1838-40, namely, 1·18, can be taken as constant for the whole decade 1831-40.[19] From this, and the recorded increase of the population, he calculates the births. In working back he uses the burials to estimate the correction that should be made to allow for changing mortality, and he checks the births for 1811-20 by reference to their survivors, the 0-10 age group in the 1821 Census. His correction for the high mortality of the eighteenth century is derived from the ratio between age groups in 1821 and 1841, on the lines indicated in the discussion of the fall in infant mortality. Having thus found a ratio of births to baptisms for 1791-1800, he treats it as a constant for the eighteenth century. This may give rather too high a ratio for the decade 1781-90, since at that time registration was deteriorating with the spread of Dissent. Further back I do not propose to go. Below are his ratios, with Farr's repeated for comparison.

### Table III

| | Brownlee | Farr |
|---|---|---|
| 1781–90 | 1·243 | 1·102 |
| 1791–1800 | 1·243 | 1·142 |
| 1801–11 | 1·276 | 1·276 |
| 1811–20 | 1·272 | 1·359 |
| 1821–30 | 1·278 | 1·278 |
| 1831–40 | 1·388 | 1·334 |

The resulting birth-rates are:

### Table IV

#### Birth-Rates per 1,000

| | |
|---|---|
| 1781–90 | 37·7 |
| 1791–1800 | 37·3 |
| 1801–10 | 37·5 |
| 1811–20 | 36·6 |
| 1821–30 | 36·6 |
| 1831–40 | 36·6 |
| 1841–50 | 33·9 |

[18] See also " The Health of London in the Eighteenth Century ", *Proceedings of the Royal Society of Medicine* (1925), XVIII, Epidemiology, 73.

[19] Mrs Hammond's criticism of Brownlee's calculation (*The Economic Journal*, Supplement (Jan. 1928), 426) is mistaken. It is true that registration was compulsory in

The steady decline throughout the most active period of the Industrial Revolution disappears. Instead, we find the abnormally high rate of the late eighteenth century maintained into the first decade of the nineteenth. Even the slight drop shown from the maximum of 37·7 would be reduced if it is true, as suggested, that this figure is slightly too high. The decade 1811-20 shows a fall of one point. This is not much for a period which saw the famines of 1811-12 and the bread riots of 1816-19. The rate then remains stable till 1831-40, after which there is a sharp drop. For the third time the country was threatened with famine, and now the birth-rate seemed to have lost its buoyancy. Is it pure coincidence that this collapse followed close on the Factory Act of 1833 and the New Poor Law of 1834? It is quite possible; but there is a *prima facie* case for the "Malthusians".

Compare with these figures the statement of Miss Blackmore and Miss Mellonie, that "the definite slump in the baptism rate comes between the years 1811 and 1821".[20] The rates per 1,000 that they quote are 33·3 and 28·6. I have failed to discover how they arrive at these figures. Taking eleven-year averages about the Census year, I get rates of 30·4 and 29·5. When, on the next page, they convert baptisms into births, the slump in the rate is equally surprising, from 38·1 to 34·1. However, the quality of our surprise changes when we observe that their estimate of the births for 1821 is well below the number of recorded baptisms. But have they not themselves written, "the most deadly alternative hypothesis that can be brought up is the charge of absolute unreliability of the figures"? We are disarmed.

It must be admitted that there are peculiar causes of uncertainty in the figures for the last two decades. The recorded baptisms in the late 'thirties fall off with unnatural rapidity, except for a phenomenally high rate for 1837, which, if not a clerical error, can only be explained on the assumption that, in that year, 50,000 baby girls who normally would not have been baptised were carried to church on a wave of patriotism and christened "Victoria". Brownlee applied statistical tests which satisfied him that the baptism rate did not fall off as a result of the introduction of civil registration. The authors of the 1851 Census Report disagree. They reject the baptism figures for 1837-40 and substitute a computed average. If we take this figure and apply Farr's ratio to calculate the births in this decade, and take Farr's estimate of the deficiency in registration in the following decade, we get the following average birth-rates:

| | |
|---|---|
| 1831-40 . . . . . . . . | 36·9 |
| 1841-50 . . . . . . . . | 34·8 |

the years 1838-40. That is why Brownlee accepts the figures in the *Civil* Registers as equalling the total deaths. It is by comparison with these figures that the "leakage" in the *Parish* Registers can be measured, and the Parish Registers were not affected by the Registration Act.     [20] *Loc. cit.* 208.

On this basis the drop is reduced, but it is still about twice as big as the interval between the highest and lowest rates recorded from 1780 to 1840.

We now turn to the death-rate. As there is no serious disagreement about the direction and extent of its movement, I take Brownlee's figures without question. They are based on a death-burial ratio of 1·2.

## TABLE V
### Death-Rates per 1,000

| | |
|---|---|
| 1781–90 | 28·6 |
| 1791–1800 | 26·9 |
| 1801–10 | 23·9 |
| 1811–20 | 21·1 |
| 1821–30 | 22·6 |
| 1831–40 | 23·4 |

There is a very marked rise in the last two decades. This, it appears, is the result chiefly of higher mortality in the early years of life. Of those born 1801-21, 75 per cent were alive at the date of the 1821 Census. Of those born 1821-41, only 71 per cent were alive at the 1841 Census. And yet the progress of medical science had not suddenly stopped. The effects of the discoveries and improved practices of the late eighteenth century should still have been spreading through the country. The death-rate from smallpox, the principal non-economic scourge of infancy, was still declining. Porter gives a Table of smallpox mortality which, though he does not say so, is presumably for London.[21] It only shows the decline of the share of smallpox in the general death-rate, not the movement in smallpox mortality. Farr's summary for London is more useful. "In 1771-80," he writes, "not less than 5 in 1,000 died annually of small-pox; in 1801-10 the mortality sank to 2; and in 1831-5 to 0·83."[22] Nor can the rise be attributed to the devastations of a new and unconquerable disease. Epidemic cholera appeared first in 1831. The mortality is unknown, but it is suggested that in London the death-rate from cholera in the period 1831-5 was no higher than it had been at the end of the seventeenth century.[23] Cholera had always taken its toll of life. The peril grew in the 'forties, and became a terrifying scourge in the seven years 1848-54, when, according to Farr, a quarter of a million people in the United Kingdom died of cholera and diarrhoea.[24] It is impossible to trace the movement in puerperal mortality. Lying-in hospitals usually include all deaths in childbed from whatever cause. General registers often include under this heading deaths consequent on childbirth only. Hospital records are not typical and vary amazingly. Mrs George quotes, from Willan, figures for the British Lying-in Hospital showing a fall from 1 death in 42 deliveries in 1749-58 to 1 in 914 in 1799-1800.[25] This is utterly misleading, as the rate for the five years

[21] *Progress of the Nation* (1912), 9.                    [22] *Vital Statistics*, 305.
[23] *Op. cit.* 305.              [24] Farr, *op. cit.* 352.              [25] *London Life*, 49.

1799-1803 was 1 in 187·5.[26]   In the Dublin Hospital the rate fell from 1 in 67 for 1761-70 to 1 in 113 for 1791-1800.   It then rose again to 1 in 66 for 1811-20, and in the 'sixties was about 1 in 32.[27]   Farr, writing in 1871, was prepared to accept Le Fort's statement that the average for all institutions, not only in England, was 1 in 29.[28]   But the Royal Maternity Charity could show a rate of 1 in 435 for the years 1875-7.[29]   Outside the hospitals we have Willan's evidence that an eminent physician lost of his private patients, between 1786 and 1800, just over 1 in 100, including all deaths in childbed,[30] and Miss Buer quotes estimates for London in 1760 and 1781 of 1 in 60 and 1 in 66,[31] which are consistent with this if Willan's friend worked only among the rich.   The official figures for England and Wales, 1847-54, are 1 in 189,[32] but Matthews Duncan, after careful research, put the general rate in 1870 at 1 in 120.[33]   But Duncan was distinctly pessimistic.   Certainly progress was made in the eighteenth century, and it seems probable that the rate of mortality was approximately halved between 1800 and 1870.   Under this head forces are favourable to a fall in the general death-rate.

Finally, we require the marriage-rate.   Below I give—(A) the number of persons married per 1,000 of the population, reckoned by taking twice the annual average of recorded marriages in each decade

## TABLE VI

### *Marriage-Rates per 1,000*

|      | (A)  | (B)   |
|------|------|-------|
| 1761 | 17·2 | 16·70 |
| 1771 | 17·0 | 16·78 |
| 1781 | 17·5 | 17·20 |
| 1791 | 17·5 | 17·46 |
| 1801 | 17·3 | 17·30 |
| 1811 | 16·4 | 16·50 |
| 1821 | 16·2 | 16·16 |
| 1831 | 16·1 | 16·32 |
| 1841 | 15·6 | 15·78 |

in proportion to the population on 1st January, the middle day of the decade.[34]   For the eighteenth century I have used Brownlee's population estimates.   (B) Mr Griffith's marriage-rate figures, based on eleven-year averages.   Mr Griffith uses his own population estimates for the eighteenth century and Rickman's figures for the nineteenth, without allowing for the different time-intervals between the Censuses.   Hence the disagreement.

[26] *Account of the British Lying-in Hospital*, 1808.
[27] J. M. Duncan, *On the Mortality of Childbed*, 93.
[28] *Op. cit.* 274.
[29] *Ibid.* 280.
[30] *Reports on the Diseases in London* (1801), 320.
[31] *Health, Wealth, etc.*, 147.
[32] Farr, 270.
[33] *Op. cit.* 24.
[34] The figures are in the Eighth Report of the Registrar-General, 30.

It will be observed that here the fall from the high level of the eighteenth century—a more consistent high level in my figures than in Mr Griffith's —is steadier and more continuous in the case of the birth-rate. In my figures it is uninterrupted. But, in interpreting this fall, we must remember that there are several possible causes of a fall in the marriage-rate which do not imply any discouragement of marriage. For instance, a steadily falling death-rate will have this effect, by increasing the average duration of married life and reducing the number of second and third marriages.[35] We know that this cause was present until about 1820. Secondly, the fall may be a mechanical after-effect of a reduction of the average age at marriage. A marriage-rate rises by anticipation and falls by postponement. It therefore moves in waves. A gradual lowering of the marriage age may produce a long wave. The rate rises at first, but, in time, automatically relapses towards its former level. For, if every girl in the country were to get married at 20 instead of, say, 25, the marriage-rate would only rise permanently in proportion to the loss by death between the two ages. It is quite possible that the hump, or wave, which has its peak about 1790, represents a change of this kind. As Mr Griffith has shown, the late eighteenth century saw a decline of apprenticeship and of the custom of living-in, both of which had made early marriage difficult for the poorer classes.[36] The Danish Census of 1787 gives clear testimony to the importance of the factor of economic and social independence in determining the marriage age. Of males between the ages of 20 and 30 the following percentages were married or widowed in various classes: journeymen and apprentices 8·2 per cent, domestic servants 4·1 per cent, handicraftsmen (*i.e.* small masters) 62·8 per cent, "other independent" 51·4 per cent.[37] There is testimony to early marriages in the Reports on the Poor Laws.[38] This, however, is less significant. It probably expresses moral horror at juvenile weddings, whereas the fact of economic importance is that certain classes, previously obliged to postpone marriage till they were past 30, were becoming free to marry at the normal age. A fall due to this cause will not indicate that a smaller proportion of the population is marrying, and, as the Census Commissioners of 1851 said, "the proportion of children to a marriage, and consequently the population, are regulated, not so much or so immediately by the numbers of the people who marry as by the age at which marriage is contracted ".[39] Thirdly, the fall may be due to a declining proportion of women of marriageable age. This possibility must be examined.

---

[35] *Cf. Sweden*, ed. J. Guinchard, i, 132: "We must here point out the extraordinary decline in the number of re-marriages, a circumstance which, no doubt, stands in connection with the decline in mortality."        [36] *Op. cit.* chap. v.

[37] M. Rubin, "Population and the Birth-Rate", *Journal of the Royal Statistical Society*, LXIII, 602.

[38] Griffith, *op cit.* Appendix II.        [39] *1851 Census*, I, ii, p. xlvi.

We know that the population began to increase rapidly about 1780, and continued to do so, at an accelerating pace, till 1820, with a high birth-rate and a falling death-rate, particularly among infants. We should expect to find from 1791 to 1821 a rising percentage of children and a falling percentage of adults. This may prove to be the most potent cause of the steady fall in the marriage-rate. If a marriage-rate is to be taken as an index of the readiness or reluctance of the people to marry, it must be reckoned in relation only to those of marriageable age. Similarly, if the birth-rate is to be taken as an index of the extent to which the population was utilising its powers of reproduction, it must be reckoned in relation, not to the total population nor to the married women of child-bearing age, but to all women of child-bearing age. When this is done, the presumed change in the age-distribution will make the fall in the rate between 1790 and 1820 diminish, and possibly disappear, and the fall after 1820 increase. This same fact will affect the interpretation which should be put on the movements of the death-rate.

The age-distribution is also, as Miss Buer has pointed out, relevant in another way. Excess in the unproductive ages throws an extra burden on active adults. A higher productivity per head is demanded of them if the standard of life is to be maintained for the whole population. Economic distress in such circumstances may be evidence, not of an excessive aggregate population, but of a relatively diminished working population. But Miss Buer does not attempt any statistical measurement of this factor.

Our starting-point is the age-figures in the Censuses for 1821 and 1841. In the former the return of age was voluntary, but the response was wide enough to allow a reasonably accurate estimate of the whole. These can be supplemented from the Tables in the 1871 Census General Report, already referred to as the source of Farr's ratio between baptisms and births. Table 58 gives the sex and age of the population from 1801 to 1871, Table 61 gives ages only, but goes back, for the younger groups, to 1761. As the calculation is based on survival in 1821 and after, the higher ages, 60-80 and over, cannot be estimated even for 1811, and the proportion of the population covered dwindles as the date recedes. The Report describes the eighteenth-century figures as "less certain" than the nineteenth, and makes no strong claim of accuracy even for the latter. The reader is consoled by the comment that "her past is of much less practical importance than her future population to England".[40] Below I give the percentage of the population falling in the age-group 20-60 at certain dates. The figure for 1801 is taken from the above estimate, and is probably slightly too high.[41]

[40] General Report, p. xiv.
[41] My rough calculations below make it 45.9 per cent.

## TABLE VII

### Age-group 20-60

|  |  |  |  |  |  |  |  |  | per cent |
|---|---|---|---|---|---|---|---|---|---|
| 1801 | . | . | . | . | . | . | . | . | 46·3 |
| 1821 | . | . | . | . | . | . | . | . | 44·0 |
| 1841 | . | . | . | . | . | . | . | . | 47·0 |
| 1861 | . | . | . | . | . | . | . | . | 47·6 |
| 1871 | . | . | . | . | . | . | . | . | 47·1 |

Obviously Miss Buer's theory has foundation. The composition of the 1821 population was abnormal. Had it been divided in the same proportions as that of 1871 there would have been about 361,000 more people alive between the ages of 20 and 60. But is it obvious that this would have been an advantage? It is probably true that a population deficient in adult members is more susceptible than the average to economic stress, but it must be remembered that this deficiency was due to an excess of the young, not of the aged, and that it coincided with a rise in the economic value of the child. The Industrial Revolution did not set children working for the first time, but it certainly did increase the productivity of child labour by linking it to the machine. We hear not only of parents overworked to support their children, but also of children working to support their parents. Secondly, one of the periods of most acute distress occurred round 1841, when the deficiency had been remedied. May it not have been due to the rapid arrival of those missing thousands to swell the ranks of the adult workers? This aspect of the phenomenon is probably even more significant than that to which Miss Buer draws attention. Here is a change rapid enough to cause a crisis, its effect magnified by concentration, while the other was weakened by diffusion; an " earthquake wave of labour supply ",[42] breaking into a labour market already invaded by women and children and weakened by many lean years of uncertain trade. Here are two forms of pressure, both derived directly from the rate at which the population had been growing, and both calculated to exert a check on that growth, the first by emphasising the burdens of parenthood, the second by discouraging early marriage among the working class. The second was probably the stronger, and I suspect that it was an important cause of the rapid fall in the marriage-rate and birth-rate after 1830.

To measure the birth-rate and marriage-rate in proportion to those capable of marrying and giving birth, I have taken as standard the number of women aged 20-40. This fits in better with the available statistics than the more correct age-group 15-50, and it gives a satisfactory index of change. To compare with the figures given in the 1871 Census, I have made a rough calculation of the numbers in this group back to 1781, avoiding the assumption of constant mortality on which those

---

[42] Beveridge, loc. cit. 466. Referring to the Edwardian age.

estimates are based.  The method by which I arrived at my guesses—
for they are little more—is as follows:

Of the total female population living in 1801, 69·3 per cent survived
in 1821.  Of the total female population living in 1821, 73·5 per cent
survived in 1841.  If we assume the same ratio between the survival
rates of age-groups, we can calculate from the recorded number of
women aged 40-60 in 1821 that the women aged 20-40 in 1801 numbered,
to the nearest thousand, 1,389,000.  A similar calculation for the two
sexes together makes the whole 20-40 group number 2,705,000.  These
estimates are likely to be on the high side.  The general survival rate
is influenced by the death-rate among infants, which was certainly
higher in 1801 than in 1821.  In the group survival rate this should not
enter.  It is true that within a few years from these starting-points the
position was reversed, and infant mortality was higher in 1831 than in
1811, but by that time even the youngest members of the populations
under consideration had left the most dangerous ages behind them.  If,
however, as is not unlikely, the death-rate among the old followed a
similar course, this would have a compensating effect.

In an attempt to correct this error, I made a second calculation on
the basis of the death-rate in the groups concerned, that is, between the
ages of 20 and 60.  Unfortunately the existing figures only allow a comparison between rates for the closing year of each period, based on an
average of seven years about that point.  We have, that is to say, burials
by ages for 1818-24, and deaths by ages for 1838-44.[43]  The returns were
not complete, and we have to begin with a proportional distribution of
the cases where age was not given.  Then the burials must be converted
into deaths.  As it is certain that failure to register was most common
in the case of infants, we cannot apply to adults the ratio found appropriate for all ages.  The crude death-rates for the seven-year periods
round 1821 and 1841 were 21·8 and 21·7.  If the deaths per 1,000 living
under five varied in the same proportion, then the ratio for converting
adult burials into deaths in 1821 works out at 1·034.  The resulting
death-rate per 1,000 living aged 20-60 for 1821 is 11·9.  The corresponding rate for 1841 is 12·25.  If we use this mortality ratio in place of the
survival ratio used previously, we arrive at a 20-40 age-group in 1801 of
2,563,000.  The same method applied to women only gives 1,316,000.
These figures set the lower limit, as no ratio more favourable to the
mortality of the earlier period is worth considering.  As I think the
second estimate is further below the mark than the first is above it, on
the grounds that the fall in the death-rate from 1801 to 1821 was not all
in infant mortality, while the rise from 1821 to 1841 probably was, I
have made my final guess by adding two-thirds of the differences to the
lower figure.  The result is:

[43] *1831 Census*, I, p. xxxviii *et seq.*  *Eighth Report of Registrar-General*, 187.

## Table VIII

*Age-group 20-40 in 1801*

|  | My estimate (000) | Census estimate (000) |
|---|---|---|
| Women . . . . . . | 1,364 | 1,371 |
| Men . . . . . . . | 1,293 | 1,351 |
| Total . . . . . | 2,657 | 2,722 |

The journey back another twenty years to 1780 is extremely hazardous. We can fill in the age-group 40-60 in 1801 by the same method,
using the ratio between survival rates just established for the 20-40 group
by means of the above estimate. The result, in thousands, is 1,559. To
find a ratio between the probable survival rates of the periods 1781-1801
and 1801-21 is difficult. I used the ratio between the general survival
rates for the whole population as in the first estimate made of the 20-40
group in 1801. I adopted Brownlee's estimate of the 1781 population,
namely, 7,531,000, and arrived at the population over 20 in 1801 by
deducting from the recorded total an estimated 0-20 age-group, the latter
being derived from the 20-40 group in 1821 by the use of the same type
of ratio. The resulting figure for the age-group 20-40 in 1781 is 2,253,000.
There is not enough evidence about age mortality to make correction of
this figure possible, and I propose to take it as it stands, remembering
that it is little more than a guess. I propose to reckon that 51 per cent
of these were women. The percentages in 1821 and 1841 were 51·61
and 51·25. This fall reflects the lower infant mortality when the second
group was born. On these grounds the eighteenth-century figure should
be higher still, but against this we have the heavy losses through puerperal mortality in this age-group.[44] It is probable that the percentage
rose slightly from 1781 to 1821. My estimates for 1801 give 51·34. For
Denmark in 1787 the percentage was 50·2, a remarkably low figure.[45]
On these grounds I take 51. I have interpolated figures for 1791, 1811
and 1831 on the assumption that the same proportion of the twenty
years' increment falls within the first decade in the case of the
group as in the case of the whole population. The results are tabulated
below.

[44] Price's age mortality estimates for the eighteenth century do not bear this out,
but they are based on insufficient evidence. His Table for Chester, 1772-81, shows
female mortality exceeding male only at ages 28-36. His Swedish Table, 1755-76, shows
no female excess, but equality from 30 to 35. (*Observations on Reversionary Payments*,
5th edn, II, Tables 40 and 42.) In Farr's figures for England and Wales, 1838-54,
female mortality exceeds male from the age of 10 to 35. (*Op. cit.* 183.) The highest
excess of female over male adult mortality in the eighteenth century is found among
French nuns, as compared with monks. (J. Milne, *Treatise on the Valuation of Annuities*,
Table XVI.)

[45] M. Rubin, "Population and the Birth-Rate", *Journal of the Royal Statistical
Society*, LXIII, 599.

## TABLE IX

### Age-group 20-40

|  | | | My estimate | | 1871 Census Tables 58 and 61 | | |
|---|---|---|---|---|---|---|---|
|  | | (1) | (2) | (3) | (1) | (2) | (3) |
| 1781 | . . . | 1,149 | 2,253 | 29·9 | 1,104 | 2,186 | 29·0 |
| 1791 | . . . | 1,242 | 2,427 | 29·4 | 1,219 | 2,414 | 29·3 |
| 1801 | . . . | 1,364 | 2,657 | 28·9 | 1,371 | 2,722 | 29·6 |
| 1811 | . . . | 1,541 | 2,990 | 28·6 | 1,561 | 3,063 | 29·2 |
| 1821 | . . . | 1,775 | 3,440 | 28·2 | 1,775 | 3,440 | 28·2 |
| 1831 | . . . | 2,157 | 4,187 | 29·8 | 2,136 | 4,181 | 29·7 |
| 1841 | . . . | 2,553 | 4,981 | 31·0 | 2,553 | 4,981 | 31·0 |

(1) Number of women in thousands.
(2) Number of both sexes in thousands.
(3) Percentage of the population contained in the age-group.
The Census Table does not distinguish the sexes for the eighteenth century. I have taken women as 50·5 per cent as a compromise between my 51 per cent and Farr's 50·36 per cent for 1801.

The next Table shows the resulting birth-rates and marriage-rates in proportion to women aged 20-40, based on eleven-year averages about the Census year and Brownlee's ratio of births to baptisms.

## TABLE X

|  | | Marriages per cent Women 20-40 | | Births per cent Women 20-40 | |
|---|---|---|---|---|---|
|  | | My estimate | 1871 census | My estimate | 1871 census |
| 1781 | . . . | 5·73 | 5·95 | 24·8 | 25·8 |
| 1791 | . . . | 5·79 | 5·89 | 25·5 | 25·9 |
| 1801 | . . . | 5·82 | 5·79 | 25·2 | 25·0 |
| 1811 | . . . | 5·61 | 5·54 | 25·6 | 25·2 |
| 1821 | . . . | 5·57 | 5·57 | 25·4 | 25·4 |
| 1831 | . . . | 5·25 | 5·31 | 24·3 | 24·5 |
| 1841 | . . . | | 4·93 | | 22·0 |
| 1851 | . . . | | 5·27 | | 21·6 |
| 1861 | . . . | | 5·35 | | 22·1 |
| 1871 | . . . | | 5·44 | | 23·1 |

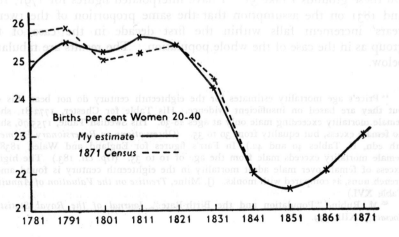

Births per cent Women 20-40
My estimate ———
1871 Census – – – –

Although the difference between the two estimates is not great, it does affect the general character of the curves. My figures put the climax both of the birth-rate and of the marriage-rate rather later than the Census figures. This makes the period 1791-1821 mark a definite peak in the birth curve rather than the first step in a fall by stages. The result depends very much on the highly speculative eighteenth-century figures. I feel convinced that Farr was wrong in putting the 20-40 age-group in 1781 as low as 29 per cent of the total population, lower, that is, than at any other date except 1821. Between 1750 and 1780 the rate of population growth had been low and constant, showing a slight slackening in the last decade. The percentage increases by decades, on Brownlee's estimates, were 7, 7·4 and 6·8. The birth-rate had risen by about 0·5 per 1,000. Brownlee's analysis of the London Bills of Mortality shows that infant mortality fell about 1750, but rose again slightly by 1770. The big fall came between 1761-70 and 1781-90. Death-rates for the country as a whole seem to have followed a similar course, with a lag of nearly ten years. The increase caused by the first fall would, in part at least, have passed into the age-group 20-40 by 1781, while the second increase would not yet have made itself felt.

At the same time the middle ages were gaining at the expense of the old. Between 1760 and 1800 the death-rate in London for ages 10-50 fell considerably, the biggest fall being one of 15·6 per cent at age 20-30. But the death-rate among persons over 50 rose slightly, the biggest rise being one of 5·9 per cent at age 50-60.[46] It is reasonably certain, therefore, that the proportion of persons aged 20-40 must have been higher in 1781 than in 1801, probably higher than in 1831. I think my figure is, if anything, too low, and under-estimates the rise in the birth-rate between 1781 and 1801.

The conclusions to be drawn from this study are mostly of the nature of hypotheses, amenable to a greater or less degree to the test of detailed research. They can be summarised as follows:

1. The crude birth-rate during the whole period 1750-1830 was remarkably high as compared both with what went before and with what followed. Its climb to these heights is not altogether surprising, since it followed close on an age when the death-rate was phenomenally high and the population stationary. The maintenance of this high rate, with only insignificant fluctuations, during the last forty years of this period is, however, very surprising, in view of three circumstances—the spectacular fall in the death-rate which began about 1780, the decline in infant mortality, itself equivalent in its economic consequences to a rise in the birth-rate, and the occurrence of a succession of acute economic

---

[46] J. Brownlee, "The Health of London in the Eighteenth Century", *Proceedings of the Royal Society of Medicine* (1925), XVIII. Epidemiology, 73 *et seq*. Especially Table VI.

crises.  It follows that, if we are seeking an explanation of the rapid increase of population, we must pay as much attention to the forces which kept the birth-rate up as to those which pulled the death-rate down.

2. If the birth-rate is reckoned in proportion to those capable of bearing children, its buoyancy is even more remarkable.  It rose steeply till 1791 and maintained its level till 1821.  Farr's estimates and my calculated figures (omitting the interpolations) agree in showing a slight rise during the first twenty years of the century.  Not until about 1830 did the rate relapse to the level of 1780.  The births on which these high rates are based stretch from 1786 to 1826.  Within these limits fall at least three severe economic crises—those associated with Speenhamland, Luddism and Peterloo.  For fully half the time the country was at war and was obliged to surrender her manhood for service at sea and on the Continent, a limitation on the national reproductive powers not allowed for in a rate based on the number of adult women.

And yet the rate in the middle of the war was 18·5 per cent higher than in 1851, and the rate for the miserable years of peace, 1816-26, was 10 per cent higher than that for 1871, the climax of the " Golden Age ".

3. The marriage-rate may have risen up to the end of the eighteenth century, but it fell in the nineteenth, and both estimates make it lower in 1821 than it had been in 1801.  This suggests that either fertility rose or illegitimacy increased, probably both.[47]  If it is true that the wave in the marriage curve which reaches its summit in 1801 represents a lowering of the average age at marriage, higher fertility would naturally follow.  It would result immediately from the fact that young marriages are more fertile in their early years, and it would intensify with time, since young marriages have a longer child-bearing period.[48]  Mr Griffith's fertility curve,[49] which shows a steep rise from 1795 to 1815, would, on this hypothesis, exaggerate the movement, since it is based on the relation of births to marriages celebrated, and the decline in the number of the latter would not, in fact, indicate a decline in the number of married couples living.  If this theory is accepted, and allowance is made for the effects of the falling death-rate, there is no need to assume a real falling-off in marriage before 1820, still less a reduction in the number of mothers, married and unmarried.

4. The crude death-rate, having reached its lowest point about 1811, began to rise a few years later, and continued to do so until the late

---

[47] No trustworthy figures for illegitimacy exist before 1842.  Rickman's estimate for 1830, from which Mr Griffith deduces that 5 per cent of the births were illegitimate, is far too low (p. 125).  The rate for 1851-60 was 6·5 per cent, and it had been falling.  (Farr, op. cit. 101.)

[48] In 1911 the highest average number of children born per year in marriages of completed fertility occurred where the mother married at 17.  Census, XIII, 354-5.

[49] Pp. 31 and 44.

'thirties. This rise coincided with a change in age-distribution favourable to a low death-rate, namely, an increase in the proportion of those
in healthy middle-life. It is therefore more serious than it appears. On
a basis of seven-year averages, the death-rates in 1821 and 1841 were 21·8
and 21·7. Had the 1841 population been constituted. as to age and sex,
in the same proportions as the 1821 population, the death-rate would
have been 22·8, an increase of 5 per cent. It seems probable that this
rise, most marked among infants and in the big towns,[50] was the result
of economic causes, using the term broadly to cover deficiency of
food-supply, housing and sanitation.

  5. Somewhere between 1820 and 1830 began a definite decline both
of the marriage-rate and of the birth-rate. By 1831 the birth-rate,
measured in proportion to women aged 20-40, got back for the first time
to the level of 1781 (this is a guess); by 1841 it had slumped far below
it (this is a fact). Now it is only fair to old theories to point out how
this fall by stages, slow at first and then rapid, reflects the history of
child labour and the Poor Law. In the 'twenties restrictions on the
employment of children had begun, though feebly, and apprenticeship
was giving place to contractual labour,[51] a system which does not relieve
the parent so completely of the responsibility for the child. From 1815
to 1834 the Speenhamland system was still widely in force, but the rates
of relief had been drastically reduced wherever possible. Justices began
to protest against the " rate in aid of wages ", and in several cases it
was pronounced illegal.[52] In the 'thirties came an effective Factory Act
and the new Poor Law.

  6. This converging of the birth- and death-rates, with its consequent
check on the rate of population growth, seems to be the result of economic pressure. Now observation has shown that the death-rate is not
quick to respond to the fluctuations of economic prosperity, whereas the
marriage-rate and birth-rate are more sensitive. This is fully discussed,
with the relevant statistics, by Mr Yule in two articles in the *Journal of
the Royal Statistical Society.*[53] In the earlier article he shows the close
correlation between the marriage-rate and various indices of national
prosperity, including foreign trade and employment. In the second
article he examines the death-rate as well, and draws certain general
conclusions. " It will be seen ", he writes, " that the death-rate shows
no tendency to vary inversely with trade and the marriage-rate. On the
contrary, over the period 1859-1908 the prosperous periods show, on the

    [50] Griffith, 186.
    [51] Redford, *Labour Migration in England*, 25-30.
    [52] S. and B. Webb, *English Poor Law History*, i, 182-9.
    [53] " On the changes in the Marriage- and Birth-Rates in England and Wales during
the Past Half-Century " in LXIX. " The Growth of Population and the Factors which
control it " in LXXXVIII. See also R. H. Hooker, " On the Correlation of the Marriage-
Rate with Trade " in LXIV.

whole, a higher death-rate than the periods corresponding to the troughs of the depression." He concludes that "all the facts seem consonant with the view that, in recent historical times and in civilised States, it is the birth-rate that must be regarded as the regulating factor in population: no other view seems possible ".[54] This may not be as true of 1800 as of 1900, but it can hardly be the exact reverse of the truth. Certainly birth-control was not widely practised, though some knowledge of it existed. Perhaps Francis Place exaggerated when, in 1822, he wrote that among the working people "the means to prevent conception" (he corrected this to " to destroy the fœtus ") " is already in use to a considerable extent ".[55] The heated interest shown in the subject in the early nineteenth century is no accident. It reflects both a desire to escape from the supposed pressure of population and a real conviction in some quarters that the use of undesirable methods by ignorant people constituted a serious danger to life and health. The main check, however, would probably come through the postponement of marriage. The fact that the birth-rate did fall rapidly in the 'thirties indicates that it was responsive to economic pressure. The previous rise in the death-rate suggests that this pressure was present at least in 1815, probably sooner. This thought again leads us to ask why it was that the birth-rate did not begin to fall earlier. Even if it suffered a check when the war began, it quickly recovered, and remained buoyant for another twenty years.

7. The economic pressure was in part a direct result of the rapidity of population growth. Urban concentration was a condition of this growth, and caused the high town mortality which drove up the national death-rate. The particular phenomena which acted most strongly to lower the birth-rate were, first, the burden of supporting the children saved by the declining infant mortality; secondly, the subsequent inrush of a wave of young adults into an already despondent labour market. These young people are unable to marry, and the birth-rate sags. These are both by-products of the population curve.

Such are the presumptions created and the hypotheses suggested by the general statistics of the period. So far as the Malthusians are concerned, it is evident that, whether they were right or wrong in the details of their analysis, their anxiety was abundantly justified and they were absolutely right to regard the birth-rate as the key to the situation. Things fell out as Malthus had feared. The preventive check was slow to act, and the positive check came into operation to arrest the pace of population growth. Malthus held that the failure of the preventive check was in part due to the evil influence of the Poor Law. Rickman

[54] Pp. 29 and 33.
[55] M. Stopes, Contraception, 273. Cf. Farr, in 1871, op. cit. 32: "The births, again, are under control to an extent which has not yet been duly appreciated, but is now rendered clear by the Census."

thought that the Poor Laws were "much less conducive to an Increase
of Population than they are usually stated to be in Argument", but he
believed that the manufacturing population was increasing rapidly,
partly "because in many Manufactures, Children are able to maintain
themselves at an early age, and so entail little expense on their Parents,
to the obvious encouragement of marriage".[56] On these views the general
statistics cannot claim to pronounce judgment, but I hope I have shown
that they can only be forced to give evidence against them under torture.

[56] *1821 Census, p.* xxx

# THE POPULATION OF ENGLAND AND WALES FROM THE INDUSTRIAL REVOLUTION TO THE WORLD WAR

### T. H. MARSHALL

THE first thing that strikes one about the population of England in the nineteenth century is the close sympathy between the rate of growth and the ebb and flow of economic prosperity. By this is not meant the trade cycle, with its almost decennial crises, but the broader movement which divides the whole period into five sections: war boom, post-war depression, Golden Years, Great Depression, and pre-war recovery. One statistician has endeavoured to express the correlation precisely by setting against the percentage increase for each decade the average of wholesale prices for the previous decade.[1] The two curves show a remarkably close correspondence, but it is not perfect. What exactly was happening before 1801 it is impossible to say. It seems probable that the rate of growth showed two bursts of speed in the eighteenth century, one from 1740 to 1760 and the other from 1780 onwards.[2] The latter continued unchecked to its peak in the decade 1811-21, as though the population had gathered enough impetus to carry it past the end of the war at increasing speed into the heart of the slump. From that point it applied the brakes, ignoring two or three commercial crises with their brief price climaxes, and steadily reduced its pace until it reached a low level in 1851-61, the decade during which prices took their decisive turn upwards. The brakes then came off for a short spurt of twenty years, a spurt in which, for the first time, there are clear signs of reckless driving. The population curve rises too high and then falls too low, and continues to zig-zag across the price curve in a definite erratic manner. A glance ahead over the horizon of the World War shows us that the two are parting company. The population is steadily slowing up in a way that suggests reasons unconnected with the price-level. It looks as though engine-trouble had developed about 1880 and had got progressively more serious ever since. The total population, which was just under nine millions in 1801, doubled itself by 1851 and doubled itself again by 1911.

[1] G. Udny Yule, *The Fall of the Birth-Rate*, 1920.
[2] G. Talbot Griffith, *Population Problems of the Age of Malthus*, 1926. An important work on all aspects of the early period.

This brief sketch directs our attention to two fundamental questions which the historian of population must try to answer. First, " Was there a causal connection in the nineteenth century between the rate of population growth and fluctuations in economic prosperity, as indicated by the price-level?" Secondly, " Did something happen about 1880 to break this causal connection, and, if so, what?" It is the duty of a " Revision " to explain with how much certainty these questions can at present be answered.

There are only three factors at work on the population side: births, deaths and migration. The first task is to disentangle them. Of the three, migration is the one which might seem to be most obviously and directly related to economic forces. But the numbers involved are small. The only figure that concerns us here is the net balance of movement inwards or outwards, because we are discussing quantity, not quality. Migration may change the character of a population far more than it affects its total, since the immigrants and emigrants who cancel out when we calculate the net gain or loss do not cancel out when we examine the effect on racial mixture. A qualitative change of this sort might modify the age-composition, health and fertility of the people, and so influence indirectly the rate of population growth. This is an important fact when we are considering migration between town and country, but it is impossible to trace any such influence on the population of England and Wales as a whole. In the first half of the century there are two movements which might have quantitative importance, the return from the wars and the immigration of the Irish. It has been estimated that, if allowance is made for the fighting forces, the phenomenally high rate of growth (18·1 per cent) for 1811-21 falls to 16·4 per cent.[3] The peace probably brought over into England a good many others besides discharged soldiers and sailors, but it seems that the natural increase of the population by excess of births over deaths cannot have been less than 15 per cent. The Irish had been coming over in ever larger numbers since the end of the American war. The famines of 1817-18 and 1822 increased the stream by expulsion, and the early railway boom and the expansion of the textile industries further increased it by attraction. By 1840 there was a considerable Irish population in Lancashire and in London, but a large proportion of the emigrants had settled in Scotland. Then came the famine, and in ten years the Irish in Great Britain had added over 300,000 to their numbers.[4] They did not all stay. For many, England was a stepping-stone to America, but over 500,000 Irish-born persons were enumerated in England and Wales at the Census of 1851. It is not surprising therefore that, whereas the total population growth for 1841-51 was 12·7 per cent,

[3] R. Price Williams, " On the Increase of Population in England and Wales " *J.R.S.S.* (*Journal of the Royal Statistical Society*), September 1880.
[4] A. Redford, *Labour Migration in England, 1800-1850*, 1926

the natural increase was probably less than 11 per cent. The effect is to put back the beginning of the second period of acceleration by ten years. Forty years passed before migration again became an important factor. In 1881-91 there was a net *loss* of some 600,000, and in 1901-11 of 500,000. The result is paradoxical. None of the return from the wars and only a small fraction of the influx of the Irish can be attributed to economic prosperity in England, but most of the exodus of the 'eighties *can* be attributed to economic depression in England, and a part of this expulsive economic force probably continued to stimulate the emigration of the early twentieth century. If, therefore, we wish to correlate population with prosperity, we ought to eliminate the effect of migration in the first period and retain it in the second. But elimination in the first period upsets the correlation, while elimination in the second period improves it by smoothing out the zig-zags and making the population curve show some signs of buoyancy in harmony with the economic revival which began in the 'nineties. The result is not satisfactory to a theory of simple economic causation.

Let us turn to the births and deaths. Registration, it will be remembered, was not instituted till 1837, and was only made compulsory by an Act of 1874. The figures, therefore, are dubious. We can, however, speak with some assurance of the general shape of the curves, and we do not find in them any clear sympathy with the movement of prices. The birth-rate was falling at the time when the population was increasing most rapidly. It began to recover before the rise of prices had had time to exert any effect, and its fall since 1880 has disregarded all economic indices. The death-rate did, as it should, trace a curve which was the inverse of the curve of population growth until 1840, but it was persistently high during the Golden Years and began to fall in the Great Depression.[5] We know, of course, *a priori*, that non-economic forces were at work in the case of the death-rate at least, and probably in the case of the birth-rate too, and a deeper analysis is therefore both possible and necessary.

It is generally agreed that the outstanding fact in the first period was a rapidly falling death-rate. The cause of the fall is to be found mainly in the progress of medicine, of which there is ample evidence. The doctors of the eighteenth century responded to the impetus which the seventeenth had given to all scientific work, and they thought naturally in terms of the health of the people rather than the ailments of the rich. The people, on their side, were becoming more receptive and teachable, and it is possible that their social habits were growing more hygienic. The terrific wave of intemperance associated with the gin shops was passing away. A great attack was made on such devastating diseases as summer diarrhoea and winter fever, on infant mortality and deaths

[5] *The Registrar-General's Statistical Review* for 1925 gives convenient summaries back to the beginning of registration.

in child-bed, and it was followed by the more spectacular discoveries which banished scurvy from our ships and relegated small-pox to the position of a minor peril.[6] There is, on the other hand, little evidence of anything that could be called an economic cause of this improvement in health. Recent researches seem to show that the diet of the agricultural poor was no better at the end of the eighteenth century than it had been at the beginning. Urban improvement was confined to London and one or two progressive towns. When the period of rapid concentration began in the 'twenties, the urban death-rate rose. It is possible that the relative decline in the importance of infectious epidemics as causes of mortality benefited the towns more than the villages, since infection spreads most easily where population is most dense; but this cannot be regarded as an economic factor.

The birth-rate is more difficult to interpret, partly because births escape registration more easily than deaths. The probability is that the rate fell slightly about 1790, remained fairly stable for some twenty-five years and fell again more decisively in the 'thirties.[7] The factors which may cause changes in the crude birth-rate are the age-composition of the population, the marriage-rate, the average age at marriage, voluntary control of births, and physiological conditions affecting fertility. Of the last, too little is known to make historical investigation possible. As for birth-control, propaganda was undoubtedly taking place, but it could not have had any appreciable effect on the national figures. The three remaining factors are more amenable to analysis. If the net rate of child-production rises, the population must get younger. It must contain a larger proportion of children. The birth-rate had probably risen in the eighteenth century, and thereafter infant mortality had declined. We must remember that small-pox had become so universal that few children escaped the infection, and Jenner's invention of vaccination in 1798 meant a further saving of young life in the early nineteenth century. The birth-rate had to fall simply because there was a smaller proportion of fertile adults from whom births could come. The fall requires no explanation in terms of economic or any other external cause. The marriage-rate had to fall for the same reason. After a time the wave of young life swept on to swell the ranks of adults, and the proportion of the reproductive classes rose, reaching its maximum about 1840. But the marriage- and birth-rates not only continued to fall, they fell faster than ever. Here, for the first time, is a clear possibility of economic causation. Can we say that the depression checked reproduction and so contributed towards retarding the rate of population growth? It depends on our interpretation of the falling

---

[6] Sir George Newman, *Health and Social Evolution*, 1931.

[7] T. H. Marshall, " The Population Problem during the Industrial Revolution ", *The Economic Journal* (Economic History Series), January, 1929. *Supra*, 306-330.

rates and on the reasons which led people to postpone marriage. (Illegitimacy was greate. then than now, but not great enough to affect the trend of the birth-rate curve.) It is thought that, in the eighteenth century, people began to marry younger because, with the decline of long apprenticeships and of the custom of "living-in" with the employer, social and economic independence came earlier. If so, the marriage-rate rose by anticipation, by drawing on the limited reservoir of marriageable persons. A rise of this kind must, other things being equal, be followed by a fall to approximately the old rate, as soon as the change of age-level is completed. For, clearly, if the same total number of girls get married, it makes no difference to the marriage-rate whether they marry at 22 or 18. It is the process of change from the one level to the other that affects it. The slight fall in the marriage-rate at the beginning of the nineteenth century may have been of this kind, and the high birth-rate may have been the natural result of having a younger married population.

But the continued fall requires further explanation. Two factors which may lead to a postponement of marriage are occupational skill and the employment of women. Unskilled men marry younger than skilled because they reach the maximum earning-power sooner. Women marry later when they can win economic independence by work outside the home. Undoubtedly there had been a degeneration of some old crafts into semi-skilled trades. It was notorious how quickly the immigrant Irish learned to be competent weavers. It is equally certain that industry in the machine age evolved new classes of highly skilled occupation. The whole movement might, theoretically, cause first a rise and then a fall in the marriage-rate. But it seems unlikely that the fall could have begun as early as the 'thirties. The employment of women outside the home, however, was already increasing and may have had some effect. But there still remains room for the simplest economic argument, that people abstained from marriage because, for the moment, they could not afford it. This argument gains support from subsequent events. We know that such abstentions are usually short-lived. The instinct for marriage is too strong to be killed by any economic depression. And we find in fact that the marriage-rate recovered very quickly. It was distinctly buoyant between 1850 and 1870, and there is definite evidence that people were marrying younger again.[8] Naturally the birth-rate rose too. Some statisticians have disputed this, on the ground that the apparent rise was probably due to the gradual improvement in registration up to its enforcement in 1874. But the fact that the Census figures show a steady increase in the proportion of persons under fifteen from 1851 to 1871, at a time when there was no significant decline in infant mortality, seems to prove that the rise was real. But it began

[8] G. Udny Yule, "On the Changes in the Marriage- and Birth-Rates in England and Wales during the Past Half-Century", *J.R.S.S.*, March 1906.

so early, almost before prices had turned upwards, and certainly before wages had started to rise, that one hesitates to attribute it to economic revival. It may simply have been that there is a natural limit to the time for which human beings can act with prudence and circumspection in these matters.

If economic depression really checked the supply of human life in the 'thirties, one naturally asks why the check did not appear earlier, at the beginning of the post-war slump. There are two possible answers. The fall in the 'thirties did not correspond with a period of low prices. Prices were high, but wages were low and unemployment was considerable, and these conditions lasted for five or six years. It is a unique phenomenon in the nineteenth century. Every other price climax of equal duration was associated with improving trade. This may explain why it was only in these ten or fifteen years that a definite reaction of economic pressure on births can be discovered. But we cannot rule out the other answer, that social policy mitigated the effects of the slump. The new Poor Law and the first effective Factory Act withdrew simultaneously two sources of maintenance for young families. The economic pressure of the high birth-rate was increased by the decline in infant mortality. The "effective" birth-rate, *i.e.* the crude birth-rate *minus* infant mortality, was rising. We feel the need of some fact to explain how this exceptional pressure was resisted. No English statistics can prove that the Poor Law did not play a part. The strongest argument against it is the comparative argument, that other countries had similar birth-rates and no Poor Law. But these two are not the only variables, and, if the Poor Law argument is rejected on *a priori* grounds, the whole case for economic causation must fall too.

The birth-rate began its great decline in the middle 'seventies. There can be no doubt that the latter part of the fall was due to voluntary control by contraception, for there are signs of a definite fall in the fertility of marriages. Mr Yule has estimated that, when every allowance has been made for the number of wives and their age-distribution, the decline in fertility between 1871 and 1911 must have been about 28 per cent, and that it took place at accelerating speed. Also, if, as we should expect, the practice of contraception spread down the social scale, the differential fertility between the middle classes and the unskilled labourers ought at first to increase and subsequently to diminish. This is apparently what happened. The differential fertility was greatest at the end of our period.[9] But it is less certain that contraception caused the beginning of the birth-rate fall. The spread of birth-control propaganda is generally dated from the Bradlaugh-Besant trial for the dissemination of indecent literature, which attracted a great

---

[9] T. H. C. Stevenson, " The Fertility of various Social Classes in England and Wales from the middle of the Nineteenth Century to 1911 ", *J.R.S.S.*, May 1920.

deal of public attention. But it took place in 1877. The early fall was associated with a rise in the age at marriage. Many fewer girls married under 20, rather fewer between 20 and 25, and rather more between 25 and 40.[10] This suggests that we might have here a recurrence of the situation in the 'thirties, when economic depression acted directly on the marriage-rate. But in the 'thirties prices were high and wages low. In the 'seventies prices fell and wages rose. Real wages, moreover, did not merely *continue* to rise. They *began* to rise. They had been more or less stationary in the twenty years during which the marriage-rate rose and took a decisive turn upwards just as the marriage-rate started to fall. A theory of simple economic causation will not do. It is possible that the explanation should be sought in changing social habits related to the growth of skilled trades and black-coated occupations, the increasing independence of women, and the effects of the gradual spread of education. But the solution of the problem remains obscure.

What, in the meantime, had happened to the death-rate? There had been a rise after 1820, and it was a rise which fell most heavily on the towns and on the children. Undoubtedly it was a product of ill-organised, unhealthy urban environment. There was no deterioration in medical skill, and the only new disease of importance was cholera, which appeared first in 1831 and returned with greater violence in 1848-54 It did not appreciably affect the mortality-curve for the whole period. The towns of those days were admirably fitted to spread such an infection, not only because some of them had as yet made no attempt to cope with the problem of urban sanitation, but also because the enterprising efforts of others were worse than useless. Bad drains, which leak into the water supply, may be more fatal than none at all. But if drains spread the cholera, cholera certainly helped to spread the drains. It gave an impetus to the movement for a scientific study of public health. It frightened the towns into taking action. But progress was very slow. There is no evidence of a general reduction of mortality until after 1870. On the contrary, the death-rate, and especially the infant death-rate, rose in most of the large towns. When the improvement began, the young and strong benefited first. Over 35 there was no gain, and over 45 a loss. A little later the middle-aged joined in, but the infants had to wait until the twentieth century.[11] The remarkable effect on the age-composition of the population of the saving of life among the very young and the definitely old is a post-war phenomenon.

The high death-rate in mid-Victorian England was a product of its economic civilisation. The situation on the medical front was improving.

[10] *Statistique Internationale du mouvement de la population* (1749-1905) (Paris, 1907), I, 109. The volume contains many useful summaries.
[11] *The Registrar-General's Decennial Supplements;* also *Statistical Review* for 1921, Tables, Part I, Table 3.

The defence grew ever stronger, while no new forces of importance appeared on the attacking side. Cholera at the beginning of the period and influenza at the end were alarming, but not statistically impressive in the long run. Influenza in the 'nineties was about one-tenth as deadly as tuberculosis in the 'fifties. The apparent increase of cancer was probably due largely to better diagnosis. The close correlation between death-rates and density does not mean that concentration is necessarily deadly. Well-planned tenement blocks, like the Peabody estates, had a lower mortality than the average for London. It is, as Professor Bowley has shown, by overcrowding, rather than by mere density, that the death-rate is governed.[12] The close correlation between death-rates and poverty breaks down when you bring in the agricultural labourer. Mortality in some occupations was extravagantly high, but the facts show clearly that it was the home, and not the job, that controlled the rates. The differences were greater as between infant than as between adult death-rates, and Manchester enjoyed, throughout the period, an unenviable pre-eminence over the more purely factory towns and over the seats of the most unhealthy occupations. The causes were, therefore, in a sense economic. But mid-Victorian England was not exactly poor, and certainly was not getting poorer. The trouble was due to ill-designed expenditure of the national wealth rather than to any deficiency in the total. The subsequent improvement was immense. In the England which had just emerged from the World War both general and infant mortality were just half what they had been at the climax of the Golden Years. Part of the progress was due to increased wealth per head and better nourishment of the poor, part to the gradual acclimatisation of the people to town life, but more to the reorganisation of the material environment through the growth of a science and a service of public health, and to the unceasing advance of medical knowledge, to Pasteur and Lister and the doctors who made their work, and the work of others, less celebrated, a means to the strengthening of human vitality and the prolongation of human life.

Although the nineteenth-century towns were, by modern standards, unhealthy, they were distinguished from those of an earlier age by the fact that they grew by the natural excess of births over deaths. They were assisted in this by the other, and older, source of growth, migration, which gave them a population strong in young adults among whom deaths are fewest and births most numerous. The general trend of internal migration is well known, but its exact measurement is extremely difficult. The official estimate that 50 per cent of the people lived in urban districts in 1851 and 78 per cent in 1911 gives a rough idea of the transformation achieved during the century. If we look at the chang-

---

[12] A. L. Bowley, " Death-rates, Density, Population and Housing ", *J.R.S.S.*, July 1923; also A. F. Weber, *The Growth of Cities in the Nineteenth Century* (New York, 1899), on this and all aspects of urban growth.

ing proportion of the total population living in each county, we find that, from 1801 to 1911, the share of Glamorgan rose by 290 per cent, that of Durham by 126 per cent and that of Lancashire by only 75 per cent. Clearly Lancashire was already an area of concentration at the time of the first Census. The periods of maximum expansion in each district reflect the familiar outline of industrial history: 1811-21 for the West Riding, the 'twenties for Lancashire and Cheshire, the 'thirties for Staffordshire, the 'fifties for Glamorgan and the 'sixties for Durham. If the whole period is divided into four parts we find that the old towns, already large in 1801, grew most rapidly in the first quarter, the new towns created by the Industrial Revolution in the second, new populous districts undistinguished by big cities in the third, while the fourth is characterised by a general slowing-up accompanied by a definite emigration out of big cities into suburban residential districts.[13] This suggests that the rising death-rate of the 'twenties may have been caused by this sudden inrush into old towns, physically and mentally unprepared to receive it; that the new towns and populous districts were a little better adapted to their task; and that the approximation of urban towards rural death-rates in and after the 'nineties may have been due in part to the urbanisation of the country-side.

It has been clearly shown by several studies that the normal process of migration was by short-distance waves, stimulated by the attraction of growing centres.[14] High wages drew people into the town from near-by, others flowed in to take their place in the surrounding country, and the ripples spread outwards in widening circles. Such a movement is ill-designed to meet a very rapid expansion of demand, since the supply immediately available is always geographically restricted. Lancashire, for example, experienced a shortage in the 'twenties and 'thirties, but the emigrants from East Anglia continued to go to London and those from the west to South Wales. Direct long-distance migration occurred too, but in much smaller quantities. It could be produced by one of two things, an exceptionally strong pull, or an exceptionally strong expulsive push. Men uprooted by acute depression in their home district prepare to move without a fixed objective and may travel far. In the 'thirties and in the 'eighties such an expulsive force existed, and in both periods it was assisted by organised effort. Even so the population was hard to move. The new Poor Law authorities managed to dispatch 2,700 migrants from East Anglia to the industrial north, but they found it easier to get them to leave the country by the neighbouring ports. In the 'eighties, too, there was much emigration, and the exodus from

[13] T. A. Welton, " On the Distribution of Population in England and Wales, 1801-1891 ", J.R.S.S., December 1901 (continued to 1911 in J.R.S.S., February 1913); also Census of 1911, Summary Tables, Table 4.
[14] E.g. Redford, op. cit.; and E. G. Ravenstein. " The Laws of Migration ", J.R.S.S., June 1885.

country to town was clearly governed more by the proximity of the town than by the degree of depression in the country.

The laws which govern the exceptionally long pull have not been sufficiently investigated. Obviously it has the best chance when assisted by a simultaneous push elsewhere. Emigration reached its peak in time of depression. Probably the response to the pull is determined, not by the rational calculation of economic advantages, but by the presence of a certain sensational quality in the appeal. There is romance in the call of London and of the Colonies. Cotton at one time, and coal at another, became the almost legendary symbols of prosperity and progress. But the legend may outlast the reality that created it, and no new legend may arise to divert the stream to other places. Middlesbrough became a legend when its population grew by 2,580 per cent in thirty years, and we find that, in 1861, 73 per cent of its people were Yorkshiremen, and only 50 per cent in 1871.[15] Huntingdon lost heavily in the agricultural depression. In 1881 one-third of the emigrants were found in the three contiguous counties and another third divided between Lancashire, Yorkshire and London.[16] The short-wave movement still went on and the long pull still set in the old directions. Glamorgan is a good example. Its growth, as we have seen, was sensational. Short-wave immigration, once started, remained constant and peculiarly insensitive to economic change. Long-distance immigration fluctuated with the rise and fall of the industry, but with a very poor measure of adjustment. In the depressed 'nineties 35,000 natives of Glamorgan left the county, but 94,000 newcomers streamed in, more than half of them coming from afar.[17] Although English industry in general was reviving, there was no new legend to check the established flow to Wales nor to create sufficient flow out of it. When times were bad the miners hung around the pits and sent their women-folk to London to seek domestic service. It is an accepted theory that casual labour flourishes where skill is low and employers are many. It would be interesting to discover whether another cause may not have been this polarisation of movement, creating chronic over-supply even in skilled trades. May it, possibly, help to explain the prevalence of casualisation in London and of endemic short-time in Lancashire and in the coal mines?

It seems clear that mobility increased during the century. The decline in the rate of urban concentration at the end does not imply a decline of mobility. Once the settled habits of an earlier age had been broken down by better transport and communications and by the new

---

[15] Ravenstein, *loc. cit.*

[16] W. Ogle, " The Alleged Depopulation of the Rural Districts of England ", *J.R.S.S.*, June 1889.

[17] Brinley Thomas, " The Migration of Labour into the Glamorganshire Coal-Field, 1861-1911 ", *Economica*, November 1930.

mental attitudes developed by the experience of migration itself, movement probably became, as it were, less linear and more circular. The purposeful streams which altered the quantitative distribution of the population between North and South, town and country, textiles and mining, became less important than the constant circulation, especially of the urban population, from town to town, producing a perpetual qualitative mingling without greatly modifying the relative numerical totals. Occupational mobility is obtained mainly by directing the stream of new human material, as it enters the labour market, into those quarters where it is most needed. It has therefore been suggested that such mobility is greatest when this stream is largest, that is, when the population is increasing most rapidly. No such correlation can be found with geographical mobility, because it proceeds in a quite different way. It is the young adults who migrate, when they have won independence from the family of their birth and have not yet shouldered heavy responsibilities for a family of their own. Such people have already taken up an occupational position. Even in the worst of the agricultural depression young men usually had a spell in agriculture before they ventured to change both their home and their job.[18] The dispatch of children from villages to factories early in the century was a peculiar phenomenon and never assumed large proportions. When, therefore, the direction of the rising stream of young humanity into new industries involves a change of locality, the social and psychological factors which govern migration constitute a serious obstacle.

Population, as a factor in economic history, must be regarded as a cause and not merely as an effect. It has its own vital principle which is only partially amenable to economic pressure. In the nineteenth century, as we have seen, the birth-rate acted with a sturdy independence. The death-rate, responding in the main to the efforts of the doctors, was, on the economic side, governed not merely by the gross production of wealth. An economic control of population growth through the death-rate would seem to be normal only in a people living on the margin of subsistence. Migration was a social process far from perfectly adapted to the needs of industry. The rapid growth of the population may have been on the whole a stimulus to economic progress, but it was at times a cause of economic friction and distress. At the beginning of the century the doctors increased the economic burden of parents by saving the lives of their children, and of adults generally by enlarging the dependent, as compared with the productive, section of the community. Then, as the children grew up, industry received an unprecedented influx of new labour which it could not easily absorb, at a time when, more than any other, the labour of the child competed with the labour of the man. The rapid growth round 1870 did not,

<hr>

[18] A. L. Bowley, " Rural Population in England and Wales ", *J.R.S.S.*, May 1914.

however, prove too much for the productive powers of the relatively diminished working population. Real income rose faster than it had ever done before. But once more, in the pre-war decade, the consequent pressure of increasing supplies of new labour seemed to cause friction, for it coincided with a period of stagnation in the welfare of the masses. Ideally the industrial machine can adapt itself to any population, growing or stable, young or old, but, in practice the population has more than once proved itself to be a master who sets severe tasks to his puzzled servant.

## POPULATION OF ENGLAND AND WALES

| | Total at beginning of decade 000s | % Increase | % Natural increase | Standardised Death rate | Deaths under 1 year p. 1,000 births | Birth-rate | Marriage-rate | Marriages p. 1,000 single women 15+ | Legitimate births p. 1,000 married women 15-45 |
|---|---|---|---|---|---|---|---|---|---|
| 1801–11 | 8,893 | 14·0 | — | — | — | — | — | — | — |
| 1811–21 | 10,164 | 18·1 | — | — | — | — | — | — | — |
| 1821–31 | 12,000 | 15·8 | — | — | — | — | — | — | — |
| 1831–41 | 13,897 | 14·3 | — | — | — | — | — | — | — |
| 1841–51 | 15,914 | 12·7 | 10·9 | 21·6 | 153 | 32·6 | 16·1 | — | — |
| 1851–61 | 17,928 | 11·9 | 12·6 | 21·2 | 154 | 34·1 | 16·9 | 51·7 | 281·0 |
| 1861–71 | 20,066 | 13·2 | 13·6 | 21·3 | 154 | 35·2 | 16·6 | 51·8 | 287·3 |
| 1871–81 | 22,712 | 14·4 | 15·1 | 20·3 | 149 | 35·4 | 16·2 | 50·7 | 295·5 |
| 1881–91 | 25,974 | 11·7 | 14·0 | 18·6 | 142 | 32·4 | 14·9 | 45·3 | 274·6 |
| 1891–1901 | 29,003 | 12·2 | 12·4 | 18·1 | 153 | 29·9 | 15·6 | 44·9 | 250·3 |
| 1901–11 | 32,528 | 10·9 | 12·4 | 15·2 | 128 | 27·2 | 15·5 | 43·2 | 221·6 |
| 1911–21 | 36,070 | 4·9 | 6·8 | 13·5 | 100 | 21·8 | 16·6 | 45·8 | 173·5 |

# THE DENOMINATION AND CHARACTER
# OF SHARES, 1855-1885

## J. B. JEFFERYS

AMONG the problems facing the promoters of limited liability
companies following the general permissive Acts of 1855 and 1856
were those of attracting the number and quality of shareholders
the company desired and of establishing a sound financial reputation.
No well-tried mechanism of company promotion and investment
existed, and the concept of limited liability had still to win acceptance
in commercial and industrial circles schooled in the concept of partnership liability " to the last shilling and the last acre ". The denomination
of the shares issued by the companies and the character of these shares,
whether fully paid up when purchased or left partly uncalled, were held
to be of great importance in the solution of these problems. " Probably
no point ought to be more anxiously weighed ", wrote an adviser to
limited companies in the 'sixties, " than the nominal amount of the
shares into which the capital of the company is to be divided."[1] An
equal concern was shown as to the proportion to be called up on each
share. By the 'eighties and 'nineties these considerations were no
longer to the fore. New companies accepted without question that the
ordinary share denomination should be between £1 and £5 nearly or
fully paid up. Instead, attention was centred on the use of varying types
of shares, such as founders' and preference, and on the use and misuse
of debenture stock. A study of this transition and of the factors leading
to it throws some light on the methods of finance of the early limited
companies and on the composition and outlook of the investing classes.

In the first ten years of general limited liability the share denomination of the majority of companies was high measured against the £1
standard. Of 3,720 companies formed between 1856 and 1865 inclusive
and believed still to be in existence in the latter year, only 597, or 16 per
cent, had shares below £5 in value; the remainder ranged between £5
and £5,000, with the largest group (52 per cent) from £10 up to £100
shares.[2] More than thirty companies had share denominations of
£1,000 and over, the chief types being iron, coal, engineering, land

---

[1] Loftus Fitz-Wygram, *Limited Liability Made Practical, Reduction of the Capital
of Companies and the Sub-Division of Shares* (1867), 7. He was a director of several
companies and well-informed on company finance.
[2] Analysis and details from the *Limited Liability Joint Stock Companies List*
(1864-6). This list does not comprise all the limited companies that were registered,
but the sample is over 60 per cent of the total and includes all the important companies.

development and cotton.   The panic of 1866, for reasons discussed later, discouraged the very high shares and the success of the cotton and "single ship" companies in raising capital easily with shares of £5 and £1 in the 'seventies and early 'eighties encouraged lower shares in other spheres.   In 1882 W. R. Skinner wrote in the preface to his *Stock Exchange Year Book and Directory*: " It is a feature of the present financial period that fully-paid shares chiefly of £1 are quite the vogue ", and by the end of the century the triumph of the £1 share was complete in almost every sphere of limited company enterprise.

The character of the share—whether fully paid up or not—followed a parallel course of development.   Shares only partly paid up were a feature of the opening years of limited company finance.   In some cases, mainly co-operative ventures, this was the result of a decision to call up the capital by instalments.   For example, the Airedale Building and Manufacturing Company Ltd. of Yorkshire had shares of £2 10s. each on which one shilling was called up monthly.   But in the majority of cases there was no intention, initially, of calling up the whole of the amount of the share and a common announcement in the prospectus of a company was: " It is not intended to call up more than 25 L per share " (£100),[3] or: " It is not anticipated that more than 10 L per share will be required " (of a £20 share).[4]   After the crisis of 1866 this system found fewer supporters.   Companies were allowed by the 1867 Companies Act to reduce their capital and share values, thereby increasing the proportion called-up, and while relatively few of the older companies took this course,[5] the new industrial and commercial companies tended to issue smaller shares with a higher proportion paid up.   In 1885 over three-quarters of the issued capital of the 661 industrial and commercial, iron and steel, coal and shipping companies listed in *Burdett's Official Intelligence* was paid up.[6]   And these companies, by reason of size or regular share quotation, were considered among the more important companies in existence.

---

Close examination of the figures reveals a tendency for the average share denomination to rise between 1856 and " the great winding up " in 1866.   Of the 2,040 formed between 1856 and 1863 inclusive, 20 per cent had shares below £5 in value and 24 per cent above £10.   Of the 1,680 formed in 1864 and 1865, 10 per cent had share values below £5 but 38 per cent above £10.   The large number of banking and finance companies formed in these two years partly accounts for this rise in denomination.

[3] Prospectus of the London and Colonial Bank Ltd. (1863).

[4] Prospectus of the East Rosedale Iron Co. Ltd. (1866).

[5] In the ten years, 1867-77, seventy-one companies reduced their issued capital, a total reduction from £56 millions to £22 millions.   *Report of the Select Committee on the Companies Acts, 1862 and 1867* (1877), VIII, Qu. 39.   (To be referred to later as the 1877 *Report*.)

[6] Percentages calculated from figures given in unpublished M. Com. thesis, University of London, 1937, by A. Essex-Crosby, " Joint Stock Companies, 1890-1930 ", and based on *Burdett's Official Intelligence* (1885).   Approximately 60 per cent of the issued capital of the 1,585 companies listed and engaged in all types of finance, industry and commerce was paid up in this year.

23

This, however, was only the average trend of all limited companies; there were wide differences between the practices in individual industries and some of these differences should be noted.

Apart from a small number of co-operative ventures engaged in retail trading or managing workmen's clubs, the companies with the lowest share denomination, fully paid, were those engaged in non-ferrous mining enterprises. In the 'sixties the shares in these companies were rarely over £10 and the £1 share was common. By the 'eighties the £1 share fully paid up was nearly universal in this group. Cotton company shares in the 'sixties ranged from shares, such as those of J. H. Bates (Albert Cotton Mills) Co. Ltd. (1864), of £1,000 each to the low shares of the co-operative cotton mills, such as the £1 fully paid shares of the Belthorpe Co-operative Manufacturing Company Ltd. (1861). But in the burst of cotton company formation between 1870 and 1875, the "Oldham Limiteds" era, the £5 share with £1 to £3 paid up became popular and shares of this type remained a characteristic of cotton companies to 1914. In shipping the companies formed to take over private shipping lines or to amalgamate lines had high share denominations. But the boom in the 'eighties led to the formation of new companies with £10 shares, and the many "single ship" companies had shares of £1 to £5 fully paid. Iron and steel, coal, and engineering and shipbuilding companies, which in nearly all important cases were conversions of existing partnerships, were the least affected by the trend to low share denomination. The share values fell slightly when some of the concerns took advantage of the 1867 Act giving them power to reduce capital, but in the 'eighties the £1 share was still practically unknown. The usual shares were between £10 and £50 with about two-thirds of this sum called up.

Banking, investment, finance, land and insurance companies had very different share characteristics from the other groups. The Bank Act of 1844 established the denomination of shares in Joint-Stock Banks at £100 each, of which one-half was to be left uncalled as reserve liability. The 1858 Act granting general liability to banks continued this regulation and although it was withdrawn by the 1862 Act the tradition of the high share, of which one-half was uncalled, remained. The land, investment and insurance companies adopted the same practice. For example, in 1867 it was reported that "nothing was more common than insurance companies . . . with shares of 100 L and only 5 L or 10 L called up ",[1] and in 1875 of 58 important banking companies only seven had fully paid-up shares, and of the remainder only one company had more than half of its shares paid up. In 1885 an analysis of the capitals of the 144 banking and 87 insurance companies listed in

[1] Report from the Select Committee on Limited Liability Acts (1867). X, Qu. 1306. (To be referred to later as the 1867 Report.)

Burdett, shows an average of only 24·6 per cent and 21·8 per cent respectively of the issued capital paid up. The shares of the finance, land and investment companies had, however, by the 'eighties begun to approximate more closely to the general trend. The share denominations fell and in 1885 61 per cent of the issued capital of the 226 listed companies in this group was paid up.[8]

The reasons for the high share denomination and uncalled character of the shares and for the variations in the practice of the different groups of companies were many. In the first place, in the absence of any experience of general limited liability, the tradition of partnership practice and, to a lesser extent, the experience of railway, canal, gas and other joint-stock organizations exerted a very powerful influence. The significant difference between a partnership and a limited liability company to a large section of founders and investors was not that less need be invested in a company but that in the event of failure liability was limited. Many early joint-stock companies, though they had a wider basis than a partnership, were established on similar lines and followed similar traditions as to what constituted an investment. To take one example, the Liverpool and Philadelphia Steam Ship Company of 1850 had shares of £9,000 each. Canal, bank and railway companies made a closer approach to the impersonal company, but even so bank shares were not less than £100 and railway and canal shares rarely less than £25 each. The influence of this tradition of high share denomination and heavy investment was seen in the 1855 Act. Clauses in this Act prohibited the issue of shares of less than £10 each and provided that " the deed of settlement shall be executed by shareholders not less than 25 in number, holding shares to the amount in the aggregate of at least three-fourths of the nominal capital of the company ".[9] This was in the spirit of the band of adventurers, known to each other before the formation of the company, investing heavily and exercising direct control of the undertaking. These provisions did not appear in the 1856 Act, but the ideas which promoted them continued.

A second factor affecting the denomination and particularly the character of the shares of the early limited companies was the current opinion as to what measures a company should take to gain stability and high financial standing. In the long drawn out and sometimes very heated discussions on the pros and cons of limited liability in the 'forties and 'fifties the danger that the limitation of responsibility for debts and actions would lead to wild speculation, panics and a decline of commercial morality had been stressed time and time again by the opponents of general limited liability.[10] The limited concept was new, and disturbing

[8] Percentages calculated from figures given in A. Essex-Crosby, *op. cit.*
[9] 18 and 19 Vict. c. 133. Section 9, 1 (4).
[10] The memories of the " railway mania " were very vivid in the minds of all taking part in the discussions in the early 'fifties, and the opponents of limited liability had

pictures of the unknown proved easy to paint. The founders and shareholders of limited companies were therefore very sensitive on the
subject of the security of their company. Advice on the measures that
should be taken to remove any suggestion of insecurity or instability
was of course legion. When a need was thought to exist for suggestions
to avoid financial weakness few could refrain from rushing into print.
But the significant feature of this advice was the underlying assumption
in every instance that the closer a limited company could approach to
the partnership system of responsibility, the greater would be its security
and the higher its standing. The Limited Liability Acts had been
passed, but partnership principles were still used as the yardstick. In
short, the advice tendered was, maintain a high reserve of uncalled
capital, fix a high share denomination, and confine the shareholdings to
those who know the trade.

John Brooke, of the Huddersfield Chamber of Commerce and an
opponent of limited liability, was one of the first to suggest the need for
maintaining uncalled capital under general limited liability. In his final
argument before the Commission on Mercantile Law in 1853 he said:
" if you limit the responsibility of joint-stock companies . . . then make
it three times the amount paid up." [11] The Commission rejected the
suggestion, but, in practice, the limited companies accepted it. Ten
years later it was held that " the unpaid portion of the shares constitutes
a continuous guarantee fund beyond the control of Directors and
managers . . . and practically establishes a security of the *highest*
order ",[12] and that " the security of the uncalled capital was one of the
chief arguments in favour of limited liability ".[13] Similarly it was
agreed that a limited company could be considered sound if it approxi-
mated to the partnership system by having high shares, heavy
individual investments and relatively few shareholders. For example,
a witness before the Select Committee on the Limited Liability Acts in

little difficulty in suggesting that the mania was due to the special facilities afforded
speculators by the limited liability of railway companies and that if this privilege
were extended to all spheres of commerce and industry the consequences would be
disastrous. One opponent, referring to the Bill of 1856, wrote: " This Limited Liability
Bill ought therefore to be called ' An Act for the better enabling Adventurers to interfere with and ruin Established Traders *without risk to themselves!* '" (E. Phillips,
*Bank of England Charter, Currency, Limited Liability and Free Trade* (1856), 36.) And
in addition to leading to financial danger, limited liability was also " immoral " and
" un-Christian ". For example: " There is a moral obligation, which it is the duty of
the laws of a civilized and Christian nation to enforce, to pay debts, perform contracts
and make reparations for wrongs. Limited liability is formed on the opposite
principles." (E. W. Cox, *The New Law and the Practice of Joint Stock Companies with
Limited Liability* (5th edn. 1862), n I.)

[11] *Report of the Commission on Mercantile Law* (1854), 159.
[12] *The Law of Limited Liability and its Application to Joint Stock Banking Advocated* (1863), 11.
[13] *Journal of the Royal Society of Arts*, XV (Dec. 1866), 52.

1867 said that when a company consults as to the value of the shares
" the answer invariably is ' if you want to have a large stable company
make your shares very large ' . . . there is not a shadow of doubt that
a company with 10 shareholders of 1,000 L each is a much more stable
company than a company with any number of shareholders with 1 L
each." [14] Attempts to appeal to a wider group of investors with lower
shares fully paid were strongly criticized. When the Great Ship Company issued shares at £1 each, an investor asked: " Is it not commercially
absurd to entrust such a vast professional structure to the fostering care
of petty tradesmen who know nothing of the technicalities of the shipbuilding and shipowning trade instead of seeking at least £100 shareholders?" [15] and the Chairman of the 1867 Select Committee summed
up this view by observing: " I suppose the lower you go in the denomination of shares the more ignorant people you catch?" [16]

Opinions as to what constituted stability or instability would by
themselves, however, have had little direct influence on the methods of
company finance. These views had a strong empirical bias based on
partnership experience, and, as will be shown later, a slight change of
fortune led to the assertion, made equally dogmatically and in some
cases by the same people, of directly contrary views. The acceptance
by the founders of limited companies of the view that uncalled capital,
high shares and few shareholders made for financial stability was due
more to the strong insistence on these measures by the creditors and to
the nature of the investment market than to the soundness of the
reasons put forward in their favour.

Creditors in the first quarter of a century following the passage of
the Acts in the 'fifties were in a very strong position vis-à-vis limited
companies. While it was true, as had been suggested by Robert Lowe
when he introduced the 1856 Act, that " the capital of a limited Company would be easier to raise [than a partnership] and therefore the
temptation to borrowing less ",[17] a large number of companies, by the
nature of their business, had to borrow both short and long term and
until the widespread use of debenture issues the usual trade creditors
were the main source for loans. The creditors, owing to the small
development of the limited system, were in a position to enforce practically the same terms on their few limited customers as were already
conceded by their numerous unlimited partnership customers. The
most important of these terms was that which demanded that in addition to paid-up capital there should be an uncalled reserve which could

[14] 1867 Report, op. cit. Qu. 2043.

[15] Journal of the Royal Society of Arts, loc. cit. 84.

[16] 1867 Report, op. cit. Qu. 786 and cf. Qu. 1388, Justice Romilly, " the smaller the
amount of shares the less ' bona fide' is the company ; that is the experience we have
in Court ".

[17] Robert Lowe, Speech of the Rt Hon. Robert Lowe on the Amendment of the Law
of Partnership and Joint Stock Companies, February, 1, 1856 (1856), 34.

be drawn upon in an emergency.[18] In 1877 David Chadwick, who, as one concerned with the formation of some of the most important limited companies in the first thirty years of limited liability, knew more about the workings of the system than any other single person, said: " In the case of a trading company I think it is very prudent and very proper to have 25 to 33 or 40 per cent uncalled out of the subscribed capital; without that they cannot stand in the market with proper credit."[19] With this view held by both creditors and promoters, an uncalled portion of the shares in those companies needing "proper credit" was inevitable and, in fact, contrary to the prophecies and fears of the opponents of limited liability, the creditors during the first two decades of the operation of the system were "in clover".[20]

The investment mechanism in the 'fifties and 'sixties was still in a very embryonic stage of development. The two main types of shareholders in the early limited companies were the successful capitalists connected with the basic and heavy industries and the wealthy traders and merchants concentrated in the large commercial centres. The former, for the most part, became shareholders when their own going concern was converted into a limited company or they took shares in other companies which had a similar partnership background. The latter were prominent in financial and credit companies and in the larger hotel and wagon companies popular in the early 'sixties. It was reported in this boom that " the great body of investors in recent undertakings do not belong to the class of simple investors but to the native trading community ",[21] and again that " successful traders have been leaving trade and going into the money-lending and financing business . . . in proof . . . refer to the lists of Directors of our Banks and Finance companies to see how largely the money-lending community consists of mercantile men ".[22] Both of these groups of investors were wealthy, were not, and were not expected to be, " interested in more than two or three companies "[23] and through their knowledge of the business took an active part in the management of the company. " Shares of high denomination " were effective with these investors " for the

[18] The existence of partly uncalled shares did not by itself of course give a complete guarantee of extra security. That would depend on whether the shareholders could meet the extra calls. It has been suggested that the provision in the 1862 Act obliging a company to keep a register of members open to public inspection was urged by creditors to enable them to obtain a complete view of the credit-worthiness of the company and sufficiency of the contribution. *Report of the Committee on Company Law Amendment* (1945), para. 77.          [19] 1877 *Report, op. cit.* Qu. 1953.

[20] *Journal of the Royal Society of Arts, loc. cit.* 24.

[21] *The Shareholders Guardian* (18 April 1864), 184. The writer did not view this development very favourably and continued: " the inadequacy of the individual requirements of trade is the very motive assigned for the formation of companies ; yet we find the whole industrial community actually denuding themselves in order to promote schemes outside their sphere."

[22] *Credit and its Bearings upon the Crisis of 1866* (1866), 16-17.

[23] *The Investors and Stock Exchange Magazine* (Jan. 1863).

reason principally that when they were placed in good hands the capital was more easily raised." [24]    Individual holdings were large and uncalled share liability did not appear a disadvantage as they had a close control on the direction of the enterprise.    There were other investors in the market; the " simple ", " safe " or " steady and legitimate " [25] investors who had been schooled in Consols, railway and other public utilities, and the frankly speculative investor interested in ready marketability of shares or high dividends.    These investors had other concepts of investment and of the denomination and character of shares, but their influence was small.    The confidence of the " safe " investor in the general limited companies was not great in the 'fifties and 'sixties and in any case the channels for bringing this class of investor into contact with the limited company were largely undeveloped.    The speculative investors, while frequently named in the course of post-mortems on limited companies, at no time, numerically or financially, constituted a significant section of investors.    Consequently, while a few companies in certain industries issued shares of a denomination and character, small and fully paid, that would make an appeal to these classes, the majority of companies catered for the wealthy investor with whom the founders had connections or who was known to the brokers and financial agents in the commercial centres.    The financial methods of these companies matched the needs, pockets and outlook of these investors.

It was the crisis of 1866 which, while confined so far as bankruptcy was concerned to the small speculative and large financial companies, first shook both founders and investors of commercial and industrial companies in their belief in the shares of high denomination with a large uncalled portion.    Heavy calls on unpaid shares were made, sometimes as much as £20 and £30 per share.    Where no calls were made, the shares were completely unrealizable at a time when liquidity was all important.    Henry Pochin, a Manchester merchant and an extensive investor in and director of many cotton and iron and coal companies, told how " the shares in many companies are incapable of being negotiated in any form . . . the bankers won't look at them as security for advances . . . and investors were forced to keep money lying in the bank at low rates of interest against future calls ".[26]    The companies also found that the calling up of unpaid portions of shares was a clumsy and disquieting method of obtaining capital at a time of emergency.

In the discussions on this crisis and at the inquest on the operation of limited companies held by a Select Committee in 1867 the existing methods of company finance still found defenders.    Elaborate reasons were advanced for the existence of uncalled liability and high shares.

[24] Fitz-Wygram, op. cit. 7.
[25] Cf. D. Morier Evans, Speculative Notes and Notes on Speculation (1864), 175, and The Shareholders Guardian, op. cit.
[26] 1867 Report, op. cit. Qus. 2298, 2301, 2311.

But for the first time grave doubts were also expressed whether the close approximation to partnership principles was the correct path for limited companies and their investors. To many shareholders the emergency call-up of unpaid share portions meant that "limited liability" had become "unlimited in fact "[27] and it was suggested that the true operation of limited liability had not been understood.[28] The high share denomination was also criticized. This device was claimed "far from making the company fall into the hands of rich shareholders . . . tends to its falling into the hands of those who have nothing to lose ".[29] Whereas "the smaller the share the larger then becomes the basis of the company. The creditor has a much better security with ten men holding 100 L each than one man holding 1,000 L." [30] And again: " I would much rather have five men at 10 L apiece than one man at 50 L." [31] The accepted basis of security was now claimed to be the source of insecurity; diametrically opposite conclusions being drawn with great facility from the same facts.

Conducted in this manner the debate was inevitably inconclusive and no sudden change in practice took place. But wealthy investors re-examined their concepts of shareholding and ten years later it was reported that wider dispersion of shareholdings, lower denominations and less uncalled liability was appealing to this class of investor.[32] A more important factor in the trend towards smaller shares, fully paid, was the entry of the middle classes into the market for shares of industrial and commercial limited companies. The confidence of these investors in the limited form increased with the evident stability of many of the companies, but heavy investment in one company, high shares and uncalled liability did not appeal to them. Observers were agreed that "high shares tended to keep out the middle classes ",[33] and that " cautious people have avoided investment because of the heavy unpaid liability ".[34] However, the usual investments of these classes, Consols and public utilities, were not expanding as fast as their savings were accumulating and did not yield as high a return as general limited companies.[35] Consequently, with the assistance of bankers, brokers

---

[27] W. Bartlett and H. Chapman, *A Handy Book for Investors* (1869), 172.

[28] *Cf.* 1867 *Report, op. cit.* evidence of W. Newmarch, Qu. 1008, " the public did not really understand what the operation of limited liability was ", and W. Hawes, *Journal of the Royal Society of Arts, loc. cit.* 23, " limited liability was not understood ".

[29] 1867 *Report*, Qu. 681.     [30] *Ibid.* Qu. 539.

[31] *Ibid.* Qu. 995.

[32] *Cf.* evidence of Bonamy Price, 1877 *Report, op. cit.* Qu. 1240, " persons are becoming accustomed to take shares in various companies rather than have a larger sum in one business ", and Qu. 1252: " You find now that nearly the whole amount of the shares has to be paid up within a reasonable time."

[33] *Cf.* Fitz-Wygram, *op. cit.* 14.

[34] *Bowyers Investment Review* (Bristol, April 1869), 159. This was one of the first investment papers outside London and catered for the middle class investor.

[35] For example, David Chadwick spoke for a number of the investors when he wrote in 1871: "We are too much alive to our own interests to place our trust in Consols

and firms like Messrs Chadwick, Adamson, Collier and Co., Joshua Hutchinson and Son of London, and Richardson, Chadbourn and Co., of Manchester, the middle classes began to take shares in limited companies.[36] And to attract the capital of these classes, and to enable them to spread their investments, company promoters offered low share denominations with no uncalled liabilities.

Two other factors influenced the development towards the lower share denomination and smaller uncalled liability. These were the use of uncalled capital in obtaining credit for the company, and the varying needs of companies and varying types of investors in the different industries. Together these factors accounted for the unevenness of the trend towards the small fully paid share.

The need to keep part of the shares uncalled in order to secure the goodwill of creditors became less imperative as the limited form proved its efficiency and stability. Further, estimates of the capital required by limited enterprises became more accurate and a reserve call in case an underestimate had been made was seldom necessary. But offsetting these developments was the new use that had been found for the uncalled capital. In the 'sixties some companies, rather than make a call on the ordinary shareholders for unpaid portions, had issued debentures to obtain additional capital.[37] Where the debentures were secured against fixed assets, the uncalled character of the shares tended to be perpetuated, but when they were secured against the uncalled capital the calling up of shares became virtually impossible. The Mortgage Debenture Act of 1865 had envisaged land companies securing their debentures in the latter fashion, but the legal position for other companies was doubtful.[38] The practice, however, developed and a discussion at the shareholders' meeting of the Bristol Wagon Co. Ltd. in 1870 (wagon companies throughout these years were in the forefront of financial experiments) illustrated the effect of the practice on uncalled share liability. The directors of this company suggested that preference shares should be issued to raise additional capital. A shareholder objected and countered with the proposal that a further call on the unpaid shares should be made. The chairman then pointed out that " as the amount of their

---

alone " (*Chadwicks Investment Circular*, issued monthly by Chadwick, Adamson, Collier and Co. (1871), 30).

[36] The firm of Chadwicks, for example, increased the number of their friends, as they called their clients, from hundreds in the 'sixties to 4,000 in 1874 and 5,000 in 1877. (1867 *Report*, Qu. 869 ; *Chadwicks Investment Circular* (1874), 257 ; 1877 *Report*, *op. cit.* Qu. 1079.)

[37] For example, the *Sixth Annual Report* of Bolckow Vaughan Iron and Steel Co. Ltd., " it is intended to receive loans and debentures in preference to making calls for the prosecution of additional works ". And the answer to the question: " May I ask what advantage it would be to a limited company to issue debentures? "—" simply that it prevents the shareholders being called upon for calls ". (1867 *Report*, *op. cit.* Qu. 1235.)

[38] Cf. 1867 *Report*, *op. cit.* Qu. 1244: " It is a question whether unpaid calls can be made a security for debentures."

shares yet unpaid was security for the debentures they had raised, a call could not be made without being applied to the reduction of the money they had borrowed ".[39] The company issued preference shares. The new companies being formed in the 'seventies and 'eighties found less tortuous methods of securing debentures, but this practice by many older companies restricted the possibilities of fully paid-up shares. At the same time it can be noted, this move to give debenture holders the first claim on uncalled capital in preference to the ordinary creditor was the first of many steps taken in the succeeding half-century to drive the ordinary creditor from the "clover" he had enjoyed when limited liability was first introduced. But that is another story.

The influence of the varying needs of companies and the changing composition of investing groups in different industries can be shown by illustration from some of the main fields of limited company development in these years.

The companies engaged in mining, tin, lead, copper and to some extent coal, had the cost-book system and transferable share tradition behind them. The investors were small local men in Wales, Devon and Cornwall taking shares in mines they knew well. Capital was small and the £1 to £10 share fully paid up suited the company and the investor. The exhaustion of British mines and the development of limited companies engaged in mining enterprises abroad changed radically the character of the companies but not the character of the shares. The overseas ventures were regarded as frankly speculative; few investors would risk much capital, and the average life of the company was short. In these circumstances the £1 fully paid share was popular and effective.

In the cotton industry, Oldham was the chief centre of the limited companies, and the shareholders in these mills consisted chiefly of the machine makers, small business men and traders of Oldham and neighbouring towns, and merchants and brokers in Manchester and to some extent Liverpool.[40] The £5 share denomination suited this miscellaneous group of investors. It was left partly unpaid as security for the large amounts of loan capital which was a feature of almost every one of these companies.[41] Promoters had found that additional money both for trading purposes and extensions of plant was far easier to raise as loan capital, repayable at call, than as share capital, and only in times of

---

[39] Reported in *Bowyers Investment Review* (29 June 1870), 203.

[40] " It is a well-known fact that the successful competitors for executing the work required in a new mill are those who will subscribe for the greatest number of shares ", J.C.A., *Limited Liability and Cotton Spinning* (1886), 9, and *Report of the Royal Commission on the Depression of Trade and Industry* (1886), VIII, Qu. 5276. Also Qu. 5134 lists shareholders, " small shopkeepers, publicans . . . lodge keepers, overlookers ", and Qus. 5507-8 for merchant interest.

[41] The issued share and loan capital of ninety mills in and around Oldham in 1885 amounted to £6,891,103. Of this £3,435,427 was loan capital, or practically 50 per cent. There was £2,807,859 uncalled capital as part security for the loans. (*Report on the Depression*, op. cit. Appendix A, 308. Statement by J. Kidger.)

expensive loan capital, *e.g.* 7 or 8 per cent interest, was it usual to raise further capital by calling on the unpaid portions of shares.[42]

In the shipping industry also an investment tradition had existed before the introduction of general limited liability. The high risk factor had tended to a dispersion of ownership through the 64ths system. In the 'fifties a share in a medium-sized ship under this system cost between £75 and £100 and the owners were chiefly merchants and ship-brokers in the larger sea-ports. This class continued to be the dominant investors in the limited shipping lines and the share denomination continued high. The shares were left one-quarter or one-third unpaid as reserve against liability through accidents. With the improvement in underwriting and insurance this reserve became less necessary, but the share denomination of the larger companies and lines, mainly passenger, tended to remain high. The shareholders in these companies were often all members of one family or drawn from a limited group of wealthy merchants. The "single ship" companies of the 'eighties, mainly cargo and tramp ships, aimed from the start at a much wider group of investors and issued shares at £1 each to be fully paid. According to contemporaries this wider group was reached, and it was reported that " the fact is notorious that even servant girls and small greengrocers all round the country have been induced to put their small savings into tonnage".[43] This dispersed shareholding in small amounts made uncalled liability difficult to operate and a "single ship" line made reserves in case of accidents unnecessary.

The limited companies in the coal, iron and engineering industries were, in the majority of cases, conversions of private mines, furnaces and works, and the shareholders were chiefly the original owners, local men of some standing and a few town investors. The capital and share-holdings were large and the number of investors relatively small. For example, the Bargoed Coal Co. Ltd., issued capital £20,000, shareholders 16 (1868); Palmers Shipbuilding and Iron Co. Ltd., capital £800,000, shareholders 350 (1868); Ebbw Vale Coal and Iron Co. Ltd., capital £2,200,000, shareholders 596 (1868); and Vickers Sons and Co. Ltd., capital £500,000, shareholders 25 (1875). The shares were taken as long-term investments and high denomination presented no obstacles to this class of investor. A large proportion of the shares was left uncalled, in some cases to act as security for loans, in others owing to mistakes in the valuation of the property when the company was formed.[44] The profits made by these companies, particularly between

---

[42] Cf. *Co-operative Wholesale Society Annual* (1883), 166. Many companies called up shares in preference to loans at high rates of interest, 1877-80.

[43] *Report on the Depression*, op. cit. Qu. 11217.

[44] Chadwick reported that in the case of companies such as Bolckow Vaughan, Palmers Shipbuilding and Ebbw Vale, the company was registered before the final report of the valuers had been made available, consequently the nominal capitals were often very high with shares largely unpaid. (1867 *Report.* op. cit. Qu. 857.)

1871 and 1875, attracted attention, and smaller companies were formed
with lower share denomination to attract a wider group of shareholders,
but the large semi-private company continued to dominate these
industries until the late 'eighties.

Banking, finance, insurance and land companies were particularly
influenced by the current view as to what constituted security and
stability in a limited company. While opinion held that high shares
meant security, the companies issued high shares. When opinion
changed, banks issued £25 and £10 shares and insurance companies in
the 'eighties shares as low as £1, but the uncalled character of the share
tended to remain. For banks and insurance companies the uncalled
capital was vital as reserve liability. In the finance and trust companies
the unpaid portion of the shares was used directly as a means of obtaining loans. Strong criticism, not entirely justified, was directed at "a
certain class of company, the main purpose of whose existence is to
borrow on the faith of their uncalled capital and to employ the money
so borrowed in trade or in making loans in the colonies and elsewhere ".[45] These factors, rather than any particular characteristics of
the investors, who were concentrated mainly in London, determined the
share issue of the finance group of companies.

By the 'eighties the trend towards the small fully paid-up share was
being established. The desire of the wealthy investor to spread his
investments and to remove " unlimited liability in fact " by paying up
more per share, and the introduction into the investment market for
limited companies of the " safe " investor interested in the security of
his capital and the marketability of his shares were factors hastening
this trend. The use of the uncalled portion of the share for raising
loans and the varied composition of investing classes and needs of
companies in different industries were factors which delayed and
rendered the operation of this trend uneven. The denomination and
character of the shares to be issued were still matters to be considered
by a new company in the 'eighties, but they had lost the position of key
importance that they held in the 'sixties.[46] A small share fully paid
was beginning to suit the majority of the companies and their investors.
The trend had not been foreseen by the originators of limited liability.
The chairman of the Institute of Bankers referred in 1884 to their dis-
appointment as they had hoped " that limited liability would be adopted
with shares of some hundreds or thousands of pounds instead of in
shares of a shilling or a pound, not for the purpose of creating capital
for speculative purposes but to enable persons to put their money into

[45] *The Accountant* (1888), 405. Report of speech by G. A. Jamieson before the
British Association.
[46] *Cf.* A. Packer, *How the Public are Plundered* (1878), 18, still refers to the use of
different share denominations to attract different types of investors, £20 to £50 for the
" monied " classes and £1 for the " industrial classes ".

well-established businesses in considerable sums without being involved in unlimited liability ".[47]    But to measure every new development in company finance by the yardstick of the Bankruptcy Court can warp judgement.   Fraud and failure accompanied both high and low shares, unpaid and fully paid.   What the originators of limited liability failed to foresee was not the increasing waywardness of economic society but the changing needs of that society.   These needs in the succeeding thirty years led to an even greater divergence between the hopes of the founders and company practice.   The remaining functions performed by variations in the denomination and character of the shares (security for loans and credit and differentiation between types of investors) were outmoded by the extensive use of founders' and preference shares and debenture stock; the overwhelming majority of investors in public companies lost all interest in, and power to control, the direction of the enterprises; and the private partnership was replaced in almost every sphere by the private limited liability company.   The development of the limited company responded to the needs of industry and trade rather than to the hopes of the founders or the warnings of Select Committees and Royal Commissions.

[47] *Journal of the Institute of Bankers*, V (1884), 13.

# THE COMING OF GENERAL LIMITED LIABILITY [1]

## H. A. SHANNON

JOINT-STOCK enterprise for trading purposes has existed in England from at least 1553, and Dr Scott has given us its history down to 1720.   But that history, and joint-stock history for more than the succeeding century, is the history of particular companies and not of a general movement.   The general movement could not take place until certain economic and legal changes had been effected.   The economic changes were the great changes in industry, commerce and transport of the second half of the eighteenth century through which the field of economic activities and the scale of individual operations were potentially enlarged.   The legal change was the substitution of the law of corporations for the law of partnership in company affairs.   Investors could then invest safely and the full exploitation of the economic changes became possible.   Law and economics were mutually interacting.   But before the legal changes of 1844 and 1855, English [2] law virtually prohibited joint-stock enterprise for ordinary trading and manufacturing purposes.

The earlier companies obtained their legal constitution either by royal charter granted under common law, or by a royal charter granted under statute, or by a special Act of Parliament, and were legal corporations.   Other trading associations remained simple partnerships.   Now the law of corporations was (and is) very different from the law of partnership, conferring many valuable privileges absent in the latter.   A corporation was a distinct legal *persona* and its own assets were, under common law, the only security for its debts.   A member, having paid his capital, had no further liability.   A corporation had perpetual succession, not being dissolved by changes in its membership.   It could act in law as a single body, in particular suing and being sued in its corporate name.   None of this was true of partnerships.   The superior form of " corporation " could be obtained only through formal application for an act or charter, a method expensive, cumbersome in procedure and uncertain of success.   Point by point the law was changed until at

---

[1] This account of the evolution of the limited company and its law in the first half of the nineteenth century is taken mainly from official material. I hope to deal both with the outside sources and with some early company statistics on another occasion.

[2] Scotch law was different and better. See R. R. C. on *Mercantile Law, 1854-55,* XVIII, 754 *et. seq.*

last an association could by mere registration have itself incorporated as a matter of right.

## (i) *The Bubble Act of 1720*

The possibility of this development coming a century earlier, even if somewhat in advance of economic progress, had been checked by the Bubble Act of 1720.[3] In the speculative mania of that time, "the pernicious art of stock-jobbing" had been largely practised at the public's expense. Governmental misdeeds, financial and moral, added to the public distress. To allay the popular clamour and to divert the public's attention, the Government passed the famous Bubble Act. Unincorporated joint-stock enterprise was prohibited under very heavy penalties. The disasters of the time probably checked of themselves any tendency of the company-form to spread generally and were a practical demonstration of its possible defects. Fifty years afterwards a theoretical demonstration of its effective field was given by Adam Smith.[4] The company-form of enterprise was in eclipse.

The Act had two parts. The first authorised special charters of incorporation to two new joint-stock companies (the London Assurance and the Royal Exchange companies). The second prohibited the creation of all unincorporated companies, but left unaffected all ordinary partnerships (except in marine insurance) "in such manner as hath hitherto usually and may be legally done". No clear definition of a company was given. The Act related that "several undertakings . . . have . . . been publicly contrived and practised. . . which manifestly tend to the common grievance and inconvenience of great numbers of your Majesty's subjects in their trade or commerce and other their affairs". Four special indicia of such undertakings were added: first, the contrivers "do presume . . . to open books for public subscription"; second, "that the said undertakers . . . have presumed to act as if they were corporate bodies"; third, "and have pretended to make their shares . . . transferable . . . without any legal authority"; and fourth, they pretended to act under obsolete charters or extended a charter beyond its true scope. The Act declared illegal and void "all and every the undertakings described . . . and all other public undertakings or attempts tending to the common grievance, prejudice and inconvenience of your Majesty's subjects or great numbers of them in their trade, commerce or other lawful affairs", together with "all . . . matters and things whatever for furthering, countenancing or proceeding in any such undertaking or attempt". Offenders were liable to two sets of punishments: first, "all such fines, penalties and punishments" prescribed by common and by statute law for such "common and public

---

[3] 6 Geo. I. c. 18 (1719), in force from June 1720.
[4] *Wealth of Nations*, bk. V, chap. i, iii.

nuisances " as companies were declared to be ; and second, forfeiture of all lands, goods and chattels and imprisonment for life under a præmunire.

This Act, in regulating a commercial matter, outlined the offence in almost unintelligible language and attached to it the gravest penalty known to English law. It seemed phrased to stultify itself. And except for a minor prosecution in 1723,[5] it remained a dead letter until 1808. Then it was revived in an action [6] apparently of trade or personal animus which was dismissed as a kind of first offence under the Act. But Lord Ellenborough, the judge, in declaring the Bubble Act still operative, hoped that the " general notoriety " given by the action to the Act would prevent any further projects. Within a few years (1808-12) five other actions took place, all petty except one. In this [7] Ellenborough decided that a company with beneficial objects was legal though it might have some of the indicia of illegality given in the Act. No more actions followed until 1825, when Lord Eldon, in a case [8] concerned with the very speculative Real del Monte Mining Company, questioned Ellenborough's decision and reopened the whole question of the illegality of companies. But by that time there were in existence unincorporated companies of standing with capital variously given [9] as £160 million and £200 million.[10] When the Bubble Act threw doubt on their legality it was repealed. Even trained lawyers had been unable to make much of it.[11] As has been shown, the judges could draw no clear principles from it and the decisions were conflicting.[12] In 1825 the Attorney-General declared that " it appears to be agreed on all hands that its meaning and effect are altogether unintelligible ".[13] The Lord Chancellor, Lord

[5] *King* v. *Cawood* (1723), 2 Ld. Raymond 1361. The Act was also referred to in deciding by-laws of the Hudson Bay Company in 1727.

[6] *King* v. *Dodd* (1808), 9 East 516. This was a case brought through a private relator. There was no accusation of fraud and the relator subscribed merely to bring the action.

[7] *King* v. *Webb* (1811), 14 East 406. This case was about a bakery with 2,500 members. The jury found in point of fact that the company was beneficial to the public but prejudicial to the bakers, and the point of law contained in " common grievance " was referred to the higher court for decision, as above.

[8] *Kinder* v. *Taylor* (1825) 3 L. J. Ch. 68.

[9] *Hansard* (1825), XII, 1279 and 1194 (Moore and Lauderdale).

[10] Moore speaks as though the capital were paid-up. But English, in his *Complete View of . . . Joint Stock Companies* (1825), gives the nominal capital of all companies existing in 1826 as some £150,000,000, and the " amount advanced " as some £49,000,000. By amount advanced he means total possible calls. But there are errors in his figures, *e.g.* in his total of the 1824 companies. I hope to deal with the statistical side on a later occasion.

[11] George, *A View of the Existing Law affecting Unincorporated Companies* (1825), declared it was " a string of non-sequiturs from first to last ", p. 53. George suggests that the Act became moribund because it had so effectively crushed companies out (p. 38), but the Attorney-General at the time of the repeal thought differently (*Hansard* (1825), XIII, 1019).

[12] Ellenborough was generally favourable to companies, Eldon quite antagonistic.

[13] *Hansard* (1825), XIII, 1019.

Eldon, declared that "the statute . . . was very ill-drawn and that it is not certain what was or was not intended to be settled ".[14]

But the Act, while prohibiting companies in this unintelligible fashion, left partnerships unaffected. The difficulties of setting up a large joint-stock enterprise under the law of partnership were set out as the leading reasons in all petitions for incorporation.[15]   They were the unlimited liability attaching to each member and the almost utter impossibility of suing and being sued.   Probably here, in creating a greater reluctance to grant charters of incorporations, the Act had its greatest influence against the joint-stock form.   To this law of partnership we must now turn.

## (ii) The English Law of Partnership

This law was specially reported on in 1837 "with regard to the difficulties which exist in suing and being sued where partners are numerous", and "whether it would be expedient to introduce a law authorising persons to become partners with a limited liability ".[16]   The evils set out in the old petitions for incorporation were being more generally felt.

The English law of partnership had been derived from the common law, the civil law and the law merchant. It was a case-law,[17] judgemade.   It was based on the conception of partnership, largely justified by the prevailing practice, as the business association of a few persons intimately known to one another and usually working together.   Each partner could then be fairly regarded as the full accredited agent of the others.   As a sharer in the profits, each could be regarded as fully liable for the losses.   And the rule had been developed for the better protection of creditors, that this liability extended to all his private property, " to his last shilling and acre ".   The exploitation of the new economic changes, however, often required a larger capital than a few individuals

[14] In *Kinder* v. *Taylor* (1825).

[15] See (*House of Commons Journals*) the petitions of the Winchelsea Cambrick and Lawn Manufactory, 1764 ; British Cast Plate Glass Company, 1733 ; Cotton and Linen Manufactory, 1779 (unsuccessful) ;  Northumberland Fishing Society, 1789 ;  Globe Insurance Company, 1799 ; London Flour Company, 1800.   These petitions sometimes make interesting reading ; *e.g.* in the second petition of the Cast Plate Glass Company (*House of Commons Journals*, XXXIX (1784), 940) is the following passage: " the petitioners have expended upwards of £100,000 without receiving the smallest dividend, owing to the variety of circumstances to which an infant manufactory upon an entire new plan must naturally be liable "—a passage interesting for the huge amount sunk in a new invention, with authenticating details, and for the earliness of its infant industry argument.   Again, the Globe Insurance Company got its Act but was refused its charter under it.   See Clifford, *Private Bill Legislation*, II, 617.

[16] 1837, XLIV (503).   It was prepared by H. Bellenden Ker, an eminent lawyer, on the instruction of the President of the Board of Trade, C. P. Thomson (see below). Ker consulted business men and economists like Tooke, Baring and Senior.

On its second term of reference see below, section (vi).

[17] Collyer, *On Partnership* (1832), refers to over 1,000 cases.

24

could raise or would risk. A different kind of association grew up, a business union with numerous members, not well known to one another, each contributing a little capital, and leaving the management in the hands of a few directors or officers. This was the unincorporated company. But the law of partnership was being applied to it without modification, and not until about 1870,[18] when companies had acquired full legal recognition, did the Courts perceive fully the essential differences between simple partnerships and unincorporated companies. The strong conservatism of the legal profession,[19] the example of a great Lord Chancellor,[20] the lingering influence of the moribund Bubble Act and its suggestion of common law prohibition,[21] the indifference of the legislature,[22] the relative novelty of the economic changes, the conservatism of many business men, the relatively small number of companies in existence—all combined to check the correction of an unsuitable body of law.[23] Ker in 1837 could report that "there was no branch of the law which is so imperfect as that relating to partnership", that its application to companies "amounted to an absolute denial of justice", and he could complain justly that the judges had done nothing to adapt it to the changing conditions.

The principal evils were three in number: first, in legal proceedings with third parties; second, in legal proceedings within the partnership; and third, in determining the partnership itself.

A third party in taking action against a partnership had to join the full and precise names of all the partners, with their description. Misjoinder or non-joinder, error or omission, no matter how arising, would invalidate the action and compel it to be reassumed corrected.[24] Without a public register of partners or any other public means of finding the necessary particulars, this technical requirement of procedure amounted by its practical impossibility to an absolute denial of justice against the creditors of a company. Given a stout technical resistance by the company, Senior's statement was true: "abatements follow which make the suit interminable". A company might maintain a partner abroad, e.g. Ireland, out of the jurisdiction of the Court, and so nullify the action.

---

[18] In re The Agriculturist Cattle Insurance Company, L. R. 5 ch. 725.

[19] See Cole's communication in the Report on Partnership at p. 76.

[20] One witness said: "The principle on which Lord Eldon appears to have proceeded . . . was that of allowing as many obstacles and difficulties as possible to be thrown in the way of unincorporated companies, evidently with a view to destroying them indirectly." Ibid. 66.

[21] The Act itself until at least 1825 and its suggestion until 1843.

[22] The Attorney-General thought "no regulation of companies was necessary". Hansard (1825), XIII, 1019.

[23] Was the state of the public finances another factor? Eldon seemed to think that the competition of companies with the Government funds might make them illegal on that ground of public policy. See the long and interesting report in George, op. cit. 47-8. Compare the war-time restrictions on capital investments.

[24] In some cases this right of several pleas in abatement was refused.

Even if, by a lucky chance, the action were maintained successfully, the technical difficulties in its execution were often insuperable.[25]

A company in taking action against a third party had its own difficulties in supplying the necessary particulars.    George [26] gives an imaginary example of a company with 2,000 members, which had twenty-five sales to a third party and 300 changes of membership in the same period.    As only those actually partners at the time of each sale could sue for it, and as with 300 transfers, some were sure to fall in between consecutive sales, the company would probably have to undertake twenty-five different actions each with its own list of 2,000 partners, fully named and described, to recover the series of sales.

Every witness concurred with Ker's condemnation of this rule of law and argued for the right of a large partnership to have a corporate or quasi-corporate name in legal proceedings.[27]

The second great defect of the law arose from the absence of any adequate remedies between the partners themselves.    Under a fairly well-established rule the Courts were not likely to interfere in any internal dispute unless at the same time ordering a dissolution.    One dissatisfied member could often destroy a company by a vexatious suit. Members with a genuine grievance had to decide if it was worth wrecking the company to have it remedied.    And where the dispute was one of account, even the dissolution of the company was not likely to afford an equitable decision.    An example will give the point vividly.[28]    " Intricate accounts are seldom understood by lawyers and can never be made clear to the judges. . . . Such questions . . . are generally very imperfectly decided, the decision turning generally on some legal technicalities and very seldom on the merits of the case.    I can state as an instance . . . some very intricate West India accounts which were upwards of thirty years in the Court of Chancery, and ultimately without a chance of the very complicated accounts . . . being made intelligible to the Court . . . and after thirty years the parties came to an agreement that they would refer the matter to Mr John Smith and myself."    Again, where [29] a shareholder sued fourteen directors it was held that each director, and if necessary each of the 300 shareholders, had the right of separate defence.    Again, if a man were a member of two companies,

[25] See the description in George, *op. cit.* 23-5.    On a collateral point he says :   " But the when, the where and the how . . . open such a prospect that the writer has not the courage . . . to contemplate it for a minute."    See also R. S. C. on *Joint Stock Companies*, 1844, VII (119), 75.                                [26] *Op. cit.* 19 ff.

[27] One witness said :   " Improper combinations by operatives . . . should not be encouraged.    If operatives were to form partnerships or associations by small and numerous contributions, the end might be to drive capitalists from their manufactories." *Report on Partnership*, 70.

[28] Evidence of Lord Ashburton, ex-President of the Board of Trade and a member of the great Baring family of bankers.  *Report*, 45.

[29] *Van Sandau* v. *Moore* (1825).    Eldon was the judge.    Moore, a company promoter, subsequently moved for the repeal of the Bubble Act.

these could not sue each other, for the same person could not be both plaintiff and defendant. Arbitration clauses were ineffective, for the Courts, if arbitration were refused, would deal with the dispute themselves.

The third defect related to the rule "that any person taking an interest in the profits became liable as a partner", with absolutely unlimited liability. It did not matter at all that the person was completely unknown to the creditors or did not share in the management. But no one knew precisely what was "taking an interest in profits". Yet the majority of opinions expressed to Ker was against any formal definition, for the difficulty was inherent in the nature of partnership. Many a partner would try to masquerade as a creditor, and it was thought best to let each case be decided on its own merits. Some very nice cases occurred.[30]

With this as the state of the law, English firms must have been small partnerships. Large partnerships simply could not carry on. Until the law was changed, full economic development was impossible. Yet this report and evidence, with all its cogency of argument, brought about only the Chartered Companies Act of 1837.[31] For a reasonably complete digest of partnership law the mercantile community had to wait until the Partnership Act of 1890. For an improvement in procedure it had to wait until the Judicature Acts of 1873-5. By that time joint-stock company law had been developed on different lines, the lines of corporations. Before returning to a consideration of the statute law which by slow degrees modified the common law, we may conclude in the words of Collyer[32] that "the principles of the law of partnership afford a field for the continual exercise of the most distinguished talents in our courts both of law and of equity".

### (iii) *Special Private Acts for Suing Powers*

To overcome some of these difficulties of the common law, many unincorporated companies, though lying within the shadow of illegality cast by the Bubble Act, had obtained special private Acts empowering them to sue and be sued in the name of an officer. This type of Act may be regarded as a first step towards modern company law.

---

[30] *E.g.* it was not clear if insurers who received back a bonus on their premiums became *ipso facto* partners with unlimited liability, though the insurance company might by private Act or special contract be a limited company. *Report*, 48 and 60.

[31] On this Act see below, section (iv). Ker later expressed himself: "Since making my Report I was so mortified that none of the points except that imperfect measure [this Act] had been taken up that . . . I have thought little on the subject." R. S. C. on *Joint Stock Companies* (1844), VII (119), 197. The defects, *e.g.* existing companies were not under the Act, maintained the practice of applying for private Acts for suing and other powers, against the desire of the Board of Trade. *Ibid.* 191.

[32] *On Partnership* (1832), preface.

Some 100 of them were passed between 1801 and 1844, some being passed before the Repeal of the Bubble Act.[33] Some sixty insurance companies and forty other companies had them before the Registration Act of 1844. These Acts are of double importance. First, it was in them that the Lords with legal experience, experts in commercial pathology, worked out several rules and safeguards that were later to be embodied in the general company law. Second, they broke the bundle of corporate rights, a bundle that was to be further loosened by the Acts of 1825, 1834 and 1837. Also the absorption of parliamentary time involved was leading up to the general Act of 1844 and (with the time involved with other private company Acts) to the Companies Clauses Act of 1845.

Their evolution was over by 1826.[34] At first, in arranging for a nominal representative, the Acts did not clearly provide that the company and its members were the parties really liable. When this was done, no provisions were made for a register of partners. When this was brought in, the register contained only the name of partners at the time of the Act. The next step was to ensure registrations of transfers and to impose some continuing liability on the transferrer. Finally, provisions were made for the internal regulation of the partnership. Here we have the beginnings of company publicity, shareholders' registers, A and B contributory lists for determining the liability of present and past members, Table A for regulating the internal affairs of the company, and, faintly, the separate identity of the company.[35]

Even this power of quasi-corporate suing power was not always granted easily, and Ker's general Bill for enabling companies to get that power by mere registration, though prepared in accordance with official directions, was ignored until 1844.

### (iv) The Repeal of the Bubble Act, 1825, and the Acts of 1834 and 1837

In 1825 the desirability of the repeal of the Bubble Act was raised by a company promoter in Parliament,[36] and in June the Attorney-General introduced the repealing Bill. The grounds were both legal and economic. The Bubble Act was unintelligible and extreme, and "still more strongly" many laudable companies were suffering from it.[37]

---

[33] See *Index to Local and Private Acts* (1801-99), 782 *et seq.* Supplementary Acts are not included in the above figure.

[34] See Lord Eldon's account in the *Report on Partnership*, 6-7.

[35] Most of these provisions were embodied in a general banking statute of 1826 (7 Geo. IV, c. 46), and the desirability of adapting this Act to all companies was urged by all Ker's witnesses.

[36] Moore, in *Hansard* (1825), XII, 1279 *et seq.* He was later accused of bubble promotions in *Hansard* (1828), XVIII, 651.

[37] The Attorney-General said, on the legal points: "that the offenders should incur the heaviest penalties for committing an offence against an unintelligible Act." *Hansard*

The Repealing Act [38] fell into two parts. The first repealed the prohibitory section of the Bubble Act, and the second conferred greater power on the Crown in granting incorporating charters. No positive regulation was proposed. The absence of any actions under the Bubble Act for so long a period was deemed to show that no necessity for such regulation existed,[39] and any regulation would be "at once difficult, unwise and impolitic". The Bill was passed with very little debate. Huskisson alone argued for something more positive.

Unincorporated companies were left to the common law, where Eldon still thought them illegal. This tendency continued until the 'forties,[40] but it has now passed away, without, however, any authoritative decision on the point.[41]

Section two of the Repealing Act, giving extra powers to the Crown, declared that an incorporating charter could prescribe individual liability on the members. Previously, this liability was by common law quite limited. The authorities had therefore "considerable reluctance" in advising the Crown to grant charters, and the new power was needed to facilitate the granting of charters. Companies *inter alia* might then obtain a corporate name, though with a regulated liability. At first sight this section, with its prescribed degree of liability instead of the older limited liability, appears far from being a step towards general limited liability. But for the first time in a general Act the bundle of common law rights possessed by a corporation, unbreakable if kept whole, was loosened; and with one right broken separately the others were to follow, until a new statutory bundle was made up. And in exercising their discretionary powers the "advisers of the Crown" were open to sharp criticism.[42]

The power of the Crown was further increased by the Trading Companies Act of 1843,[43] which was passed without debate though amended by the Commons and the Lords.[44] It was "to enable his Majesty to invest trading and other companies with the powers necessary

---

(1825), XIII, 1019; and on the economic points, "joint-stock companies . . . formed for the most useful and laudable purposes . . . advantageous to the public . . . were said to be illegal . . . and it was highly expedient to repeal part of the existing law". *Ibid.*

[38] 6 Geo. IV, c. 91.

[39] The Attorney-General added: "It could not be objected to this view . . . that it [the Bubble Act] had not been exercised, because it had accomplished the objects for which it was passed, because this [the accomplishment] had been done before and companies were established shortly afterwards which had continued ever since." *Hansard* (1825), XIII, 1020.

[40] See *Garrard* v. *Hardey* (1843), 5 Man. and Gr. 471.

[41] Lindley, *On Companies* (1902), thinks them legal.

[42] See below, section (vi).          [43] 4 & 5 Will. IV, c. 94.

[44] *House of Commons Journals* (1834), LXXXIX, 532 and 598. The Lord's amendments on the charter terms followed the safeguards brought into the private Acts for suing power.

for the due conduct of their affairs and for the security of the rights and interests of their creditors ". Its rehearsal stated that companies were being formed which it would be inexpedient to incorporate either in the full common law sense or in the truncated sense of the 1825 Act, and yet which it would be expedient " to endow with some of the privileges of incorporation ". The special privilege named and intended was, not the higher privilege of a corporate name, but that of suing and being sued through officers.

The Crown could then, on special application and approval, create an association that at common law was neither a partnership nor a corporation. But the Courts construed the grants very strictly and the Acts were found ineffectual by 1837. The then President of the Board of Trade [45] was interested in financial and legal reform and knew from business experience the better law on the Continent. He had brought in the 1834 Act. During the speculative outburst in 1836 he had become further interested in companies and had a record kept of the new formations. While critical of extensions of the company-form to objects he thought more fit for individual enterprise, he saw the good and the bad and he was anxious that there should not be a wholesale condemnation.[46] Here no doubt we have the origin of the Report on Partnership.

The Report's immediate effect, however, was only the passing of the Chartered Companies Act of 1837,[47] "an Act for the better enabling Her Majesty to confer certain powers and immunities on trading and other companies ". The very title showed a considerable advance. The Act repealed section two of the Bubble Act Repeal and all of the Trading Companies Act, only to re-enact them with modifications and additions. Corporate rights were again conferrable on unincorporated companies, especially the suing rights and regulated liability of individual members. The limiting clause ran : "to such extent only per share as shall be declared and limited"[48]—the first mention of limitation by shares. A member's liability ceased immediately on an official return of his transfer, and not after three years as under the 1834 Act. The rights of members against the company were improved. On all points of publicity and procedure there was marked advance. Companies under it became quasi-corporations.[49]

It was then possible for the President of the Board of Trade to open or shut the floodgates of general limited liability. A charter still required special application and a discretionary judgement. Practice

[45] C. P. Thomson. See the *Dictionary of National Biography*, XIX, 716. He had been a director in several of the 1825 companies.

[46] *Hansard* (1836), XXXIII, 688 *et seq.*     [47] 1 Vict., c. 73.

[48] In at least one company the liability was double the subscribed capital. See (1854), LXV (299), 595—a special return of the grants.

[49] They are treated under that heading in Halsbury's *Laws of England*, V, 751.

varied under different Presidents,[50] but consent was never too freely given. Charters conferring suing powers were difficult to obtain, and charters conferring limited liability were seldom granted at all.[51] The Board of Trade in 1834 had declared [52] that the new powers, even the suing powers, would not be conferred indiscriminately so long at least as the partnership law remained unchanged,[53] for unfair competition might ensue. They might be conferred where the nature and objects of the company justified their grant on grounds of public policy. The examples given were: first, where the object was hazardous and deterrent to small partnerships, as in mining; second, where the capital was beyond the resources of a few individuals, as in railways; third, where extended responsibility was desirable, as in insurance; and where a numerous membership was necessary, as in literary societies. These general principles were still applied in 1850 [54] and later. The expense of obtaining a charter remained quite high.

Dissatisfaction with the Board's policy was rising in the 'fifties,[55] and when the dissatisfaction with the law of partnership came to a head in 1854, at least in the matter of its unlimited liability, the Board seemed glad of an excuse to stop. Companies had then the right to suing powers by mere registration, and their next step was to have limited liability. We must therefore retrace our steps to the new Registration Act.

## (v) *The Registration Act of 1844*

Within four years from Ker's ignored recommendation for the registration of partnerships " merely to bring them within the effectual reach of the law ", parliamentary attention was drawn to some notorious frauds quite outside that reach. In 1841 a Committee was set up " to inquire into the state of the law respecting joint-stock companies (banking companies excepted), with a view to the prevention of fraud ",[56] but it seems only to have collected three days' evidence. Revived in 1843, in finally reported in 1844, under the chairmanship of Gladstone.[57]

Considerable time was devoted to the cases of fraudulent practice which started the inquiry. Much of the evidence is here irrelevant, but it is interesting to note that the Committee classified bubble companies [58] into those naturally unsound, those unsound through bad management, and those clearly fraudulent. For the first nothing could

---

[50] R. S. C. on *Savings of the Middle and Working Classes* (1850), XIX (508), 200.
[51] At least in domestic trades. *Ibid.* 201.
[52] See R. S. C. on *Joint Stock Companies* (1844), VIII (119), 333.
[53] This would suggest that Thomson was dissatisfied with it in 1834.
[54] R. S. C. on *Savings of the Middle and Working Classes*, 200.
[55] See below, section (vi).                    [56] *Hansard* (1841), LVII, 842.
[57] Report 119 in 1844, VII. It is called a " first report ", but no more appeared, though one on insurance companies seemed half promised.
[58] The phrase was still used.

be done, and for the others the great remedy was publicity.[59] Some witnesses, however, had not too much faith in mere enlightened self-interest.[60] The Committee had their own doubts too, but felt, " by the proposed plan of registration trustworthy evidence for any further necessary action would be obtained ".[61]

On the law of partnership the Committee accepted Ker's report [62] in its entirety. The concocters of the frauds were " practically unamenable to any judicature, civil or criminal ". The lessons learnt in railway legislation, from the darker side of railway promotions, and from enlarged experience of scrip-jobbing in railway companies, had also much influence.[63] Early railway experiences, like the experience under private bills for suing powers, have passed into company law.

The Board of Trade had found their discretionary power, even in giving suing rights, under the Act of 1837 extremely irksome and beyond their competence.[64] As a result of this and of the Report in 1844, the Registration Act of 1844 [65] was passed, " an Act for the registration, incorporation and regulation of joint-stock companies " a further improvement in title. It did not apply, and did not much need to be applied, to Scotland. With it and beyond Ker's recommendation came the first Winding-Up Act.[66] The Registration Act declared it was expedient to provide for the due registration of companies, and the Winding-Up Act declared it was expedient to extend the remedies of their creditors and to provide for the discovery of abuses and the causes of failures.

A joint-stock company was defined as a commercial partnership with more than twenty-five members or with a capital divided into freely transferable shares. Insurance companies [67] (and some friendly societies) were included as such without test of membership or transferability, but banking companies were excluded as being under other Acts.[68] All such companies were compelled to register under fines.

[59] " Publication of the directors, of the shareholders, of the deed of settlement, of the amount of capital and whether subscribed or not, nominal or real, would baffle every case of fraud which has come under the notice of your Committee. . . . Periodical accounts, if honestly made and fairly audited, cannot fail to excite attention to the real state of the company." *Report*, v.

[60] " Parties who become shareholders in very many cases never think of reading the deed of settlement, and indeed are not often competent to understand it." *Ibid.* 11.

[61] *Ibid.* p. vi. Ironically enough their report was used in 1856 as a reason for removing all official checks. See below, section (vi).

[62] But in 1844 Ker had become converted to Eldon's doctrines of restriction or prohibition of companies. *Ibid.* 185 *et seq.*

[63] See the long and valuable evidence of Duncan, *ibid.* 162 and 208 *et seq.* and of Parkes, 225 *et seq.* Both had legal experience with railways.

[64] See Gladstone's frank statement in *Hansard* (1844), LXXVI, 276.

[65] 7 & 8 Vict., c. 110.                    [66] *Ibid.* c. 111.

[67] Insurance frauds had been particularly scandalous.

[68] Their old right to suing powers by mere registration was repealed at the time it was given to companies generally. They had now to make special application. See 7 & 8 Vict., c. 113.

The Act partially applied to existing companies, including parliamentary companies, in order to have complete records.

The intention of the Acts was to safeguard companies, shareholders and creditors. A company, before doing anything public, had, through its promoters, to register with the Registrar of Joint Stock Companies, its name and objects together with their names, addresses and descriptions. It then received "provisional registration", and the promoters could assume its name, accept allotments limited to 10s. per cent, and contract for necessaries, but could not trade. Prospectuses had to be registered together with any changes. Returns of officers, provisional committee-men (i.e. directors), subscribers, etc., had to be made. Directors had to consent in writing to their appointment and take one share, that is, assume legal liability.

For "complete registration", other particulars were required. Of special importance was the execution of a deed of settlement. Members were called "subscribers" until they signed this deed, when they were called "shareholders". The deed to be recognised required the signatures of at least one-fourth of the subscribers and covering at least one-fourth of the shares. This is not quite the same thing as "minimum subscription" which Ker had anticipated in his discussion, that "a certain part of the capital should be paid up", for this refers to numbers of shares and not to value of capital subscribed for. As a double hurdle its effect can be seen in the early statistics.[69] The deed had to provide for internal regulation along lines given in the Act. It was the duty of the Registrar to reject any deeds which were incomplete or repugnant to the Act or to the law generally.[70] This is not laissez-faire but administrative or quasi-administrative law, and all in 1844. Model rules were given to investors to safeguard them from their own incompetence in the liberty of contract, and in addition a watch-dog to see they were adopted. The Registrar was appointed eleven years after the first factory inspector. An analogous provision had been enacted in 1829 for the better protection of members of friendly societies,[71] but there is a wide gap between members of a joint-stock company and members of a friendly society. Other returns of membership, transfers, etc., were also required periodically. Directors were prohibited from dealing in the company's shares and from certain contractings with it, unless notice was given. Books of accounts, audit, balance sheets, and a right of inspection were statutorily provided for.

On complete registration the company was incorporated by name for the objects registered. Members had the unlimited liability of a simple

[69] But also compare the criticisms given lower in this section.

[70] On this point see below, section (vi), and Economica, June 1930.

[71] 10 Geo. IV, c. 56. One witness suggested that some of its provisions would be valuable in a joint-stock Act. Report, 233.

partnership, and liability continued for three years after a transfer of interest.

But there had been dishonest investors as well as promoters, and these practised "scrip-jobbing". Roughly, they became subscribers with a title to shares called "scrip". They would sell this for what premium it would fetch and leave the transferees to become the shareholders. If no premium was forthcoming, they would not proceed further, and not having signed the deed (which probably because of them could not be completed) they were free from legal obligation. Companies often stuck fast at this stage of having issued scrip-receipts for the first deposit, and a call could not be obtained. Months might pass before the deed could be completed. The company would die a natural death from lack of funds or the promoters be compelled to return the deposit money, since a start could not be made.[72] Such dealings in scrip were prohibited until registration had been completed and the deed signed by the transferrer.

But the whole Act was very defective on its penal side. Failure to make the enumerated returns was punishable by fines; false statements in them were apparently misdemeanours. But it was no one's duty to prosecute; action was left to the common informer.[73] The continued registration of prospectuses was repealed in 1847 without any advice whatever to the Registrar.[74] Companies could therefore be formed with objects quite different from those registered and no one could easily trace the steps in the changes. The important proviso for ensuring *bona fide* operation that required the deed to be signed by one-fourth of the shareholders holding one-fourth of the shares was frequently evaded by false signatures or signatures bought at 1s. a time.[75] Or a small capital would be registered and then subsequently by special resolution it would be increased.[76] The balance-sheets were often deliberatively manufactured "for the return".[77] Though balancing, they contained arithmetical errors.[78] Registration itself was frequently ignored.[79] Scrips were dealt in.[80] Yet "an immense mass of benefit" resulted to the public from the Act.[81]

Companies were now legally recognised and regulated. The first great requirement, the corporate suing capacity of a trading association,

---

[72] See the interesting evidence of Duncan, *ibid.* 164 *et seq.*
[73] R. S. C. on *Assurance Associations* (1852-3), XXI, (965), 4.
[74] "When the Amendment Act was passed, I knew nothing of the Act . . . nothing of any stipulation in it ; I never had a word said to me upon the subject of it ; I never saw it or heard of it until the Act was actually passed and I sent for a copy of it." *Ibid.* 13. The Act was 10 & 11 Vict., c. 78. The old provisions were "very burdensome to promoters ".
[75] R. S. C. on *Assurance Associations* (1852-53), XXI (965), 4, p. 18, "or a pot of beer ", 270.          [76] *Ibid.*, p. 23.          [77] *Ibid.*, p. 5.
[78] See the score of examples in *Return of Assurance Accounts* (1852), LI (171).
[79] R. S. C. on *Savings of the Middle and Working Classes*, 203.
[80] *Hansard* (1856), CXL, 119.          [81] R. S. C. on *Assurance Associations*, 19.

had at last been met. The first great modification in the law of partnership had been made. We have now to see how the second modification, the elimination of unlimited liability, came about.

### (vi) *The Achievement of General Limited Liability, 1855-6-7*

English law had no objection to limited liability in itself, and the Courts would enforce an agreed clause that the discharge of the contract or damages in lieu would be confined to a stated corpus of assets. Where contracts were commonly reduced to writing, they frequently gave no recourse against the partners, but only against the capital of the company as such. All insurance policies had this protecting clause.[82] Trading contracts often had a similar clause, and sometimes directors were prohibited from contracting without it.[83] Limited liability was therefore only a matter of notice and agreement. To give that notice on all occasions, however, was very clogging in business and a simple public notice was required.

One way of giving it was by incorporation under Act or charter. Incorporation by private Act was well-nigh impossible. Under a Standing Order of the Lords, a company had to have three-fourths of its capital " deposited in the Bank of England or invested in Exchequer Bonds " before its Bill could pass the Standing Committee.[84] People who might have subscribed if limited liability was ensured had first to subscribe in the hope of getting it, and it was impossible to break the circle.

The first approach to a simple public notice of limited liability was argued in the long discussions on *en commandite* partnership. In this form the liability of certain members is limited to their subscribed capital, and the liability of the others is left unlimited as in simple partnership. The limited members have no right of management. Public notice, with particulars of the deed of partnership, and especially the capital subscribed by the limited members, had to be given. This form had been developed in Italy, was legalised in France in 1671, in Ireland in 1782, and on the Continent and in America early in the nineteenth century. An extension of the Irish Act passed the Commons in 1818 but got no further.[85] Huskisson mentioned it in the Bubble Act debate. Leave to introduce a Bill for England was refused in 1847.[86]

Though such a compromise form might be thought particularly congenial to English minds, the sturdy individualism of traders in the first half of the nineteenth century was against it. The clash of

---

[82] Report on *Partnership*, 60 ; on *Joint Stock Companies*, 168, 180, etc. This destroyed the " extended responsibility " thought desirable by the Board of Trade in 1834 ; see above.

[83] R. S. C. on *Joint Stock Companies*, 167 ; *Hansard* (1854), CXXXIV, 766.

[84] *Hansard* (1824), XI, 856 and 1076 ; and *ibid.* (1855), CXXXVIII, 867 *et seq.*

[85] *Hansard* (1818), XXXVIII, 22 and *House of Commons Journals* (1818), LXXIII, 391.

[86] See *Hansard* (1852), CXIX, 677.

opinions, of statements of fact, the arguments for and against, ran on
*ad nauseam* through the reports of 1837,[87] 1850,[88] 1851 [89] and 1854.[90]
Ker left the question undecided, deferring to the clash in his witnesses.
The Committee of 1844 thought the point, "though worthy of consideration", outside their reference. The Committee of 1850 condemned
as serious obstacles to small investments both unlimited liability and the
remediless state of partners *inter se*,[91] but only recommended an extension of the charter system of 1837 and an improvement in partnership
remedies. The Committee of 1851 also recommended that extension
and more strongly condemned general unlimited liability. They
recommended a further inquiry. A Royal Commission on Mercantile
Law was set up,[92] and in 1854 they by a majority reported against any
change in unlimited liability and for a slight extension of the charter
system. On the main question of liability they had found "great
contrariety of opinion" and "conclusions diametrically opposite", and
had great difficulty in deciding on which side the weight of authority
rested. Some thirty of their witnesses were strongly against any change,
some forty in favour of some form of *en commandite* partnership.[93]
The two nominees of the Dundee Chamber of Commerce and the five
directors of the Bank of England were divided in opinion. The differences in details, in conditions and in safeguards were as numerous as
the witnesses.

It is to be noted that hardly anywhere in these reports was a pure
measure of limited liability discussed. What was discussed at great
length was this mixed form with unlimited and limited partners.[94]
Only some fifteen witnesses out of seventy in 1854 were in favour of
general limited liability.[95] The adoption of this general limited liability
came almost with a jump in 1855.

One main argument of the supporters of *en commandite* partnerships
(or, rarely, of limited companies) was that much capital was lying idle
or not employed to the best advantage. Capitalists, not able or inclined
to enter business as active partners by reason, *e.g.* of age, sex or training,
had no way of safely investing any part of their wealth in productive

[87] Ker's Report on *Partnership Law* (1837), XLIV (530).
[88] R. S. C. on *Savings of the Middle and Working Classes* (1850), XIX (508).
[89] R. S. C. on the *Law of Partnership* (1851), XVIII (509).
[90] R. R. C. on *Mercantile Law* (1854), XXVII (1791).
[91] They were concerned with apparently workers' co-operations, which were not,
though they should have been, under the Act of 1844.
[92] The difference between English and Scotch law was the second reason for this
Commission. Traders had been complaining. *Hansard* (1853), CXXV, 123.
[93] Per *Hansard* (1854), CXXXIV, 764, Goderich said: "The Commissioners stated
they had taken the opinions of 69 persons . . . 37 of whom expressed themselves
decidedly in favour of a law of limited liability, while some of the remaining 32 were
of opinion that a considerable change should be made." I cannot trace any such
statement.         [94] See Lord Curriehill's very definite statement, *Report*, 11 *et seq.*
[95] One vigorous merchant suggested the designation of a limited company should
be "The Greedy Big Percentage Cut-and-Run Company". *Ibid.* 107.

enterprise without risking all their possessions.  Poor but able men were unable to get support from richer men, for these would thereby risk their entire fortunes.  Not every Watt found his Boulton.  Capital and enterprise were divorced and both were suffering.  The answer of opponents was simply to deny that such a set of facts or such a disposition existed or to assert them insignificant.  If, in France, capital was abundant and enterprise sluggish; or if, in America, capital was scarce and enterprise " go-ahead ";[96] or if, in Ireland, there was neither capital nor enterprise—then the encouragement of both by limited liability was perhaps desirable and necessary.  But England had both capital and enterprise in abundance and no such encouragement was necessary.  At times something like a pæan of English greatness in capital and character runs through the evidence.[97]

To the opponents any form of limited liability was likely to lead to speculation, over-trading and fraud.  English enterprise was so spirited that it must be curbed by unlimited liability, " kept within salutary bounds by the dread of loss ".  If men were allowed to subscribe £100 to a company and be no further liable, a spirit of gambling would develop, to the detriment of the country and its tradition of sober judgement.  Limited liability would endanger the reputation of British merchants as reducing the security behind their engagements  Credit would be more difficult to obtain at home and abroad.  Limited partners, ignorant and functionless, would always be liable to fraud.  Again came the usual series of flat contradictions from the other side.  The examples of foreign countries with limited liability disproved any tendency to excessive speculation.  Credit would not suffer, as the relevant facts would be publicly known; excessive and unwise credit resulted indeed from the supposed security of a long list of unlimited partners.  Fraud, either against partners or creditors, could be minimised by suitable provisions and by an improvement of the admittedly bad state of English bankruptcy law.[98]

Opinions differed on the relative efficiencies of limited and simple partnerships and were generally against the efficiency of the limited company.[99]  Yet opponents appeared to dread unfair competition with their partnerships.

[96] The phrase was used in 1844, VII (119), 178.

[97] One illustration out of many may be given: " Although the details of our mercantile law may require correction, yet while there is on every side such evidence of satisfactory progress and national prosperity, it would be unwise to interfere with principles which . . . have proved beneficial to the general industry of the country." R. R. C. on *Mercantile Law*, 7.

[98] Bankruptcy badly needs its economic historian.  For a reasoned estimate of insolvencies in the 'forties, see (1851), XVIII (509), 157.

[99] Relaxation of the Usury Laws to permit a loan to bear interest at a rate varying with the profit had been urged for the promotion of capital and enterprise by the 1851 Committee.  The Royal Commission by majority rejected this recommendation, but suggested the entire repeal of those laws in matters of personal property. *Report*, 7.

But in all this babel of opinion and in all these contradictions in point of fact among the merchant princes and the captains of industry, the humble voice of small capitalists was not quite unheard. Both the 1850 and the 1851 Committees emphasised the growing wealth of the country. The 1851 Report gave the following Table [100] to illustrate the growth of property (annual values for assessment purposes):

|  | 1814-15 | 1848 |
|---|---|---|
| Land . . . . . . | £39,405,000 | £47,981,000 |
| Messuages or chiefly houses . . | 16,259,000 | 42,314,000 |
| Railways, gas-works and other personal property . . . | 636,000 | 8,885,000 |

They added that not only had personal property increased so disproportionately to realty, but also it was more widely diffused. While unlimited liability might be advantageous in the larger transactions of the nation, carried out by firms of a few rich partners, limited liability was needed for local enterprises of a useful kind, financed by numerous passive small investors under the guidance of their richer neighbours. The Health of Cities Report in 1845 had shown the need for such local improvements. Some rich philanthropists, in endeavouring to carry them out, were, for their own safety, driven to obtain a limited charter at high expense, but others, with support from local investors, had been unable to pay for one and were deterred. Some safe field of investment must be opened.

All this time no one seemed to have queried the right of railway companies to have limited liability. It was taken for granted that where a large capital beyond the means of a few partners was needed for a work of acknowledged public usefulness, the subscribers should be given that privilege. Even the size of the capital was not always looked at.[101] As the members had no real control over the company, limited control must be balanced by limited responsibility, if the capital was to be raised. But it was only rarely seen [102] that the same argument applied to all registered companies. By that registration their social usefulness was admitted, but at the same time their members' active control was removed, the Act prohibiting shareholders to act except through the directors in set form. Here was limited control but unlimited responsibility. It would almost seem that the railways, a new form of enterprise, were allowed to work out their proprietary form as they found best, but that companies, working in the field hitherto developed by small partnerships, were expected to keep close to the older proprietary form. Railways had no old traditions to hamper their freedom, nor, in this

[100] *Report*, p. iv.
[101] "The Acts . . . have always considered railway companies . . . as entitled as a matter of course to be non-liable companies . . . whether they be large or small." R. S. C. on *Joint Stock Companies*, 217.
[102] But see Ludlow's communication in R. R. C. on *Mercantile Law*, 144.

matter, vested interests to fight. All railways having limited liability, there could be no accusation of unfair competition on this ground. It was the railways that won the acceptance of general limited liability.

The conservatism of successful big business men in their vested interests, proud of their triumphs in life and of their ability to bear the honourable burden of unlimited liability, or of lawyers to whom all change was distasteful, was not found so universally among members of a free-trade Parliament. To most of these the law of unlimited liability was a species of protection, either through actual wealth and active management or through the high expense of avoiding it by expensive charters or Acts conceded on no clear principle. It came up for debate in 1851,[103] 1852 [104] and 1854.[105]

The debate in 1851 [106] was influenced by the 1850 Report on Savings. The law of partnership was an obstacle to philanthropy and an irritant in social and industrial relations, checking local improvements, e.g. in housing, and the attempts at workers' co-operation of the new 1848 French type. In the debate of 1852,[107] following the 1851· Report on Partnership, the same line of argument was more prominently in the forefront. The need of safe investments for small capitalists was being felt, and " the very intelligent people on the other side of Temple Bar " could look after themselves in active partnerships. The big debate in 1854 [108] swung over to more general lines. Most of the conflicting arguments found in the reports reappeared, but Parliament took a wider view of national requirements than the business men had done. The anomalies in the law were all too patent: private Acts, charters,[109] and special contract terms conferred every day the " protection " of limited liability on some companies; the Registration Act, with its common law unlimited liability, denied it to all others. Such differentiation was inconsistent with " the spirit of recent laws ". There had been an artificial diversion of natural sources into the protected companies or even into foreign countries which had limited liability. This bounty of

[103] Hansard (1851), CXIV, 842 et seq.                    [104] Ibid. (1852), CXIX, 688 et seq.
[105] Ibid. (1854), CXXXIV, 752 et seq.

[106] The motion was: " to consider the law of partnership and the expediency of facilitating the limitation of liability with a view to encourage useful enterprise and the additional employment of labour ".

[107] Motion: " For a Standing Committee or unpaid Commission to consider, suggest and report . . . measures to remove legal and other obstacles which impede the investments and industry of the humbler classes."

[108] Motion: " that the law of partnership which renders every person who, though not an ostensible partner [i.e. was a mere investor], shares in the profit of a trading concern liable to the whole of its debts is unsatisfactory and should be so far modified as to permit persons to contribute to the capital of such concerns on terms of sharing their profits without incurring liability beyond a certain amount."

[109] " Of all systems the worst is . . . to forbid limited liability and then vest in a minister . . . the power of suspending the law. I should as soon think of allowing the Secretary of the Treasury to grant dispensations for smuggling or the Attorney-General licences to commit murder." Quoted from Lowe's evidence, R. R. C. on Mercantile Law, 85.

limited liability had been a cause, if not the cause, of the manias in railway and foreign investments. But limited liability was good.[110] The only safe investments for small passive capitalists had been the canals and the railways. The latter were almost completed and would afford no further outlet, but limited liability would open the general field of industry to such investments and further national prosperity would result. The motion was passed against the wishes of the Government.

It stopped any further grant of charters. These had been criticised on special occasions, when it had been admitted that the course of precedent had not been uniform and the principles of grant not easy in application. Following the motion of 1854, this " safety-valve " was shut down.[111]

Towards the end of 1855 the Government introduced two Bills, one to enable loans to partnerships to bear interest varying with the profits, and the second to confer limited liability by registration. The law of corporations was at last to be applied. The first Bill lapsed at the end of the session, but the Bill for limited liability was rushed through, despite a protest from the Lords. There was little debate[112] and only one new contribution. This was that the Board of Trade had found its duty under the Act of 1837, " a duty it was incompetent to perform ". The public advantages of limited liability could be tested only by actual success or failure of the companies and not at all by the rules of the Board. Limited liability was to be a right by regulations laid down by Parliament and not by charter conferred by the Board. Thus, the argument of 1844 for a general grant of suing powers was again urged.

That Parliament had the opinion of the country with it was quite clear. The opponents said that the Government, knowing the Bill was popular " out of doors ", had made concessions to the popular desire. In the Lords, the mover claimed that " the almost universal opinion . . . as indicated by the public press was in its favour ".[113] The protests of a few Chambers of Commerce, e.g. of Manchester, were ignored.

This Limited Liability Act [114] was really only an addendum to the Registration Act. Companies had to go through its forms of registration but claiming limited liability. They must have 15 per cent of their nominal capital actually paid up, have at least twenty-five shareholders and three-quarters of the capital subscribed. Their name must end with "Limited".

---

[110] See the panegyrical outburst in *Hansard* (1854), CXXXIV, 755, by Collier, the mover.

[111] On charters, see *Hansard* (1852), CXXIII, 1071 ; (1853), CXXIV, 348 ; CXXIX, 652 and 1598 ; (1855), CXXXVII, 943.

[112] *Hansard* (1855), CXXXIX, 310, 1378 and 1896 *et seq.*

[113] He added it was only a temporary measure and a new Bill would be introduced later. *Hansard* (1855), CXXXIX, 2038.

[114] 18 & 19 Vict., c. 133. It did not apply to Scotland.

25

Some forty-six companies had been registered under it when it was repealed in 1856. Lowe had become President of the Board of Trade, and he was an ardent advocate of limited liability. The 1855 Act was based on the Registration Act, and this Act had been shown by the Committee on Assurance Associations to be highly defective. Lowe was convinced that the law relating to companies needed revision. In introducing his own Bill,[115] he traced the evolution of the law as from prohibition to privilege and then to right, and brought out all the defects of the Act of 1844, and the great uncertainty of law that existed between provisional and complete registration. Roundly denying the power, or even the desirability, of Government of attempting to supply mankind with common-sense and contending that 100 honest companies should not be regulated to prevent the 101st from perpetrating fraud, he proposed the substantial removal of all restriction, except a measure of publicity. There was no debate—there could hardly be any after his speech—and the Bill passed easily.

By this Joint Stock Companies Act of 1856,[116] any seven or more persons could by registering a " memorandum of association " become a body corporate with limited liability. All that was required was the seven signatures to the memorandum. This had to declare, inter alia, the name and objects of the company and whether to be limited or not. For the internal regulation of the company a model set of rules, drawn and consolidated from the ordinary rules adopted by companies, was given. This had to be adopted unless the company proposed its own, which it could freely do.[117] No further formality was required and the old safeguards of a minimum paid-up capital, the registration of prospectuses, the scrutiny of the Registrar, were done away with.[118] Seven

---

[115] *Hansard* (1856), CXL, 111-38. His speech was by far the soundest ever given to the House on the subject.

[116] 19 & 20 Vict., c. 47. It was slightly amended on points of construction in 1857 by 20 & 21 Vict., cc. 14 ad 80. It did not apply to banking or insurance companies, which had their own Acts.

[117] " Having given them a pattern, the State . . . had no desire to force on these little republics any particular constitution " (p. 134).

[118] Under the Act of 1844 the Registrar had to approve the deed as consistent with the Act and with law generally. His refusal to accept a deed might be challenged by mandamus, but his acceptance was evidence that the Act had been met. Under the Act of 1862 his certificate was conclusive. The then Registrar constructively construed this to give him some judicial powers. Some witnesses at the 1867 Committee would have formally extended this power. How near the proposals were to administrative law may be seen from the following answer of Lord Romilly: " I think that that is open to this objection, that it must be a judicial function he performs. If he performs a judicial function he must be allowed to hear counsel to explain the matter, whether solicitors or whether barristers or whether the parties themselves. And if so, considering the importance of the matter, it would be difficult to allow that to be done without an appeal to some higher tribunal. It would seem to be an unwise thing to make a new judicial tribunal for the purpose of ascertaining whether in their returns they [companies] had strictly told the truth or not." R. S. C. on *Limited Liability Acts* (1867), X (329), 82. By 1876 the Registrar was made purely ministerial, and (from the 1895 Report) it would seem that whatever judicial power might be in the post was

people each holding a farthing share could become a corporation.  But one right, a " minority right ", was given: shareholders, if one-fifth in number and in value, could have the company inspected by accountants appointed by the Board of Trade.  And the model rules required a balance-sheet to be presented at the annual meeting of shareholders.

General limited liability had come, and with it the modern era of investment.  The effect can be seen in the statistics below.

By 1862, when a great consolidating Act was passed, 2,479 companies had registered under the 1856 Act with limited liability.[119]  Their paid-up capital amounted in 1864 to £31,310,000, of which, however, some 16·5 per cent had been invested in companies then dissolved or being wound up.  The total number of all companies officially known to exist in 1844 when the Registration Act was passed was 994, and the total number registered in the eleven years of its existence was 966.[120]  The great increase under this Act of 1856, though only six years in existence, shows the popularity of the limited form and clearly demonstrates both the need and usefulness of this form as a factor of enterprise.

But, as the above account shows, the legislature at first saw in the company-form only a dangerous and unworthy innovation that should be suppressed.  When companies were accepted as inevitable, perhaps laudable, in certain branches of business, no attempt was made to adapt the general law of the land to them, but they were left either largely remediless or forced to obtain a better standing by a private Act for suing powers.  Other companies, thought more desirable, might be given superior privileges after a special application and examination.  When it was realised that the defective state of the law left in companies and in company promotion an undesirably large and easy field for fraud, the legislature after twenty years' experience brought them into more effective control through compulsory registration.  This, however, was meant more as surveillance than as encouragement.  Unlimited liability was still insisted upon.  After another ten years, and after at least twenty years of discussion and reports, the legislature was moved, by the realisation of the amount of capital not most productively employed, to accept the limited company as a desirable form of business enterprise.  In its new-found faith it removed some old checks and gave companies an almost unwise degree of freedom.  Subsequent legislation, however, has limited that freedom.  The history of company law, like that of railways, shows the slow and uncertain attempts of the legislature to regulate and control a new economic form—a history, too, that has not yet reached its last chapter.

---

" somewhere " in the Board of Trade, probably in the law officers.  See (1877), VIII (365), 437, and 1895 ; LXXXVIII (7779), 51.

[119] Registrar's Return (1864), LVIII (452), 516 *et seq.*  Two errors (nos. 407 and 1148) have been corrected.  In addition, twelve companies had private Acts.

[120] Return (1846), XLIII (504), 55, and the annual returns.

# THE LIMITED COMPANIES OF 1866-1883

## H. A. SHANNON

THE limited system extended with increasing rapidity during 1866-83. In nine-year periods, the registration of companies in London as limited by shares and formed under the Acts was 25 per cent higher in 1866-74 than in 1856-65, and 55 per cent higher in 1875-83 than in 1866-74. Two general developments in the period, affecting the interpretation of the statistics, may be conveniently treated before the detailed figures.[1]

### I

The first is the growth of the private limited company. All the economic characteristics of this type are those of partnership proper, whether the company was merely the adoption of the corporate form by an old partnership or the registration of, intrinsically, a new partnership. In both there would be no appeal to the general public for funds, and a fair amount of personal acquaintance among the members may be presumed. The technique and the fraudulent possibilities, unforeseen by the early advocates of limited liability and longer ignored, were pointed out quite clearly by a legal expounder of the Act of 1856.[2] A few obvious examples were found incidentally in the early 'sixties under the consolidating Act of 1862,[3] but it is likely that the general discredit of the limited form after the events of 1863-5 and the revelations of 1866 checked any strong movement this way. That came with the early 'seventies. For practical reasons, however, the date taken here for the start of the movement is 1875.[4]

---

[1] I am indebted to the Comptroller of Companies and the authorities and staff at Somerset House for permission and courtesy in the matter of records; and to Miss D. W. Young for assistance in the abstraction of certain preliminary data.

[2] See E. W. Cox, *The Joint Stock Companies Act* (1856), p. vii.

[3] *Economic History*, II (1932), 408.

[4] My earliest reference is *The Banker's Magazine*, XXXIII (1873), 787. The first legal textbook (F. B. Palmer's) was in 1877. A well-known company agent says 1874 (H. W. Jordan, *Sixty Years of Company Registration* [1925], 14). *Cf.* J. H. Clapham, *Economic History of Modern Britain* (1932), II, 360-1.
There was then no distinction between public and private companies, and the determination had to be made, file by file, according to its often mixed material. The one-man company was already (1875) in existence. My main criteria were the number and nature of the shareholdings, names and addresses of members, nominal value of shares. The absence of a restricted transfer clause was not found helpful. Something might be gleaned from vendor contracts, but the physical conditions in the vaults precluded their study.

The second development, though more legalistic, is of considerable importance. The legal limits of a company's activities are determined by its object clause, but the deeper implications of *ultra vires* were not fully realized until 1874.[5] Early object clauses had often been short and simple, and the investor, knowing the object of his investment, could be thought of with some precision as an entrepreneur. With the elaboration of objects to suffice, as far as legal ingenuity could ensure, for all time and for almost every conceivable purpose, the investor as an er.'repreneur becomes a more shadowy figure. He may have picked the jockeys and the stable; he did not know which horse would be ridden. Indeed, there was nothing in the law to tell him who the jockeys were.[6]

Connected with this is the fact that the Acts were available to associations " for *any* lawful purpose ", being wider than the Act of 1844. Deductions of a trade-cycle kind from the total registrations can only be made cautiously. Part of the rise in the early 'seventies came simply from a change in electioneering law. The Ballot Act of 1872 was followed by numerous registrations of local political clubs—here, with hesitation, classified as " local halls ". A temperance wave in the late 'seventies, with scores and scores of tea and coffee taverns, accounts for the enormous rise in the class called " hotels, restaurants, etc." The outburst of skating-rinks (then glorified as " glaciariums ") round 1875 is hardly in direct trade-cycle line. Single-ship companies present many difficulties. Starting in Liverpool about 1878, they were being registered in the early 'eighties at the rate of three or four a week and " with a taint from their birth ", as the *Economist* says.[7] And for a later period it warns us that the rise in registrations is not unconnected with promoters' attempts to forestall an impending improvement in law.[8] Further, the true significance of companies will vary with their capital —here ignored in a study of mere numbers.[9]

[5] In this year the doctrine was emphatically laid down in *Ashbury Railway Co.* v. *Riche* (L.R., 7 H.L., 671), though adumbrated earlier.

[6] Under common law and by articles of association the directors had the power of choice between objects. If a shareholder did not attend the meetings (and most did not, perhaps could not, by sex or residence), he would not know his directors—and there are cases where the director did not know his companies (*Economist*, XLII (1884), 570)—and no lists had to be filed for *limited* companies.

For general comment on " the principle of giving the company every imaginable power and leaving [choice] to the directors ", see *Economist*, XLVI (1888), 1440. *Cf. In re Crown Bank* (1890, 44 Ch. 641) where the judge said this bank " might set up in a line of balloons between the earth and the moon ".

Widely drafted clauses were sometimes found difficult to classify. I have generally followed the official summary as given in the office registers, but have supplemented from the files.

[7] *Economist*, XLIV (1886), 1350 and 1440 ; and below. This development forced me to abandon my old classification of shipping companies as " coastal " or " ocean ".

[8] *Economist* XLVI (1888), 821.

[9] *E.g.* many of the coffee taverns and political clubs were " small ", and the unclassified companies contain many schools and other non-commercial types. The general range in registrations is enormous, literally from " bee-keeping " to " worldwide capitalists ".

## II

These numbers are considerable.   The first nine years odd of limited liability (1856-65) saw the registration of 4,859 companies in London as formed under the Acts and limited by shares.   The first nine years of the present study (1866-74) saw 6,111 such registrations, and the second nine years (1875-83) no less than 9,551.   The total is 20,521, or 15,662 for the present period.[10]

## III

Many of them were "abortive" or "small", and have to be eliminated.   Of the 6,111 companies in 1866-74, some 1,878 were abortive or small—say, 31 per cent ranging from 36 per cent in 1866-8 through 32 per cent in 1869-71 to 28 per cent in 1872-4.   The high abortive rate after the shock of 1866 is as noticeable as the low rate in 1872-4, when a boom was on.

For 1875-83 an allowance must first be made for the private companies.   By definition their registrations can hardly ever be abortive, though sometimes small.   In determining the proportion of immediate promoting failures the observed cases of private companies must be removed.   The 9,551 companies of 1875-83 contain 1,391 private companies (14½ per cent), leaving 8,160 as public.   The abortives and smalls, numbering 3,311, equal 40 per cent of the public companies or 35 per cent of all registrations.   These proportions suggest that the earlier period (1866-74) may contain a fair number of private companies. By sub-periods of three years the percentages of abortives against public companies are:  1875-7, 33 per cent; 1878-80, 45 per cent; 1881-3, 43 per cent; or against all registrations, 29 per cent, 38 per cent, 36 per cent. With the 36 per cent abortive rate for 1856-65, we may say that in the first quarter century or so of limited liability the investor rejected more or less out of hand about one-third of the proposals submitted to him.

## IV

We may turn now to the companies deemed effectively formed, treating first those considered "public".   Their dissolutions have been grouped into four classes: sold, amalgamated and reconstructed; wound up compulsorily, or under supervision, or by reason of liabilities—in short, insolvent; wound up voluntarily, without reason assigned; and those which dissolved in disregard of legal form, or "unknown".

---

[10] These are the official totals adjusted for transfers, etc.   My own working totals were three short for 1856-65, three over for 1866-74, and one over for 1875-83, and have been adjusted through miscellaneous abortives.   The files extend for nearly half a mile— usually unpleasant and often awkwardly stacked.

For a comparable study of the companies of 1856-65, see *Economic History*, II (1932), 396-424, which also gives further explanations on method and technical terms.

In the detailed analyses, however, companies for gas and water and for public halls and political clubs will be omitted.   They have obvious peculiarities, which suggest their omission, and they have been falling in relative importance over the whole period, from 26 per cent in 1856-9 to some 5 per cent in 1881-3, which compels their omission to maintain comparability.

The effective public companies thus left in number 3,827 for 1866-74 and 4,513 for 1875-83.

## V

Small percentages of these companies (ranging from 3·2 to 6·1) sold themselves *en bloc* within five years of their registration.   More generally, about one-sixth of the public companies were sold, amalgamated or reconstructed before 1929, the lowest percentage (13·1) arising from the formations of 1875-7 and the highest (18·3) from those of 1881-3.   Half of such liquidations in the companies formed 1866-74 occurred within the first fifteen years of their existence, and half of those formed 1875-83 within their first ten years.   Resolutions for such disposal were usually uninformative, frequently merely confirming schemes privately circulated but not publicly filed.   Where details were given, their fuller meaning might have been guessed at from, *e.g.* market quotations of shares—but such study is impracticable.   It is not possible to say from the official material whether these disposals *en bloc* were made with profit.   One's impression of the majority of cases where particulars were given is that they were unprofitable,[11] but it is not possible to be more definite.

Before turning to the chronological aspect of these dissolutions, a general point of methodology must be made clear.   The factors playing on the death-rate of companies can be thought of as two groups: age and chronological.   When companies are young, they will die in batches; when times are bad, much the same can be said, though the coincidence is not perfect.   On occasions the factors will mingle, crest adding to crest.   In times of boom many new companies are formed which are still young when the slump comes.   The causation is different.   But a measure of the play of each group will appear if only companies of about the same age are studied together.   The data will be reasonably homogeneous, and events occurring at the beginning of a time series can be attributed largely to the age-factor, and events occurring afterwards to the chronological factor.   It seems misleading to compare, *e.g.* the dissolutions of one year with all companies subject to risk (*i.e.* existing) that year irrespective of the age distribution of the dissolutions and of the companies existing.   Here the public *home* companies of 1866-74 will be taken together, to be followed by those of 1875-83—using a base

[11] Professor D. H. Macgregor estimates that 40 per cent of the reconstructions in 1896 were at a loss (*The Economic Journal*, XXXIX (1929), 499).

unit of nine years. Material for this study is given in Table F, which can be easily turned into appropriate percentage form.[12]

When graphed, the percentages representing the sales, amalgamations and reconstructions of companies formed 1866-74 lie consistently round the 2½ per cent line until the middle of the 'eighties (1883-6). Then the graph, like that of the earlier base period 1856-65, rises steadily to the 5 per cent line, pausing there in the late 'nineties before descending to low levels for the years before the war. The rising graph dips slightly after the Baring crisis. In the immediate post-war years it, or rather the industrial section of it, soars up to almost 19 per cent, reflecting the cotton boom. Both variations also appear in the corresponding graph of the companies formed 1856-65.

The chronological behaviour of disposals *en bloc* among the companies formed 1875-83 clearly belongs to the same family. The average curve rises steadily through the 'eighties, the industrial section keeping level, however, and rising only from 1883-6; then the average curve and its components, "industrial" and "general", follow much the same course on higher levels throughout the 'nineties. Again there is a dip after the Baring crisis and during the long liquidation of its affairs by the Bank of England and guarantors—when the Stock Exchange and the Money Market would be both warned and nervous. From the present century the disposals *en bloc* have a steady downward trend until the post-war boom. Then again the industrial curve, heavily weighted by cotton companies, shows an enormous peak.

Thus, three sets of companies (1856-65, 1866-74, 1875-83), with age factors eliminated or minimized, teach the same lesson; a rise in sales, amalgamations and reconstructions during the late 'eighties and 'nineties.

## VI

The figures for companies wound up compulsorily or under supervision or by reason of liabilities are of more interest and instruction. They afford a measure of the economic wisdom of our grandfathers under *laissez-faire*.

They show that insolvencies within five years of registration had a fairly steady upward trend from the beginning. The figure for the formations of 1856-9, which is 6·6 per cent, is not quite comparable with succeeding particulars and is likely to be too low.[13] From the formations of 1860-2 it rises steadily from 9·5 to 21·5 per cent of 1878-80, except for 1866-8 formations deemed naturally sound after the scare of 1866, and

---

[12] See *Economic History, loc. cit.* 406.

It will be noted that the home survivals of companies formed 1866-74, like those of 1856-65, follow two Pareto curves, broken at 1883. For 1877-83 and 1883-1910 the equations are: (i) $y = 3464 \cdot x^{-\cdot712604}$ and (ii) $y = 4011 \cdot x^{-\cdot818304}$. The survivals of companies formed 1875-83 follow, from 1892, the equation: $y = 4583 \cdot x^{-\cdot787562}$.

[13] Owing to a small change in law; see *Economic History, loc. cit.* 400.

drops a little to 19·5 for the formations of 1881-3. It is reasonable to assume that in these cases investors lost all, or almost all, the capital sunk; indeed, if we remember premiums and heavy calls through the Courts and liquidators on subscribed but unpaid capital, the assumption takes on the character of a certainty. This will not be modified even for those cases where the liquidators subsequently disposed of the assets *en bloc* as the best way of meeting liabilities.

The weighted average for the formations of 1856-65 is some 12 per cent; for 1866-74, some 15 per cent; for 1875-83, some 20 per cent; for the whole period 1856-83, it is 17 per cent. It may be admitted generally that companies which so failed, failed from fraud or gross mismanagement amounting to fraud. The factor of fraud, then, for more than the first quarter century of limited liability, or one-third of its total history, is some one-sixth. Readers who look on this as hard definition will admit a general undeniable validity to corresponding failures within *three* years of promotion. That test yields a factor of one-ninth.[14]

The rise in trend is most marked. Three causes may be suggested: investors may have been cutting losses sooner, creditors giving shorter shrift, promoters being more fraudulently active. The first may have been assisted by the growth of the small £1 share, which rose from 7 per cent of the shares offered in 1863-5 to 12½ per cent in 1873-5 and 32½ per cent in 1883-5. Where capital was fully paid, directors without the power of further calls would be stopped short and credit would be harder to get. The second cause is quite likely: with increasing experience of limited debtors creditors would act more quickly.

The third can stand elaboration. An ignorant popularity was attaching to the limited system; the *Economist* remarked in 1882 that "every year must have its mania"; hits are known and remembered when misses are concealed and unpublished. Capital was here as often blind as lynx-eyed; the investor, like any unorganized casual, could be sweated. The unfortunate Bills, piloted by Chadwick who was an investing agent with a good reputation,[15] showed the discontent of 160 Chambers of Commerce in the middle 'seventies.[16] The changed tone of the *Economist* may be as much due to wide fraud as to a new editor.

[14] My own preference is for the one-sixth. A student of companies is likely to be cynical, but I do think that the factor of fraud is much too minimized generally.
The number of companies is a better measure here than the capital value. Some preliminary results of an unfinished study of the latter suggest, however, no modification for the text. See *Economist*, XXXVII (1879), 1254: "If a balance sheet could be drawn up of the losses and gains to Great Britain from the establishment of companies on the limited principle to work industrial undertakings, we have no doubt the balance would be largely on the wrong side." Compare *The Banker's Magazine*, LVII (1894), 685.
[15] I think this may stand despite some evidence in *Smith* v. *Chadwick* (1882) and the profit record of the Ebbw Vale Company.
[16] *Hansard* (1876), CCXXXI, 1065 *et seq*. One Bill passed the Commons with the approval of the Government but was rejected in the Lords, largely through erroneous parallels by the Lord Chancellor.

The Royal Commission on the Depression was futilely vexed by "promoters whose interest lies rather in the creation of an industrial undertaking and the speedy sale of its shares at a premium than in its permanent prosperity". A valuable report into foreign company law in 1889[17] showed uneasiness in high quarters. Fraud in companies had reached the dignity of the Queen's Speech in 1888.[18] But no important change in law occurred until 1890.

The Courts too moved slowly, despite such judgments as *Twycross* v. *Grant* (1873). What might have been a valuable, if badly drafted, clause in the Act of 1867 received, by majority, a narrow construction in *Gover's Case* (1875). The decision of the Law Lords in *Peek* v. *Derry* (1887) required an amending Act in 1890 to make the law more acceptable, though Buckley says of it, "Conceived as a terror to the prospectus-maker and calculated to increase the income of the competent expert who has no scruples". For licence, miscalled liberty, they hamstrung the Winding Up Act in *ex parte Barnes* (1896)—confirming two earlier cases of 1892. The attitude of even Lord Justice Brett is worth rescuing from oblivion: "I must confess to such an abhorrence of fraud in business that I am always most unwilling to come to a conclusion that a fraud has been committed" (*Wilson* v. *Clinch*, 1879).[19]

Wrecking of companies and collusion in liquidation still continued in face of attempts by the Courts to check abuses. Evidence can be found in the pages of the *Economist* and the *Statist* and from asides in the law reports. Facts killing fictions, the *Economist* by 1879 was out for State intervention: "All windings up should be under the direct management of the Court; all liquidators . . . should be official . . .; the expenses [a public charge]." This would kill collusion in the "bubble companies blown by men of strong lungs and brazen countenances", who paid a young lordling £100 per titled director introduced. The *Statist* quoted with approval the official memorial of the London bankers in 1879: "winding up of joint-stock companies—a branch of insolvent business of increasing extent and unfortunately of increasing notoriety for scandals and failures of justice". It later added its own opinion of "these days, when the practice of presenting wrecking peti-

---

[17] In LXXVII (5627).

[18] *Hansard* (1888), CCCXXII, 8 and 14: "Liability will also, I trust, be laid on promoters of public limited companies in order to put down the evil which has grown of late years", with the apologetic addendum, "and which could not have been provided against at the time" (*i.e.* the legislation of 1862).

[19] Formal references to these cases can be had from any standard legal text-book, say, Mew's *Digest*. The quotations are from the full legal reports.

Marshall was dissatisfied with the Courts: "If judges could be induced to treat more severely fraud whenever it is found in the high ranks of business, particularly among promoters of companies, the industry of the country would become steadier" (in *Remuneration of Capital and Labour* [ed. Dilke] (1885), 177). The implication seems sounder than the later gloss in *Industry and Trade* (1919), 314.

Lawyers and the City were content with England as the New Jersey of Europe; see *Economist*, XLVI (1888), 1472, and, inferentially, *Banker's Magazine*, LX (1895), 740.

tions is almost becoming a branch of business with a certain class of legal practitioners ". An attempt was once made against Bolckow Vaughans! A judge casually remarked in 1876 that he had " the usual contest " in his Chambers as to who should be the official liquidator; and another declared in 1879 that " I have on the suggestion of my chief clerks, founded on their experience, directed them in no case whatever to appoint any official of the company, liquidator. They are always under some improper influences." [20] The conclusion reached above, of small returns (if any) to shareholders in short-lived companies, stands unshaken. Even Vice-Chancellor Woods quickly retraced his opinion that companies should not wind up in Court. [21]

A comforting bubble may be pricked. The departmental Committee of 1895 said that the majority of businesses were honestly run, and the Lords Committee of 1896-9 accepted the statement that " the great mass of companies are honest ", one eminent witness putting dishonesty at 2 or 3 per cent. [22] This has been followed by some writers. [23] The statement in that form may be correct. The argument and the implication appear fallacious, depending on an unjustifiable comparison of flow and stock. It has been shown, more evidence can be adduced, [24] and it is acceptable to common-sense that fraudulent companies are short-lived and honest companies more long-lived. Hence, fraudulent companies coming into existence, new and short-lived, will arithmetically form a small proportion of all companies in existence mostly old and honest. But, compared with the flow of companies coming into existence at the same time, fraudulent companies will form a high proportion. *This* is the true comparison for testing the beneficial working of the Acts, and optimism here is misplaced. The dead as well as the living must be remembered.

The general facts of insolvency may now be stated briefly. In all, 30·3 per cent of the companies formed 1866-74 and 33·4 per cent of 1875-83 ended in insolvency, the figures for three-yearly periods showing a general rise. The corresponding figure for the formations of 1856-65 was 25·6 per cent. For the whole period 1856-83, it is just over 30 per cent. But whereas half of these liquidations took place within the first six years of existence with the formations of 1856-65, half took place within the first five years with those of 1866-74, and within the first four years with those of 1875-83.

[20] *Economist*, XXXVII (1879), 1449 and XLII (1884), 350; *Statist*, II (1879), 452, III (1879), 95, and IV (1880), 275; *In re Lisbon Steam Tramways* (1876) and *In re Gold Company* (1879)—a mere selection of references. Space does not permit a discussion of the prolific "guinea-pig" directors.

[21] His early opinion is given in *Economic History, loc. cit.* 414, quoting the Report of 1867; the recantation is in *London Flour Company* (1868).

[22] See (1895), LXXXVIII (7779), VI, and (1898), IX (392), Qs. 106-7.

[23] *E.g.* Mr Todd in *Economic History*, IV (1932), 53. This is one of the points where I think the weight of evidence is against his statements.

[24] See any Report under the Winding Up Act of 1890.

The chronological behaviour of insolvencies fulfilled expectation. The insolvencies among home companies formed 1866-74 were low until after 1870, when the memory of " Black Friday, 1866 ", was fading; then they rose sharply, the industrial insolvencies in the three years 1877-80 being 13 per cent of industrial companies existing in 1877. Throughout the 'eighties they were, proportionately, fallir ⁊ fast, and from the 'nineties they were a mere trickle. Since the war they have shown a slight upward trend, with receivers on behalf of banks showing importance. After the high peak of the late 'seventies (which reflects the age-factors) the graph reveals a long faint cyclical movement with industrial peaks about the middle 'nineties, about 1905 and just before the war.

The behaviour of insolvencies in companies formed 1875-83 starts differently and then broadly conforms to type. There is no opening peak but a precipitous drop from the late 'seventies to the early 'nineties. But whereas the companies formed 1856-65 had a little run before being caught by the crash of 1866 and those formed 1866-74 another run before boom and crash round 1875-8, the companies formed 1875-83 were caught at the opening of their career by the City of Glasgow crash. Their subsequent course is marked by faint cyclical peaks and a sharp rise in post-war times, showing the conformity to type.

## VII

Unexplained voluntary resolutions—the third type of dissolution among public companies—remain for discussion.

Their interpretation is especially difficult, as the bare resolutions tell us little of causes. Again, however, the companies which so found it necessary to wind up within three or five years of starting may be thought of as failures, this time *perhaps* from ignorance and misjudgment. Then we see that 13·9 per cent of the companies formed 1866-74 wound up in this unexplained fashion within five years from promotion and 9·7 per cent of those formed 1875-83. With the 14·4 per cent from the formations of 1856-65, the average for the whole period 1856-83 becomes 12·3 per cent. Looked at in this way, the factor of ignorance and misdirection in the investment of capital was about one-eighth. If looked at from the three-year windings up, instead of the five-year, it becomes 7·6 per cent—say, a factor of one-thirteenth.

The more detailed averages do not show any very definite trend. The formations of the sub-period 1866-8 had an unusually low figure, a result to be expected when we remember that only sound companies would dare be offered immediately after the crisis of 1866; the same is true of the sub-period 1878-80, the crash of the City of Glasgow Bank teaching a lesson previously forgotten. On the whole, however, the trend is downward.

The chronological graph of the voluntary windings up in the home companies formed 1866-74 is much smoother than the corresponding graph of those formed 1856-65. It is a much flattened-out version of the insolvencies described above. From its peak in the 'seventies it falls slowly to the war, with a small industrial peak at the beginning of this century. It rises, however, into a sharp peak immediately after 1919, and for this part of its course it resembles, not its contemporary "insolvencies" graph, but its contemporary "sold *en bloc*" graph. The explanation is easy and almost certain here: companies, using the voluntary form of resolution, were winding up for sale or reconstruction. It is difficult to believe anything else of voluntary windings up in the cotton industry around 1920, which are proportionately important here.

The behaviour, in voluntary windings up, of the formations of 1875-83 presents puzzles, to be explained largely by vagaries in heavily weighted groups, especially shipping and hotels. The voluntary graph on the whole resembles that of the corresponding sales, especially in showing a maintained high peak centred on 1900 for the " industrials " group. The fuller data suggest the cause: the peculiar behaviour of the *interlinked* " single-ship companies ". Against 228 shipping companies existing in 1892, no less than 72 had wound up voluntarily by the end of 1900; the corresponding totals in the " industrials " group were 534 and 97. The upsetting effect on the average is obvious. Their behaviour during the war was also peculiar, as might be expected. The voluntary graph, like its predecessors, jumps immediately after the war. But here the rise is mainly in the " general " group, and the disturbing factor lies in the " hotel " group. Out of 104 hotels, etc., existing in 1919, some 29 had voluntarily wound up by the end of 1924, against the " general " group totals of 426 and 61 respectively.

So far, a complication in the chronological studies has been ignored. In some cases it will be important and must be brought into clear light. Company shares need not necessarily be fully paid up, and where the nominal value is high they are likely not to be fully paid. Particulars of nominal value, based on a 20 per cent random sample, are interesting and pertinent. They are, as percentages of the sample run over three years in each case:

|  | 1863–5 (Per cent) | 1873–5 (Per cent) | 1883–5 (Per cent) |
|---|---|---|---|
| £1 | 7 | 12½ | 32¼ |
| £5 | 19 | 29 | 19 |
| £10 | 31 | 32½ | 26¼ |
| £10–£25 | 19 | 7 | 4 |
| Over £25 | 18 | 11 | 12 |
| (£100 and over | 8 | 7 | 7½) |

Some intermediate values (*e.g.* £2 and £4) are omitted here. The general downward shift is obvious and is very marked by the 'eighties. It is surprising that there was no greater shift by the 'seventies, seeing what a lesson was taught at the Overend Gurney crash; it seems to have taken the (unlimited) City of Glasgow crash to drive the lesson home.[25] Some influence on the figures comes from the mining companies whose shares, being rather speculative, would be small. The growth of closely private companies, such as family conversions, maintained the percentages of very high value shares—some being as high as £1,000.

Limited companies have added rigidity to the economic system. Single traders or partners, with income arising solely from their business, will react immediately to the bankruptcy necessary for a flexible capitalism. Limited companies, whose shareholders presumably have supplementary incomes, will not. The timing with general economic conditions will be less perfect. Further, with reserves of capital subscribed and unpaid, a common result with high value shares, limited companies will be given a buoyancy which will carry them through storm, even if leaving them to sink in the calm or just letting them limp home to port. Again, the timing is less perfect; the marginal company is harder to push over the brink. Shareholders may be faced with embarrassing alternatives: an immediate winding up with the certainty of losing both capital and extra calls, or the financing of current trade deficits by instalments through calls.[26] Like Belial in Pandemonium, their philosophy might be:

> Besides what hope the never-ending flight
> Of future days may bring—what chance, what change
> Worth waiting . . .
> If we procure not to ourselves more woe.

## VIII

The gap in official sources of companies which dissolved in disregard of legal form,[27] leaving us without information, can merely be described statistically. With the companies of 1866-74, some 7·9 per cent so ended within five years of registration: with the companies of 1875-83, some 6·1 per cent. These compare with the 9·6 per cent of companies formed 1856-65. The Registrar intermittently circularized companies defaulting in returns; from 1880, under the Act of that year, his power of inquiry was strengthened and a regular routine of circularization was set up. This may account for the falling trend. One's impression of the companies so dissolving was of smallness, but some big cases were noticed, e.g. one of almost £900,000. The percentages for companies within three years of promotion are: 1856-65, 7·4; 1866-74, 5·3; 1875-83, 5·1. These short-lived and informally dissolved companies are likely to have been unsatisfactory promotions at least.

[25] Giffen, however, considered that large unpaid capitals were rare after 1866. This sample would suggest a later date.

[26] This seems to be the position of the Lancashire cotton industry today.

For interesting examples of " hanging-on ", see Professor G. W. Daniel's instructive article in Manchester School, III (1932), 77-84.

[27] Where letters were filed I have taken them as equal to formal resolutions.

## IX

The results of these public companies may now be combined. Those relating to voluntary disposals *en bloc* will be omitted, as the subsequent history of the company taking over has not been abstracted. This leaves the insolvencies, the voluntaries and the unknowns which, with at least short-lived companies, are akin.

Within five years of promotion they amounted to 35·9 per cent for companies formed 1856-65, to 37·1 per cent for companies formed 1866-74, and to 36·2 per cent for companies formed 1875-83. The factor of fraud, ignorance and misjudgment generally is a steady one-third. The investor, it seems, was neither *homo economicus* nor *homo sapiens*. From a quarter century of experience investors had learnt nothing—a result which is not at all surprising when the circumstances are considered realistically. For a decade or so they could not even trust *The Times*.[28] The factor of fraud, ignorance and gross mis-judgment as measured by dissolutions within three years of promotion is, for the main periods in order, 22·3 per cent, 23·2 per cent and 25·6 per cent—say, one-fourth. The investor went badly wrong once in every three or four times he acted. If a duration of more than ten years is taken as the test, he was wrong in more than half his investments.

## X

We may now turn to the companies which have been considered " private " on the special search from 1875. They were one-seventh of the registrations and about one-fifth of the effective formations—both higher figures than were expected. With a narrower definition, almost equivalent to " family businesses ", the Registrar estimated that private companies were about one-third of the registrations during 1890.[29] Assuming, from the particulars of " abortives " given above, that some one-third of the total registrations were then abortive, his estimate shows that about one-half of the effective formations fell within his definition of " private ". This would have surprised the early doctrinaire advocates of limited liability whose deductions of its advantages never reached this point.[30]

Details of the distribution of private companies in the different indus-tries can be easily had from the tables. In 1875-7, the earliest sub-period, the coal, iron and allied industries contained just over a quarter of all private companies, but by 1881-3 their proportion (of formations) had sunk to one-sixth. This group had the earliest important private com-panies, arising perhaps from their usually high capitals and from the slump in coal and iron. Pride of place in 1881-3 was taken by the

[28] See *Rubery* v. *Grant and Sampson* (1875)—an instructive tale of rogues who fell out. Sampson was the City Editor.

[29] 1895, LXXXVIII (7779), 54.          [30] *E.g.* Lowe, *Hansard* (1856), CXL, 113.

private single-ship companies which formed almost one-sixth of the private formations.

On the whole their behaviour was better than that of the public companies. For the formations of 1875-83, a tenth had become insolvent within three years of registration and one-seventh within five years. Even so, these figures are high. Partly it may be due to defects in the difficult classification; some companies, even where the shares were strongly held by a few members, may have been public companies unsuccessfully floated and their short existence gave the criteria little grip. More likely, however, the high figures were due to the ubiquitous factor of fraud—here on creditors. In 1877 Chadwick told the Committee on the Companies Act that thirty-nine out of forty propositions to him for flotation came from firms on the down grade.[31] The arithmetic was perhaps specious, but its lesson is clear. Partnerships which saw little chance of passing on their liabilities to the public would be tempted to make the transfer to their creditors, especially as a judicious use of debentures could enable them to sweep back into their own pockets assets that should have gone to their creditors.[32] Where creditors continued to trade with the same people, once partners, now shareholders, they could only look to the limited company for payment; indeed, if they accepted the company in lieu of the partnership, the same applied to old debts.

Another one-tenth of the private companies wound up voluntarily within three years, and something under one-sixth within five years. Informal dissolutions were rather high, as might be expected where a company consisted of a few friends; one private company in twelve so dissolved within three years and one in ten within five years.

More summarily, 29·7 per cent dissolved within three years in any form and 40·1 per cent within five years. Young private companies died more quickly than public ones. They were, however, sold more slowly, only 3·9 per cent within five years when 4·3 per cent of the public companies had changed form.

## XI

There remains for some brief notes the rich field of manias. The committee member who thought a "crop of fools" every ten years a natural phenomenon was too optimistic:[33] the crop was more often annual. When, however, we remember their occasional "premium-hunting", our sympathy must wane.[34]

---

[31] (1877), VIII (365), Q. 2092.
[32] The classical case is *Salomon* v. *Salomon and Company* (1897).
[33] (1877), VIII (365), Q. 1536.
[34] See, however, *Report on the Stock Exchange* (1877), XIX (2157), *e.g.* Qs. 4015 *et seq.* The public strongly tended to accept a company whose shares were at a premium as one good for investment; indeed, a premium before allotment was almost

Typically enough for the times, Lancashire led the way. In 1860 and 1861 cotton companies were effectively forming at a rate of one a week, but the movement stopped dead with the Cotton Famine. With 1863-5 came the well-known general mania, centring round companies for financing, banking, insurance and hotels, to end on Black Friday, 1866. The salutary Life Assurance Act of 1870—passed to the great disgust of Bagehot's *Economist*—stopped the formation of new life companies with its stringent provisions for the policy holder's safety. Another crop came to harvest with the first mining boom—if we ignore the constant procession of lead and other mines still trailing their Phoenician glory. This was the foreign boom round 1871 when, in July, the *Economist* remarked, " Already the state of our advertising columns reminds us of 1863 and 1864 ". In three years (1871-3) 135 companies were effectively started for foreign mines, of which 56 were in 1871. Gold and silver claimed *at least* 52; lead, copper, etc., 17; coal and iron, 18; and companies with wide power to search for minerals unspecified, but likely on the whole to be " gold and silver ", 48. Ignoring sales, etc., 65 of these companies were dissolved within five years of promotion. This boom was marked by the extension of two financial devices: founders' shares and debentures, the once easy manner of 1863-5 having become, as the *Economist* remarked, rather difficult. The promoters took the shares in consideration of the mine, the public subscribed for the debentures—without, be it noted, even the legal control of a shareholding. After this, founders' shares largely disappear until round 1890 and debentures (where there were legal difficulties in drafting as negotiable instruments) until the early 'eighties.

Before this boom was decently interred, the rise in coal and iron prices set going a home one on a much greater scale. Starting with 78 effective promotions in coal and iron mines in 1872, two effective formations a week ruled throughout 1873, followed by a total of 84 in 1874. In addition to these 271 effective companies, another 52 were attempted unsuccessfully, giving the public an embarrassing choice between 323 companies. As the tables show, the heavy trades generally followed suit. This simple faith in the permanency of prosperity kept very much at home: the " speculators of all sorts [who] rushed off to Spain " (Lowthian Bell) formed no companies. The rocket had fallen before they got back. Within three years, 76 of the 271 companies were dead; within five years, 128; within ten years, 176; out of the three-year total, 45 had died insolvent; out of the five-year, 76; out of the ten-year, 108.

---

necessary to ensure a company's flotation at all. And the luring beacon was easily lighted. Good companies which refused to stoop to the market devices sometimes found it difficult to get started. The evil was, therefore, intensified. See Giffen's evidence, Qs. 7461 *et seq.*

26

The cotton industry became active as the iron and coal boom slackened. In 1873, when the movement began, 38 companies were successfully floated; then 99 in 1874; and 69 in 1875. The " Oldham Limiteds " had arrived. After 1875 only the usual trickle of cotton companies came into the limited system, over half being private. Perhaps "mania" is too opprobious here: out of the 206 cotton companies started 1873-5, only 37 were compelled to retire within five years of promotion.

Land and building companies accompanied the general boom as they had in 1863-5. But from coal and cotton the fancy turned to ice and coffee. In 1876, 29 skating rinks were effectively floated, while 21 stranded as abortive or small; and the movement quickly ceased.[35] As it was fading away, coffee taverns and hotels came in. Their numbers were much higher; the effective formations of 1878-80 inclusive were 191, and others, as small or abortive, 147—a total of 338; in the next three years, 1881-3, the corresponding registrations were 118 and 185—a total of 303. In addition, 26 private companies were formed in this group after 1878. These formations are economically of little importance.

The fall of the (unlimited) City of Glasgow Bank caused a lull. Three outbursts finally remain for note: overseas mines and lands, electricity and single-ships.

The colonies, as much neglected by the promoter as by the politician, received their first boom in 1880 when new gold was discovered in India and diamonds in South Africa.[36] Companies for colonial mines, especially gold, silver and diamonds, boomed in 1880-1 inclusive. Twenty-two companies for gold and silver, with 2 for diamonds, were effectively floated—one can hardly say started—in 1880; and 19 for gold and 13 for diamonds in 1881. But, as the Statist remarked of the boom generally, the mine was more often than not situated in Bucklersbury, E.C. Of these 56 companies, 22 were dissolved within three years and 29 within five years. Seven of the 15 diamond companies were sold in the late 'eighties (round 1887-8). Colonial land and plantations, too, became popular, 33 being effectively formed in 1880-1—with 7 dead within five years. The Statist alleged that the colonial and foreign land companies were formed to " relieve some Anglo-colonial and foreign banks of the burden of heavy and otherwise unreliable advances " and in some cases the movement was part of the liquidation of the City of Glasgow.[37]

---

[35] The " amusement " class, having been small 1866-74, was dropped and merged in " unclassified ". These skating rinks and some other amusements, like aquariums, therefore unfortunately swell the unclassified—a group which I have tried to keep low.

[36] " South Africa " has been consistently classified as " colonial ".

[37] Statist, IV (1879), 273, and VIII (1881), 599. The ranching mania had its centre, however, north of the Tweed—one company registered in London even obtaining a private Act to be transferred to Edinburgh where no doubt its true headquarters were.

The boom in foreign mines and land, starting too in 1880, got into swing in 1881 and was still strong in 1883. It was mostly in land and gold and silver, with some lead and copper. Land and plantations, especially ranches, gathered 46 effective companies and 30 abortive between 1881-3 inclusive, with—an interesting point, reminiscent of some British investment in the far-off 'thirties—11 private companies. Gold and silver had 71 effective formations in the same three years and 63 abortive registrations. Between land and gold, therefore, the public were offered 210 companies and accepted 117. The 71 gold and silver companies fared badly: 24 died within three years and 36 within five years. The 46 land companies were a little better: 11 died within three years and 17 within five years.

Of more permanent significance was the mania in electrical companies, to be dated with some precision in 1882, though companies trickle in from 1878. The *Statist*, referring to 1878-82, estimated that some £4¼ million of capital had gone for ever, that £1¼ million had been sunk in plant, etc., remaining, and that the amount of fees to directors paid over the period (£160,000) would by 1884 have bought up all the concerns on the Stock Exchange.[38] It was a litigious time, too, with disputes over patent rights. The formation of subsidiary companies, buying foreign rights, is noteworthy as the first important appearance of such activity.[39] Between 1881-3 (three years) 126 companies publicly offered themselves, of which 73 were in 1882. Of the former, 51 were abortive; of the latter, 28. Out of the 75 effective public formations 1881-3, 32 were dead within three years of promotion and 36 within five years—the scythe swinging immediately. Twelve were sold or otherwise amalgamated within three years from starting.

Finally, there was a mania in single-ship companies, which was still raging in 1883. The first effective case noted was a Liverpool one in 1878, then 9 in 1879 and 20 in 1880. Thereafter the numbers rose rapidly: 66 in 1881, 96 in 1882, 111 in 1883—a total in three years of 273 companies with the trend rising. Within three years from promotion 66 out of this 273 had dissolved, 40 being voluntary, 17 compulsory, etc., and 9 unknown; in the fourth and fifth years, an extra 26 dissolved, of which 15 were voluntary, 8 compulsory, etc., and 3 unknown. In other words, one-third died within five years (92 out of 273), the majority by their own hand, so to speak.

Accompanying this public outburst went private registrations—frequently the splitting up of partnership fleets, each ship being made a separate company. In 1880 there were 25 such registrations, all on the same day; in 1881, 23; in 1882, 34; in 1883, 38.

---

[38] *Statist*, XIV (1884), 151.
[39] The pioneer was a fraudulent company for making coffee out of dates.

TABLE

COMPANIES, LIMITED BY SHARES, ATTEMPTED IN 1866–74, AND REGISTERED

| Description | R. | A.S. | Effective | | | | 3 Years and Under | | | | 4–5 Years | | | | 6–10 Years | | | |
|---|---|---|---|---|---|---|---|---|---|---|---|---|---|---|---|---|---|---|
| | | | 1866–74 | 1866–68 | 1869–71 | 1872–74 | S | C | V | U | S | C | V | U | S | C | V | U |
| Coal and Iron Mines | 490 | 90 | 400 | 69 | 60 | 271 | 8 | 56 | 26 | 17 | 11 | 39 | 19 | 11 | 6 | 49 | 14 | 9 |
| Lead, etc., Mines | 323 | 86 | 237 | 48 | 96 | 93 | 10 | 32 | 29 | 20 | 8 | 25 | 16 | 9 | 7 | 29 | 15 | 9 |
| Quarries | 136 | 52 | 84 | 29 | 17 | 38 | 2 | 7 | 6 | 2 | 2 | 4 | 8 | 5 | 5 | 14 | 5 | 4 |
| Iron Manufacturing and Engineering | 182 | 17 | 165 | 26 | 33 | 106 | 6 | 16 | 12 | 5 | 1 | 9 | 4 | 1 | 2 | 26 | 4 | 3 |
| Iron and Steel Products | 73 | 16 | 57 | 14 | 10 | 33 | 1 | 4 | 3 | — | 1 | 6 | 2 | — | 3 | 3 | 5 | 1 |
| Specialized Engineering | 133 | 37 | 96 | 19 | 21 | 56 | 4 | 9 | 11 | 12 | 2 | 7 | 5 | 4 | 3 | 6 | 4 | 4 |
| Railway, etc., Equipment | 57 | 19 | 38 | 8 | 6 | 24 | 1 | 1 | — | 1 | — | 4 | 1 | 2 | — | 2 | 2 | 1 |
| Shipbuilding, etc. | 28 | 7 | 21 | 1 | 7 | 13 | — | 2 | 1 | — | — | 3 | 2 | — | 1 | 1 | 1 | — |
| Lead, etc., Manufacture | 18 | 1 | 17 | 5 | 3 | 9 | — | 5 | 2 | — | — | 1 | — | 1 | 1 | 1 | — | — |
| Coal By-Products | 33 | 18 | 15 | 2 | 5 | 8 | — | 3 | — | 2 | — | 3 | — | 1 | — | 2 | — | 1 |
| Bricks, Tiles, Cement | 181 | 42 | 139 | 25 | 29 | 85 | 3 | 15 | 10 | 9 | 1 | 9 | 4 | 4 | 4 | 16 | 6 | 5 |
| Coastal Shipping | 101 | 21 | 80 | 13 | 25 | 42 | 2 | 6 | 11 | 3 | 1 | 3 | 6 | 2 | 3 | 1 | 8 | 1 |
| Ocean Shipping | 51 | 10 | 41 | 9 | 8 | 24 | 1 | 4 | 7 | 1 | — | 4 | — | 1 | — | 1 | 2 | — |
| Trams, Buses, etc. | 131 | 68 | 63 | 6 | 23 | 34 | 3 | 9 | 6 | 2 | 1 | 8 | 1 | 2 | 2 | 4 | 5 | 1 |
| Cables, Telegraphy | 74 | 35 | 39 | 6 | 18 | 15 | 5 | 2 | 2 | 2 | 2 | 5 | — | 2 | 1 | 1 | 3 | 2 |
| Cotton Manufacture | 201 | 10 | 191 | 19 | 25 | 147 | 2 | 4 | 9 | 2 | 1 | 12 | 5 | 2 | 3 | 7 | 9 | 2 |
| Woollens, etc. | 37 | 7 | 30 | 5 | 10 | 15 | — | 1 | 2 | — | 1 | 1 | 1 | 1 | — | 3 | 4 | — |
| Miscellaneous Textiles | 100 | 26 | 74 | 14 | 12 | 48 | 1 | 5 | 12 | 2 | — | 6 | 6 | 2 | 3 | 3 | 3 | 1 |
| Household, etc., Goods | 145 | 53 | 92 | 18 | 18 | 56 | — | 12 | 12 | 4 | — | 6 | 3 | 2 | 1 | 8 | 2 | 3 |
| Food and Provisions | 259 | 104 | 155 | 28 | 40 | 87 | 3 | 16 | 23 | 13 | 5 | 10 | 13 | 1 | 4 | 10 | 8 | 7 |
| Breweries, Flour Mills, etc. | 83 | 28 | 55 | 11 | 8 | 36 | 1 | 7 | 4 | 3 | 2 | 2 | 3 | 2 | 1 | — | 5 | 1 |
| Hotels, Restaurants, etc. | 161 | 59 | 102 | 31 | 28 | 43 | 2 | 4 | 7 | 1 | 2 | 4 | 2 | 2 | 2 | 8 | 5 | 1 |
| Land and Buildings | 284 | 72 | 212 | 76 | 40 | 96 | 2 | 7 | 10 | 3 | 2 | 5 | 6 | 3 | 2 | 11 | 25 | 5 |
| Newspapers | 134 | 61 | 73 | 19 | 18 | 36 | 3 | 7 | 3 | 2 | 1 | 2 | 6 | 3 | 1 | 7 | 2 | 6 |
| Printing and Paper | 86 | 28 | 58 | 6 | 15 | 37 | 1 | 10 | 8 | 4 | 1 | 2 | 1 | 2 | 1 | 4 | 2 | — |
| Chemicals, etc. | 98 | 18 | 80 | 17 | 12 | 51 | 3 | 8 | 10 | 3 | — | 7 | 3 | 3 | 3 | — | 4 | 1 |
| Farming Accessories | 103 | 24 | 79 | 8 | 31 | 40 | 5 | 5 | 8 | 4 | — | 4 | 5 | 2 | — | 4 | 6 | 2 |
| Petty Lending | 117 | 35 | 82 | 26 | 28 | 28 | — | 3 | 2 | 4 | — | 3 | 4 | — | 2 | 7 | 3 | 5 |
| Insurance | 162 | 67 | 95 | 35 | 34 | 26 | 3 | 9 | 7 | 10 | 2 | 7 | 5 | 1 | 2 | 11 | 2 | 2 |
| Financing, etc.: Home | 103 | 39 | 64 | 13 | 12 | 39 | 2 | 6 | 10 | 6 | — | 3 | 3 | 1 | 2 | 4 | 3 | 1 |
| Financing, etc.: Colonial | 6 | 2 | 4 | 1 | 2 | 1 | — | — | — | 1 | — | — | — | — | — | — | 1 | 1 |
| Financing, etc.: Foreign | 23 | 10 | 13 | 3 | 2 | 8 | — | 1 | 1 | 2 | — | 1 | 1 | — | — | 2 | — | — |
| Banking: Home | 43 | 15 | 28 | 8 | 6 | 14 | 1 | 4 | 1 | 2 | — | — | — | — | 3 | 4 | — | — |
| Banking: Colonial | 10 | 4 | 6 | 4 | 0 | 2 | — | — | — | 1 | — | 1 | — | — | — | — | — | — |
| Banking: Foreign | 23 | 8 | 15 | 2 | 3 | 10 | 1 | 1 | 1 | — | — | — | — | — | 2 | 1 | 3 | — |
| Mines and Lands: Colonial | 133 | 45 | 88 | 14 | 28 | 46 | 2 | 7 | 14 | 6 | 1 | 4 | 6 | 4 | 4 | 6 | 6 | 5 |
| Mines and Lands: Foreign | 358 | 105 | 253 | 45 | 99 | 109 | 12 | 19 | 23 | 27 | 5 | 19 | 20 | 12 | 11 | 24 | 15 | 10 |
| Miscellaneous: Colonial | 34 | 15 | 19 | 3 | 5 | 11 | 2 | 3 | 1 | — | — | 1 | — | — | — | 2 | 1 | — |
| Miscellaneous: Foreign | 60 | 34 | 26 | 5 | 8 | 13 | — | 6 | 2 | 1 | — | 2 | 1 | 1 | — | 2 | 2 | 1 |
| Public Utilities: Colonial | 22 | 9 | 13 | 2 | 9 | 2 | 2 | — | 2 | — | 1 | 1 | — | — | 1 | 1 | — | — |
| Public Utilities: Foreign | 123 | 55 | 68 | 15 | 23 | 30 | 1 | 3 | 5 | 3 | — | 6 | 2 | 2 | 3 | 5 | 3 | 2 |
| Mercantile and Trading | 184 | 76 | 108 | 27 | 21 | 60 | 4 | 8 | 9 | 9 | 1 | 4 | 9 | 2 | 2 | 5 | 7 | 2 |
| Unclassified | 448 | 196 | 252 | 59 | 50 | 143 | 10 | 15 | 30 | 15 | 5 | 11 | 9 | 8 | 4 | 15 | 14 | 7 |
| (1) General Totals | 5551 | 1724 | 3827 | 794 | 948 | 2085 | 109 | 342 | 342 | 203 | 64 | 242 | 189 | 100 | 96 | 309 | 211 | 104 |
| Local Halls and Clubs | 238 | 79 | 159 | 42 | 47 | 70 | 1 | — | 2 | 1 | 1 | 2 | 3 | 3 | 2 | 8 | 7 | 1 |
| Gas and Water | 322 | 75 | 247 | 104 | 93 | 50 | 8 | 5 | 4 | 6 | 4 | — | — | — | 12 | 6 | 6 | 2 |
| (2) Grand Totals | 6111 | 1878 | 4233 | 940 | 1088 | 2205 | 118 | 347 | 348 | 210 | 69 | 244 | 192 | 103 | 110 | 323 | 224 | 107 |

Notes : R = registered ; A.S. = abortive and small ; S = sold, amalgamated or reconstructed ; C = wound up omitted from tenth year but included in total) ; E = existing 1929 ; $Q_1$, M, $Q_3$ = Quartiles and Medians of companies

## A

IN LONDON, WITH DURATION AND MODE OF DISSOLUTION

| 11–15 Years | | | 16–20 Years | | | 21–30 Years | | | 31–40 Years | | | 41–50 Years | | | Over 50 Years | | | Totals | | | | E. | C-V-U | | |
|---|---|---|---|---|---|---|---|---|---|---|---|---|---|---|---|---|---|---|---|---|---|---|---|---|---|
| S | C | V | S | C | V | S | C | V | S | C | V | S | C | V | S | C | V | S | C | V | U | 1929 | Q₁ | M | Q₃ |
| 5 | 27 | 10 | 5 | 4 | 6 | 5 | 7 | 3 | 1 | 3 | 5 | 3 | 1 | — | 1 | 1 | 2 | 45 | 187 | 85 | 43 | 40 | 2 | 5 | 10 |
| 2 | 6 | 1 | 2 | 2 | 1 | — | 2 | 1 | — | — | 1 | — | — | — | — | — | — | 29 | 96 | 64 | 47 | 1 | 2 | 4 | 7 |
| 2 | 1 | 2 | 1 | — | — | 1 | — | 1 | — | — | 1 | 1 | — | 1 | — | — | — | 14 | 26 | 24 | 16 | 4 | 3 | 5 | 8 |
| 4 | 7 | 4 | 2 | 4 | 4 | 4 | 2 | 5 | 2 | 1 | 3 | 7 | 1 | — | 3 | — | — | 31 | 66 | 36 | 12 | 20 | 3 | 7 | 12 |
| 2 | 1 | 4 | 1 | — | — | 5 | 2 | — | — | — | — | 1 | — | — | 2 | — | — | 16 | 16 | 14 | 4 | 7 | 4 | 6 | 11 |
| 2 | 5 | — | 3 | 1 | 2 | 4 | — | — | — | — | — | — | 1 | — | — | — | — | 18 | 29 | 22 | 21 | 6 | 2 | 4 | 7 |
| — | 2 | 2 | 1 | 1 | 2 | 5 | 1 | 2 | 1 | — | — | — | — | 1 | — | — | 2 | 8 | 11 | 12 | 4 | 3 | 5 | 10 | 20 |
| — | 1 | 1 | — | 1 | — | 2 | — | 3 | — | 1 | 1 | — | — | — | — | — | — | 3 | 8 | 8 | 0 | 2 | 4 | 5 | 12 |
| — | 1 | — | — | — | — | 1 | — | 1 | — | 1 | 1 | — | — | — | — | — | — | 2 | 8 | 6 | 1 | 0 | 2 | 5 | 13 |
| — | — | — | — | — | 1 | 1 | — | 1 | — | 1 | 1 | — | — | — | — | — | — | 0 | 10 | 1 | 4 | 0 | 3 | 4 | 7 |
| — | 3 | 3 | 4 | 4 | 2 | 4 | 2 | 3 | 2 | 2 | 3 | 1 | — | 2 | 2 | — | 1 | 19 | 52 | 33 | 24 | 11 | 3 | 6 | 11 |
| 2 | 2 | 4 | 4 | — | 4 | — | — | 3 | 1 | 1 | 1 | 1 | — | 1 | 2 | — | 2 | 16 | 13 | 38 | 6 | 7 | 3 | 5 | 11 |
| 1 | 3 | 1 | — | 1 | 1 | 1 | 1 | 2 | — | — | 2 | — | 1 | 2 | — | — | 2 | 4 | 10 | 23 | 2 | 4 | 3 | 8 | 21 |
| — | — | 1 | — | 1 | 1 | 4 | — | 3 | — | — | 1 | — | — | 2 | — | — | — | 10 | 22 | 20 | 7 | 3 | 2 | 5 | 9 |
| — | — | 1 | 1 | 1 | 1 | 1 | — | 1 | 1 | — | — | — | — | — | — | — | — | 14 | 5 | 7 | 3 | 10 | 3 | 5 | 7 |
| 2 | 11 | 4 | 2 | 2 | 5 | 6 | 7 | 6 | 2 | 2 | 2 | 31 | 3 | 7 | 3 | 2 | 2 | 52 | 50 | 49 | 9 | 31 | 5 | 11 | 22 |
| 1 | 1 | 2 | — | — | 1 | 7 | 2 | 1 | 1 | — | — | — | — | — | 2 | — | — | 6 | 7 | 13 | 1 | 3 | 5 | 7 | 12 |
| 1 | 1 | 6 | 1 | 1 | — | 7 | — | 2 | 2 | — | — | — | — | 2 | 2 | — | 1 | 14 | 16 | 33 | 6 | 5 | 3 | 5 | 11 |
| 2 | 1 | 1 | 1 | 1 | 3 | 4 | — | 4 | 1 | — | — | — | — | 2 | 1 | 1 | 1 | 9 | 29 | 28 | 13 | 13 | 2 | 5 | 10 |
| 2 | 2 | 8 | 1 | 2 | 3 | 5 | 1 | 1 | 1 | — | 2 | 1 | 1 | — | 2 | — | 2 | 24 | 42 | 60 | 24 | 5 | 2 | 4 | 7 |
| — | 2 | 2 | 2 | — | 1 | 6 | — | 3 | — | — | 1 | 1 | — | 3 | — | — | 1 | 13 | 11 | 22 | 6 | 3 | 3 | 5 | 13 |
| 3 | 4 | 1 | — | 2 | 4 | 4 | 1 | 8 | 3 | 1 | 1 | — | — | 4 | 2 | — | 1 | 18 | 24 | 33 | 9 | 18 | 5 | 10 | 21 |
| 2 | 4 | 21 | 2 | 5 | 7 | 7 | 4 | 12 | 3 | — | 4 | — | 1 | 7 | 1 | 1 | 1 | 20 | 37 | 93 | 17 | 45 | 6 | 10 | 18 |
| 4 | 1 | — | 1 | 1 | — | 3 | — | 1 | 3 | 1 | 1 | 1 | — | 1 | 1 | — | — | 18 | 19 | 14 | 14 | 8 | 3 | 6 | 9 |
| 2 | 7 | 2 | — | 2 | — | 2 | 1 | 2 | 1 | — | 1 | — | — | — | — | — | — | 7 | 24 | 14 | 7 | 6 | 2 | 4 | 10 |
| 4 | 7 | 6 | 7 | 1 | 2 | 3 | 1 | 2 | 1 | — | 1 | 1 | 1 | 1 | — | — | — | 21 | 19 | 28 | 7 | 5 | 2 | 4 | 10 |
| 1 | 3 | 3 | — | — | 3 | 3 | 1 | 4 | — | 2 | 6 | — | — | — | — | — | — | 10 | 19 | 32 | 11 | 7 | 3 | 6 | 12 |
| — | 9 | — | — | — | 1 | 3 | 2 | 4 | — | 2 | 6 | — | — | 1 | — | — | — | 5 | 27 | 30 | 13 | 7 | 6 | 11 | 16 |
| 2 | 1 | 5 | 2 | 1 | — | 5 | 2 | 1 | 1 | — | 1 | — | — | 1 | — | — | — | 17 | 31 | 22 | 17 | 8 | 2 | 5 | 10 |
| 2 | — | 4 | 3 | 3 | 1 | — | — | 1 | 1 | — | 1 | — | — | — | — | — | — | 9 | 17 | 23 | 10 | 5 | 2 | 4 | 10 |
| — | 4 | 1 | — | — | — | — | — | — | — | — | — | — | — | — | — | — | 1 | 0 | 0 | 2 | 2 | 0 | 2 | 6 | 7 |
| — | 1 | 1 | — | — | 1 | — | — | 1 | — | — | — | — | — | — | — | — | — | 0 | 2 | 7 | 3 | 1 | 3 | 4 | 11 |
| 1 | 1 | — | 2 | 1 | — | 2 | 1 | — | 2 | — | 2 | 2 | — | — | — | — | — | 13 | 10 | 1 | 2 | 2 | 2 | 3 | 9 |
| — | — | — | 1 | — | 1 | — | — | 1 | 1 | — | — | — | — | — | — | — | — | 2 | 0 | 2 | 0 | 2 | — | — | — |
| — | — | — | — | — | — | — | — | 1 | 1 | — | — | 1 | — | 1 | 1 | — | — | 6 | 2 | 5 | 1 | — | 3 | 6 | — |
| 2 | 1 | — | 3 | 2 | 1 | 3 | 2 | 2 | — | 2 | 1 | 1 | — | 1 | — | — | 1 | 15 | 24 | 31 | 17 | 1 | 2 | 5 | 8 |
| 3 | 6 | 4 | 5 | 1 | 2 | 3 | 3 | 3 | 4 | 1 | 2 | 1 | — | 1 | — | — | 1 | 42 | 72 | 71 | 55 | 13 | 3 | 5 | 9 |
| — | 1 | — | — | — | 1 | 1 | 1 | 1 | 1 | — | 2 | 1 | — | — | — | — | — | 5 | 6 | 6 | 0 | 2 | 3 | 7 | 12 |
| — | 1 | — | — | — | 1 | 1 | — | 1 | 1 | — | 2 | — | — | — | — | — | — | 1 | 11 | 9 | 3 | 3 | 3 | 5 | 9 |
| — | 1 | — | — | — | 1 | 1 | — | 1 | 1 | — | — | 1 | — | — | — | — | — | 5 | 3 | 4 | 0 | 1 | 3 | 9 | 15 |
| 2 | 2 | 1 | — | 1 | 1 | 3 | — | 2 | — | 3 | 1 | — | — | — | 1 | — | 1 | 15 | 17 | 17 | 10 | 9 | 3 | 6 | 11 |
| 3 | 1 | 5 | 2 | — | — | 3 | — | 4 | 1 | 2 | 2 | 1 | — | — | 1 | — | 1 | 18 | 20 | 37 | 15 | 18 | 3 | 5 | 10 |
| 4 | 8 | 10 | 7 | 2 | 6 | 6 | 6 | 12 | 6 | 2 | 3 | 1 | — | 2 | 2 | 1 | 1 | 45 | 60 | 87 | 34 | 26 | 2 | 6 | 13 |
| 63 | 131 | 132 | 66 | 46 | 70 | 118 | 50 | 105 | 44 | 21 | 52 | 57 | 10 | 43 | 22 | 7 | 22 | 639 | 1158 | 1166 | 500 | 364 | — | 21 | 39 |
| 8 | 4 | 1 | 11 | 5 | 1 | 15 | 4 | 7 | 29 | 2 | 8 | 13 | 2 | 10 | 5 | 2 | 2 | 105 | 23 | 71 | 11 | 33 | 10 | 23 | 38 |
| — | 1 | 5 | 1 | 1 | 9 | 4 | 3 | 9 | 4 | 1 | 18 | 3 | 3 | 9 | 7 | — | 9 | 23 | 26 | 39 | 9 | 66 | 7 | 23 | 38 |
| 71 | 136 | 138 | 78 | 52 | 80 | 137 | 57 | 121 | 77 | 24 | 78 | 73 | 15 | 62 | 34 | 9 | 33 | 767 | 1207 | 1276 | 520 | 463 | — | — | — |

by or under the Courts and through liabilities ; V = unexplained voluntary winding up ; U = unknown (details under C, V, and U.

TABLE

COMPANIES, LIMITED BY SHARES, ATTEMPTED IN 1875–83 AND

(ONLY PUBLIC

| Description | R. | A.S. | Effective | | | | | 3 Years and Under | | | | 4–5 Years | | | | 6–10 Years | | | |
|---|---|---|---|---|---|---|---|---|---|---|---|---|---|---|---|---|---|---|---|
| | | | Private | Public | 1875–77 | 1878–80 | 1881–83 | S | C | V | U | S | C | V | U | S | C | V | U |
| Coal and Coal Mines | 310 | 61 | 96 | 153 | 81 | 33 | 39 | 3 | 38 | 7 | 7 | 1 | 10 | 2 | 1 | 5 | 17 | 5 | 2 |
| Lead, etc., Mines . | 366 | 129 | 27 | 210 | 69 | 67 | 74 | 4 | 54 | 8 | 26 | 8 | 25 | 9 | 5 | 10 | 27 | 10 | 7 |
| Quarries . . | 135 | 49 | 29 | 57 | 32 | 14 | 11 | — | 9 | 2 | 5 | 1 | 7 | 5 | 1 | 1 | 3 | 6 | 1 |
| Iron Manufacture and General Engineering | 203 | 39 | 70 | 94 | 47 | 23 | 24 | — | 13 | 3 | 4 | 1 | 10 | 3 | 2 | — | 16 | 4 | — |
| Iron and Steel Products . | 140 | 34 | 49 | 57 | 21 | 10 | 26 | — | 10 | 3 | — | 2 | 4 | 2 | 2 | 1 | 8 | 3 | |
| Specialized Engineering . | 260 | 87 | 71 | 102 | 27 | 22 | 53 | 2 | 19 | 4 | 7 | 1 | 11 | 4 | — | 3 | 7 | 4 | 3 |
| Railway, etc., Equipment . | 69 | 16 | 14 | 39 | 16 | 7 | 16 | — | 4 | 1 | 4 | 1 | 5 | 2 | 1 | 1 | 4 | 5 | — |
| Shipbuilding, etc. . | 64 | 21 | 8 | 35 | 7 | 8 | 20 | 1 | 1 | | 5 | 4 | 1 | 1 | — | — | 1 | 2 | 1 | — |
| Lead, etc., Manufacturing | 33 | 13 | 8 | 12 | 3 | 2 | 7 | 2 | 2 | 3 | 1 | | | | 1 | | | | |
| Electrical . . | 161 | 65 | 9 | 87 | — | 12 | 75 | 13 | 22 | 9 | 6 | — | 2 | 4 | — | 7 | 1 | 4 | 1 |
| Coal By-Products . | 20 | 9 | — | 11 | 4 | 3 | 4 | — | 2 | | 1 | 1 | — | 2 | — | 1 | | | 1 |
| Bricks, Tiles, Cement | 289 | 86 | 76 | 127 | 57 | 25 | 45 | 1 | 27 | 7 | 6 | 2 | 13 | 3 | 2 | 3 | 10 | 7 | 1 |
| Shipping . . | 682 | 92 | 141 | 449 | 36 | 67 | 346 | 8 | 23 | 52 | 14 | 11 | 11 | 25 | 4 | 21 | 10 | 43 | 3 |
| Trams, Omnibuses . | 225 | 93 | 14 | 118 | 38 | 40 | 40 | 6 | 11 | 9 | 9 | 3 | 8 | 2 | — | 9 | 7 | 5 | 3 |
| Telegraphy, Cables . | 21 | 9 | — | 12 | 6 | 5 | 1 | 2 | 1 | 1 | 1 | | | | | | | | |
| Cotton Manufacture | 238 | 14 | 86 | 138 | 89 | 13 | 36 | 1 | 10 | 7 | 1 | 1 | 10 | 4 | — | 1 | 9 | 3 | 3 |
| Woollen Manufacture | 48 | 10 | 14 | 24 | 11 | 7 | 6 | — | 3 | 3 | 1 | — | | | | | 1 | 3 | 2 |
| Miscellaneous Textiles | 72 | 20 | 18 | 34 | 16 | 7 | 11 | — | 8 | | — | | 2 | 1 | 1 | 1 | 1 | 4 | — |
| Household, etc., Goods | 463 | 204 | 96 | 163 | 54 | 50 | 59 | 5 | 25 | 10 | 11 | 3 | 6 | 7 | 1 | 5 | 12 | 11 | 3 |
| Food and Provisions | 544 | 254 | 78 | 212 | 52 | 61 | 99 | 6 | 62 | 16 | 12 | 3 | 15 | 5 | 1 | 7 | 14 | 12 | 3 |
| Breweries . . | 136 | 45 | 22 | 69 | 24 | 20 | 25 | 1 | 18 | 4 | 2 | 3 | 6 | 3 | — | 2 | 6 | 2 | — |
| Hotels, Restaurants, etc. | 812 | 375 | 33 | 404 | 95 | 191 | 118 | 5 | 26 | 13 | 7 | 1 | 20 | 16 | 4 | 3 | 19 | 30 | 3 |
| Land and Buildings | 539 | 169 | 60 | 310 | 148 | 58 | 104 | 4 | 19 | 5 | 9 | 3 | 10 | 7 | 3 | 7 | 18 | 25 | 7 |
| Newspapers . . | 189 | 82 | 33 | 74 | 34 | 13 | 27 | 3 | 11 | 9 | 4 | 2 | 1 | 1 | — | 5 | 5 | 4 | 2 |
| Paper and Printing | 208 | 63 | 46 | 99 | 40 | 20 | 39 | — | 16 | 7 | 8 | 2 | 11 | 1 | 1 | 2 | 5 | 4 | 1 |
| Chemicals, etc. . | 134 | 35 | 36 | 63 | 26 | 12 | 25 | 1 | 15 | 6 | 4 | — | 8 | 1 | — | 2 | 5 | 3 | 1 |
| Farming Accessories | 126 | 45 | 25 | 56 | 27 | 14 | 15 | 1 | 7 | 2 | 3 | — | 1 | 2 | — | 1 | 4 | 5 | 2 |
| Petty Lending . | 157 | 66 | 17 | 74 | 22 | 17 | 35 | — | 8 | 4 | 1 | — | 2 | 5 | 1 | — | 7 | 12 | 1 |
| Insurance . . | 184 | 84 | 6 | 94 | 31 | 32 | 31 | 3 | 13 | 7 | 4 | 4 | 5 | 6 | 1 | 8 | 5 | 4 | — |
| Investment, etc.: Home | 140 | 70 | 21 | 49 | 6 | 14 | 29 | 1 | 10 | 3 | 7 | 3 | 1 | — | — | 3 | 5 | 2 | — |
| Investment, etc.: Colonial | 9 | 2 | — | 7 | 1 | 2 | 4 | — | 1 | | — | | | | | — | 1 | 1 | — |
| Investment, etc.: Foreign | 40 | 22 | 1 | 17 | 2 | 5 | 10 | — | 3 | 1 | 1 | — | | 1 | — | 1 | 1 | 1 | — |
| Banks: Home . | 55 | 18 | — | 37 | 10 | 17 | 10 | — | 10 | 1 | 1 | 1 | 2 | 1 | — | 2 | 3 | — | — |
| Banks: Colonial . | 6 | 5 | — | 1 | — | 1 | — | — | | | | | | | | | | | |
| Banks: Foreign . | 34 | 20 | — | 14 | 5 | 5 | 4 | — | 3 | 1 | 1 | — | | | | 2 | 3 | — | — |
| Mines and Lands: Colonial | 252 | 68 | 15 | 169 | 26 | 61 | 82 | 11 | 26 | 7 | 7 | 7 | 10 | 6 | 2 | 16 | 7 | 6 | 1 |
| Mines and Lands: Foreign | 476 | 172 | 36 | 268 | 51 | 64 | 153 | 10 | 39 | 24 | 19 | 9 | 21 | 12 | 3 | 12 | 25 | 17 | 8 |
| Miscellaneous: Colonial | 44 | 15 | 7 | 22 | 7 | 6 | 9 | 2 | 3 | 2 | — | — | 3 | 2 | — | — | 2 | — | — |
| Miscellaneous: Foreign | 95 | 36 | 16 | 43 | 9 | 8 | 26 | 2 | 9 | 2 | 2 | 2 | 6 | 1 | 1 | — | 4 | 1 | — |
| Public Utilities: Colonial | 37 | 10 | 1 | 26 | 1 | 6 | 19 | — | — | 3 | — | 3 | — | — | — | 2 | 2 | — |
| Public Utilities: Foreign | 160 | 65 | 11 | 84 | 18 | 27 | 39 | 1 | 6 | 5 | — | 2 | 5 | — | — | 1 | 3 | 5 | 1 |
| Mercantile and Trading . | 209 | 84 | 52 | 73 | 26 | 19 | 28 | 1 | 12 | 4 | 5 | 1 | 7 | 4 | — | 2 | 4 | 3 | 1 |
| Unclassified . . | 640 | 271 | 43 | 326 | 150 | 86 | 90 | 9 | 46 | 20 | 26 | 2 | 18 | 9 | 6 | 14 | 20 | 21 | 4 |
| (1) General Totals . | 9025 | 3127 | 1385 | 4513 | 1425 | 1174 | 1914 | 109 | 645 | 280 | 231 | 85 | 277 | 158 | 44 | 158 | 299 | 281 | 61 |
| Local Halls and Clubs | 373 | 144 | 4 | 225 | 80 | 62 | 83 | 3 | 4 | 3 | 2 | 2 | 4 | 3 | 1 | 3 | 8 | 15 | 5 |
| Gas and Water . | 153 | 40 | 2 | 111 | 49 | 30 | 32 | 2 | — | 2 | — | 1 | 2 | — | — | 5 | 3 | 1 | — |
| (2) Grand Totals . | 9551 | 3311 | 1391 | 4849 | 1554 | 1266 | 2029 | 114 | 649 | 285 | 233 | 88 | 283 | 161 | 45 | 166 | 310 | 297 | 66 |
| Private Companies . | — | — | — | — | 336 | 401 | 654 | 36 | 146 | 152 | 116 | 18 | 49 | 59 | 35 | 44 | 65 | 108 | 26 |
| (3) Final Totals . | 9551 | 3311 | 6240 | | 1890 | 1667 | 2683 | 150 | 795 | 437 | 349 | 106 | 332 | 220 | 80 | 210 | 375 | 405 | 92 |

Notes : See

**B**

REGISTERED IN LONDON, WITH DURATION AND MODE OF DISSOLUTION
IN DETAIL)

| 11-15 Years | | | 16-20 Years | | | 21-30 Years | | | 31-40 Years | | | 41-50 Years | | | Over 50 Years | | | Totals | | | | E. | C-V-U | | |
|---|---|---|---|---|---|---|---|---|---|---|---|---|---|---|---|---|---|---|---|---|---|---|---|---|---|
| S | C | V | S | C | V | S | C | V | S | C | V | S | C | V | S | C | V | S | C | V | U | 1929 | $Q_1$ | M | $Q_3$ |
| 1 | 6 | 2 | 2 | 2 | 3 | 5 | 3 | 3 | 1 | 2 | 4 | 3 | 2 | 1 | — | — | — | 21 | 80 | 27 | 10 | 15 | 2 | 4 | 10 |
| 1 | 6 | 3 | 1 | 1 | — | 1 | 1 | 1 | — | 2 | — | — | — | — | — | — | — | 25 | 114 | 31 | 39 | 1 | 2 | 4 | 6 |
| — | 2 | 1 | — | — | 1 | — | 2 | — | 2 | 1 | — | — | — | — | — | — | — | 4 | 24 | 15 | 7 | 7 | 3 | 4 | 8 |
| 3 | 3 | 4 | 4 | — | — | 3 | 1 | 2 | — | — | — | 2 | — | 2 | 1 | — | — | 14 | 43 | 18 | 6 | 13 | 3 | 5 | 9 |
| — | 1 | 1 | 2 | 1 | 1 | 1 | 1 | 1 | 1 | 2 | 2 | — | — | — | — | — | — | 7 | 27 | 13 | 2 | 8 | 3 | 5 | 10 |
| 6 | 1 | 1 | 4 | — | 1 | 1 | 1 | 2 | 2 | 2 | — | — | 1 | 2 | — | — | — | 19 | 40 | 18 | 12 | 13 | 2 | 4 | 8 |
| — | — | — | — | — | — | — | 3 | — | — | — | — | — | — | 1 | — | — | — | 2 | 13 | 12 | 6 | 6 | 3 | 5 | 8 |
| 1 | — | 5 | 3 | — | — | — | 1 | — | — | — | — | 1 | 1 | — | 1 | — | — | 8 | 5 | 13 | 4 | 5 | 2 | 4 | 12 |
| — | — | — | 1 | — | — | — | 1 | — | — | — | — | — | — | — | — | — | — | 3 | 3 | 3 | 3 | — | 2 | 3 | 4 |
| 3 | 1 | 2 | 1 | 1 | 3 | 2 | — | 1 | — | — | — | — | — | — | — | — | — | 25 | 27 | 23 | 9 | 3 | 2 | 3 | 7 |
| — | 2 | — | — | 2 | 1 | — | — | — | — | — | — | 1 | — | — | — | — | — | 2 | 5 | 3 | 1 | — | 2 | 4 | 11 |
| 3 | 5 | 8 | 1 | 2 | 3 | 5 | 2 | 4 | 1 | — | 3 | 3 | — | 1 | — | — | — | 19 | 59 | 36 | 9 | 4 | 2 | 5 | 11 |
| 16 | 14 | 51 | 10 | 3 | 27 | 13 | 5 | 27 | 10 | — | 17 | — | 2 | 2 | — | — | — | 89 | 68 | 244 | 22 | 26 | 3 | 8 | 15 |
| 3 | 3 | 3 | 1 | 1 | 5 | 3 | — | 10 | 1 | 4 | 2 | 2 | — | 1 | — | — | — | 28 | 34 | 36 | 12 | 8 | 3 | 6 | 16 |
| — | — | 1 | 1 | — | 1 | — | — | — | — | — | — | — | — | — | — | — | — | 3 | 1 | 3 | 1 | 4 | — | — | — |
| — | 3 | 1 | 1 | 8 | 2 | — | 2 | 6 | 15 | 1 | 2 | 10 | 2 | 2 | — | 1 | — | 29 | 46 | 27 | 4 | 32 | 4 | 8 | 20 |
| 1 | — | 1 | — | — | 1 | 1 | 1 | 1 | — | — | — | — | 2 | 2 | — | — | — | 2 | 5 | 10 | 3 | 4 | 3 | 6 | 25 |
| 1 | 2 | 1 | — | 2 | 3 | 2 | 1 | 1 | 1 | 1 | 2 | — | — | — | — | — | — | 4 | 14 | 9 | 1 | 6 | 3 | 5 | 14 |
| 6 | 2 | 3 | 2 | 2 | 7 | 9 | 1 | 5 | 1 | — | 4 | 1 | — | 3 | — | — | — | 27 | 48 | 46 | 15 | 27 | 2 | 5 | 9 |
| 1 | 1 | 3 | 5 | 1 | 1 | 4 | 2 | — | — | 3 | 5 | 1 | — | — | — | 3 | — | 29 | 103 | 53 | 14 | 13 | 2 | 3 | 7 |
| — | — | — | — | — | — | — | — | — | 2 | — | — | 1 | — | 3 | — | — | — | 13 | 32 | 16 | 3 | 5 | 2 | 4 | 8 |
| 7 | 12 | 33 | 12 | 5 | 13 | 6 | 14 | 26 | 5 | 7 | 19 | 2 | 2 | 25 | — | — | — | 41 | 105 | 175 | 20 | 63 | 5 | 11 | 24 |
| 10 | 23 | — | 3 | 1 | 1 | 1 | 2 | 21 | 1 | 2 | 11 | 2 | 1 | 7 | — | — | 1 | 21 | 67 | 114 | 26 | 82 | 5 | 11 | 17 |
| 2 | 1 | 3 | 1 | 1 | 2 | 2 | 3 | 1 | 1 | 1 | 1 | — | 2 | 2 | — | — | 1 | 16 | 21 | 21 | 8 | 8 | 2 | 4 | 11 |
| 2 | 4 | 1 | 1 | 2 | 2 | 1 | 3 | 2 | 1 | 1 | 2 | — | 2 | 2 | — | — | 1 | 9 | 44 | 22 | 11 | 13 | 3 | 5 | 11 |
| 3 | — | 1 | 2 | 2 | 2 | 1 | — | 2 | — | 1 | 1 | — | — | 2 | — | — | — | 7 | 28 | 17 | 6 | 5 | 2 | 4 | 10 |
| — | 4 | 2 | 2 | 1 | 1 | — | 1 | 1 | — | — | 2 | — | — | — | — | — | — | 4 | 18 | 16 | 5 | 13 | 3 | 7 | 14 |
| — | 3 | 6 | 1 | 1 | 1 | 3 | — | 2 | — | 4 | 1 | — | — | 1 | — | — | — | 2 | 25 | 32 | 8 | 7 | 4 | 8 | 13 |
| 5 | 1 | — | 4 | — | 2 | 3 | — | 2 | 2 | — | — | — | — | — | — | — | — | 29 | 24 | 23 | 5 | 13 | 2 | 4 | 6 |
| 1 | — | 5 | 1 | 1 | 1 | 1 | — | 1 | — | — | — | — | — | — | — | — | 2 | 10 | 17 | 14 | 7 | 1 | 2 | 5 | 11 |
| — | — | — | 1 | — | — | — | — | — | — | — | — | — | — | — | — | — | — | 1 | 2 | 1 | — | 3 | — | — | — |
| — | — | — | 1 | 1 | 1 | — | — | — | — | — | — | — | — | 1 | — | — | — | 2 | 5 | 5 | 1 | 4 | 2 | 5 | 18 |
| 3 | — | — | 2 | — | 1 | 3 | — | 1 | 2 | 1 | — | — | — | — | — | — | — | 13 | 16 | 4 | 1 | 3 | 2 | 3 | 10 |
| 1 | — | — | — | — | — | 1 | 1 | — | — | 1 | — | — | — | — | — | — | — | 1 | — | — | — | — | — | — | — |
| 1 | — | — | — | — | — | 1 | 1 | — | — | 1 | — | 1 | 1 | — | — | — | — | 3 | 6 | 4 | 1 | — | 3 | 7 | 9 |
| 8 | 6 | 3 | 2 | — | 4 | 3 | 2 | 5 | 2 | — | 4 | 2 | — | 2 | — | — | — | 51 | 51 | 37 | 10 | 20 | 3 | 5 | 11 |
| 5 | 5 | 8 | 1 | 2 | 4 | 4 | 4 | 7 | 1 | 4 | 10 | — | 2 | 2 | — | — | — | 42 | 102 | 84 | 33 | 7 | 2 | 5 | 10 |
| 1 | 1 | 1 | — | — | — | 1 | 2 | — | — | — | — | 1 | — | — | — | — | — | 4 | 10 | 7 | — | 1 | 3 | 5 | 8 |
| 1 | — | 2 | — | 1 | 2 | — | 1 | 2 | — | — | — | 1 | 1 | — | — | — | — | 7 | 21 | 10 | 4 | 1 | 3 | 5 | 12 |
| 1 | 1 | — | 1 | — | — | — | — | 2 | — | 1 | 1 | — | — | — | — | — | — | 6 | 3 | 9 | — | 8 | 3 | 8 | 25 |
| 3 | 4 | 1 | 2 | — | 4 | 5 | 1 | 9 | 2 | — | 2 | 1 | 1 | 1 | — | — | — | 17 | 20 | 27 | 3 | 17 | 4 | 10 | 25 |
| 2 | 2 | 1 | 2 | — | 1 | 5 | — | 4 | 1 | — | — | — | 1 | — | — | — | 1 | 14 | 25 | 18 | 6 | 10 | 2 | 4 | 7 |
| 6 | 7 | 10 | 8 | 6 | 5 | 6 | 4 | 13 | 2 | 5 | 6 | 1 | 2 | 5 | — | — | — | 48 | 108 | 89 | 41 | 40 | 2 | 5 | 12 |
| 98 | 118 | 199 | 85 | 53 | 116 | 93 | 57 | 172 | 58 | 39 | 104 | 33 | 20 | 72 | 2 | 1 | 3 | 721 | 1509 | 1385 | 379 | 519 | — | — | — |
| 1 | 3 | 9 | 3 | 8 | 9 | 5 | 5 | 6 | 4 | 2 | 16 | 6 | 4 | 12 | 1 | — | 1 | 28 | 38 | 74 | 13 | 72 | 7 | 16 | 33 |
| 6 | 1 | 1 | 8 | — | 2 | 10 | — | 6 | 1 | — | 2 | 5 | 3 | 1 | 1 | — | 1 | 39 | 9 | 16 | 1 | 46 | 8 | 32 | 40 |
| 105 | 122 | 209 | 96 | 61 | 127 | 108 | 62 | 184 | 63 | 41 | 122 | 44 | 27 | 85 | 4 | 1 | 5 | 788 | 1556 | 1475 | 393 | 637 | — | — | — |
| 24 | 26 | 72 | 28 | 14 | 40 | 22 | 12 | 48 | 8 | 8 | 26 | 10 | 10 | 14 | — | 3 | 1 | 190 | 333 | 520 | 206 | 142 | — | — | — |
| 129 | 148 | 281 | 124 | 75 | 167 | 130 | 74 | 232 | 71 | 49 | 148 | 54 | 37 | 99 | 4 | 4 | 6 | 978 | 1889 | 1995 | 599 | 779 | — | — | — |

Table A

TABLE

"Effective" Yearly Formations, 1856–83, of Companies, Registered

| Description | '56 | '57 | '58 | '59 | '60 | '61 | '62 | '63 | '64 | '65 | '66 | '67 | '68 | '69 | '70 | '71 | '72 | '73 | '74 | '75 |
|---|---|---|---|---|---|---|---|---|---|---|---|---|---|---|---|---|---|---|---|---|
| Coal and Iron Mines | 11 | 10 | 10 | 9 | 8 | 7 | 10 | 25 | 41 | 30 | 31 | 19 | 19 | 11 | 18 | 31 | 78 | 109 | 84 | 44 (13) |
| Lead, etc., Mines | 8 | 33 | 28 | 31 | 31 | 28 | 48 | 23 | 22 | 21 | 12 | 18 | 18 | 23 | 43 | 30 | 33 | 32 | 28 | 22 (2) |
| Quarries | 2 | 8 | 3 | 3 | 9 | 12 | 8 | 19 | 28 | 15 | 13 | 9 | 7 | 7 | 5 | 5 | 12 | 17 | 9 | 10 (1) |
| Iron Manufacturing and General Engineering | 3 | 4 | 2 | 2 | 2 | 6 | 5 | 4 | 27 | 23 | 13 | 5 | 8 | 9 | 9 | 15 | 34 | 37 | 35 | 21 (13) |
| Iron and Steel Products | — | — | — | — | 1 | 3 | 2 | 6 | 5 | 5 | 8 | 4 | 2 | 1 | 6 | 3 | 8 | 14 | 11 | 10 (4) |
| Specialized Engineering | 2 | — | 1 | 2 | 2 | 3 | 5 | 3 | 16 | 5 | 7 | 10 | 2 | 4 | 11 | 6 | 15 | 17 | 24 | 12 (7) |
| Railway, etc., Equipment | — | 2 | — | — | 5 | — | 7 | 5 | 3 | 5 | 6 | 1 | 1 | 3 | 2 | 1 | 8 | 12 | 4 | 6 (2) |
| Shipbuilding, etc. | — | 3 | — | 1 | — | 2 | 3 | 4 | 7 | 6 | 1 | — | — | 1 | 1 | 5 | 3 | 8 | 2 | 1 (—) |
| Electrical | — | — | — | — | — | — | — | — | — | — | — | — | — | — | — | — | — | — | — | — (—) |
| Lead, etc., Manufacturing | — | 1 | 1 | 1 | 2 | — | 3 | 3 | 3 | 1 | 4 | 1 | — | — | 2 | 1 | 2 | 3 | 4 | 1 (—) |
| Coal By-Products | — | 1 | — | 1 | 1 | 5 | 5 | 6 | 4 | 11 | 1 | 1 | — | 1 | — | 4 | — | 5 | 3 | 3 (—) |
| Bricks, Tiles, Cement | 2 | 3 | 2 | 1 | 4 | 3 | 7 | 2 | 6 | 11 | 10 | 5 | 10 | 9 | 9 | 11 | 28 | 26 | 31 | 16 (7) |
| Coastal Shipping | 4 | 13 | 4 | 2 | 7 | 1 | 5 | 8 | 3 | 9 | 7 | 5 | 1 | 5 | 14 | 6 | 10 | 20 | 12 | 11 (1) |
| Ocean Shipping | 5 | 1 | 4 | — | 2 | 5 | 1 | 3 | 11 | 5 | 5 | 2 | 2 | 1 | 3 | 4 | 13 | 5 | 6 | 6 (3) |
| Trams, Buses, etc. | 2 | 1 | 2 | 2 | 3 | 5 | 1 | 3 | 5 | 5 | 4 | 2 | — | 3 | 6 | 14 | 12 | 14 | 8 | 16 (—) |
| Cables, Telegraphy | — | 2 | 3 | 1 | 2 | 1 | — | 2 | 2 | 2 | 1 | — | 5 | 9 | 7 | 2 | 6 | 8 | 1 | 2 (—) |
| Cotton Manufacture | 1 | 1 | — | 9 | 45 | 53 | 3 | 2 | 7 | 12 | 11 | 6 | 2 | 4 | 8 | 13 | 10 | 38 | 99 | 69 (12) |
| Woollens and Worsteds | — | — | — | 2 | — | 1 | — | 3 | 2 | 6 | 3 | — | 2 | 2 | 3 | 5 | 5 | 5 | 5 | 3 (2) |
| Miscellaneous Textiles | 6 | 4 | 3 | 1 | — | 3 | 5 | 1 | 10 | 10 | 11 | 2 | 1 | 4 | 1 | 7 | 14 | 17 | 17 | 7 (1) |
| Household, etc., Goods | 8 | 7 | 2 | 5 | 3 | 7 | 7 | 7 | 9 | 24 | 8 | 7 | 3 | 5 | 3 | 10 | 16 | 22 | 18 | 19 (4) |
| Food, Provisions, etc. | 9 | 10 | 4 | 5 | 7 | 4 | 2 | 7 | 18 | 12 | 10 | 6 | 12 | 6 | 15 | 19 | 31 | 29 | 27 | 22 (3) |
| Breweries, Flour Mills, etc. | 1 | 6 | 6 | 3 | 2 | 6 | 11 | 5 | 8 | 27 | 8 | 3 | — | 2 | 4 | 2 | 9 | 12 | 15 | 10 (2) |
| Hotels, Restaurants, etc. | — | 3 | 4 | 8 | 5 | 6 | 13 | 45 | 34 | 22 | 12 | 7 | 12 | 8 | 7 | 13 | 14 | 13 | 16 | 23 (1) |
| Land and Buildings | — | 10 | 2 | 7 | 13 | 19 | 14 | 25 | 36 | 42 | 40 | 12 | 24 | 13 | 13 | 14 | 19 | 39 | 38 | 54 (7) |
| Newspapers | 3 | 3 | 5 | 2 | 3 | 1 | 3 | 2 | 7 | 7 | 9 | 8 | 2 | 3 | 6 | 9 | 9 | 18 | 9 | 16 (1) |
| Paper and Printing | 1 | 3 | 1 | 2 | 1 | 2 | 8 | 4 | 8 | 7 | 2 | 2 | 2 | 2 | 5 | 8 | 11 | 12 | 14 | 23 (6) |
| Chemicals, etc. | 2 | 3 | 2 | 2 | 2 | 1 | 1 | 8 | 8 | 9 | 8 | 5 | 4 | 5 | 1 | 6 | 23 | 8 | 20 | 11 (7) |
| Farming Accessories | 8 | 7 | 2 | 7 | 2 | 5 | — | 6 | 8 | 7 | 3 | 3 | 2 | 6 | 10 | 15 | 19 | 13 | 8 | 8 (2) |
| Petty Lending | 11 | 11 | 5 | 7 | 8 | 8 | 4 | 8 | 11 | 11 | 11 | 8 | 7 | 13 | 2 | 13 | 7 | 11 | 10 | 10 (1) |
| Insurance | — | — | — | — | — | — | 3 | 14 | 17 | 14 | 12 | 10 | 13 | 10 | 16 | 8 | 6 | 8 | 12 | 10 (3) |
| Finance, Investment : Home | 1 | — | — | 1 | — | — | — | 4 | 7 | 5 | 8 | 4 | 1 | 2 | 1 | 9 | 8 | 11 | 20 | 5 (2) |
| Finance, Investment: Colonial | — | — | — | — | 1 | — | 1 | 5 | 7 | 4 | — | 1 | — | — | — | 2 | — | 1 | — | — (—) |
| Finance, Investment: Foreign | — | — | — | — | — | — | — | 3 | 8 | 4 | 3 | — | — | — | 1 | 1 | 5 | — | 3 | — (—) |
| Banking : Home | — | — | — | — | — | 4 | 10 | 10 | 8 | 5 | 5 | — | 3 | 1 | 1 | 4 | 8 | 3 | 3 | 7 (—) |
| Banking : Colonial | — | — | — | — | — | — | 5 | 2 | 2 | 1 | 3 | 1 | — | — | — | 1 | 2 | — | — | — (—) |
| Banking : Foreign | — | — | — | — | — | — | 2 | 9 | 8 | 5 | 1 | 1 | — | — | — | 3 | 5 | 4 | 1 | 1 (—) |
| Mines and Lands : Colonial | — | 5 | 8 | 5 | 6 | 8 | 16 | 11 | 18 | 11 | 7 | 3 | 4 | 9 | 2 | 17 | 11 | 18 | 17 | 8 (1) |
| Mines and Lands : Foreign | 3 | 10 | 8 | 5 | 4 | 9 | 10 | 20 | 14 | 15 | 16 | 16 | 13 | 18 | 25 | 56 | 43 | 40 | 26 | 22 (—) |
| Miscellaneous : Colonial | 2 | — | — | — | — | 2 | 2 | 5 | 2 | 2 | 2 | — | 1 | 1 | 3 | 4 | 3 | 4 | 4 | 4 (1) |
| Miscellaneous : Foreign | — | 1 | 1 | — | — | 1 | 4 | 7 | 4 | 2 | — | 3 | 4 | 1 | — | 9 | 2 | 2 | 5 | — (—) |
| Public Utilities : Colonial | 2 | 4 | — | 1 | — | 3 | 7 | 2 | 2 | — | — | 2 | — | 5 | 2 | 2 | 1 | 1 | — | 1 (—) |
| Public Utilities : Foreign | 1 | 2 | 2 | 1 | 3 | 3 | 6 | 9 | 13 | 7 | 6 | 4 | 5 | 4 | 3 | 16 | 15 | 7 | 8 | 9 (—) |
| Mercantile and Trading | 2 | 2 | 1 | 1 | — | 2 | 1 | 3 | 9 | 12 | 14 | 7 | 6 | 6 | 7 | 8 | 13 | 25 | 22 | 11 (8) |
| Unclassified | 8 | 8 | 5 | 6 | 12 | 10 | 14 | 20 | 29 | 35 | 26 | 15 | 18 | 12 | 19 | 19 | 37 | 49 | 57 | 51 (3) |
| (1) General Totals | 108 | 182 | 123 | 136 | 196 | 238 | 259 | 360 | 500 | 474 | 364 | 215 | 215 | 232 | 293 | 423 | 616 | 736 | 733 | 590 (120) |
| Halls and Clubs | 7 | 16 | 11 | 11 | 11 | 16 | 11 | 15 | 13 | 14 | 14 | 15 | 13 | 13 | 19 | 15 | 20 | 25 | 25 | 30 (—) |
| Gas and Water | 33 | 41 | 34 | 39 | 39 | 25 | 39 | 43 | 54 | 56 | 41 | 31 | 32 | 33 | 36 | 24 | 18 | 12 | 20 | 14 (1) |
| (2) Grand Totals | 148 | 239 | 168 | 186 | 246 | 279 | 309 | 418 | 567 | 544 | 419 | 261 | 260 | 278 | 348 | 462 | 654 | 773 | 778 | 634 (121) |

Notes : Public Companies, unbracketed ; Private Companies, bracketed.

C

IN LONDON AS FORMED UNDER THE ACTS AND LIMITED BY SHARES

| '76 | '77 | '78 | '79 | '80 | '81 | '82 | '83 | Totals |
|---|---|---|---|---|---|---|---|---|
| 25 (12) | 12 (6) | 7 (6) | 8 (10) | 18 (8) | 15 (7) | 11 (16) | 13 (18) | 714 (96) |
| 28 (2) | 19 (3) | 16 (3) | 16 (3) | 35 (2) | 42 (5) | 21 ( 3) | 11 (4) | 720 (27) |
| 13 (4) | 9 (3) | 3 (4) | 4 (3) | 7 (—) | 5 (2) | 3 (7) | 3 (5) | 248 (29) |
| 12 (7) | 14 (6) | 9 (6) | 2 (8) | 12 (6) | 10 (4) | 9 (9) | 5 (11) | 337 (70) |
| 6 (2) | 5 (5) | 3 (4) | 1 (8) | 6 (3) | 11 (10) | 7 (3) | 8 (10) | 136 (49) |
| 5 (5) | 10 (9) | 6 (7) | 8 (5) | 8 (7) | 20 (9) | 16 (7) | 17 (15) | 237 (71) |
| 6 (—) | 4 (2) | 2 (2) | 3 (—) | 2 (1) | 7 (1) | 6 (2) | 3 (4) | 104 (14) |
| 2 (1) | 4 (1) | 2 (1) | — (—) | 6 (—) | 3 (1) | 5 (1) | 12 (3) | 82 (8) |
| — (—) | — (—) | 3 (—) | 4 (—) | 5 (—) | 16 (—) | 45 (3) | 14 (6) | 87 (9) |
| 1 (2) | 1 (1) | — (—) | 2 (—) | — (1) | 5 (—) | 2 (1) | — (3) | 44 (8) |
| 1 (—) | — (—) | 1 (—) | 2 (—) | — (—) | — (—) | 1 (—) | 3 (—) | 60 (—) |
| 25 (8) | 16 (9) | 6 (12) | 14 (6) | 5 (8) | 11 (3) | 21 (11) | 13 (12) | 307 (76) |
| 9 (2)<br>— (—) | 7 (—)}<br>3 (—) | 10 (1) | 20 (3) | 37 (29) | 96 (25) | 123 (38) | 127 (39) | 663 (141) |
| 7 (3) | 15 (—) | 15 (2) | 10 (1) | 15 (2) | 16 (1) | 9 (2) | 15 (3) | 210 (14) |
| 1 (—) | 3 (—) | 1 (—) | 1 (—) | 3 (—) | — (—) | — (—) | 1 (—) | 66 (—) |
| 12 (6) | 8 (5) | 2 (8) | 3 (4) | 8 (9) | 9 (16) | 17 (14) | 10 (12) | 464 (86) |
| 5 (1) | 3 (—) | — (1) | 1 (3) | 6 (—) | 1 (2) | — (1) | 5 (4) | 68 (14) |
| 7 (1) | 2 (6) | 2 (1) | 3 (1) | 2 (3) | 3 (1) | 5 (1) | 3 (3) | 151 (18) |
| 13 (7) | 22 (14) | 15 (7) | 20 (7) | 15 (12) | 18 (12) | 22 (8) | 19 (25) | 334 (96) |
| 13 (3) | 17 (2) | 11 (7) | 19 (7) | 31 (16) | 40 (14) | 31 (11) | 28 (15) | 445 (78) |
| 9 (2) | 5 (1) | 7 (3) | 7 (—) | 6 (6) | 8 (2) | 14 (3) | 3 (3) | 199 (22) |
| 30 (5) | 42 (1) | 67 (2) | 75 (4) | 49 (6) | 52 (5) | 34 (5) | 32 (4) | 646 (33) |
| 48 (7) | 46 (7) | 20 (5) | 19 (5) | 19 (4) | 41 (3) | 35 (8) | 28 (14) | 690 (60) |
| 11 (2) | 7 (—) | 1 (3) | 7 (3) | 5 (4) | 9 (4) | 14 (4) | 4 (12) | 183 (33) |
| 6 (1) | 11 (2) | 3 (2) | 5 (10) | 12 (3) | 22 (5) | 8 (3) | 9 (14) | 194 (46) |
| 6 (1) | 9 (8) | 4 (2) | 1 (4) | 7 (3) | 13 (2) | 4 (4) | 8 (5) | 181 (36) |
| 9 (3) | 10 (3) | 5 (1) | 4 (5) | 5 (2) | 6 (3) | 8 (2) | 1 (4) | 187 (25) |
| 5 (2) | 7 (—) | 5 (4) | 3 (3) | 9 (3) | 12 (2) | 13 (1) | 10 (1) | 240 (17) |
| 10 (—) | 11 (—) | 9 (—) | 11 (2) | 12 (1) | 14 (—) | 7 (—) | 10 (—) | 237 (6) |
| — (1) | 1 (—) | 3 (3) | 5 (2) | 6 (2) | 11 (1) | 9 (3) | 9 (7) | 131 (21) |
| — (—) | 1 (—) | 1 (—) | 1 (—) | — (—) | 1 (—) | 2 (—) | 1 (—) | 29 (—) |
| — (—) | 2 (—) | 1 (—) | 2 (—) | 2 (—) | 2 (—) | 5 (1) | 3 (—) | 45 (1) |
| 1 (—) | 2 (—) | 3 (—) | 9 (—) | 5 (—) | 4 (—) | 6 (—) | — (—) | 102 (—) |
| — (—) | — (—) | — (—) | 1 (—) | — (—) | — (—) | — (—) | — (—) | 17 (—) |
| 1 (—) | 3 (—) | — (—) | 2 (—) | 3 (—) | 3 (—) | 1 (—) | — (—) | 53 (—) |
| 5 (1) | 13 (2) | 12 (1) | 7 (1) | 42 (1) | 51 (3) | 18 (—) | 13 (5) | 345 (15) |
| 15 (1) | 14 (1) | 14 (5) | 19 (3) | 31 (6) | 54 (3) | 49 (5) | 50 (12) | 619 (36) |
| 2 (—) | 1 (—) | 3 (—) | 3 (—) | — (2) | 2 (1) | 3 (2) | 4 (1) | 56 (7) |
| 3 (1) | 1 (3) | 1 (1) | 2 (1) | 5 (2) | 11 (4) | 10 (1) | 5 (3) | 87 (16) |
| — (—) | — (—) | 1 (1) | 2 (1) | 3 (—) | 4 (—) | 11 (—) | 4 (—) | 60 (1) |
| 6 (1) | 3 (—) | 6 (1) | 14 (1) | 7 (1) | 13 (—) | 12 (1) | 14 (6) | 199 (11) |
| 7 (2) | 8 (6) | 2 (2) | 6 (5) | 11 (7) | 12 (7) | 7 (6) | 9 (9) | 214 (52) |
| 62 (7) | 37 (5) | 28 (3) | 25 (7) | 33 (3) | 34 (2) | 28 (4) | 28 (9) | 725 (43) |
| 427 (103) | 408 (111) | 310 (110) | 371 (126) | 493 (163) | 707 (160) | 652 (191) | 555 (301) | 10916 (1385) |
| 24 (1) | 26 (1) | 16 (1) | 19 (1) | 27 (1) | 24 (—) | 30 (1) | 29 (1) | 509 (4) |
| 14 (—) | 21 (—) | 10 (—) | 7 (—) | 13 (—) | 9 (—) | 11 (—) | 12 (1) | 761 (2) |
| 465 (104) | 455 (111) | 336 (111) | 397 (126) | 533 (164) | 740 (160) | 693 (192) | 596 (302) | 12186 (1391) |

" Unclassified " here includes " amusements, theatres, etc.," throughout.

## TABLE D

### ANALYSIS OF DURATIONS AND MODES OF DISSOLUTION OF ALL "EFFECTIVE" COMPANIES, LIMITED BY SHARES, FORMED 1866-74 AND REGISTERED IN LONDON, BY SUB-PERIODS

**(1) Cumulative percentages of all Companies deemed "effectively formed".**

| Duration | Sold, etc. | | | | Compulsory, etc. | | | | Voluntary | | | | Unknown | | | | Totals | | | |
|---|---|---|---|---|---|---|---|---|---|---|---|---|---|---|---|---|---|---|---|---|
| | '66-'68 | '69-'71 | '72-'74 | '66-'74 | '66-'68 | '69-'71 | '72-'74 | '66-'74 | '66-'68 | '69-'71 | '72-'74 | '66-'74 | '66-'68 | '69-'71 | '72-'74 | '66-'74 | '66-'68 | '69-'71 | '72-'74 | '66-'74 |
| Over 50 years | 19·9 | 19·8 | 16·5 | 18·1 | 24·0 | 25·4 | 32·0 | 28·5 | 31·7 | 29·8 | 29·6 | 30·2 | 12·7 | 13·5 | 11·5 | 12·3 | 88·3 | 88·5 | 89·7 | 89·1 |
| Existing | | | | | | | | | | | | | | | | | 11·7 | 11·5 | 10·3 | 10·9 |

**(2) Cumulative Percentages of all "Effective" Companies, except Gas, Water and Local Halls and Clubs.**

| Duration | Sold, etc. | | | | Compulsory, etc. | | | | Voluntary | | | | Unknown | | | | Totals | | | |
|---|---|---|---|---|---|---|---|---|---|---|---|---|---|---|---|---|---|---|---|---|
| | '66-'68 | '69-'71 | '72-'74 | '66-'74 | '66-'68 | '69-'71 | '72-'74 | '66-'74 | '66-'68 | '69-'71 | '72-'74 | '66-'74 | '66-'68 | '69-'71 | '72-'74 | '66-'74 | '66-'68 | '69-'71 | '72-'74 | '66-'74 |
| 3 years and under | 2·6 | 3·6 | 2·6 | 2·8 | 7·0 | 7·4 | 10·3 | 8·9 | 8·9 | 9·3 | 9·9 | 6·0 | 5·0 | 6·5 | 4·8 | 5·3 | 20·7 | 26·8 | 27·7 | 26·0 |
| 5 " | 4·3 | 6·1 | 4·5 | 3·9 | 11·2 | 13·9 | 17·4 | 15·3 | 13·9 | 15·5 | 14·2 | 11·2 | 7·2 | 8·5 | 7·9 | 7·9 | 33·9 | 44·0 | 43·4 | 41·6 |
| 10 " | 6·9 | 8·9 | 7·0 | 6·2 | 17·1 | 22·2 | 26·2 | 23·3 | 19·4 | 19·9 | 19·2 | 19·3 | 10·2 | 12·3 | 10·0 | 10·6 | 53·5 | 63·3 | 61·6 | 60·3 |
| 15 " | 7·9 | 11·1 | 8·7 | 7·8 | 21·1 | 25·8 | 29·3 | 26·8 | 22·8 | 23·4 | 22·3 | 23·7 | 12·3 | 13·8 | 10·8 | 11·9 | 65·0 | 74·1 | 70·2 | 70·2 |
| 20 " | 9·7 | 12·7 | 9·6 | 8·7 | 23·3 | 26·8 | 30·2 | 27·9 | 24·7 | 25·7 | 23·9 | 25·4 | 13·7 | 14·3 | 11·3 | 12·6 | 72·0 | 79·6 | 75·0 | 75·5 |
| 30 " | 13·5 | 14·9 | 10·3 | 9·6 | 25·4 | 27·9 | 31·4 | 29·3 | 27·4 | 28·0 | 26·6 | 28·8 | 14·3 | 14·7 | 11·6 | 12·9 | 82·0 | 85·6 | 82·4 | 83·1 |
| 40 " | 15·8 | 16·1 | 13·5 | 12·8 | 25·6 | 28·2 | 32·2 | 30·1 | 28·8 | 29·1 | 27·9 | 30·8 | 14·5 | | 11·7 | 13·0 | 86·7 | 88·1 | 85·3 | 86·2 |
| 50 " | 16·4 | 17·2 | 14·6 | 13·5 | 25·8 | | 32·5 | 30·3 | 30·0 | 29·7 | 29·4 | 31·4 | 14·6 | | | | 88·2 | 89·9 | 89·1 | 89·2 |
| Over 50 years | 17·6 | 17·5 | 16·1 | 15·5 | 25·9 | | 32·8 | | 30·5 | 30·2 | 29·6 | 33·0 | | | | | 91·2 | 90·7 | 90·1 | 90·5 |
| Existing | | | 16·7 | 16·0 | | | | | | | | | | | | | 8·8 | 9·2 | 9·9 | 9·5 |

## TABLE E

### Analysis of Durations and modes of Dissolution of all "Effective" Companies, Limited by Shares Formed 1875-83 and Registered in London, by Sub-Periods

| Duration | Sold, etc. | | | | Compulsory, etc. | | | | Voluntary | | | | Unknown | | | | Totals | | | |
|---|---|---|---|---|---|---|---|---|---|---|---|---|---|---|---|---|---|---|---|---|
| | '75-'77 | '78-'80 | '81-'83 | '75-'83 | '75-'77 | '78-'80 | '81-'83 | '75-'83 | '75-'77 | '78-'80 | '81-'83 | '75-'83 | '75-'77 | '78-'80 | '81-'83 | '75-'83 | '75-'77 | '78-'80 | '81-'83 | '75-'83 |
| **(1) Cumulative Percentages of all Companies deemed "effectively formed":** | | | | | | | | | | | | | | | | | | | | |
| Over 50 years | 13·9 | 14·6 | 17·6 | 15·7 | 32·0 | 30·8 | 28·7 | 30·3 | 30·6 | 32·2 | 32·7 | 32·0 | 10·4 | 9·2 | 9·3 | 9·0 | 87·0 | 86·8 | 88·3 | 87·6 |
| Existing | | | | | | | | | | | | | | | | | 13·0 | 13·2 | 11·7 | 12·4 |
| **(2) Cumulative Percentages of all Public Companies "effectively formed".** | | | | | | | | | | | | | | | | | | | | |
| Over 50 years | 14·2 | 15·7 | 18·1 | 16·3 | 32·9 | 33·0 | 30·9 | 32·0 | 30·0 | 29·9 | 31·1 | 30·4 | 9·7 | 7·0 | 7·5 | 8·1 | 86·8 | 85·6 | 87·7 | 86·9 |
| Existing | | | | | | | | | | | | | | | | | 13·2 | 14·4 | 12·3 | 13·1 |
| **(3) Cumulative Percentages of all "Effective" Public Companies except, Gas, Water, and Local Halls and Clubs.** | | | | | | | | | | | | | | | | | | | | |
| 3 years and under | 1·3 | 2·3 | 3·3 | 2·4 | 13·5 | 15·5 | 14·1 | 14·2 | 6·5 | 5·8 | 6·5 | 6·2 | 6·2 | 3·8 | 5·1 | 5·1 | 27·5 | 26·9 | 29·0 | 28·0 |
| 5 " " | 3·2 | 3·8 | 5·4 | 4·3 | 20·8 | 21·5 | 19·5 | 20·4 | 10·0 | 8·9 | 10·0 | 9·7 | 7·3 | 4·8 | 5·9 | 6·1 | 41·3 | 39·0 | 40·8 | 40·5 |
| 10 " " | 4·8 | 7·7 | 7·8 | 7·8 | 28·6 | 27·6 | 25·6 | 27·1 | 16·4 | 14·5 | 16·5 | 15·9 | 9·3 | 6·4 | 6·7 | 7·4 | 59·1 | 56·1 | 58·9 | 58·2 |
| 15 " " | 6·7 | 9·5 | 12·7 | 10·0 | 30·4 | 30·0 | 28·9 | 29·7 | 20·1 | 17·7 | 22·1 | 20·3 | 10·0 | 6·5 | 7·1 | 7·9 | 67·2 | 63·7 | 70·8 | 67·9 |
| 20 " " | 8·5 | 11·7 | 14·4 | 11·8 | 32·1 | 31·2 | 29·7 | 30·8 | 22·4 | 20·4 | 24·9 | 22·9 | 10·2 | 6·8 | 7·4 | 8·2 | 73·2 | 70·1 | 76·5 | 73·7 |
| 30 " " | 10·5 | 13·9 | 16·4 | 13·9 | 33·3 | 32·9 | 30·7 | 32·1 | 26·4 | 24·6 | 28·4 | 26·7 | — | 7·1 | 7·5 | 8·3 | 80·3 | 78·6 | 83·0 | 80·9 |
| 40 " " | 11·6 | 15·1 | 17·9 | 15·2 | 34·3 | 34·2 | 31·2 | 32·9 | 27·9 | 27·4 | 30·8 | 29·0 | — | 7·2 | 7·7 | — | 84·0 | 83·9 | 87·5 | 85·5 |
| 50 " " | 12·9 | 15·7 | 18·3 | 15·9 | 34·7 | 34·7 | 31·6 | 33·4 | 30·0 | 29·7 | 31·6 | 30·7 | — | 7·3 | — | — | 87·8 | 87·4 | 89·2 | 88·2 |
| Over 50 years | 13·1 | — | 16·0 | — | 34·7 | — | — | 33·4 | 30·1 | — | — | 30·7 | — | — | — | — | 88·1 | — | — | 88·5 |
| Existing | | | | | | | | | | | | | | | | | 11·8 | 12·6 | 10·8 | 11·5 |
| **(4) Cumulative Percentages of all Private Companies—all deemed "effective".** | | | | | | | | | | | | | | | | | | | | |
| 3 years and under | 2·9 | 2·0 | 2·7 | 2·7 | 10·7 | 13·3 | 8·5 | 10·5 | 12·2 | 11·0 | 10·2 | 10·9 | 7·8 | 8·5 | 8·5 | 8·3 | 33·6 | 34·9 | 30·0 | 32·4 |
| 5 " " | 4·5 | 2·0 | 4·7 | 3·9 | 14·9 | 16·9 | 11·8 | 14·0 | 16·1 | 14·7 | 15·0 | 15·1 | 10·1 | 11·5 | 10·9 | 10·9 | 45·6 | 45·1 | 42·4 | 44·0 |
| 10 " " | 6·0 | 5·2 | 8·7 | 7·0 | 19·1 | 21·9 | 16·5 | 18·7 | 21·4 | 23·5 | 23·4 | 22·9 | 11·9 | 13·4 | 12·7 | 12·7 | 58·4 | 64·1 | 61·4 | 61·3 |
| 15 " " | 7·1 | 6·7 | 8·8 | 8·8 | 22·9 | 23·7 | 18·2 | 20·6 | 25·9 | 31·4 | 27·2 | 28·1 | 12·5 | 13·4 | 13·9 | 13·8 | 66·9 | 76·0 | 69·8 | 70·9 |
| 20 " " | 8·6 | 7·7 | 10·8 | 10·8 | 23·2 | 24·2 | 19·3 | 21·4 | 28·0 | 34·5 | 30·3 | 31·0 | 13·1 | 15·2 | 14·1 | 14·1 | 72·6 | 81·7 | 77·4 | 77·4 |
| 30 " " | 11·0 | 9·8 | 14·7 | 13·8 | 25·0 | — | 21·0 | 22·6 | 30·4 | 38·0 | 34·4 | 34·4 | 13·1 | 16·0 | 14·6 | 14·6 | 77·7 | 88·0 | 84·6 | 83·6 |
| 40 " " | 11·0 | 10·0 | 15·8 | 14·7 | 26·5 | — | 21·3 | 23·0 | 32·7 | 38·8 | 36·7 | 36·3 | 13·4 | — | 14·6 | 14·6 | 81·8 | 89·0 | 88·5 | 86·8 |
| 50 " " | 12·2 | 11·0 | 16·1 | 16·1 | 27·4 | — | 22·0 | 23·8 | 33·3 | 39·5 | 38·1 | 37·3 | 13·7 | — | 14·7 | 14·7 | 85·4 | 90·6 | 90·9 | 89·4 |
| Over 50 years | — | — | — | — | — | — | — | 23·9 | 33·6 | — | — | 37·4 | — | — | — | — | 86·7 | — | — | 89·7 |
| Existing | | | | | | | | | | | | | | | | | 13·1 | 9·4 | 9·1 | 10·3 |

## TABLE F

PUBLIC HOME "INDUSTRIAL" AND "GENERAL" COMPANIES (EXCEPT GAS, WATER, LOCAL HALLS AND CLUBS) FORMED 1866-74 AND 1875-83, EXISTING AT THREE-YEARLY INTERVALS, WITH ANALYSIS OF DISSOLUTIONS IN INTERVALS.

| Date | Formed 1866-74 | | | | | | | | | | Formed 1875-83 | | | | | | | | | |
|---|---|---|---|---|---|---|---|---|---|---|---|---|---|---|---|---|---|---|---|---|
| | Industrials | | | | | General | | | | | Industrials | | | | | General | | | | |
| | E | S | C | V | U | E | S | C | V | U | E | S | C | V | U | E | S | C | V | U |
| 1868 | 216 | 7 | 11 | 11 | 7 | 467 | 10 | 31 | 28 | 27 | | | | | | | | | | |
| 1871 | 423 | 12 | 24 | 35 | 19 | 881 | 29 | 63 | 79 | 36 | | | | | | | | | | |
| 1874 | 1178 | 27 | 116 | 97 | 38 | 1650 | 44 | 158 | 158 | 76 | | | | | | | | | | |
| 1877 | 900 | 25 | 118 | 56 | 31 | 1214 | 32 | 111 | 77 | 78 | 382 | 7 | 69 | 26 | 19 | 887 | 9 | 112 | 50 | 50 |
| 1880 | 670 | 18 | 53 | 34 | 8 | 916 | 28 | 80 | 60 | 15 | 474 | 7 | 63 | 35 | 11 | 1419 | 38 | 188 | 76 | 41 |
| 1883 | 557 | 13 | 41 | 22 | 8 | 733 | 21 | 41 | 47 | 20 | 954 | 14 | 81 | 70 | 26 | 2001 | 61 | 249 | 128 | 62 |
| 1886 | 473 | 18 | 24 | 22 | 5 | 604 | 20 | 14 | 32 | 13 | 763 | 26 | 61 | 48 | 10 | 1501 | 48 | 116 | 113 | 32 |
| 1889 | 404 | 16 | 8 | 16 | — | 525 | 19 | 13 | 19 | 7 | 618 | 24 | 16 | 41 | 3 | 1192 | 51 | 53 | 75 | 9 |
| 1892 | 364 | 11 | 5 | 11 | 2 | 467 | 20 | 11 | 23 | 4 | 534 | 15 | 20 | 29 | 2 | 1004 | 29 | 50 | 59 | 5 |
| 1895 | 335 | 17 | 9 | 9 | 1 | 409 | 18 | 7 | 21 | 2 | 468 | 25 | 19 | 35 | 2 | 861 | 33 | 27 | 51 | 5 |
| 1898 | 299 | 17 | 3 | 5 | — | 361 | 15 | 3 | 16 | 2 | 387 | 16 | 3 | 33 | 2 | 745 | 31 | 13 | 34 | 3 |
| 1901 | 274 | 5 | 1 | 8 | — | 325 | 20 | 2 | 9 | — | 333 | 13 | 8 | 24 | — | 664 | 16 | 10 | 35 | — |
| 1904 | 260 | 3 | 3 | 6 | — | 294 | 4 | 2 | 11 | — | 288 | 6 | 3 | 14 | — | 603 | 12 | 11 | 26 | 3 |
| 1907 | 248 | 1 | 2 | 1 | — | 277 | 3 | 3 | 6 | 1 | 265 | 5 | 6 | 10 | — | 551 | 14 | 8 | 19 | 1 |
| 1910 | 244 | 2 | 3 | 4 | — | 264 | 2 | 4 | 8 | — | 244 | 3 | 2 | 7 | — | 509 | 10 | 13 | 17 | — |
| 1913 | 235 | 5 | 5 | 4 | — | 250 | 4 | 1 | 6 | 1 | 232 | 2 | 3 | 8 | — | 469 | 6 | 11 | 13 | 1 |
| 1916 | 221 | 2 | — | 1 | 1 | 238 | 3 | — | 2 | — | 219 | 5 | 2 | 10 | — | 438 | 2 | — | 8 | 2 |
| 1919 | 217 | 41 | 1 | 11 | — | 233 | 2 | — | 14 | — | 202 | 33 | — | 9 | — | 426 | 6 | 2 | 40 | 2 |
| 1922 | 164 | 1 | 2 | 6 | — | 217 | 1 | 2 | 4 | — | 160 | 2 | 3 | 1 | — | 378 | 2 | 4 | 21 | — |
| 1925 | 155 | 3 | 2 | 1 | — | 210 | 5 | 3 | 2 | — | 154 | 2 | 4 | 7 | — | 349 | 6 | 1 | 11 | — |
| 1928 | 149 | | | | | 200 | | | | | 141 | | | | | 331 | | | | |

Notes : See Table A.

The advantages of limited liability will be part of the causes for this outburst.[40]    A kind of shipbuilding for stock, especially on the North-East Coast, will be another.    Again and again, the memorandums declared that the company is to acquire a ship "now building".    Firms of shipbrokers seem to have signed the original contracts with shipbuilders (frequently through the same solicitors) and then formed a company to take over the contract.    Here comes the taint at birth, as the *Economist* describes it—and the point is worth noting by those who think that shareholders need have even any legal control over their company.    These shipbrokers made themselves, through the articles they themselves drafted and registered on the company, the ship's "husband" or manager, dismissible only in the event of misappropriation of funds, and fixed their own remuneration.[41]    No doubt they earned many a comfortable income when the shareholders got nothing.

[40] Especially in damages for collision, home *and* foreign.

[41] See the very accurate remarks in *The Economist*, XLIV (1886), 1350 and 1440, which are fully substantiated from the files. *Cf.* the *Statist*, XIII (1884), 265: "The whole tendency of single-ship companies is distinctly bad", especially in dodging insurance.

As one firm of shipbrokers may have been the "husband" to as many as a dozen single-ship companies, erratic behaviour occurs in this group not easily to be correlated with current conditions.

## XII

This survey suggests one clear conclusion; that limited liability was no unmixed blessing, that it little deserves the panegyrics so often bestowed on it. No important improvement in behaviour is discernible from the statistics; none, perhaps, ought to be expected. England never reformed her law, as Germany did. No Committee of Inquiry has yet worked from the wide basis of ascertainable facts buried in the vaults. And it must be deemed unfortunate that limited liability was moulded by that able doctrinaire, Robert Lowe, whose spirit lived long after him and is not dead today.

# THE "GREAT DEPRESSION" IN INDUSTRY AND TRADE

## H. L. BEALES

THERE is something enigmatic about the "great depression". It parades in our textbooks with all the assurance of an established generalisation, yet in the lecture room its historical reality is openly scouted. Has a legend come to roost in the former which will be driven out in due season—the time-lag between lecture room and textbook has not been accurately measured!—from the latter?

The textbooks tell us that the economic history of the nineteenth century divides itself off into phases, the turning-points being set at Waterloo, the repeal of the Corn Laws (or sometimes at the Great Exhibition five years later), the financial crisis of 1873, and the publication of the final report of the Royal Commission on the Depression of Trade and Industry in 1886. The first phase, from 1815 to 1846, has not yet acquired a generally accepted distinguishing label; the second, from 1846 to 1873, is known as "the good years"; the third, from 1873 to 1886, as "the great depression"; the fourth, from 1886 to 1914, or even unto now, as "the end of *laissez-faire*". There is something to be said for the description in terms of prosperity of early Victorian experience, after the disastrous famine when "those damned rotten potatoes", as Wellington put it, temporarily rendered the maintenance of agricultural protection impossible. Something, but not too much. "The good years" were not equally good for everybody, and they were punctuated by events and behaviour which were not consistent with the benevolent busy-bee character usually ascribed to our Victorian ancestors. Readers of, for example, Goschen's *Essays and Addresses* (1905) will not forget his vivid description, reprinted from the *Edinburgh Review* of 1868, of "the era of two per cent"—the collapse in railway finance; the inflated operations of 1864 and 1865 which led to the crisis of 1866 and the long financial, commercial, industrial, and railway crisis of 1867; the decreased exports; the Court of Chancery "blocked with the liquidation of companies bankrupt or dying of atrophy"; the depreciation in the value of foreign stock; the phenomenon of "capital on strike" against limited liability, railways, promoters, contractors and engineers, and against foreign governments, complaining of the deficiencies of the law and of the shortcomings of those to whom it had entrusted its fortunes; and the blocking of the conduit pipes through which the reservoirs of English capital were opened to foreign borrowers. That there was some soul of evil in the goodness of "the good years" is apparent if one examines the history of agricultural labourers, or recalls the coffin ships against which Plimsoll later on crusaded, or penetrates into schoolrooms with Matthew Arnold and the school inspectors, or searches out the ravages of occupational diseases which miners and metal-workers had been complaining of for half a century. Still, the buoyancy of trade figures shows the greatest expansion of economic activity that any country had known so far in history. Let the term "the good years" stand till someone has thought of a better. But "the great depression" is a more ambiguous label. Was it great? If so, great in relation to what? Was it depression? If so, what interests felt its malign influence? And how long did it last—was 1886 really the end of it? Was it a British phenomenon, or did Greater Britain, as Dilke called the overseas empire in 1868, and the outer world share its baleful effects? And anyhow, if there was a great depression, what were its causes and consequences?

The term "depression" is difficult. It is sometimes used as a synonym of "slump", as descriptive, that is, of the downward swing of the trade cycle. Sometimes it is employed to characterise the short-lived group of events that follow immediately upon a panic or crisis. This word has no established technical meaning. Economists and economic historians might with advantage set up a committee of terminology which would come to agreement upon the definition of terms common to both their disciplines. Wanting that, we may employ the term here for the whole long period from 1873 onwards, during which our business leaders thought they were "depressed", whether economists and statisticians agreed with them or not, and found politicians ready to voice their uneasiness.

The continuous ululations of business people, like the repeated groanings of working people, are never mere flatulence. It may be admitted that 1873 was a turning-point, though there are some who would like to put that turning-point further back—in 1866, say, or even in 1864. If an earlier date be sought there seems to be no valid reason for choosing 1864 or 1866 rather than the Cotton Famine; or for choosing the Cotton Famine, which to non-Marxians looks like an unexpected intrusion of an extraneous political determinant, rather than the speculative "over-production" that preceded it. We know that every year is in some sense a turning-point just as all periods are periods of transition. But the special appropriateness of 1873 as an initial date for a recognisable phase of the nineteenth century is that it was a year of financial crisis, marking the beginning of the end of an excited spasm of foreign-loan making, and initiating a period of falling prices. The business leaders, in finance, trade and industry, began their depression in 1873. But when did that depression end? Will the textbook year 1886 stand? That year undoubtedly derives its currency from the fact that in 1886

the Royal Commission on the Depression of Trade and Industry issued
its three interim and its final reports.  That Commission was appointed
in 1885 "to inquire and report upon the extent, nature, and probable
cause of the depression now or recently prevailing in various branches
of trade and industry, and whether it can be alleviated by legislative or
other measures".  These terms of reference may indicate a certain
scepticism of the reality of the phenomena of depression and a certain
uneasiness as to the finality of the maxims of *laissez-faire* as the inevitable basis of public economic policy.  Particularly, Sir Robert Giffen,
our leading statistician, openly disavowed the validity of the epithet
"depression" as an adequate description of current experience; and
foreign competition was leading to a demand, swelling at times to a
clamour, for the revival of protection.[1]  But Royal Commissions,
imposing as they are, command no magic powers; that of 1886 had no
secret incantation, no "open sesame", which broke the evil spell of
depression.  The same manifestations recurred, and ten years later the
word "depression" was still on men's lips and in their thoughts.  If we
retain the term "great depression" we cannot retain the year 1886 as its
terminus.  The melancholy span must be extended for another decade,
until 1896, when prices at last began to rise again.

That fact of nearly a quarter-century of falling prices gives a unity
to these years, and removes a first misconception about "the great
depression".  Mrs Knowles used to say, with undue modesty, that her
history ended in 1886.  It was her *Industrial and Commercial Revolutions of the Nineteenth Century* that established the textbook vogue of
the year 1886 as the end of the depression.  The final report of the Royal
Commissioners does, indeed, stress certain phenomena which were
outstanding—the absence of profit or its meagreness, supply of commodities outstripping demand, protectionist policies in other countries,
the decay in agrarian purchasing power, a falling away of the demand
for railway material, and other factors—but in no way suggested that
the depression was at an end.  The early 'nineties bore an almost
equally lugubrious character, and the change in business psychology
does not come till 1896, when at last prices began again to rise.

If it be feasible, on the ground of falling prices,[2] to regard the years
from 1873 to 1896 as a unity, is it reasonable to describe them as "the
great depression"?

Falling prices are uncomfortable to producers of all ranks.  Profits
are hard to come by and unemployment is rife.  Contemporary
observers and later commentators are agreed that there was a depression
of profits in the years subsequent to 1873, and that in this respect the

---

[1] The "fair trade" movement began in 1881 with the formation of the Fair Trade
League to prevent foreign countries compassing the destruction of British sugar refineries.
[2] Sauerbeck's index-number of British wholesale prices (1867-77 = 100) shows an
unbroken fall from 111 in 1873 to 61 in 1896, save for 1880 to 1882 and 1889 to 1891.

contrast with "the good years" is unmistakable. Cunningham used the phrase "the great divide" of the decade 1870-80 because in those years Cobdenite free trade was abandoned in one country after another; the futility of the Cobdenite vision of universal peace resting on the basis of national interdependence had been thoroughly exposed.[3] An era of meagre profits and a widespread return to policies of protection are certainly features of the last quarter of the nineteenth century. The special circumstances that had given so buoyant a character to "the good years" no longer prevailed. That this country would not permanently enjoy the lucrative position of *tertium gaudens* while other countries were engaged in wars of unification—a phrase which applies to the U.S.A. as well as Europe—was only to be expected. An observant eye might have concluded at the International Exhibition of 1867, too, that British predominance in the world's industrial markets would be considerably modified in days to come: the competitive quality of the machinery, the chemicals, even the textiles of some other countries was visible then. In 1867, moreover, a somewhat disturbed House of Commons had appointed a committee to investigate our methods of technical education, or rather, their absence, and startling evidence was given of the great progress that was being made by the industry of some continental countries.[4] Even earlier the achievement as well as the promise of American engineers was observed by English experts.[5]

But these revelations had not seriously ruffled our optimism. It was the continued elusiveness of profits which provoked us to economic introspection and which convinced business men and politicians of the greatness of the prevalent depression. No index of business profits was available, and economists and statisticians frequently qualified the talk of depression by awkward demonstrations of increasing national wealth derived from income tax figures. That was one reason why, as Cunningham put it, in 1885, "the science of Political Economy speaks with far less authority and receives less respectful attention than it did some years ago". What, too, would be the opinion of politician or business man, unused to scientific examination of economic phenomena, who read, say, Giffen's essay on *The Liquidation of 1873-1876*? He would read there these words: "To anyone who has even glanced at the economic history of England during the present century, the common talk now about the 'unusual' depression of our trade appears simply ludicrous. The people who indulge in it have simply never thought of what depression of trade is. There has probably never been a great commercial crisis in England which caused so little suffering to the mass

[3] W. Cunningham, *The Rise and Decline of the Free Trade Movement* (1904), 92.
[4] See *Report of Select Committee on Scientific Instruction* in Parliamentary Papers, 1867-8, XV.
[5] See D. L. Burn, "The Genesis of American Engineering Competition" in *Economic History*, II, no. 6 (January 1931).

of the nation."[6]   Giffen complained that politicians had fomented the
outcry about depression "in a somewhat unintelligent manner", and that
unjustified emphasis was laid on the assumption that depression was an
unusual and bewildering phenomenon, instead of being the most natural
thing in the world.   Such opinions must have seemed sheer perversity
to men whose incomes had dwindled.   They would have felt more at
home in the gloomy pages of A. J. Wilson's *Resources of Modern
Countries* (1878).   " Everywhere ", he wrote, " there is a stagnation and
a negation of hope.   The low present condition of business enterprise
and possibilities is at present nearly universal. . . . Month by month
English exports have been declining, and month by month producers
are content to take lower prices. . . . Our only consolation is that our
near neighbours are no better off than ourselves. . . . On all grounds I
look for a further depression in the trade of this country, and when I
consider how unprepared we are by our habits and social conditions for
a prolonged time of retrogression, I confess the prospect is to me an
alarming one. . . . This is not a period like those which followed ordinary panics.   It is, more likely, the beginning of a new era for ourselves
and the world."

Confirmation from a different source of the prevalent mood of
depression might be gathered from the discussions of bodies as different
as the Political Economy Club and the House of Commons.   The
former, from June 1877, repeatedly returned to the discussion of the
features and causes of depression.   The " present stagnation of trade "
was debated in 1877; the " commercial depression of Europe and
America of the last five years ", in 1878; agricultural depression in 1881;
over-production in 1882; the " fall of wholesale prices in recent years "
in 1885; and in 1887, 1888 and 1895, industry, agriculture and limited
liability were analysed in terms of expansion and depression.   Discussions in Parliament were recurrent.   The Queen's Speech of 1880
rejoiced at some revival in trade but bemoaned a lack of buoyancy in
the revenue; in 1883 the Government was assailed for the absence of
any reference in the Queen's Speech to " the marked, continued and
apparently hopeless depression of the trade of the country ".   Gladstone
and Chamberlain refused the reiterated demand for a Royal Commission
of Inquiry, but it had to be conceded in 1885; and it was followed by
the Gold and Silver Commission (1888), and the Inquiry into Technical
Education (1887).   The reports of all three Commissions were vigorously
discussed and the material they collected provides most valuable docu-
mentation for the 'eighties.   There was, in fact, a continuous output of
discussions, speeches, books, reports and pamphlets, which prove, at
least, that people thought they were depressed, whether in fact they
were or not.   We can, at any rate, say that the period of falling prices

[6] Sir R. Giffen, *Economic Inquiries and Studies* (1904), I, 112.   This illuminating
essay provides an admirable diary of events in the years analysed.

from 1873 to 1896 was a period when people said there was a great depression.

The true character of the period of "the great depression" cannot be gathered simply from echoes of the mournful dirges that were chanted on the general theme of bad times. Actually the period embraces three slumps and two intervening recoveries. The peak of the good years was reached in 1872, and the succeeding slump lasted till 1879. Three years of improvement then followed. The second spasm of depression lasted from 1882 to 1886. It was succeeded by four years of recovery, after which the third phase of depression pursued its course, lasting from 1890 till 1896.

The expansion of "the good years" reached its peak in 1872. Exports had risen from £97 million in 1854 to £256 million; imports from £152 million to £355 million; re-exports from £19 million to £58 million.[7] No other country could show a similar record, and such indices of advancing industrialism as coal production, cotton consumption, and pig-iron output, as well as figures of shipping and shipbuilding, reflected the striking conquest of markets achieved by the great industry that had issued from the industrial revolution. As The Times put it in 1871, "We can . . . look on the present with undisturbed satisfaction. Our commerce is extending and multiplying its world-wide ramifications without much regard for the croaking of any political or scientific Cassandras. . . . Turn where we may, we find in our commerce no traces of decadence."[8] Not only was the ubiquitous British trader busy in every corner of the world, but the contractor of railways and public works, the concessionaire, the financier, were ceaselessly planting the material equipment and amenities of Victorian industrialism in western Europe and America. If there were no traces of decadence in our commerce, our economic cosmopolitanism was helping towards the advance of industrialism elsewhere, and a break in prosperity would show that advance as effective foreign competition. That result was in the nature of things. Industrialism could not remain insular, and revived economic nationalism was round the corner though The Times did not discern it in 1871. It was difficult to believe that the good days were over, and in the early years after the break, prophecies were frequent of the imminence of recovery. But the annual trade return silenced the optimists, and general gloom set in. An occasional voice protested, Giffen's or Leone Levi's, whose History of Commerce appeared in 1880, but optimism was not the mood of the day.

The pessimism was overdone. In coal and cotton export, prices had fallen but quantities were maintained; in the metallurgical and woollen

[7] These figures are taken from the tables in British and Foreign Trade and Industry, Cd. 4954 (1909), an invaluable summary of official figures.
[8] Leading article of 26 September 1871, quoted by R. J. S. Hoffman, Great Britain and the German Trade Rivalry, 1875-1914 (1933), 5.

industries, the position was more disturbing. On the other hand, railway receipts were rising until 1877, and shipping clearances to 1880. Income assessments rose to a peak in 1876, and then fell steadily for five years Assessments of profits under Schedule D—which included the Law, the Church, the Stage, the Press, the public-house, as well as business—were falling between 1876 and 1883. The boom that had culminated in 1873 involved so much excitement that liquidations were inevitable. The industries which had figured most prominently in the boom, figured most prominently in the slump. Furnaces went out of blast, and the plight of the heavy industries was reflected in reduced demand for coal and in the gradual spread of the contagion of depression. On the other hand, the Birmingham jewellery and brass trades maintained their strength, while the manufacture of small-arms and buttons wilted.[9] In the first slump, too, Birmingham and the Black Country maintained their saddlery and harness trades, their edge-tool manufacture, and their tinplate and japanned-ware industries; their bad times came with the second visitation of depression. Nail-making in the Black Country suffered from successful foreign competition at the very time when the wire nail was coming on to the market, but Birmingham's loss in this case was Leeds's gain.

The tide of depression turned in 1880. The brief fall in the output of pig-iron, steel and coal was arrested. Railway receipts rose again, and bank clearings in 1881 passed their previous high-water mark of 1873. Employment improved after the black year 1879 had passed. Exports rose again—cotton piece-goods by 28 per cent, woollen goods by 6 per cent, coal by 35 per cent, iron and steel by 90 per cent in quantity between 1879 and 1881. Wholesale prices rose slightly and things generally were brighter. But the gloom returned all too soon. Between 1882 and 1886 the brief interlude of improvement was forgotten in a new visitation of depression. Unemployment mounted again. Export and import figures fell sharply. Cotton goods had their worst year in 1885, iron and steel exports decreased again. The make of pig-iron dropped from 8·6 million tons in 1882 to 7 million in 1886, though steel production was higher in 1886 than ever before. In this phase the depression, however, was more narrowly confined: its baleful effects were most marked in the cotton and metal trades. So careful an observer as Goschen, addressing the Manchester Chamber of Commerce in 1885, admitted that in coal and iron the Continent had been gaining on us, and that the consumption of cotton had been relatively much larger both on the Continent and in the United States than in this country. " An examination", he commented, "of the present state of things points to the conclusion that a part of the advantages on which the supremacy in

[9] A useful account of the depression in the Birmingham area is available in G. C. Allen's *The Industrial Development of Birmingham and the Black Country* (1929), 209 et seq.

trade and manufactures of this country depends are, to a certain degree, imperilled by some of the changed conditions of the general situation."[10] Goschen, however warmed to the theme of expanding imperial markets, and it is noteworthy that since the onset of the depression British possessions had increased their absorption of our exported products from 25·6 to 35 per cent of the total.

The remaining phases of the period of falling prices may be quickly summarised. Boom conditions returned in 1886. Exports and imports rose, industrial activity expanded, unemployment dropped. All the indices showed a welcome buoyancy until 1890, when the tendencies were reversed again. For the succeeding four years the exports of cotton piece-goods declined, while woollens and iron and steel dropped heavily both in quantity and value. There was some improvement between 1894 and 1896, and again a falling away between 1896 and 1898. By then it was clear that the phase of Britain's easy leadership among the industrial nations of the world was over. It was equally clear that immense changes had been effected in the internal habits and standards of life of the community.

A narrative of the period from 1873 to 1896, however brief, suggests the unsuitability of the term "great depression" as a generalised description. As was frequently pointed out, the conditions that prevailed were universal. There may have been, as Giffen suggested, a slight falling off in the real rate of material progress in this country, but the outstanding fact, or group of facts, in the quarter-century was the rapid industrialisation of other countries and the further industrialisation of this. Between 1870 and 1900 astonishing progress was made in the United States, Germany and France. A single illustration must suffice. In 1870 the coal production of the United Kingdom was 110 million tons, of the U.S.A. 30 millions, of Germany 26 millions, of France 13 millions; in 1900 the figures were for the United Kingdom 225, the U.S.A. 241, Germany 108, and France 32. Export figures may be given in more detail. In £ millions, they were as follows:

| Average | | U.K. | Germany | U.S.A. | France |
|---|---|---|---|---|---|
| 1870–4 | . . | 235 | 114 (1872–4) | 96 | 135 |
| 1875–9 | . . | 202 | 132 | 125 | 138 |
| 1880–4 | . . | 234 | 153 | 165 | 138 |
| 1885–9 | . . | 226 | 151 | 146 | 132 |
| 1890–4 | . . | 234 | 153 | 185 | 137 |
| 1895–9 | . . | 238 | 181 | 213 | 144 |

The British foreign investment of the period recovered after the shock of 1875, and by the end of the century had reached a figure of £2,000 million. Goschen pointed out in 1885 that " we drink now only ten glasses of spirits for every thirteen that we drank in the largest drinking year, which was the year 1875, . . . and we have cut off one

[10] Viscount Goschen, *Essays and Addresses on Economic Questions, 1865-1893* (1905), 208.

pipe or one cigar out of every thirty-five ", but more houses were being
built, twice as much tea was being consumed, and even the working-
classes were eating imported meat, oranges and dairy produce in quantities unprecedented.   Our exports were able to command more imports
than before, even if they were roughly stationary in quantities and
values.   Further, there was a great increase in productivity as well as a
gain in comforts—offset, of course, by recurrent short time and
unemployment.

The determining factors which govern the character of the period
from the British standpoint, were first the improving mechanism of
industrialism, and second the advance of other countries to competitive
power.   The former can be traced in detail (up to 1886) in Dr Clapham's
second volume, or if contemporary accounts be desired in, for example,
Dr D. A. Wells's *Recent Economic Changes* (1890) or, in slighter form,
in the section on Industrial Wealth in Sir Lyon Playfair's *Subjects of
Social Welfare* (1889).   Wells was content to explain most, if not all, of
the economic disturbance by man's increased powers of control over the
forces of nature.   He rejected the explanations which exercised most
contemporary minds—including the majority and the minorities
who reported in 1886 on our depression of trade and industry—
over-production, the scarcity and appreciation of the precious metals,
commercial restrictions, excessive speculation, changes in wealth-
distribution, and agricultural depression.[11]   He was more concerned to
analyse the saving of time and labour in production and distribution
that had been effected since 1860—the Suez Canal, the telegraph, the
steamer, Bessemer steel, and the rest—and to see these as more potent
than variations in the volumes and values of the precious metals.   The
explanation of the fall in prices certainly cannot be given solely in terms
of gold and silver and their mutual relationships: it must, in part at
least, be in terms of increasing productive efficiency.   The advancing
technique and the improving mechanism of industrialism were formative
factors between 1873 and 1896.   That at least can be said with certainty.

The competitive efficiency of other countries, itself a function of the
progressiveness of industrialism, played its part in the British depression.
When E. E. Williams published his *Made in Germany* in 1896, it
promptly ran through several editions.   " Take observations ", advised
its author, " in your own surroundings. . . . You will find that the
material of some of your own clothes was probably woven in Germany.
Still more probable is it that some of your wife's garments are German
importations; while it is practically beyond a doubt that the magnificent
mantles and jackets wherein her maids array themselves on their

[11] The depression in agriculture receives a bare mention only in this article.   Difficulties in that branch of our national economy had their own special character and
causes.   Though serious, they are one among many factors in the making of depression
in the period under review.

Sundays out are German-made and German-sold, for only so could they be done at the figure. Your governess's fiancé is a clerk in the city; but he also was made in Germany. The toys and the dolls and the fairy books . . ." and so on, through a list which includes the piano, the mug inscribed "A Present from Margate", the drain-pipes, the poker, the opera and its singers, the texts on the wall, and the German band that rouses you from sleep in the morning—all made in Germany.

It was the invasion of the home market that disturbed people most in these years, and led to the revival of the protectionist agitation. The truth was that conditions of world economy had come to fruition at an awkward time. Rapid technological changes rendered the problem of obsolescent capital peculiarly difficult here, and the general environment of falling prices increased our difficulties more, perhaps, than those of our younger rivals.

Only a few considerations may be stressed in one brief article. Insular economic history has ceased in the last quarter of the nineteenth century to have more than an insular significance. If the general monetary factors may seem to have been under-valued, that is due, perhaps, to a desire to avoid thinking of yesterday in terms of today. The period of the so-called "great depression" was a period of progress in circumstances of great difficulty. It might be dubbed a period of "lean years" in contrast with the preceding good years, if profit were the main criterion of welfare. In no final sense, however, was that period one of retrogression. "Wreck'd on a reef of visionary gold" would make an epitaph for its textbook writers rather than for its entrepreneurs.

# THE ECONOMIC FACTORS IN
# THE HISTORY OF THE EMPIRE

## RICHARD PARES

SOME vague and misleading things have been said about economic imperialism in late years; but there is no reason for doubting that there is such a thing, or rather that there are such things. Colonisation and empire-building are above all economic arts, undertaken for economic reasons and very seldom for any others. At some times in the history of England and France, as in that of the Greek cities, emigration has appeared to proceed from στάσις—political or religious discord. But such exceptions as the Pilgrim Fathers are not so complete as they look. Even the conscious founder of a new City of God, like John Winthrop, thought it a material consideration that " My means here are so shortened (now my 3 eldest sons are come to age) as I shall not be able to continue in this place and employment where I now am . . . and with what comfort can I live with 7 or 8 servants in that place and condition where for many years I have spent 3 or 400*li.* per ann. and maintain as great a charge?"[1]   No doubt there were in the English and French Civil Wars some people who emigrated for religious or political reasons though they had enough economic inducement to stay at home. But such exiles probably did not make up a majority, though they may have been the dominant political caste, even in their own colonies, while in other colonies they were hardly to be found at all.

It is therefore necessary to look first of all for the economic motives of imperial expansion and exploitation.  Since these motives probably have not remained the same throughout the history of empires, no theory will suit every age and type of empire.  Certainly the modern Marxist theories are subject to this limitation, as their wiser authors admit.

The best method of discussing the matter will be, I think, to describe the successive theories of empire, and the practice with which they corresponded—or did not correspond.  This method has one advantage: it helps us to remember, or does not prevent us from remembering, that the most important thing in the history of an empire is the history of its mother-country.  Colonial history is made at home: given a free

---

[1] *Winthrop Papers* (1931 edn.), II, 126. It may be objected that this is not a perfect instance because Winthrop had just been deprived of a small office on account of his politics ; but it is not the reason he gives, and his latest editor even doubts the fact (*ibid.* 100).

hand, the mother-country will make the kind of empire it needs. This
is particularly true of the British Empire, because England, more than
any other colonial power, has had such a free hand. Others may have
had to content themselves, up to now, with the kind of empire they could
get; we have been able—after many struggles, indeed—to make the kind
of empire we wanted. It is important, therefore, to know what kinds of
empire have we wanted, and why? For this reason and because it is the
empire about which I can generalise with most confidence, I shall confine
myself to discussing the British Empire.

\*       \*       \*

# I

The great object of the mercantilist was to create employment.[2] So
long as he did so he was curiously indifferent to the productivity of the
labour employed. Hence, for example, Cary congratulated himself on
the fact that in the colonial trade " the commodities exported and imported being generally bulky do thereby employ more ships, and
consequently more sailors, which leaves more room for other labouring
people to be kept at work in husbandry and manufactures, whilst they
consume the product of the one, and the effects of the other in an
employment of a distinct nature from either ".[3]

It is not necessary here to explain this preoccupation with employment, or the pessimistic attitude which Professor Heckscher has labelled
" Fear of Goods ". As a result of this attitude, the average mercantilist
was almost equally preoccupied with foreign trade.[4] The first enthusiasts judged a colonial adventure as they would have judged an extremely
" favourable " branch of foreign trade. A colony was to yield raw
materials and dispose of English manufactures, in order, as the younger
Hakluyt said, that " what in the number of things to go out wrought,
and to come in unwrought, there need not one poor creature to steal, to
starve, or to beg as they do ".[5] How this was to come about, and in

---

[2] It has been justly doubted whether the economic historian ought to speak of " The
mercantilists ". When I use the phrase, I mean the mercantilist " man in the street ",
of whom, I think, a fairly consistent picture can be drawn.

[3] J. Cary, An Essay on Trade (Bristol, 1695), 69. Perhaps most people would have
given a military reason for encouraging sailors ; Cary prefers to argue that sailors are
kept from competing for other people's jobs. He is not quite consistent, for he praises
labour-saving devices and denounces unproductive employments such as alehouse-
keeping. This is a point on which even the best mercantilist writers were far from
clear ; they thought of national wealth so much in terms of international trade that
they did not attend enough to the distribution of industry and rewards within the
nation. (See Mun's curious reflections on lawyers, and his ambiguous handling of the
question of luxury.)

[4] Mr Keynes has explained this connection of thought very ingeniously in terms of
his own theory (General Theory of Employment, Interest, and Money, 334-8).

[5] " Discourse of Western Planting ", printed in Original Writings and Correspondence
of the two Richard Hakluyts, ed. Hakluyt Society, 238.

particular how an effective demand for English manufactures was to be discovered or created, the prophets did not always stop to answer. In their ignorance they could not yet distinguish colonies of settlement and of exploitation from trading-stations, and they seem to have imagined that the demand for woollens among, for example, the Red Indians of North America would be immense. Few of them asked themselves how the Red Indians would pay for their purchases; and of those who did, like the elder Hakluyt, still fewer could give anything like a satisfactory answer.[6] Only time was to show which of the countries open to imperialist exploitation were to be valued for the markets and the products of their native inhabitants, and which were not. The former, such as the East Indies, were destined to furnish the basis of a trading empire; the latter had to be used another way, if they were to be used at all.

When they talked of raw materials and markets, of course, the mercantilists meant, above all, the raw materials of industry and markets for industrial products. In fact, most of them seem to have assumed without question that the national interest of England in economic affairs was the interest of a trading, or rather an industrial nation. This is curious, because her main source of wealth was still agriculture, and the fact was recognised in a great deal of her policy. The mercantilists usually assumed that the duty or the destiny of colonies was to confine themselves to griculture and leave industry to the mother-country. This was even true of Ireland, which was treated as a colony and sometimes even called one. Cary set out to prove to the Irish that their true interest was in agriculture. He did not produce any economic arguments, nor could he have done so, for he obviously thought that industry was in itself more eligible than agriculture: it was so much less "laborious" and provided so much more "easy" a subsistence that nobody, according to Cary, would remain on the land if he saw a chance of employment in a town. Finally, Cary gave away his case by conceding that if Ireland could find an industry—the linen industry—which did not compete with our own, Englishmen would be very glad.[7]

There were certain difficulties about this division of labour between England and Ireland. Cary recognised that if England was to have a monopoly of industry, Ireland must be free to make a living by engaging in every form of agriculture. But he knew it would be hard to persuade the English land-owning class that this was not contrary to its interest. Ireland competed with England in cattle-raising. The English Parliament, dominated by landowners, and ready to protect agriculture quite as much as industry, therefore passed the famous Act of Limitation, which forbade the importation of Irish cattle—the counterpart in agriculture to the various measures for putting down manufactures in the colonies. Cary thought this Act ought to be repealed. How did he set about per-

[6] "Inducements to the liking of the voyage intended towards Virginia" (*Original Writings*, 332-3).     [7] Cary, *op. cit.* 91-4.

suading the English agriculturalists that they would suffer no injury? By arguing that the prohibition had driven the Irish into pasturing sheep, and selling their wool abroad or manufacturing it for themselves; this diminished the export from England—not, indeed, of wool for that might not be exported, but of woollen manufactures; this in turn lessened the profits of our woollen industry, and lowered the rents of English lands. " Nothing ", said Cary, " will advance their lands like trade and manufactures, therefore whatever turns the stream of these elsewhere lessens the number of inhabitants who should consume their provisions, and when these increase, so do the others." [8] In other words, the destiny of English agriculture was to supply the home market of an industrial nation, in free competition with colonial agriculture; all were to receive their reward from the high prices or large exports of the workshop of the world. The English landed interest, however, was not convinced by this kind of imperialism (no more it is now), and preferred to deal with the matter by a further increase of the restrictions upon Irish enterprise; it kept up the prohibition against Irish cattle, and tried to avoid the predicted results by preventing the growth of the woollen industry in Ireland and the export of Irish wool to foreign parts.[9]

In the American colonies and colonial trades, the merchants and industrialists were better able to impose their idea of an imperial division of labour without the same opposition from the landed interest. Although writers like Child growled occasionally at New England for producing foodstuffs which might compete with the products of our own agriculture in our West India markets, this was not a serious grievance.[10] The English farmer more or less willingly resigned the markets of the sugar islands to the North American farmer. Those islands received very little of their food from England in the eighteenth century, before the American Revolution. Conversely, the North American wheat-grower had hardly begun to compete with the English exporter in the markets of Europe. Difficulties of transportation were the reason for this. Had New England and the bread colonies been as near as Ireland, no doubt the English landlord would have obtained protection against their wheat as he obtained it against Irish cattle.[11] But he had good markets nearer at hand which they could not share, and the only articles

[8] Cary, op cit. 100-7.
[9] As Professor G. N. Clark points out, the only effect of the Act of Limitation was to turn the thwarted Irish exporter of cattle into a very successful producer of beef and butter. He also doubts whether the Irish woollen industry would have grown very much if the English Parliament had let it alone. (The Later Stuarts, 289, 303-7.) He is right; but this legislation, though ineffectual, shows how an imperial Parliament thought fit to treat a colonial dependency.
[10] A Discourse about Trade (1690 edn.), 204.
[11] When the agricultural interests of an imperial nation are strong enough politically, they may put an end to the imperial connection altogether, as the very powerful sugar interest in the United States has helped to bring about the dis-annexation of the Philippines.

in which the farmers of the old and the new world competed were beef and dairy produce; since it was Irish, not English, beef and butter that competed against the American, the English Parliament saw no reason for favouring either side against the other.

Competition between the agriculture of the mother-country and that of the colonists was the last thing the mercantilists intended. Unlike the nineteenth-century theorists, they never meant to send colonists abroad to produce in the new world what they had produced in the old. The object of colonisation was to obtain goods which were complementary to the products of the mother-country—raw materials of industry such as silk, cotton, and dyewoods, and articles of consumption which could not be grown at home. True, unexpected and unwelcome articles of consumption, such as Virginia tobacco, were sometimes thus brought into common use. But other commodities were more respectable; and one of the oftenest-repeated arguments for colonisation was the phenomenal fall in the price of sugar which we believed—perhaps wrongly—to have been caused by the production of our sugar islands after 1640.

This was the more important because we considered that we had thereby emancipated ourselves from the national monopoly of the Portuguese. It was a commonplace of many mercantilist writers that a nation which had a monopoly of an article could and would squeeze the consumers of the world. It could be done by crop restriction (as the Dutch burnt half their spices to sell the rest at a better price [12]). But the mere existence of a " staple " might be enough in itself.[13] In fact, no sooner were we free from the Portuguese monopoly of sugar than we tried to come to terms with the Portuguese government in order to set up an English one.[14] The mercantilists did not explain what was the point of these national monopolies; they did not think it needed explaining. Presumably, given an inelastic demand (which the mercantilists, with their " fear of goods ", mostly assumed) the monopoly would increase the " favourable " trade balance.

The schemes for world monopolies of colonial products broke down through the competition of empires. The English and French rivalled each other in many branches of American production, the English and Dutch in many branches of Eastern trade; tobacco was the only colonial industry in which we obtained a dominating position, and even there we had competitors. But even without the monopolies, the colonies were

[12] Cary proposed that we should get the " staple " of wool and destroy what we could not sell at a good profit.

[13] Some of the wilder journalists proposed that we should contrive to charge higher prices to the foreigners than to the home consumer (very unlike the modern cartel or state monopoly which dumps abroad to sell high at home). It is hard to see how the merchant could do this without the help of the government ; and the government was generally too much afraid of losing the trade to squeeze the foreigner—hence the large and frequent drawbacks of duty on exportation.

[14] Hist. MSS. Comm., Heathcote MSS., 19, 23.

well worth while. The emphasis which pamphleteers laid upon rich tropical commodities was justified by the great fortunes which the sugar-planters made in the seventeenth century. Here was an article for which the demand was great and increased all the time. Although the British sugar islands went through a period of depression after 1720, when their produce was beaten out of the world market by the French, the home demand grew so consistently that it had certainly caught up with the supply by 1740, and in the 'fifties the refiners were beginning to ask for free trade in raw sugars. Here was a new kind of monopoly which the founders of colonies had hardly contemplated: geographical limitations and (according to some conjectures) a deliberate policy of restriction had put a certain class of colonists in a position to lay a monopoly tax on the English consumer. The obvious remedy was expansion of sugar cultivation in the empire. But that required conquests, which the planters did their best to prevent for many years, until experience convinced them that they would gain more in safety from certain strategic annexations than they would lose by increasing the competition within the empire.[15] Even after the Peace of Paris had added to our sugar acreage, the home market could take all that the planters could grow; this probably accounts for the disproportionate development of the sugar industry in the Ceded Islands, at the expense of the other forms of production.[16]

Those who, like the sugar planters, applied themselves to raising the tropical goods for which Western Europe was crying out, became rich enough to buy the English manufactures which they could never have bought if they had stayed in England. This, according to the mercantilists, was the second great justification of colonies. America, unlike Asia, had disappointed us by the insufficiency of her native markets, but she compensated us by making rich customers out of Englishmen. Child estimated that " every Englishman in Barbadoes or Jamaica creates employment for four men at home ".[17] As Child could see, the Englishmen in those colonies were somewhat exceptional, for each of them represented, besides himself, eight or ten negroes whose labour he exploited. For this reason their value as consumers threw into the shade the humbler colonists north of Maryland. The West India colonists were, in the mass, England's best customers per head of white population, and for a long time they were her best customers absolutely. The immense increase of the North American population changed the situation about the middle of the eighteenth century. But if we distinguish the colonies of exploitation from the colonies of settlement within the mercantilist empire—a much more real distinction, economically,

[15] I have discussed this subject at length in my book, *War and Trade in the West Indies*, chap. iii and v.
[16] L. J. Ragatz, *The Fall of the Planter Class in the British Caribbean*, 38-9, 119-20.
[17] *A Discourse about Trade*, 176, 208.

than the more popular one between North America and the West Indies—it can easily be seen that the colonies of exploitation, which alone possessed staple export crops, remained until the American Revolution the most important part of the empire in every respect; they employed more shipping, produced more valuable goods, consumed more English manufactures.[18]

With few exceptions, theorists and governments disliked the other colonies or ignored them. They did not fit into the picture. They consumed, it is true, a great deal of English manufactures; but they paid for them by somewhat dubious means, such as competing with English fishermen or with English ships in the West India trade, or—worse still —trading to the enemy in war-time. The government tried to make honest men of them by introducing them to a staple crop which should really supplement the resources of the empire; but it did not succeed. The extension of this kind of colony was a very doubtful benefit. Some politicians like Bedford and the elder Pitt were willing to gain popularity by taking up the cause of these people against the French; but at other times the government questioned the wisdom or necessity of letting them penetrate the hinterland too freely.[19]  Above all, it was economically a matter of comparative indifference, because it did not much affect any class of people in England.  General farming was about as much use to the community whether it was conducted in Suffolk, Ulster or Massachusetts; in fact, as it was more likely to be pure subsistence farming on the frontier than in the settled parts of the empire, the move from Suffolk to Massachusetts was a retrograde step.  The colonist without a staple crop, and therefore without an easy method of paying for English goods, was almost worse than useless to a mercantilist empire.  Small wonder, then, that a mercantilist government usually regarded him with indifference or vexation.  And not only a mercantilist government; for the *trekboers* of the nineteenth century were even more of a political liability to the empire than the American backwoodsmen of the eighteenth, and no more of an economic asset.  This kind of imperialism, which consists in the advance of the subsistence-farmer into lands claimed by native tribes, has very often been partly or entirely involuntary, so far as the home government is concerned.

Another disadvantage was thought likely to result from the frontiersman's lack of resources: already, since he found such difficulty in selling and therefore in buying, he was in the habit of making his own clothes, no matter how cheap they might be had from England.  It was feared that he would soon manufacture for a market.  This was not likely to happen in a hurry, as Adam Smith argued and later American history

---

[18] The line would be drawn between the colonies north of Maryland with the hinterland of the Southern mainland colonies, on the one hand, and the sugar islands with the coastal districts of the Southern colonies on the other.

[19] As in the celebrated Board of Trade Report of 7 March 1768.

showed; but the Imperial government left nothing to chance, for colonial manufactures were the great bugbear of economists. Hence the several Acts of Parliament which struck at the development of manufactures in the colonies. Some of them, like the Hatters' Act, were procured by blindly selfish interests. Others, like the Iron Act of 1750, implied a coherent, though perhaps equally selfish, conception of the imperial division of labour.

Something of the same kind might be said of the Calico Acts which tried to restrain the use of certain East India textiles in the interest of the English woollen industry. After some false starts, the trade between England and India had become an unusual and perhaps an objectionable one for a mercantilist country: since the vogue of chintzes and calicoes, more manufactures were imported than exported, and those of a kind to interfere with our chief industry at home. Naturally the woollen interests demanded protection and got it. It did not succeed in protecting them, nor did it destroy the Indian textile industries directly; but it unintentionally established the English cotton industry which destroyed them a hundred years later. The Calico Acts were certainly framed without any regard to the interests of India; but it would be a mistake to represent this as a breach of England's imperial obligations to a dependency, for India was not yet part of our empire, and there was little reason for thinking she ever would be. We behaved to India as we would have behaved to any other foreign country—in fact, very much as we did behave to France.

The part played by capital in imperial expansion was seldom discussed. This is not surprising. The mercantilists were only beginning to see what capital was, and what part it played in production. Moreover, there is little evidence that England was, or wanted to be, a capital-exporting country. True, there were many complaints of unemployment and decay of trade, which might be interpreted in a modern capitalist society as symptoms of the capitalists' uneasiness and desire for expansion; but it is doubtful if mercantilist England was such a society as to make this argument admissible. It is true, again, that the very miscellaneous activities of such early colonial and foreign trade magnates as Sir Thomas Smith and Sir Martin Noell are a little reminiscent of the modern finance-capitalist in search of new worlds to conquer. But such men were few and their resources cannot have gone far, even with the joint-stock companies which some of them controlled. Again, it is true that colonisation and overseas trade call for exceptional concentrations of capital. Indeed, the greatest trouble of colonies was getting enough capital; the undertakers had no idea of the amount that would be wanted, and many a colony starved or came near starving because the "adventurers" [20] at home had run out of money or patience,

[20] It is significant that the name "adventurer" was used for the capitalist who stayed at home and ventured his money, not the planter who ventured his person.

and could not finance the undertaking any further without impossibly large return cargoes.[21]  That, to be sure, does not prove that these inadequate capitalists were not impelled by capitalistic motives.  But the best proof that mercantilist England had no surfeit of capital waiting to be released abroad, is that she was a capital-importing country.  There was a great deal of foreign, especially Dutch, capital in England.  In the eighteenth century the Dutch capitalists specialised in government loans, but in the seventeenth they seem to have taken a part in commerce and industry.  Their participation was sometimes strangely resented in England.[22]  In the colonies it was more welcome to settlers, but the government tried hard to reject it.  There were later occasions when the exclusive attitude had to be relaxed; the planters were glad to borrow Dutch money after a financial crisis in 1773, and Parliament was glad to let them do it.[23]

Although it is unlikely that English capitalists badly needed an outlet in the mercantilist age, a great deal of capital was exported to the colonies, for colonisation is impossible without it.  Of course the advance of capital need not imply the export of capital goods.  That might be usual in such heavily capitalised forms of tropical agriculture as sugar-planting, where a capital investment might take the form of machinery and slaves; but it was inappropriate to such enterprises as the first planting of Virginia and New England.  There it was more necessary to advance food and consumers' goods to the colonists while they devoted themselves to building up their own capital equipment.  The chief effort, therefore, of such capitalists as the Virginia Company was to send out successive " supplies ".  Unfortunately they could not see that they were contributing to the formation of capital in the colonies, and too often rebelled against what they regarded as a waste of money without any commercial returns.  Perhaps, though it may seem strange, the best capitalised ventures were those which were least inspired by capitalist motives  When a man like Winthrop resolved to remove for New England, he sold out, if he could, in the old country and took with him, or ordered after him, enough articles of consumption and some necessary tools to start a career as a farmer in the new world.[24]

---

[21] Sartorius von Waltershausen attributed the financial difficulties of modern German colonial enterprises to the impatience of small investors for dividends (*Das Volkswirtschaftliche System der Kapitalanlage im Auslande*, 136).

[22] See the documents in the Timmerman case, 1616 (State Papers, 14/87, no. 74). Timmerman's desire to set up a sugar refinery was opposed because he had " combined with divers strangers beyond seas, and hath there so great a stock of money, as if he should be suffered to use this art, it would suck out the heart and power of this business from the English ".  In 1635 some applicants for leave to refine sugar promised not to " employ stranger's estates ", but only their own (State Papers, 16/279, no. 79).

[23] 13 Geo. III, c. 14.

[24] A comparison of Plymouth and Massachusetts Bay shows, to some degree, that the colonists were best off where they had least to do with English merchants.

But Winthrop and his like were well-to-do men. Few emigrants could afford such a degree of independence; the others were beholden to capitalists for the effort of transplanting them and starting them in their new careers. Those who could not even pay their passage had to sell themselves to the shipowners, to be resold in the colonies as indentured servants for a term of years. Many young merchants were set up in business in the colonies with stock advanced them from England; and they dispensed part of the credit they received to the consumer in the backwoods, who might not pay for years, so that the merchants of England, and the bankers and manufacturers who credited them, must at all times have had a large floating capital outstanding in the colonies. Even the rich planter of sugar and tobacco was deeply in debt to his factor, and indirectly to his factor's banker. The factors had to keep by them a great capital for paying duties, answering bills of exchange, and executing orders for goods; besides this, they must advance large sums upon bond and mortgage if they were to have any business at all, for many planters expected to have the benefit of their consignments requited by loans.

Since the capital invested permanently or currently in the colonies must have been very large, it is surprising that the writers upon colonisation did not say more about it. Perhaps this is because they did not consider it an advantage. It was not thought advantageous to the nation because nobody believed that the nation needed to get rid of capital. It was not much advantage to the individual who gave a great deal of this credit involuntarily or very reluctantly. A few families like the Beckfords and the Lascelles lived by lending money to planters rather than by planting; they might even consider it an injury to be repaid by a safe debtor.[25] But they were exceptional. Most of the people concerned in the colonies were only anxious to see their money again; and well they might be, for what with paper currency in North America and serious restrictions upon alienation or division of estates in the West Indies, the colonies did all that debtor communities can do to frustrate their creditors. No public loans were floated for the colonies in England, so the capital invested there was all private; but perhaps, *mutatis mutandis*, the government's suppression of colonial paper money in 1751 and 1764, and the disallowance of countless laws for the purpose of protecting debtors, may be compared with such later measures as the Colonial Stocks Acts and some of the Indian financial safeguards.

Since the colonies absorbed as much capital as they could get, they cannot have done much to build up capital in England and thereby to promote the Industrial Revolution. It has been suggested that the profits made by merchants in the colonial trade had this effect; but since the most lucrative and important branches of colonial trade were those

[25] Henry Lascelles occasionally tried to avoid receiving payment of a good debt, but he pressed for repayment far oftener.

28

in which the English merchants acted as factors for the planters, and since, whatever the size of their commissions, these men had to employ all their capital and all they could get from their bankers in financing the trade itself, they can hardly have had much to spare for the Industrial Revolution.   Indeed, the manufacturers were lucky if they did not have to give them credit.   The planters themselves seem to have been recipients of capital rather than sources of it.   True, if a Beckford could build Fonthill or buy a borough seat, he could have set up a factory; but from what can be learnt of the way the West India millionaires spent their money there seem to have been more Fonthills than factories among them, and more overdrafts and protested bills than either. Some of the Bristol and Liverpool banks arose from the wealth accumulated in the colonies or colonial trades, but few or none of the great London houses; and it is beginning to be clear that it was the agricultural rather than the colonial wealth of England that was tapped for industrial development in the later eighteenth century.

## II

As England became industrialised, a very different way of thinking about empires began to prevail.   Historians have generally concerned themselves with its negative side—the rejection of mercantilism.   It undoubtedly had such a negative side, ranging from the qualified negation of Adam Smith to the more complete negation of Bentham and Cobden.   But it had also a positive side, which is sometimes forgotten; and this positive theory of empire is the better worth discussing because the free trade era was the great age of colonisation and colonial trade.

The positive theory of empire dealt chiefly with the emigration of capital and labour.   The chief writers on the subject—especially Wakefield, Merivale and J. S. Mill—were dominated by Ricardo's law of rent.   They believed that increases of population and manufacturing technique were of little use to capital and labour if the only result was to put money in the landlord's pocket by causing more food to be produced from inferior English soils.   So far, they kept company with the adversaries of the Corn Laws.   But they did not stop short at admitting foreign food free of duty.   Wakefield, at least, believed that the whole world supplied too little available corn for industrial England, and that if we merely obtained more "use of land"—that is, food—from foreigners, we should have to wait upon their very slow agricultural improvements.   It was not more "use of land", but more land, and above all more first-class land, that was wanted.[26]   J. S. Mill wrote, in

---

[26] *The Art of Colonization*, Letter xvi.   There are similar passages in *England and America*.

sentences which the others quoted with approval, " Much has been said of the good economy of importing commodities from the places where they can be bought cheapest; while the good economy of producing them where they can be produced cheapest is comparatively little thought of. If to carry consumable goods from the places where they are superabundant to those where they are scarce is a good pecuniary speculation, is it not an equally good speculation to do the same thing with regard to labour and instruments?" [27]

Judged historically, this was very good sense. England, and indeed all Western Europe, needed cheap food and raw materials in order to pursue its career of industrialisation. Not all the increase has come from new lands; a great deal of it has proceeded from agricultural improvements in Europe itself. But that would not have been enough, as Wakefield saw. Again, it may be objected, and was objected at the time, that many of the emigrants from the British Isles went to the half-urban United States rather than the purely agricultural colonies. That is true; but the United States were less than half-urban before 1860, and moreover the immigration into the settled districts was still being balanced by some emigration from the settled districts to the frontier.

The same theory of colonisation had certain important corollaries. Capital and labour were said to be too thick on the ground at home. Mill and Merivale believed that the competition of capitals with each other might lower the rate of profit to such a point that accumulation would cease. Wakefield thought capital was redundant with respect to the " field of employment ". It was not merely that capital was tempted abroad by a higher rate of profit; capital must get away from home at any cost. The theorists did not quite agree on the question whether it was necessary to export more capital than labour. Merivale gave two different answers; Mill was sure that it did not matter. Wakefield was preoccupied with another side of the question—the proportion of capital to labour arriving in the colony. He was one of the first to see how much the new Englands overseas differed from the old. He wanted to reproduce in Australasia and North America the old England with something like its class-stratification; he was therefore shocked by the half-barbarous equality of the one-class society in the backwoods. He could only realise his ideal by making the colonies safe for capitalists and wage-earners, which he hoped to do by his celebrated land system. It was not so important to him that England should be relieved of her plethora of capital, as that the colonists should not be starved of it. Merivale criticised his theory as too sweeping. Capitalisation of colonies could not be an end in itself; there must be some inducement, and that must come from the profitable nature of the product. He thought

[27] *Principles of Political Economy*, book V, chap. xi, § 14.

Wakefield's system would only work in a colony with a staple export. That, again, was roughly true. Capitalism itself causes, to some extent, the production of commercial crops, because it demands a payment in some currency that can be realised at home; but it is equally true, or more so, to say that commercial crops invite capitalism.

Of course the capital and labour that went overseas had, and were meant to have, an effect upon the capital and labour that stayed behind. It was not only by the relief of simple evacuation, but by the new markets which the colonies afforded. The increased productivity of the labour of transplanted Englishmen has, in fact, given more employment to Englishmen at home than any extension of markets in other parts of the Empire. That is how, in spite of their small populations, the development of their own industries, and the increasing proportion of their trade which has fallen to foreigners, the self-governing dominions have taken off a great and increasing proportion of English exports.[28]

This is only one side of the story. Another great development was taking place in the Empire at the same time. The transformation of the economic relations between England and India in the nineteenth century throws a strong light on the nature of free-trade imperialism.

Towards the end of the eighteenth century England's trade with the East was very largely a reciprocal exchange of manufactures—woollens and hardware for cottons and silks; the East India Company was exporting a smaller proportion of bullion than it had done fifty years earlier. In the first half of the nineteenth century this state of affairs was much changed: England exported more manufactures than ever, though of a different kind, and her imports from India consisted more and more of raw materials. Some Indians have concluded from this that England systematically destroyed the industries of India and reduced her from a manufacturing to an agricultural country. Their complaint is the more bitter because the English cotton industry, which so reversed the fortunes of India, had grown up under a protective system aimed at the cotton industry of India.

There is no doubt that the change took place: it is less certain that it was deliberate. Certainly the abolition of the East India Company's trade monopoly in 1813 was in some ways unfortunate for the Indian cotton weavers. The Company had aimed at exporting as much English woollen manufactures as possible (for which reason the older-established woollen interests supported it, almost alone, against the private traders),

[28] Professor Flux called attention to this in 1899 (*Journal of the Royal Statistical Society*, LXII, 496-8). Mr J. A. Hobson controverted him (*Imperialism*, 39). It was a matter of classification: Mr Hobson classed the South African colonies with the tropical dependencies, Professor Flux with the self-governing dominions. It is a nice question which of them is right; for my own part I prefer Professor Flux's view. The economic and social affinities of South Africa with the tropical colonies are strong, but not, in my opinion, decisive. Compare both these sets of figures with Table XXXIX in Grover Clark's *Balance Sheets of Imperialism*.

and importing as much Indian textiles as the European market would take. (This, perhaps, was because its greatest commercial strength in India was its command over the cotton-weaving industry, which it maintained by almost feudal means.) The directors were monopolists of the old school. Like all monopolists, they were pessimistic about the chances of increasing the volume of the trade; they could handle a luxury article for which the possible demand was limited, but they could not, and perhaps would not, drive a new kind of trade which might upset the social and economic conditions in a sub-continent. The Company's tenacious conservatism, therefore, gave the Indian weavers some sort of protection; and when the private traders, heavily backed by the cotton towns and other comparatively new export industries, succeeded in getting the trade opened, the immediate result was a rush of English cotton goods to India, the cessation of India's cotton textile exports to England, and a gradual increase of her exports of raw materials, especially raw cotton. The Lancashire cotton interests made it clear that when their goods were excluded from the European markets by the Continental System and their supplies of raw material interfered with by the War of 1812 with the United States, they looked to India to make good both deficiencies. A few people on both sides of the controversy saw that the final result might be the transformation of India from a manufacturing to a raw-material producing country. Most Englishmen saw nothing to regret in this; but a few conservative eccentrics regretted it, like Tierney and, some years later, the colonial historian Montgomery Martin.[29]

But it would be temerarious to pronounce that agriculture was substituted for industry in India by the policy of the English government or the enterprise of the English merchant. In the first place India was not an industrial country to begin with, and Indian weaving was not wholly destroyed. The finest and best manufactures, such as those of Dacca, appear indeed to have been ruined; and such dislocation as was caused in this way must have been unusually cruel and disastrous among Hindus because their caste-system prohibited industrial transference. But the coarser kinds of weaving survived, and suffered comparatively little from English competition. A division of labour was maintained during the rest of the century: India imported her finer goods from Lancashire and made her coarser goods at home. Moreover, so far as the fine Indian craftsmen were ruined, it was chiefly by English competition in neutral markets. Indian weavers did not depend wholly or even principally upon the English market. Bengal, at least, exported more cotton goods to the United States, Portugal and the Far East, and it was the failure of these markets too, about 1818, that so

[29] For Tierney's speech, see *Hansard*, 1st series, XXVI, 525; Montgomery Martin's evidence before the Select Committee of 1840, *Parliamentary Papers*, 1840, viii, especially question 3920.

much damaged the industry.[30]   True, it was English competition that had this result; but it can hardly be thought a Satanic policy for a manufacturing nation to undersell its dependencies in neutral markets. Nevertheless, the Indians had some cause to complain of the heavy internal transit-duties which crippled the development of manufactures until they were removed in 1836, and the protective duties levied in England not only on Indian silks, which competed with English industry but on cottons which could no longer hope to undersell the English weavers in any circumstances.   These duties were materially lowered by Peel's reformed tariff, but only after the employers and still more the workers in the silk manufacture had showed how far a backward industry was from appreciating the beauties of free trade in the year of grace 1840.[31]

As for the swollen imports of raw cotton from India, the English merchants do not seem to have stimulated its production in the early part of the century so much as to have diverted India's exports of this article from other markets to England.   In the American cotton famine of the 'sixties the Lancashire cotton interest was indeed very much to blame for encouraging an injudicious extension of cotton-growing in India and then returning to American cotton as soon as it could, leaving India with a serious over-production.   But that was partly because, in spite of the Cotton Supply Association's measures for improving the quality of Indian cotton, India could not, in the time, produce material good enough for the Lancashire machines—which is shown by the fact that a great deal of Indian cotton was re-exported at the height of the famine.   Still, though it may have been nobody's fault, it was a disaster for India.[32]   The only compensation was that the glut of cotton probably helped the Bombay spinners to develop their industry.

The influence of Lancashire was soon afterwards exercised again in a manner which was uncongenial if not positively injurious to Indian industrialists.   This was in the celebrated controversy of the 'seventies over the Indian cotton duties.   Lancashire was beginning for the first time to foresee the exclusion of its cottons from some of the protected markets of Europe, and claimed the right, once more, to fall back on India as a market as well as a source of raw materials.   At the same time a large-scale cotton industry was just beginning to develop in India itself.   The Indian government let itself in for a pretty quarrel by refusing to abolish the cotton import duties before it had lowered the general import duties or removed certain more burdensome forms of

<hr>

[30] See the table in *Parliamentary Papers*, 1832, x, part ii, 883-7 ; also the interesting letter quoted by Larpent in answer to question 2776, *Parliamentary Papers*, 1840, viii.

[31] A great deal of the evidence before the Committees of 1840 is very interesting ; that of Thomas Cooper, silk-weaver of Macclesfield, before the Commons Committee is particularly so (*Parliamentary Papers*, 1840, viii).

[32] Isaac Watts, *The Cotton Supply Association ; its Origin and Progress* (1871), *passim*.

taxation. The matter was really one of revenue, and as such it was finally treated; but since the cotton duties were in fact though not in intention protective, the Lancashire members of parliament, regardless of party, pressed continually to have them removed before any other kind of tax was remitted in India. The discussion was interesting, if only because it was one of the few occasions when Gladstone spoke almost disrespectfully of free trade: he contrasted the merciless vigour with which we applied free trade principles "against the feeling of the Indian people", with our acquiescence in the protective policy of the self-governing colonies.[33] The contrast, which Lansdowne later described as "swallowing the colonial camel and straining at the Indian gnat", was indeed invidious. But the complete free trader replied that though we could not prevent the Australians from making fools of themselves, we might and should restrain India. At the same time it was argued (for instance, in a strong minute of Sir Henry Maine) that we had a right to expect from India an open market for our goods as a compensation for the very serious liabilities which her possession and defence had laid upon our foreign policy.[34] (This was just after the Eastern crisis of 1875-8, in which our connection with India was felt to have been an important element.)

The duties do not seem to have been serious economically; they were more important as a symbol of India's dependence upon the commercial policy of Great Britain and the interests which could so easily dominate that policy. For it was apparent before the world that the government had capitulated to Lancashire, and had imposed its will on the very reluctant authorities in India. Again, in 1894-5, when the Liberal Secretaries of State forced the Indian government to impose a countervailing excise duty on Indian yarn in order to mollify Lancashire's aversion to the reimposition of the cotton duties, it was plain that the opinions of India's responsible authorities could easily be overridden by interested parties in England. This incident, even more than the other, was a very important one in the development of Indian nationalism.

It cannot exactly be said that in these tariff controversies Lancashire tried consciously to force India out of industry into agriculture, but it is true that Lancashire only began rather late in the day to insist upon a fair field for competition between England and India. The case of India is a rather exceptional one, because an industrial power does not often conquer another power with a very similar export industry. The history of Lancashire and India shows, to some degree, what is likely to happen when it does so.

[33] *Hansard*, 3rd Ser., CCXLVI, 1746.

[34] *Parliamentary Papers*, no. 392 of 1879, 9-10. Sir John Strachey made some rather similar remarks in his Financial Statement of 1877 (*Parliamentary Papers*, no. 241 of 1879, 3).

## III

The exchange of commodities, however, is not the whole story. Recent theorists of various schools have insisted on the capitalist nature of modern imperialism.

Most of them connect it with capital export in particular; but not all do so. Rosa Luxemburg explains why imperialism is immanent in capitalism without laying much stress on the necessity of exporting capital. She tries to show, by a very elaborate analysis of the schemata at the end of volume II of Marx's *Capital*, that capitalist accumulation cannot take place unless the capitalist can sell to somebody outside the capitalist system that part of the surplus value which he means to capitalise as an addition to what he has already accumulated. This is one way of saying that capitalism needs markets and finds them, for preference, in those classes at home, and those foreign nations, which are not yet producing on a capitalist basis. That is a truism. Imperialism, both capitalist and pre-capitalist, has always tried to exploit, to control, and even to create such markets.

Another similar explanation comes from other Marxist sources. One effect of capitalist competition, to which Marx often drew attention, was the necessity of cutting costs of production by producing on an ever larger and more efficient scale. In fact, schemata or no schemata, the capitalist would have to accumulate, and to multiply his products and his markets for this reason alone.[35] This argument, however, does not offer so much reason as the other for the necessity of selling the product to "non-capitalists". Professor Flux suggested a somewhat similar explanation of economic imperialism, when he wrote that industrialists might prefer "markets for standard lines of products", which should bring about a profitable "expansion of production on lines similar to those which long experience has smoothed", to speculating upon the latent demands of their own countrymen for new lines of goods.

The other Marxists do not altogether deny Rosa Luxemburg's thesis; indeed, they adopt it, in part, for their own. Bukharin says that one kind of imperialism (one kind only) may be compared to a vertical trust, where "a state capitalist trust includes an economically supplementary unit, an agrarian country for instance". Lenin did not disdain the comparison; but when Kautsky defined imperialism as "the striving of every industrial capitalist nation to bring under its control

---

[35] Adam Smith saw the connection between industrial development and the size of the market, but applied it somewhat perversely to the case of colonies, for he attacked our concentration on the colonial trade as making us depend too much on a single market. His arguments were political. In so far as the American colonies were a single market, they must have contributed to the growth of large-scale industry; but the very great social diversity of colonial life—planters, slaves and backwoodsmen—made it impossible to describe them as a single market for this purpose.

and to annex increasingly big *agrarian* regions ", he had his nose bitten off by Lenin for saying so. Lenin replied that "The characteristic feature of imperialism is *not* industrial capital but finance capital. . . . The characteristic feature is that it strives to annex *not only* agricultural regions, but even highly industrial regions."[36] His proof of the last proposition was weak, for he was thinking of purely strategic conquests; but the distinction of finance capital and industrial capital is a more serious one.

While Rosa Luxemburg argues that capitalism requires an ever-increasing export of goods, other Marxists say rather that it demands an export of capital. Not necessarily capital goods; they do not agree to lay stress on that. Rosa Luxemburg seems to have thought that consumers' goods would be exported, rather than producers' goods; indeed it must be so, if Marx's schema was to be taken literally, but she did not insist on it—in fact, she thought that now more goods of the one kind would be sent abroad, now more of the other. This is true. It is not necessary to export capital goods in order to export capital, and capital export has often taken the form of advances of consumers' goods; on the other hand, at certain important epochs, when capital has been exported at a great rate, capital goods, especially railways, have been the principal exports. Bukharin and Lenin, however, laid more stress on the export of capital goods. Lenin had a particular reason for doing so. Whereas Rosa Luxemburg saw imperialism as the necessary result of capitalist competition, Lenin saw it rather as the necessary consequence of capitalist monopoly. He connected it with cartels and tariffs, which were particularly prominent in the capital-goods industries: when once a cartel has obtained a monopoly of the home market, its need and its power to export some of its produce will increase, and by limiting the amount of capital which can be profitably employed within the monopoly area it will force capital—that of its possible competitors, or its own surplus—to leave the country in search of occupation elsewhere. The argument is put rather more explicitly by Bukharin than by Lenin.[37]

It is an interesting point of view. No doubt trusts and cartels may make it more worth while to dispose of surplus products abroad than to raise the standard of life at home. They may also make it more profitable to invest surplus capital in developing foreign industries than to work up for the home market the products of cartels upon which an excessively high price has been fixed. But this theory does not explain the largest empire which exists at present. The development of the British Empire and the movements of capital within it cannot be ascribed to cartels, tariffs or monopolies. In spite of the efforts of Chamberlain (whose Imperial Preference schemes were represented by

---

[36] N. Bukharin, *Imperialism and World Economy*, 120; Lenin, *Imperialism, the Highest Stage of Capitalism*, chaps. vi and vii.

[37] Bukharin, *op. cit.* 97.

Lenin as a retort to the cartellised national monopolies of other industrial countries), the British Empire cannot really be said to have entered
the monopoly stage before 1932

Lenin and Bukharin insist upon the exportation not only of capital
goods but also of capital. Why does capital emigrate? Partly in order
to smooth the path for the emigration of goods: this is particularly true
of the capital-goods industries, for there have been many occasions when
the flotation of foreign loans, especially for armaments and railways, has
gone hand in hand with large orders for capital goods. In these cases
capital may be identified with capital goods; capital emigrates chiefly in
order that capital goods may do so.[38] Apart from this special case, the
export of capital is explained from two ends: either capital has got to
emigrate because it cannot stay at home, or it is tempted abroad because
it finds better employment there. Neither the second nor even the first
of these explanations is the peculiar property of the Marxists. J. S. Mill
and Wakefield thought that capital could be absolutely redundant at
home, so that it must either go abroad or cease to be capital, *i.e.* must be
consumed instead of being accumulated.

I am not qualified to discuss, as an economist, the analysis of the
formation of capital upon which these explanations of imperialism
depend. It is certain that in the last hundred years a great deal of
capital has been exported from England. The amount and pace of the
flow are difficult to determine. L. H. Jenks and C. K. Hobson agree in
naming 1875 as the epoch when the " primary " export of capital ceased
and only secondary export remained: that is, when we ceased to build
up our foreign investments by a surplus of exported over imported goods
and services, and only added to them by reinvesting part of our income
from earlier investments. According to Hobson there was no "primary"
export of capital in any year between 1875 and 1907; Hobson's table
depends indeed on a reduction of Giffen's allowance for shipping earnings, but even if Giffen's original figures are accepted the year 1875 still
appears to have been something of a turning point. The greatest era
of English railway-building abroad was past, though there was still
plenty to do, especially in South Africa; the greatest exports of railway
materials were therefore over too. This is important, because railways
seem to have been the great basis of England's foreign investments;
there are still countries, such as India and Argentina, where the railways
account for more than half the English capital invested, and the United
States was such a country before the repatriation of English capital in

<hr />

[38] Sartorius von Waltershausen thought it was the national economist's duty to see
that the export of capital was used as a means of pushing the foreign sales of capital
goods. Not every flotation of a foreign railway or mining loan results in a corresponding
export of material ; most of the early ones did, but according to C. K. Hobson (*The
Export of Capital,* 7) the English railway loans to the Argentine did not in 1910-13 ;
moreover, few of the later United States railway loans floated in the London market
can have done so.

the last war.    Therefore the passing of the age of overseas railway-building is one of the significant dates of English history.

Another important development in the tendency of English foreign investment is noticed after 1875: before that date it was cosmopolitan, but afterwards it appears to have been concentrated to a greater degree within the boundaries of the empire.    Foreign railway and government securities must have been sold and the proceeds reinvested in similar securities within the empire.    This process is hard to trace or to explain, but it is there.    C. K. Hobson suggested that the British capitalist was the frontiersman or pioneer who opened up a new and difficult field of enterprise, developed it to some degree, then sold out to foreigners who liked a steady investment in an established concern, and himself moved on to new adventures.    This has an element of truth in it; certainly the pioneer British enterprises in France and America were generally bought out by the natives as going concerns.    Whatever the causes, the relative concentration of capital—it has never been more than that—is yet a third example of the usefulness of a political empire as a standby: the investor, like the seeker for a market or the consumer of raw materials, is glad to turn to the empire when, for one reason or another, the more fully developed independent countries begin to be less attractive than they were.

Capitalist imperialism has certain important secondary consequences. It tends to replace the self-sufficient economy and subsistence-agriculture of the colonial lands by production for the world market.    Colonies of exploitation and, indeed, colonies of settlement, so far as they are obliged to make a return upon invested capital, must produce for a market. Hence, perhaps, the persistent monoculture of the most highly capitalised tropical countries—and before the abolition of slavery all tropical agriculture in the British colonies and the United States was highly capitalised. Where the loan is granted on condition that the borrower shall give the lender the benefit of his consignments or his orders—which was common in the eighteenth-century sugar business—this effect is even more obvious.    The railway is another important agent of capitalism which tends to produce similar results.    Sometimes, as in the American prairies, railways cause or promote production for a market; at other times, however, production for a market has caused railways.    The efforts of the Cotton Supply Association to goad the India Office into sanctioning or undertaking railways are interesting in this respect.    Of course the Association was concerned only with the promotion of cotton-growing, so that some critics were unkind enough to suggest that its efforts had caused, or were likely to cause, a shortage of food in certain districts; presumably this accusation was founded on the fact that the Madras Irrigation and Canal Company, which was much patronised by the Association, was at work in some of the districts where the dreadful Orissa famine broke out in 1866.    The Association defended itself, and claimed to have proposed nothing but what would promote the general development of India. There was not much in its earlier memorials to the India Office to substantiate the claim; and it is obvious that a capitalist industry in search of raw material might easily, in a poor country with patchy communications, cause subsistence farming to be replaced by commercial crops to an unhealthy extent. The government of India had been aware of the danger, and sometimes vetoed provincial measures for the undue encouragement of cotton-growing by remission of taxes. At the same time it is fair to say that the railways which were designed to carry cotton to the ports could also, in an emergency, bring food supplies to the cotton districts.

The Cotton Supply Association contemplated, at one time, an attack on the whole system of landholding in India; but on second thoughts it decided that the existing systems would enable cotton to be grown without much change. Capitalist imperialism is often charged with destroying communal land tenure for its own purposes; and there is no doubt that in many parts of Asia and Africa it has resulted in, or been accompanied by, a revolution in the native landholding system. Capitalistic motives have not always been responsible for this; for example, they do not account for the injudicious rigour with which the *ryotwari* system was pressed upon some communal economies in Madras, or the policy of Sir George Grey which turned British Kaffraria into a slum. White imperialism has had more effect on the native's way of life, especially in Africa, by limiting the quantity of his land than by altering the tenures. This has not always been the doing of capitalism. It was the white farmer who first deprived the African native of his land, partly that he might own it himself, partly that he might dispose of the labour of the landless man. This limitation of native resources and an often deliberate policy of high taxation have undoubtedly played into the hands of industrial capitalism as well—Kimberley and Johannesburg are largely founded upon such policies. But the policies were not invented, in the first place, for the sake of Kimberley and Johannesburg; they were not even invented by the type of capitalist agriculture which uses them, to some extent, in Kenya today. They were invented by the Boer—a curious kind of capitalist, for most of his capital consisted in cows, whose accumulation became almost an end in itself.

This brings us to the last of the criticisms directed against capitalist imperialism. Capital is said to leave the country of its origin, where high wages, Factory Acts and limitation of hours reduce its profits, and fly to new countries, where it carries on the same industries that it carried on at home, with the advantage of cheaper labour and fewer restrictions. This certainly happens, sometimes even within the limits of a single country like the United States. The spectre of "raising up foreign competitors" has been conjured up very freely; and just as mercantilists tried to prevent wool, skilled labour or machinery from being exported to a possible competitor, special taxes upon foreign investments were discussed before the last war. But it is difficult to be sure how much English capital has been applied to the development abroad of England's own staple industries. Some part of this foreign investment takes the form of banking capital, or loans to foreign governments for general industrial development; the further application of this capital is not easily traced, statistically. Moreover there have lately been many instances, even within the empire, of capital establishing itself where it may take the benefit of protective duties instead of paying them. Apart from these, capital does not appear to prefer investment in the staple industries which compete with those of its mother-country. The typical British investments in the United States were once railways; in India, railways again, and tea plantations—certainly not cotton mills, which British capital has avoided in a remarkable way. In China? Again, not cotton mills, for the British-owned mills are a small proportion of the foreign mills, while British capital is a much higher proportion of foreign capital as a whole. In South Africa, gold mines; in Argentina, railways again.[39] Ordinarily, therefore, foreign investment more often contributes to the general development of colonial lands than to " raising up foreign competitors ". This consideration is strengthened by the fact that the industrial and capital-exporting lands (which are, in spite of certain variations, roughly the same) lend little to each other but a great deal to the agrarian countries. The United States are no exception to this rule, for in the days when they were great borrowers they were an agricultural nation.

The secondary effects of imperialism upon the mother-country are also important, but cannot be discussed here at length. Obviously they tend to create a " labour aristocracy " and a *rentier* nation. The great improvement of the English workman's standard of life after 1850 was helped, though not solely caused, by the development of the industries which flourished on capital export. This in its turn did something to create a *rentier* class by the expansion of industrial towns and increase of ground-rents. But the returns upon capital invested abroad have done

[39] In Argentina, the British investment in railways is currently estimated at £277 million, the total British investment at £500-£600 million; in the United States before the war, £616 million in railways, total British long-term publicly issued investment, £750 million (Feis, *Europe, the World's Banker*, 23, 27). In India the estimates vary. Feis gives, for 1914, £140 million in railways, total British investment £378 million; but this is very misleading, as most of the government loans were contracted for railway building; D. H. Buchanan (*The Development of Capitalist Enterprise in India*, 154) puts the capital outlay on railways, 1914-15 at 65·6 per cent of the total investment in India. This includes Indian as well as British capital; for the British capital alone, probably the figure would be higher. According to figures quoted by Buchanan (206), only 9 cotton mills out of 345 were entirely owned by Europeans in 1921, against 322 entirely owned by Indians. In China, according to figures quoted by G. E. Hubbard (*Eastern Industrialization and its Effect on the West*, 223), British Investments in 1931 stood in the ratio of 54:40 to Japanese investments (the next largest), but British investments in cotton mills stood as 4:39 to Japanese in spindles, as 8:44 in looms.

far more in that respect; ever since the days of the Nabob and the sugar millionaire, the luxury trades at home have received a stimulus from the imperial *rentier*. This parasitical imperialism was transforming the economy of London and the home counties even before the war.[40] England's " tribute " is not exactly similar in its origin to that of Imperial Rome,[41] but its internal effect is not unlike, and if there are no shocks from outside, the finance empire shows signs of outliving the industrial and the political empire. As the colonial lands become industrialised and independent, it is the only kind of imperial relation that remains appropriate.

To sum up, it is pretty clear that imperialism is above all a process— and, to some degree, a policy—which aims at developing complementary relations between high industrial technique in one land and fertile soils in another. These relations are pre-capitalist relations; they are also capitalist relations. Not all the Marxist teachings apply to all the facts, but many of them open the eyes of colonial historians to things which they ought to have seen before.

[40] See the eloquent description in J. A. Hobson's *Imperialism*.
[41] I have not been able to discuss at length the so-called " tribute " of India. The earliest fortunes brought back from India were not returns to capital in India, but were gained in India itself by privileged though illicit trade, and often by sheer oppression. It was remitted home, not, I think, as dividends but as repatriated capital. When the East India Company's servants ceased to make money in this way, there were still considerable remittances of savings from the very generous salaries (Macaulay saved a competence for life out of four years' salary as Law Member), the still more generous pensions, and the heavy military charges payable by India to England. Later again, this " tribute " was increased by the normal payment of interest on British capital invested in India. That does not call for special comment, but I think the " tribute " does, because it is almost the only instance I know which supports the Marxist view that pre-capitalist imperialism was designed, like the Roman and other ancient empires, to extract tribute from the subject peoples. (Incidentally, the Romans were not above investing in their empire—there was Seneca with his *usuria per totam Britanniam exercita*.)

far more in that respect; ever since the days of the Nabob and the sugar millionaire, the luxury trades at home have received a stimulus from the imperial tenure. This parasitical imperialism was transforming the economy of London and the home counties even before the war.[40] England's " tribute " is not exactly similar in its origin to that of imperial Rome,[41] but its internal effect is not unlike, and if there are no shocks from outside, the finance empire shows signs of outliving the industrial and the political empire. As the colonial lands become industrialised and independent, it is the only kind of imperial relation that remains appropriate.

To sum up, it is pretty clear that imperialism is above all a process — and, to some degree, a policy — which aims at developing complementary relations between high industrial technique in one land and fertile soils in another. These relations are pre-capitalist relations; they are also capitalist relations. Not all the Marxist teachings apply to all the facts, but many of them open the eyes of colonial historians to things which they ought to have seen before.

[40] See the eloquent description in J. A. Hobson's Imperialism.

[41] I have not been able to discuss at length the so-called " tribute " of India. The earliest fortunes brought back from India were not returns to capital in India, but were gained in India itself by privileged though illicit trade, and often by sheer oppression. It was remitted home, not, I think, as dividends but as repatriated capital. When the East India Company's servants ceased to make money in this way, there were still considerable remittances of savings from the very generous salaries (Macaulay saved a competence for life out of four years' salary as Law Member), the still more generous pensions, and the heavy military charges payable by India to England. Later again, this " tribute " was increased by the normal payment of interest on British capital invested in India. That does not call for special comment, but I think the " tribute " does, because it is almost the only instance I know which supports the Marxist view that pre-capitalist imperialism was designed, like the Roman and other ancient empires, to extract tribute from the subject peoples. (Incidentally, the Romans were not above investing in their empire — there was Seneca with his usuria per totam Britanniam exercita.)